LYNN ALTENBERND and LESLIE L. LEWIS

Introduction to Literature:

STORIES / POEMS / PLAYS

Introduction to Literature:
PLAYS

SECOND EDITION

Edited, with a Handbook
for the Study of Drama, by
LYNN ALTENBERND,
University of Illinois, and
LESLIE L. LEWIS,
University of Colorado

THE MACMILLAN COMPANY

PRINTING 5678910 YEAR 3456789

Earlier edition © 1963 by The Macmillan Company.

Library of Congress catalog card number: 69–20452

THE MACMILLAN COMPANY
866 THIRD AVENUE, NEW YORK, NEW YORK 10022
Collier-Macmillan Canada, Ltd., Toronto, Ontario

Printed in the United States of America

CREDITS AND ACKNOWLEDGMENTS

Copyrighted works, listed in the order of appearance, are reprinted in the United States, its possessions and dependencies, and Canada by permission of the following.

Antigone, by Sophocles, translated by Dudley Fitts and Robert Fitzgerald. THE ANTIGONE OF SOPHOCLES: An English Version by Dudley Fitts and Robert Fitzgerald, copyright, 1939, by Harcourt, Brace & World, Inc. and reprinted with their permission.

Amphitryon, by Plautus, translated by Lionel Casson. "Amphitryon," copyright © 1963 by Lionel Casson, from *Six Plays of Plautus* translated by Lionel Casson. Reprinted by permission of Doubleday & Company, Inc.

Everyman, anonymous, translated by C. G. Child. Reprinted from THE SECOND SHEPHERD'S PLAY, EVERYMAN & OTHER EARLY PLAYS, translated by C. G. Child, by courtesy of Houghton Mifflin Company.

The Misanthrope, by Molière, translated by Richard Wilbur. © copyright 1954, 1955, by Richard Wilbur. Reprinted by permission of Harcourt, Brace & World, Inc.
CAUTION: Professionals and amateurs are hereby warned that this translation, being fully protected under the copyright laws of the United States of America, the British Empire, including the Dominion of Canada, and all other countries which are signatories to the Universal Copyright Convention and the International Copyright Union, is subject to royalty. All rights, including professional, amateur, motion picture, recitation, lecturing, public reading, radio broadcasting, and television, are strictly reserved. Particular emphasis is laid on the question of readings, permission for which may be secured from the author's agent in writing. Inquiries on professional rights (except for amateur rights) should be addressed to Mr. Gilbert Parker, Agency for the Performing Arts, Inc., 120 West 57 Street, New York, New York 10019; inquiries on translation rights should be addressed to Harcourt, Brace & World, Inc.; 757 Third Avenue, New York, New York 10017.
The amateur acting rights of THE MISANTHROPE are controlled exclusively by the Dramatists Play Service, Inc., 440 Park Avenue South, New York, New York. No amateur performance of the play may be given without obtaining in advance the written permission of the Dramatists Play Service, Inc., and paying the requisite fee.

Ghosts, by Henrik Ibsen, translated by William Archer. "Ghosts" is reprinted with the permission of Charles Scribner's Sons from THE COLLECTED WORKS OF HENRIK IBSEN, Volume VII, translated by William Archer.

Man of Destiny, by George Bernard Shaw. By permission of The Shaw Estate and The Society of Authors.

Preface

This second edition of *Introduction to Literature: STORIES, POEMS*, and *PLAYS* retains the essential features described in the preface to the first edition.

The three parts present an abundance and variety of material in such a way that the teacher can construct his own course to serve the students' needs, his own interests, and his department's program. The authors have chosen not to suggest interpretations of the selections in introductory notes and have omitted exercises following the selections. The space so saved has been used to increase the number of selections, affording a freer choice in course organization for the teacher and more generous opportunities for extensive related reading by the student. The editors have made their selections with regard for enduring literary merit, usefulness in introductory courses, and range of techniques and themes representing the highest achievement in each of the literary types. The books are intended primarily for courses that aim at developing mature reading skill, but they do not restrict the teacher to a single means of attaining this end.

The handbooks are intended to facilitate rather than forestall classroom discussion. Hence they set forth their principles briefly, without elaboration, and with modest illustration. The editors have concentrated on preliminary and elementary suggestions for reading literary works. The student with little earlier experience in these matters may thus find help in getting started, while the more advanced student will find the handbooks useful for review. Often the teacher may wish to develop points beyond our discussion of them or, if the class procedure is inductive, to use the handbooks as references that summarize the discussion succinctly. They are, of course, no substitute for the guidance of an intelligent and sympathetic teacher.

The preface to the first edition recorded our indebtedness to our colleagues, to our editor, Mr. J. G. Case of The Macmillan Company, and to our wives. The intervening years have only increased these debts. The death of Professor Leslie L. Lewis as the preparation of this second edition neared completion moves the surviving partner in the enterprise to record the passing of a wise collaborator who became a good friend.

L. A.

Contents

INTRODUCTION xi

A HANDBOOK FOR THE STUDY OF DRAMA 1

PLAYS 25

SOPHOCLES / 495–405 B.C.
Antigone 26
(An English Version by Dudley Fitts and Robert Fitzgerald)
PLAUTUS / 250?–184 B.C.
Amphitryon 49
(Translated by Lionel Casson)
ANONYMOUS / 1500?
Everyman 80
(Translated by C. G. Child)
WILLIAM SHAKESPEARE / 1564–1616
The Tragedy of Hamlet, Prince of Denmark 97
MOLIÈRE / 1622–1673
The Misanthrope 166
(Translated by Richard Wilbur)
RICHARD BRINSLEY SHERIDAN / 1751–1816
The School for Scandal 200

HENRIK IBSEN / 1828–1906
Ghosts 251
(Translated by William Archer)
GEORGE BERNARD SHAW / 1856–1950
The Man of Destiny 291
ANTON CHEKHOV / 1860–1904
The Cherry Orchard 319
(Translated by Constance Garnett)
LUIGI PIRANDELLO / 1867–1936
It Is So! (If You Think So) 351
(English Version by Arthur Livingston)
JOHN MILLINGTON SYNGE / 1871–1909
Riders to the Sea 391
EUGENE O'NEILL / 1888–1953
Desire Under the Elms 400
FEDERICO GARCÍA LORCA / 1898–1936
Blood Wedding 436
(Translated by James Graham-Luján and Richard L. O.'Connell)
JEAN ANOUILH / 1910–
Becket or The Honor of God 467
(Translated by Lucienne Hill)
EUGENE IONESCO / 1912–
The Chairs 518
(Translated by Donald M. Allen)

INDEX OF AUTHORS, TITLES, AND LITERARY TERMS 545

Introduction

Because the aim of *Introduction to Literature* is to provide material for instruction in reading the various literary forms, *PLAYS* includes examples of various dramatic effects from farce to tragedy, in works representing many countries, centuries, and theatrical modes. This enlarged second edition adds *Amphitryon, Hamlet,* and *The Man of Destiny,* while dropping only two short plays of Yeats. The substitution of *The Misanthrope* for *The Miser* of Molière permits us to present an unusually deft and sparkling translation by Richard Wilbur. The arrangement of plays in the order of the authors' birth dates gives the student a suggestion of the period of the play as he takes it up, and allows the instructor freedom to assign the plays in accordance with his own approach.

In predominantly verse plays we have numbered every fifth line or an adjacent line if space did not permit numbering the proper line. Each line of verse has been counted but once even where there is a change of speaker midline. For *Hamlet* we have followed the standard numbering of the Globe text, with the result that the numbering of prose passages will appear to be arbitrary because the column width of this volume differs from that of the original Globe edition.

The headnotes impose no analysis, interpretation, or exercises upon the play introduced. Each headnote enables the student to place the dramatist in his social and theatrical milieu. Each also supplies suggestions for further reading of plays by the same dramatist, in the hope that the student will proceed on his own and gain experience enough to profit from dramatic criticism.

The handbook concentrates on overcoming the initial difficulties in reading plays, supplies some principles of dramatic structure, and introduces some terms useful in discussion. Being elementary, it may directly benefit the less experienced student and save the instructor's time for developing its points further.

L. A.

L. L. L.

Introduction to Literature: PLAYS

A Handbook
for the Study
of Drama

I. The Nature of Drama

Drama is a narrative art, one of several modes in which mankind has learned to present a story. Stories are presented to give pleasure, to entertain. In addition, they have a wide range of functions in a society; they may, for example, conserve its legends, order its laws, explore its problems, demonstrate its codes, ridicule its weaknesses, or extend its knowledge. Stories must in some way happen within the range of human nature; the emotions of the characters, their reasons for doing as they do, and how it feels to them to be in such situations must seem plausible, or at least possible, to the listener or reader of the story. If the story is of an age and order of ideas different from his own, he must be able to transplant himself—to be an ancient Greek, a medieval man, a renaissance man—but he still can reasonably expect the story to deal with human affairs recognizably like those of his own direct experience. Stories may be heard as recited by a storyteller, read as a short story or novel by a solitary reader, or seen and heard in the dramatic mode by a spectator in a theater. Our concern here is with a fourth mode of enjoying a story—reading a play.

Drama is composed not for a reader, as fiction and poetry are, but for spectators. The playwright works with a knowledge of the limitations and advantages of a specific kind of theater. He then entrusts his play to a director and actors, who produce the play before an audience. The production is interpreted and executed for a given kind of stage in a given kind of theater, the particular kind varying from one period of history to another. The audience reacts as a group, interprets, and varies its interpretations not only from age to age but also from night to night, from matinee to evening. What the playwright sets down in words is usually restricted to directions for setting and costuming, directions for acting, and the speeches of the characters. The result is "an imitation of an action," a story acted by its characters with a vividness beyond the reach of other literary forms. In ideal completeness, the result comes to a spectator who as one in an audience sees, hears, and feels the total effect of the performed play in the *dramatic present*.

The dramatic present is a complex spell cast over the spectators as they unite in *seeing* and *hearing* a story which is happening *there,* on the stage before them. Playwrights are at one with actors, directors, and technicians in dedication to living performances, with each performance, ideally, happening for the first time, and with no one aware of the conclusion until the conclusion appears. Reflection and criticism must wait until the final curtain; immediacy and intensity are re-created in each performance before each audience. Even though the spectator is aware that he is in a theater, watching a performance, and that he knows the outcome of the play, the pull of the dramatic present is forward.

The amount of story presented is foreshortened in a play; the action is initiated as close as possible to its final issue. The incidents are of high tension to start with, and the tension increases rapidly. The sense of finality, of hurrying to a conclusion, increases with each of the few incidents which can be exhibited in the limited time for a performance. The characters, under the pressure of the action, make discoveries and decisions rapidly. The pace and in-

2

tensity of drama give it its characteristic "dramatic" effect, an effect calculated for projection through an audience.

According to Aristotle, the playwright is combining six elements in a play: action, character, thought, language, music, and spectacle. Plays are not miscellaneous, episodic, or accidental, but artfully calculated and wrought, each one unified and made probable under its own assumptions and totality. Unity and probability, the pervasive qualities of plays, are produced within each play by careful harmonizing of the dramatic elements. A play is, in the best sense of the word, artificial, the work of an artificer, and of an artificer working with many arts and many nonverbal, as well as verbal, resources.

II. The Drama as Literature

With a theater, a stage, actors, an audience, and with resources of music and spectacle, dance and pantomime, gesture, action, costume, and setting to draw upon in the creation of a unified and plausible play, the playwright is obviously composing a work of art with more than words. The playwright does use words, though, and his product is thus a form of literature. Like fiction, it tells a story; like poetry, it makes imaginative use of language. And like other literary forms a play exists on paper, before and after its performance; hence it can be read. Shakespeare's plays were first printed in 1623; his readers have subsequently far outnumbered his spectators.

It is a paradoxical tribute to the power and permanence of great plays that they will have a reading audience long after, and far distant from, the specific theatrical conditions under which they were first produced—just as they will be produced under theatrical conditions far different from those for which they were composed. Aristotle in the *Poetics* analyzed, partly on the basis of reading, the tragedies of Aeschylus, Sophocles, and Euripides, which had been composed and produced more than a half century before. The tragedies he analyzed were composed for performance in an outdoor amphitheater, but they have subsequently been produced indoors on proscenium stages. Similarly, Shakespeare's plays have been read by people who have never seen them performed, and have been performed in outdoor theaters resembling the Greek and in indoor theaters resembling everything from a barn to an opera house, although the nature of the Elizabethan stage influenced the form of Shakespeare's plays.

Editors now supply the reader of early plays with helpful initial information which compensates for the bareness of the original text. Increasingly in modern times the playwright knows that if his play makes a genuine impact in the theater, it will be read by a great number of people who follow the drama as readers, whether they can be spectators or not. Playwrights have thus become somewhat more considerate of the reader in supplying external guidance to the time, place, setting, and characters than older dramatists were. With a touch of the whimsical essayist in his nature, J. M. Barrie first broke the rule of subtracting the playwright from the play in his published versions by inserting in his stage directions comments which were not expected to be directions to his actors. In *What Every Woman Knows* he remarks that there is nothing more comfortable than a horsehair chair if it has a good slit down the middle, and that Maggie, who is not good-looking, enters with her throat cut, so to speak, from ear to ear. George Bernard Shaw developed both the descriptive and interpretive support of the dialogue in the versions of his plays published to be read. His prefaces, often expanded after the play had been performed, draw the reader's attention to values in the play and to the significance of such values in society and life.

More important to the reader of a play than such post-mortem discussion are the expanded descriptions of scenes and characters in modern published plays. The playwright here has an opportunity to reach the reader with clues to the interpretation he hopes for, in the knowledge that his play, in this version, is to be read by a solitary spectator, who needs assistance in endowing the action with its full dramatic effect.

The solitary spectator poring over the text of a play is certainly not in the same relation to the play that he would be in if he were one of an audience watching a performance. Neither, however, is he quite in the position of the reader of a novel or of a poem. A play heavily equipped with interpretive prefaces (even by Shaw) is, as a novel, a bad novel. It is true that there is a kind of novel reader who tries to skip all the text except the dialogue, and a kind of novelist who tries to write the so-called dramatic novel—one which reduces the text as far as possible to dialogue. The novelist, however, is still composing for his art form, one which permits extension, omniscience, authorial intrusion, and many other devices forbidden to the playwright by the nature of the dramatic mode. The novelist may do all the work for the reader, even to telling him what he has read. The dramatist may do something for the reader by his title, informative stage directions, and descriptive cast of characters. The rest is dialogue, out of which the solitary spectator must make his play himself. He may—or may not—perform in his mind all the functions usually attended to on the stage by the set designer, the director, and the actors.

Whether the play reader should stage the play in his imagination as he reads it, to overcome the disadvantage of being at home rather than at the theater, or take advantage of his opportunity to read it as he reads a novel, is a question for which there is no dogmatic answer. The entire force of the playwright's art has been directed toward making the reader perform the play on a stage— even, if the reader is well-enough informed, on the particular kind of stage for which the playwright composed it: the open-air arena for Sophocles, the unlocalized and fluid Elizabethan stage for Shakespeare, the room with one wall removed for Ibsen. However, the stage to any playwright is a physical facility upon which he calculates how to reveal a story. The story will owe its vitality, finally, to our ability to relate it to life. The reader may therefore read through the stage to reality or directly from the page to reality. In reading *Romeo and Juliet* he may re-create "fair Verona, where we lay our scene," as a town in medieval Italy, as the stage of the Globe Theatre in Shakespeare's London, or as some ideal stage of his own designing. Whether he identifies himself with the protagonist or the director, whether he reads *to* the stage, *through* the stage, or *without* the stage, he is invited even by the printed play to yield to the unfolding situation, to see and hear, to form an active imaginative equivalent to the play. A more complete appreciation of the playwright's skill in overcoming the difficulties of the complex dramatic medium may come only with a second reading; certainly the perception of the artistry of a playwright is a rich addition to the first natural apprehension of a play.

Offering the play reader any alternative to "staging" the play as he reads is treason to the theater. By way of amends, the editors offer their belief that the play reader, starting with that degree of familiarity with the dramatic process he has gained from seeing plays and films and from reading poetry and fiction, will find a double enrichment in seeing plays produced as often as he can. His experiences as a reader will make him a more receptive and sensitive theatergoer; and his theater experience will make him a fuller reader. We do not really agree with George Jean Nathan, that inveterate playgoer, when he said (in an introduction to an anthology, of course), "Plays are meant to be acted well; if they are not thus well acted it is better that they be read than seen." We believe it is better to read a good play than neither to see it nor read it; we also believe that reading a play either before or after seeing it performed on stage or screen is a source of pleasure and understanding equal to that provided by reading fiction and poetry. Drama makes powerful comments on human nature and the human condition; it reveals human truth arising out of characters under the pressure of situation; it is a persuasive and memorable mode of conveying truth. Every civilized society has provided itself with the means of projecting itself, testing itself, exploring and judging itself in its theater.

III. The Elements of Drama

A. DRAMATIC CONVENTIONS

A play is manifestly not a real but an artificial representation of life. It asks from the audience an active adoption of the rules of the game—an acceptance of a good many dramatic conventions, in the spirit of "willing suspension of disbelief." Spectators know that they are in a theater; they bought tickets and found their seats. They know that the scene is only a scene on a stage; they saw the curtain drawn to reveal it. Within the play itself they accept conventions of time and space: a presentation of scenes years apart compressed into two hours, events most unnaturally uninterrupted by accidental distractions, and speech dealing unnaturally with one subject. They accept arrested time while they walk about between acts. They accept as whispers speeches loud enough to be heard in the balcony, asides heard by them and not by characters on the stage a few feet away from the speaker, soliloquies in which a character tells them more of himself than his fellow characters know, and so on ad infinitum. Some conventions are inherent in all drama; some are "dated" to conditions and modes in particular times. All conventions are a testimony to the pleasure the audience expects to receive by adopting them. The reader of a play should similarly adopt them, insofar as the printed play calls for their adoption, as concessions made to have an imaginatively or dramatically true experience of a play. Within the play, unity and probability are built upon the dramatic conventions.

B. THE PLAY STORY

A play compels "willing suspension of disbelief" for the artificial nature of the dramatic mode by offering a *story* that is clear, strong, and progressive enough to be plausible within the dramatic world. The story base of a play may be original with the dramatist or borrowed from legend, history, or fiction. Greek and Elizabethan dramatists commonly took a story already well known. The Joan of Arc story has been used by Shaw in *Saint Joan* and by Anouilh in *The Lark*. Oedipus of Thebes, Richard II, Mary, Queen of Scots, and Antigone, among others, have had more than one play constructed from their stories. Lorca is said to have developed *Blood Wedding* from a newspaper clipping he had kept for years.

Many stories are the original invention of the playwright. He may draw on his own life experiences, his memories, his reactions to the kind of life led by the people in places he has known. He may invent the story to express the characters or to protest against their environment. His initial impulse may come from an interest in situation, character, or theme.

Nowadays a short story or novel may become the basis of a play; an original play story or a novel or a short story may become the basis of a motion picture; any or all of them may become the basis of a television play. A good story, one into which perceptive interpretation of human life has been packed, will give pleasure in all four forms, but we must not expect the derivative form to be a precise equivalent of the original.

A natural but superficial complaint of the reader of a novel who subsequently sees it in play or screenplay form is that it has been changed. The dramatist left out a character; he suppressed a subplot; he changed the *reasons* for the actions of the characters. To note *why* the dramatist made the changes— how the total of the changes accounts for a good play made from a good novel or a good screenplay from a good play—is an illuminating exercise, but it should start from a recognition that changes *will be made* in any story as it is handled in a different medium. The dramatist may change many elements in a novel: the number and order of incidents, the number and the motives of characters, the atmosphere of the scenes, even, sometimes, the theme. More than one play is thus possible from a single life or a single story, more than one screenplay from a single play. Each has required an artist concentrated on making an intensely particular use of the source story within his mode.

What the playwright sees in a story, from whatever source, is a chance to develop it in a particular way to create the effect and express the meaning he has decided it can be made to have in his play. As playwright he has been called an artificer, joiner, chess player, architect—all terms calling attention to the necessity of careful workmanship to get a story constructed for the stage. Henry James has said: "The fine thing in a real drama, generally speaking, is that more than any other work of literary art, it needs a masterly structure. It needs to be shaped and fashioned and laid together, and this process makes a demand upon an artist's rarest gifts. He must combine and arrange, interpolate and eliminate, play the joiner with the most attentive skill; and yet at the end effectually bury his tools and his sawdust, and invest his elaborate skeleton with the smoothest and most polished integument."

1. DIALOGUE AND ACTION

A character in a play appears made-up for his part and at once starts talking and acting. The talking is the dialogue, the language resource of the playwright. The acting is not only the manner of delivery of the dialogue but the entire accompanying movement, gesture, pantomime, and stage business. Dialogue itself is, in a sense, a form of action, and the talking and the accompanying action are so fused that they seem one. We shall separate them for your attention and then combine them, for to a play reader the heart of the dramatic illusion is the realization of the fusion of dialogue and action so that each character seems to be himself, operating naturally under the circumstances of the play.

Dramatic dialogue is artfully concentrated, selected, and heightened for economy and intensity. The demands upon it in a play are many and various: it must explain, anticipate, and with the help of action execute the play story, but its existence, even with the support of dramatic conventions, depends upon its seeming to be the natural speech of particular characters. Speech is pervasively characteristic—voice, enunciation, pronunciation, accent, dialect, speech rate, vocabulary range, the fund of image-bearing knowledge revealed—all these and more attributes of speech daily tell us things about everyone we listen to. Coming to us from a made-up character accompanied by his actions, speech is both characteristic and characterizing. Speech is such a strong individualizing attribute that contrasts amounting to antitheses between protagonist and antagonist are often audibly reinforced by language. Richard II and Bolingbroke are men of the same class and time, as are Brutus and Marc Antony, but they are at opposite poles in speech as well as in principles.

Dialogue is supported constantly by its physical accompaniment, action, by movement, and in the total scene, by the settings or scenery. Characters in a play are seldom stationary for long—an unfolding play on a stage is a carefully patterned continuity of movement. Scenes expand and contract with the addition and subtraction of characters; groups form and dissolve; attention shifts from side to side or from upstage to downstage. Characters welcome callers, speed parting guests, answer telephones, pass teacups, lose tempers, draw swords, or swing fists—talking all the while. Stage business, as it is called, is an active accompaniment of and supplement to the dialogue. It may set out the speeches or overwhelm them in calculated violence and confusion, but a careful fusing of action and dialogue is the joint preoccupation of playwright, director, and actor. Reading an acting version of a play will supply reminders of the perpetual necessity of leading from one speech to the next by patterned movement, gesture, exits, and entrances to support the dialogue.

An excerpt from Sheridan's *The Rivals* will supply some simple illustrations of the efforts of the dramatist to fuse natural and characterizing dialogue with action in dramatic situations. Lydia and Julia, who have been exchanging confidences about their lovers, are surprised by the unexpected arrival of Sir Anthony Absolute and Mrs. Malaprop, the chief obstacles to the pursuit of their inclinations. Observe how the qualities suggested by the characters' names are developed by the dialogue.

(*Enter* LUCY *in a hurry.*)

LUCY. O Ma'am, here is Sir Anthony Absolute just come home with your aunt.

LYDIA. They'll not come here—Lucy, do you watch.

(*Exit* LUCY.)

JULIA. Yet I must go. Sir Anthony does not know I am here, and if we meet, he'll detain me, to show me the town. I'll take another opportunity of paying my respects to Mrs. Malaprop, when she shall treat me, as long as she chooses, with her select words so ingeniously *misapplied,* without being *mispronounced.*

(*Re-enter* LUCY.)

LUCY. O lud! Ma'am, they are both coming upstairs.

LYDIA. Well, I'll not detain you, coz. Adieu, my dear Julia. I'm sure you are in haste to send to Faulkland. There—through my room you'll find another staircase.

JULIA. Adieu.—(*Embrace.*)

(*Exit* JULIA.)

LYDIA. Here, my dear Lucy, hide these books. Quick, quick! Fling *Peregrine Pickle* under the toilet—throw *Roderick Random* into the closet—put *The Innocent Adultery* into *The Whole Duty of Man*—thrust *Lord Aimworth* under the sofa—cram *Ovid* behind the bolster—there—put *The Man of Feeling* into your pocket—so, so—now lay *Mrs. Chapone* in sight, and leave *Fordyce's Sermons* open on the table.

LUCY. Oh burn it, Ma'am! the hairdresser has torn away as far as *Proper Pride.*

LYDIA. Never mind—open at *Sobriety.*—Fling me *Lord Chesterfield's Letters*—Now for 'em.

(*Enter* MRS. MALAPROP, *and* SIR ANTHONY ABSOLUTE.)

MRS. MALAPROP. There, Sir Anthony, there sits the deliberate simpleton who wants to disgrace her family, and lavish herself on a fellow not worth a shilling!

LYDIA. Madam, I thought you once——

MRS. MALAPROP. You thought, Miss! I don't know any business you have to think at all. Thought does not become a young woman. But the point we would request of you is, that you will promise to forget this fellow—to illiterate him, I say, quite from your memory.

LYDIA. Ah! Madam! our memories are independent of our wills. It is not so easy to forget.

MRS. MALAPROP. But I say it is, Miss; there is nothing on earth so easy as to *forget,* if a person chooses to set about it. I'm sure I have as much forgot your poor dear uncle as if he had never existed—and I thought it my duty so to do; and let me tell you, Lydia, these violent memories don't become a young woman.

SIR ANTHONY. Why sure she won't pretend to remember what she's ordered not!—aye, this comes of her reading!

LYDIA. What crime, Madam, have I committed to be treated thus?

MRS. MALAPROP. Now don't attempt to extirpate yourself from the matter; you know I have proof controvertible of it. But tell me, will you promise to do as you're bid? Will you take a husband of your friend's choosing?

LYDIA. Madam, I must tell you plainly, that had I no preference for anyone else, the choice you have made would be my aversion.

MRS. MALAPROP. What business have you, Miss, with *preference* and *aversion?* They don't become a young woman; and you ought to know, that as both always wear off, 'tis safest in matrimony to begin with a little *aversion.* I am sure I hated your poor dear uncle before marriage as if he'd been a blackamoor—and yet, Miss, you are sensible what a wife I made!—and when it pleased heaven to release me from him, 'tis unknown what tears I shed! But suppose we were going to give you another choice, will you promise us to give up this Beverley?

LYDIA. Could I belie my thoughts so far as to give that promise, my actions would certainly as far belie my words.

MRS. MALAPROP. Take yourself to your room. You are fit company for nothing but your own ill-humours.

LYDIA. Willingly, Ma'am—I cannot change for the worse.

(*Exit* LYDIA.)

MRS. MALAPROP. There's a little intricate hussy for you!

SIR ANTHONY. It is not to be wondered at, Ma'am—all this is the natural consequence of teaching girls to read. Had I a thousand daughters, by heaven! I'd as soon have them taught the black art as their alphabet!

MRS. MALAPROP. Nay, nay, Sir Anthony, you are an absolute misanthropy.

SIR ANTHONY. In my way hither, Mrs. Malaprop, I observed your niece's maid coming forth from a circulating library! She had a book in each hand—they were half-bound volumes, with marble covers! From that moment I guessed how full of duty I should see her mistress!

MRS. MALAPROP. Those are vile places, indeed!

SIR ANTHONY. Madam, a circulating library in a town is as an evergreen tree of diabolical knowledge! It blossoms through the year! And depend on it, Mrs. Malaprop, that they who are so fond of handling the leaves, will long for the fruit at last.

MRS. MALAPROP. Fie, fie, Sir Anthony, you surely speak laconically!

SIR ANTHONY. Why, Mrs. Malaprop, in moderation, now, what would you have a woman know?

MRS. MALAPROP. Observe me, Sir Anthony. I would by no means wish a daughter of mine to be a progeny of learning; I don't think so much learning becomes a young woman; for instance— I would never let her meddle with Greek, or Hebrew, or Algebra, or Simony, or Fluxions, or Paradoxes, or such inflammatory branches of learning—neither would it be necessary for her to handle any of your mathematical, astronomical, diabolical instruments;—but, Sir Anthony, I would send her, at nine years old, to a boarding-school, in order to learn a little ingenuity and artifice. Then, Sir, she should have a supercilious knowledge in accounts—and as she grew up, I would have her instructed in geometry, that she might know something of the contagious countries—but above all, Sir Anthony, she should be mistress of orthodoxy, that she might not misspell, and mispronounce words so shamefully as girls usually do; and likewise that she might reprehend the true meaning of what she is saying. This, Sir Anthony, is what I would have a woman know— and I don't think there is a superstitious article in it.

Here, in a comedy with a love-under-difficulties plot, is the first appearance of Sir Anthony Absolute and Mrs. Malaprop, who have been indirectly characterized previously, the first as "hasty in everything" and the second as "an old tough aunt in the way." Julia's remarks, as she exits, about Mrs. Malaprop's ingenious misapplication of words, are addressed in part to the audience and prepare for that singularity. Lydia's spunky resourcefulness in deceit is shown by the disposition of the books, in a violent outburst of activity—fling, throw, thrust, cram—accompanied by a list of titles that direct satirical laughter at the popular novels of the day. In one brief encounter, the three characters are sorted out as two against one, but against a clever one; a cross intrigue is hinted at; and three characterizing speech mannerisms are exhibited.

In this illustrative scene, uncomplicated and low-pitched though it is, the reader is reminded of movement, given a chance to hear dialogue as action, and invited to fill in the full scene. The constant fusing of dialogue and action in the reader's mind as he sees and hears what he reads is what "lifts" the play, endows it with movement, shapes an active imaginative equivalent, and so enriches its significance and meaning that the play comes to seem more real than life itself.

2. PLOT

The playwright orders and connects the events in a story to form a *plot,* a causal or motivated sequence of actions which introduce a conflict into the lives of a group of characters, cause them to decide on certain courses of conduct in relation to the change, follow the alternating efforts of the two sides to a conclusion, and give a glimpse of the new state of affairs which arises as a result of the struggle.

That *conflict* is the basis of plot is another "rule rather than exception" in dramatic theory; many more plays have conflict plots than not. Most plays initiate a "purposive will," or free choice of a course of action by the challenged character; it is the pursuit of this purpose to its conclusion which gives coherence to the plot. The kind of person he is and the kind of persons he is engaged with and against in a conflict thus become premises of the plot at the time of its inception, and characters, the agents of the plot, often seem to be what the play is about.

In analyzing a plot, we will give most of our space not to its general nature, which is already familiar, but to the methods forced upon the playwright by the nature of the dramatic form. The common parts of a plot are:

1. The exposition, or preliminary situation.
2. The inciting or exciting force, or challenge.
3. The rising action, or complication.
4. The climax, or turning point (sometimes preceded by the crisis, which makes the direction of the turn final).
5. The denouement, resolution, or (in tragedy) catastrophe.

a. Exposition and Inciting Force. The *exposition* is all the information necessary for the reader to grasp the initial situation, to be able to go on with the play. A novelist may supply a "long foreground," a section of plain narrative dealing in a leisurely way with the preliminary situation, full of characterizing incidents that familiarize the reader with the potentials of the various characters before pressure is put upon them by the complication. The dramatist has no time for this; the time of a play is limited; the plot and not the preconditions of the plot is the heart of the matter. The members of the audience want to see and hear the situation develop as fast as their information allows them to grasp it. There was a time, in Thebes, when Antigone's brother had not been denied burial, and a time in Denmark when Hamlet's uncle had not murdered the king. *Antigone,* however, opens after the death of Polyneices, with Antigone already confronted with the edict of Creon against burying her dead brother; *Hamlet* opens with the king's ghost inciting the prince to revenge. The reader is hard pressed to get things sorted out, the people placed. He scents a future conflict between Antigone and Creon, between young Hamlet and his uncle. He is carried forward, is then delayed for further exposition, is then carried forward again.

Yet from the outset the exposition must be clear; who are these people, where are they, when is it, who is speaking to whom about what? The first revelations about the characters are also a matter of exposition. They must be "placed" by the reader before he can respond to the complication. The playwright, in developing exposition in a forward-moving situation, extends knowledge of the preliminary situation backward, and rounds out characters gradually by material that extends their pasts, reveals their secrets, or multiplies examples of their reactions. The presence of the past in the present or the pressure of a plot situation to force out of the characters secrets from their past lives is particularly suited to the dramatic mode. Ibsen, especially, often begins very late in the situation and makes disclosures both expository and dramatic of the difference between the initial glimpse of the character and the final truth.

The play reader is at no time at a greater disadvantage as compared with the spectator than at the opening of the play. On the stage the spectator can *see* the place, *see and hear* the characters, quickly sort them out, size them up, and move forward with the unfolding situation. Because the taking hold of a play by the reader at the outset is the key to his catching up with the spectator, the reader must give particular attention to the aids supplied by the playwright.

The first of these aids are the printed preliminaries. The title of the play, the time and place of the action, the setting, and the cast of characters—as much preconditioning of the imagination as possible—are usually given before the first scene. The reader will do well to start slowly, assimilating in advance what to expect. Prologues were formerly used to furnish a clue to the play's unifying idea as well as to its initial situation. Thus "scandal" is the Prologue's subject in Sheridan's *The School for Scandal*, preceding an opening scene in which Lady Sneerwell is conferring with Snake on the ruining of reputations in general and of Charles Surface's reputation in particular. Two servants talking about their masters, a time-honored device now out of fashion but still charmingly clear and direct, took care of the opening of many fine old plays. This "furniture-dusting," as it was called in derogation, did not complete the exposition, but initiated it with some arousing of expectation, as in Sheridan's *The Rivals:*

SCENE: *A street in Bath.*

(COACHMAN *crosses the stage.—Enter* FAG, *looking after him.*)

FAG. What!—Thomas!—Sure, 'tis he? —What!—Thomas!—Thomas!

COACHMAN. Hey!—Odd's life!—Mr. Fag!—give us your hand, my old fellow-servant.

FAG. Excuse my glove, Thomas:— I'm dev'lish glad to see you, my lad: why, my prince of charioteers, you look as hearty!—but who the deuce thought of seeing you in Bath!

COACHMAN. Sure, Master, Madam Julia, Harry, Mrs. Kate, and the postilion be all come!

FAG. Indeed!

COACHMAN. Aye! Master thought another fit of the gout was coming to make him a visit: so he'd a mind to gi't the slip, and whip! we were all off at an hour's warning.

FAG. Aye, aye! hasty in everything,

or it would not be Sir Antony Absolute!

COACHMAN. But tell us, Mr. Fag, how does young master? Odd! Sir Anthony will stare to see the Captain here!

FAG. I do not serve Captain Absolute now.

COACHMAN. Why sure!

FAG. At present I am employed by Ensign Beverley.

COACHMAN. I doubt, Mr. Fag, you ha'n't changed for the better.

FAG. I have not changed, Thomas.

COACHMAN. No! why, didn't you say you had left young master?

FAG. No.——Well, honest Thomas, I must puzzle you no farther: briefly then —Captain Absolute and Ensign Beverley are one and the same person.

COACHMAN. The devil they are!

FAG. So it is indeed, Thomas; and the *Ensign*-half of my master being on guard at present—the *Captain* has nothing to do with me.

COACHMAN. So, so!—What, this is some freak, I warrant!——Do tell us, Mr. Fag, the meaning o't—you know I ha' trusted you.

FAG. You'll be secret, Thomas?

COACHMAN. As a coach-horse.

FAG. Why then the cause of all this is—LOVE—Love, Thomas, who (as you may get read to you) has been a masquerader ever since the days of Jupiter.

COACHMAN. Aye, aye;—I guessed there was a lady in the case: but pray, why does your master pass only for

Ensign? Now if he had shammed *General*, indeed——

FAG. Ah! Thomas, there lies the mystery o' the matter. Hark'ee, Thomas, my master is in love with a lady of a very singular taste: a lady who likes him better as a *half-pay Ensign* than if she knew he was son and heir to Sir Anthony Absolute, a baronet of three thousand a year!

COACHMAN. That is an odd taste indeed!—but has she got the stuff, Mr. Fag? is she rich, hey?

FAG. Rich!—why, I believe she owns half the stocks—Z——ds! Thomas, she could pay the national debt as easily as I could my washerwoman! She has a lap-dog that eats out of gold—she feeds her parrot with small pearls—and all her thread-papers are made of bank-notes!

COACHMAN. Bravo!—Faith!—Odd! I warrant she has a set of thousands at least. But does she draw kindly with the Captain?

FAG. As fond as pigeons.

COACHMAN. May one hear her name?

FAG. Miss Lydia Languish. But there is an old tough aunt in the way; though, by the bye, she has never seen my master, for he got acquainted with Miss while on a visit in Gloucestershire.

COACHMAN. Well—I wish they were once harnessed together in matrimony. ——But pray, Mr. Fag, what kind of a place is this Bath? I ha' heard a deal of it—here's a mort o' merry-making, hey?

With this preparation, the affair of Ensign Beverley and Lydia Languish is in train: the inciting force, love; the complication, a tough old aunt and a hasty father named Absolute.

The *inciting force* is the first part of the exposition which is dynamic— that is, which contains a challenge, threat, or danger to the condition of the protagonist as first glimpsed. The characteristic most inciting forces have in common is that they confront the main character or protagonist with a situation he will not accept without resistance. The threat may be from an enemy or rival, from the protagonist's past, from another aspect of the protagonist's nature, from any source that arouses his will. A purposive course to defeat the threat is chosen by the protagonist. Recognizing from the preliminary situation what the inciting force is, and having seen the protagonist choose means to contest it, the reader is in a position to follow the rising action. Against Creon's edict forbidding burial for her brother is set Antigone's "I, then, will go to heap the earth above the brother whom I love." The ensuing course of the action may surprise, shock or baffle the first expectation, but it will not depart from the exposition base in a way unintelligible under the conditions offered.

b. Complication, Climax, and Denouement. The *rising action,* sometimes called the *complication* because it "ties the preliminary situation into a knot," consists of the actions taken by the protagonist and by the forces against him. The rising action usually consists of incidents in pairs, a move and a counter-move, the countermove producing the next move. Or each action is a consequence of the antecedent action and becomes in turn an antecedent for another consequence. The diversity of the forces that can be made to operate in a dramatic conflict, and of the dramatic effects that arise from the kind and order of the incidents, is so great that no rule can be offered except that the sequence should rise in intensity and finally resolve itself within the potential of the situation and characters. Any last-minute intervention of an unestablished force in order to extricate the protagonist from the consequences of the preceding action will mar both the probability and necessity of the action and break the spell of the dramatic present. Such interventions most often occur in comedy and melodrama: last-minute pardons from the king, unexpected inheritances from unmentioned grandmothers, deathbed confessions from unsuspected guilty parties. They are called *deus ex machina* after the old custom of lowering a god upon the stage to settle human affairs.

The *climax,* or *turning point,* is the event that determines how the conflict will end, favorably or unfavorably for the protagonist. The *denouement* or *catastrophe* presents the outcome, disposes of subplots, and gives a glimpse of a new, stable situation.

That the basis of a play (the unifying center to which the other dramatic elements contribute) is its action, the thing done, is a rule that supplies the reader his best connection with most plays. From Aristotle, again: "The plot, being an imitation of an action, must imitate one action and that a whole, the structural union of the parts being such that, if any one of them is displaced or removed, the whole will be disjointed and disturbed."

C. CHARACTERS

A good play, however, does not give the impression that it is a plot being acted out but that it is a group of characters acting as they must. The emotions of the characters give interest to the plot; the story seems to be what it has to be because the characters are as they are. The sense of probability (that these things could have happened under the conditions revealed by the play) and the sense of necessity (that they had to happen as they did) are alike served by the intimate or organic fusion of characters and action. As Brander Matthews said, "The conjunction of character and action is no chance mechanical mixture; it is rather an intimate chemical union." To put this another way: that some critics hold emotion rather than action to be the true stuff of drama is a tribute to the fusion of character and plot achieved by the playwright. The plot governs, but imperceptibly, because its development is conceived as necessary for its particular agents.

The cast of characters in a play will usually be as small as the dramatist can manage for unfolding his story. Having only two or three hours for the play, and needing to develop and exhibit the *essentials* of the situation fully, he will restrict himself not only in time (starting late in the story) but in characters. Some time must go to establishing any character; if too many characters are introduced, the principals are not fully enough developed to produce a sharp impression. Just as the action of the play is compressed, the number of characters is limited, so that each must carry his share of the action and be a representative figure in the representative world of the play.

Not all of the characters even in a selective cast will achieve an equal distinctness and individuality. Because the action must move as fast as characterization will let it, or impel it, the action must center on a few principal characters. No formula for major and minor characters holds for all plays, but the play reader will find it helpful to distinguish as quickly as possible between major, individualized characters and minor, more typical characters. It is not a reproach to a playwright to note that some of his characters are quickly established types—the play is not about them, and the time saved in characterizing them briefly by establishing the type pattern can be spent on the major characters and the major action.

Some modern playwrights, William Saroyan and William Inge, for example, do try to distribute the interest over a larger number of characters, which also means they try to distribute the action or the theme over a larger number, but there are still some type characters. Older dramatists worked in a social and intellectual milieu that was proud of its skill in assigning typical traits to many of the members of the society: Molière and Shakespeare drew freely upon the types their own age and society had identified and created characteristic behavior for: the pedant, the fop, the braggart, the soldier, the hypocrite, the gallant.

The main character in a plot—the one the dramatic pressure centers upon —is called the *protagonist;* his opponent is called the *antagonist,* or if not a person, the *antagonistic force.* Other roles which recur in drama because their functions are inherent in the nature of plot are the *confidant* (feminine *confidante*), in whom a major character confides; and the *foil,* who contrasts with, or is the opposite of, the protagonist. These last two roles may be combined in a single character. The dramatic mode tends to isolate the characters in a play from all interpretation of themselves except that which they give to one another in the play situation of which they are a part. To create a sense of what they were like before the play began and will be like after it has ended calls for a reach and insight on the dramatist's part to realize them, and a rich manipulation of language and action to project them. Many ephemeral plays contain characters who merely act the part the plot calls for and drop from memory with the fall of the curtain. Characters who so complete themselves that they are remembered as persons outside the details of their stories, as the creators rather than the victims of the dramatic necessity they served, give permanence to the play: Hamlet, Oedipus, Caliban, Shylock, Antigone, Hedda Gabler, Cyrano, Lear, Joan of Arc.

The playwright has several ways in which to characterize. He has, first of all, the appearance of the character, which he often specifies in stage directions. The age, sex, size, dress, and general physical type are instantly visible, probably more effectively so on the stage than in the descriptive characterizations of fiction. Each character appears "made up" for his part, perhaps exactly as the dramatist has specified, or perhaps as the imagination of the director has supplemented or interpreted the indications given by the playwright. The type or mold is quickly established. He then starts talking and acting. He may talk to the audience in asides and soliloquies, or to another character about a third. Language—not only what a character says but how he says it—is an intimate characteristic. In the interplay of characters, what each says about the others becomes indirect characterization of himself as well as direct characterization of his subjects. As the characters in a play talk and move about the stage, the interdependence of action and dialogue further develops characterization. What kind of person would decide to do this for that reason? Attraction, repulsion, or objectivity toward the characters is created in the audience by what they seem to be, what they seem to be doing, and why.

D. MEANING IN DRAMA

The meaning, or *theme,* of a play—that truth about human life, nature, or experience the playwright has founded his play story upon and adhered to in selecting and rejecting the psychology, language, and actions of his characters—is sometimes stated, phrased, or explicitly dramatized in the play. The play story may literally contain, and in its representation express, all that the play means. Or the play story may be a provocative, symbolic, or allusive means of leading the audience to the perception of a universal truth beyond or above its particulars. The theme of a play is often a basic truism about human nature's knowledge of itself and of the ordering of that moral world which is possible to it. Conflicts and their resolutions as precipitated between men and women, love and hate, tradition and revolt, desire and duty, passion and law, for example, stick close to our wisdom about ourselves and our universe.

The meaning of a specific play, grounded by a playwright in the unity of its subject, lies in the total response of the audience to the story and its agents, the characters. His plotting of the story, the dialogue, and other actions of the characters are among his means of leading the reader to the meaning. He may give a clue in the title of the play: *Everyman, Ghosts, Purgatory, The Green Pastures, The Sins of the Fathers, Pygmalion.* Within the play, action is meaningful—gesture, facial expressions, pauses, things *not* said. Dialogue also expresses the feelings, decisions, and conclusions of the character. Sometimes the meaning is in the interaction or conjunction of the lines, or in *how* they are spoken. Sometimes the speeches are directly thematic. In problem plays or thesis plays opposing lines of argument may be obtrusive, just as opposing sides of the conflict are, but under any dramatic tension characters speak not only as agents in an action but as human beings discovering principles and convictions as a result of that action. Here the reader is at home; he has formed his opinion of the characters; he responds to what is said in terms of who is saying it and why. He can recognize the thoughts the dramatist agrees with and those he introduces to discredit. Many good things are said in dramatic dialogue in this incidental fashion, some of them by the antagonistic characters or by characters on the wrong side of the central issue.

Perception of irony by the reader also stimulates his discovery of meaning.

Whenever he feels sure that two remarks are in contrast, with the truth in neither, whenever he is ahead of a character because he knows more than the character does, he is discovering meaning. Dramatic, or Sophoclean, irony, in which an outcome is foreknown by the reader but not by the character, directs the reader toward the meaning of the play as a whole.

The final meaning of a play, however, is the product of its total impression. In this sense, theme is structural; it is led up to and affirmed by the effect upon the reader of all the elements of the play. A play often "stages" its final conclusion about human life; if it does not, such a conclusion will be implicitly formulated by the reader. "What fools these mortals be" is a thematic statement by Puck. "As flies to wanton boys are we to the Gods, They kill us for their sport" is a thematic statement by Lear. The total meaning, however, is not suddenly impressed upon a play in its most conclusive speech or scene, but is the product of the emphasis, repetition, language, and structural guidance of the dramatist. That *unity* which Aristotle insisted a dramatic action should have, the unity we have stressed in the sections on the nature of drama, on plot, and on tragedy, is in part, certainly, a unity of subject. All the elements of a play contribute to making it probable that its particular meaning would emerge within the characters under the conditions offered.

IV. Traditional Types of Plays

Plays, like other works of art, nourish themselves on the subjects and forms of expression that are part of the surrounding society. Plays are distinctly contemporary upon their first appearance; sometimes they are trying to lead their society, and they collide with it; sometimes they are hand in glove with the tastes, ideas, and attitudes of their day. Greek tragedies were composed and performed for a national religious festival; mystery and morality plays were created by and for the medieval world; the Elizabethans flocked to their wooden O's to see their players show "the very age and body of the time his form and pressure."

Plays are as subject to imitation as other art forms; in any period, more plays like those already being welcomed are likely to appear. The common features of any successful type of play get assembled into something like a formula or set of rules. It is not true, of course, that two plays of the same type, whether by the same or different dramatists, are identical. The *Oedipus the King* and *Antigone* of Sophocles are not identical, though both are classical tragedies; *The Boor* and *The Proposal* of Chekhov are not identical, though both are farces. Yet plays can be classified into types, and a particular type of play, with the scope it affords for unified, probable, particular examples, may satisfy both dramatist and society for long periods of time.

Foreknowledge of the type of play he intends to create can be both a focus for the playwright's selection and combination of dramatic elements and a restraint upon his imagination. If he destroys the delicate balance between the frame and the individual creation within it the product may be rejected—and father no imitations. Audiences have been puzzled, shocked, and even infuriated by elements of novelty in plays, sometimes by the ideas, sometimes by the treatment. A battle between the defenders of the traditional, neoclassical mode and enthusiasts for a new romantic mode broke out during the performance of Victor Hugo's *Hernani* in Paris in 1830. The Abbey Theatre in Dublin had been the scene of so many riots against the religious, moral, or national implications of plays that W. B. Yeats, in trying to quiet the uproar over Sean O'Casey's *The Plough and the Stars,* told the audience, "You have once more rocked the cradle of a reputation." However, dramatists are often trying not only to please their age but to teach it, lead it, or advance it. They experiment, innovate, stretch or change the prevailing mode in order to say more or to say it in a new way; originality often wins after the initial shock wears off. But when elements of novelty do appear successfully in a familiar type of play, they will be noted, imitated, and formulated into rules for the new type. So by a mingled process of imitation and innovation, of model and experiment, of convention and revolt, drama progresses, keeps contemporary, keeps up with or ahead of its age. In a close study of the development of drama each emerging type in each social period is precisely defined; the degree and kind of adaptation and innovation are noted.

The recommendation of the players given by Polonius to Hamlet

The best actors in the world, either for tragedy, comedy, history, pastoral, pastoral-comical, historical-pastoral, tragical-historical, tragical-comical-historical-pastoral, scene individable, or poem unlimited: . . .

is often taken as Shakespeare's satirical comment on the overminute classification of plays, but the serious student of dramatic literature will need to know many of them, Polonius or no.

We offer here a division of drama into farce, comedy, melodrama, and tragedy, according to the response intended. Although drama runs the gamut from the lightest laughter to the proudest tears, these four responses underlie the specific types of plays in all periods. As points of reference, they will help orient the reader in any play.

A. FARCE

Farce aims at laughter, provoked by outrageous assaults on decorum and restraint. Farce uses violent or slapstick behavior, exaggerated pantomime, clowning, absurd situations, gags, and wisecracks, usually combined in a fast-paced uproar of cross-purposes and misunderstandings. Situations are nonsensical or iconoclastic in farce—identical twins mistaken for one another, the right people in the wrong bedrooms, the "chase," in which everybody chases everybody else without knowing why, the beating and berating of people under false impressions, abused marital misunderstandings. The whole is offered for its display of human behavior out of control. Physical impropriety and violence are not the only means of farcing; release of restrictive bonds may be plotted into quiet, underplayed displays of hilarious escapes from the fetters of decorum.

Farce has an ancient and honorable history; it is an artistic medium when it serves its limited, but salutary, aims with successful means. Its "thoughtless laughter" is one response that drama seems endlessly suited to evoke. It is difficult to name farces without trespassing upon farce-comedy, for involvement with the characters, or relation of the situation to a serious view of life, moves the farce out of orbit. However, the "fine old art of farce" may, by careful treatment of its materials, rise far above slapstick. It is an art in itself and a contributor to high comedy. Shakespeare's *The Comedy of Errors*, Oscar Wilde's *The Importance of Being Earnest*, Chekhov's *The Boor* and *The Proposal*, Anatole France's *The Man Who Married a Dumb Wife*, Molière's *Scapin*, and Feydeau's *Keep an Eye on Amélie* are a few examples of farces given immortality by skilled exploitation of the resources of the type.

B. COMEDY

Comedy grows out of farce by almost imperceptible gradations. The farcical element, the resort to hamming, clowning, wisecracking, or wide-open absurdity to stimulate laughter, is the spice of life to many comedies. Laughter engenders laughter; a little thoughtless laughter may engender some thoughtful laughter. Light comedy or farce-comedy are serviceable terms covering a wide middle band between farce and high comedy. In general, comedy presents plot situations more probable than those of farce, more serious and believable, but not threatening or fatal. The characters are not the complete stereotypes that people farces; they are socially recognizable, slightly individualized; we can laugh at or with them with some concern for their predicaments. However, they do not compel our identification with them or cause us to think of grave issues through them. The laughter of comedy may be the "warm laughter" of secure and affectionate faith in the imperfect but admirable world in which good people have passing troubles with one another, as in Shakespeare's *A Midsummer Night's Dream* or *As You Like It*, Eugene O'Neill's *Ah! Wilderness*, Lindsay and Crouse's *Life with Father*. It may be the "corrective laughter" of satire, from gentle to savage, directed at a ridiculous incongruity, abnormality, or excess of a human trait, as in Molière's *Tartuffe* and Ben Jonson's *Volpone*. The laughter of comedy may be laughter at wit, the epigram, the telling exchange, the contest for cleverness between sophisticated people, as in comedy of manners. Intellectual comedy, or the comedy of ideas, uses situations and characters to produce "thoughtful laughter," not on the gravest issues of life, but on irrationalities in the society. Whether overlapping with farce or extending to a vision of humor as a socially healthful force, comedy is a dramatic effect that engenders many subtypes as societies change, for it is a distinctly social mirror. All comedy is perhaps related, as the branches of a tree are related to the trunk, by being rooted in a *comic vision*, a mood in which the world seems manageable, somehow, by treating its passing difficulties with a sense of humor, with gaiety, with a protective wit aimed partly at ourselves.

C. MELODRAMA, DRAME, AND PROBLEM PLAY

Melodrama used as a term for a type of play applies not only to the mystery-thriller, but to plays of strong plot situations and strong emotions, full of possible but usually averted disaster for the sympathetic characters. It enlists identification rather than detachment. It often exploits "poetic justice" and engenders pity for the protagonist and hate for the antagonist. It poses serious consequences for the protagonist, but sometimes does not pose them quite honestly. They are external and will be escaped or evaded somehow.

The honest melodrama, which offers such excitements as are made possible by a few easy assumptions about the characters and about the element of chance, luck, or coincidence in solving situations, is, of course, a perfectly legitimate dramatic type that does not need to apologize for itself. The common statement that farce is to comedy what melodrama is to tragedy sometimes implies that farce and melodrama are lower forms of artistic endeavor, and from one point of view they are, but in very few periods would the theater have survived if farce and melodrama had been subtracted from it. All ages seem to like to laugh and to escape. Since both farce and melodrama produce strong reactions by visible means, they are at home in motion pictures, and their appeal there is perennial; but they often arrive on the screen from the stage.

At the top of its possibilities, melodrama overlaps with serious drama, or *drame,* and with the problem play and approaches tragedy. The problem play, which uses melodramatic effects to protest a social evil, is a serious drama with an immediate social purpose; it uses the strong emotions of melodrama to compel action. Some problem plays outlast their immediate applicability and live on the human values the problem reveals, and thus received seem to be *drame* or tragedy. The characters, again, mark the difference.

D. TRAGEDY

The tragic effect is the hardest of the dramatic effects to define and the one that is subjected to the greatest defining effort. So much effort, in fact, has gone into the theory of tragedy that the reader may be diverted to theory before he has enough experience with tragedies to have a foundation in his own responses. We therefore simplify in terms of the rule rather than the exceptions, and recommend postponing the refining of tragic theory until many tragedies have been read.

*Trage*dy represents characters whose wills are set on courses necessary to their own moral natures and who are overpowered by the forces against them. The following paragraph from Aristotle's *Poetics* (which was translated by S. H. Butcher) states the effect to be produced as pity and fear and indicates the nature of the tragic protagonist.

A perfect tragedy should imitate actions which excite pity and fear, this being the distinctive function of tragic imitation. It follows plainly, in the first place, that the change of fortune presented must not be the spectacle of a virtuous man brought from prosperity to adversity, for this moves neither pity nor fear; it merely shocks us. Nor, again, that of a bad man passing from adversity to prosperity, for nothing can be more alien to the spirit of Tragedy; it possesses no single tragic quality; it neither satisfies the moral sense nor calls forth pity or fear. Nor, again, should the downfall of an utter villain be exhibited. A plot of this kind would doubtless satisfy the moral sense, but it would inspire neither pity nor fear; for pity is aroused by unmerited misfortune, fear by the misfortune of a man like ourselves. Such an event, therefore, will be neither pitiful nor terrible. There remains, then, the character between these two extremes—that of a man who is not eminently good and just, yet whose misfortune is brought about not by vice or depravity, but by some error or frailty. He must be one who is highly renowned and prosperous—a personage like Oedipus, Thyestes, or other illustrious men of such families.

The tragic protagonist, by the strength of his will, the sincerity of his choice of a course of action, and the strenuousness of his efforts, compels extreme identification. We pity the impotence of the highest human powers in an imperfect individual imbued with them, and watch fearfully while forces stronger than such a protagonist overwhelm him. His destruction is inescapable, unacceptable, and should produce a painful resentment at the moral imperfection or poetic injustice in the universe.

Instead, tragedy "through pity and fear effects the proper katharsis of those emotions." Aristotle's phrase has been analyzed through the centuries; does *katharsis* mean "purgation," or does it mean "purification"; does it mean to empty the mind of the spectator of pity and fear or to raise the mind above them, replace them by exaltation, admiration, reconciliation?

The tragic protagonist contests the external and dramatically visible forces arrayed against him, but this visible and particular contest is only an outward representation of his internal conflict. He has responded to a compelling moral challenge by a decision reached alone. He often answers to his defeat with a defiant affirmation of the rightness of his choice. Under the particulars of any tragedy lies the universal principle that soul-searching catastrophes are a part of the human situation in a universe not committed to indulging the individual will. Individuals who have power to defy and rise above the catastrophic repudiation of their wills exalt mankind.

The effects of tragedy being the most profound and elevating of all dramatic effects, and the achievement of tragedy the highest reach of dramatic art, it is natural that dramatic criticism concentrates on the nature, laws, and purity of tragedy. Tragedy that passes the most exacting tests is rare. In his *The Anatomy of Drama,* Alan Reynolds Thompson finds only three eras in which great tragedies have been produced: in Athens in the fifth century B.C., in Elizabethan England, and in the Paris of Louis XIV. He then lists twenty supreme tragedies for all the centuries represented, with none after Racine, although Ibsen's *Ghosts* would be his next choice.

As noted above, the interplay between the theater and its society is very close; the possibility or impossibility of achieving supreme tragedies has therefore been used as a test for societies. Currently we are debating whether little men rather than highly renowned men are possible tragic protagonists, whether the modern world is capable of producing true tragedies, whether we have a sense of a moral order to ground them in.

However, the acute dissection of tragedy should follow upon an acquaintance with many of them; with, say, the twenty in Professor Thompson's list. A slightly less than supreme tragedy is still a wonderfully rewarding play to read, and the "foothills of tragedy," which slope down from the lofty peaks to the plain of ordinary melodrama, are well worth exploring also.

Viewed structurally, tragedies vindicate fully the causal plot structure we have sketched, since inevitability must be demonstrated out of challenge and response to force us to accept the tragic outcome. They are unified, made probable and inevitable, by harmonizing a strong character, capable of searching and revealing emotions we can identify as universal, with a tragic world which declares through tone, spectacle, language, and action that it is antagonistic, violent, and destructive. We enter into the kind of pity and fear which will lead to purgation of those emotions through extreme identification or empathy with the protagonist. We contest his fate, and so will accept no easy means or artificial circumstances. The plot does govern a tragedy, but the illusion that we are watching people acting as they must, having their moral natures, being themselves in their circumstances, must survive our own desire to break with the illusion. The inevitability of defeat under the conditions offered, and the recognition of internal triumph in external defeat, are the two fused elements in the tragic effect.

V. Modern Plays

Until modern times, the playwright's efforts were directed toward unifying the elements of drama to produce the effect of farce, comedy, melodrama, or tragedy in some pure or acceptably blended form. He had before him, also, a prevailing theatrical style. One theatrical style succeeded another: romantic tragedy gave way to neoclassical tragedy; neoclassical comedies gave way to realistic comedies. The whole society was permeated with the changed beliefs, tastes, and attitudes that the changing theatrical styles derived from and expressed.

The modern age, however, is not unified in acceptance of any one set of basic concepts; it has had too many shocks, too rapid an assault on the old, and too many rival claimants for the new. Roughly, the vigorous transformation of the play, the stage, and acting was directed first at greater realism, in the sense of a more exact external representation of the internal life the playwright felt his characters to have.

Naturalism is a term used for a deterministic realism, one in which the characters are the products of their environment, and the forces that play upon the characters are what the play is really about. Revelations of the conditioning of characters by heredity, economic circumstances, and the mores, codes, and loyalties of cultures, sometimes coupled with theses directed at modifying them, mark naturalistic plays. Realism in the sense of fidelity to fact or detail is a method that can be employed either in naturalistic plays or in plays of non-deterministic ideology.

Under the impetus toward realistic depiction of life, stage settings were made painstakingly exact replicas of the environmental envelope that had engendered the play story. The room-with-one-wall-removed concept went hand in hand with a new realistic school of ensemble acting, spreading from Konstantin Stanislavsky's directing of Chekhov's plays at the Moscow Art Theater. Ignoring the audience, each actor carried out his identity as a character, dealing with other characters in a group in a room, unaware that one wall had been removed. Dialogue and costume became realistic also.

Developments in modern drama came very rapidly once the stage set out to catch up with the previous responses of the other arts to the changed conditions in modern society. Ibsen is usually regarded as the pioneer in naturalistic treatments of middle-class lives in middle-class environments. But segments of society far below those depicted by Ibsen followed on the stage: ordinary life as lived by common people, working-class people, and down-and-out people was represented with realistic fidelity to the hovel, tenement, farmhouse, dive or water front that was their world in such plays as Gorky's *The Lower Depths,* Rice's *Street Scene,* O'Neill's *Desire Under the Elms,* O'Casey's *Juno and the Paycock.*

Realism, whether associated with deterministic themes or not, continued as the dominant theatrical style in modern drama, but the conviction that much of the truth of life cannot be equated with its externals led to various anti-realistic or presentational styles: symbolism, expressionism, theatricalism. The invisible inner life, sometimes shockingly or absurdly at variance with the objectively demonstrated product-of-forces interpretation, received dramatic expression in antirealistic ways, ways that made the invisible visible according to laws other than materialistic.

Both realism and antirealism took advantage of a series of brilliant, zealous enlargements of the possibilities of stagecraft. The stage has been made revolving, has been surrounded by spectators in arena staging, or theater in the round, has been made flexible and unlocalized. Increased command over lighting and sound has aided all the arts contributing to theater in capturing on the stage a more complete illusion of life.

Traditional drama would have been suffused with the modern cast of man, with the modern view of society, and with the effects of the new theatrical resources even if it had continued to produce farces, comedies, melodramas, and tragedies in some familiar form. But the modern playwright is himself part of the diversity and uncertainty of modern man's views of himself and his universe. He resists creating a pure or traditional effect (comedy or tragedy) and resists a single style. He blends, crosses, and combines both diverse dramatic effects and diverse theatrical styles in the same play. Perhaps the most disconcerting aspect of modern drama to audiences and readers first exposed to it was its *mixed* nature: naturalism dissolved into fantasy, every character had his own story, the brutal and the tender were juxtaposed, the most limiting realism was succeeded by symbols universalizing the implications, characters dropped from a present action into a flashback of childhood. The modern playwright, however, has not abandoned unity or harmony. By remaining free to manipulate many dramatic elements, he tries to achieve an illusion of life in a play full of its own nature, carrying its own seal of dramatic probability upon it. He is still an artificer, but one working with many more tools.

The reader encounters in antirealistic plays the same mingling of farce and pathos, of internal and external states of mind, of symbol and action, that is offered him in antirealistic fiction and poetry. The structure of conflict, however, still underlies most antirealistic plays and provides the reader with his best lead through the play. Only when language itself is subordinated or dispensed with, as in the theater of the absurd, will the reader find that the unity-of-action lead is unprofitable to follow. The various types of nonrealistic settings and the interpretative use of music and spectacle will challenge the reader's imaginative powers, but his orientation in the modern ideas and arts that underlie the new theater will be a compensating aid.

For Further Reading

A. COLLECTIONS OF PLAYS, SOME WITH TREATMENTS OF DRAMA OR OF THE DRAMATISTS REPRESENTED

ALLISON, ALEXANDER W., ARTHUR J. CARR, and ARTHUR M. EASTMAN. 1957, 1966. *Masterpieces of the Drama*. New York: The Macmillan Company.

BROOKS, CLEANTH, and ROBERT B. HEILMAN. 1960. *Understanding Drama.* New York: Holt, Rinehart & Winston.

REINERT, OTTO. 1961. *Drama: An Introductory Anthology.* Boston: Little, Brown and Company.

———. 1961. *Modern Drama.* Boston: Little, Brown and Company.

BLOCK, HASKELL M., and ROBERT G. SHEDD (eds.). 1962. *Masters of Modern Drama.* New York: Random House.

HOGAN, ROBERT, and SVEN ERIC MOLIN, 1962. *Drama: The Major Genres.* New York: Dodd, Mead & Company.

CORRIGAN, ROBERT W. 1964. *The Modern Theatre.* New York: The Macmillan Company.

B. DRAMATIC THEORY AND CRITICISM

BENTLEY, ERIC. 1946. *The Playwright As Thinker.* New York: William Morrow and Company; Meridian Books, 1957.

CLARK, BARRETT H. 1947. *European Theories of the Drama.* Rev. ed. New York: Crown Publishers, Inc.

THOMPSON, ALAN REYNOLDS. 1948. *The Anatomy of Drama.* 2nd ed. Berkeley, Calif.: University of California Press.

———. 1948. *The Dry Mock, A Study of Irony in Drama.* Berkeley, Calif.: University of California Press.

POTTS, L. J. 1949. *Comedy.* London: Hutchinson University Library.

BUTCHER, S. H. 1951. *Aristotle's Theory of Poetry and Fine Art.* New York: Dover Publications, Inc.

KRUTCH, JOSEPH WOOD. 1953. *"Modernism" in Modern Drama.* Ithaca, N. Y.: Cornell University Press.

GASSNER, JOHN. 1954. *Masters of the Drama.* 3rd ed. New York: Dover Publications, Inc.

KITTO, H. D. F. 1955. *Greek Tragedy.* Garden City, N. Y.: Doubleday & Company, Inc.

MEYERS, HENRY ALONZO. 1956. *Tragedy, A View of Life.* Ithaca, N. Y.: Cornell University Press.

SYPHER, WYLIE (ed.). 1956. *Comedy: An Essay on Comedy, by George Meredith. Laughter, by Henri Bergson. The Meaning of Comedy, by Wylie Sypher.* Garden City, N. Y.: Doubleday & Company, Inc.

HARTNOLL, PHYLLIS (ed.). 1957. *Oxford Companion to the Theatre.* 2nd ed. rev. London: Oxford University Press.

McCOLLUM, WILLIAM C. 1957. *Tragedy.* New York: The Macmillan Company.

NICOLL, ALLARDYCE. 1958. *An Introduction to Dramatic Theory.* 4th ed. rev. London: G. G. Harrap.

SEWALL, RICHARD BENSON. 1959. *The Vision of Tragedy.* New Haven, Conn.: Yale University Press.

COLE, TOBY (ed.). 1960. *Playwrights on Playwriting.* New York: Hill & Wang.

ROWE, KENNETH THORPE. 1960. *A Theatre in Your Head.* New York: Funk & Wagnalls Company.

GASSNER, JOHN. 1964. *Ideas in the Drama.* New York: Columbia University Press.

Plays

SOPHOCLES / 495–405 B.C.

Sophocles was born at Colonus, near Athens, and grew up into the golden age of Pericles. For about a half century before the birth of Sophocles, Athens had held an annual Dionysia, a national religious festival developed out of earlier choric dances in honor of Dionysus (Bacchus), the god of wine and vegetation. By the time of Sophocles, three dramatists competed in an outdoor theater before audiences of up to fifteen thousand. The seats were arranged in a semicircle rising above a level acting area in front of a long, low building which served as palace facade and dressing room. The actors wore masks, long robes, and perhaps raised shoes. Between the acting area and the audience a chorus was stationed. It reacted to and interpreted the action. The leader of the chorus (choragos) spoke.

The stories of Greek tragedy were familiar to the Greek audience; the presentation could be new to them, and could be made to interpret and comment on underlying matters—the relation of gods to men, the individual in conflict with the state, the difference between prophecy and predetermination. The acting out of mythological stories had developed from within the earlier choric dance; when first one, then two, then (by Sophocles) three actors were added, the dramatic had gained ascendancy over the lyrical. To Sophocles, the chorus was still an important part of the action, but the imitation of a tragic conflict between the will of man and the will of the gods was the major issue.

Sophocles was in his twenties when he first won the prize over Aeschylus, an older tragic dramatist, and in his long life Sophocles also competed against his great successor, Euripides. Sophocles wrote over a hundred plays, of which seven survive; he won the prize some twenty times; and like Aeschylus and Euripides he was honored and rewarded by the city for his talents.

We present *Antigone* here; *Oedipus the King* and *Electra* of Sophocles, the *Agamemnon* and *Prometheus Bound* of Aeschylus, and the *Medea* and *The Trojan Women* of Euripides are other treasured examples of Greek tragedy.

Antigone*

AN ENGLISH VERSION BY DUDLEY FITTS
AND ROBERT FITZGERALD

THE CHARACTERS

ANTIGONE, *daughter of Œdipus, former banished king.*

ISMENE, *her elder sister.*

CREON, *their maternal uncle, now King of Thebes.*

* There is no standard reference for the line numbering of *Antigone*. We have numbered verse every five lines. A continued line of verse, regardless of a change in speakers midline or regardless of a break midline, still counts as one line. The prose has been numbered approximately every five lines typographically set. When the width of a line has not permitted the inclusion of a line number, either the previous line or the following line has been numbered.

26

HAIMON, *Creon's son, beloved of An-tigonê.*

EURYDICE, *the Queen, his mother, whose other son has just been killed defending Thebes from attack.*

TEIRESIAS, *the old and blind seer or prophet.*

A SENTRY *and* A MESSENGER

THE CHORUS *of fifteen Thebans, elder citizens, among whom the* CHORAGOS *is the leader.*

TIME: *The legendary past of Ancient Greece.*

PLACE: *The walled city of Thebes with its seven gates.*

PROLOGUE

(*Scene: Before the palace of* CREON, *King of Thebes. A central double door, and two lateral doors. A platform extends the length of the façade, and from this platform three steps lead down into the 'orchestra,' or chorus-ground. Time: Dawn of the day after the repulse of the Argive army from the assault on Thebes.*)

(ANTIGONE *and* ISMENE *enter from the central door of the Palace.*)

ANTIGONE. Ismenê, dear sister,
You would think that we had already suffered enough
For the curse on Œdipus:
I cannot imagine any grief
That you and I have not gone through. And now—   5
Have they told you of the new decree of our King Creon?
  ISMENE. I have heard nothing: I know
That two sisters lost two brothers, a double death
In a single hour; and I know that the Argive army
Fled in the night; but beyond this, nothing.   10
  ANTIGONE. I thought so. And that is why I wanted you

To come out here with me. There is something we must do.
  ISMENE. Why do you speak so strangely?
  ANTIGONE. Listen, Ismenê:
Creon buried our brother Eteoclês   15
With military honours, gave him a soldier's funeral,
And it was right that he should; but Polyneicês,
Who fought as bravely and died as miserably,—
They say that Creon has sworn
No one shall bury him, no one mourn for him,   20
But his body must lie in the fields, a sweet treasure
For carrion birds to find as they search for food.
That is what they say, and our good Creon is coming here
To announce it publicly; and the penalty—
Stoning to death in the public square!
                    There it is,   25
And now you can prove what you are:
A true sister, or a traitor to your family.
  ISMENE. Antigonê, you are mad! What could I possibly do?
  ANTIGONE. You must decide whether you will help me or not.
  ISMENE. I do not understand you. Help you in what?   30
  ANTIGONE. Ismenê, I am going to bury him. Will you come?
  ISMENE. Bury him! You have just said the new law forbids it.
  ANTIGONE. He is my brother. And he is your brother, too.
  ISMENE. But think of the danger! Think what Creon will do!
  ANTIGONE. Creon is not strong enough to stand in my way.   35
  ISMENE. Ah sister!
Œdipus died, everyone hating him
For what his own search brought to light, his eyes
Ripped out by his own hand; and Iocastê died,

His mother and wife at once: she twisted
    the cords   40
That strangled her life; and our two
    brothers died,
Each killed by the other's sword. And we
    are left:
But oh, Antigonê,
Think how much more terrible than
    these
Our own death would be if we should go
    against Creon   45
And do what he has forbidden! We are
    only women,
We cannot fight with men, Antigonê!
The law is strong, we must give in to the
    law
In this thing, and in worse. I beg the
    Dead
To forgive me, but I am helpless: I must
    yield   50
To those in authority. And I think it is
    dangerous business
To be always meddling.

    ANTIGONE.   If that is what you think,
I should not want you, even if you asked
    to come.
You have made your choice, you can be
    what you want to be.   54
But I will bury him; and if I must die,
I say that this crime is holy: I shall lie
    down
With him in death, and I shall be as dear
To him as he to me.
                 It is the dead,
Not the living, who make the longest
    demands: 59
We die for ever. . .
                You may do as you like,
Since apparently the laws of the gods
    mean nothing to you.

    ISMENE.   They mean a great deal to
    me; but I have no strength
To break laws that were made for the
    public good.

    ANTIGONE.   That must be your ex-
    cuse, I suppose. But as for me,
I will bury the brother I love.

    ISMENE.   Antigonê,   65
I am so afraid for you!

    ANTIGONE.   You need not be:

You have yourself to consider, after all.

    ISMENE.   But no one must hear of
    this, you must tell no one!
I will keep it a secret, I promise!

    ANTIGONE.   Oh, tell it! Tell every-
    one!   70
Think how they'll hate you when it all
    comes out
If they learn that you knew about it all
    the time!

    ISMENE.   So fiery! You should be
    cold with fear.

    ANTIGONE.   Perhaps. But I am doing
    only what I must.

    ISMENE.   But can you do it? I say
    that you cannot.   75

    ANTIGONE.   Very well: when my
    strength gives out, I shall do no
    more.

    ISMENE.   Impossible things should
    not be tried at all.

    ANTIGONE.   Go away, Ismenê:
I shall be hating you soon, and the dead
    will too,
For your words are hateful. Leave me
    my foolish plan: 80
I am not afraid of the danger; if it means
    death,
It will not be the worst of deaths—
    death without honour.

    ISMENE.   Go then, if you feel that
    you must.
You are unwise,
But a loyal friend indeed to those who
    love you.   85

*(Exit into the Palace. ANTIGONE goes
off, L.)*

(Enter the CHORUS.)

PÁRODOS

    CHORUS.   *[strophe 1]*
Now the long blade of the sun, lying
Level east to west, touches with glory
Thebes of the Seven Gates. Open,
    unlidded
Eye of golden day! O marching light
Across the eddy and rush of Dircê's
    stream,   5
Striking the white shields of the enemy

Thrown headlong backward from the
    blaze of morning!
  CHORAGOS.   Polyneicês   their   com-
    mander
Roused them with windy phrases,
He the wild eagle screaming   10
Insults above our land,
His wings their shields of snow,
His crest their marshalled helms.

    CHORUS.   [*antistrophe 1*]
Against our seven gates in a yawning
    ring
The famished spears came onward in the
    night;   15
But before his jaws were sated with our
    blood,
Or pinefire took the garland of our
    towers,
He was thrown back; and as he turned,
    great Thebes—
No tender victim for his noisy power—
Rose like a dragon behind him, shouting
    war.   20
  CHORAGOS.   For God hates utterly
The bray of bragging tongues;
And when he beheld their smiling,
Their swagger of golden helms,
The frown of his thunder blasted   25
Their first man from our walls.

    CHORUS.   [*strophe 2*]
We heard his shout of triumph high in
    the air
Turn to a scream; far out in a flaming arc
He fell with his windy torch, and the
    earth struck him.
And others storming in fury no less than
    his   30
Found shock of death in the dusty joy of
    battle.
  CHORAGOS.   Seven captains at seven
    gates
Yielded their clanging arms to the god
That bends the battle-line and breaks it.
These two only, brothers in blood,   35
Face to face in matchless rage,
Mirroring each the other's death,
Clashed in long combat.

  CHORUS.   [*antistrophe 2*]
But now in the beautiful morning of
    victory
Let Thebes of the many chariots sing for
    joy!   40
With hearts dancing we'll take leave of
    war:
Our temples shall be sweet with hymns
    of praise,
And the long night shall echo with our
    chorus.

SCENE 1

  CHORAGOS.   But now at last our new
    King is coming:
Creon of Thebes, Menoiceus' son.
In this auspicious dawn of his reign
What are the new complexities   4
That shifting Fate has woven for him?
What is his counsel? Why has he sum-
    moned
The old men to hear him?
  (*Enter* CREON *from the Palace, C. He
addresses the* CHORUS *from the top step.*)
  CREON.   Gentlemen: I   have   the
honour to inform you that our Ship of
State, which recent storms have threatened to destroy, has come safely to   *11*
harbour at last, guided by the merciful
wisdom of Heaven. I have summoned
you here this morning because I know
that I can depend upon you: your devotion to King Laïos was absolute;   *16*
you never hesitated in your duty to our
late ruler Œdipus; and when Œdipus
died, your loyalty was transferred to his
children. Unfortunately, as you know, his
two sons, the princes Eteoclês and   *21*
Polyneicês, have killed each other in
battle; and I, as the next in blood, have
succeeded to the full power of the
throne.   25
  I am aware, of course, that no Ruler
can expect complete loyalty from his
subjects until he has been tested in office. Nevertheless, I say to you at the
very outset that I have nothing but contempt for the kind of Governor who is
afraid, for whatever reason, to fol-   *32*

low the course that he knows is best for
the State; and as for the man who sets
private friendship above the public welfare,—I have no use for him, either. I
call God to witness that if I saw my   37
country headed for ruin, I should not be
afraid to speak out plainly; and I need
hardly remind you that I would never
have any dealings with an enemy of the
people. No one values friendship   42
more highly than I; but we must remember that friends made at the risk of
wrecking our Ship are not real friends
at all.   46

These are my principles, at any rate,
and that is why I have made the following decision concerning the sons of
Œdipus: Eteoclês, who died as a man
should die, fighting for his country, is to
be buried with full military honours,   52
with all the ceremony that is usual when
the greatest heroes die; but his brother
Polyneicês, who broke his exile to come
back with fire and sword against his   56
native city and the shrines of his fathers'
gods, whose one idea was to spill the
blood of his blood and sell his own
people into slavery—Polyneicês, I say,
is to have no burial: no man is to touch
him or say the least prayer for him;
he shall lie on the plain, unburied;   63
and the birds and the scavenging dogs
can do with him whatever they like.

This is my command, and you can see
the wisdom behind it. As long as I am
King, no traitor is going to be   68
honoured with the loyal man. But whoever shows by word and deed that he is
on the side of the State,—he shall have
my respect while he is living, and my
reverence when he is dead.

CHORAGOS.   If that is your will, Creon
    son of Menoiceus,
You have the right to enforce it: we are
    yours.   75
CREON.   That is my will. Take care
    that you do your part.
CHORAGOS.   We are old men: let the
    younger ones carry it out.

CREON.   I do not mean that: the sen-
    tries have been appointed.
CHORAGOS.   Then what is it that you
    would have us do?
CREON.   You will give no support to
    whoever breaks this law.   80
CHORAGOS.   Only a crazy man is in
    love with death!
CREON.   And death it is; yet money
    talks, and the wisest
Have sometimes been known to count a
    few coins too many.
(*Enter* SENTRY *from L.*)
SENTRY.   I'll not say that I'm out of
breath from running, King, because every
time I stopped to think about what I
have to tell you, I felt like going back.
And all the time a voice kept saying,   88
'You fool, don't you know you're walking straight into trouble?'; and then another voice: 'Yes, but if you let somebody else get the news to Creon first, it
will be even worse than that for   93
you!' But good sense won out, at least I
hope it was good sense, and here I am
with a story that makes no sense at all;
but I'll tell it anyhow, because, as they
say, what's going to happen's going   98
to happen, and—
CREON.   Come to the point. What
    have you to say?   100
SENTRY.   I did not do it. I did not
    see who did it. You must not punish
    me for what someone else has done.
CREON.   A comprehensive defence!
    More effective, perhaps,
If I knew its purpose. Come: what is it?
SENTRY.   A dreadful thing . . . I
    don't know how to put it—
CREON.   Out with it!
SENTRY.   Well, then;   105
The dead man—
                    Polyneicês—
(*Pause. The* SENTRY *is overcome,
fumbles for words.* CREON *waits im-
passively.*)
                    out there—
                    someone,—
New dust on the slimy flesh!

(*Pause. No sign from* CREON.)
Someone has given it burial that way, and
Gone . . .

(*Long pause.* CREON *finally speaks
with deadly control.*)

CREON.   And the man who dared do
this?

SENTRY.   I swear I
Do not know! You must believe me!

                              Listen: *110*
The ground was dry, not a sign of dig-
ging, no,
Not a wheeltrack in the dust, no trace of
anyone.
It was when they relieved us this morn-
ing: and one of them,
The corporal, pointed to it.

                              There it was,
The strangest—

            Look: *115*
The body, just mounded over with light
dust: you see?
Not buried really, but as if they'd cov-
ered it
Just enough for the ghost's peace. And
no sign
Of dogs or any wild animal that had
been there.
And then what a scene there was! Every
man of us   *120*
Accusing the other: we all proved the
other man did it,
We all had proof that we could not have
done it.
We were ready to take hot iron in our
hands,
Walk through fire, swear by all the gods,
It was not I!
*I do not know who it was, but it was
not I!*   *125*

(CREON's *rage has been mounting
steadily, but the* SENTRY *is too intent
upon his story to notice it.*)

And then, when this came to nothing,
someone said
A thing that silenced us and made us
stare
Down at the ground: you had to be told
the news,

And one of us had to do it! We threw
the dice,
And the bad luck fell to me. So here I
am,   *130*
No happier to be here than you are to
have me:
Nobody likes the man who brings bad
news.

CHORAGOS.   I have been wondering,
King: can it be that the gods have
done this?

CREON (*furiously*).   Stop.
Must you doddering wrecks
Go out of your heads entirely? 'The
gods!'   *135*
Intolerable!
The gods favour this corpse? Why? How
had he served them?
Tried to loot their temples, burn their
images,
Yes, and the whole State, and its laws
with it!
Is it your senile opinion that the gods
love to honour bad men?   *140*
A pious thought!—

                  No, from the very beginning
There have been those who have whispered together,
Stiff-necked anarchists, putting their
heads together,
Scheming against me in alleys. These are
the men,
And they have bribed my own guard to
do this thing.   *145*

(*Sententiously.*)   Money!
There's nothing in the world so demoral-
ising as money.
Down go your cities,
Homes gone, men gone, honest hearts
corrupted,
Crookedness of all kinds, and all for
money!   *150*

(*To* SENTRY.)   But you—!
I swear by God and by the throne of
God,
The man who has done this thing shall
pay for it!
Find that man, bring him here to me, or
your death

Will be the least of your problems: I'll
   string you up   155
Alive, and there will be certain ways to
   make you
Discover your employer before you
   die;
And the process may teach you a lesson
   you seem to have missed:
The dearest profit is sometimes all too
   dear:
That depends on the source. Do you
   understand me?   160
A fortune won is often misfortune.
    SENTRY.   King, may I speak?
    CREON.   Your very voice distresses
   me.
    SENTRY.   Are you sure that it is my
   voice, and not your conscience?
    CREON.   By God, he wants to analyse
   me now!
    SENTRY.   It is not what I say, but what
   has been done, that hurts you.   165
    CREON.   You talk too much.
    SENTRY.   Maybe; but I've done noth-
   ing.
    CREON.   Sold your soul for some
   silver: that's all you've done.
    SENTRY.   How dreadful it is when the
   right judge judges wrong!
    CREON.   Your figures of speech   170
May entertain you now; but unless you
   bring me the man,
You will get little profit from them in
   the end.
    (Exit CREON into the Palace.)
    SENTRY.   'Bring me the man'—!
I'd like nothing better than bringing him
   the man!
But bring him or not, you have seen the
   last of me here.   175
At any rate, I am safe!
    (Exit SENTRY.)

ODE I

CHORUS.   [strophe 1]
Numberless are the world's wonders, but
   none

More wonderful than man; the storm-
   gray sea
Yields to his prows, the huge crests bear
   him high;   179
Earth, holy and inexhaustible, is graven
With shining furrows where his plows
   have gone
Year after year, the timeless labour of
   stallions.

                    [antistrophe 1]
The lightboned birds and beasts that
   cling to cover,
The lithe fish lighting their reaches of
   dim water,
All are taken, tamed in the net of his
   mind;   185
The lion on the hill, the wild horse
   windy-maned,
Resign to him; and his blunt yoke has
   broken
The sultry shoulders of the mountain
   bull.

                    [strophe 2]
Words also, and thought as rapid as air,
He fashions to his good use; statecraft is
   his,   190
And his the skill that deflects the arrows
   of snow,
The spears of winter rain: from every
   wind
He has made himself secure—from all
   but one:
In the late wind of death he cannot
   stand.

                  [antistrophe 2]
O clear intelligence, force beyond all
   measure!   195
O fate of man, working both good and
   evil!
When the laws are kept, how proudly
   his city stands!
When the laws are broken, what of his
   city then?
Never may the anárchic man find rest at
   my hearth,

Never be it said that my thoughts are
his thoughts. *200*

SCENE 2

(*Re-enter* SENTRY *leading* ANTIGONE.)

CHORAGOS. What does this mean?
Surely this captive woman
Is the Princess, Antigonê. Why should
she be taken?
SENTRY. Here is the one who did it!
We caught her
In the very act of burying him.—Where
is Creon?
CHORAGOS. Just coming from the
house.
(*Enter* CREON, *C.*)
CREON. What has happened? *5*
Why have you come back so soon?
SENTRY (*expansively*). O King,
A man should never be too sure of any-
thing:
I would have sworn
That you'd not see me here again: your
anger
Frightened me so, and the things you
threatened me with; *10*
But how could I tell then
That I'd be able to solve the case so soon?
No dice-throwing this time: I was only
too glad to come!
Here is this woman. She is the guilty one:
We found her trying to bury him. *15*
Take her, then; question her; judge her
as you will.
I am through with the whole thing now,
and glad óf it.
CREON. But this is Antigonê! Why
have you brought her here?
SENTRY. She was burying him, I tell
you! *19*
CREON (*severely*). Is this the truth?
SENTRY. I saw her with my own eyes.
Can I say more?
CREON. The details: come, tell me
quickly!
SENTRY. It was like this:
After those terrible threats of yours, King,

We went back and brushed the dust away
from the body. *24*
The flesh was soft by now, and stinking,
So we sat on a hill to windward and kept
guard.
No napping this time! We kept each
other awake.
But nothing happened until the white
round sun
Whirled in the centre of the round sky
over us:
Then, suddenly, *30*
A storm of dust roared up from the
earth, and the sky
Went out, the plain vanished with all its
trees
In the stinging dark. We closed our eyes
and endured it.
The whirlwind lasted a long time, but it
passed;
And then we looked, and there was
Antigonê! *35*
I have seen
A mother bird come back to a stripped
nest, heard
Her crying bitterly a broken note or two
For the young ones stolen. Just, so, when
this girl
Found the bare corpse, and all her love's
work wasted, *40*
She wept, and cried on heaven to damn
the hands
That had done this thing.
And then she brought more dust
And sprinkled wine three times for her
brother's ghost.
We ran and took her at once. She was
not afraid,
Not even when we charged her with what
she had done. *45*
She denied nothing.
And this was a comfort to me,
And some uneasiness: for it is a good
thing
To escape from death, but it is no great
pleasure
To bring death to a friend.
Yet I always say

There is nothing so comfortable ,as your
   own safe skin!   *50*
  CREON (*slowly, dangerously*). And
  you, Antigonê?
You with your head hanging,—do you
  confess this thing?
  ANTIGONE.   I do. I deny nothing.
  CREON (*to* SENTRY). You may go.
  (*Exit* SENTRY.)
  (*To* ANTIGONE.) Tell me, tell me
  briefly: *55*
Had you heard my proclamation touch-
  ing this matter?
  ANTIGONE.   It was public. Could I
  help hearing it?
  CREON.   And yet you dared defy the
  law.
  ANTIGONE.   I dared.
It was not God's proclamation. That final
  Justice
That rules the world below makes no
  such laws.   *60*
Your edict, King, was strong,
But all your strength is weakness itself
  against
The immortal unrecorded laws of God.
They are not merely now: they were,
  and shall be,   *64*
Operative for ever, beyond man utterly.
I knew I must die, even without your
  decree:
I am only mortal. And if I must die
Now, before it is my time to die,
Surely this is no hardship: can anyone
Living, as I live, with evil all about me, *70*
Think Death less than a friend? This
  death of mine
Is of no importance; but if I had left my
  brother
Lying in death unburied, I should have
  suffered.
Now I do not.
          You smile at me. Ah Creon,
Think me a fool, if you like; but it may
  well be   *75*
That a fool convicts me of folly.
  CHORAGOS.   Like father, like daugh-
  ter: both headstrong, deaf to reason!
She has never learned to yield.
  CREON.   She has much to learn.

The inflexible heart breaks first, the
  toughest iron
Cracks first, and the wildest horses bend
  their necks   *80*
At the pull of the smallest curb.
               Pride? In a slave?
This girl is guilty of a double insolence,
Breaking the given laws and boasting of
  it.
Who is the man here,   *84*
She or I, if this crime goes unpunished?
Sister's child, or more than sister's child,
Or closer yet in blood—she and her sister
Win bitter death for this!
  (*To* SERVANTS.)   Go, some of you,
Arrest Ismenê. I accuse her equally.
Bring her: you will find her sniffling in
  the house there.   *90*
Her mind's a traitor: crimes kept in the
  dark
Cry for light, and the guardian brain
  shudders;
But how much worse than this
Is brazen boasting of barefaced anarchy!
  ANTIGONE.   Creon, what more do you
  want than my death?
  CREON.   Nothing.   *95*
That gives me everything.
  ANTIGONE.   Then I beg you: kill me.
This talking is a great weariness: your
  words
Are distasteful to me, and I am sure that
  mine
Seem so to you. And yet they should not
  seem so:
I should have praise and honour for what
  I have done.   *100*
All these men here would praise me
Were their lips not frozen shut with fear
  of you.
  (*Bitterly.*)   Ah the good fortune of
  kings,
Licensed to say and do whatever they
  please!
  CREON.   You are alone here in that
  opinion.   *105*
  ANTIGONE.   No, they are with me.
  But they keep their tongues in leash.
  CREON.   Maybe. But you are guilty,
  and they are not.

ANTIGONE. There is no guilt in reverence for the dead.

CREON. But Eteoclês—was he not your brother too?

ANTIGONE. My brother too.   *109*

CREON. And you insult his memory?

ANTIGONE (*softly*). The dead man would not say that I insult it.

CREON. He would: for you honour a traitor as much as him.

ANTIGONE. His own brother, traitor or not, and equal in blood.

CREON. He made war on his country. Eteoclês defended it.

ANTIGONE. Nevertheless, there are honours due all the dead.   *115*

CREON. But not the same for the wicked as for the just.

ANTIGONE. Ah Creon, Creon.
Which of us can say what the gods hold wicked?

CREON. An enemy is an enemy, even dead.

ANTIGONE. It is my nature to join in love, not hate.   *120*

CREON (*finally losing patience*).
Go join them, then; if you must have your love,
Find it in hell!

CHORAGOS. But see, Ismenê comes:
(*Enter* ISMENE, *guarded.*)
Those tears are sisterly, the cloud
That shadows her eyes rains down gentle sorrow.

CREON. You too, Ismenê,   *125*
Snake in my ordered house, sucking my blood
Stealthily—and all the time I never knew
That these two sisters were aiming at my throne!
        Ismenê,
Do you confess your share in this crime, or deny it?
Answer me.

ISMENE. Yes, if she will let me say so. I am guilty.   *130*

ANTIGONE (*coldly*). No, Ismenê.
You have no right to say so.
You would not help me, and I will not have you help me.

ISMENE. But now I know what you meant; and I am here
To join you, to take my share of punishment.

ANTIGONE. The dead man and the gods who rule the dead   *135*
Know whose act this was. Words are not friends.

ISMENE. Do you refuse me, Antigonê? I want to die with you:
I too have a duty that I must discharge to the dead.

ANTIGONE. You shall not lessen my death by sharing it.

ISMENE. What do I care for life when you are dead?   *140*

ANTIGONE. Ask Creon. You're always hanging on his opinions.

ISMENE. You are laughing at me. Why Antigonê?

ANTIGONE. It's a joyless laughter, Ismenê.

ISMENE.   But can I do nothing?

ANTIGONE. Yes. Save yourself. I shall not envy you.
There are those who will praise you; I shall have honour, too.   *145*

ISMENE. But we are equally guilty!

ANTIGONE.   No more, Ismenê.
You are alive, but I belong to Death.

CREON (*to the* CHORUS). Gentlemen, I beg you to observe these girls:
One has just now lost her mind; the other,
It seems, has never had a mind at all.   *150*

ISMENE. Grief teaches the steadiest minds to waver, King.

CREON. Yours certainly did, when you assumed guilt with the guilty!

ISMENE. But how could I go on living without her?

CREON.   You are.
She is already dead.

ISMENE.   But, your own son's bride!

CREON. There are places enough for him to push his plow.   *155*
I want no wicked women for my sons!

ANTIGONE. O dearest Haimon, how your father wrongs you!

CREON. I've had enough of your childish talk of marriage!

CHORAGOS. Do you really intend to steal this girl from your son?

CREON. No; Death will do that for me.   *159*

CHORAGOS.   Then she must die?

CREON (*ironically*). You dazzle me.
          —But enough of this talk!

(*To* GUARDS.)   You, there, take them away and guard them well:

For they are but women, and even brave men run

When they see Death coming.

(*Exeunt* ISMENE, ANTIGONE, *and* GUARDS.)

ODE II

CHORUS.   [*strophe 1*]

Fortunate is the man who has never tasted God's vengeance!   *165*

Where once the anger of heaven has struck, that house is shaken

For ever: damnation rises behind each child

Like a wave cresting out of the black northeast,

When the long darkness under sea roars up

And bursts drumming death upon the windwhipped sand.   *170*

                              [*antistrophe 1*]

I have seen this gathering sorrow from time long past

Loom upon Œdipus' children: generation from generation

Takes the compulsive rage of the enemy god.

So lately this last flower of Œdipus' line

Drank the sunlight! but now a passionate word   *175*

And a handful of dust have closed up all its beauty.

                              [*strophe 2*]

What mortal arrogance
Transcends the wrath of Zeus?

Sleep cannot lull him, nor the effortless long months

Of the timeless gods: but he is young for ever,   *180*

And his house is the shining day of high Olympos.

All that is and shall be,

And all the past, is his.

No pride on earth is free of the curse of heaven.

                              [*antistrophe 2*]

The straying dreams of men   *185*
May bring them ghosts of joy:

But as they drowse, the waking embers burn them;

Or they walk with fíxed éyes, as blind men walk.

But the ancient wisdom speaks for our own time:

Fate works most for woe   *190*
With Folly's fairest show.

Man's little pleasure is the spring of sorrow.

SCENE 3

CHORAGOS. But here is Haimon, King, the last of all your sons.

Is it grief for Antigonê that brings him here,

And bitterness at being robbed of his bride?

(*Enter* HAIMON.)

CREON. We shall soon see, and no need of diviners.

                    —Son,

You have heard my final judgment on that girl: *5*

Have you come here hating me, or have you come

With deference and with love, whatever I do?

HAIMON. I am your son, father. You are my guide.

You make things clear for me, and I obey you.

No marriage means more to me than your continuing wisdom.   *10*

CREON. Good. That is the way to behave: subordinate

Everything else, my son, to your father's will.

This is what a man prays for, that he may get

Sons attentive and dutiful in his house,

Each one hating his father's enemies,   15

Honouring his father's friends. But if his sons

Fail him, if they turn out unprofitably,

What has he fathered but trouble for himself

And amusement for the malicious?

                    So you are right

Not to lose your head over this woman.   20

Your pleasure with her would soon grow cold, Haimon,

And then you'd have a hellcat in bed and elsewhere.

Let her find her husband in Hell!

Of all the people in this city, only she

Has had contempt for my law and broken it.   25

Do you want me to show myself weak before the people?

Or to break my sworn word? No, and I will not.

The woman dies.

I suppose she'll plead 'family ties.' Well, let her.

If I permit my own family to rebel,   30

How shall I earn the world's obedience?

Show me the man who keeps his house in hand,

He's fit for public authority.

                    I'll have no dealings

With law-breakers, critics of the government:

Whoever is chosen to govern should be obeyed—   35

Must be obeyed, in all things, great and small,

Just and unjust! O Haimon,

The man who knows how to obey, and that man only,

Knows how to give commands when the time comes.

You can depend on him, no matter how fast   40

The spears come: he's a good soldier, he'll stick it out.

Anarchy, anarchy! Show me a greater evil!

This is why cities tumble and the great houses rain down,

This is what scatters armies!

No, no: good lives are made so by discipline   45

We keep the laws then, and the lawmakers,

And no woman shall seduce us. If we must lose,

Let's lose to a man, at least! Is a woman stronger than we?

CHORAGOS. Unless time has rusted my wits,

What you say, King, is said with point and dignity.   50

HAIMON (*boyishly earnest*). Father.

Reason is God's crowning gift to man, and you are right

To warn me against losing mine. I cannot say—

I hope that I shall never want to say—that you

Have reasoned badly. Yet there are other men   55

Who can reason, too; and their opinions might be helpful.

You are not in a position to know everything

That people say or do, or what they feel:

Your temper terrifies them—everyone   59

Will tell you only what you like to hear.

But I, at any rate, can listen; and I have heard them

Muttering and whispering in the dark about this girl.

They say no woman has ever, so unreasonably,

Died so shameful a death for a generous act:

'She covered her brother's body. Is this indecent?   65

'She kept him from dogs and vultures. Is this a crime?

'Death?—She should have all the honour that we can give her!'

This is the way they talk out there in the
city.

You must believe me:

Nothing is closer to me than your happiness.   70

What could be closer? Must not any son

Value his father's fortune as his father
does his?

I beg you, do not be unchangeable:

Do not believe that you alone can be
right.

The man who thinks that,   75

The man who maintains that only he has
the power

To reason correctly, the gift to speak, the
soul—

A man like that, when you know him,
turns out empty.

It is not reason never to yield to reason!

In flood time you can see how some trees
bend,   80

And because they bend, even their twigs
are safe,

While stubborn trees are torn up, roots
and all.

And the same thing happens in sailing:

Make your sheet fast, never slacken,—
and over you go,

Head over heels and under: and there's
your voyage.   85

Forget you are angry! Let yourself be
moved!

I know I am young; but please let me say
this:

The ideal condition

Would be, I admit, that men should be
right by instinct;

But since we are all too likely to go
astray,   90

The reasonable thing is to learn from
those who can teach.

CHORAGOS.   You will do well to listen
to him, King,

If what he says is sensible. And you,
Haimon,

Must listen to your father.—Both speak
well.

CREON.   You consider it right for a
man of my years and experience   95

To go to school to a boy?

HAIMON.   It is not right
If I am wrong. But if I am young, and
right,

What does my age matter?

CREON.   You think it right to stand
up for an anarchist?

HAIMON.   Not at all. I pay no respect
to criminals.   100

CREON.   Then she is not a criminal?

HAIMON.   The City would deny it, to
a man.

CREON.   And the City proposes to
teach me how to rule?

HAIMON.   Ah. Who is it that's talking
like a boy now?

CREON.   My voice is the one voice
giving orders in this City!   105

HAIMON.   It is no City if it takes
orders from one voice.

CREON.   The State is the King!

HAIMON.   Yes, if the State is a desert.
(Pause.)

CREON.   This boy, it seems, has sold
out to a woman.

HAIMON.   If you are a woman: my
concern is only for you.   110

CREON.   So? Your 'concern'! In a
public brawl with your father!

HAIMON.   How about you, in a public
brawl with justice?

CREON.   With justice, when all that
I do is within my rights?

HAIMON.   You have no right to
trample on God's right.

CREON (completely out of control).
Fool, adolescent fool! Taken in by
a woman!   115

HAIMON.   You'll never see me taken
in by anything vile.

CREON.   Every word you say is for
her!

HAIMON (quietly, darkly).   And for
you.

And for me. And for the gods under the
earth.

CREON.   You'll never marry her while
she lives.   120

HAIMON.   Then she must die.—But
her death will cause another.

CREON.   Another?

Have you lost your senses? Is this an
  open threat?
　HAIMON.　There is no threat in speak-
  ing to emptiness.
　CREON.　I swear you'll regret this
  superior tone of yours! 　　　*125*
You are the empty one!
　HAIMON.　If you were not my father,
I'd say you were perverse.
　CREON.　You girlstruck fool, don't
  play at words with me!
　HAIMON.　I am sorry. You prefer
  silence.
　CREON.　Now, by God—! 　　*130*
I swear, by all the gods in heaven above
  us,
You'll watch it, I swear you shall!
　(*To the* SERVANTS)　Bring her out!
Bring the woman out! Let her die before
  his eyes!
Here, this instant, with her bridegroom
  beside her!
　HAIMON.　Not here, no; she will not
  die here, King. 　　　*135*
And you will never see my face again.
Go on raving as long as you've a friend
  to endure you.
　(*Exit* HAIMON.)
　CHORAGOS.　Gone, gone.
Creon, a young man in a rage is danger-
ous!
　CREON.　Let him do, or dream to do,
  more than a man can. 　　　*140*
He shall not save these girls from death.
　CHORAGOS.　　　These girls?
You have sentenced them both?
　CREON.　　　No, you are right.
I will not kill the one whose hands are
  clean.
　CHORAGOS.　But Antigonê?
　CREON (*somberly*).　I will carry her
  far away 　　　*145*
Out there in the wilderness, and lock her
Living in a vault of stone. She shall have
  food,
As the custom is, to absolve the State of
  her death.
And there let her pray to the gods of
  hell:
They are her only gods: 　　　*150*

Perhaps they will show her an escape
  from death,
Or she may learn,
　　　　　though late,
That piety shown the dead is pity in vain.
　(*Exit* CREON.)

ODE III

　CHORUS.　　　　　[*strophe*]
Love, unconquerable
Waster of rich men, keeper 　　　*155*
Of warm lights and all-night vigil
In the soft face of a girl:
Sea-wanderer, forest-visitor!
Even the pure Immortals cannot escape
  you, 　　　*159*
And mortal man, in his one day's dusk,
Trembles before your glory.

　　　　　　　[*antistrophe*]
Surely you swerve upon ruin
The just man's consenting heart,
As here you have made bright anger
Strike between father and son— 　*165*
And none has conquered but Love!
A girl's glánce wórking the will of heaven:
Pleasure to her alone who mocks us,
Merciless Aphroditê.

SCENE 4

　CHORAGOS (*as* ANTIGONE *enters
  guarded*).
But I can no longer stand in awe of this,
Nor, seeing what I see, keep back my
  tears.
Here is Antigonê, passing to that chamber
Where all find sleep at last.

　ANTIGONE.　　　[*strophe 1*]
Look upon me, friends, and pity me 　*5*
Turning back at the night's edge to say
Goodbye to the sun that shines for me
  no longer;
Now sleepy Death
Summons me down to Acheron, that
  cold shore:
There is no bridesong there, nor any
  music. 　　　*10*

CHORUS. Yet not unpraised, not without a kind of honour,
You walk at last into the underworld;
Untouched by sickness, broken by no sword.
What woman has ever found your way to death?

ANTIGONE.   [antistrophe 1]
How often I have heard the story of Niobê,   15
Tantalos' wretched daughter, how the stone
Clung fast about her, ivy-close: and they say
The rain falls endlessly
And sifting soft snow; her tears are never done.   19
I feel the loneliness of her death in mine.
    CHORUS.   But she was born of heaven, and you
Are woman, woman-born. If her death is yours,
A mortal woman's, is this not for you
Glory in our world and in the world beyond?

ANTIGONE.   [strophe 2]
You laugh at me. Ah, friends, friends,
Can you not wait until I am dead? O Thebes,   26
O men many-charioted, in love with Fortune,
Dear springs of Dircê, sacred Theban grove,
Be witness for me, denied all pity,
Unjustly judged! and think a word of love   30
For her whose path turns
Under dark earth, where there are no more tears.
    CHORUS. You have passed beyond human daring and come at last
Into a place of stone where Justice sits.
I cannot tell   35
What shape of your father's guilt appears in this.

ANTIGONE.   [antistrophe 2]
You have touched it at last: that bridal bed
Unspeakable, horror of son and mother mingling:
Their crime, infection of all our family!
O Œdipus, father and brother!   40
Your marriage strikes from the grave to murder mine.
I have been a stranger here in my own land:
All my life
The blasphemy of my birth has followed me.
    CHORUS.   Reverence is a virtue, but strength   45
Lives in established law: that must prevail.
You have made your choice,
Your death is the doing of your conscious hand.

ANTIGONE.   [epode]
Then let me go, since all your words are bitter,
And the very light of the sun is cold to me.   50
Lead me to my vigil, where I must have
Neither love nor lamentation; no song, but silence.
    (CREON interrupts impatiently.)
    CREON.   If dirges and planned lamentations could put off death,
Men would be singing for ever.
    (To the SERVANTS)   Take her, go!
You know your orders: take her to the vault   55
And leave her alone there. And if she lives or dies,
That's her affair, not ours: our hands are clean.
    ANTIGONE.   O tomb, vaulted bride-bed in eternal rock,
Soon I shall be with my own again
Where Persephonê welcomes the thin ghosts underground: 60
And I shall see my father again, and you, mother,
And dearest Polyneicês—dearest indeed

To me, since it was my hand
That washed him clean and poured the
    ritual wine: 64
And my reward is death before my time!
And yet, as men's hearts know, I have
    done no wrong,
I have not sinned before God. Or if I
    have,
I shall know the truth in death. But if
    the guilt
Lies upon Creon who judged me, then,
    I pray,
May his punishment equal my own.
    CHORAGOS.   O passionate heart, 70
Unyielding, tormented still by the same
    winds!
    CREON.   Her guards shall have good
    cause to neglect their delaying.
    ANTIGONE.   Ah! That voice is like the
    voice of death!
    CREON.   I can give you no reason to
    think you are mistaken.
    ANTIGONE.   Thebes, and you my
    fathers' gods,   75
And rulers of Thebes, you see me now,
    the last
Unhappy daughter of a line of kings,
Your kings, led away to death. You will
    remember
What things I suffer, and at what men's
    hands,
Because I would not transgress the laws
    of heaven.   80
    (*To the* GUARDS, *simply*) Come: let
us wait no longer.
    (*Exit* ANTIGONE, *L., guarded.*)

ODE IV

CHORUS.   [*strophe 1*]
All Danaê's beauty was locked away
In a brazen cell where the sunlight could
    not come:
A small room, still as any grave, enclosed
    her.
Yet she was a princess too,   85
And Zeus in a rain of gold poured love
    upon her.

O child, child,
No power in wealth or war
Or tough sea-blackened ships
Can prevail against untiring Destiny! 90

[*antistrophe 1*]
And Dryas' son also, that furious king,
Bore the god's prisoning anger for his
    bride:
Sealed up by Dionysos in deaf stone,
His madness died among echoes.
So at the last he learned what dreadful
    power   95
His tongue had mocked:
For he had profaned the revels,
And fired the wrath of the nine
Implacable Sisters that love the sound of
    the flute.

[*strophe 2*]
And old men tell a half-remembered
    tale   100
Of horror done where a dark ledge splits
    the sea
And a double surf beats on the gréy
    shóres:
How a king's new woman, sick
With hatred for the queen he had im-
    prisoned,
Ripped out his two sons' eyes with her
    bloody hands   105
While grinning Arês watched the shuttle
    plunge
Four times: four blind wounds crying for
    revenge,

[*antistrophe 2*]
Crying, tears and blood mingled.—Pit-
    eously born,
Those sons whose mother was of heav-
    enly birth!
Her father was the god of the North
    Wind   110
And she was cradled by gales,
She raced with young colts on the glit-
    tering hills
And walked untrammeled in the open
    light:

But in her marriage deathless Fate found
    means   *114*
To build a tomb like yours for all her joy.

SCENE 5

(*Enter blind* TEIRESIAS, *led by a boy.
The opening speeches of* TEIRESIAS
*should be in singsong contrast to the
realistic lines of* CREON.)

TEIRESIAS. This is the way the blind
    man comes, Princess, Princess,
Lock-step, two heads lit by the eyes of
    one.
  CREON. What new thing have you to
    tell us, old Teiresias?
TEIRESIAS. I have much to tell you:
    listen to the prophet, Creon.
  CREON. I am not aware that I have
    ever failed to listen.   *5*
TEIRESIAS. Then you have done
    wisely, King, and ruled well.
  CREON. I admit my debt to you. But
    what have you to say?
TEIRESIAS. This, Creon: you stand
    once more on the edge of fate.
  CREON. What do you mean? Your
    words are a kind of dread.
TEIRESIAS. Listen, Creon: *10*
I was sitting in my chair of augury, at the
    place
Where the birds gather about me. They
    were all a-chatter,
As is their habit, when suddenly I heard
A strange note in their jangling, a
    scream, a
Whirring fury; I knew that they were
    fighting,   *15*
Tearing each other, dying
In a whirlwind of wings clashing. And I
    was afraid.
I began the rites of burnt-offering at the
    altar,
But Hephaistos failed me: instead of
    bright flame,
There was only the sputtering slime of
    the fat thigh-flesh   *20*
Melting: the entrails dissolved in grey
    smoke,

The bare bone burst from the welter.
    And no blaze!
This was a sign from heaven. My boy
    described it,
Seeing for me as I see for others.
I tell you, Creon, you yourself have
    brought   *25*
This new calamity upon us. Our hearths
    and altars
Are stained with the corruption of dogs
    and carrion birds
That glut themselves on the corpse of
    Œdipus' son.
The gods are deaf when we pray to them,
    their fire
Recoils from our offering, their birds of
    omen   *30*
Have no cry of comfort, for they are
    gorged
With the thick blood of the dead.
                      O my son,
These are no trifles! Think: all men make
    mistakes,
But a good man yields when he knows his
    course is wrong,
And repairs the evil. The only crime is
    pride.   *35*
Give in to the dead man, then: do not
    fight with a corpse—
What glory is it to kill a man who is
    dead?
Think, I beg you:
It is for your own good that I speak as
    I do.
You should be able to yield for your own
    good.   *40*
  CREON. It seems that prophets have
    made me their especial province.
All my life long
I have been a kind of butt for the dull
    arrows
Of doddering fortune-tellers!
                    No, Teiresias:
If your birds—if the great eagles of God
    himself   *45*
Should carry him stinking bit by bit to
    heaven,
I would not yield. I am not afraid of pol-
    lution:

No man can defile the gods.
                    Do what you will,
Go into business, make money, speculate
In India gold or that synthetic gold from
    Sardis,   50
Get rich otherwise than by my consent
    to bury him.
Teiresias, it is a sorry thing when a wise
    man
Sells his wisdom, lets out his words for
    hire!
    TEIRESIAS. Ah Creon! Is there no
    man left in the world—
    CREON. To do what—Come, let's
    have the aphorism!   55
    TEIRESIAS. No man who knows that
    wisdom outweighs any wealth?
    CREON. As surely as bribes are baser
    than any baseness.
    TEIRESIAS. You are sick, Creon! You
    are deathly sick!
    CREON. As you say: it is not my
    place to challenge a prophet.
    TEIRESIAS. Yet you have said my
    prophecy is for sale.   60
    CREON. The generation of prophets
    has always loved gold.
    TEIRESIAS. The generation of kings
    has always loved brass.
    CREON. You forget yourself! You are
    speaking to your King.
    TEIRESIAS. I know it. You are a king
    because of me.
    CREON. You have a certain skill; but
    you have sold out.   65
    TEIRESIAS. King, you will drive me
    to words that—
    CREON.   Say them, say them!
Only remember: I will not pay you for
    them.
    TEIRESIAS. No, you will find them
    too costly.
    CREON.   No doubt. Speak:
Whatever you say, you will not change
    my will.
    TEIRESIAS. Then take this, and take
    it to heart!   70
The time is not far off when you shall
    pay back

Corpse for corpse, flesh of your own
    flesh.
You have thrust the child of this world
    into living night,
You have kept from the gods below the
    child that is theirs:
The one in a grave before her death, the
    other,   75
Dead, denied the grave. This is your
    crime:
And the Furies and the dark gods of Hell
Are swift with terrible punishment for
    you.
Do you want to buy me now, Creon?
                    Not many days,
And your home will be full of men and
    women weeping,   80
And curses will be hurled at you from
    far
Cities grieving for sons unburied, left to
    rot
Before the walls of Thebes.
These are my arrows, Creon: they are all
    for you.
    (*To* BOY) But come, child: lead me
    home   85
Let him waste his fine anger upon
    younger men.
Maybe he will learn at last
To control a wise tongue in a better
    head.
    (*Exit* TEIRESIAS.)
    CHORAGOS. The old man has gone,
    King, but his words
Remain to plague us. I am old, too,   90
But I cannot remember that he was ever
    false.
    CREON. That is true. . . . It troubles
    me.
Oh, it is hard to give in! but it is worse
To risk everything for stubborn pride.
    CHORAGOS. Creon: take my advice.
    CREON.   What shall I do? 95
    CHORAGOS. Go quickly: free Anti-
    gonê from her vault
And build a tomb for the body of Poly-
    neicês.
    CREON. You would have me do this?
    CHORAGOS.   Creon, yes!

And it must be done at once: God moves
Swiftly to cancel the folly of stubborn
    men.   *100*
    CREON.   It is hard to deny the heart!
    But I
Will do it: I will not fight with destiny.
    CHORAGOS. You must go yourself,
    you cannot leave it to others.
    CREON.   I will go.
                —Bring axes, servants:
Come with me to the tomb. I buried
    hear, I   *105*
Will set her free.
           Oh, quickly!
My mind misgives—
The laws of the gods are mighty, and a
    man must serve them
To the last day of his life!
    (*Exit* CREON.)

P Æ A N

                  [*strophe 1*]
CHORAGOS.   God of many names
CHORUS.   O Iacchos
                        son
of Cadmeian Sémelê
             O born of the Thunder!
Guardian of the West
                    Regent
of Eleusis' plain
          O Prince of mænad Thebes
and the Dragon Field by rippling Is-
    menos: *5*

                  [*antistrophe 1*]
CHORAGOS.   God of many names
CHORUS.   the flame of torches
flares on our hills
          the nymphs of Iacchos
dance at the spring of Castalia:
from the vine-close mountain
            come ah come in ivy:
Evohé evohé! sings through the streets
    of Thebes   *10*

                  [*strophe 2*]
CHORAGOS.   God of many names

CHORUS.   Iacchos of Thebes
heavenly Child
    of Sémelê bride of the Thunderer!
The shadow of plague is upon us:
                    come
with clement feet
          oh come from Parnasos
down the long slopes
    across the lamenting water   *15*

              [*antistrophe 2*]
CHORAGOS.   Iô Fire! Chorister of the
    throbbing stars!
O purest among the voices of the night!
Thou son of God, blaze for us!
    CHORUS. Come with choric rapture
    of circling Mænads
Who cry *Iô Iacche!*
           God of many names!   *20*

É X O D O S

(*Enter* MESSENGER, *L.*)

MESSENGER.   Men of the line of
    Cadmos, you who live
Near Amphion's citadel:
                I cannot say
Of any condition of human life 'This is
    fixed,
This is clearly good, or bad.' Fate raises
    up,
And Fate casts down the happy and
    unhappy alike: *5*
No man can foretell his Fate.
           Take the case of Creon:
Creon was happy once, as I count happi-
    ness:
Victorious in battle, sole governor of the
    land,
Fortunate father of children nobly born.
And now it has all gone from him! Who
    can say   *10*
That a man is still alive when his life's
    joy fails?
He is a walking dead man. Grant him
    rich,
Let him live like a king in his great
    house:

If his pleasure is gone, I would not give
So much as the shadow of smoke for all
    he owns.   *15*
    CHORAGOS. Your words hint at sor-
    row: what is your news for us?
    MESSENGER. They are dead. The
    living are guilty of their death.
    CHORAGOS. Who is guilty? Who is
    dead? Speak!
    MESSENGER.   Haimon.
Haimon is dead; and the hand that killed
    him
Is his own hand.   *19*
    CHORAGOS. His father's? or his own?
    MESSENGER. His own, driven mad
    by the murder his father had done.
    CHORAGOS. Teiresias, how clearly
    you saw it all!
    MESSENGER. This is my news: you
    must draw what conclusions you
    can from it.
    CHORAGOS. But look: Eurydicê, our
    Queen:
Has she overheard us?   *25*
(Enter EURYDICE *from the Palace, C.)*
    EURYDICE. I have heard something,
    friends:
As I was unlocking the gate of Pallas'
    shrine,
For I needed her help today, I heard a
    voice
Telling of some new sorrow. And I
    fainted
There at the temple with all my maidens
    about me.   *30*
But speak again: whatever it is, I can
    bear it:
Grief and I are no strangers.
    MESSENGER.   Dearest Lady,
I will tell you plainly all that I have seen.
I shall not try to comfort you: what is
    the use,
Since comfort could lie only in what is
    not true?   *35*
The truth is always best.
                I went with Creon
To the outer plain where Polyneicês was
    lying,

No friend to pity him, his body shredded
    by dogs.
We made our prayers in that place to
    Hecatê
And Pluto, that they would be merciful.
And we bathed   *40*
The corpse with holy water, and we
    brought
Fresh-broken branches to burn what was
    left of it,
And upon the urn we heaped up a tower-
    ing barrow
Of the earth of his own land.
             When we were done, we ran
To the vault where Antigonê lay on her
    couch of stone.   *45*
One of the servants had gone ahead,
And while he was yet far off he heard a
    voice
Grieving within the chamber, and he
    came back
And told Creon. And as the King went
    closer,
The air was full of wailing, the words
    lost,   *50*
And he begged us to make all haste. 'Am
    I a prophet?'
He said, weeping, 'And must I walk this
    road,
'The saddest of all that I have gone be-
    fore?
'My son's voice calls me on. Oh quickly,
    quickly!
'Look through the crevice there, and
    tell me   *55*
'If it is Haimon, or some deception of
    the gods!'
We obeyed; and in the cavern's farthest
    corner
We saw her lying:
She had made a noose of her fine linen
    veil
And hanged herself. Haimon lay beside
    her,   *60*
His arms about her waist, lamenting her,
His love lost under ground, crying out
That his father had stolen her away from
    him.

When Creon saw him the tears rushed
    to his eyes
And he called to him: 'What have you
    done, child? Speak to me.   65
'What are you thinking that makes your
    eyes so strange?
'O my son, my son, I come to you on
    my knees!'
But Haimon spat in his face. He said not
    a word,
Staring—
            And suddenly drew his sword
And lunged. Creon shrank back, the
    blade missed; and the boy,   70
Desperate against himself, drove it half
    its length
Into his own side, and fell. And as he
    died
He gathered Antigonê close in his arms
    again,
Choking, his blood bright red on her
    white cheek.
And now he lies dead with the dead, and
    she is his   75
At last, his bride in the houses of the
    dead.
    (*Exit* EURYDICE *into the Palace.*)
CHORAGOS.   She has left us without a
    word. What can this mean?
MESSENGER.   It troubles me, too; yet
    she knows what is best,
Her grief is too great for public lamenta-
    tion,
And doubtless she has gone to her cham-
    ber to weep   80
For her dead son, leading her maidens in
    his dirge.
CHORAGOS.   It may be so: but I fear
    this deep silence.
    (*Pause.*)
MESSENGER.   I will see what she is
    doing. I will go in.
    (*Exit* MESSENGER *into the Palace.*)
    (*Enter* CREON *with attendants, bear-
ing* HAIMON'S *body.*)
CHORAGOS.   But here is the King him-
    self: oh look at him,   84
Bearing his own damnation in his arms.

CREON.   Nothing you say can touch
    me any more.
My own blind heart has brought me
From darkness to final darkness. Here
    you see
The father murdering, the murdered
    son—
And all my civic wisdom!   90
Haimon my son, so young, so young to
    die,
I was the fool, not you; and you died
    for me.
CHORAGOS.   That is the truth; but you
    were late in learning it.
CREON.   This truth is hard to bear.
    Surely a god
Has crushed me beneath the hugest
    weight of heaven,   95
And driven me headlong a barbaric way
To trample out the thing I held most
    dear.
The pains that men will take to come to
    pain!
    (*Enter* MESSENGER *from the Palace.*)
MESSENGER.   The burden you carry
    in your hands is heavy,
But it is not all: you will find more in
    your house.   100
CREON.   What burden worse than
    this shall I find there?
MESSENGER.   The Queen is dead.
CREON.   O port of death, deaf world,
Is there no pity for me? And you, Angel
    of evil,
I was dead, and your words are death
    again.   105
Is it true, boy? Can it be true?
Is my life dead? Has death bred death?
MESSENGER.   You can see for your-
    self.
    (*The doors are opened, and the body
of* EURYDICE *is disclosed within.*)
CREON.   Oh pity!
All true, all true, and more than I can
    bear!   110
O my wife, my son!
MESSENGER.   She stood before the
    altar, and her heart

Welcomed the knife her own hand
  guided,
And a great cry burst from her lips for
  Megareus dead,
And for Haimon dead, her sons; and her
  last breath   *115*
Was a curse for their father, the mur-
  derer of her sons.
And she fell, and the dark flowed in
  through her closing eyes.
  CREON.   O God, I am sick with fear.
Are there no swords here? Has no one a
  blow for me?
  MESSENGER.   Her curse is upon you
  for the death of both.   *120*
  CREON.   It is right that it should be.
  I alone am guilty.
I know it, and I say it. Lead me in,
Quickly, friends.
I have neither life nor substance. Lead
  me in.
  CHORAGOS.   You are right, if there
  can be right in so much wrong. *125*
The briefest way is best in a world of
  sorrow.
  CREON.   Let it come,
Let death come quickly, and be kind to
  me.

I would not ever see the sun again.
  CHORAGOS.   All that will come when
  it will; but we, meanwhile,   *130*
Have much to do. Leave the future to
  itself.
  CREON.   All my heart was in that
  prayer!
  CHORAGOS.   Then do not pray any
  more: the sky is deaf.
  CREON.   Lead me away. I have been
  rash and foolish.
I have killed my son and my wife.   *135*
I look for comfort; my comfort lies here
  dead.
Whatever my hands have touched has
  come to nothing.
Fate has brought all my pride to a
  thought of dust.

(*As* CREON *is being led into the house,
the* CHORAGOS *advances and speaks directly to the audience.*)

  CHORAGOS.   There is no happiness
  where there is no wisdom;   *139*
No wisdom but in submission to the
  gods.
Big words are always punished,
And proud men in old age learn to be
  wise.

PLAUTUS / 250?–184 B.C.

What little is known about the life of Titus Maccius Plautus is not entirely verified, though it does suggest some of the conditions that shaped his career as a playwright. He was born in the Umbrian hill town of Sarsina, went as a boy to Rome, and learned there the Latin of the capital, which varied significantly from his native language. He worked in a theater in some kind of assistant's position and perhaps acted, went into business and failed, worked as a miller's helper, and during years of real poverty gained a knowledge of Greek drama and wrote several plays. These brought enough income to permit him to return to the theater as playwright and actor. Something like 130 plays have been attributed to Plautus, but only 20 and a fragment—those declared by the critic M. Terentius Varro to be authentic—now survive.

Plautus based his plays upon the Greek New Comedy of the fourth century B.C., but because little survives of the Greek originals it is impossible to say whether Plautus translated, adapted, or imitated them. It is probable that he borrowed stereotyped plots and imitated stock characters, while infusing both with new vitality derived from his close sympathetic observation of contemporary Roman life. It is, at any rate, through Plautus and his successor in the writing of Roman comedy, Terence, that we derive such character types as the lovelorn young man, the virtuous maiden, the formidable matron, the lecherous old man, the braggart soldier, and the abused, impudent slave.

Theater buildings as such were unknown in Rome in the time of Plautus. His plays were staged in an open arena or on improvised platforms with little or no scenery. Hence the dialogue includes a good many indications of the actors' movements in the playing area and of their "business" with buildings, furniture, and other properties. Such stage directions as appear in modern versions are the additions of editors and translators, as are the act divisions.

Amphitryon has been the most often imitated and acted of Plautus's comedies, though some critics regard *The Rope* (*Rudens*) as a finer play. Molière and Dryden are among those who have based plays on the *Amphitryon* of Plautus. Jean Giraudoux titled his play *Amphitryon 38* (1929), on the pretext that it was the thirty-eighth version of the original, though the count is not to be taken too seriously.

This play is the only one in which Plautus used materials from mythology. Yet it is clear that he is primarily interested in depicting human foibles—in showing, that is, the human weakness in gods and mortals rather than the divinity in man. In other respects the play is typical of Roman comedy in its use of type characters, its carefree implausibility of plot (not to mention the liberties it takes with geography and biology), its stress upon the comic scene rather than the consistent development of theme, and its liberal use of jokes, wisecracks, puns, comic alliterations, and grotesque figures of speech.

Our translator, Lionel Casson, describes his version as a free prose translation designed to retain the spirit of the verse original, to sound like contemporary comedy, and yet to remain a translation rather than become an adaptation.

Amphitryon

TRANSLATED BY LIONEL CASSON

DRAMATIS PERSONAE

MERCURY.
SOSIA, *servant of Amphitryon (slave).*
JOVE.
ALCMENA, *wife of Amphitryon.*
AMPHITRYON, *Alcmena's husband, commander in chief of the Theban army.*
BLEPHARO, *captain of Amphitryon's ship.*
BROMIA, *maid of Alcmena (slave).*
[THESSALA, *maid of Alcmena (slave)*].

SCENE

In front of AMPHITRYON'S *house in Thebes.*

PROLOGUE

(*The door of* AMPHITRYON'S *house opens, and a figure emerges, to all outward appearances a typical slave of the comic stage: short, slight, bearded, and with a countenance that reveals equal parts of wiliness and self-interest. Besides the standard servant's garb, he has on his head the broad-brimmed hat the Greeks wore against the sun when traveling. He walks downstage and addresses the audience.*)

PROLOGUE. Do you want me to be bighearted and see that your business transactions, all your buying and selling, make money? Do you want my help in general? Do you want me to expedite your business speculations, foreign and domestic, at present in operation or scheduled for the future, and have them produce steady, fat profits? Do you want me to see that you and all friends and relatives get only good news, and to deliver only messages that will best promote the public welfare? (*Importantly.*) I hardly need remind you that the other gods have assigned *me* the responsibility for handling all messages and profits. (*Resuming his former tone.*) So, if you want me to aid and abet the pouring of perennial profits into your pockets, please, all of you, don't make any noise during this performance and be fair and honest critics after it's over.

Now let me tell you who ordered me to come here and why, and at the same time give you my name: the orders come from Jove, and my name is Mercury. The reason my father's sent me here is to ask a favor of you. Of course, he's perfectly aware that you'll take whatever he tells you as an order, since he knows you respect and fear the name of Jove, as you should. Nevertheless, he specifically instructed me to put this to you as a request, in nice, polite language. (*Confidentially, gesturing toward the dressing room.*) After all, the Jove who told me to come here is just as much afraid of getting into trouble as any of you: his mother was flesh and blood and so was his father, so it's no wonder that he worries about his own skin. The same goes for me: I'm Jove's son and, if he should get in trouble, I'm afraid of catching the disease.

So, that being the case, I come to you in peace, and I bring a peaceful message. The favor I want to ask is simple and perfectly proper: I'm here as a proper person to put a proper request to proper people. After all, it's not proper to ask for improper things from proper people, and it's stupid to ask for proper things from improper people—they're a criminal bunch who don't know what right is and don't hold by it.

Now, please, all of you, pay attention to what I'm going to say. Our wish should be your command—we deserve this from you and the nation, Father and I. In tragedies I've seen all the others—Father Neptune, Lady Virtue, Lady Victory, Lord Mars, Lady War—reel off all the favors they've done for you, but do I really have to give you a list of the good that my father, King of Heaven, has designed and constructed for all of you? And Father's never been one to nag good people about the good he's done them. He takes it for granted you're all grateful for it.

Now then, first I'll tell you the favor I've come here to ask, and then I'll explain the plot of this tragedy. (*As if taken aback.*) What are these frowns for? (*As if a light has suddenly dawned.*) Because I said the play was going to be a tragedy? (*Airily.*) I'm a god—I'll have everything changed. If you want, I'll turn it from a tragedy to a comedy without altering a line. Well, do you want me to or not? (*Suddenly grinning foolishly.*) How stupid of me! I'm a god! I know what you want, I understand your feelings in the matter perfectly. I'll make it into a comedy with some tragedy mixed in. After all, with kings and gods appearing in it, I don't think it would be right to make it pure comedy. But, let's face it, a servant *does* play an important part. So, as I said just before, I'll make it a tragicomedy.

But to get back to the favor Jove instructed me to ask of you. He wants detectives to go through every seat in every row of the house. If they spot a claque working for any actor, they're to strip each offender of his coat, right here in the house, and hold it as bail. (*Mimicking the manner of a court clerk.*) If anyone tries to fix the awarding of prizes for the actors or other artists, either in writing or in person or through third parties, or if the government officials in charge do the fixing themselves, Jove hereby rules that the guilty parties be sentenced under the statute applicable had said parties been convicted of malfeasance in seeking public office. (*Indignantly.*) Victors survive struggles through strength not sneakiness and subterfuge; why shouldn't an actor be liable to the same legal penalties as holders of our highest office? Men ought to compete on the basis of character not claques. Good, honest performances will create their own claques—*if* the men who do the judging are honest.

Here's another order I've received: detectives are to be assigned to actors, too. Any actor who arranges for a claque to applaud for himself, or who arranges to cut down on a competitor's applause, is to get the whip till it makes tatters of his hide along with his costume. Now, don't be surprised that Jove is taking such good care of actors today. Nothing to be surprised about: Jove himself is going to act in this play. (*Pauses and looks over the whole audience.*) What are you so surprised about? As if we're introducing anything new in having Jove on the stage! Why, just last year, right in this theater, the actors prayed to Jove, and he came down on stage to rescue them.[1] And then, of course, he's always appearing in tragedy. So, as I say, he'll act in the play today, and I will too. And now your attention please, while I explain the plot of this comedy.

(*Gesturing toward the backdrop.*) The city here is Thebes. (*Pointing to* AMPHITRYON's *house.*) In that house there, lives Amphitryon; he was actually born at Argos, the son of a citizen of Argos. He's married to Alcmena, King Elec-

[1] Apparently last year's play ended with a *deus ex machina.*

tryon's daughter. At the moment Amphitryon is on active duty as commander in chief of the army, since Thebes is at war with the Teleboans.

When Amphitryon went off to the front his wife was pregnant. (*Grinning knowingly.*) Now, I think you're all aware by this time of the way my father carries on, the liberties he allows himself in this sort of thing, what a lover he can become once his affections have found an object. He began carrying on an affair with Alcmena behind her husband's back. He borrowed her husband's looks for himself, made love to her, and made her pregnant on his own. I want you to be sure to get Alcmena's situation straight: she's pregnant by the both of them, by her husband and by almighty Jove. (*Gesturing toward the house.*) Father's inside there right now in bed with her. That's why tonight's running longer than usual: it'll go on till he's had his pleasure from where he wants it. He's doing all this, of course, disguised to look like Amphitryon. Incidentally, don't be surprised at this get-up I'm wearing, at the way I've come here dressed like a servant. I'm introducing you to an age-old story, but in a new garb—that's why I've come here (*Pointing to his costume.*) in this new get-up.

All right. Father's inside there at this very moment; yes, Jove himself right there. He's changed himself into the image of Amphitryon, and all the servants who see him think that that's who he is. (*Smiling.*) He can be a real quick-change artist when the spirit moves him. I've changed myself to look like Sosia, Amphitryon's servant, who's off at the front with his master. This way I can be Father's servant during his affair, and the household won't want to know who I am when they see me running around the place all day. They'll think I'm a servant, one of themselves, and won't question who I am or what I'm here for.

(*Confidentially.*) Father's inside now, (*Rapturously.*) lolling in the lap of the lovely lady he loves. He's busy telling Alcmena all about what happened to Amphitryon at the front. There she is, in the arms of her seducer, and she thinks she's with her husband! Right now he's telling her how Amphitryon routed the enemy's troops and was given a pile of presents as reward. (*As if telling a secret.*) We've absconded with all the gifts he got out there. (*Airily.*) Father can do whatever he wants to, with no trouble at all.

Now, today Amphitryon's coming home from the front along with the servant whose looks I'm using. (*Taking out a cluster of feathers and sticking them in his hat.*) To make it easier for you to tell us apart, I'll always have these little feathers in my hat, while Father, under his hat, will have a little gold tassel, which Amphitryon won't have. None of the household here will be able to see these marks of identification, but you will.

(*His attention caught, looks toward the wings, stage right.*) There's Amphitryon's servant Sosia now, carrying a lantern. He's just come from the waterfront. As soon as he gets to the house, I'll drive him away. You pay attention: it'll be well worth your while to see Jove and Mercury do an act!

(*He steps back and hides in the shadows near the door of the house.*)

Act I

(*Enter* SOSIA *carrying a lantern. He is the spitting image of the disguised* MERCURY *except for the telltale feathers in the hat.*)

SONG

SOSIA.
For guts and nerve no man alive comes
    close to me right now.

I'm walking alone this time of night
   though I know damned well just how
Young kids carry on. Or the cops might
   see me and clap me into jail.
And then next morning I'd be sprung—
   to report to the whipping detail!
With no chance to plead my case in
   court, and the master not around,
They'll all be absolutely convinced the
   case against me is sound;
Eight bruisers then will make me an
   anvil and pound me full of dents.
Arriving home from overseas, I'll be welcomed at public expense!

(*Shaking his head mournfully.*)
The sweat my master was in! I had to go
From the dock this time of night though
   I said no.
   (*Bitterly.*)
He couldn't wait till day to send me
   from there!
No easy job, this serving a millionaire;
A rich man's servant leads a lousy life.
All his nights and days it's just a constant
   strife
To keep up with the errands and jobs
   he has to do,
With never a moment's peace or rest for
   you.
What wealthy master's done work him-
   self? Not one!
So whatever a man can think up, he
   thinks can be done.
"It's all right," he thinks, and never
   thinks how long
The job may be. But whether the order's
   all *wrong*
And *not* all right, will never enter his
   mind.
So a slave runs into wrongs of every
   kind.
You have to sweat—and shrug and be
   resigned.
   MERCURY (*to the audience*). Hey,
   I'm the one who should complain
   that way!
Till Papa pressed me into service today
I'd no idea what slavery meant.
Now, *he's* been used to being a slave

Since birth—and listen to him rave!
   SOSIA (*working himself up*). I'm a
   stupid slob of a slave, I am! I got
   the idea too soon
To pray to the gods on my safe return,
   and thank them for the boon.
If the gods should ever return the thanks
   in the way that I deserve,
They'd commission a guy to welcome my
   face as a private punching preserve.
   (*Shaking his head bitterly.*)
That safe return they blessed me with,
   like an ingrate I upset!
   MERCURY (*to the audience*). Not
   many are like this fellow here—he
   knows just what he should get.
   SOSIA. No Theban thought, and
   neither did I, that things would
   turn out the way
They did turn out: that, safe and sound,
   we'd make it home one day.
Our conquering army's conquered the
   foe, and now we're home again;
A bitter battle's been fought and won,
   and all the enemy slain.
Our men by their morale and might have
   stormed and won the town
Of the nation that so often cruelly cut
   our people down.
We owe it most to Amphitryon, who led
   us like a wonder:
He's brought to all his countrymen new
   lands, renown, and plunder,
And Creon he's put upon the throne as
   king of Thebes for life.
Now me he's sent ahead from the dock
   to go home and tell his wife
How, by leading, guiding, ordering, her
   husband served the state.
   (*Thoughtfully.*)
Now, how to tell her once I'm there—
   just let me concentrate.
I can, of course, just think up lies, the
   way I usually do,
Since, when the fight was at its height,
   my running speed was, too.
   (*Shrugging.*)
I'll simply pretend that I was there and
   tell her things I've heard.

But to figure a way to spin this yarn
  and think up every word
Is what I want to work out first.
(*After a moment's deep thought,
brightly.*)
I'll say that this occurred.
(*In a burlesque of the tragic stage,*
Sosia *clears his throat resoundingly,
strikes a histrionic pose, and launches
into a dramatic recitative à la grand
opera.*)
When we first arrived at the enemy's
  land, the minute we came ashore,
Amphitryon at once picked out the
  leaders on his staff,
And these he sent to the Teleboans to
  make his position clear:
If they were willing to come to terms
  and, avoiding violence,
Would apprehend and deliver up the
  bandits with their booty,
Would give us back what they'd carried
  off, he'd start for home at once,
He'd lead his forces out of the land and
  leave the foe in peace.
But if they intended otherwise, and refused what he was asking,
Then with all the might and men he had,
  he'd attack and storm their town.
The delegates Amphitryon sent repeated
  this word for word.
The Teleboan people, though, brave men
  with confidence
In both their fighting spirit and strength,
  got very arrogant
And proceeded to tell our delegates off
  in no uncertain terms:
They answered that, when it came to
  war, they could well defend themselves,
So Thebes had better leave their land,
  get the army out, and fast.
The minute this word was brought to
  him, Amphitryon drew up
His whole great force in front of the
  camp; the enemy likewise
Mobilized his men in front of the town,
  magnificently armed.
(*Working himself up.*)

Once the armies were out in full force
  on each side,
All the men took their stations, the ranks
  were drawn up.
We deployed our platoons as we usually do,
And the enemy lined up his forces
  against us.
Then both the commanders, advancing
  into
No man's land, held a parley away from
  the ranks.
Whichever side lost in the fight, they
  agreed,
Would surrender their city, their temples,
  their fields,
Their houses, their hearths, their own
  bodies and souls.
Once agreed, they went back, and the
  trumpets blared forth.
The earth echoed the sound. From each
  side came a yell.
Each commander, both their man and
  ours, said his prayers
To great Jove, and exhorted his soldiers
  to fight.
(*With great excitement.*)
In the struggle each man gave his all.
Swords clanged; lances broke; and the
  shouts
Of the men rose as high as the sky.
And an actual cloud floated up
From the breath given off as they
  gasped.
Scores of soldiers succumbed to their
  wounds.
Then at last, as we hoped for, our men
See that victory's coming their way.
More and more of the enemy fall.
In we charge to drive home the attack.
Like furies we fight—and they crack!
(*Pauses, then resumes with great feel-
ing.*)
Yet not one of the foe turned to flee
  from the field.
They kept standing their ground, never
  breaking the lines.
Sooner die than abandon their posts, was
  their thought.

Each fell where he stood; the very
  corpses kept ranks.
(*Excitedly again.*)
When Amphitryon notices this,
He immediately orders a charge
Of his cavalry on the right flank.
Like a flash they obey the command.
With a terrible yell they attack,
At a gallop they charge on the right,
And they shatter and trample the foe.
The enemy yields all along—
A triumph of right over wrong!
(SOSIA *stands immobile, transfixed by
his own eloquence.*)
MERCURY.   Not a word he's said so
  far is false, every bit of it is true.
For I was there when the fight was
  fought, and Father was there too.
SOSIA.   The Teleboans took to their
  heels, and we got added courage.
We fired away at the fleeing foe, and
  filled their bodies with darts.
And Pterelas, their king, was killed by
  Amphitryon's own hand.
The fight we fought out there that day
  went on from dawn to night.
(I remember because, the whole day
  long, I hadn't had a bite.)
The dark at last separated us, and broke
  the fighting off.
Next day their leaders, bathed in tears,
  came from town to us in camp.
They beg, with olive branch outstretched,
  our pardon for their sins.
They surrender unconditionally: they,
  each and every one,
Give up to Thebes to treat as it will their
  city, children, homes.
Amphitryon, for his bravery, was
  awarded the golden cup
That Pterelas their king once used.
(*Nodding with great satisfaction.*)
          I'll tell all this to his spouse.
(*Abruptly turns and walks toward the
door.*)
Now to carry out the master's orders.
      Forward march and into the house!
(*The following speeches are all asides:*

*each speaker, though at times he seems
to address the other, actually talks to the
audience.*)
MERCURY.   Aha! He's heading this
way. I'll get going and head him off. I'm
not letting him get anywhere near this
house today. We look exactly alike, so
I'll play a game with him, that's what I'll
do. As a matter of fact, since I took his
face and figure, it's only right to give
myself his character. And that means I
have to be canny, tricky, and nasty, and
use his own medicine, some nasty trick,
to get him away from the door. (*Turning away to look at* SOSIA.) What's going
on? He's looking up at the sky! I'll keep
an eye on him and see what he's after.
SOSIA (*staring at the sky, puzzled*).   I
swear to god, if there's one thing in this
world I'm convinced of beyond any
doubt, it's that tonight the Patron God
of Night got tight and is sleeping it off.
The Big Dipper hasn't budged in the
sky, and the moon's in exactly the same
place it was when it rose. Orion, Vesper,
the Pleiades—none of them has set. All
the stars are standing in the same spot;
tonight's not moving aside for tomorrow
anywhere.
MERCURY (*to the heavens*).   Keep it
up, Night. Do what Daddy wants. Do
what you might with all your might for
the almighty. Best investment you could
make.
SOSIA (*as before*).   I don't think I've
ever seen a longer night than this. Well,
maybe just once, when I got flogged
and strung up from dusk till dawn. But,
I swear, even that night wasn't as long
as this one. If you ask me, the sun's
sleeping off a drunk. Did a little over-
indulging at dinner last night, probably.
MERCURY.   Is that so? You stinker,
you think gods are like you? Damn you,
I'll fix you for such talk—*and* for your
bad habits! Just step over here and
you'll get what you're not going to like.
SOSIA (*grinning*).   Where are those

woman chasers who can't stand going
to bed alone? What a chance to give a
workout to a high-priced whore who
charges by the night!

MERCURY. Judging by what this fellow says, Father's doing the best and
smartest thing. He's lying in bed with
Alcmena making love, doing what he
likes doing most.

SOSIA. Well, I'll go in and give
Alcmena the report the master ordered
me to. (*Starts walking toward the door,
catches sight of the figure of* MERCURY,
and comes to an abrupt halt.) Hey—
who's that I see standing in front of the
house? At this time of night? I don't
like this!

MERCURY (*with a contemptuous gesture in* SOSIA'S *direction*). Nobody
scares as easily as this one here.

SOSIA (*nervously*). I get it: here I am
all dressed up—and he wants to dress
me down!

MERCURY (*grinning*). He's scared
stiff. I'll have some fun with him.

SOSIA (*as before*). I'm a goner! My
jaw has that pre-sock sensation. He's
going to greet the homecomer with a
kiss from a fist, I know it. He probably
feels sorry for me: because my master
made me stay awake last night, his
knuckles will see to it I get some sleep
today. I'm a goner, an absolute goner!
I ask you now, look at the size of that
bruiser!

MERCURY (*confidentially*). I'll talk
out loud in front of him. He'll hear what
I say, and get even more scared.
(*Loudly.*) Come on, fists, it's been ages
since you've given me something to slug
away in the stomach. That last time—
was it only yesterday? Seems like ages
ago! You laid four men out. Knocked
them stiff.

SOSIA. I'm scared he's going to make
a change in my family: here I am, an
only child, and he's going to make me a
quintuplet! He says he knocked out four

men; I'm afraid I'm going to raise the
figure.

MERCURY (*rolling up his sleeves and
taking a boxer's stance, with satisfaction*). There, that's more like it.

SOSIA. He's rolling up his sleeves—
getting ready for the kill!

MERCURY (*between his teeth*). He's
not going to get away from here without a good licking.

SOSIA. Who isn't?

MERCURY (*promptly*). Whoever
comes this way—he'll eat knuckles!

SOSIA (*hurriedly*). Not me. I don't
like eating this late. I already had dinner.
Why don't you be smart and serve that
dish to people who are hungry?

MERCURY (*caressing one of his fists,
with satisfaction*). Real weight in this
here fist.

SOSIA. Figuring the poundage in his
punch! Poor me!

MERCURY (*thoughtfully*). What if I
put him to sleep with a soft, slow sock on
the jaw?

SOSIA. You'll save my life—I haven't
been to bed for three nights running.

MERCURY (*throwing a practice hay-
maker, disgustedly*). Awful! We're not
doing well at all. These knuckles just
won't learn how to sock a jaw. One tap
with this fist, and I should be able to
change a man's looks.

SOSIA. He's like the fellows who fix
up statues! He's going to make me a
new face!

MERCURY (*to his fist*). If you really
hit a man, you should knock every bone
out of his head.

SOSIA. Say, maybe he's thinking of
filleting my face like a fish! Keep me
from a fellow who fillets folks! If he
catches sight of me, I'm done for!

MERCURY (*elaborately sniffing the
air*). I smell someone—and he'll be
sorry!

SOSIA. Oh, my God, did he get a
whiff of me?

MERCURY (*with more intensive sniffing*). He was far away before, but he can't be very far now.

SOSIA (*flabbergasted*). This guy's a magician!

MERCURY (*throwing a series of fast jabs*). These fists are bucking like a bronco.

SOSIA. If you're going to give them a workout on me, please break them in on the wall first!

MERCURY (*suddenly stops his shadow boxing and stands still, cocking an ear; burlesquing the style of grand opera*). Somebody's words have winged their way to mine ears!

SOSIA. What rotten luck! Why didn't I clip its wings? *I* have to have a voice like a bird!

MERCURY (*snarling*). He's going to get it from me. I'll fix his wagon.

SOSIA (*promptly*). I haven't got a wagon.

MERCURY (*as before*). I'll give him a load of fist.

SOSIA (*resentfully*). I'm all worn out from the trip back on the boat, I'm still seasick, I can barely walk *without* carrying anything, so don't get the idea I can take any loads.

MERCURY. No question about it—I hear somebody talking.

SOSIA. Saved! He doesn't see me. He says Somebody's talking. One thing I know: my name's Sosia, not Somebody.

MERCURY (*turning toward* SOSIA, *burlesquing the style of grand opera*). Here from the right, methinks a voice strikes mine ears.

SOSIA (*despondently*). My voice struck him, eh? I'm afraid *I'll* get struck to even the score. (*Takes a tentative step away.*)

MERCURY (*ironically*). He's coming my way. Perfect.

SOSIA (*stopping dead in his tracks*). I'm so scared, I'm numb all over! I swear, I couldn't tell you where in the

world I am right now, if you asked me. I'm so scared I can't even move! This is it: this is the end of the master's orders —and Sosia along with them. (*Eyes* MERCURY *uncertainly, notices that he is not moving, and screws up his courage.*) All right. My mind's made up: I'll talk back to him. That way I'll look like someone with guts, and he'll keep his hands off me.

(SOSIA, *swinging his lantern jauntily, swaggers up to the door. The two now address each other instead of the audience.*)

MERCURY (*in his grand opera style*). Whither away, O stranger with Vulcan's fire in that piece of horn?

SOSIA (*belligerently*). What do you want to know for, O stranger who fillets faces with his fists?

MERCURY (*menacingly*). Are you a slave or not?

SOSIA (*shrugging*). Whichever I like.

MERCURY (*arms akimbo, jaw out*). Is that so?

SOSIA (*arms akimbo, jaw out*). Yeah, that's so.

MERCURY (*contemptuously*). You deserve a good licking.

SOSIA. That's a lie!

MERCURY (*rolling up his sleeves and making other ominous preparations*). You're going to tell me it's the truth. I'll see to that right now.

SOSIA (*his courage rapidly becoming unscrewed*). Now, why do you have to do that?

MERCURY (*ominously*). I want to know where you're going, who you belong to, and what you came for. How about it?

SOSIA (*blandly*). I came here, and I'm my master's servant. Any the wiser now?

MERCURY (*as before*). Damn you, I'll stop that mouth of yours!

SOSIA (*girlishly fluttering his eyes, and demurely putting his hands over his lips*).

Oh sir, you can't! It's a very proper mouth, and I take good care of it.

MERCURY (*grimly*). More nonsense out of you? What are you doing around this house?

SOSIA. What are *you* doing here?

MERCURY. Orders from King Creon. One man stands guard all night every night.

SOSIA (*grandly*). Very nice of him. Takes good care of the house because he knows we're away. (*Taking a step forward and airily waving* MERCURY *aside*.) You can leave now. Tell him the family's back.

MERCURY (*blocking the way*). I don't know how you can belong to this family. And, "family man," unless you take off this minute, you're not going to get treated like one of the family!

SOSIA (*stubbornly*). I tell you I live here. I'm a servant here.

MERCURY. Do you know what's going to happen to you? If you don't get out of here, I'm going to make you into a real aristocrat.

SOSIA. How's that?

MERCURY. Once I get my hands on a club, you won't walk away from here, you'll be carried.

SOSIA (*desperately*). But I tell you I'm one of the family! A family servant.

MERCURY. You're not leaving this minute? Then kindly figure out how soon you want your licking.

SOSIA. You think you're going to keep me out of this house after I came all the way here from overseas?

MERCURY (*incredulously*). This is your house?

SOSIA. Of course.

MERCURY. Then who's your master?

SOSIA. Amphitryon. He's off now commanding the Theban army. Alcmena's his wife.

MERCURY. Tell me, what's your name?

SOSIA (*drawing himself up; in the grand opera style*). Men call me Sosia. Sprung from the loins of Davus am I.[2]

MERCURY (*eying him distastefully*). You've got a nerve! You'll pay for this. Coming here this way with a pack of lies, and dirty schemes on foot!

SOSIA (*reproachfully*). I came here with my shoes on foot, not dirty schemes.

MERCURY (*promptly*). Still lying— you came here with your feet on shoes. (*Roars at his joke*.)

SOSIA (*deciding it would be politic to acknowledge this sally, roaring too*). You're absolutely right.

MERCURY (*suddenly switching off the laughter*). Then you're absolutely going to get a beating for telling lies.

SOSIA. But I absolutely don't want one.

MERCURY. But you're absolutely going to get one, whether you want it or not. When I say "absolutely," my mind's made up; there's no room for discussion. (*Starts clobbering* SOSIA.)

SOSIA. Don't! Please! I beg you!

MERCURY (*continuing the clobbering*). Where do you get the nerve to say you're Sosia when I'm Sosia?

SOSIA. He's murdering me!

MERCURY. Murder isn't anything compared with what's coming. Who's your master?

SOSIA (*hurriedly*). You are. Those fists of yours have given you right of possession. (*At the top of his lungs*.) Men of Thebes! Help!

MERCURY (*silencing him with a punch*). So you'll yell, will you, you stinker! Now speak up! What did you come here for?

SOSIA (*bitterly*). So you could have somebody to beat to a pulp.

MERCURY. Who's your master?

SOSIA (*doggedly*). Amphitryon. I'm his servant Sosia.

[2] "Men call me Joe. Sprung from the loins of Mike, etc." will give some idea of the joke.

MERCURY. That means you're going to get beaten up even more for talking nonsense. *I'm* Sosia, not you.

SOSIA (*muttering to himself*). God, do I wish it! You be me, and then I'll beat *you* up.

MERCURY (*snarling*). What are you muttering about?

SOSIA (*hurriedly*). I'll keep quiet.

MERCURY. Who's your master?

SOSIA. Whoever you say.

MERCURY. Now tell me this: what's your name?

SOSIA. Whatever name you say.

MERCURY (*glowering*). You told me you were Amphitryon's Sosia.

SOSIA. I made a mistake. I meant to say I was Amphitryon's *associate*.

MERCURY (*nodding satisfiedly*). I knew darn well the family had only one Sosia—me. You dropped the ball there.

SOSIA (*aside*). I wish to god you'd do that with those fists!

MERCURY (*emphatically*). I'm the Sosia you were trying to tell me a minute ago you were.

SOSIA (*in desperation*). Will you do me a favor? Will you *please* let me talk to you in peace, without getting beaten up?

MERCURY. No peace—just a temporary truce, if there's something you want to say.

SOSIA (*quickly*). I don't talk without a treaty of peace—you're stronger than I am, you can lick me.

MERCURY (*with an air of magnanimity*). Say what you want. I won't hurt you.

SOSIA. You give me your word?

MERCURY. Word of honor.

SOSIA (*suspiciously*). What if you go back on it?

MERCURY (*in his grand opera style*). Then may the wrath of Mercury fall upon Sosia!

SOSIA (*suddenly regaining his aplomb*). Well, now that I can say what I want to, you listen here: *I'm* Amphitryon's servant Sosia.

MERCURY (*advancing on him menacingly*). What, again?

SOSIA (*doggedly*). We made peace, we signed a treaty, so I'm telling you the truth.

MERCURY. I'm going to beat you up!

SOSIA (*as before*). You can do whatever you like with me, because you're stronger than I am, you can lick me. (*At the top of his lungs.*) But, no matter what you do to me, this is one thing, damn it all, I'm not going to keep quiet about!

MERCURY (*grimly*). You're not going to stop me from being Sosia, not as long as you live.

SOSIA. And, damn it all, you're not going to make me be somebody different from myself. I'm the only servant Sosia we've got in the family. I'm the fellow who went off with Amphitryon to the front.

MERCURY (*to the world at large*). This fellow's out of his mind!

SOSIA. That's what's wrong with you, not me! (*To himself.*) What the devil! Ain't I Amphitryon's servant Sosia? Didn't our ship arrive just tonight from the port of the Teleboans with me aboard? Didn't my own master send me here? Ain't I standing in front of my own house right this minute? Don't I have a lantern in my hand? Ain't I talking? Ain't I awake? Didn't this fellow here just now beat me up? (*Groaning.*) He sure did! My jaw still aches. (*Resolutely.*) What am I waiting for? Why don't I go right into my house?

MERCURY. What do you mean, *your* house?

SOSIA (*doggedly*). That's what I said.

MERCURY. Oh no. Every word you just said is a lie. *I'm* Amphitryon's Sosia. Tonight our ship cleared the land of the Teleboans with *me* on board. It was after we stormed and took King Pterelas' town and beat the Teleboan army by some hard fighting, and Amphitryon killed King Pterelas with his own hands during the battle.

SOSIA (*to the audience, flabbergasted*). Even I don't believe I'm me when I hear him say these things! No doubt about it —this fellow's got everything that happened there down pat! (*To* MERCURY.) Tell me this: what was Amphitryon presented with out of the booty from the Teleboans?

MERCURY (*promptly*). The gold cup King Pterelas used to drink out of.

SOSIA (*to the audience, glumly*). That's the right answer. (*To* MERCURY.) Where's the cup now?

MERCURY (*as before*). In a chest. Locked and sealed with Amphitryon's seal.

SOSIA. What is his seal?

MERCURY. The rising sun in a four-horse chariot. (*Snarling.*) You trying to catch me, damn you?

SOSIA (*to the audience, in despair*). He's convinced me. I'll have to find another name! I don't know where he could have seen all this. (*Stands glumly for a moment, then is electrified by an idea.*) Wait! Now I'll get him. After all, what I did all by myself in the tent, with no one else around, that's something he'll never be able to tell me, *never.* (*To* MERCURY, *brimming with confidence.*) Well, if you're Sosia, what were you busy doing in the tent when the fighting was going on fast and furious? You tell me that, and I give up.

MERCURY (*slowly and with great precision*). There was a keg of wine. I filled a jug from it.

SOSIA (*to the audience, nervously*). He's on the right track.

MERCURY. Then I put away the whole jugful, neat, just the way it came from mother grape.

SOSIA (*to the audience, dumb struck*). That's just what happened! I put away a jugful of wine, neat. (*Savagely.*) I'll bet he was hiding there inside that jug.

MERCURY. Well? Have I convinced you you're not Sosia?

SOSIA (*belligerently*). You're telling me I'm not, eh?

MERCURY (*shrugging*). What else can I tell you, when *I* am?

SOSIA (*with hand over heart*). I swear by Jove that *I* am, and I swear that's no lie.

MERCURY (*with hand over heart*). And I swear by Mercury that Jove doesn't believe you. Take my word, he'll sooner believe me without an oath than you with.

SOSIA (*desperately*). Well then, who am I, if I'm not Sosia? Answer me that!

MERCURY. When I'm done being Sosia, you go right ahead and be Sosia. But right now *I'm* Sosia, so either you beat it or get a beating, Anonymous!

(SOSIA *goes up to him, looks him over, and then steps back scratching his head.*)

SOSIA (*to the audience, baffled*). So help me, when I look at him I recognize all my features, there's no doubt about it! I've seen myself in the mirror lots of times, and he's exactly like me. He's got the same hat and clothes. (*Peering harder.*) He's my spitting image! Legs, feet, height, haircut, eyes, nose, lips, jaws, chin, beard, neck, everything. What else is there to say? If he's got whip-scars all over his back, no two items in this world could be more alike. (*Clutching his head.*) Yet, when I think it over, I'm the same person I've always been, no question about it! I know my master's name, I know our house, I can use my head, and I've got all my senses. (*Plucking up courage.*) I won't pay any attention to what he says; I'll knock on the door. (*Starts walking up to the door.*)

MERCURY (*blocking the way*). Where do you think you're going?

SOSIA. Home.

MERCURY (*grimly*). You could climb aboard Jove's own magic chariot this minute to try to get away, but it wouldn't do you a bit of good: you're in for trouble and you're going to get it!

SOSIA (*weakly*). Can't I give my mistress the report my master ordered me to?

MERCURY. You can give *your* mistress whatever you want. But I'm not letting you get anywhere near mine. (*Thundering.*) Now, don't get me sore or you'll be carried out of here with those legs of yours stove in!

SOSIA (*with alacrity*). Oh no! I'm going. (*Raising his eyes to heaven.*) God in heaven, please! Where did I lose myself? Where did I get changed over? Where did I drop my looks? Did I forget myself and leave myself at the pier? Because this fellow here's got hold of the exact same looks I used to have. He's my statue—something nobody'll ever give me when I'm dead, I've already got while alive! (*Eyes* MERCURY *standing resolutely in front of the door and shrugs helplessly.*) I'll go back to the pier and tell the master everything that's happened. (*Mournfully.*) Maybe he won't recognize me either. (*Brightening.*) I hope to god he doesn't! I'll have these slave clothes off me and a free man's on, in no time! (*Dashes off, stage right.*)

MERCURY (*to the audience, with great satisfaction*). This job went off very nicely. *Very* nicely. I got that blamed nuisance away from the door, and (*Gesturing toward the house.*) Father can stay on in her arms in peace. (*Grinning.*) When that fellow gets back there to his master, he'll tell Amphitryon that Sosia the servant drove him away from the door. Amphitryon'll think he's lying and that he disobeyed orders and never even came here. (*Gleefully.*) I'll get both of them all mixed up and drive them and Amphitryon's whole household crazy, until Father's had enough of his inamorata. Then, when it's all over, they'll all find out what happened, and Jove at the end will restore Alcmena and her husband to their former married bliss. You see, Amphitryon is going to raise an awful ruckus with his wife and accuse her of adultery, but Father will step in and put down the insurrection.

(*Starts to go toward the door, then suddenly stops, struck by a new idea.*) There's something I didn't mention before about Alcmena. She's going to give birth today to twins, two boys. One will be a full-term baby, the other just a six-month baby. One is Amphitryon's, the other Jove's; the littler baby has the greater father, and vice versa. You all sure you understand the situation?

(*Looks the faces over anxiously and, reassured, continues.*) For the sake of Alcmena's reputation, Father's fixed it so there'll be only one confinement: she'll be done with two birth pangs in one labor. That way no one'll suspect anything illicit, and this clandestine cohabiting will stay a secret. However, as I mentioned before, Amphitryon will be told the whole story. What's the difference? Alcmena's reputation won't be hurt the least little bit. After all, it wouldn't do for a god to let *his* sin and guilt fall on the head of a mortal. (*His attention caught, looks toward the door.*) I'll shut up now—there's a sound at the door. Here comes the fake Amphitryon with Alcmena, the wife he has on loan.

(*The door opens and* JOVE *and* ALCMENA *step out.*

ALCMENA, *a ravishingly beautiful woman, perhaps in her early thirties, has more than mere good looks: her face shines with a candor and purity that add a special radiance to her loveliness.*

Her consort is a strongly built, handsome man in his forties. By the way he carries himself you can sense immediately that he is used to giving, not taking orders. He carries a stick, and is dressed in traveling clothes topped off by a broad-brimmed hat that has a tiny gold tassel dangling down behind.)

JOVE (*holding both her hands, tenderly*). Good-by, Alcmena dear. Take good care of our household, as you're doing. And please take things easy! You can see for yourself that your time is very near now. I've got to run along. (*Gravely.*) Whether it's a girl or a boy —I want the child to be brought up.

ALCMENA (*plaintively*). What's come up, dear, to make you leave home so suddenly?

JOVE (*tenderly*). Believe me, it's not because I'm tired either of you or of being home. But, when the commander in chief isn't with his troops, things that don't need doing get done with lots more dispatch than things that do.

MERCURY (*to the audience, gesturing toward* JOVE). A smooth operator, this one here. (*Grinning.*) And why not? He's *my* father.[3] Watch how he's going to butter the girl up.

ALCMENA (*pouting*). Well! I can certainly see how much *you* care for your wife.

JOVE (*kissing her*). Isn't it enough for you that I love you more than any other woman in the world?

MERCURY (*aside, gesturing toward the sky where presumably* JUNO *is*). If that one up there finds out that you're busy with things like this, believe me, you'll wish you were Amphitryon instead of Jove!

ALCMENA (*as before*). I'd rather find out for myself than be told. Before your place in bed has had time to get warm, you're on your way! You arrived just yesterday in the middle of the night, and now you're leaving. Do you think I like this?

MERCURY (*to the audience*). I'll go up and have a word with her. Play Helpful Henry for Papa. (*Walking up to* ALCMENA *and addressing her.*) So help me, I don't think there's a man on earth who's as mad about his wife as he's mad about you. (*Glances covertly to observe the effect of this on* JOVE.)

JOVE (*to* MERCURY, *thundering*). God damn you! Think I don't know what you're up to! Out of my sight!

[3] Mercury was patron god of thieves.

What do you think you're doing, messing into my affairs? What do you think you're doing, opening that big mouth of yours? (*Brandishing his stick.*) Why, I'll take this stick and I'll—

ALCMENA (*interrupting in alarm*). Don't, please!

. JOVE (*snarling*). Just let him open that big mouth of his!

MERCURY (*to the audience, grinning*). My debut as Helpful Henry was almost a fiasco.

JOVE (*conciliatorily*). But to get back to what you were saying, dear. You really shouldn't be angry with me. I sneaked away from headquarters. I stole this chance to see you, so I could be the first to tell you, and you the first to hear, how I served my country. And now you've heard all about it. Would I do such a thing if I didn't love you very, very much?

MERCURY (*to the audience, chuckling*). Didn't I tell you he'd do this? A little buttering up, and he has the poor girl eating out of his hand.

JOVE. And now I've got to sneak back, so the men won't find out and say I think more of my wife than my country.

ALCMENA (*starting to cry*). You have your poor wife in tears by going away like this.

JOVE (*tenderly*). Sh! Don't spoil those pretty eyes. I'll be back very soon.

ALCMENA (*sobbing*). That "very soon" is such a long, long time!

JOVE (*as before*). Believe me, I'm not very happy about going away and leaving you.

ALCMENA (*bitterly*). Oh sure—that's why you're leaving the same night you came. (*She reaches out to hold him by the arm.*)

JOVE (*gently taking her hand away*). You mustn't hold me back. It's getting late. I want to be out of the city before dawn. (*He holds up a box.*) Here's the cup which was awarded to me for gallantry in action. King Pterelas used to own it; I killed him with my own hands. (*Handing it to her.*) It's a present for you, Alcmena.

ALCMENA (*smiling radiantly through her tears*). You're always doing things like that! It's a wonderful gift, as wonderful as the giver.

MERCURY (*bowing gallantly*). Say rather a wonderful gift, as wonderful as the *getter*.

JOVE (*turning on him*). Still at it? Damn you, can't I get rid of you!

ALCMENA (*stroking his cheek*). Please, Amphitryon, don't be angry at Sosia. For my sake.

JOVE (*grumbling*). Well, anything to please you.

MERCURY (*to the audience, gesturing toward* JOVE). What love does to him! So touchy!

JOVE (*kissing her good-by*). Anything you want before I go?

ALCMENA. Yes. Love me even though I'm far away—since I'm all yours, even though you're far away.

MERCURY (*impatiently*). Let's go, Amphitryon! It's already getting light.

JOVE. You go ahead, Sosia. I'll be along in a minute. (MERCURY *leaves, stage left.* JOVE *kisses* ALCMENA *again.*) Nothing I can do for you?

ALCMENA. Yes—come back soon. (*She waves a last good-by, then swiftly turns and runs into the house.*)

JOVE (*calling after her*). All right. (*Winking at the audience.*) I'll be back sooner than you think! So cheer up.

(*He turns and, raising his head, addresses the sky.*)

Night, you waited very patiently. You're dismissed; make way for Day. Let Day now spread its clear bright light over the earth. And, Night, to even things up I'll make the day shorter by exactly as much time as you were longer than the night before. Go now—let the dark give way to light!

(*To the audience.*)

And now I'll go and follow Mercury. (*He exits, stage left, and the stage is now empty.*)

Act II

(*It is now some hours later, and day has dawned. Enter stage right,* AMPHITRYON, *then* SOSIA, *then some porters carrying baggage.* AMPHITRYON *is identical in appearance with the* JOVE *of the last act, save for the telltale tassel.*)

SONG

AMPHITRYON (*impatiently*).
Come on! Shake a leg and follow me!
SOSIA (*hurrying to keep up*).
I am, I'm right behind you, see?
AMPHITRYON (*stopping and eying him distastefully*).
You're a worthless good-for-nothing, I'd say.
SOSIA (*innocently*).
But why? What makes you feel that way?
AMPHITRYON (*angrily*).
Because you stand there telling me
What never was and never will be.
SOSIA (*shaking his head despondently*).
You see? You're always doing it.
You won't trust any of us one bit.
AMPHITRYON (*working himself up*).
Now what do you mean by that! I swear,
You good-for-nothing, I'm going to tear
That good-for-nothing tongue of yours out!
SOSIA (*doggedly*).
I belong to you, so I've no doubt
You'll do to me what it suits you to.
But nothing you can possibly do
Will make me say this isn't true.
AMPHITRYON (*exploding*).
You're standing here and yet, you louse,
You've the nerve to tell me you're now in the house!
SOSIA (*as before*).
That's true.
AMPHITRYON.
          Well, god will punish you—
And, damn it all, *I* will too.
SOSIA (*sulkily*).
You're master here. All I do is serve.

AMPHITRYON (*in a towering rage*).
I want to know where you get the nerve
  To play your jokes on me,
To tell me a thing no man has seen,
  A thing which just can't be.
Of all the barefaced impudence!
  Of all the brazen stunts!
To tell me that the selfsame man
  Can be in two places at once!

SOSIA (*as before*).
I tell you that's what happened to me.

AMPHITRYON.
Oh, you be damned!

SOSIA (*reproachfully*).
              But I don't see
What I've done to earn these threats
  from you.

AMPHITRYON.
You dare to ask, you stinker, you,
  When you stand there laughing in my
    face?

SOSIA (doggedly).
If what I'd said was not the case,
  Then I'd deserve these damns from you.
But it's not a lie. Every word is true,
  I'm giving you the story straight.

AMPHITRYON (*looking at him in disgust*).
The fellow's drunk, as sure as fate.

SOSIA (*despairingly*).
I wish I were!

AMPHITRYON (*acidly*).
          You wish to do
What's already done?

SOSIA (*bewildered*).
            Who me?

AMPHITRYON (*icily*).
               Yes you.
Just where did you find the liquor, pray?

SOSIA.
Me? Nowhere. Haven't touched a drop
  today.

AMPHITRYON (*to the world at large, throwing up his hands helplessly*).
What kind of man is this, anyway!

SOSIA (*expostulating, pointing to the house*).
By now I've said it ten times, I swear.
  Must I holler in your ear?
I tell you I'm in that house over there,
  And also beside you here.
You think that now the situation
  Is sufficiently plain and clear?

AMPHITRYON (*shouting*).
Stand back from me! Why, this is outrageous!

SOSIA.
Why, what's the matter now?

AMPHITRYON (*witheringly*).
              You're contagious—
You've caught the plague.

SOSIA (*reproachfully*).
           Why say such a thing?
I'm in the pink, my health's just flourishing!

AMPHITRYON (*snarling*).
I'll bet it doesn't stay that way!
  You'll get what's coming to you today:
If I make it home, I guarantee
  You'll live a life of misery!

(*He glares at* SOSIA *balefully in silence for a moment, and then resumes.*)

(*Icily.*) Follow me, faithful servant who makes a fool of his master by talking drivel, who, on top of neglecting to carry out his master's orders, deliberately comes to laugh in his master's face, who hands his master an impossible story, something no one's ever heard of even through hearsay—AND whose back, believe you me, will pay for every last one of his lies.

SOSIA (*reproachfully*). Amphitryon, I can't tell you how unhappy it makes an honest servant, one who tells his master the honest truth, to see the truth take a beating.

AMPHITRYON (*as before*). Then let's you and I figure it out: how the devil is it possible for you, at this very moment, to be right here and also in the house? That's what I want to know.

SOSIA. It's absolutely true: I'm here and I'm there. If this sounds like a miracle, it's just as much a miracle to me as it is to you.

AMPHITRYON. How's that?

SOSIA (*grinning*). Since it's no less a miracle to me than to you. (*Becoming serious again.*) So help me, at first I didn't believe in my other me, until my other me convinced me to believe in him. He reeled off the whole story, down to the last detail, of what happened at the front. And he stole my looks along with my name: two drops of milk aren't as alike as my other me is to me. (*Thoughtfully.*) You see, when you sent me home from the pier before daybreak a little while ago—

AMPHITRYON (*interrupting impatiently*). Well, what about it?

SOSIA (*ignoring the interruption*). —I'd already been standing in front of the house long before I arrived there.

AMPHITRYON (*throwing up his hands*). What the devil is this nonsense! Are you in your right mind?

SOSIA (*glumly*). See for yourself.

AMPHITRYON (*tapping his temple significantly; to himself, portentously*). After he left me, he must have seen the evil eye. Had some evil strike him.

SOSIA (*promptly*). I sure did: I got beaten to a pulp.

AMPHITRYON. Who beat you?

SOSIA (*as before*). I did myself. (*As* AMPHITRYON *looks at him bewildered.*) The me who's in the house now.

AMPHITRYON (*with deadly calm*). Now watch out. I want only answers to my questions, nothing more. First of all —this other Sosia of yours, who is he? That's what I want to know.

SOSIA. Your servant.

AMPHITRYON (*groaning*). Even one of you is more than I want! (*Pounding his fist into the palm of his hand.*) I've owned only one Sosia in all my life, and that's you!

SOSIA (*shaking his head stubbornly*). I'll tell you right here and now, Amphitryon: I bet you, when you get home, you'll run into another servant Sosia in addition to me in the house. His father's name was Davus just like mine, he looks exactly like me, and he's the same age. To put it in a nutshell, your Sosia's become twins.

AMPHITRYON (*baffled*). This is a very strange story. (*After a moment's thought.*) Did you get to see my wife?

SOSIA. How? I wasn't allowed into the house.

AMPHITRYON. Who stopped you?

SOSIA. The other Sosia I've been telling you about, the one who beat me up.

AMPHITRYON (*thundering*). Who is that Sosia?

SOSIA. Me, I tell you! How many times must I say it?

AMPHITRYON (*suddenly struck by a thought, eying him suspiciously*). Say, tell me this—you weren't asleep a little while ago, were you?

SOSIA (*shaking his head vigorously*). Not the least little bit.

AMPHITRYON. I was wondering whether maybe you had seen some Sosia in a dream.

SOSIA (*in high dudgeon*). I am not in the habit of carrying out my master's orders in a comatose condition. I was wide awake when I saw him, I'm wide awake now seeing you, I'm wide awake now telling you this story, and I was wide awake a little while ago when I got beaten up. He was wide awake too.

AMPHITRYON. Who was?

SOSIA (*wearily*). The other Sosia, I tell you. (*Pleadingly.*) Please! Can't you understand?

AMPHITRYON (*helplessly*). How the devil could anyone understand! You talk such drivel!

SOSIA (*grimly*). You'll understand soon enough, when you see that Sosia standing in front of your eyes.

AMPHITRYON (*starting off toward the door, grimly*). Then follow me. The first thing I've got to do is look into this whole business.

(*He strides up to the door and looks it over. Then, with* SOSIA *and the porters at his heels, he moves away to examine the rest of the house from the outside. As they do so, the door opens and, unnoticed by them,* ALCMENA *steps out.*)

SONG

ALCMENA (*to the audience, sadly*).
As we go through life, how rare is happiness

Compared with misery! It's part of life
For everyone, it's heaven's pleasure that
Sorrow travel hand in hand with joy,
That, once some good has happened, on
   its heels
There follow even more of toil and
   trouble.
You see, just now I learned this for my-
   self,
I know it from my own experience.
I was given a moment of joy, the chance
   I had
To see my husband. It lasted just a night;
Before the day had come, he suddenly
Arose and went away. And now I feel
I'm utterly alone, since he whom I
Love best of all no longer is with me.
His leaving brought me more of sorrow
   than
His coming brought me joy.
(*Pauses, and then, her countenance
brightening, resumes proudly.*)
Yet one thing's made me happy: he
   conquered his foes
And came back home bearing a crown
   of glory.
This is my consolation; he may always
   leave
My side if it is to return to me a hero.
The parting will hurt, but I will bear the
   hurt
With strength and resolution if this one
Reward I get: to see my husband hailed
By all as victor on the field of battle.
For me just this is enough. Our greatest
   prize
Is courage—courage takes, beyond all
   doubt,
First place among all things upon this
   earth.
Our lives, our liberty, safety, all we own,
Our parents, children, homes, and father-
   land—
Courage is the guardian of them all.
For courage embraces every good
   there is:
If a man has courage, every good is his!

(*She falls silent. A moment later,*
AMPHITRYON *and his entourage return
from their inspection of the house.* ALC-
MENA, *unnoticed, remains buried in
thought near the door.*)
AMPHITRYON (*to* SOSIA, *enthusiasti-*

cally). I know my wife will be overjoyed to see me back. (*Smiling happily,
half to himself.*) We're very much in
love with each other. (*To* SOSIA) Especially since everything's gone so well—
I led the army to victory, I defeated at
the first encounter an enemy everyone
thought invincible. Yes, I'm sure of it;
she simply can't wait to see me back.
SOSIA. What about me? You think
that lady friend of mine won't be glad
to see *me?*
ALCMENA (*her attention caught by
the sound of voices, in surprise*). There's
my husband!
AMPHITRYON (*to* SOSIA, *heading for
the door*). Follow me.
ALCMENA (*to herself*). What's he
coming back for? A little while ago he
was saying he was in a hurry to get
away. (*Puzzled.*) Is he deliberately trying to test me? Does he want to see for
himself how I miss him when he's away?
(*Smiling happily.*) Well, I certainly have
no objections to having him back!
SOSIA (*suddenly catching sight of*
ALCMENA *and stopping in his tracks*).
Amphitryon, we'd better go back to the
ship.
AMPHITRYON (*also stopping; puzzled*).
Why?
SOSIA. Because no one's going to give
us homecomers breakfast.
AMPHITRYON (*as before*). Now what
put that idea in your head?
SOSIA. We're too late.
AMPHITRYON. How's that?
SOSIA. There's Alcmena in front of
the door. And I can see she's got a full
belly.
AMPHITRYON (*looking and smiling*).
Oh, she was pregnant when I left.
SOSIA (*groaning*). My god! That's
the end of me!
AMPHITRYON. What's the matter?
SOSIA. If I follow your figuring, she
must be in her ninth month. That means
I've come home just in time to start
hauling water!

AMPHITRYON (*smiling*). Come on, cheer up.

SOSIA. Cheer up? Oh, sure! (*Savagely.*) Just let me get my hands on a bucket. God damn it, never believe a word I say from this minute on if I don't draw the last drop of life out of that damn well once I get started!

AMPHITRYON. Come along. Don't worry; I'll give someone else the job.

ALCMENA (*to herself, excitedly*). I think I really should run up to meet him.

(*She walks swiftly up to him, holding out her hands. He takes them in his and looks at her, smiling blissfully.*)

AMPHITRYON (*warmly*). Joyful greetings from Amphitryon to his darling wife—the finest wife in all Thebes, in her husband's considered opinion, and a good woman too, as every husband in Thebes will tell you. (*Drawing her closer, tenderly.*) How have you been, dear? Are you glad to see me?

(*There is a moment of silence as* ALCMENA *stares at him uncomprehendingly.*)

SOSIA (*aside, acidly*). Never saw anybody more glad. Giving him about as warm a greeting as you would a stray mutt!

AMPHITRYON (*as before*). And to see you pregnant this way and so near your time! I'm simply delighted!

ALCMENA (*bewildered*). Will you please tell me why you must make fun of me like this with these salutations and greetings? As if you didn't see me just a little while ago! As if you've just this minute come back from the front! (*Curiously.*) Why this greeting me as if you hadn't seen me for ages?

AMPHITRYON (*taken aback*). Why, I haven't laid eyes on you until just now!

ALCMENA (*as before*). Now what makes you say that?

AMPHITRYON (*as before*). Because I've learned to tell the truth!

ALCMENA (*annoyed*). Well, a man who unlearns what he's learned is not behaving well at all! Are you two trying to test my feelings? (*Softening her tone as she notices their genuine bewilderment.*) What brings you back so quickly? A bad omen hold you back? The weather keeping you from sailing to the front, as you said you were going to do a little while ago?

AMPHITRYON. "A little while ago?" How little a while ago was this little while ago?

ALCMENA (*resentfully*). You're trying to catch me! (*With a careless wave of the hand, irritably.*) Some time ago. Just before.

AMPHITRYON (*throwing up his hands*). Now will you kindly explain how that's possible? (*Mimicking her.*) "Some time ago. Just before."

ALCMENA (*acidly*). What do you think? That, because you're making fun of me, I'm making fun of you? Imagine telling me that this is the first I've seen of you when you just left here a little while ago!

AMPHITRYON (*to* SOSIA, *incredulously*). She's talking raving nonsense!

SOSIA (*to* AMPHITRYON, *with an I-understand-the-whole-business air*). Just wait a little while, until she sleeps off this dream.

AMPHITRYON. You mean she dreams while she's wide awake?

ALCMENA (*to* AMPHITRYON, *sharply*). I most certainly am wide awake, and I'm telling you what happened with these eyes of mine wide open. A little while ago, just before daybreak, I saw both you and (*gesturing contemptuously toward* SOSIA) him.

AMPHITRYON. Where?

ALCMENA. Here, in your own house.

AMPHITRYON (*brusquely*). You never did!

SOSIA (*to* AMPHITRYON). Wait a second. (*Eagerly.*) What if the ship brought us from the dock to the door here in our sleep?

AMPHITRYON (*witheringly*). Are you on her side too?

SOSIA (*whispering urgently*). What

do you expect? Don't you understand? If you try to say no to a madwoman, you'll make the crazy thing crazier, and she'll keep clobbering you. Say yes to her, and she'll let you off with only one sock.

AMPHITRYON (*to* SOSIA, *grimly*). There's one thing that's going to happen right now: I'm going to give her a piece of my mind for not giving me a greeting on my return home.

SOSIA (*to* AMPHITRYON). You'll stir up a hornet's nest!

AMPHITRYON (*to* SOSIA). Quiet! (*To* ALCMENA.) Alcmena, I want to ask you something.

ALCMENA (*shrugging*). Go ahead. Anything you like.

AMPHITRYON (*angrily*). Have you had an attack of stupidity? Or an overdose of the feeling that no one's good enough for you?

ALCMENA (*helplessly*). My dear husband, whatever put the idea in your head to ask me a question like that?

AMPHITRYON (*bitterly*). Because, up to now, you always used to come up and greet me the way any decent, loving wife would greet a husband. Now I come home and find you completely changed!

ALCMENA (*earnestly*). But I did! My dear, the very moment you arrived yesterday, I greeted you. I asked how you were, I took your hand, and I kissed you.

SOSIA (*to* ALCMENA, *uncomprehendingly*). You greeted him yesterday?

ALCMENA. You too, Sosia.

SOSIA (*to* AMPHITRYON, *shaking his head mournfully*). Amphitryon, I had hoped she would bear you a son, but she's not big with child.

AMPHITRYON. With what, then?

SOSIA. With bats in her belfry!

ALCMENA (*to* SOSIA, *acidly*). I am perfectly sound, and god willing, I'll be safe when I give birth. (*Gesturing toward* AMPHITRYON.) And if he'd only do his duty, you'd get a good smack of the whip! (*Raising her voice.*) You'd get

what you deserve for putting a jinx like that on me, you jinxer you!

SOSIA (*muttering to himself, sullenly*). Yeah? A pregnant woman should get a good smack—(*catching* ALCMENA'S *glare and switching abruptly to bright innocence*) a snack, I mean. You know, something to nibble on in case she starts to feel nauseous.

AMPHITRYON (*to* ALCMENA). You saw me here yesterday?

ALCMENA (*wearily*). If you must be told for the tenth time, yes!

AMPHITRYON (*hopefully*). In a dream, maybe?

ALCMENA (*as before*). No. I was wide awake, and so were you.

AMPHITRYON (*to the world at large*). The troubles I have!

SOSIA. What's the matter?

AMPHITRYON. My wife's gone crazy!

SOSIA (*gloomily, nodding knowledgeably*). Sudden attack of manic depression. Nothing like it for driving people mad.

AMPHITRYON (*solicitously*). When did you first feel this coming on, Alcmena?

ALCMENA (*preserving an icy calm*). I tell you, I am *not* crazy.

AMPHITRYON. Then why do you say you saw me yesterday, when I only arrived in port last night? I had dinner there, and I slept all night on board. (*Emphatically.*) I haven't put foot inside this house since the day I left with the army to fight the Teleboans. And, what's more, defeated them.

ALCMENA (*as before*). That's not so. You had dinner with me, and you slept with me.

AMPHITRYON (*roaring*). What did you say?

ALCMENA (*as before*). The truth.

AMPHITRYON (*grimly*). Not about that, it isn't. About anything else, I wouldn't know.

ALCMENA (*as before*). And, at the crack of dawn, you left for the front.

AMPHITRYON (*frantically*). How can this be?

SOSIA (*promptly*). She's telling it just as she remembers it. It's a dream she's telling you. (*To* ALCMENA, *shaking his head regretfully*.) But, after you woke up, Alcmena, you should have offered special prayers to Jove. He's our patron god of miracles, you know.

ALCMENA (*disgusted*). Oh, go to the devil!

SOSIA (*muttering to himself*). No, you go—(*Catching her glare and switching abruptly to bright innocence.*) and take care of those prayers. Do you good.

ALCMENA (*to* AMPHITRYON, *grimly*). That's the second time he's insulted me, and you let him get away with it.

AMPHITRYON (*to* SOSIA). Shut up! (*To* ALCMENA.) Now tell me: today, at the crack of dawn, I went away from you, did I?

ALCMENA (*shrugging*). If it wasn't you two, then who told me the story of how the battle went?

AMPHITRYON (*flabbergasted*). You mean to say you know about that?

ALCMENA. Of course! I heard from you all about how you stormed and took a great city and how you killed King Pterelas yourself.

AMPHITRYON (*as before*). *I* told you that?

ALCMENA. Yes, you. And Sosia was there with us.

AMPHITRYON (*to* SOSIA). Did you hear me tell her all this today?

SOSIA (*with a how-silly-can-you-get tone of voice*). Now where would I have heard you?

AMPHITRYON (*to* SOSIA, *throwing up his hands*). Ask *her,* not me.

ALCMENA (*to* AMPHITRYON, *witheringly*). Strange, isn't it, that he won't contradict you.

AMPHITRYON. Sosia! Look at me.

SOSIA. I'm looking.

AMPHITRYON. Now, don't just yes me; I want you to tell me the truth. Did you hear me tell her today these things she said I did?

SOSIA (*scornfully*). Please! Are you crazy too? Asking me a question like that! This is the first I've seen of her, just like yourself.

AMPHITRYON (*grimly*). Well, Alcmena? Did you hear him?

ALCMENA (*calmly*). I certainly did —telling lies!

AMPHITRYON. So you don't trust either him or your own husband, eh?

ALCMENA (*as before*). Only because I trust myself most of all, and I know that everything happened exactly as I've told it to you.

AMPHITRYON. You say that I arrived here yesterday?

ALCMENA. You deny that you left here today?

AMPHITRYON (*exploding*). Of course I do! I tell you, this is the first and only time I've been home!

ALCMENA (*tossing her head*). Then I'd like to know whether you're also going to deny that this morning you gave me the gold cup you said you received as an award?

AMPHITRYON (*snorting*). I did not give you that cup, nor did I mention a word about it! I'll admit I had in mind to give it to you, and I still do. (*Doing a double take.*) Who told you about it, anyway?

ALCMENA (*coldly*). You told me about it with your own lips and gave it to me with your own hands.

AMPHITRYON (*in desperation*). Wait here. Don't move. Please! (*Turning and whispering to* SOSIA.) This is incredible, Sosia! How could she have known that I was awarded a gold cup? (*Menacingly.*) Unless you met her before and told her the whole story.

SOSIA (*hastily*). I never said a word to her! The first time I laid eyes on her was when you did.

AMPHITRYON (*clutching his head in despair*). What kind of person is she!

ALCMENA (*patiently*). Would you like me to show you the cup?

AMPHITRYON. Yes, I would!

ALCMENA. Very well. (*She goes to the door and claps her hands. A moment later a maid appears in the doorway.*) Thessala, go back in and bring out the cup my husband gave me this morning.

AMPHITRYON (*pulling* SOSIA *off to the side*). Come over here, Sosia. (*Sotto voce, nervously.*) Listen, if she has that cup, that'll be the miracle to end all miracles.

SOSIA (*sotto voce, incredulously*). You mean you believe her? (*Pointing to a box in the hands of one of the porters.*) But it's in this chest here. Locked and sealed with your own seal.

AMPHITRYON (*as before*). Is the seal intact?

SOSIA (*sotto voce*). Take a look.

AMPHITRYON (*doing so; sotto voce, relieved*). Perfect. Just the way I sealed it.

SOSIA (*sotto voce*). Listen, why don't you have her treated for lunacy?

AMPHITRYON (*sotto voce, gloomily*). Damn it all, I'll have to. She's crazy as a loon, damn it!

(*The maid reappears carrying a cup which she hands to* ALCMENA, *who turns and calls to* AMPHITRYON.)

ALCMENA. No need for any more talk. Here's your cup. (*Holding it up.*) See?

AMPHITRYON (*striding over*). Let's have it.

ALCMENA (*handing it to him*). Here you are. And take a good look. Since you insist on denying cold facts, I'll make it as plain as day for you. (*Sternly.*) Is this the cup that was awarded to you?

AMPHITRYON (*dumb struck*). In the name of Jove! What *is* this I see? It's the cup all right! (*To* SOSIA, *dumbly.*) Sosia, I'm a ruined man!

SOSIA (*grimly*). Either this woman is the greatest witch that ever lived, or your cup must still be in that box.

AMPHITRYON (*grimly*). Then hurry and open that box.

SOSIA (*throwing up his hands*). Why bother? The seal's still intact. (*Wildly.*) Everything's working out perfectly: you've produced a second Amphitryon, I've produced a second Sosia, and now, if the cup comes up with a cup, we've all become twins!

AMPHITRYON (*as before*). We're opening that chest and having a look, and that's that!

SOSIA. Will you please just check the seal first, so you don't start blaming me afterwards?

AMPHITRYON (*thundering*). Open it! This woman wants to drive us both insane with these stories of hers! (SOSIA *starts fumbling with the chest.*)

ALCMENA (*helplessly*). Where would I have gotten it except from you? It was your gift to me!

AMPHITRYON (*grimly*). I've got to look into this business.

SOSIA (*emitting a war whoop*). By Jove! By Jove almighty!

AMPHITRYON (*startled*). What's the matter?

SOSIA (*pointing to the chest, shaking like a leaf*). There's no cup in this chest!

AMPHITRYON. What's that you say?

SOSIA. The truth!

AMPHITRYON (*between his teeth*). It better turn up, or you'll pay for it with your hide.

ALCMENA (*holding out the cup, calmly*). It has turned up—here.

AMPHITRYON (*to* ALCMENA, *as before*). All right. Who gave it to you?

ALCMENA (*as before*). The man who's asking me the question.

SOSIA (*to* AMPHITRYON, *dancing with rage*). Trying to trick me, eh? You sneaked away from the ship, you ran ahead by a different road, you took the cup out, you gave it to her, and then you sneaked the seal back on!

AMPHITRYON (*clutching his head*).

Oh, my god! Are you out to help this madwoman too? (*To* ALCMENA, *wearily*.) So you say we arrived here yesterday?

ALCMENA (*quietly and calmly*). Yes, I do. And the minute you arrived, you greeted me. I greeted you and gave you a kiss.

SOSIA (*to the audience, shaking his head dolefully*). Right away, I don't like the way it begins. Bad stuff, this kiss business.

AMPHITRYON. Go on.

ALCMENA. Then you took a bath.

AMPHITRYON. And after my bath?

ALCMENA. You sat down to table.

SOSIA (*to* AMPHITRYON). Good! Perfect! Get to the bottom of this.

AMPHITRYON (*to* SOSIA, *brusquely*). Don't interrupt! (*To* ALCMENA.) Go on with your story.

ALCMENA. Dinner was served. We ate together. I sat alongside you.

AMPHITRYON. On the same couch?

ALCMENA. On the same couch.

SOSIA (*shaking his head dolefully*). I don't like the sound of this dinner party!

AMPHITRYON (*turning on him*). Let her go on with her explanations. (*To* ALCMENA.) And after we finished dinner?

ALCMENA. You said you were sleepy. The table was cleared, and we went off to bed.

AMPHITRYON. Where did you sleep?

ALCMENA. With you. In the same room. In the same bed.

AMPHITRYON (*gasping convulsively*). You've done for me!

SOSIA (*in alarm*). What's the matter?

AMPHITRYON. This woman's just murdered me!

ALCMENA (*agitated*). What did I do? Please!

AMPHITRYON (*turning his back on her*). Don't you talk to me!

SOSIA. What's the matter?

AMPHITRYON (*dramatically*). I'm ruined! Her honor—while I was away, it was stained!

ALCMENA (*wounded*). God in heaven! My dear husband, how can you say a thing like that about me!

AMPHITRYON (*wildly*). Your husband? I? Don't you call me by that name! False woman, it's a false name!

SOSIA (*to the audience, grinning*). This is a pretty sticky state of affairs if (*gesturing toward* AMPHITRYON) he's become a woman and isn't her man.

ALCMENA (*helplessly*). What did I do to make you say such things to me?

AMPHITRYON (*in a cold fury*). You've just presented the facts yourself. You have to ask *me* what you did wrong?

ALCMENA (*bewildered*). How could I have done anything wrong, when I was with you, the man I married?

AMPHITRYON (*screaming*). You were with me? (*To the world at large.*) There isn't a woman alive as brazen as this one! (*Icily.*) If you have no sense of shame, the very least you can do is act as if you did.

ALCMENA (*her eyes flashing*). Neither I nor anyone in my family would ever stoop to the behavior you're accusing me of. Is it your idea to catch me in adultery? You never will!

AMPHITRYON (*throwing up his arms in despair*). Oh, my god in heaven! (*Turning to* SOSIA.) Sosia, you at least recognize me, don't you?

SOSIA (*looking him over, coolly*). Just about.

AMPHITRYON. Didn't I have dinner yesterday aboard ship in port?

ALCMENA (*coldly*). I have witnesses, too, to back up what *I* say.

SOSIA (*to* AMPHITRYON, *scratching his head*). I really don't know what to say about this whole business except that, maybe, there's some other Amphitryon who takes over your affairs while you're away and (*delicately, with a glance in* ALCMENA'S *direction*) discharges your duties for you in your absence. If a fake Sosia is a miracle, believe you me, this other Amphitryon of yours is an even bigger one!

AMPHITRYON (*desperately*). Some witch must have driven her out of her wits.

ALCMENA (*passionately*). In the name of the supreme god of the heavens, in the name of Our Lady Juno, whom I reverence and worship with all my heart as I should, I swear to you that, outside of yourself, no man's body has touched mine to rob me of my honor!

AMPHITRYON (*dully*). I only wish it were true.

ALCMENA (*resentfully*). It *is* true. But that doesn't mean a thing because you don't want to believe it.

AMPHITRYON (*sneering*). You're a woman, you're quick to swear.

ALCMENA (*proudly*). A woman who's done no wrong can be quick to swear. She can speak up for herself with confidence and without fear.

AMPHITRYON (*muttering*). You're quick to swear, all right.

ALCMENA (*as before*). As any good woman should be!

AMPHITRYON (*as before*). Good, eh? That's what you *say*.

ALCMENA (*gravely*). What people generally mean by the word "dowry" is not what I consider my dowry to be. No —mine is decency and honor and self-control; respect for heaven, love for my parents, and good relations with all my family; to carry out your wishes, to give to the good, and to help the honest.

SOSIA. So help me, if everything she says is true, this woman's a paragon of virtue!

AMPHITRYON (*unhappily*). I'm so mixed up, I don't even know my own name!

SOSIA (*promptly*). You're Amphit-

ryon, all right. But be careful: the way people have been changing ever since we got back, you might lose your right title to it if you don't watch out.

AMPHITRYON (*wearily*). Alcmena, I must look into this matter, I can't just drop it.

ALCMENA. I'd be very glad if you would.

AMPHITRYON (*as before*). Now what do you say to this? Your cousin Naucrates came over on the same ship with me. Suppose I bring him here from the dock. If he denies that things happened as you say they did, what do you think would be the fair thing to do? Can you give me any good reason why I shouldn't divorce you?

ALCMENA. None at all—*if* I've done something wrong.

AMPHITRYON. Agreed. (*To* SOSIA, *gesturing toward the porters.*) Take them inside. I'm going back to the ship to get Naucrates.

(AMPHITRYON *shuffles off despondently, stage right.* SOSIA *gestures to the porters, who file into the house. He is about to follow them when, struck by a thought, he turns back to* ALCMENA.)

SOSIA (*confidentially*). Look, there's no one around now besides us two. Tell me the honest truth: is there another Sosia inside who looks exactly like me?

ALCMENA. Oh, get away from me! (*Disgustedly.*) Like master, like man!

SOSIA (*grumbling*). If that's the way you want it, I'll go. (*Enters the house.*)

ALCMENA (*to the audience, shaking her head sadly*). A strange way for my husband to be acting. To get pleasure out of falsely accusing me of misconduct! (*Shrugging.*) Well, whatever it is, I'll find out soon enough from Cousin Naucrates.

(*She turns and enters the house. The stage is now empty.*)

Act III

(*Enter* JOVE, *stage left. He walks downstage and addresses the audience.*)

JOVE. I'm the Amphitryon with the servant Sosia who turns into Mercury when it's convenient, the Amphitryon who lives in (*pointing toward the sky*) the penthouse and sometimes becomes Jove when the spirit moves him. But the minute I arrive here, quick as a flash I change my clothes and become Amphitryon.

(*With a respectful bow.*) This time I'm here for your sakes: I didn't want to leave this comedy only half done. At the same time, I wanted to come to Alcmena's rescue, since her husband (*gesturing in the general direction of the port*), *that* Amphitryon, is accusing her of adultery though she's done nothing wrong. After all, I'd be to blame if what I alone was responsible for should fall on the head of poor, innocent Alcmena. (*Grinning.*) I'll pass myself off now as Amphitryon, as I did before, and drive the whole household crazy. (*Becoming grave.*) However, after it's all over, I'll reveal the secret, and I'll help Alcmena when her time comes: I'll see to it that she delivers both the child her husband conceived and the one I conceived with only one confinement and without any pain.

(*Looking about.*) I told Mercury to stand by me immediately in case I had orders for him. (*With a wave of his hand, draws the audience's attention to the door of the house. The next second it opens, and* ALCMENA *appears in the doorway.*) I'll speak to her right now.

(ALCMENA *emerges from her house carrying a bag. She slams the door shut behind her and, not noticing* JOVE, *walks downstage and puts down the bag.*)

ALCMENA (*to the audience, in a rage*). I simply can't stay in this house. To have my own husband accuse me this way of adultery, of shame and dishonor! Things that happened he shouts to high heaven never happened, and the next minute accuses me of things that never happened, that were none of my doing. What's more, he imagines I'll shrug all this off as just so much water under the bridge. I will not! He can't falsely accuse me of adultery—I won't stand for it! Either I leave him, or he gives me full satisfaction, and, what's more, swears to me that he takes back every word he's uttered against his wife's innocence!

JOVE (*to the audience*). I'll have to arrange things the way she wants if I'm ever to get her to take back her fond lover. Amphitryon is an innocent victim: my doings have fallen on his neck, and my love affair let him in for a lot of trouble a little while ago. But now the tongue-lashing and cursing she got from him is falling on *my* neck, and *I'm* the innocent victim! (*Walks up to her.*)

ALCMENA (*to the audience*). There's the man who's made his wife miserable by accusing her of shame and dishonor.

(*Turns her back on him as he comes up.*)

JOVE (*tenderly*). My dear wife, I want to talk to you. Why do you turn your back on me?

ALCMENA (*furiously*). It's my nature. I can't stand the sight of an enemy.

JOVE. Hey, what's this! An enemy?

ALCMENA (*as before*). Exactly. It's the truth—unless you're ready to accuse me of calling you by a false name this time too!

JOVE (*putting his arm about her; meltingly*). You're so angry!

ALCMENA (*thrusting his arm away*). You keep your hands off me! (*Witheringly.*) After all, if you had any sense and were in your right mind, you'd hardly want to hold a conversation, serious or otherwise, with a woman you consider and call immoral. Not unless you're stupider than the stupidest!

JOVE (*earnestly*). My calling you so doesn't make you any more so, and I *don't* consider you immoral. I've come here for only one purpose: to apologize to you. I've never felt so badly about anything as I did when I heard you were angry with me. "Why did you say such things?" you'll ask. I'll tell you why. It was not, I swear it, that I thought you were immoral; I was just testing your feelings, what you'd do, how you'd be inclined to take it. What I said to you before wasn't serious—it was all a joke! Just ask Sosia.

ALCMENA (*glaring at him*). You go ahead and bring my Cousin Naucrates, just as you said you were going to do, to be your witness that you hadn't been here before.

JOVE (*reproachfully*). Now, if something's said in a joke, it's not fair to take it seriously.

ALCMENA (*bitterly*). A joke that cut me to the very heart, as I know only too well.

JOVE (*on his knees*). Alcmena, I beg you! On my knees! Please! Forgive me! Pardon me! Don't be angry with me!

ALCMENA (*coldly*). My character makes everything you've said against me simply meaningless. (*Turning from him.*) Since I've never had anything to do with immorality in deed, I want nothing to do with it in word. I'm saying good-by now. Keep your part of the property, and arrange to return mine. And now, if you please, send some servants to escort me.

JOVE (*frantically*). Are you in your right mind?

ALCMENA (*picking up her bag, as before*). If you won't send any, I'll go by myself. (*Proudly.*) My honor will be my escort! (*Starts walking away.*)

JOVE (*urgently*). Wait! (*As she stops.*) I will swear any oath you want that I believe you are a faithful wife. (*Dramatically.*) And if I swear falsely (*raising his eyes to heaven*) Almighty Jove, I call on you to bring heaven's wrath upon Amphitryon for all time!

ALCMENA (*shuddering*). No! Heaven's blessing!

JOVE (*dryly*). I'm sure it will be that, because that was no false oath I gave you. (*Taking her gently by the arm.*) Now, are you still angry with me?

ALCMENA (*reluctantly*). No.

JOVE. Good! (*Gently.*) You know, in life things like this happen all the time. We have our joys, and then again our sorrows. We have fights, and then we make up again. Yet, whenever we have fights of this kind and make up again, we're twice as good friends as we were before.

ALCMENA (*reproachfully*). You should have been careful and not said such a thing in the first place. (*Smiling at him.*) But, since you've apologized completely for everything, well, I'll let it go.

(*They embrace and stand for a moment smiling happily at each other.*)

JOVE (*as if suddenly remembering something*). Listen, you must have the ritual utensils made ready for me. When I was at the front I made some vows about what I'd do if I returned safe and sound, and I want to carry them out.

ALCMENA. I'll take care of it. (*Claps her hands, and two maid servants appear at the door.*)

JOVE (*to the servants*). Call Sosia out here. (*They re-enter the house. He turns to* ALCMENA.) I want him to bring Blepharo—he was captain of my ship— here to have lunch with me. (*To the audience, grinning.*) Blepharo is not only going to get no lunch—he's going to be one surprised man when I haul Amphitryon out of here by the neck!

ALCMENA (*to the audience*). I wonder what he's up to, talking to himself like that? (*Her attention caught, glances toward the door.*) Someone's coming out. It's Sosia.

(SOSIA *emerges from the house and walks up to* JOVE.)

SOSIA (*to* JOVE, *seriously*). Here I

am, Amphitryon. Anything to be done, just say the word and I'll do it.

JOVE. Sosia, you've come just at the right time.

SOSIA (*looking from the one to the other*). Have you two made peace? (*Breaking into a smile.*) Well, I'm delighted! It's a pleasure to see you two relaxed! (*Seriously again.*) The system a good servant should follow is this: whatever your owners do, you do, you take your expression from them. If they're sad, you be sad; if they're gay, you be gay. (*Switching on the smile again.*) So, tell me: you've made up, have you?

JOVE (*eyeing him piercingly*). What are you making jokes for? You know very well everything I said a while back was just in fun.

SOSIA (*bewildered*). Just in fun was it? I thought you were dead serious!

JOVE (*smiling at* ALCMENA). I've apologized for everything, and now there's peace between us.

SOSIA. Fine!

JOVE. And now I want to go in and take care of those vows I made.

SOSIA. Good idea.

JOVE. You go to the pier and invite Captain Blepharo to lunch for me. We'll eat just as soon as I'm done with my prayers.

SOSIA (*over his shoulder as he dashes off, stage right*). By the time you think I've just arrived there, I'll already be back here.

JOVE (*calling after him*). Just hurry back.

ALCMENA. You don't want me for anything, do you? Then I'll go in and get ready whatever you need.

JOVE. You run along and get everything set up as quickly as you can.

ALCMENA. You can come in whenever you want. I'll see to it there are no delays.

JOVE (*kissing her tenderly*). That's the way an attentive wife should talk.

(*She goes into the house, and he turns to the audience.*) I fooled them both, mistress and servant. They think I'm Amphitryon—are they ever wrong! (*Looking upward.*) Hey there! You, the immortal Sosia! Put in an appearance here. You hear what I say even though you're not here in the flesh. When Amphitryon gets back, keep him away from the house. Use any trick you can think of. I want you to play around with him till I've had my pleasure with this wife of his I'm borrowing. Now, please see that you do all this just the way you know I want it done. And I want you to stand by and help while I (*grinning*) offer up prayers to myself!

(*He enters the house. A moment later* MERCURY *dashes in at top speed, stage left.*)

SONG

MERCURY (*yelling*).
Hey, gangway everyone, clear the road!
    Out of my way, I say!
No man alive better have the nerve to
    stand and block my way!
(*Pulling up, in normal tones.*)
Why shouldn't the right to threaten the
    public be given gods, like me.
When two-bit slaves do it all the time,
    in every comedy?
They rush to yell, "The boat's come in!
    Your father's home, and mad!"
But *I'm* obeying Jove himself; I'm here
    on orders from Dad.
So *I've* an even greater right to holler
    "Clear the way"—
My father calls and, quick, I run; one
    word, and I obey.
With Jove I'm just as dutiful as any
    father's pet.
When he's in love, I'm Helpful Henry; I
    aid, advise, abet,
And share his joys—the times he's happy
    are when I'm happiest.
He has affairs. That's good. He's smart:
    he does as he likes best.
And everyone of you should too—of
    course, with moderation.
Now, Father wants Amphitryon fooled.
    You'll see a presentation,

A spectacle for spectators, of fooling at
its height.
I'll put a garland on my head, and make
believe I'm tight,
Then climb to the roof and, when he
comes, get rid of him from there:
Though he hasn't had a drop to drink,
he'll end up soused for fair.
(*Chuckling.*)
And then his servant Sosia will pay for
what I've done—
Amphitryon will demonstrate that *he's*
the guilty one.
What's that to me? My job is Jove, to be
at his beck and call.
(*His attention caught, he looks off, stage
right.*)
Well, look who's here—Amphitryon. May
I kindly ask you all
To give me your attention while I take
him for a ride.
It involves my acting out a part, so now
I'll go inside
And fix myself to look as though I'd tied
one on somewhere.
Then up I go to the top of the roof to
drive him off from there.

(MERCURY *dashes inside. A moment
later* AMPHITRYON *enters, shuffling along
disconsolately.*)

AMPHITRYON (*to the audience, irritably*). I went to get Naucrates, but
I couldn't. He wasn't on the ship, he
wasn't at home, and I wasn't able to find
a soul in town who had seen him. I've
been all over: up and down every street,
in the gyms, in the drugstores, the
bazaar, the market, the athletic field, the
main square, all the doctors' offices, all
the barbers', every temple in town—I'm
worn out with looking, and I can't find
him any place.
(*Falls silent a moment, shaking his
head bitterly. Then, resolutely.*) I'll go
home, get Alcmena, and go further into
this matter of who it was who made her
disgrace herself. I'm going to get to the
bottom of this business or die in the
attempt!
(*Strides up to the door, tries it, and
steps back in surprise.*) The door's bolted!
(*Bitterly.*) Great! Just like everything
else that's been going on around here.
Well, I'll just bang on it. (*Pounding
away.*) Open up! Hey, isn't anyone
going to open this door?
(MERCURY *suddenly appears on the
roof, a garland sitting askew on his head,
and leans over.*)
MERCURY (*as if drunk*). Who'z 'at
at the door?
AMPHITRYON (*shouting*). I am.
MERCURY (*with drunken incompre-
hension*). Wha' d'ya mean, "I am?"
AMPHITRYON (*snarling*). You heard
me!
MERCURY (*waggling a finger at him,
playfully reproachful*). Breaking down
doors this way! God will punish you.
AMPHITRYON (*taken aback, incredulously*). What's that?
MERCURY (*piously*). It's that He'll
make you unhappy your whole life long.
AMPHITRYON (*recognizing the face, in
a voice of thunder*). Sosia!
MERCURY (*brightly*). That's right.
I'm Sosia. (*Belligerently.*) Think I'd forgotten it? What do you want?
AMPHITRYON (*dancing with rage*).
You good-for-nothing, you have to *ask*
me what I want?
MERCURY (*belligerently*). Sure, I'm
asking. You almost banged that door off
its hinges, dumbbell. You think the gov-
ernment supplies us with doors? What
are you looking at me for, stupid? What
do you want? Who are you, anyway?
AMPHITRYON (*between his teeth*).
God damn you, you'll be the death of
every whip I own! Asking me who I am!
I'll warm your god-damned hide for you
for talking like that!
MERCURY (*sadly*). You must have
been a bad boy when you were young.
AMPHITRYON. How so?
MERCURY. Because, in your old age,
you're begging for a beating.
(*Roars at his own joke.*)
AMPHITRYON (*between his teeth*).

I'll torture the life out of you for those words.

MERCURY (*piously*). I'm going to pray for you.

AMPHITRYON. How's that?

MERCURY. I'm going to pray you come to a bad end.

[At this point there was a large gap, perhaps three hundred verses, in the lost manuscript from which all our surviving copies of the *Amphitryon* derive. However, from some twenty random lines cited in ancient grammars and similar works, we can reconstruct what took place. Mercury dumps a bucket of water on Amphitryon, and the slapstick between them continues until the noise draws Alcmena out of the house; whereupon she and Amphitryon renew their quarrel. At some point Sosia enters; he had carried out Jove's orders, and has Captain Blepharo in tow. Amphitryon, of course, immediately wades into Sosia, but Jove appears on the scene, disguised as Amphitryon, and wades into *him,* accusing him of lechery and seduction. The argument between them grows hot and heavy, each claiming that he is the real thing and the other an impostor, until both agree to put the problem in Blepharo's hands: he is to test them and decide. Blepharo makes a number of attempts, gets nowhere, and, at the point where he admits defeat, the text resumes. Jove, Amphitryon, and Blepharo are on stage; we are now in Act IV.]

Act IV

BLEPHARO. Look—you two divide yourselves up by yourselves. I'm leaving, I've got things to do. (*Shaking his head.*) I don't think I've ever seen anything as queer as all this anywhere.

AMPHITRYON (*desperately*). Blepharo, I beg you: stand by me; don't go away!

BLEPHARO (*resolutely*). Good-by! What's the good of my standing by if I can't tell which one of you to stand by? (*Leaves, stage right, still shaking his head.*)

JOVE (*to the audience, excitedly*). I'm going into the house. Alcmena's giving birth! (*Turns and rushes inside.*)

AMPHITRYON (*to the audience, watching* BLEPHARO *go off and not noticing* JOVE'S *departure*). Oh, my god! Now what do I do? My friends and allies have all run out on me! (*Grimly.*) By god, he's not going to make a fool of me like this and get away with it, whoever he is! I'm going straight to King Creon this minute and tell him about the whole business. I'll get even on that witch doctor who's turned my whole household into lunatics. (*Turning to carry out his threat and seeing no one; startled.*) Where is he? By god, I'll bet he's inside, with my wife! (*Clutching his head.*) I'll swear, not another man in all Thebes has such misery! Now what do I do? Nobody knows who I am. Everybody plays any joke he feels like on me. (*Wildly.*) I'll break into the house, that's what I'll do. Anyone I lay eyes on—maid or servant, wife or seducer, my own father or grandfather—I'll cut their throats right there in the house! All the gods in heaven, including Jove himself, can't stop me even if they want to. I've made up my mind and I'm going to do it! Here I go into the house!

(*He makes a mad dash for the door but a sudden tremendous clap of thunder and blinding flash of lightning stop him dead in his tracks; he falls flat on the ground, unconscious.*)

Act V

(AMPHITRYON *is still unconscious, sprawled full length on the ground in front of his house. The thunder and lightning continue for a few moments and then gradually cease. Suddenly the door flies open, and* BROMIA, ALCMENA'S

maid, *her hair disheveled and her clothes
in disarray, bursts out. Without noticing
AMPHITRYON, she rushes downstage and
addresses the audience.*)

SONG

BROMIA (*hysterically*).
  My mind has given up the thought that
    I've any chance to survive,
  My heart's abandoned every hope—I'll
    never stay alive!
  It seems to me that everything—the
    earth, the air, the sky—
  Have all conspired against my life, have
    willed to see me die.
  The strangest things went on in the
    house! God knows what I should do!
  (*Gasping for breath.*)
  Oh, god! I'm sick! Some water, please!
    My end is near, I'm through!
  My head aches so, my hearing's gone,
    my vision's not what it should be.
  No other woman's this miserable, no
    other ever *could* be!
  (*Stops, gets hold of herself, and re-
  sumes much more calmly.*)
  It's what Alcmena had happen to her.
    Once in labor, she prayed to god.
  Then, bang and crash! Thunder and
    lightning! So sudden, so near, so hard!
  The sound knocked over all of us; we
    fell in our tracks, struck dumb.
  And then a mighty voice called out,
    "Alcmena, help has come!
  Don't fear! A god from heaven's on
    hand to shed his favor on thee."
  "And rise, all you," it said to us, "who
    fell through fear of me."
  I rose, since I had fallen too. The light-
    ning gleamed so, I
  Was sure our house had caught on fire.
    Then I heard Alcmena's cry.
  For a moment, horror held me fast—
    but fear for her won out.
  I ran to see what she'd called me for.
    Amazed, I look about:
  She'd given birth to twins, two boys. It
    was all a mystery,
  A birth none saw or had foreseen.

(*Suddenly noticing* AMPHITRYON.)
      My god, what's this I see?

Who is the gentleman stretched out here,
    before our very door!
Some victim of Jove's thunderbolt? By
    Jove, he looks it, for
He's laid out there as if he's dead. I think
    I'd better run
And check. Perhaps I know the man.
  (*Rushing up to* AMPHITRYON *and tak-
ing a look; startled.*)
         My master, Amphitryon!
  (*Shouting in his ear.*)
Amphitryon!
  AMPHITRYON   (*groaning*).   I'm
dead.
  BROMIA.   Get up!
  AMPHITRYON   (*as   before*).   A
corpse.
  BROMIA (*reaching out and taking his
hand*).   Here, let me have your hand.
  AMPHITRYON (*feebly*). Who's hold-
ing me?
  BROMIA.   Your Bromia.
  (*She hauls mightily and succeeds in
pulling him to his feet.*)
  AMPHITRYON (*holding his head, his
eyes closed; dazedly*). But *I* don't un-
derstand—
That crack from Jove has me numb with
    fear. I feel as if I died
And have just come back from the un-
    derworld.
  (*Finally pulling out of his stupor and
looking at her curiously.*)
        But what brings *you* outside?
  BROMIA (*nervously*). The same fear
and dread gripped all of us.
  (*Pointing to the door; dramatically.*)
    In there, the house where you dwell,
I saw such a wonder I'm still unnerved.
  (*Covering her face, hysterically.*)
         Amphitryon, it's hell!
  AMPHITRYON (*pulling her hands from
her face and forcing her to look at him*).
Now answer this: am I your master? Am
I Amphitryon?
  BROMIA. Of course you are.
  AMPHITRYON.   No, look again.
  BROMIA (*as before*).   Of course
you're Amphitryon.

AMPHITRYON (*to the world at large, bitterly*). The only one of my household here who's preserved her sanity.

BROMIA (*reproachfully*). No sir, we're all completely sane.

AMPHITRYON (*as before*). There's one exception—me.
The shameful conduct of my wife has driven *me* insane.

BROMIA (*passionately*).
But you, yourself, will admit you're wrong as soon as I explain!
(*Stops for a moment to make sure he is willing to listen, then continues gently.*) Yes, you'll realize that your wife is a decent and honorable woman. It will take me only a moment to tell you some things that will prove it beyond any doubt.
(*She pauses, then begins again, observing him keenly to note the effect of her words.*) To begin with, Alcmena has just given birth to twins, two boys.

AMPHITRYON (*blankly*). Twins, you say?

BROMIA. Twins.

AMPHITRYON (*hopelessly*). God help me!

BROMIA (*impatiently*). Please let me go on—I want to show you that god *is* helping both you and your wife.

AMPHITRYON. Go on.

BROMIA (*excitedly*). When her time came, and she went into labor, your wife, as women in childbirth always do, washed her hands, covered her head, and prayed to god to help her. The next second, there was a mighty clap of thunder. At first we all thought your house would come crashing down; the lightning gleamed so, the whole place looked as though it were made of gold.

AMPHITRYON (*savagely*). Will you kindly let me go as soon as you're through having fun with me? (*Shrugs as BROMIA gestures helplessly and falls silent.*) All right, what happened next?

BROMIA (*resuming excitedly*). During all this, not one of us heard your wife utter a groan or a cry. It was a completely painless delivery.

AMPHITRYON (*grudgingly*). Well, I'm glad to hear that—in spite of all she's done to me.

BROMIA (*impatiently*). Forget all that and just listen to what I'm going to tell you. (*Resuming her excited narrative tone.*) When it was all over, she told us to wash the babies down. We started right in. Well, I can't tell you how big and strong the baby was that I was bathing! There wasn't one of us who could pin the diapers and clothes around him.

AMPHITRYON (*scratching his head*). This is an incredible story. If it's true, my wife certainly received a lot of help from heaven.

BROMIA (*eagerly*). Believe me, what comes next you'll say is even more incredible. (*Resuming her narrative tone.*) I had just put him in his cradle when there slithered down through the skylight two serpents with crests, both of them simply enormous. The next minute, there they were, the two of them, with heads raised looking about.

AMPHITRYON (*shuddering*). Oh, my god!

BROMIA (*reassuringly*). Nothing to be afraid about. (*Resuming her narrative tone.*) The serpents eyed everyone there. As soon as they spotted the children, they made a rush for them. I pulled the cradles back and steered them away; I was frightened for myself but even more afraid for the babies. The snakes followed after, fiercer than ever. Then that child, the one I had bathed, saw them. He jumped right out of his cradle, went straight for them, and, in a flash, had one gripped in each hand.

AMPHITRYON. Incredible! This is a very dangerous deed you've described! Just hearing about it gives me the shudders! What then? Go on?

BROMIA. The baby strangled both those serpents. And, while he was doing it, a mighty voice was heard calling to Alcmena—

AMPHITRYON (*interrupting angrily*). Who was the man?

BROMIA. Man? It was the lord of men and of gods, almighty Jove! He announced that he had had intercourse with Alcmena in secret and that the child that had killed the snakes was his. (*As an afterthought.*) The other, he said was yours.

(*For a full moment* AMPHITRYON *stands buried in thought.*)

AMPHITRYON (*suddenly his old vibrant self*). Well, I certainly have no cause for complaint when I'm given the chance to share my goods with Jove. Go inside and have the ritual utensils made ready for me right away. I want to pray hard and long, and beg almighty Jove for peace. And I'll call in Tiresias, the prophet, and ask what he thinks I should do. At the same time I'll tell him how this whole business happened. (*A tremendous clap of thunder is heard.*) What's that? Thunder—but so loud! (*Falling to his knees.*) Oh god, help me, please!

VOICE FROM OFF STAGE (*slowly and impressively*). Take heart, Amphitryon. I am here to help you and your family. There is nothing to be afraid of. Prophets, fortune tellers—don't bother with any of them. I will tell you both the future and the past much better than they, for I am Jove.

To begin with, I borrowed your Alcmena's body, slept with her, and conceived a son by her. You too conceived a son, when you left to go to the front. She has brought forth both together, in one birth. The one sprung from my seed will do deeds that will make your name great forever. Go back now to Alcmena and live with her in the harmony you two have always known. She deserves no reproaches; *I* forced her to do what she did. And now I must return to the heavens.

AMPHITRYON. I'll do as you command—but I beg you: don't forget your promises. I'll go inside now to my wife, and I won't bother with Tiresias. (*He rises from his knees, walks downstage and addresses the audience.*) And now, ladies and gentlemen, for Jove's sake, a good loud round of applause!

ANONYMOUS / 1500?

During the Middle Ages in Europe the drama, as in ancient Greece, developed out of formal religious practices. Chanted dialogue, action, and spectacle were introduced into the liturgy. The *Quem Quaeritis,* a resurrection playlet or trope of the tenth century, is the earliest preserved example. The public response was so great that the plays were moved into the churchyard, then into the town squares. In 1264 the church committed its dramatic activities, which had been growing more secular, popular, and responsive to the folk imagination, to a special festival of *Corpus Christi.* In England the guilds assumed responsibility for the Biblical plays, called *miracles.* The growth of the miracles into cycles of from thirty-two to forty-eight plays, requiring three to six days for performance, in various cities such as York, Wakefield, Chester, and Coventry, attests the natural attraction of medieval drama to its age. The responses of the audience gradually shaped the material of the plays; farce, buffoonery, and some social satire were intermingled with the basic and familiar Bible stories. *Noah, The Second Shepherds' Play,* the *Killing of Abel,* and *Abraham and Isaac* are among the best of the miracle plays.

The morality plays, of which *Everyman* is the finest example, overlapped with and succeeded the miracles. Freed from the traditional necessity of enacting Bible stories, the moralities dramatized abstract conflicts: Good *vs.* Evil; Mercy *vs.* Mischief; Pauper *vs.* Landlord; Life *vs.* Death. Allegory, or concrete representation of abstractions, is the prevailing method; as in all allegory, the ability to give a human and particular character to the abstract determines the degree of interest created.

Everyman (about 1500) so far surpasses the typical morality plays that it survives for its own merit, while such others as *The Castle of Perseverance, The Satire of the Three Estates,* and *Mankind* are of interest primarily to historians and scholars. *Everyman* is Bunyan on the stage, long before Bunyan's time. It has many touches of humor and of humanity, a true dramatic structure, and a theme as universal as the name of the protagonist.

Allegorical plays reappear in subsequent drama, as in *Experience* and *Everywoman;* touches or suggestions of allegory are present in such more recent plays as Elmer Rice's *The Adding Machine* and Archibald MacLeish's *J. B.*

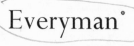

Everyman*

TRANSLATED BY C. G. CHILD

Here beginneth a treatise how the High Father of Heaven sendeth Death to summon every creature to come and give an account of their lives in this world, and is in manner of a moral play.

(The MESSENGER *enters.)*

* There is no standard reference for the line numbering of *Everyman*. We have numbered verse every five lines. A continued line of verse, regardless of a change in speakers midline or regardless of a break midline, still counts as one line. When the width of a line has not permitted the inclusion of a line number, either the previous line or the following line has been numbered.

MESSENGER. I pray you all give your audience,
And hear this matter with reverence,
In form a moral play.
The Summoning of Everyman it is called so,
That of our lives and ending maketh show   5
How transitory we be every day.
This matter is wondrous precious,
But the meaning of it is more gracious
And sweet to bear away.   9
The story saith: Man, in the beginning
Watch well, and take good heed of the ending,
Be you never so gay!
Ye think sin the beginning full sweet,
Which, in the end, causeth the soul to weep,
When the body lieth in clay.   15
Here shall you see how Fellowship and Jollity,
Both Strength, Pleasure, and Beauty,
Will fade from thee as flower in May,
For ye shall hear how our Heaven's King   19
Calleth Everyman to a general reckoning.
Give audience and hear what he doth say.
(*The* MESSENGER *goes.*)
GOD *speaketh.* I perceive, here in my majesty,
How that all creatures be to me unkind,
Living, without fear, in worldly prosperity.
In spiritual vision the people be so blind,   25
Drowned in sin, they know me not for their God;
In worldly riches is all their mind.
They fear not my righteousness, the sharp rod.
My law that I disclosed, when I for them died,
They clean forget, and shedding of my blood red. 30
I hung between two it cannot be denied,

To get them life I suffered to be dead,
I healed their feet, with thorns was hurt my head.
I could do no more than I did truly,
And now I see the people do clean forsake me;   35
They use the seven deadly sins damnable
In such wise that pride, covetousness, wrath, and lechery,
Now in this world be made commendable,
And thus they leave of angels the heavenly company.
Every man liveth so after his own pleasure,   40
And yet of their lives they be nothing sure.
The more I them forbear, I see
The worse from year to year they be;
All that live grow more evil apace;
Therefore I will, in briefest space,   45
From every man in person have a reckoning shown.
For, if I leave the people thus alone
In their way of life and wicked passions to be,
They will become much worse than beasts, verily.
Now for envy would one eat up another, and tarry not, 50
Charity is by all clean forgot.
I hoped well that every man
In my glory should make his mansion,
And thereto I made them all elect,
But now I see, like traitors abject,   55
They thank me not for the pleasure that I for them meant,
Nor yet for their being that I them have lent.
I proffered the people great multitude of mercy,
And few there be that ask it heartily.
They be so cumbered with worldly riches, thereto   60
I must needs upon them justice do,—
On every man living without fear.
Where art thou, Death, thou mighty messenger?
(DEATH *enters.*)

DEATH.   Almighty God, I am here at
   your will,
Your commandment to fulfill.   65
   GOD.   Go thou to Everyman,
And show him in my name
A pilgrimage he must on him take,
Which he in no wise may escape,
And that he bring with him a sure reck-
   oning   70
Without delay or any tarrying.
   DEATH.   Lord, I will in the world go
   run over all,
And cruelly search out both great and
   small.
Every man will I beset that liveth beastly
Out of God's law, and doth not dread
   folly.   75
He that loveth riches I will strike with
   my dart
His sight to blind and him from heaven
   to part—
Except if Alms be his good friend—
In hell for to dwell, world without end.
Lo, yonder I see Everyman walking.   80
Full little he thinketh on my coming!
His mind is on fleshly lusts and his
   treasure,
And great pain it shall cause him to
   endure
Before the Lord, of Heaven the King.
Everyman, stand still! Whither art thou
   going   85
Thus gayly? Hast thou thy Maker forgot?
(EVERYMAN enters.)
   EVERYMAN.   Why askest thou?
Wouldest thou know? For what?
   DEATH.   Yea, sir, I will show you
   now.
In great haste I am sent to thee   90
From God, out of his majesty.
   EVERYMAN.   What, sent to me!
   DEATH.   Yea, certainly.
Though thou hast forgot him here,
He thinketh on thee in the heavenly
   sphere,   95
As, ere we part, thou shalt know.
   EVERYMAN.   What desireth God of
   me?

DEATH.   That shall I show thee.
A reckoning he will needs have
Without any longer respite.   100
   EVERYMAN.   To give a reckoning
   longer leisure I crave.
This blind matter troubleth my wit.
   DEATH.   Upon thee thou must take a
   long journey,
Therefore, do thou thine accounting-
   book with thee bring.   104
For turn again thou canst not by no way,
   And look thou be sure in thy reck-
   oning,
For before God thou shalt answer, and
   show true
Thy many bad deeds and good but a few,
How thou hast spent thy life and in what
   wise
Before the Chief Lord of Paradise.   110
Get thee prepared that we may be upon
   that journey,
For well thou knowest thou shalt make
   none for thee attorney.
   EVERYMAN.   Full unready I am such
   reckoning to give.
I know thee not. What messenger art
   thou?
   DEATH.   I am Death that no man
   fear,   115
For every man I arrest and no man
   spare,
For it is God's commandment
That all to me should be obedient.
   EVERYMAN.   O Death, thou comest
   when I had thee least in mind!   119
In thy power it lieth to save me yet;—
Thereto of my goods will I give thee, if
   thou wilt be kind,—
   Yea, a thousand pounds shalt thou
   get!—
And defer this matter till another day.
   DEATH.   Everyman, it may not be in
   any way.
I set no store by gold, silver, riches, or
   such gear,   125
Nor by pope, emperor, king, prince, or
   peer.
For, if I would receive gifts great,
All the world I might get,

But my custom is clean the contrary way.
I give thee no respite. Come hence, nor
delay!   *130*
  EVERYMAN. Alas, shall I have no
long respite!
I may say Death giveth no warning!
To think on thee, it maketh my heart
sick,
  For all unready is my book of reck-
oning.
  But if I might have twelve years of
waiting,   *135*
My accounting-book I would make so
clear
That my reckoning I should not need to
fear.
Wherefore, Death, I pray thee, for God's
mercy,
Spare me till I be provided with a
remedy!
  DEATH. It availeth thee not to cry,
weep, and pray,   *140*
But haste thee lightly, that thou mayest
be on thy journey,
And make proof of thy friends, if thou
can,
For, know thou well, time waiteth for
no man,
And in the world each living creature
Because of Adam's sin must die by na-
ture.   *145*
  EVERYMAN. Death, if I should this
pilgrimage take,
And my reckoning duly make,
Show me, for Saint Charity,
Should I not come again shortly?
  DEATH. No, Everyman, if once thou
art there,   *150*
Thou mayest nevermore come here,
Trust me, verily.
  EVERYMAN. O gracious God, in the
high seat celestial,
Have mercy on me in this utmost
need!
Shall I no company have from this vale
terrestrial   *155*
Of mine acquaintance that way me to
lead?
  DEATH. Yea, if any be so hardy

As to go with thee and bear thee com-
pany.
Haste thee that thou mayest be gone to
God's magnificence,
Thy reckoning to give before his pres-
ence.   *160*
What, thinkest thou thy life is given thee,
And thy worldly goods also?
  EVERYMAN. I had thought so, verily.
  DEATH. Nay, nay, it was but lent to
thee,
For, as soon as thou dost go,   *165*
Another a while shall have it and then
even so,
Go therefore as thou hast done.
Everyman, thou art mad! Thou hast thy
wits five,
And here on earth will not amend thy
life,
For suddenly I do come!   *170*
  EVERYMAN. O wretched caitiff,
whither shall I flee
That I may escape endless sorrow!
Nay, gentle Death, spare me until
to-morrow
That I may amend me
With good avisement!   *175*
  DEATH. Nay, thereto I will not con-
sent,
Nor no man respite, if I might,
But to the heart suddenly I shall smite
Without any "advisement."   *179*
And now out of thy sight I will me hie,
See that thou make thee ready speedily,
For thou mayest say this is the day
Wherefrom no man living may escape
away.
  EVERYMAN. Alas, I may well weep
with sighs deep!   *184*
Now have I no manner of company
To help me on my journey and me to
keep,
And also my writing is all unready.
What can I do that may excuse me!
  I would to God I had never been
begot!   *189*
To my soul a full great profit it would be.
  For now I fear pains huge and great,
God wot!

The time passeth—help, Lord, that all
    things wrought!
For, though I mourn, yet it availeth
    naught.
The day passeth and is almost through,
I wot not well of aught that I may do.
To whom were it best that I my plaint
    should make?   196
What if to Fellowship I thereof spake,
And what this sudden chance should
    mean disclosed?
For surely in him is all my trust re-
    posed—   199
We have in the world so many a day
Been good friends in sport and play.
I see him yonder certainly—
I trust that he will bear me company;
Therefore to him will I speak to ease my
    sorrow.
Well met, good Fellowship, and a good
    morrow!   205
    (*Enter* FELLOWSHIP)
FELLOWSHIP *speaketh*. I wish thee
    good morrow, Everyman, by this
    day!
Sir, why lookest thou so piteously?
If anything be amiss, prithee to me it
    say
    That I may help in remedy.
EVERYMAN. Yea, good Fellowship,
    yea,   210
I am in great jeopardy!
FELLOWSHIP. My true friend, show
    to me your mind.
I will not forsake thee to my life's end,
In the way of good company.
    EVERYMAN. That was well spoken
    and lovingly.   215
FELLOWSHIP. Sir, I must needs know
    your heaviness.
I have pity to see you in any distress.
If any have wronged you, revenged ye
    shall be,
Though I upon the ground be slain for
    thee,
Even should I know before that I should
    die.   220
    EVERYMAN. Verily, Fellowship, gra-
    mercy!

FELLOWSHIP. Tush! By thy thanks I
    set not a straw.
Show me your grief and say no more.
    EVERYMAN. If I my heart should you
    unfold,
And you then were to turn your heart
    from me,   225
And no comfort would give when I had
    told,
    Then should I ten times sorrier be.
FELLOWSHIP. Sir, I say as I will do
    indeed!
EVERYMAN. Then you be a good
    friend at need.
I have found you true heretofore.   230
    FELLOWSHIP. And so ye shall ever-
    more,
For, in faith, if thou goest to hell,
    I will not forsake thee by the way.
EVERYMAN. Ye speak like a good
    friend—I believe you well.
I shall deserve it, if so I may!   235
FELLOWSHIP. I speak of no deserv-
    ing, by this day,
For he that will say, and nothing do,
Is not worthy with good company to go.
Therefore show me the grief of your
    mind,   239
As to your friend most loving and kind.
    EVERYMAN. I shall show you how
    it is:
Commanded I am to go a journey,
A long way hard and dangerous,
    And give a strict account without
    delay
Before the High Judge, Adonai.   245
Wherefore, I pray you, bear me com-
    pany.
As ye have promised, on this journey.
    FELLOWSHIP. That is matter, indeed!
    Promise is duty—
But if I should take such a voyage on
    me,   249
I know well it should be to my pain;
Afeard also it maketh me, for certain.
But let us take counsel here as well as
    we can,
For your words would dismay a strong
    man.

EVERYMAN. Why, if I had need, ye said

Ye would never forsake me, quick nor dead, 255

Though it were to hell truly!

FELLOWSHIP. So I said certainly,

But such pleasant things be set aside, the truth to say;

And also, if we took such a journey,

When should we come again? 260

EVERYMAN. Nay, never again till the day of doom.

FELLOWSHIP. In faith, then, will I not come there.

Who hath you these tidings brought?

EVERYMAN. Indeed, Death was with me here.

FELLOWSHIP. Now, by God that all hath bought, 265

If Death were the messenger,

For no man living here below

I will not that loathly journey go—

Not for the father that begat me!

EVERYMAN. Ye promised otherwise, pardy! 270

FELLOWSHIP. I know well I do say so, truly,

And still, if thou wilt eat and drink and make good cheer,

Or, haunt of women the merry company,

I would not forsake you while the day is clear,

Trust me, verily. 275

EVERYMAN. Yea, thereto ye would be ready!

To go to mirth, solace, and play,

Your mind would sooner persuaded be

Than to bear me company on my long journey.

FELLOWSHIP. Now, in good sooth, I have no will that way— 280

But if thou would'st murder, or any man kill,

In that I will help thee with a good will.

EVERYMAN. Oh, that is simple advice, indeed!

Gentle Fellowship, help me in my necessity!

We have loved long, and now I am in need! 285

And now, gentle Fellowship, remember me!

FELLOWSHIP. Whether ye have loved me or no,

By Saint John, I will not with thee go!

EVERYMAN. Yes, I pray thee, take this task on thee and do so much for me,

As to bring me forward on my way for Saint Charity, 290

And comfort me till I come without the town.

FELLOWSHIP. Nay, if thou wouldest give me a new gown,

I will not a foot with thee go.

But, if thou hadst tarried, I would not have left thee so.

And so now, God speed thee on thy journey, 295

For from thee I will depart as fast as I may!

EVERYMAN. Whither away, Fellowship? Will you forsake me?

FELLOWSHIP. Yea, by my faith! I pray God take thee.

EVERYMAN. Farewell, good Fellowship,—for thee my heart is sore.

Adieu forever, I shall see thee no more! 300

FELLOWSHIP. In faith, Everyman, farewell now at the ending.

For you I will remember that parting is grieving.

(FELLOWSHIP *goes*.)

EVERYMAN. Alack! Shall we thus part indeed?

Ah, Lady, help! Lo, vouchsafing no more comfort,

Fellowship thus forsaketh me in my utmost need. 305

For help in this world whither shall I resort?

Fellowship heretofore with me would merry make,

And now little heed of my sorrow doth he take.

It is said in prosperity men friends may
    find
Which in adversity be full unkind. *310*
Now whither for succor shall I flee,
Since that Fellowship hath forsaken me?
To my kinsmen will I truly,
Praying them to help me in my neces-
    sity.
I believe that they will do so   *315*
For "Nature will creep where it may not
    go."
    (KINDRED *and* COUSIN *enter.*)
I will go try, for yonder I see them go.
Where be ye now, my friends and kins-
    men, lo?
    KINDRED. Here we be now at your
    commandment.   *319*
Cousin, I pray you show us your intent
In any wise and do not spare.
    COUSIN. Yea, Everyman, and to us
    declare
If ye be disposed to go any whither,
For, wit you well, we will live and die
    together!
    KINDRED. In wealth and woe we will
    with you hold,   *325*
For "with his own kin a man may be
    bold."
    EVERYMAN. Gramercy, my friends
    and kinsmen kind!
Now shall I show you the grief of my
    mind.
I was commanded by a messenger
That is a High King's chief officer. *330*
He bade me go a pilgrimage to my pain,
And I know well I shall never come
    again;
And I must give a reckoning strait,
For I have a great enemy that lieth for
    me in wait,
Who intendeth me to hinder.   *335*
    KINDRED. What account is that
    which you must render?—
That would I know.
    EVERYMAN. Of all my works I must
    show
How I have lived and my days have
    spent,
    Also of evil deeds to which I have
    been used   *340*

In my time, since life was to me lent,
    And of all virtues that I have refused.
Therefore, I pray you, go thither with me
To help to make my account, for Saint
    Charity!
    COUSIN. What, to go thither? Is that
    the matter?   *345*
Nay, Everyman, I had liefer fast on
    bread and water
All this five year and more!
    EVERYMAN. Alas, that ever my
    mother me bore!
For now shall I never merry be,
If that you forsake me!   *350*
    KINDRED. Ah, sir, come! Ye be a
    merry man!
Pluck up heart and make no moan.
But one thing I warn you, by Saint Anne,
    As for me, ye shall go alone!
    EVERYMAN. My cousin, will you not
    with me go?   *355*
    COUSIN. No, by our Lady! I have the
    cramp in my toe.
Trust not to me, for, so God me speed,
I will deceive you in your utmost need.
    KINDRED. It availeth not us to coax
    and court.
Ye shall have my maid, with all my
    heart.   *360*
She loveth to go to feasts, there to make
    foolish sport
    And to dance, and in antics to take
    part.
To help you on that journey I will give
    her leave willingly,
If so be that you and she may agree.
    EVERYMAN. Now show me the very
    truth within your mind—   *365*
Will you go with me or abide behind?
    KINDRED. Abide behind? Yea, that I
    will, if I may—
Therefore farewell till another day!
    EVERYMAN. How shall I be merry or
    glad?—   *369*
For fair promises men to me make,
But, when I have most need, they me
    forsake!
I am deceived—that maketh me sad!
    COUSIN. Cousin Everyman, farewell
    now, lo!

For, verily, I will not with thee go.   *374*
Also of mine own an unready reckoning,
I have to give account of, therefore I
    make tarrying.
Now God keep thee, for now I go!
    (KINDRED *and* COUSIN *go.*)
    EVERYMAN.   Ah, Jesus, is all to this
        come so?
Lo, "fair words make fools fain,"   *379*
They promise, and from deeds refrain.
My kinsmen promised me faithfully
For to abide by me stedfastly,
And now fast away do they flee.
Even so Fellowship promised me.
What friend were it best for me to pro-
    vide?   *385*
I am losing my time longer here to
    abide.
Yet still in my mind a thing there is,
All my life I have loved riches.
If that my Goods now help me might,
He would make my heart full light.   *390*
To him will I speak in my sorrow this
    day.
My Goods and Riches, where art thou,
    pray?
    (GOODS *is disclosed hemmed in by*
chests and bags.)
    GOODS.   Who calleth me? Everyman?
        Why this haste thou hast?
    I lie here in corners trussed and piled
        so high,
And in chests I am locked so fast,   *395*
    Also sacked in bags, thou mayest see
        with thine eye,
I cannot stir; in packs, full low I lie.
What ye would have, lightly to me say.
    EVERYMAN.   Come hither, Goods,
        with all the haste thou may,
For counsel straightway I must ask of
    thee.   *400*
    GOODS.   Sir, if ye in this world have
        sorrow or adversity,
That can I help you to remedy shortly.
    EVERYMAN.   It is another disease that
        grieveth me;
In this world it is not, I tell thee so,
I am sent for another way to go,   *405*
To give a strict account general
Before the highest Jupiter of all.

And all my life I have had joy and pleas-
    ure in thee,
Therefore I pray thee go with me,
For, peradventure, thou mayest before
    God Almighty on high   *410*
My reckoning help to clean and purify,
For one may hear ever and anon
That "money maketh all right that is
    wrong."
    GOODS.   Nay, Everyman, I sing an-
        other song—
I follow no man on such voyages,   *415*
For, if I went with thee,
Thou shouldest fare much the worse for
    me,
For, because on me thou didst set thy
    mind,
Thy reckoning I have made blotted and
    blind,
So that thine account thou canst not
    make truly—   *420*
And that hast thou for the love of me.
    EVERYMAN.   That would be to me
        grief full sore and sorrowing,
When I should come that fearful an-
    swering.
Up, let us go thither together!
    GOODS.   Nay, not so! I am too brittle,
        I may not endure,   *425*
I will follow no man one foot, be ye sure.
    EVERYMAN.   Alas! I have thee loved,
        and had great pleasure
All the days of my life in goods and
    treasure.
    GOODS.   That is to thy damnation, I
        tell thee a true thing,
For love of me is to the love everlasting
    contrary.   *430*
But if thou hadst the while loved me
    moderately,
In such wise as to give the poor a part
    of me,
Then would'st thou not in this dolor be,
Nor in this great sorrow and care.
    EVERYMAN.   Lo, now was I deceived
        ere I was ware,   *435*
And all I may blame to misspending of
    time.
    GOODS.   What, thinkest thou I am
        thine?

EVERYMAN. I had thought so.

GOODS. Nay, Everyman, I say no.

Just for a while I was lent to thee,   *440*

A season thou hast had me in prosperity.

My nature it is man's soul to kill,

If I save one, a thousand I do spill.

Thinkest thou that I will follow thee?

Nay, from this world not, verily!   *445*

EVERYMAN. I had thought otherwise.

GOODS. So it is to thy soul Goods is a thief,

For when thou art dead I straightway devise

Another to deceive in the same wise

As I have done thee, and all to his soul's grief.   *450*

EVERYMAN. O false Goods, cursed may thou be!

Thou traitor to God that hast deceived me,

And caught me in thy snare.

GOODS. Marry, thou broughtest thyself to this care,—

Whereof I am glad!   *455*

I must needs laugh, I cannot be sad!

EVERYMAN. Ah, Goods, thou hast had long my hearty love.

I gave thee that which should be the Lord's above.

But wilt thou not go with me, indeed?—

I pray thee truth to say!   *460*

GOODS. No, so God me speed!

Therefore farewell, and have good-day.

(GOODS *is hidden from view*.)

EVERYMAN. Oh, to whom shall I make my moan

For to go with me on that heavy journey!

First Fellowship, so he said, would have with me gone,   *465*

His words were very pleasant and gay,

But afterwards he left me alone;

Then spake I to my kinsmen, all in despair,

And they also gave me words fair,

They lacked not fair speeches to spend,

But all forsook me in the end;   *471*

Then went I to my Goods that I loved best,

In hope to have comfort, but there had I least,

For my Goods sharply did me tell

That he bringeth many into hell.   *475*

Then of myself I was ashamed,

And so I am worthy to be blamed.

Thus may I well myself hate.

Of whom shall I now counsel take?

I think that I shall never speed   *480*

Till I go to my Good Deeds.

But, alas! she is so weak,

That she can neither move nor speak.

Yet will I venture on her now.

My Good Deeds, where be you?   *485*

(GOOD DEEDS *is shown*.)

GOOD DEEDS. Here I lie, cold in the ground.

Thy sins surely have me bound

That I cannot stir.

EVERYMAN. O Good Deeds, I stand in fear!

I must pray you for counsel,   *490*

For help now would come right well!

GOOD DEEDS. Everyman, I have understanding

That ye be summoned your account to make

Before Messias, of Jerusalem King.

If you do my counsel, that journey with you will I take.   *495*

EVERYMAN. For that I come to you my moan to make.

I pray you that ye will go with me.

GOOD DEEDS. I would full fain, but I cannot stand, verily.

EVERYMAN. Why, is there something amiss that did you befall?

GOOD DEEDS. Yea, Sir, I may thank you for all.   *500*

If in every wise ye had encouraged me,

Your book of account full ready would be.

Behold the books of your works and your deeds thereby.

Ah, see, how under foot they lie

Unto your soul's deep heaviness.   *505*

EVERYMAN. Our Lord Jesus his help vouchsafe to me,

For one letter here I cannot see.

GOOD DEEDS. There is a blind reckoning in time of distress!

EVERYMAN. Good Deeds, I pray you
help me in this need,
Or else I am forever damned indeed. *510*
Therefore help me to make reckoning
Before him, that Redeemer is of every-
thing,
That is, and was, and shall ever be, King
of All.
GOOD DEEDS. Everyman, I am sorry
for your fall, *514*
And fain would I help you, if I were able.
EVERYMAN. Good Deeds, your coun-
sel, I pray you, give me.
GOOD DEEDS. That will I do, verily.
Though on my feet I may not go,
I have a sister that shall with you be, also,
Called Knowledge, who shall with you
abide, *520*
To help you to make that dire reck-
oning.
(KNOWLEDGE *enters*.)
KNOWLEDGE. Everyman, I will go
with thee and be thy guide,
In thy utmost need to go by thy side.
EVERYMAN. In good condition I am
now in every thing,
And am wholly content with this good
thing, *525*
Thanks be to God, my creator!
GOOD DEEDS. And when he hath
brought thee there,
Where thou shalt heal thee of thy
smart,
Then go with thy reckoning and thy
good deeds together,
For to make thee joyful at heart *530*
Before the Holy Trinity.
EVERYMAN. My Good Deeds, gra-
mercy!
I am well content, certainly,
With your words sweet.
KNOWLEDGE. Now go we together
lovingly *535*
To Confession, that cleansing river fair.
EVERYMAN. For joy I weep—I would
we were there!
But, I pray you, give me cognition,
Where dwelleth that holy man, Confes-
sion?

KNOWLEDGE. In the House of Salva-
tion. *540*
We shall find him in that place,
That shall us comfort by God's grace.
(CONFESSION *enters*.)
Lo, this is Confession. Kneel down, and
ask mercy,
For he is in good favor with God Al-
mighty.
EVERYMAN. O glorious fountain that
all uncleanness doth clarify, *545*
Wash from me the spots of vice unclean,
That on me no sin be seen!
I come with Knowledge for my redemp-
tion,
Redeemed with heartfelt and full con-
trition,
For I am commanded a pilgrimage to
take, *550*
And great accounts before God to make.
Now I pray you, Shrift, Mother of Sal-
vation,
Help my good deeds because of my
piteous exclamation!
CONFESSION. I know your sorrow
well, Everyman,
Because with Knowledge ye come to
me. *555*
I will you comfort as well as I can,
And a precious stone will I give thee,
Called penance, voice-voider of adver-
sity.
Therewith shall your body chastened be
Through abstinence and perseverance in
God's service. *560*
Here shall you receive that scourge of me
That is penance strong, that ye must
endure,
To remember thy Saviour was scourged
for thee
With sharp scourges, and suffered it
patiently—
So must thou ere thou escape from that
painful pilgrimage. *565*
Knowledge, do thou sustain him on this
voyage,
And by that time Good Deeds will be
with thee.
But in any case be sure of mercy,

For your time draweth on fast, if ye will
    saved be.
Ask God mercy, and he will grant it
    truly.   570
When with the scourge of penance man
    doth him bind,
The oil of forgiveness then shall he find.
    (CONFESSION *goes*.)
    EVERYMAN.   Thanked be God for his
    gracious work,
    For now will I my penance begin.
This hath rejoiced and lightened my
    heart,   575
    Though the knots be painful and hard
    within.
    KNOWLEDGE. Everyman, see that ye
    your penance fulfil,
Whatever the pains ye abide full dear,
And Knowledge shall give you counsel at
    will,
    How your account ye shall make full
    clear.   580
    EVERYMAN. O eternal God, O heav-
    enly being,
O way of righteousness, O goodly vision,
Which descended down into a virgin pure
Because he would for every man redeem
    That which Adam forfeited by his dis-
    obedience—   585
O blessed God, elect and exalted in thy
    divinity,
    Forgive thou my grievous offence!
    Here I cry thee mercy in this presence.
O spiritual treasure, O ransomer and re-
    deemer,
Of all the world the hope and the gov-
    ernor,   590
Mirror of joy, founder of mercy,
Who illumineth heaven and earth
    thereby,
Hear my clamorous complaint, though
    late it be,
Receive my prayers, unworthy in this
    heavy life!   594
Though I be a sinner most abominable,
Yet let my name be written in Moses'
    table.
O Mary, pray to the Maker of everything
To vouchsafe me help at my ending,

And save me from the power of my
    enemy,
For Death assaileth me strongly!—   600
And, Lady, that I may, by means of thy
    prayer,
In your Son's glory as partner share,
Through the mediation of his passion I
    it crave.
I beseech you, help my soul to save!
Knowledge, give me the scourge of pen-
    ance;   605
My flesh therewith shall give acquittance.
I will now begin, if God give me grace.
    KNOWLEDGE. Everyman, God give
    you time and space!
Thus I bequeath you into the hands of
    our Saviour,   609
Now may you make your reckoning sure.
    EVERYMAN.   In the name of the Holy
    Trinity,
My body sorely punished shall be.
Take this, body, for the sin of the flesh.
As thou delightest to go gay and fresh,
And in the way of damnation thou didst
    me bring,   615
Therefore suffer now the strokes of pun-
    ishing.
Now of penance to wade the water clear
    I desire,
To save me from purgatory, that sharp
    fire.
    GOOD DEEDS. I thank God now I
    can walk and go,
And am delivered of my sickness and
    woe!   620
Therefore with Everyman I will go and
    not spare;
His good works I will help him to declare.
    KNOWLEDGE. Now, Everyman, be
    merry and glad,
Your Good Deeds cometh now, ye may
    not be sad.
Now is your Good Deeds whole and
    sound,   625
Going upright upon the ground.
    (GOOD DEEDS *rises and walks to
them*.)
    EVERYMAN.   My heart is light and
    shall be evermore.

Now will I smite faster than I did before.

GOOD DEEDS. Everyman, pilgrim, my special friend,

Blessed be thou without end! 630

For thee is prepared the eternal glory.

Now thou hast made me whole and sound this tide,

In every hour I will by thee abide.

EVERYMAN. Welcome, my Good Deeds! Now I hear thy voice,

I weep for sweetness of love. 635

KNOWLEDGE. Be no more sad, but ever rejoice!

God seeth thy manner of life on his throne above.

Put on this garment to thy behoof,

Which wet with the tears of your weeping is,

Or else in God's presence you may it miss, 640

When ye to your journey's end come shall.

EVERYMAN. Gentle Knowledge, what do you it call?

KNOWLEDGE. A garment of sorrow it is by name,

From pain it will you reclaim.

Contrition it is, 645

That getteth forgiveness,

Passing well it doth God please.

GOOD DEEDS. Everyman, will you wear it for your soul's ease?

(EVERYMAN *puts on the robe of contrition.*)

EVERYMAN. Now blessed be Jesu, Mary's son,

For now have I on true contrition! 650

And let us go now without tarrying.

Good Deeds, have we all clear our reckoning?

GOOD DEEDS. Yea, indeed, I have them here.

EVERYMAN. Then I trust we need not fear. 654

Now, friends, let us not part in twain!

KNOWLEDGE. Nay, Everyman, that will we not, for certain.

GOOD DEEDS. Yet must thou lead with thee

Three persons of great might.

EVERYMAN. Who should they be?

GOOD DEEDS. Discretion and Strength they hight. 660

And they Beauty may not abide behind.

KNOWLEDGE. Also ye must call to mind

Your Five Wits as your counsellors beside.

GOOD DEEDS. You must have them ready at every tide.

EVERYMAN. How shall I get them hither? 665

KNOWLEDGE. You must call them all together,

And they will hear you immediately.

EVERYMAN. My friends, come hither and present be,

Discretion, Strength, my Five Wits, and Beauty.

(*They enter.*)

BEAUTY. Here at your will be we all ready. 670

What will ye that we should do?

GOOD DEEDS. That ye should with Everyman go,

And help him in his pilgrimage.

Advise you—will you with him or not, on that voyage?

STRENGTH. We will all bring him thither, 675

To help him and comfort, believe ye me!

DISCRETION. So will we go with him all together.

EVERYMAN. Almighty God, beloved mayest thou be!

I give thee praise that I have hither brought

Strength, Discretion, Beauty, Five Wits —lack I nought— 680

And my Good Deeds, with Knowledge clear,

All be in my company at my will here.

I desire no more in this my anxiousness.

STRENGTH. And I, Strength, will stand by you in your distress,

Though thou wouldest in battle fight on the ground. 685

FIVE WITS. And though it were
through the world round,
We will not leave you for sweet or sour.
BEAUTY. No more will I unto Death's
hour,
Whatsoever thereof befall.
DISCRETION. Everyman, advise you
first of all.   690
Go with a good advisement and deliber-
ation.
We all give you virtuous monition
That all shall be well.
EVERYMAN. My friends, hearken what
I will tell.
I pray God reward you in his heavenly
sphere.   695
Now hearken all that be here,
For I will make my testament
Here before you all present.
In alms, half my goods will I give
with my hands twain,   699
In the way of charity with good intent,
And the other half still shall remain
In bequest to return where it ought to
be.
This I do in despite of the fiend of hell,
Out of his peril to quit my well
For ever after and this day.   705
KNOWLEDGE. Everyman, hearken what
I say.
Go to Priesthood, I you advise,
And receive of him in any wise
The Holy Sacrament and Unction to-
gether,   709
Then see ye speedily turn again hither.
We will all await you here, verily.
FIVE WITS. Yea, Everyman, haste thee
that ye may ready be.
There is no emperor, king, duke, nor
baron bold,
That from God such commission doth
hold
As he doth to the least priest in this
world consign,   715
For of the Blessed Sacraments, pure and
benign,
He beareth the keys, and thereof hath
the cure

For man's redemption, it is ever sure,
Which God as medicine for our souls'
gain   719
Gave us out of his heart with great pain,
Here in this transitory life for thee and
me.
Of the Blessed Sacraments seven there be,
Baptism, Confirmation, with Priesthood
good,
And the Sacrament of God's precious
Flesh and Blood,
Marriage, the Holy Extreme Unction, and
Penance.   725
These seven are good to have in remem-
brance,
Gracious Sacraments of high divinity.
EVERYMAN. Fain would I receive that
holy body.
And meekly to my spiritual father will I
go.
FIVE WITS. Everyman, that is best
that ye can do.   730
God will you to salvation bring,
For Priesthood exceedeth every other
thing.
To us Holy Scripture they do teach,
And convert men from sin, heaven to
reach.
God hath to them more power given   735
Than to any angel that is in heaven.
With five words he may consecrate
God's body in flesh and blood to make,
And handleth his Maker between his
hands.
The priest bindeth and unbindeth all
bands   740
Both in earth and heaven.—
Thou dost administer all the Sacraments
seven.
Though we should kiss thy feet, yet
thereof thou worthy wert.
Thou art the surgeon that doth cure of
mortal sin the hurt.
Remedy under God we find none   745
Except in Priesthood alone.—
Everyman, God gave priests that dignity,
And setteth them in his stead among us
to be,

Thus be they above angels in degree.

KNOWLEDGE.   If priests be good, it is
   so surely;   *750*

But when Jesus hung on the cross with
   grievous smart,

There he gave out of his blessed heart

That same Sacrament in grievous torment.—

He sold them not to us, that Lord omnip-
   otent.

Therefore Saint Peter the apostle doth
   say   *755*

That Jesus' curse have all they

Which God their Saviour do buy or sell,

Or if they for any money do "take or
   tell."

Sinful priests give sinners bad example
   in deed and word,

Their children sit by other men's fires, I
   have heard,   *760*

And some haunt of women the company,

With life unclean as through lustful acts
   of lechery—

These be with sin made blind.

FIVE WITS.   I trust to God no such
   may we find.   *764*

Therefore let us do Priesthood honor,

And follow their doctrines for our souls'
   succor.

We be their sheep, and they shepherds
   be,

By whom we all are kept in security.

Peace! for yonder I see Everyman come,

Who unto God hath made true satisfaction.   *770*

GOOD DEEDS.   Methinketh it is he
   indeed.

EVERYMAN.   Now may Jesus all of
   you comfort and speed!

I have received the Sacrament for my
   redemption,

And also mine extreme unction.

Blessed be all they that counselled me to
   take it!   *775*

And now, friends, let us go without longer
   respite.

I thank God ye would so long waiting
   stand.

Now set each of you on this rood your
   hand,

And shortly follow me.

I go before where I would be.   *780*

God be our guide!

STRENGTH.   Everyman, we will not
   from you go,

Till ye have gone this voyage long.

DISCRETION.   I, Discretion, will abide
   by you also.

KNOWLEDGE.   And though of this pilgrimage the hardships be never so
   strong,   *785*

No turning backward in me shall you
   know.

Everyman, I will be as sure by thee,

As ever I was by Judas Maccabee.

EVERYMAN.   Alas! I am so faint I may
   not stand,

My limbs under me do fold.   *790*

Friends, let us not turn again to this land,
   Not for all the world's gold,

For into this cave must I creep,

And turn to the earth, and there sleep.

BEAUTY.   What—into this grave! Alas!
   Woe is me!   *795*

EVERYMAN.   Yea, there shall ye con-
   sume utterly.

BEAUTY.   And what,—must I smother
   here?

EVERYMAN.   Yea, by my faith, and
   never more appear!

In this world we shall live no more at all,

But in heaven before the highest lord of
   all.   *800*

BEAUTY.   I cross out all this! Adieu,
   by Saint John!

I take "my tap in my lap" and am gone.

EVERYMAN.   What, Beauty!—whither
   go ye?

BEAUTY.   Peace! I am deaf, I look not
   behind me,

Not if thou wouldest give me all the gold
   in thy chest.   *805*

(BEAUTY *goes, followed by the others,
as they speak in turn.*)

EVERYMAN.   Alas! in whom may I
   trust!

Beauty fast away from me doth hie.
She promised with me to live and die.
  STRENGTH. Everyman, I will thee also
    forsake and deny,
Thy game liketh me not at all!   810
  EVERYMAN. Why, then ye will for-
    sake me all!
Sweet Strength, tarry a little space.
  STRENGTH. Nay, Sir, by the rood of
    grace,
I haste me fast my way from thee to
    take,   814
Though thou weep till thy heart do break.
  EVERYMAN. Ye would ever abide by
    me, ye said.
  STRENGTH. Yea, I have you far
    enough conveyed.
Ye be old enough, I understand,
Your pilgrimage to take in hand.
I repent me that I thither came.   820
  EVERYMAN. Strength, for displeasing
    you I am to blame.
Will ye break "promise that is debt"?
  STRENGTH. In faith, I care not!
Thou art but a fool to complain,
You spend your speech and waste your
    brain.   825
Go, thrust thyself into the ground!
  EVERYMAN. I had thought more sure
    I should you have found,
But I see well, who trusteth in his
    Strength,
She him deceiveth at length.
Both Strength and Beauty have forsaken
    me,   830
Yet they promised me fair and lovingly.
  DISCRETION. Everyman, I will after
    Strength be gone—
As for me, I will leave you alone.
  EVERYMAN. Why, Discretion, will ye
    forsake me!
  DISCRETION. Yea, in faith, I will go
    from thee,   835
For when Strength goeth before
I follow after, evermore.
  EVERYMAN. Yet, I pray thee, for love
    of the Trinity
Look in my grave once in pity of me.

  DISCRETION. Nay, so nigh will I not
    come, trust me well!   840
Now I bid you each farewell.
  EVERYMAN. Oh, all things fail save
    God alone—
Beauty, Strength, and Discretion!
For when Death bloweth his blast,
They all run from me full fast.   845
  FIVE WITS. Everyman, my leave now
    of thee I take.
I will follow the others, for here I thee
    forsake.
  EVERYMAN. Alas! then may I wail
    and weep,
For I took you for my best friend.
  FIVE WITS. I will thee no longer
    keep.   850
Now farewell, and here's an end!
  EVERYMAN. O Jesu, help! All have
    forsaken me.
  GOOD DEEDS. Nay, Everyman, I will
    abide by thee,
I will not forsake thee indeed!
Thou wilt find me a good friend at
    need.   855
  EVERYMAN. Gramercy, Good Deeds,
    now may I true friends see.
They have forsaken me everyone,
I loved them better than my Good Deeds
    alone.
Knowledge, will ye forsake me also?
  KNOWLEDGE. Yea, Everyman, when
    ye to death shall go,   860
But not yet, for no manner of danger.
  EVERYMAN. Gramercy, Knowledge,
    with all my heart!
  KNOWLEDGE. Nay, yet will I not from
    hence depart,
Till whereunto ye shall come, I shall see
    and know.
  EVERYMAN. Methinketh, alas! that I
    must now go   865
To make my reckoning, and my debts
    pay,
For I see my time is nigh spent away.
Take example, all ye that this do hear
    or see,
How they that I love best do forsake me,

Except my Good Deeds that abideth
    faithfully.   *870*
    GOOD DEEDS. All earthly things are
    but vanity.
Beauty, Strength and Discretion do man
    forsake,
Foolish friends and kinsmen that fair
    spake,
All flee away save Good Deeds, and that
    am I!
    EVERYMAN. Have mercy on me, God
    most mighty,   *875*
And stand by me, thou Mother and
    Maid, holy Mary!
    GOOD DEEDS. Fear not, I will speak
    for thee.
    EVERYMAN. Here I cry God mercy!
    GOOD DEEDS. Shorten our end and
    minish our pain,
Let us go and never come again.   *880*
    EVERYMAN. Into thy hands, Lord, my
    soul I commend—
Receive it, Lord, that it be not lost!
As thou didst me buy, so do thou me
    defend,
    And save me from the fiend's boast
That I may appear with that blessed
    host   *885*
That shall be saved at the day of doom.
    In manus tuas, of mights the most,
Forever *commendo spiritum meum.*
    (EVERYMAN *goes into the grave.*)
    KNOWLEDGE. Now that he hath suf-
    fered that we all shall endure,
The Good Deeds shall make all sure;
Now that he hath made ending,   *891*
Methinketh that I hear angels sing,
And make great joy and melody,
Where Everyman's soul shall received be!
    (THE ANGEL *appears.*)
    THE ANGEL. Come, excellent elect
    spouse to Jesu!   *895*
    Here above shalt thou go,
Because of thy singular virtue.

Now thy soul from thy body is taken,
    lo!
Thy reckoning is crystal clear.
Now shalt thou into the heavenly sphere,
Unto which ye all shall come   *901*
That live well before the day of doom.
    (THE ANGEL *goes and the* DOCTOR
enters.)
    DOCTOR. This moral men may have
    in mind,—
    Ye hearers, take it as of worth, both
    young and old,
And forsake Pride, for he deceiveth you
    in the end, as ye will find,   *905*
    And remember Beauty, Five Wits,
    Strength, and Discretion, all told,
They all at the last do Everyman forsake
Save that his Good Deeds there doth he
    take.
But beware, if they be small,
Before God he hath no help at all,   *910*
None excuse for Everyman may there
    then be there.
Alas how shall he then do and fare!
For after death amends may no man
    make,
For then Mercy and Pity do him forsake.
If his reckoning be not clear when he
    doth come,   *915*
God will say, *Ite, maledicti, in ignem
    æternum.*
And he that hath his account whole and
    sound,
High in heaven he shall be crowned,
Unto which place God bring us all thither
That we may live, body and soul, to-
    gether!   *920*
Thereto their aid vouchsafe the Trinity—
Amen, say ye, for holy Charity!

FINIS

*Thus endeth this moral play of Every-
man.*

WILLIAM SHAKESPEARE / 1564–1616

So little is known of the life of William Shakespeare, and so inadequately does that little seem to explain the versatile genius manifested in the poetry and the plays, that generations of skeptics have striven to attribute their authorship to a host of other—usually minor—writers. Yet the results of scholarship, some old and some quite recent, leave little doubt that about thirty-eight plays were in fact written by the man from Stratford. We do know that Shakespeare had a sound lower-school education in his native town, and that after his move to London, probably at the age of twenty-one, he was a practical theater man, acting in popular plays and sharing in their production. His own scripts were designed for immediate production to exploit the prevailing tastes of renaissance England and to appeal to the broadest possible audience.

Shakespeare's plays may be classified in a number of ways. One useful classification groups them as histories (e.g., *Richard III, Henry V*), farces and comedies (*The Comedy of Errors, As You Like It*), tragedies (*Hamlet, Othello, King Lear, Macbeth*), dark comedies (*All's Well that Ends Well, Measure for Measure*), and romances (*The Winter's Tale, The Tempest*). This listing represents, in a very general way, the chronological order in which each of these modes was most prominent in Shakespeare's work.

Hamlet (probably 1601) is frequently regarded as Shakespeare's—and the English theater's—greatest play, though some thoughtful readers favor each of the other three mature tragedies: *Othello, King Lear,* and *Macbeth*. Over the centuries *Hamlet* has been a stage favorite, and its leading role has provided the climactic achievement of a long succession of great actors. Yet the play is baffling in many ways, for it bursts the bounds of every definition of successful tragedy, and it has given rise to a remarkable diversity of interpretations.

Like most of Shakespeare's plays, *Hamlet* is an adaptation of older materials. Its genesis may be traced from a tale in the *Historia Danica* of Saxo Grammaticus (about 1200), through the French *Histoires Tragiques* of Belleforest (1576), and through another English *Hamlet* of the 1580's, now lost and possibly by Thomas Kyd, author of *The Spanish Tragedy,* the most prominent English example of the revenge tragedy. As in every other instance of his borrowing, Shakespeare transfigures his materials by the majestic power of his blank verse and by his poetic imagination. More importantly, he plunges deeper into the dungeons of human thought than ever the revenge tragedy was able to do, and produces a profoundly disturbing drama of the thoughtful man's grappling with the ambiguities of action and contemplation, virtue and corruption, illusion and reality. From his sources Shakespeare retains the broadest outlines of a traditional plot; from his own brooding upon man's condition he draws Hamlet's internal conflict over the nature and value of existence. The popularity of the play may be attributed to its mingling of many elements: complex characterization, mystery, comedy both light and grim, satire, suspense, elevated poetry, pageantry, and the dramatization of the puzzle of existence. The stage has little more to offer.

The Tragedy of Hamlet, Prince of Denmark*

DRAMATIS PERSONÆ

CLAUDIUS, *king of Denmark.*

HAMLET, *son to the late, and nephew to the present king.*

POLONIUS, *lord chamberlain.*

HORATIO, *friend to Hamlet.*

LAERTES, *son to Polonius.*

VOLTIMAND,
CORNELIUS,
ROSENCRANTZ,
GUILDENSTERN, } *courtiers.*
OSRIC,
A Gentleman,

A Priest.

MARCELLUS, } *officers.*
BERNARDO,

FRANCISCO, *a soldier.*

REYNALDO, *servant to Polonius.*

Players.

Two clowns, grave-diggers.

FORTINBRAS, *prince of Norway.*

A Captain.

English Ambassadors.

GERTRUDE, *queen of Denmark, and mother to Hamlet.*

OPHELIA, *daughter to Polonius.*

Lords, Ladies, Officers, Soldiers, Sailors, Messengers, and other Attendants.

Ghost of Hamlet's Father.

* The line numbering of *Hamlet* corresponds to the line numbering of the Globe edition, which is the reference used by most scholars. We have numbered verse every five lines. A continued line of verse, regardless of a change in speakers midline or regardless of a break midline, still counts as one line. Because the Globe prose matter was numbered according to the number of lines typographically set, and because the width of the columns in this book is not the same as the Globe's, the prose line numbers here can only be approximated. Generally, in prose, we have numbered only at the ends of speeches, so that the lines that do get numbered also have the same number in the Globe. When the width of a line has not permitted the inclusion of a line number, either the previous line or the following line has been numbered.

SCENE—DENMARK

Act I

SCENE 1—ELSINORE

(*A platform before the castle.*)
(FRANCISCO *at his post. Enter to him* BERNARDO.)

BERNARDO. Who's there?

FRANCISCO. Nay, answer me: stand, and unfold yourself.

BERNARDO. Long live the king!

FRANCISCO. Bernardo?

BERNARDO. He. 5

FRANCISCO. You come most carefully upon your hour.

BERNARDO. 'Tis now struck twelve; get thee to bed, Francisco.

FRANCISCO. For this relief much thanks: 'tis bitter cold,
And I am sick at heart. 9

BERNARDO. Have you had quiet guard?

FRANCISCO. Not a mouse stirring.

BERNARDO. Well, good night.
If you do meet Horatio and Marcellus,
The rivals[1] of my watch, bid them make haste.

FRANCISCO. I think I hear them. Stand, ho! Who's there?

[1] partners

97

(*Enter* HORATIO *and* MARCELLUS.)

HORATIO.   Friends to this ground.

MARCELLUS.   And liegemen to the
Dane.   15

FRANCISCO.   Give you good night.

MARCELLUS.   O, farewell, honest
soldier:

Who hath relieved you?

FRANCISCO.   Bernardo   has   my
place.

Give you good night.   (*Exit.*)

MARCELLUS.   Holla! Bernardo!

BERNARDO.   Say,

What, is Horatio there?

HORATIO.   A piece of him.

BERNARDO.   Welcome, Horatio; welcome, good Marcellus.   20

MARCELLUS.   What, has this thing appear'd again to-night?

BERNARDO.   I have seen nothing.

MARCELLUS.   Horatio says 'tis but
our fantasy,

And will not let belief take hold of him

Touching this dreadful sight, twice seen
of us: 25

Therefore I have entreated him along

With us to watch the minutes of this
night,

That if again this apparition come,

He may approve[2] our eyes and speak
to it.

HORATIO.   Tush, tush, 'twill not appear.

BERNARDO.   Sit down a while;   30

And let us once again assail your ears,

That are so fortified against our story,

What we have two nights seen.

HORATIO.   Well, sit we down,

And let us hear Bernardo speak of this.

BERNARDO.   Last night of all,   35

When yond same star that's westward
from the pole

Had made his course to illume that part
of heaven

Where now it burns, Marcellus and myself,

The bell then beating one,—

(*Enter* GHOST.)

2 confirm

MARCELLUS.   Peace, break thee off;
look, where it comes again!   40

BERNARDO.   In the same figure, like
the king that's dead.

MARCELLUS.   Thou   art   a   scholar;
speak to it, Horatio.

BERNARDO.   Looks it not like the
king? mark it, Horatio.

HORATIO.   Most like: it harrows me
with fear and wonder.

BERNARDO.   It would be spoke to.

MARCELLUS.   Question it, Horatio.

HORATIO.   What   art   thou,   that
usurp'st this time of night,   46

Together with that fair and warlike form

In which the majesty of buried Denmark

Did   sometimes   march? by heaven I
charge thee, speak!

MARCELLUS.   It is offended.

BERNARDO.   See, it stalks away!   50

HORATIO.   Stay! speak, speak!   I
charge thee, speak!

(*Exit* GHOST.)

MARCELLUS.   'Tis gone, and will not
answer.

BERNARDO.   Now now, Horatio! you
tremble and look pale:

Is not this something more than fantasy?

What think you on't?   55

HORATIO.   Before my God, I might
not this believe

Without the sensible and true avouch

Of mine own eyes.

MARCELLUS.   Is it not like the
king?

HORATIO.   As thou art to thyself:

Such was the very armor he had on   60

When he the ambitious Norway com-
bated;

So frown'd he once, when, in an angry
parle,

He smote the sledded Polacks on the ice.

'Tis strange.

MARCELLUS.   Thus twice before, and
jump at this dead hour,   65

With martial stalk hath he gone by our
watch.

HORATIO.   In what particular thought
to work I know not;

But, in the gross and scope' of my opinion,
This bodes some strange eruption to our state.

MARCELLUS. Good now, sit down, and tell me, he that knows, 70
Why this same strict and most observant watch
So nightly toils the subject of the land,
And why such daily cast of brazen cannon,
And foreign mart for implements of war;
Why such impress of shipwrights, whose sore task 75
Does not divide the Sunday from the week;
What might be toward, that this sweaty haste
Doth make the night joint-laborer with the day:
Who is't that can inform me?

HORATIO.   That can I;
At least the whisper goes so. Our last king, 80
Whose image even but now appear'd to us,
Was, as you know, by Fortinbras of Norway,
Thereto prick'd on by a most emulate[3] pride,
Dared to the combat; in which our valiant Hamlet—
For so this side of our known world esteem'd him— 85
Did slay this Fortinbras; who by a seal'd compact
Well ratified by law and heraldry,
Did forfeit, with his life, all those his lands
Which he stood seized of, to the conqueror: 89
Against the which, a moiety competent
Was gagèd[4] by our king; which had return'd
To the inheritance of Fortinbras,
Had he been vanquisher; as, by the same covenant,

And carriage[5] of the article design'd,
His fell to Hamlet. Now, sir, young Fortinbras, 95
Of unimprovèd metal hot and full,
Hath in the skirts of Norway here and there
Shark'd up a list of lawless resolutes,
For food and diet, to some enterprise
That hath a stomach in't; which is no other— 100
As it doth well appear unto our state—
But to recover of us, by strong hand
And terms compulsatory, those foresaid lands
So by his father lost: and this, I take it,
Is the main motive of our preparations,
The source of this our watch and the chief head 106
Of this post-haste and romage[6] in the land.

BERNARDO. I think it be no other but e'en so:
Well may it sort, that this portentous figure
Comes armèd through our watch; so like the king 110
That was and is the question of these wars.

HORATIO. A mote it is to trouble the mind's eye.
In the most high and palmy state of Rome,
A little ere the mightiest Julius fell,
The graves stood tenantless and the sheeted dead 115
Did squeak and gibber in the Roman streets:
As stars with trains of fire and dews of blood,
Disasters in the sun; and the moist star
Upon whose influence Neptune's empire stands,
Was sick almost to doomsday with eclipse: 120
And even the like precurse of fierce events
As harbingers preceding still the fates

[3] enviously ambitious
[4] pledged

[5] import
[6] rummage; turmoil

And prologue to the omen coming on,
Have heaven and earth together demon-
    strated   *124*
Unto our climatures and countrymen.—
But soft, behold! lo, where it comes
    again!
    (*Re-enter* GHOST.)
I'll cross[7] it, though it blast me. Stay,
    illusion!
If thou hast any sound, or use of voice,
Speak to me: *129*
If there be any good thing to be done,
That may to thee do ease and grace to
    me,
Speak to me:
If thou art privy to thy country's fate,
Which, happily, foreknowing may avoid,
O, speak!   *135*
Or if thou hast uphoarded in thy life
Extorted treasure in the womb of earth,
For which, they say, you spirits oft walk
    in death,
Speak of it: stay, and speak! (*The cock
    crows.*) Stop it, Marcellus.
    MARCELLUS.   Shall I strike at it with
    my partisan?[8]   *140*
    HORATIO.   Do, if it will not stand.
    BERNARDO.   'Tis here!
    HORATIO.   'Tis here!
    MARCELLUS.   'Tis gone!
                    (*Exit* GHOST.)
We do it wrong, being so majestical,
To offer it the show of violence;
For it is, as the air, invulnerable,   *145*
And our vain blows malicious mockery.
    BERNARDO.   It was about to speak,
    when the cock crew.
    HORATIO.   And then it started like a
    guilty thing
Upon a fearful summons. I have heard,
The cock, that is the trumpet to the
    morn,   *150*
Doth with his lofty and shrill-sounding
    throat

[7] cross its path—dangerous if the ghost is an
evil spirit
[8] a pike; a long-handled weapon with an
ax-like blade

Awake the god of day; and at his warn-
    ing,
Whether in sea or fire, in earth or air,
The extravagant and erring spirit hies
To his confine: and of the truth herein
This present object made probation. *156*
    MARCELLUS.   It faded on the crowing
    of the cock.
Some say that ever 'gainst that season
    comes
Wherein our Saviour's birth is celebrated,
The bird of dawning singeth all night
    long: *160*
And then, they say, no spirit dare stir
    abroad,
The nights are wholesome; then no
    planets strike,
No fairy takes, nor witch hath power to
    charm,
So hallow'd and so gracious is the time.
    HORATIO.   So have I heard and do in
    part believe it.   *165*
But look, the morn, in russet mantle clad,
Walks o'er the dew of yon high eastward
    hill:
Break we our watch up; and by my
    advice,
Let us impart what we have seen to-night
Unto young Hamlet; for, upon my life,
This spirit, dumb to us, will speak to
    him.   *171*
Do you consent we shall acquaint him
    with it,
As needful in our loves, fitting our duty?
    MARCELLUS.   Let's do't, I pray; and I
    this morning know
Where we shall find him most con-
    veniently.   (*Exeunt.*)   *175*

SCENE 2

(*A room of state in the castle.*)
(*Flourish. Enter the* KING, QUEEN,
HAMLET, POLONIUS, LAERTES, VOL-
TIMAND, CORNELIUS, LORDS, *and* AT-
TENDANTS.)

    KING.   Though yet of Hamlet our
    dear brother's death

The memory be green, and that it us
befitted
To bear our hearts in grief and our
whole kingdom
To be contracted in one brow of woe,
Yet so far hath discretion fought with
nature   *5*
That we with wisest sorrow think on him,
Together with remembrance of ourselves.
Therefore our sometime sister, now our
queen,
The imperial jointress to this warlike
state,
Have we, as 'twere with a defeated
joy,—   *10*
With an auspicious and a dropping eye,
With mirth in funeral and with dirge in
marriage,
In equal scale weighing delight and
dole,—
Taken to wife: nor have we herein
barr'd
Your better wisdoms, which have freely
gone   *15*
With this affair along. For all, our
thanks.
Now follows, that you know, young
Fortinbras,
Holding a weak supposal of our worth,
Or thinking by our late dear brother's
death
Our state to be disjoint and out of
frame,   *20*
Colleagued with this dream of his ad-
vantage,
He hath not fail'd to pester us with
message,
Importing the surrender of those lands
Lost by his father, with all bonds of
law,
To our most valiant brother. So much for
him.   *25*
Now for ourself and for this time of
meeting:
Thus much the business is: we have here
writ
To Norway, uncle of young Fortinbras,—
Who, impotent and bed-rid, scarcely
hears

Of this his nephew's purpose,—to sup-
press   *30*
His further gait herein; in that the levies,
The lists and full proportions, are all
made
Out of his subject: and we here dispatch
You, good Cornelius, and you, Volti-
mand,
For bearers of this greeting to old Nor-
way;   *35*
Giving to you no further personal power
To business with the king, more than the
scope
Of these delated articles allow.
Farewell, and let your haste commend
your duty.

CORNELIUS.⎫ In that and all things
VOLTIMAND.⎭ will we show our
           duty.   *40*

KING. We doubt it nothing: heartily
farewell.
(*Exeunt* VOLTIMAND *and* CORNELIUS.)
And now, Laertes, what's the news with
you?
You told us of some suit; what is't,
Laertes?
You cannot speak of reason to the Dane,
And lose your voice: what wouldst thou
beg, Laertes,   *45*
That shall not be my offer, not thy ask-
ing?
The head is not more native to the heart,
The hand more instrumental to the
mouth,
Than is the throne of Denmark to thy
father.
What wouldst thou have, Laertes?
     LAERTES. My dread lord,   *50*
Your leave and favor to return to
France;
From whence though willingly I came to
Denmark,
To show my duty in your coronation,
Yet now, I must confess, that duty done,
My thoughts and wishes bend again
toward France   *55*
And bow them to your gracious leave
and pardon.
     KING. Have you your father's leave?

What says Polonius?

POLONIUS. He hath, my lord, wrung
from me my slow leave
By laborsome petition, and at last
Upon his will I seal'd my hard con-
sent: 60
I do beseech you, give him leave to go.

KING. Take thy fair hour, Laertes;
time be thine,
And thy best graces spend it at thy will!
But now, my cousin Hamlet, and my
son,—

HAMLET (aside). A little more than
kin, and less than kind.[9]   65

KING. How is it that the clouds still
hang on you?

HAMLET. Not so, my lord; I am too
much i' the sun.

QUEEN. Good Hamlet, cast thy
nighted color off,
And let thine eye look like a friend on
Denmark.
Do not for ever with thy vailèd lids   70
Seek for thy noble father in the dust:
Thou know'st 'tis common; all that lives
must die,
Passing through nature to eternity.

HAMLET. Aye, madam, it is common.

QUEEN.   If it be,   74
Why seems it so particular with thee?

HAMLET. Seems, madam! nay, it is;
I know not "seems."
'Tis not alone my inky cloak, good mother,
Nor customary suits of solemn black,
Nor windy suspiration of forced breath,
No, nor the fruitful river in the eye,   80
Nor the dejected 'havior of the visage,
Together with all forms, moods, shapes
of grief,
That can denote me truly: these indeed
seem,
For they are actions that a man might
play:
But I have that within which passeth
show;   85

9 true child

These but the trappings and the suits of
woe.

KING. 'Tis sweet and commendable
in your nature, Hamlet,
To give these mourning duties to your
father:
But, you must know, your father lost a
father,
That father lost, lost his, and the survivor
bound   90
In filial obligation for some term
To do obsequious sorrow: but to per-
sèver
In obstinate condolement is a course
Of impious stubbornness; 'tis unmanly
grief;
It shows a will most incorrect to
heaven,   95
A heart unfortified, a mind impatient,
An understanding simple and un-
school'd:
For what we know must be and is as
common
As any the most vulgar thing to sense,
Why should we in our peevish opposi-
tion   100
Take it to heart? Fie! 'tis a fault to
heaven,
A fault against the dead, a fault to
nature,
To reason most absurd; whose common
theme
Is death of fathers, and who still hath
cried,
From the first corse till he that died
to-day,   105
"This must be so." We pray you, throw
to earth
This unprevailing woe, and think of us
As of a father: for let the world take
note,
You are the most immediate to our
throne;
And with no less nobility of love   110
Than that which dearest father bears his
son,
Do I impart toward you. For your intent
In going back to school in Wittenberg,

It is most retrograde to our desire:
And we beseech you, bend you to re-
  main   *115*
Here in the cheer and comfort of our
  eye,
Our chiefest courtier, cousin, and our son.
  QUEEN.   Let not thy mother lose
    her prayers, Hamlet:
I pray thee, stay with us; go not to Witten-
  berg.
  HAMLET.   I shall in all my best obey
    you, madam.   *120*
  KING.   Why, 'tis a loving and a fair
    reply:
Be as ourself in Denmark. Madam,
  come;
This gentle and unforced accord of
  Hamlet
Sits smiling to my heart: in grace
  whereof,
No jocund health that Denmark drinks
  to-day,   *125*
But the great cannon to the clouds shall
  tell,
And the king's rouse the heaven shall
  bruit again,
Re-speaking earthly thunder. Come away.
    (*Flourish. Exeunt all but* HAMLET.)
  HAMLET.   O, that this too too solid
    flesh would melt,
Thaw and resolve itself into a dew!   *130*
Or that the Everlasting had not fix'd
His canon 'gainst self-slaughter! O God!
  God!
How weary, stale, flat and unprofitable
Seem to me all the uses of this world!
Fie on't! ah fie! 'tis an unweeded garden,
That grows to seed; things rank and
  gross in nature   *136*
Possess it merely. That it should come to
  this!
But two months dead: nay, not so much,
  not two:
So excellent a king; that was, to this,
Hyperion[10] to a satyr: so loving to my
  mother   *140*

That he might not beteem[11] the winds of
  heaven
Visit her face too roughly. Heaven and
  earth!
Must I remember? why, she would hang
  on him,
As if increase of appetite had grown
By what it fed on: and yet, within a
  month—   *145*
Let me not think on't—Frailty, thy
  name is woman!—
A little month, or ere those shoes were old
With which she follow'd my poor father's
  body,
Like Niobe,[12] all tears:—why she, even
  she—
O God! a beast that wants discourse of
  reason   *150*
Would have mourn'd longer—married
  with my uncle,
My father's brother, but no more like my
  father
Than I to Hercules:[13] within a month;
Ere yet the salt of most unrighteous tears
Had left the flushing in her gallèd eyes,
She married. O, most wicked speed, to
  post   *156*
With such dexterity to incestuous sheets!
It is not, nor it cannot come to good:
But break, my heart, for I must hold my
  tongue.
    (*Enter* HORATIO, MARCELLUS, *and*
BERNARDO.)
  HORATIO.   Hail to your lordship!
  HAMLET.   I am glad to see you
    well: *160*
Horatio,—or I do forget myself.
  HORATIO.   The same, my lord, and
    your poor servant ever.
  HAMLET.   Sir, my good friend; I'll
    change[14] that name with you:

---

[10] Apollo, the sun god

[11] permit
[12] Apollo killed Niobe's children to punish
her pride in their number. Turned into stone,
she wept endlessly at their loss.
[13] hero of Greek myth noted for strength
and courage
[14] exchange

And what make you from Wittenberg,
Horatio?
Marcellus?   *165*
MARCELLUS. My good lord—
HAMLET. I am very glad to see you.
(*To* BERNARDO.) Good even, sir.
But what, in faith, make you from
Wittenberg?
HORATIO. A truant disposition, good
my lord.
HAMLET. I would not hear your
enemy say so,   *170*
Nor shall you do my ear that violence,
To make it truster of your own report
Against yourself; I know you are no
truant.
But what is your affair in Elsinore?
We'll teach you to drink deep ere you
depart.   *175*
HORATIO. My lord, I came to see
your father's funeral.
HAMLET. I pray thee, do not mock
me, fellow-student;
I think it was to see my mother's wed-
ding.
HORATIO. Indeed, my lord, it fol-
low'd hard upon.
HAMLET. Thrift, thrift, Horatio! the
funeral baked-meats   *180*
Did coldly furnish forth the marriage
tables.
Would I had met my dearest foe in
heaven
Or ever I had seen that day, Horatio!
My father!—methinks I see my father.
HORATIO. Where, my lord?
HAMLET.   In my mind's eye, Ho-
ratio.
HORATIO. I saw him once; he was a
goodly king.   *186*
HAMLET. He was a man, take him
for all in all,
I shall not look upon his like again.
HORATIO. My lord, I think I saw
him yesternight.
HAMLET. Saw? who?   *190*
HORATIO. My lord, the king your
father.
HAMLET.   The king my father!

HORATIO. Season your admiration
for a while
With an attent ear, till I may deliver,
Upon the witness of these gentlemen,
This marvel to you.
HAMLET.   For God's love, let me
hear.   *195*
HORATIO. Two nights together had
these gentlemen,
Marcellus and Bernardo, on their watch,
In the dead vast and middle of the night,
Been thus encounter'd. A figure like your
father,
Armed at point exactly, cap-a-pe,[15]   *200*
Appears before them, and with solemn
march
Goes slow and stately by them: thrice he
walk'd
By their oppress'd and fear-surprisèd
eyes,
Within his truncheon's length; whilst
they, distill'd
Almost to jelly with the act of fear,   *205*
Stand dumb, and speak not to him. This
to me
In dreadful secrecy impart they did;
And I with them the third night kept the
watch:
Where, as they had deliver'd, both in
time,
Form of the thing, each word made true
and good,   *210*
The apparition comes: I knew your
father;
These hands are not more like.
HAMLET.   But where was this?
MARCELLUS. My lord, upon the plat-
form where we watch'd.
HAMLET. Did you not speak to it?
HORATIO.   My lord, I did;
But answer made it none: yet once me-
thought   *215*
It lifted up its head and did address
Itself to motion, like as it would speak:
But even then the morning cock crew
loud,
And at the sound it shrunk in haste away

15 from head to foot

And vanish'd from our sight.

HAMLET.   'Tis very strange. *220*

HORATIO.   As I do live, my honor'd
lord, 'tis true,

And we did think it writ down in our duty

To let you know of it.

HAMLET.   Indeed, indeed, sirs, but
this troubles me.

Hold you the watch to-night?

MARCELLUS.⎫
BERNARDO.   ⎬ We do, my lord. *225*

HAMLET.   Arm'd, say you?

MARCELLUS.⎫
BERNARDO.   ⎬   Arm'd, my lord.

HAMLET.   From top to toe?

MARCELLUS.⎫ My lord, from head to
BERNARDO.   ⎭ foot.

HAMLET.   Then saw you not his face?

HORATIO.   O, yes, my lord; he wore
his beaver[16] up.   *230*

HAMLET.   What, look'd he frowningly?

HORATIO.   A countenance more in
sorrow than in anger.

HAMLET.   Pale, or red?

HORATIO.   Nay, very pale.

HAMLET.   And fix'd his eyes upon
you?

HORATIO.   Most constantly. *234*

HAMLET.   I would I had been
there.

HORATIO.   It would have much
amazed you.

HAMLET.   Very like, very like. Stay'd
it long?

HORATIO.   While one with moderate
haste might tell a hundred.

MARCELLUS. ⎫
BERNARDO.   ⎬ Longer, longer.

HORATIO.   Not when I saw't.

HAMLET.   His beard was grizzled,
—no?   *240*

HORATIO.   It was, as I have seen it in
his life,

A sable silver'd.

HAMLET.   I will watch to-night;
Perchance 'twill walk again.

HORATIO.   I warrant it will.

HAMLET.   If it assume my noble
father's person,

I'll speak to it, though hell itself should
gape   *245*

And bid me hold my peace. I pray you
all,

If you have hitherto conceal'd this sight,

Let it be tenable in your silence still,

And whatsoever else shall hap to-night,

Give it an understanding, but no tongue:

I will requite your loves. So fare you
well: *251*

Upon the platform, 'twixt eleven and
twelve,

I'll visit you.

ALL.   Our duty to your honor.

HAMLET.   Your loves, as mine to
you: farewell.

(*Exeunt all but* HAMLET.)

My father's spirit in arms! all is not
well;   *255*

I doubt[17] some foul play: would the
night were come!

Till then sit still, my soul: foul deeds will
rise,

Though all the earth o'erwhelm them, to
men's eyes.

(*Exit.*)

SCENE 3

(*A room in* POLONIUS'S *house.*)
(*Enter* LAERTES *and* OPHELIA.)

LAERTES.   My necessaries are em-
bark'd: farewell:

And, sister, as the winds give benefit

And convoy is assistant, do not sleep,

But let me hear from you.

OPHELIA.   Do you doubt that?

LAERTES.   For Hamlet and the trifling
of his favor,   *5*

Hold it a fashion and a toy in blood,

A violet in the youth of primy nature,

Forward, not permanent, sweet, not lasting,

[16] visor   [17] suspect

The perfume and suppliance of a minute;
No more.

 OPHELIA. No more but so?

 LAERTES. Think it no more: *10*
For nature, crescent, does not grow alone
In thews and bulk, but, as this temple
 waxes,
The inward service of the mind and soul
Grows wide withal. Perhaps he loves you
 now;
And now no soil nor cautel[18] doth be-
 smirch *15*
The virtue of his will: but you must fear,
His greatness weigh'd, his will is not his
 own;
For he himself is subject to his birth:
He may not, as unvalued persons do,
Carve for himself, for on his choice de-
 pends *20*
The safety and health of this whole state,
And therefore must his choice be circum-
 scribed
Unto the voice and yielding of that body
Whereof he is the head. Then if he says
 he loves you,
It fits your wisdom so far to believe
 it *25*
As he in his particular act and place
May give his saying deed; which is no
 further
Than the main voice of Denmark goes
 withal.
Then weigh what loss your honor may
 sustain,
If with too credent[19] ear you list his
 songs, *30*
Or lose your heart, or your chaste trea-
 sure open
To his unmaster'd importunity.
Fear it, Ophelia, fear it, my dear sister,
And keep you in the rear of your affec-
 tion,
Out of the shot and danger of de-
 sire. *35*
The chariest maid is prodigal enough,
If she unmask her beauty to the moon:

Virtue itself 'scapes not calumnious
 strokes:
The canker galls the infants of the spring
Too oft before their buttons be dis-
 closed, *40*
And in the morn and liquid dew of youth
Contagious blastments are most im-
 minent.
Be wary then; best safety lies in fear:
Youth to itself rebels, though none else
 near.

 OPHELIA. I shall the effect of this
 good lesson keep, *45*
As watchman to my heart. But, good
 my brother,
Do not, as some ungracious pastors do,
Show me the steep and thorny way to
 heaven,
Whilst, like puff'd and reckless libertine,
Himself the primrose path of dalliance
 treads *50*
And recks not his own rede.[20]

 LAERTES.   O, fear me not.
I stay too long; but here my father
 comes.

 (*Enter* POLONIUS.)
A double blessing is a double grace;
Occasion smiles upon a second leave.

 POLONIUS. Yet here, Laertes! Aboard,
 aboard, for shame! *55*
The wind sits in the shoulder of your sail,
And you are stay'd for. There; my bles-
 sing with thee!
And these few precepts in thy memory
See thou charàcter.[21] Give thy thoughts
 no tongue, *59*
Nor any unproportion'd thought his act.
Be thou familiar, but by no means vul-
 gar.
Those friends thou hast, and their adop-
 tion tried,
Grapple them to thy soul with hoops of
 steel,
But do not dull thy palm with entertain-
 ment

---

[18] deceit
[19] credulous

[20] advice
[21] inscribe

Of each new-hatch'd unfledged comrade. Beware 65
Of entrance to a quarrel; but being in,
Bear't, that the opposèd may beware of thee.
Give every man thy ear, but few thy voice:
Take each man's censure, but reserve thy judgment. 69
Costly thy habit as thy purse can buy,
But not express'd in fancy; rich, not gaudy:
For the apparel oft proclaims the man,
And they in France of the best rank and station
Are of a most select and generous chief in that.
Neither a borrower nor a lender be: 75
For loan oft loses both itself and friend,
And borrowing dulls the edge of husbandry.
This above all: to thine own self be true,
And it must follow, as the night the day,
Thou canst not then be false to any man. 80
Farewell: my blessing season this in thee!
LAERTES. Most humbly do I take my leave, my lord.
POLONIUS. The time invites you; go, your servants tend.
LAERTES. Farewell, Ophelia, and remember well
What I have said to you. 84
OPHELIA. 'Tis in my memory lock'd,
And you yourself shall keep the key of it.
LAERTES. Farewell. (*Exit.*)
POLONIUS. What is't, Ophelia, he hath said to you?
OPHELIA. So please you, something touching the Lord Hamlet. 89
POLONIUS. Marry, well bethought:
'Tis told me, he hath very oft of late
Given private time to you, and you yourself
Have of your audience been most free and bounteous:

If it be so—as so 'tis put on me,
And that in way of caution—I must tell you, 95
You do not understand yourself so clearly
As it behooves my daughter and your honor.
What is between you? give me up the truth.
OPHELIA. He hath, my lord, of late made many tenders
Of his affection to me. 100
POLONIUS. Affection! pooh! you speak like a green girl,
Unsifted in such perilous circumstance.
Do you believe his tenders, as you call them?
OPHELIA. I do not know, my lord, what I should think.
POLONIUS. Marry, I'll teach you: think yourself a baby, 105
That you have ta'en these tenders for true pay,
Which are not sterling. Tender yourself more dearly;
Or—not to crack the wind of the poor phrase,
Running it thus—you'll tender me a fool.
OPHELIA. My lord, he hath importuned me with love 110
In honorable fashion.
POLONIUS. Aye, fashion you may call it; go to, go to.
OPHELIA. And hath given countenance to his speech, my lord,
With almost all the holy vows of heaven.
POLONIUS. Aye, springes to catch woodcocks. I do know, 115
When the blood burns, how prodigal the soul
Lends the tongue vows: these blazes, daughter,
Giving more light than heat, extinct in both,
Even in their promise, as it is a-making,
You must not take for fire. From this time 120
Be something scanter of your maiden presence;

Set your entreatments at a higher rate
Than a command to parley. For Lord
   Hamlet,
Believe so much in him, that he is young,
And with a larger tether may he
   walk   *125*
Than may be given you: in few, Ophelia,
Do not believe his vows; for they are
   brokers,
Not of that dye which their investments
   show,
But mere implorators of unholy suits,
Breathing like sanctified and pious
   bawds,   *130*
The better to beguile. This is for all:
I would not, in plain terms, from this
   time forth,
Have you so slander any moment leisure,
As to give words or talk with the Lord
   Hamlet.   *134*
Look to't, I charge you: come your ways.
   OPHELIA.   I shall obey, my lord.
                               (*Exeunt.*)

                 SCENE 4

(*The platform.*)
(*Enter* HAMLET, HORATIO, *and* MAR-
CELLUS.)

   HAMLET.   The air bites shrewdly; it
      is very cold.
   HORATIO.   It is a nipping and an
      eager air.
   HAMLET.   What hour now?
   HORATIO.   I think it lacks of
      twelve.
   MARCELLUS.   No, it is struck.
   HORATIO.   Indeed? I heard it not: it
      then draws near the season   *5*
Wherein the spirit held his wont to walk.
   (*A flourish of trumpets, and ordnance
shot off within.*)
What doth this mean, my lord?
   HAMLET.   The king doth wake to-
      night, and takes his rouse,
Keeps wassail, and the swaggering up-
   spring reels;
And as he drains his draughts of Rhenish
   down,   *10*

The kettle-drum and trumpet thus bray
   out
The triumph of his pledge.
   HORATIO.   Is it a custom?
   HAMLET.   Aye, marry, is't:
But to my mind, though I am native
   here   *14*
And to the manner born, it is a custom
More honor'd in the breach than the
   observance.
This heavy-headed revel east and west
Makes us traduced and tax'd of other
   nations:
They clepe us drunkards, and with
   swinish phrase   *19*
Soil our addition; and indeed it takes
From our achievements, though per-
   form'd at height,
The pith and marrow of our attribute.
So, oft it chances in particular men,
That for some vicious mole of nature in
   them,
As, in their birth,—wherein they are not
   guilty,   *25*
Since nature cannot choose his origin,—
By the o'ergrowth of some complexion,
Oft breaking down the pales and forts of
   reason,
Or by some habit that too much o'er-
   leavens
The form of plausive manners, that these
   men,—   *30*
Carrying, I say, the stamp of one defect,
Being nature's livery, or fortune's star,—
Their virtues else—be they as pure as
   grace,
As infinite as man may undergo—
Shall in the general censure take corrup-
   tion   *35*
From that particular fault: the dram of
   eale[22]
Doth all the noble substance often dout[23]
To his own scandal.
   HORATIO.   Look, my lord it comes!
   (*Enter* GHOST.)
   HAMLET.   Angels and ministers of
      grace defend us!

[22] evil (?)
[23] do out; put out

Be thou a spirit of health or goblin
    damn'd,   *40*
Bring with thee airs from heaven or
    blasts from hell,
Be thy intents wicked or charitable,
Thou comest in such a questionable
    shape
That I will speak to thee: I'll call thee
    Hamlet,
King, father, royal Dane: O, answer
    me!   *45*
Let me not burst in ignorance; but tell
Why thy canónized bones, hearsèd in
    death,
Have burst their cerements; why the
    sepulchre,
Wherein we saw thee quietly interr'd,
Hath oped his ponderous and marble
    jaws,   *50*
To cast thee up again. What may this
    mean,
That thou, dead corse, again, in cómplete
    steel,
Revisit'st thus the glimpses of the moon,
Making night hideous; and we fools of
    nature
So horridly to shake our disposition *55*
With thoughts beyond the reaches of our
    souls?
Say, why is this? wherefore? what should
    we do?
            (GHOST *beckons* HAMLET.)
HORATIO.   It beckons you to go away
    with it,
As if it some impartment did desire
To you alone.
    MARCELLUS.   Look, with what cour-
    teous action   *60*
It waves you to a more removèd ground:
But do not go with it.
    HORATIO.   No, by no means.
    HAMLET.   It will not speak; then I
    will follow it.
    HORATIO.   Do not, my lord.
    HAMLET.   Why, what should be the
    fear?
I do not set my life at a pin's fee; *65*
And for my soul, what can it do to that,
Being a thing immortal as itself?

It waves me forth again: I'll follow it.
    HORATIO.   What if it tempt you to-
    ward the flood, my lord,   *69*
Or to the dreadful summit of the cliff
That beetles o'er his base into the sea,
And there assume some other horrible
    form,
Which might deprive your sovereignty
    of reason
And draw you into madness? think of it:
The very place puts toys of despera-
    tion,   *75*
Without more motive, into every brain
That looks so many fathoms to the sea
And hears it roar beneath.
    HAMLET.   It waves me still.
Go on; I'll follow thee.
    MARCELLUS.   You shall not go, my
    lord.   *79*
    HAMLET.   Hold off your hands.
    HORATIO.   Be ruled; you shall not go.
    HAMLET.   My fate cries out,
And makes each petty artery in this body
As hardy as the Nemean lion's nerve.
Still am I call'd. Unhand me, gentlemen.
By heaven, I'll make a ghost of him that
    lets[24] me: *85*
I say, away! Go on; I'll follow thee.
            (*Exeunt* GHOST *and* HAMLET.)
    HORATIO.   He waxes desperate with
    imagination.
    MARCELLUS.   Let's follow; 'tis not fit
    thus to obey him.
    HORATIO.   Have after. To what issue
    will this come?
    MARCELLUS.   Something is rotten in
    the state of Denmark.   *90*
    HORATIO.   Heaven will direct it.
    MARCELLUS.   Nay, let's follow him.
                              (*Exeunt.*)

            SCENE 5

(*Another part of the platform.*)
(*Enter* GHOST *and* HAMLET.)

    HAMLET.   Where wilt thou lead me?
    speak; I'll go no further.

[24] hinders

GHOST.   Mark me.

HAMLET.   I will.

GHOST.   My hour is almost come,
When I to sulphurous and tormenting
flames
Must render up myself.

HAMLET.   Alas, poor ghost!

GHOST.   Pity me not, but lend thy
serious hearing   5
To what I shall unfold.

HAMLET.   Speak; I am bound to
hear.

GHOST.   So art thou to revenge, when
thou shalt hear.

HAMLET.   What?

GHOST.   I am thy father's spirit;
Doom'd for a certain term to walk the
night,   10
And for the day confined to fast in fires,
Till the foul crimes done in my days of
nature
Are burnt and purged away. But that I
am forbid
To tell the secrets of my prison-house,
I could a tale unfold whose lightest
word   15
Would harrow up thy soul, freeze thy
young blood,
Make thy two eyes, like stars, start from
their spheres,
Thy knotted and combinèd locks to part
And each particular hair to stand on end,
Like quills upon the fretful porpen-
tine: 20
But this eternal blazon must not be
To ears of flesh and blood. List, list, O,
list!
If thou didst ever thy dear father love—

HAMLET.   O God!

GHOST.   Revenge his foul and most
unnatural murder.   25

HAMLET.   Murder!

GHOST.   Murder most foul, as in the
best it is,
But this most foul, strange, and unnatural.

HAMLET.   Haste me to know't, that
I, with wings as swift
As meditation or the thoughts of love,

May sweep to my revenge.   31

GHOST.   I find thee apt;
And duller shouldst thou be than the fat
weed
That roots itself in ease on Lethe[25]
wharf,
Wouldst thou not stir in this. Now, Ham-
let, hear:
'Tis given out that, sleeping in my
orchard,   35
A serpent stung me; so the whole ear
of Denmark
Is by a forgèd process of my death
Rankly abused: but know, thou noble
youth,
The serpent that did sting thy father's
life
Now wears his crown.   39

HAMLET.   O my prophetic soul!
My uncle!

GHOST.   Aye, that incestuous, that
adulterate beast,
With witchcraft of his wit, with traitor-
ous gifts,—
O wicked wit and gifts, that have the
power
So to seduce!—won to his shameful
lust   45
The will of my most seeming-virtuous
queen.
O Hamlet, what a falling-off was there
From me, whose love was of that dignity
That it went hand in hand even with the
vow
I made to her in marriage; and to de-
cline   50
Upon a wretch, whose natural gifts were
poor
To those of mine!
But virtue, as it never will be moved,
Though lewdness court it in a shape of
heaven,
So lust, though to a radiant angel
link'd,   55
Will sate itself in a celestial bed
And prey on garbage.

[25] the river of forgetfulness in the underworld

But, soft! methinks I scent the morning
air;
Brief let me be. Sleeping within my
orchard,
My custom always of the afternoon,   60
Upon my secure hour thy uncle stole,
With juice of cursèd hebenon[26] in a vial,
And in the porches of my ears did pour
The leperous distilment; whose effect
Holds such an enmity with blood of
man   65
That swift as quicksilver it courses
through
The natural gates and alleys of the body;
And with a sudden vigor it doth posset[27]
And curd, like eager droppings into milk,
The thin and wholesome blood: so did it
mine;   70
And a most instant tetter[28] bark'd about,
Most lazar-like,[29] with vile and loath-
some crust,
All my smooth body.
Thus was I, sleeping, by a brother's hand
Of life, of crown, of queen, at once
dispatch'd: 75
Cut off even in the blossoms of my sin,
Unhousel'd, disappointed, unaneled;
No reckoning made, but sent to my ac-
count
With all my imperfections on my head:
O, horrible! O, horrible! most hor-
rible!   80
If thou hast nature in thee, bear it not;
Let not the royal bed of Denmark be
A couch for luxury and damnèd incest.
But, howsoever thou pursuest this act,
Taint not thy mind, nor let thy soul
contrive   85
Against thy mother aught: leave her to
heaven,
And to those thorns that in her bosom
lodge,
To prick and sting her. Fare thee well
at once!

The glow-worm shows the matin to be
near,   89
And 'gins to pale his uneffectual fire:
Adieu, adieu! Hamlet, remember me.
(*Exit.*)
    HAMLET.   O all you host of heaven!
    O earth! what else?
And shall I couple hell? O, fie! Hold,
hold, my heart;
And you, my sinews, grow not instant
old,   94
But bear me stiffly up. Remember thee!
Aye, thou poor ghost, while memory
holds a seat
In this distracted globe. Remember thee!
Yea, from the table of my memory
I'll wipe away all trivial fond records,
All saws of books, all forms, all pres-
sures past,   100
That youth and observation copied there;
And thy commandment all alone shall
live
Within the book and volume of my
brain,
Unmix'd with baser matter: yes, by
heaven!
O most pernicious woman!   105
O villain, villain, smiling, damnèd vil-
lain!
My tables,[30]—meet it is I set it down,
That one may smile, and smile, and be a
villain;
At least I'm sure it may be so in Den-
mark.   (*Writing.*)
So, uncle, there you are. Now to my
word;   110
It is "Adieu, adieu! remember me."
I have sworn't.
    HORATIO.   ⎫ (*within*). My lord, my
    MARCELLUS. ⎭   lord!
    MARCELLUS (*within*).   Lord Ham-
    let!
    HORATIO (*within*).   Heaven secure
    him!
    HAMLET.   So be it!
    MARCELLUS (*within*).   Hillo, ho, ho,
    my lord!   115

[26] henbane
[27] curdle
[28] a rash
[29] leper-like

[30] tablet; notebook

HAMLET. Hillo, ho, ho, boy! come, bird, come.[31]

(*Enter* HORATIO *and* MARCELLUS.)

MARCELLUS. How is't, my noble lord?

HORATIO.   What news, my lord?

HAMLET. O, wonderful!

HORATIO. Good my lord, tell it.

HAMLET.   No; you'll reveal it.

HORATIO. Not I, my lord, by heaven.

MARCELLUS.   Nor I, my lord. *120*

HAMLET. How say you, then; would heart of man once think it?

But you'll be secret?

HORATIO. ⎫ Aye, by heaven, my
MARCELLUS. ⎭ lord.

HAMLET. There's ne'er a villain dwelling in all Denmark

But he's an arrant knave.

HORATIO. There needs no ghost, my lord, come from the grave *125*

To tell us this.

HAMLET.   Why, right; you are i' the right;

And so, without more circumstance at all,

I hold it fit that we shake hands and part:

You, as your business and desire shall point you; *129*

For every man has business and desire,

Such as it is; and for my own poor part,

Look you, I'll go pray.

HORATIO. These are but wild and whirling words, my lord.

HAMLET. I'm sorry they offend you, heartily;

Yes, faith, heartily.

HORATIO.   There's no offense, my lord. *135*

HAMLET. Yes, by Saint Patrick, but there is, Horatio,

And much offense too. Touching this vision here,

It is an honest ghost, that let me tell you:

For your desire to know what is between us,

O'ermaster't as you may. And now, good friends, *140*

As you are friends, scholars and soldiers,

Give me one poor request.

HORATIO.   What is't, my lord? we will.

HAMLET. Never make known what you have seen tonight.

MARCELLUS. ⎫
HORATIO.   ⎭ My lord, we will not.

HAMLET.   Nay, but swear't.

HORATIO.   In faith, *145*

My lord, not I.

MARCELLUS.   Nor I, my lord, in faith.

HAMLET. Upon my sword.

MARCELLUS.   We have sworn, my lord, already.

HAMLET. Indeed, upon my sword, indeed.

GHOST (*beneath*).   Swear.

HAMLET. Ah, ha, boy! say'st thou so? art thou there, true-penny? *150*

Come on: you hear this fellow in the cellarage:

Consent to swear.

HORATIO.   Propose the oath, my lord.

HAMLET. Never to speak of this that you have seen,

Swear by my sword.

GHOST (*beneath*). Swear. *155*

HAMLET. Hic et ubique?[32] then we'll shift our ground.

Come hither, gentlemen,

And lay your hands again upon my sword:

Never to speak of this that you have heard,

Swear by my sword. *160*

GHOST (*beneath*). Swear.

HAMLET. Well said, old mole! canst work i' the earth so fast?

A worthy pioneer![33] Once more remove, good friends.

HORATIO. O day and night, but this is wondrous strange!

HAMLET. And therefore as a stranger give it welcome. *165*

---

[31] cries from falconry

[32] here and everywhere?

[33] a sapper, or military engineer skilled in undermining

There are more things in heaven and
　　earth, Horatio,
Than are dreamt of in your philosophy.
But come;
Here, as before, never, so help you
　　mercy,
How strange or odd soe'er I bear my-
　　self,　　　　　　　　　　　　　*170*
As I perchance hereafter shall think meet
To put an antic disposition on,
That you, at such times seeing me, never
　　shall,
With arms encumber'd thus, or this head-
　　shake,
Or by pronouncing of some doubtful
　　phrase,　　　　　　　　　　　*175*
As "Well, well, we know," or "We could,
　　an if we would,"
Or "If we list to speak," or "There be,
　　an if they might,"
Or such ambiguous giving out, to note
That you know aught of me: this not
　　to do,
So grace and mercy at your most need
　　help you,　　　　　　　　　　*180*
Swear.
　　GHOST (*beneath*).　Swear.
　　HAMLET.　Rest, rest, perturbèd spirit!
　　　　　　　　　　　　　(*They swear.*)
So, gentlemen,
With all my love I do commend me to
　　you:　　　　　　　　　　　　*184*
And what so poor a man as Hamlet is
May do, to express his love and friend-
　　ing to you,
God willing, shall not lack. Let us go in
　　together;
And still your fingers on your lips, I
　　pray.
The time is out of joint: O cursèd spite,
That ever I was born to set it right!　*190*
Nay, come, let's go together.　(*Exeunt.*)

Act II

SCENE 1

(*A room in* POLONIUS'S *house.*)
(*Enter* POLONIUS *and* REYNALDO.)

POLONIUS.　Give him this money and
　　these notes, Reynaldo.
REYNALDO.　I will, my lord.
POLONIUS.　You shall do marvelous
　　wisely, good Reynaldo,
Before you visit him, to make inquire
Of his behavior.　　　　　　　　*4*
REYNALDO.　My lord, I did in-
　　tend it.
POLONIUS.　Marry, well said, very
　　well said. Look you, sir,
Inquire me first what Danskers are in
　　Paris,
And how, and who, what means, and
　　where they keep,
What company, at what expense; and
　　finding
By this encompassment and drift of ques-
　　tion　　　　　　　　　　　　*10*
That they do know my son, come you
　　more nearer
Than your particular demands will
　　touch it:
Take you, as 'twere, some distant knowl-
　　edge of him,
As thus, "I know his father and his
　　friends,
And in part him": do you mark this,
　　Reynaldo?　　　　　　　　　*15*
REYNALDO.　Aye, very well, my lord.
POLONIUS.　"And in part him; but,"
　　you may say, "not well:
But if 't be he I mean, he's very wild,
Addicted so and so"; and there put on
　　him
What forgeries you please; marry, none
　　so rank　　　　　　　　　　*20*
As may dishonor him; take heed of that;
But, sir, such wanton, wild and usual
　　slips
As are companions noted and most known
To youth and liberty.
REYNALDO.　　　As gaming, my lord.
POLONIUS.　Aye, or drinking, fencing,
　　swearing, quarreling,　　　　*25*
Drabbing:[34] you may go so far.
REYNALDO.　My lord, that would dis-
　　honor him.

[34] whoring

POLONIUS. 'Faith, no; as you may season it in the charge.
You must not put another scandal on him,
That he is open to incontinency;   30
That's not my meaning: but breathe his faults so quaintly
That they may seem the taints of liberty,
The flash and outbreak of a fiery mind,
A savageness in unreclaimèd blood,
Of general assault.   34
   REYNALDO.   But, my good lord,—
   POLONIUS.   Wherefore should you do this?
   REYNALDO.   Aye, my lord,
I would know that.
   POLONIUS.   Marry, sir, here's my drift,
And I believe it is a fetch of warrant:
You laying these slight sullies on my son,
As 'twere a thing a little soil'd i' the working,   40
Mark you,
Your party in converse, him you would sound,
Having ever seen in the prenominate[35] crimes
The youth you breathe of guilty, be assured   44
He closes with you in this consequence;
"Good sir," or so, or "friend," or "gentleman,"
According to the phrase or the addition
Of man and country.
   REYNALDO.   Very good, my lord.
   POLONIUS.   And then, sir, does he this—he does—what was I about to say? By the mass, I was about to say something: where did I leave?   50
   REYNALDO.   At "closes in the consequence," at "friend or so," and "gentleman."
   POLONIUS.   At "closes in the consequence," aye, marry;   54
He closes thus: "I know the gentleman;
I saw him yesterday, or t' other day,

Or then, or then, with such, or such, and, as you say,
There was a' gaming, there o'ertook in 's rouse,
There falling out at tennis": or perchance,   59
"I saw him enter such a house of sale,"
Videlicet,[36] a brothel, or so forth.
See you now;
Your bait of falsehood takes this carp of truth:
And thus do we of wisdom and of reach,
With windlasses and with assays of bias,   65
By indirections find directions out:
So, by my former lecture and advice,
Shall you my son. You have me, have you not?
   REYNALDO.   My lord, I have.
   POLONIUS.   God be wi' you; fare you well.
   REYNALDO. Good my lord!   70
   POLONIUS.   Observe his inclination in yourself.
   REYNALDO.   I shall, my lord.
   POLONIUS.   And let him ply his music.
   REYNALDO.   Well, my lord.
   POLONIUS. Farewell!
          (*Exit* REYNALDO.)
(*Enter* OPHELIA.)
How now, Ophelia! what's the matter?
   OPHELIA.   O, my lord, my lord, I have been so affrighted!   75
   POLONIUS.   With what, i' the name of God?
   OPHELIA.   My lord, as I was sewing in my closet,
Lord Hamlet, with his doublet all unbraced,
No hat upon his head, his stockings foul'd,
Ungarter'd and down-gyvèd to his ankle;
Pale as his shirt, his knees knocking each other,   81
And with a look so piteous in purport
As if he had been loosèd out of hell
To speak of horrors, he comes before me.

---

[35] aforementioned

[36] namely

POLONIUS. Mad for thy love?

OPHELIA. My lord, I do not know,
But truly I do fear it. 86

POLONIUS. What said he?

OPHELIA. He took me by the wrist
and held me hard;
Then goes he to the length of all his arm,
And with his other hand thus o'er his
brow,
He falls to such perusal of my face 90
As he would draw it. Long stay'd he so;
At last, a little shaking of mine arm,
And thrice his head thus waving up and
down,
He raised a sigh so piteous and profound
As it did seem to shatter all his bulk 95
And end his being: that done, he lets
me go:
And with his head over his shoulder
turn'd,
He seem'd to find his way without his
eyes,
For out o' doors he went without their
helps, 99
And to the last bended their light on me.

POLONIUS. Come, go with me: I will
go seek the king,
This is the very ecstasy of love;
Whose violent property fordoes itself
And leads the will to desperate undertak-
ings
As oft as any passion under heaven 105
That does afflict our natures. I am sorry.
What, have you given him any hard
words of late?

OPHELIA. No, my good lord, but, as
you did command,
I did repel his letters and denied
His access to me. 109

POLONIUS. That hath made him
mad.
I am sorry that with better heed and
judgment
I had not quoted him: I fear'd he did
but trifle
And meant to wreck thee; but beshrew
my jealousy!
By heaven, it is as proper to our age
To cast beyond ourselves in our opinions

As it is common for the younger sort 116
To lack discretion. Come, go we to the
king:
This must be known; which, being kept
close, might move
More grief to hide than hate to utter
love.

(*Exeunt.*)

SCENE 2

(*A room in the castle.*)

(*Flourish. Enter* KING, QUEEN, RO-
SENCRANTZ, GUILDENSTERN, *and* AT-
TENDANTS.)

KING. Welcome, dear Rosencrantz
and Guildenstern!
Moreover that we much did long to see
you,
The need we have to use you did pro-
voke
Our hasty sending. Something have you
heard
Of Hamlet's transformation; so call it, 5
Sith nor the exterior nor the inward man
Resembles that it was. What it should be,
More than his father's death, that thus
hath put him
So much from the understanding of him-
self,
I cannot dream of: I entreat you both,
That, being of so young days brought up
with him 11
And sith so neighbor'd to his youth and
behavior,
That you vouchsafe your rest here in our
court
Some little time: so by your companies
To draw him on to pleasures, and to
gather 15
So much as from occasion you may glean,
Whether aught to us unknown afflicts
him thus,
That open'd lies within our remedy.

QUEEN. Good gentlemen, he hath
much talk'd of you,
And sure I am two men there are not
living 20

To whom he more adheres. If it will
please you
To show us so much gentry and good
will
As to expend your time with us awhile
For the supply and profit of our hope,
Your visitation shall receive such thanks
As fits a king's remembrance.   26
  ROSENCRANTZ.   Both your majesties
Might, by the sovereign power you have
of us,
Put your dread pleasures more into com-
mand
Than to entreaty.
  GUILDENSTERN.   But we both obey,
And here give up ourselves, in the full
bent   30
To lay our service freely at your feet,
To be commanded.
  KING.   Thanks, Rosencrantz and gen-
tle Guildenstern.
  QUEEN.   Thanks, Guildenstern and
gentle Rosencrantz:
And I beseech you instantly to visit   35
My too much changèd son. Go, some of
you,
And bring these gentlemen where Ham-
let is.
  GUILDENSTERN.   Heavens make our
presence and our practices
Pleasant and helpful to him!
  QUEEN.   Aye, amen!
  (*Exeunt* ROSENCRANTZ, GUILDEN-
STERN, *and some* ATTENDANTS.)
  (*Enter* POLONIUS.)
  POLONIUS.   The ambassadors from
Norway, my good lord,   40
Are joyfully return'd.
  KING.   Thou still hast been the father
of good news.
  POLONIUS.   Have I, my lord? I assure
my good liege,
I hold my duty as I hold my soul,   44
Both to my God and to my gracious king:
And I do think, or else this brain of mine
Hunts not the trail of policy so sure
As it hath used to do, that I have found
The very cause of Hamlet's lunacy.
  KING.   O, speak of that; that do I
long to hear.   50

  POLONIUS.   Give first admittance to
the ambassadors;
My news shall be the fruit to that great
feast.
  KING.   Thyself do grace to them, and
bring them in.
                (*Exit* POLONIUS.)
He tells me, my dear Gertrude, he hath
found
The head and source of all your son's
distemper.   55
  QUEEN.   I doubt it is no other but
the main;
His father's death and our o'erhasty mar-
riage.
  KING.   Well, we shall sift him.
  (*Re-enter* POLONIUS, *with* VOLTIMAND
and CORNELIUS.)
                    Welcome, my good friends!
Say, Voltimand, what from our brother
Norway?
  VOLTIMAND.   Most fair return of
greetings and desires.   60
Upon our first, he sent out to suppress
His nephew's levies, which to him ap-
pear'd
To be a preparation 'gainst the Polack,
But better look'd into, he truly found
It was against your highness: whereat
grieved,   65
That so his sickness, age and impotence
Was falsely borne in hand, sends out
arrests
On Fortinbras; which he, in brief, obeys,
Receives rebuke from Norway, and in
fine   69
Makes vow before his uncle never more
To give the assay of arms against your
majesty.
Whereon old Norway, overcome with
joy,
Gives him three thousand crowns in an-
nual fee
And his commission to employ those
soldiers,   74
So levied as before, against the Polack:
With an entreaty, herein further shown,
                (*Giving a paper.*)
That it might please you to give quiet
pass

Through your dominions for this enter-
prise,
On such regards of safety and allowance
As therein are set down.
KING.   It likes us well, 80
And at our more consider'd time we'll
read,
Answer, and think upon this business.
Meantime we thank you for your well-
took labor:
Go to your rest; at night we'll feast to-
gether:
Most welcome home!
(*Exeunt* VOLTIMAND *and* CORNELIUS.)
POLONIUS.   This business is well
ended.
My liege, and madam, to expostulate 86
What majesty should be, what duty is,
Why day is day, night night, and time is
time,
Were nothing but to waste night, day
and time.   89
Therefore, since brevity is the soul of wit
And tediousness the limbs and outward
flourishes,
I will be brief. Your noble son is mad:
Mad call I it; for, to define true madness,
What is't but to be nothing else but mad?
But let that go.   94
QUEEN.   More matter, with less art.
POLONIUS.   Madam, I swear I use no
art at all.
That he is mad, 'tis true: 'tis true 'tis pity,
And pity 'tis 'tis true: a foolish figure;
But farewell it, for I will use no art.
Mad let us grant him then: and now
remains   100
That we find out the cause of this effect,
Or rather say, the cause of this defect,
For this effect defective comes by cause:
Thus it remains and the remainder thus.
Perpend.³⁷   105
I have a daughter,—have while she is
mine,—
Who in her duty and obedience, mark,
Hath given me this: now gather and sur-
mise.
(*Reads.*)

³⁷ consider

"To the celestial, and my soul's idol, the
most beautified Ophelia,"—   110
That's an ill phrase, a vile phrase; "beauti-
fied" is a vile phrase; but you shall
hear.
Thus:
(*Reads.*)
"In her excellent white bosom, these," &c.
QUEEN.   Came this from Hamlet to
her?
POLONIUS.   Good madam, stay awhile;
I will be faithful.   115
(*Reads.*)

Doubt thou the stars are fire;
  Doubt that the sun doth move;
Doubt truth to be a liar;
  But never doubt I love.

"O dear Ophelia, I am ill at these numbers;   120
I have not art to reckon my groans: but
that
I love thee best, O most best, believe it.
Adieu. Thine evermore, most dear lady,
whilst this machine is to him,
                      HAMLET."

This in obedience hath my daughter
shown me;   125
And more above, hath his solicitings,
As they fell out by time, by means and
place,
All given to mine ear.
KING.   But how hath she
Received his love?
POLONIUS.   What do you think of
me?
KING.   As of a man faithful and hon-
orable.   130
POLONIUS.   I would fain prove so.
But what might you think,
When I had seen this hot love on the
wing,—
As I perceived it, I must tell you that,
Before my daughter told me,—what
might you,
Or my dear majesty your queen here,
think,   135
If I had play'd the desk or table-book,
Or given my heart a winking, mute and
dumb,

Or look'd upon this love with idle sight;
What might you think? No, I went round
    to work,
And my young mistress thus I did be-
    speak: *140*
"Lord Hamlet is a prince, out of thy
    star;
This must not be:" and then I prescripts
    gave her,
That she should lock herself from his
    resort,
Admit no messengers, receive no tokens.
Which done, she took the fruits of my
    advice;   *145*
And he, repulsed—a short tale to make—
Fell into a sadness, then into a fast,
Thence to a watch, thence into a weak-
    ness,
Thence to a lightness, and by this de-
    clension
Into the madness wherein now he raves
And all we mourn for.   *151*
    KING.   Do you think 'tis this?
    QUEEN.   It may be, very likely.
    POLONIUS.   Hath there been such a
    time, I'd fain know that,
That I have positively said " 'tis so,"
When it proved otherwise?   *154*
    KING.   Not that I know.
    POLONIUS (*pointing to his head and
    shoulder*).   Take this, from this, if
    this be otherwise:
If circumstances lead me, I will find
Where truth is hid, though it were hid
    indeed
Within the center.
    KING.   How may we try it further?
    POLONIUS.   You know, sometimes he
    walks four hours together   *160*
Here in the lobby.
    QUEEN.   So he does, indeed.
    POLONIUS.   At such a time I'll loose
    my daughter to him:
Be you and I behind an arras then;
Mark the encounter: if he love her not,
And be not from his reason fall'n thereon,
Let me be no assistant for a state,   *166*
But keep a farm and carters.

    KING.   We will try it.
    QUEEN.   But look where sadly the
    poor wretch comes reading.
    POLONIUS.   Away, I do beseech you,
    both away:
I'll board him presently.
    (*Exeunt* KING, QUEEN, *and* ATTEND-
ANTS.)
    (*Enter* HAMLET, *reading.*)
                  O, give me leave:
How does my good Lord Hamlet?   *171*
    HAMLET.   Well, God-a-mercy.
    POLONIUS.   Do you know me, my
    lord?
    HAMLET.   Excellent well; you are a
    fishmonger.
    POLONIUS.   Not I, my lord.   *175*
    HAMLET.   Then I would you were so
    honest a man.
    POLONIUS.   Honest, my lord!
    HAMLET.   Aye, sir; to be honest, as
this world goes, is to be one man picked
out of ten thousand.   *179*
    POLONIUS.   That's very true, my lord.
    HAMLET.   For if the sun breed mag-
gots in a dead dog, being a god kissing
carrion—Have you a daughter?
    POLONIUS.   I have, my lord.
    HAMLET.   Let her not walk i' the
sun; conception is a blessing; but not
as your daughter may conceive,—friend,
look to 't.   *187*
    POLONIUS (*aside*).   How say you by
that? Still harping on my daughter: yet
he knew me not at first; he said I was a
fishmonger: he is far gone, far gone:
and truly in my youth I suffered much
extremity for love; very near this. I'll
speak to him again.—What do you read,
my lord?
    HAMLET.   Words, words, words.
    POLONIUS.   What is the matter, my
lord?   *195*
    HAMLET.   Between who?
    POLONIUS.   I mean, the matter that
you read, my lord.
    HAMLET.   Slanders, sir: for the satiri-
cal rogue says here that old men have

gray beards, that their faces are wrinkled, their eyes purging thick amber and plum-tree gum, and that they have a plentiful lack of wit, together with most weak hams: all which, sir, though I most powerfully and potently believe, yet I hold it not honesty to have it thus set down; for yourself, sir, shall grow old as I am, if like a crab you could go backward. *206*

POLONIUS (*aside*). Though this be madness, yet there is method in 't.—Will you walk out of the air, my lord?

HAMLET. Into my grave. *210*

POLONIUS. Indeed, that is out o' the air. (*Aside.*) How pregnant sometimes his replies are! a happiness that often madness hits on, which reason and sanity could not so prosperously be delivered of. I will leave him, and suddenly contrive the means of meeting between him and my daughter.—My honorable lord, I will most humbly take my leave of you. *218*

HAMLET. You cannot, sir, take from me anything that I will more willingly part withal: except my life, except my life, except my life.

POLONIUS. Fare you well, my lord.

HAMLET. These tedious old fools.

(*Re-enter* ROSENCRANTZ *and* GUILDENSTERN.)

POLONIUS. You go to seek the Lord Hamlet; there he is.

ROSENCRANTZ (*to* POLONIUS). God save you, sir! *225*

(*Exit* POLONIUS.)

GUILDENSTERN. My honored lord!

ROSENCRANTZ. My most dear lord!

HAMLET. My excellent good friends! How dost thou, Guildenstern? Ah, Rosencrantz! Good lads, how do you both?

ROSENCRANTZ. As the indifferent children of the earth. *231*

GUILDENSTERN. Happy, in that we are not over-happy; On Fortune's cap we are not the very button.

HAMLET. Nor the soles of her shoe?

ROSENCRANTZ. Neither, my lord. *235*

HAMLET. Then you live about her waist, or in the middle of her favors?

GUILDENSTERN. Faith, her privates we.

HAMLET. In the secret parts of Fortune? Oh, most true; she is a strumpet. What's the news? *240*

ROSENCRANTZ. None, my lord, but that the world's grown honest.

HAMLET. Then is doomsday near: but your news is not true. Let me question more in particular: what have you, my good friends, deserved at the hands of Fortune, that she sends you to prison hither? *247*

GUILDENSTERN. Prison, my lord!

HAMLET. Denmark's a prison.

ROSENCRANTZ. Then is the world one. *250*

HAMLET. A goodly one; in which there are many confines, wards and dungeons, Denmark being one o' the worst.

ROSENCRANTZ. We think not so, my lord.

HAMLET. Why, then, 'tis none to you; for there is nothing either good or bad, but thinking makes it so: to me it is a prison.

ROSENCRANTZ. Why, then your ambition makes it one; 'tis too narrow for your mind. *259*

HAMLET. O God, I could be bounded in a nut-shell and count myself a king of infinite space, were it not that I have bad dreams.

GUILDENSTERN. Which dreams indeed are ambition; for the very substance of the ambitious is merely the shadow of a dream. *265*

HAMLET. A dream itself is but a shadow.

ROSENCRANTZ. Truly, and I hold ambition of so airy and light a quality that it is but a shadow's shadow.

HAMLET. Then are our beggars bodies, and our monarchs and out-stretched heroes the beggars' shadows. Shall we to the court? for, by my fay,

I cannot reason.   *272*

ROSENCRANTZ. ⎫
GUILDENSTERN. ⎭ We'll wait upon you.

HAMLET. No such matter: I will not sort you with the rest of my servants; for, to speak to you like an honest man, I am most dreadfully attended. But, in the beaten way of friendship, what make you at Elsinore?

ROSENCRANTZ. To visit you, my lord; no other occasion.   *279*

HAMLET. Beggar that I am, I am even poor in thanks; but I thank you: and sure, dear friends, my thanks are too dear a halfpenny. Were you not sent for? Is it your own inclining? Is it a free visitation? Come, deal justly with me: come, come; nay, speak.

GUILDENSTERN. What should we say, my lord?   *286*

HAMLET. Why, any thing, but to the purpose. You were sent for; and there is a kind of confession in your looks, which your modesties have not craft enough to color: I know the good king and queen have sent for you.

ROSENCRANTZ. To what end, my lord?   *292*

HAMLET. That you must teach me. But let me conjure you, by the rights of our fellowship, by the consonancy of our youth, by the obligation of our ever-preserved love, and by what more dear a better proposer could charge you withal, be even and direct with me, whether you were sent for, or no.

ROSENCRANTZ (*aside to* GUILDEN-STERN). What say you?   *300*

HAMLET (*aside*). Nay then, I have an eye of you.—If you love me, hold not off.

GUILDENSTERN. My lord, we were sent for.

HAMLET. I will tell you why; so shall my anticipation prevent your discovery, and your secrecy to the king and queen moult no feather. I have of late—but wherefore I know not—lost all my mirth, forgone all custom of exercises; and in-

deed it goes so heavily with my disposition that this goodly frame, the earth, seems to me a sterile promontory; this most excellent canopy, the air, look you, this brave o'erhanging firmament, this majestical roof fretted with golden fire, why, it appears no other thing to me than a foul and pestilent congregation of vapors. What a piece of work is a man! how noble in reason! how infinite in faculty! in form and moving how express and admirable! in action how like an angel! in apprehension how like a god! the beauty of the world! the paragon of animals! And yet, to me, what is this quintessence of dust? man delights not me; no, nor woman neither, though by your smiling you seem to say so.   *323*

ROSENCRANTZ. My lord, there was no such stuff in my thoughts.

HAMLET. Why did you laugh then, when I said "man delights not me"?   *327*

ROSENCRANTZ. To think, my lord, if you delight not in man, what lenten entertainment the players shall receive from you: we coted[38] them on the way; and hither are they coming, to offer you service.   *331*

HAMLET. He that plays the king shall be welcome; his majesty shall have tribute of me; the adventurous knight shall use his foil and target; the lover shall not sigh gratis; the humorous man shall end his part in peace; the clown shall make those laugh whose lungs are tickle o' the sere,[39] and the lady shall say her mind freely, or the blank verse shall halt for't. What players are they?   *340*

ROSENCRANTZ. Even those you were wont to take such delight in, the tragedians of the city.

HAMLET. How chances it they travel? their residence, both in reputation and profit, was better both ways.   *345*

ROSENCRANTZ. I think their inhibi-

---

38 passed
39 easily fired, like a gun on a hair-trigger; i.e., easily moved to laughter

tion comes by the means of the late innovation.

HAMLET. Do they hold the same estimation they did when I was in the city? are they so followed? *350*

ROSENCRANTZ. No, indeed, are they not.

HAMLET. How comes it? do they grow rusty?

ROSENCRANTZ. Nay, their endeavor keeps in the wonted pace: but there is, sir, an eyrie of children, little eyases,[40] that cry out on the top of question and are most tyrannically clapped for 't: these are now the fashion, and so berattle the common stages—so they call them—that many wearing rapiers are afraid of goose-quills, and dare scarce come thither. *360*

HAMLET. What, are they children? who maintains 'em? how are they escoted?[41] Will they pursue the quality no longer than they can sing? will they not say afterwards, if they should grow themselves to common players,—as it is most like, if their means are no better,— their writers do them wrong, to make them exclaim against their own succession? *368*

ROSENCRANTZ. Faith, there has been much to-do on both sides, and the nation holds it no sin to tarre[42] them to controversy: there was for a while no money bid for argument unless the poet and the player went to cuffs in the question. *373*

HAMLET. Is't possible?

GUILDENSTERN. O, there has been much throwing about of brains.

HAMLET. Do the boys carry it away?

ROSENCRANTZ. Aye, that they do, my lord; Hercules and his load too.[43] *379*

HAMLET. It is not very strange; for my uncle is king of Denmark, and those that would make mows at him while my father lived, give twenty, forty, fifty, a hundred ducats a-piece, for his picture in little. 'Sblood, there is something in this more than natural, if philosophy could find it out. *385*

(*Flourish of trumpets within.*)

GUILDENSTERN. There are the players.

HAMLET. Gentlemen, you are welcome to Elsinore. Your hands, come then: the appurtenance of welcome is fashion and ceremony: let me comply with you in this garb, lest my extent to the players, which, I tell you, must show fairly outwards, should more appear like entertainment than yours. You are welcome: but my uncle-father and aunt-mother are deceived.

GUILDENSTERN. In what, my dear lord? *395*

HAMLET. I am but mad north-north-west: when the wind is southerly I know a hawk from a handsaw.[44]

(*Re-enter* POLONIUS.)

POLONIUS. Well be with you, gentlemen!

HAMLET. Hark you, Guildenstern; and you too: at each ear a hearer: that great baby you see there is not yet out of his swaddling clouts. *401*

ROSENCRANTZ. Happily he's the second time come to them; for they say an old man is twice a child.

HAMLET. I will prophesy he comes to tell me of the players; mark it. You say right, sir: o' Monday morning; 'twas so, indeed. *407*

POLONIUS. My lord, I have news to tell you.

HAMLET. My lord, I have news to tell you. When Roscius was an actor in Rome,—

[40] young hawks. The reference is to one or another of the companies of child actors in Shakespeare's time.
[41] supported
[42] incite
[43] the sign of Shakespeare's theater, the Globe

[44] It has been suggested that *handsaw* is a misreading for *hernshaw,* a heron. It is more likely that a hawk is, like a handsaw, a tool, namely, the plasterer's mortar-board.

POLONIUS. The actors are come hither, my lord.

HAMLET. Buz, buz!

POLONIUS. Upon mine honor,— *413*

HAMLET. Then came each actor on his ass,—

POLONIUS. The best actors in the world, either for tragedy, comedy, history, pastoral, pastoral-comical, historical-pastoral, tragical-historical, tragical-comical-historical-pastoral, scene individable, or poem unlimited: Seneca cannot be too heavy, nor Plautus[45] too light. For the law of writ and the liberty, these are the only men.   *421*

HAMLET. O Jephthah,[46] judge of Israel, what a treasure hadst thou!

POLONIUS. What a treasure had he, my lord?

HAMLET. Why,

One fair daughter, and no more,
    The which he loved passing well.

POLONIUS (*aside*). Still on my daughter.

HAMLET. Am I not i' the right, old Jephthah?

POLONIUS. If you call me Jephthah, my lord, I have a daughter that I love passing well.   *431*

HAMLET. Nay, that follows not.

POLONIUS. What follows, then, my lord?

HAMLET. Why,

As by lot, God wot,

and then you know,

"It came to pass, as most like it was,"
—the first row of the pious chanson will show you more; for look, where my abridgment comes.   *439*

(*Enter four or five* PLAYERS.)

You are welcome, masters; welcome, all. I am glad to see thee well. Welcome, good friends. O, my old friend! thy face is valanced since I saw thee last; comest thou to beard me in Denmark? What, my young lady and mistress! By'r lady, your ladyship is nearer to heaven than when I saw you last, by the altitude of a chopine.[47] Pray God, your voice, like a piece of uncurrent gold, be not cracked within the ring.[48] Masters, you are all welcome. We'll e'en to 't like French falconers, fly at any thing we see: we'll have a speech straight: come, give us a taste of your quality; come, a passionate speech.   *452*

FIRST PLAYER. What speech, my good lord?

HAMLET. I heard thee speak me a speech once, but it was never acted; or, if it was, not above once; for the play, I remember, pleased not the million; 'twas caviare to the general; but it was—as I received it, and others, whose judgments in such matters cried in the top of mine —an excellent play, well digested in the scenes, set down with as much modesty as cunning. I remember, one said there were no sallets[49] in the lines to make the matter savory, nor no matter in the phrase that might indict the author to affectation; but called it an honest method, as wholesome as sweet, and by very much more handsome than fine. One speech in it I chiefly loved: 'twas Æneas' tale to Dido; and thereabout of it especially, where he speaks of Priam's slaughter: if it live in your memory, begin at this line; let me see, let me see;   *471*

The rugged Pyrrhus, like th' Hyrcanian beast,

---

[45] Roman playwrights. Seneca was primarily a tragedian; Plautus, a writer of comedies.
[46] Jephthah vowed that if the Lord granted him victory in battle he would sacrifice as a burnt offering whatever came forth from his house to meet him upon his return. He was greeted by his virgin daughter, whom he duly sacrificed. (Judges, 11:29–40)
[47] a clog or high shoe
[48] Old coins had a ring surrounding the design, though the metal extended beyond the ring. A common practice was to remove this excess metal and collect it for melting down. When a coin was cracked (or clipped) "within the ring," it was regarded as unfit to be accepted at full value.
[49] tasty bits

It is not so: it begins with "Pyrrhus."

The rugged Pyrrhus, he whose sable arms,
Black as his purpose, did the night re-
    semble   475
When he lay couchèd in the ominous horse,
Hath now this dread and black complexion
    smear'd
With heraldry more dismal: head to foot
Now is he total gules;[50] horridly trick'd
With the blood of fathers, mothers, daugh-
    ters, sons,   480
Baked and impasted with the parching
    streets,
That lend a tyrannous and a damnèd light
To their lord's murder: roasted in wrath
    and fire,
And thus o'er-sized with coagulate gore,
With eyes like carbuncles, the hellish
    Pyrrhus   485
Old grandsire Priam seeks.

So, proceed you.
    POLONIUS. 'Fore God, my lord, well
spoken, with good accent and good discretion.
    FIRST PLAYER.

Anon he finds him   490
Striking too short at Greeks; his antique
    sword,
Rebellious to his arm, lies where it falls,
Repugnant to command; unequal match'd,
Pyrrhus at Priam drives; in rage strikes
    wide;
But with the whiff and wind of his fell
    sword   495
The unnerved father falls. Then senseless
    Ilium,
Seeming to feel this blow, with flaming top
Stoops to his base, and with a hideous crash
Takes prisoner Pyrrhus' ear: for, lo! his
    sword,
Which was declining on the milky head   500
Of reverend Priam, seem'd i' the air to
    stick:
So, as a painted tyrant, Pyrrhus stood,
And like a neutral to his will and matter,
Did nothing.   504
But as we often see, against some storm,
A silence in the heavens, the rank stand still,
The bold winds speechless and the orb be-
    low

As hush as death, anon the dreadful thun-
    der
Doth rend the region, so after Pyrrhus'
    pause   509
Arousèd vengeance sets him new a-work;
And never did the Cyclops' hammers fall
On Mars's armor, forged for proof eterne,
With less remorse than Pyrrhus' bleeding
    sword
Now falls on Priam.
Out, out, thou strumpet, Fortune! All you
    gods,   515
In general synod take away her power,
Break all the spokes and fellies[51] from her
    wheel,
And bowl the round nave down the hill of
    heaven
As low as to the fiends!

    POLONIUS. This is too long.   520
    HAMLET. It shall to the barber's,
with your beard. Prithee, say on: he's
for a jig or a tale of bawdry, or he
sleeps: say on: come to Hecuba.
    FIRST PLAYER.

But who, O, who had seen the mobled[52]
    queen—   525

    HAMLET. "The mobled queen"?
    POLONIUS. That's good; "mobled
queen" is good.
    FIRST PLAYER.

Run barefoot up and down, threatening the
    flames
With bisson rheum;[53] a clout upon that
    head
Where late the diadem stood; and for a
    robe,   530
About her lank and all o'er-teemèd loins,
A blanket, in the alarm of fear caught up:
Who this had seen, with tongue in venom
    steep'd
'Gainst Fortune's state would treason have
    pronounced:
But if the gods themselves did see her
    then,   535
When she saw Pyrrhus make malicious
    sport
In mincing with his sword her husband's
    limbs,

[51] felloes; the segments of a wheel-rim
[52] muffled
[53] blinding tears

[50] the heraldic term for red

124

WILLIAM SHAKESPEARE

The instant burst of clamor that she made,
Unless things mortal move them not at all,
Would have made milch the burning eyes
   of heaven   *540*
And passion in the gods.

POLONIUS. Look, whether he has not
turned his color and has tears in 's eyes.
Prithee, no more.

HAMLET. 'Tis well; I'll have thee
speak out the rest soon. Good my lord,
will you see the players well bestowed?
Do you hear, let them be well used, for
they are the abstracts and brief chronicles
of the time: after your death you were
better have a bad epitaph than their
ill report while you live.   *551*

POLONIUS. My lord, I will use them
according to their desert.

HAMLET. God's bodykins, man,
much better: use every man after his
desert, and who should 'scape whipping?
Use them after your own honor and
dignity: the less they deserve, the more
merit is in your bounty. Take them in.

POLONIUS. Come, sirs.   *559*

HAMLET. Follow him, friends: we'll
hear a play to-morrow. (*Exit* POLONIUS
with all the PLAYERS *but the first.*) Dost
thou hear me, old friend; can you play
the Murder of Gonzago?

FIRST PLAYER. Aye, my lord.

HAMLET. We'll ha 't to-morrow
night. You could, for a need, study a
speech of some dozen or sixteen lines,
which I would set down and insert in 't,
could you not?

FIRST PLAYER. Aye, my lord.   *569*

HAMLET. Very well. Follow that
lord; and look you mock him not. (*Exit*
FIRST PLAYER.) My good friends, I'll
leave you till night: you are welcome to
Elsinore.

ROSENCRANTZ. Good my lord!

HAMLET. Aye, so, God be wi' ye!
(*Exeunt* ROSENCRANTZ *and* GUILDEN-
STERN.) Now I am alone.   *575*
O, what a rogue and peasant slave am I!
Is it not monstrous that this player here,
But in a fiction, in a dream of passion,

Could force his soul so to his own con-
   ceit
That from her working all his visage
   wann'd;   *580*
Tears in his eyes, distraction in 's aspect,
A broken voice, and his whole function
   suiting
With forms to his conceit? and all for
   nothing!
For Hecuba!   *584*
What's Hecuba to him, or he to Hecuba,
That he should weep for her? What
   would he do,
Had he the motive and the cue for pas-
   sion
That I have? He would drown the stage
   with tears
And cleave the general air with horrid
   speech,   *589*
Make mad the guilty and appal the free,
Confound the ignorant, and amaze in-
   deed
The very faculties of eyes and ears.
Yet I,
A dull and muddy-mettled rascal, peak,
Like John-a-dreams, unpregnant of my
   cause,   *595*
And can say nothing; no, not for a king,
Upon whose property and most dear life
A damn'd defeat was made. Am I a cow-
   ard?
Who calls me villain? breaks my pate
   across?
Plucks off my beard, and blows it in my
   face?   *600*
Tweaks me by the nose? gives me the lie
   i' the throat,
As deep as to the lungs? who does me
   this?
Ha!
'Swounds,[54] I should take it: for it can-
   not be   *604*
But I am pigeon-liver'd and lack gall
To make oppression bitter, or ere this
I should have fatted all the region kites
With this slave's offal: bloody, bawdy
   villain!

[54] God's wounds—a moderately strong oath

Remorseless, treacherous, lecherous,
kindless⁵⁵ villain!

O, vengeance!   *610*

Why, what an ass am I! This is most
brave,

That I, the son of a dear father murder'd,

Prompted to my revenge by heaven and
hell,

Must, like a whore, unpack my heart
with words,

And fall a-cursing, like a very drab,   *615*
A scullion!

Fie upon 't! foh! About, my brain! I
have heard

That guilty creatures, sitting at a play,

Have by the very cunning of the scene

Been struck so to the soul that presently   *620*

They have proclaim'd their malefactions;

For murder, though it have no tongue,
will speak

With most miraculous organ. I'll have
these players

Play something like the murder of my
father   *624*

Before mine uncle; I'll observe his looks;

I'll tent him to the quick: if he but blench,

I know my course. The spirit that I have
seen

May be the devil; and the devil hath
power

To assume a pleasing shape; yea, and
perhaps   *629*

Out of my weakness and my melancholy,

As he is very potent with such spirits,

Abuses me to damn me. I'll have grounds

More relative than this. The play's the
thing

Wherein I'll catch the conscience of the
king.   (*Exit.*)

Act III

SCENE 1

(*A room in the castle.*)
(*Enter* KING, QUEEN, POLONIUS,
OPHELIA, ROSENCRANTZ, *and* GUILD-
ENSTERN.)

KING. And can you, by no drift of
circumstance,

Get from him why he puts on this confusion,

Grating so harshly all his days of quiet

With turbulent and dangerous lunacy?

ROSENCRANTZ. He does confess he
feels himself distracted,   *5*

But from what cause he will by no means
speak.

GUILDENSTERN. Nor do we find him
forward to be sounded;

But, with a crafty madness, keeps aloof,

When we would bring him on to some
confession   *9*

Of his true state.

QUEEN.   Did he receive you well?

ROSENCRANTZ. Most like a gentleman.

GUILDENSTERN. But with much forcing of his disposition.

ROSENCRANTZ. Niggard of question,
but of our demands

Most free in his reply.

QUEEN.   Did you assay him

To any pastime?   *15*

ROSENCRANTZ. Madam, it so fell out
that certain players

We o'er-raught⁵⁶ on the way: of these
we told him,

And there did seem in him a kind of joy

To hear of it: they are about the court,

And, as I think, they have already
order   *20*

This night to play before him.

POLONIUS.   'Tis most true:

And he beseech'd me to entreat your
majesties

To hear and see the matter.

KING. With all my heart, and it doth
much content me

To hear him so inclined.   *25*

Good gentlemen, give him a further
edge,

⁵⁵ unnatural   ⁵⁶ overtook

And drive his purpose on to these de-
lights.
ROSENCRANTZ.   We shall, my lord.
(*Exeunt* ROSENCRANTZ *and* GUILDEN-
STERN.)
KING.   Sweet Gertrude, leave us
too;
For we have closely sent for Hamlet
hither,
That he, as 'twere by accident, may
here   *30*
Affront Ophelia:
Her father and myself, lawful espials,
Will so bestow ourselves that, seeing un-
seen,
We may of their encounter frankly judge,
And gather by him, as he is behaved,
If't be the affliction of his love or no   *36*
That thus he suffers for.
QUEEN.   I shall obey you:
And for your part, Ophelia, I do wish
That your good beauties be the happy
cause
Of Hamlet's wildness: so shall I hope
your virtues   *40*
Will bring him to his wonted way again,
To both your honors.
OPHELIA.   Madam, I wish it may.
(*Exit* QUEEN.)
POLONIUS.   Ophelia, walk you here.
Gracious, so please you,
We will bestow ourselves. (*To* OPHELIA.)
Read on this book;
That show of such an exercise may
color   *45*
Your loneliness. We are oft to blame in
this,—
'Tis too much proved—that with devo-
tion's visage
And pious action we do sugar o'er
The devil himself.
KING (*aside*).   O, 'tis too true!
How smart a lash that speech doth give
my conscience!   *50*
The harlot's cheek, beautied with plaster-
ing art,
Is not more ugly to the thing that helps
it

Than is my deed to my most painted
word:
O heavy burthen!
POLONIUS.   I hear him coming: let's
withdraw, my lord.   *55*
        (*Exeunt* KING *and* POLONIUS.)
(*Enter* HAMLET.)
HAMLET.   To be, or not to be: that is
the question:
Whether 'tis nobler in the mind to suffer
The slings and arrows of outrageous
fortune,
Or to take arms against a sea of troubles,
And by opposing end them? To die: to
sleep;   *60*
No more; and by a sleep to say we end
The heart-ache, and the thousand natural
shocks
That flesh is heir to, 'tis a consummation
Devoutly to be wish'd. To die, to sleep;
To sleep: perchance to dream: aye,
there's the rub;   *65*
For in that sleep of death what dreams
may come,
When we have shuffled off this mortal
coil,
Must give us pause: there's the respect
That makes calamity of so long life;
For who would bear the whips and
scorns of time,   *70*
The oppressor's wrong, the proud man's
contumely,
The pangs of déspised love, the law's
delay,
The insolence of office, and the spurns
That patient merit of the unworthy takes,
When he himself might his quietus make
With a bare bodkin? who would fardels[57]
bear,   *76*
To grunt and sweat under a weary life,
But that the dread of something after
death,
The undiscover'd country from whose
bourn
No traveler returns, puzzles the will,   *80*
And makes us rather bear those ills we
have

[57] burdens

Than fly to others that we know not of?
Thus conscience does make cowards of
    us all,
And thus the native hue of resolution
Is sicklied o'er with the pale cast of
    thought,   *85*
And enterprises of great pitch and mo-
    ment
With this regard their currents turn awry
And lose the name of action. Soft you
    now!
The fair Ophelia! Nymph, in thy orisons
Be all my sins remember'd.

OPHELIA.   Good my lord,   *90*
How does your honor for this many a
    day?

HAMLET.   I humbly thank you: well,
well, well.

OPHELIA.   My lord, I have remem-
brances of yours,
That I have longed to re-deliver;
I pray you, now receive them.

HAMLET.   No, not I;   *95*
I never gave you aught.

OPHELIA.   My honor'd lord, you
know right well you did;
And with them words of so sweet breath
    composed
As made the things more rich: their per-
    fume lost,   *99*
Take these again; for to the noble mind
Rich gifts wax poor when givers prove
    unkind.
There, my lord.

HAMLET.   Ha, ha! are you honest?

OPHELIA.   My lord?

HAMLET.   Are you fair?   *105*

OPHELIA.   What means your lordship?

HAMLET.   That if you be honest and
fair, your honesty should admit no discourse to your beauty.

OPHELIA.   Could beauty, my lord,
have better commerce than with honesty?   *110*

HAMLET.   Aye, truly; for the power
of beauty will sooner transform honesty
from what it is to a bawd than the force
of honesty can translate beauty into his

likeness: this was sometime a paradox,
but now the time gives it proof. I did
love you once.   *116*

OPHELIA.   Indeed, my lord, you made
me believe so.

HAMLET.   You should not have believed me; for virtue cannot so inoculate
our old stock, but we shall relish of it: I
loved you not.   *120*

OPHELIA.   I was the more deceived.

HAMLET.   Get thee to a nunnery:
why wouldst thou be a breeder of sinners? I am myself indifferent honest; but
yet I could accuse me of such things that
it were better my mother had not borne
me: I am very proud, revengeful, ambitious; with more offenses at my beck
than I have thoughts to put them in,
imagination to give them shape, or time
to act them in. What should such fellows
as I do crawling between heaven and
earth! We are arrant knaves all; believe
none of us. Go thy ways to a nunnery.
Where's your father?   *133*

OPHELIA.   At home, my lord.

HAMLET.   Let the doors be shut upon
him, that he may play the fool no where
but in 's own house. Farewell.   *137*

OPHELIA.   O, help him, you sweet
heavens!

HAMLET.   If thou dost marry, I'll give
thee this plague for thy dowry: be thou
as chaste as ice, as pure as snow, thou
shalt not escape calumny. Get thee to a
nunnery, go: farewell. Or, if thou wilt
needs marry, marry a fool; for wise men
know well enough what monsters you
make of them. To a nunnery, go; and
quickly too. Farewell.   *146*

OPHELIA.   O heavenly powers, restore him!

HAMLET.   I have heard of your
paintings too, well enough; God has
given you one face, and you make yourselves another: you jig, you amble, and
you lisp, and nick-name God's creatures
and make your wantonness your ignorance. Go to, I'll no more on 't; it hath

made me mad. I say, we will have no
more marriages: those that are married
already, all but one, shall live; the rest
shall keep as they are. To a nunnery,
go.   (*Exit.*)   *157*
OPHELIA.   O, what a noble mind is
     here o'erthrown!
The courtier's, soldier's, scholar's, eye,
     tongue, sword:
The expectancy and rose of the fair
     state,   *160*
The glass of fashion and the mold of
     form,
The observed of all observers, quite,
     quite down!
And I, of ladies most deject and
     wretched,
That suck'd the honey of his music vows,
Now see that noble and most sovereign
     reason,   *165*
Like sweet bells jangled, out of tune and
     harsh;
That unmatch'd form and feature of
     blown youth
Blasted with ecstasy: O, woe is me,
To have seen what I have seen, see what
     I see!
     (*Re-enter* KING *and* POLONIUS.)
     KING.   Love! his affections do not
          that way tend;   *170*
Nor what he spake, though it lack'd
     form a little,
Was not like madness. There's something
     in his soul
O'er which his melancholy sits on brood,
And I do doubt the hatch and the dis-
     close
Will be some danger: which for to pre-
     vent,   *175*
I have in quick determination
Thus set it down:—he shall with speed
     to England,
For the demand of our neglected tribute:
Haply the seas and countries different
With variable objects shall expel   *180*
This something-settled matter in his
     heart,
Whereon his brains still beating puts him
     thus

From fashion of himself. What think
     you on 't?
     POLONIUS.   It shall do well: but yet
          do I believe
The origin and commencement of his
     grief   *185*
Sprung from neglected love. How now,
     Ophelia!
You need not tell us what Lord Hamlet
     said;
We heard it all. My lord, do as you
     please;
But, if you hold it fit, after the play,
Let his queen mother all alone entreat
     him   *190*
To show his grief: let her be round with
     him;
And I'll be placed, so please you, in the
     ear
Of all their conference. If she find him
     not,
To England send him, or confine him
     where
Your wisdom best shall think.
     KING.   It shall be so: *195*
Madness in great ones must not un-
     watch'd go.   (*Exeunt.*)

SCENE 2

(*A hall in the castle.*)
(*Enter* HAMLET *and* PLAYERS.)

HAMLET.   Speak the speech, I pray
you, as I pronounced it to you, trippingly
on the tongue: but if you mouth it, as
many of your players do, I had as lief
the town-crier spoke my lines. Nor do
not saw the air too much with your
hand, thus; but use all gently: for in the
very torrent, tempest, and, as I may say,
whirlwind of your passion, you must acquire and beget a temperance that may
give it smoothness. O, it offends me to
the soul to hear a robustious periwig-
pated fellow tear a passion to tatters, to
very rags, to split the ears of the ground-
lings, who, for the most part, are capable

of nothing but inexplicable dumb-shows and noise: I would have such a fellow whipped for o'er doing Termagant; it out-herods Herod: pray you, avoid it.

FIRST PLAYER. I warrant your honor.   *17*

HAMLET. Be not too tame neither, but let your own discretion be your tutor: suit the action to the word, the word to the action; with this special observance, that you o'erstep not the modesty of nature: for anything so overdone is from the purpose of playing, whose end, both at the first and now, was and is, to hold, as 'twere, the mirror up to nature; to show virtue her own feature, scorn her own image, and the very age and body of the time his form and pressure. Now this overdone or come tardy off, though it make the unskillful laugh, cannot but make the judicious grieve; the censure of the which one must in your allowance o'erweigh a whole theater of others. O, there be players that I have seen play, and heard others praise, and that highly, not to speak it profanely, that neither having the accent of Christians nor the gait of Christians, pagan, nor man, have so strutted and bellowed, that I have thought some of nature's journeymen had made men, and not made them well, they imitated humanity so abominably.

FIRST PLAYER. I hope we have reformed that indifferently with us, sir. *41*

HAMLET. O, reform it altogether. And let those that play your clowns speak no more than is set down for them: for there be of them that will themselves laugh, to set on some quantity of barren spectators to laugh too, though in the mean time some necessary question of the play be then to be considered: that's villainous, and shows a most pitiful ambition in the fool that uses it. Go, make you ready.   *50*

(*Exeunt* PLAYERS.)

(*Enter* POLONIUS, ROSENCRANTZ, *and* GUILDENSTERN.)

How now, my lord! will the king hear this piece of work?

POLONIUS. And the queen too, and that presently.

HAMLET. Bid the players make haste.

(*Exit* POLONIUS.)

Will you two help to hasten them?

ROSENCRANTZ. ⎫
GUILDENSTERN. ⎬ We will, my lord.

(*Exeunt* ROSENCRANTZ *and* GUILDENSTERN.)

HAMLET. What ho! Horatio!

(*Enter* HORATIO.)

HORATIO. Here, sweet lord, at your service.

HAMLET. Horatio, thou art e'en as just a man   *59*

As e'er my conversation coped withal.

HORATIO. O, my dear lord,—

HAMLET. Nay, do not think I flatter;

For what advancement may I hope from thee,

That no revénue hast but thy good spirits,

To feed and clothe thee? Why should the poor be flatter'd?

No, let the candied tongue lick absurd pomp,   *65*

And crook the pregnant hinges of the knee

Where thrift may follow fawning. Dost thou hear?

Since my dear soul was mistress of her choice,

And could of men distinguish, her election

Hath seal'd thee for herself: for thou hast been   *70*

As one, in suffering all, that suffers nothing;

A man that fortune's buffets and rewards

Hast ta'en with equal thanks: and blest are those

Whose blood and judgment are so well commingled

That they are not a pipe for fortune's finger   *75*

To sound what stop she please. Give me
    that man
That is not passion's slave, and I will
    wear him
In my heart's core, aye, in my heart of
    heart,
As I do thee. Something too much of
    this.   79
There is a play to-night before the king;
One scene of it comes near the circum-
    stance
Which I have told thee of my father's
    death:
I prithee, when thou sees that act a-foot,
Even with the very comment of thy soul
Observe mine uncle: if his occulted
    guilt   85
Do not itself unkennel in one speech
It is a damnèd ghost that we have seen,
And my imaginations are as foul
As Vulcan's stithy. Give him heedful
    note;   89
For I mine eyes will rivet to his face,
And after we will both our judgments
    join
In censure of his seeming.

    HORATIO.   Well, my lord:
If he steal aught the whilst this play is
    playing,
And 'scape detecting, I will pay the theft.

    HAMLET. They are coming to the
    play: I must be idle: 95
Get you a place.

    (*Danish march. A flourish. Enter* KING,
QUEEN, POLONIUS, OPHELIA, ROSEN-
CRANTZ, GUILDENSTERN, *and other*
LORDS *attendant, with the* GUARD *carry-
ing torches.*)

    KING. How fares our cousin Ham-
let?

    HAMLET. Excellent, i' faith; of the
chameleon's dish: I eat the air, promise-
crammed: you cannot feed capons so.

    KING. I have nothing with this *101*
answer, Hamlet; these words are not
mine.

    HAMLET. No, nor mine now. (*To*
POLONIUS) My lord, you played once i'
the university, you say?

    POLONIUS. That did I, my lord, and
was accounted a good actor.   *106*

    HAMLET. What did you enact?

    POLONIUS. I did enact Julius Cæsar:
I was killed i' the Capitol; Brutus killed
me.

    HAMLET. It was a brute part of him
to kill so capital a calf there. Be the
players ready?   *111*

    ROSENCRANTZ. Aye, my lord; they
stay upon your patience.

    QUEEN. Come hither, my dear Ham-
let, sit by me.   *115*

    HAMLET. No, good mother, here's
metal more attractive.

    POLONIUS (*to the* KING). O, ho! do
you mark that?

    HAMLET. Lady, shall I lie in your lap?
    (*Lying down at* OPHELIA'S *feet.*)

    OPHELIA. No, my lord.   *120*

    HAMLET. I mean, my head upon
your lap?

    OPHELIA. Aye, my lord.

    HAMLET. Do you think I meant
country matters?

    OPHELIA. I think nothing, my lord.

    HAMLET. That's a fair thought to lie
between maids' legs.   *126*

    OPHELIA. What is, my lord?

    HAMLET. Nothing.

    OPHELIA. You are merry, my lord.

    HAMLET. Who, I?   *130*

    OPHELIA. Aye, my lord.

    HAMLET. O God, your only jig-
maker. What should a man do but be
merry? for, look you, how cheerfully
my mother looks, and my father died
within these two hours.

    OPHELIA. Nay, 'tis twice two months,
my lord.   *136*

    HAMLET. So long? Nay then, let the
devil wear black, for I'll have a suit of
sables. O heavens! died two months ago,
and not forgotten yet? Then there's hope
a great man's memory may outlive his
life half a year: but, by 'r lady, he must
build churches then; or else shall he
suffer not thinking on, with the hobby-
horse, whose epitaph is, 'For, O, for, O,

the hobby-horse is forgot.'   145
(*Hautboys play. The dumb-show enters.*)

(*Enter a* KING *and a* QUEEN *very lovingly; the* QUEEN *embracing him and he her. She kneels, and makes show of protestation unto him. He takes her up, and declines his head upon her neck; lays him down upon a bank of flowers: she, seeing him asleep, leaves him. Anon comes in a fellow, takes off his crown, kisses it, and pours poison in the* KING'S *ears, and exit. The* QUEEN *returns; finds the* KING *dead, and makes passionate action. The* POISONER, *with some two or three* MUTES *comes in again, seeming to lament with her. The dead body is carried away. The* POISONER *woos the* QUEEN *with gifts: she seems loath and unwilling awhile, but in the end accepts his love.*)

(*Exeunt.*)

OPHELIA. What means this, my lord?

HAMLET. Marry, this is miching mallecho;[58] it means mischief.

OPHELIA. Belike this show imports the argument of the play.   150

(*Enter* PROLOGUE.)

HAMLET. We shall know by this fellow: the players cannot keep counsel; they'll tell all.

OPHELIA. Will he tell us what this show meant?

HAMLET. Aye, or any show that you'll show him: be not you ashamed to show, he'll not shame to tell you what it means.

OPHELIA. You are naught, you are naught: I'll mark the play.

PROLOGUE.

> For us, and for our tragedy,
> Here stooping to your clemency, 160
> We beg your hearing patiently.

HAMLET. Is this a prologue, or the posy of a ring?

OPHELIA. 'Tis brief, my lord.

[58] sneaking mischief

HAMLET. As woman's love.

(*Enter two* PLAYERS, KING *and* QUEEN.)

PLAYER KING. Full thirty times hath Phœbus' cart gone round   165
Neptune's salt wash and Tellus' orbèd ground,
And thirty dozen moons with borrowed sheen
About the world have times twelve thirties been,
Since love our hearts and Hymen did our hands   169
Unite commutual in most sacred bands.

PLAYER QUEEN. So many journeys may the sun and moon
Make us again count o'er ere love be done!
But, woe is me, you are so sick of late,
So far from cheer and from your former state,
That I distrust you. Yet, though I distrust,   175
Discomfort you, my lord, it nothing must:
For women's fear and love holds quantity,
In neither aught, or in extremity.
Now, what my love is, proof hath made you know,   179
And as my love is sized, my fear is so:
Where love is great, the littlest doubts are fear,
Where little fears grow great, great love grows there.

PLAYER KING. Faith, I must leave thee, love, and shortly too;
My operant powers their functions leave to do:
And thou shalt live in this fair world behind,   185
Honor'd, beloved; and haply as one as kind
For husband shalt thou—

PLAYER QUEEN.   O, confound the rest!
Such love must needs be treason in my breast:
In second husband let me be accurst!

None wed the second but who kill'd the
    first.   *190*
HAMLET (*aside*).   Wormwood, worm-
    wood.
PLAYER QUEEN.   The instances that
    second marriage move
Are base respects of thrift, but none of
    love:
A second time I kill my husband dead,
When second husband kisses me in bed.
    PLAYER KING.   I do believe you think
    what now you speak,   *196*
But what we do determine oft we break.
Purpose is but the slave to memory,
Of violent birth, but poor validity:
Which now, like fruit unripe, sticks on
    the tree,   *200*
But fall unshaken when they mellow be.
Most necessary 'tis that we forget
To pay ourselves what to ourselves is
    debt:
What to ourselves in passion we propose,
The passion ending, doth the purpose
    lose.   *205*
The violence of either grief or joy
Their own enactures with themselves de-
    stroy:
Where joy most revels, grief doth most
    lament;
Grief joys, joy grieves, on slender acci-
    dent.
This world is not for aye, nor 'tis not
    strange   *210*
That even our loves should with our for-
    tunes change,
For 'tis a question left us yet to prove,
Whether love lead fortune or else for-
    tune love.
The great man down, you mark his
    favorite flies;
The poor advanced makes friends of
    enemies: *215*
And hitherto doth love on fortune tend;
For who not needs shall never lack a
    friend,
And who in want a hollow friend doth
    try
Directly seasons him his enemy.

But, orderly to end where I begun,   *220*
Our wills and fates do so contrary run,
That our devices still are overthrown,
Our thoughts are ours, their ends none
    of our own:
So think thou wilt no second husband
    wed,
But die thy thoughts when thy first lord
    is dead.   *225*
    PLAYER QUEEN.   Nor earth to me
    give food nor heaven light!
Sport and repose lock from me day and
    night!
To desperation turn my trust and hope!
An anchor's cheer in prison be my scope!
Each opposite, that blanks the face of
    joy,   *230*
Meet what I would have well and it de-
    stroy!
Both here and hence pursue me lasting
    strife,
If, once a widow, ever I be wife!
    HAMLET.   If she should break it now!
    PLAYER KING.   'Tis deeply sworn.
    Sweet, leave me here a while;   *235*
My spirits grow dull, and fain I would
    beguile
The tedious day with sleep.   (*Sleeps.*)
    PLAYER QUEEN.   Sleep rock thy
    brain;
And never come mischance between us
    twain!   (*Exit.*)
    HAMLET.   Madam, how like you this
play?
    QUEEN.   The lady doth protest too
much, methinks.   *240*
    HAMLET.   O, but she'll keep her word.
    KING.   Have you heard the argument?
Is there no offense in 't?
    HAMLET.   No, no, they do but jest,
poison in jest; no offense i' the world.
    KING.   What do you call the play?
    HAMLET.   The Mouse-trap. Marry,
how? Tropically. This play is the image
of a murder done in Vienna: Gonzago
is the duke's name; his wife, Baptista:
you shall see anon; 'tis a knavish piece
of work; but what o' that? your majesty,

and we that have free souls, it touches us not: let the galled jade wince, our withers are unwrung.

(*Enter* LUCIANUS.)

This is one Lucianus, nephew to the king.

OPHELIA. You are as good as a chorus, my lord.   255

HAMLET. I could interpret between you and your love, if I could see the puppets dallying.

OPHELIA. You are keen, my lord, you are keen.

HAMLET. It would cost you a groaning to take off my edge.   260

OPHELIA. Still better, and worse.

HAMLET. So you must take your husbands. Begin, murderer; pox, leave thy damnable faces, and begin. Come: "the croaking raven doth bellow for revenge."   265

LUCIANUS. Thoughts black, hands apt, drugs fit, and time agreeing; Confederate season, else no creature seeing; Thou mixture rank, of midnight weeds collected, With Hecate's[59] ban thrice blasted, thrice infected,   269 Thy natural magic and dire property, On wholesome life usurp immediately.

(*Pours the poison into the sleeper's ear.*)

HAMLET. He poisons him i' the garden for 's estate. His name's Gonzago: the story is extant, and writ in very choice Italian: you shall see anon how the murderer gets the love of Gonzago's wife.   275

OPHELIA. The king rises.

HAMLET. What, frighted with false fire!

QUEEN. How fares my lord?

POLONIUS. Give o'er the play.

KING. Give me some light. Away!

POLONIUS. Lights, lights, lights!   281

(*Exeunt all but* HAMLET *and* HORATIO.)

HAMLET.

Why, let the stricken deer go weep,
  The hart ungallèd play;
For some must watch, while some must
    sleep:
So runs the world away.   285

Would not this, sir, and a forest of feathers—if the rest of my fortunes turn Turk with me—with two Provincial roses[60] on my razed[61] shoes, get me a fellowship in a cry of players, sir?

HORATIO. Half a share.   290

HAMLET. A whole one, I.

For thou dost know, O Damon dear,
  This realm dismantled was
Of Jove himself; and now reigns here
  A very, very—pajock.[62]   295

HORATIO. You might have rhymed.

HAMLET. O good Horatio, I'll take the ghost's word for a thousand pounds. Didst perceive?

HORATIO. Very well, my lord.

HAMLET. Upon the talk of the poisoning?   300

HORATIO. I did very well note him.

HAMLET. Ah, ha! Come, some music! come, the recorders!

For if the king like not the comedy,
Why then, belike, he likes it not,
    perdy.[63]   305

Come, some music!

(*Re-enter* ROSENCRANTZ *and* GUILDENSTERN.)

GUILDENSTERN. Good my lord, vouchsafe me a word with you.

HAMLET. Sir, a whole history.

GUILDENSTERN. The king, sir,—   310

HAMLET. Aye, sir, what of him?

GUILDENSTERN. Is in his retirement marvelous distempered.

59 an earth-goddess associated with night and evil
60 rosettes of ribbon
61 openwork
62 peacock
63 French *pardieu* = by God, but milder than the English form

HAMLET. With drink, sir?

GUILDENSTERN. No, my lord, rather with choler.[64]   *315*

HAMLET. Your wisdom should show itself more richer to signify this to the doctor; for, for me to put him to his purgation would perhaps plunge him into far more choler.   *319*

GUILDENSTERN. Good my lord, put your discourse into some frame, and start not so wildly from my affair.

HAMLET. I am tame, sir: pronounce.

GUILDENSTERN. The queen, your mother, in most great affliction of spirit, hath sent me to you.

HAMLET. You are welcome.   *325*

GUILDENSTERN. Nay, good my lord, this courtesy is not of the right breed. If it shall please you to make me a wholesome answer, I will do your mother's commandment: if not, your pardon and my return shall be the end of my business.

HAMLET. Sir, I cannot.   *331*

GUILDENSTERN. What, my lord?

HAMLET. Make you a wholesome answer; my wit's diseased: but, sir, such answer as I can make, you shall command; or rather, as you say, my mother: therefore no more, but to the matter: my mother, you say,—

ROSENCRANTZ. Then thus she says; your behavior hath struck her into amazement and admiration.[65]   *339*

HAMLET. O wonderful son, that can so astonish a mother! But is there no sequel at the heels of this mother's admiration? Impart.

ROSENCRANTZ. She desires to speak with you in her closet, ere you go to bed.

HAMLET. We shall obey, were she ten times our mother. Have you any further trade with us?

ROSENCRANTZ. My lord, you once did love me.

HAMLET. So I do still, by these pickers and stealers.   *349*

ROSENCRANTZ. Good my lord, what is your cause of distemper? you do surely bar the door upon your own liberty, if you deny your griefs to your friend.

HAMLET. Sir, I lack advancement.

ROSENCRANTZ. How can that be, when you have the voice of the king himself for your succession in Denmark?

HAMLET. Aye, sir, but "while the grass grows,"[66]—the proverb is something musty.   *359*

(*Re-enter* PLAYERS *with recorders.*)

O, the recorders! let me see one. To withdraw with you:—why do you go about to recover the wind of me, as if you would drive me into a toil?

GUILDENSTERN. O, my lord, if my duty be too bold, my love is too unmannerly.   *364*

HAMLET. I do not well understand that. Will you play upon this pipe?

GUILDENSTERN. My lord, I cannot.

HAMLET. I pray you.

GUILDENSTERN. Believe me, I cannot.

HAMLET. I do beseech you.   *370*

GUILDENSTERN. I know no touch of it, my lord.

HAMLET. It is as easy as lying: govern these ventages with your fingers and thumb, give it breath with your mouth, and it will discourse most eloquent music. Look you, these are the stops.

GUILDENSTERN. But these cannot I command to any utterance of harmony; I have not the skill.   *378*

HAMLET. Why, look you now, how unworthy a thing you make of me! You would play upon me; you would seem to know my stops; you would pluck out the heart of my mystery; you would sound me from my lowest note to the top of my compass: and there is much music, excellent voice, in this little organ; yet cannot you make it speak. 'Sblood, do you think I am easier to be played on than a pipe? Call me what instrument you will, though you can fret me, yet you cannot play upon me.

[64] anger

[65] wonder

[66] . . . oft starves the silly steed.

(*Re-enter* POLONIUS.)

God bless you, sir!   *390*

POLONIUS.   My lord, the queen would speak with you, and presently.[67]

HAMLET.   Do you see yonder cloud that's almost in shape of a camel?

POLONIUS.   By the mass, and 'tis like a camel, indeed.

HAMLET.   Methinks it is like a weasel.

POLONIUS.   It is backed like a weasel.

HAMLET.   Or like a whale?

POLONIUS.   Very like a whale.   *399*

HAMLET.   Then I will come to my mother by and by. They fool me to the top of my bent. I will come by and by.

POLONIUS.   I will say so.

HAMLET.   By and by is easily said.

(*Exit* POLONIUS.)

Leave me, friends.

(*Exeunt all but* HAMLET.)

'Tis now the very witching time of night,
When churchyards yawn, and hell itself breathes out
Contagion to this world: now could I drink hot blood,
And do such bitter business as the day
Would quake to look on. Soft! now to my mother.   *410*
O heart, lose not thy nature: let not ever
The soul of Nero enter this firm bosom:
Let me be cruel, not unnatural: *413*
I will speak daggers to her, but use none;
My tongue and soul in this be hypocrites;
How in my words soever she be shent,[68]
To give them seals never, my soul, consent!   (*Exit.*)

SCENE 3

(*A room in the castle.*)

(*Enter* KING, ROSENCRANTZ, *and* GUILDENSTERN.)

KING.   I like him not, nor stands it safe with us
To let his madness range. Therefore prepare you;

[67] at once
[68] rebuked

I your commission will forthwith dispatch,
And he to England shall along with you:
The terms of our estate may not endure
Hazard so near us as doth hourly grow   *6*
Out of his lunacies.

GUILDENSTERN.   We will ourselves provide:
Most holy and religious fear it is
To keep those many many bodies safe
That live and feed upon your majesty.

ROSENCRANTZ.   The single and peculiar life is bound,   *11*
With all the strength and armor of the mind,
To keep itself from noyance; but much more
That spirit upon whose weal depend and rest   *14*
The lives of many. The cease of majesty
Dies not alone, but like a gulf doth draw
What's near it with it; it is a massy wheel,
Fix'd on the summit of the highest mount,
To whose huge spokes ten thousand lesser things
Are mortised and adjoin'd; which, when it falls,   *20*
Each small annexment, petty consequence,
Attends the boisterous ruin. Never alone
Did the king sigh, but with a general groan.

KING.   Arm you, I pray you, to this speedy voyage,
For we will fetters put upon this fear,
Which now goes too free-footed.   *26*

ROSENCRANTZ. } We will haste us.
GUILDENSTERN. }

(*Exeunt* ROSENCRANTZ *and* GUILDENSTERN.)

(*Enter* POLONIUS.)

POLONIUS.   My lord, he's going to his mother's closet:
Behind the arras I'll convey myself,
To hear the process: I'll warrant she'll tax him home:
And, as you said, and wisely was it said,
'Tis meet that some more audience than a mother,   *31*

Since nature makes them partial, should
   o'erhear
The speech, of vantage. Fare you well,
   my liege:
I'll call upon you ere you go to bed,
And tell you what I know.
    KING.   Thanks, dear my lord. *35*
               (*Exit* POLONIUS.)
O, my offense is rank, it smells to heaven;
It hath the primal eldest curse upon 't,
A brother's murder. Pray can I not,
Though inclination be as sharp as will:
My stronger guilt defeats my strong in-
   tent,   *40*
And like a man to double business bound,
I stand in pause where I shall first begin,
And both neglect. What if this cursèd
   hand
Were thicker than itself with brother's
   blood,
Is there not rain enough in the sweet
   heavens   *45*
To wash it white as snow? Whereto
   serves mercy
But to confront the visage of offense?
And what's in prayer but this twofold
   force,
To be forestallèd ere we come to fall,
Or pardon'd being down? Then I'll look
   up;   *50*
My fault is past. But O, what form of
   prayer
Can serve my turn? "Forgive me my foul
   murder"?
That cannot be, since I am still possess'd
Of those effects for which I did the mur-
   der,
My crown, mine own ambition and my
   queen.   *55*
May one be pardon'd and retain the
   offense?
In the corrupted currents of this world
Offense's gilded hand may shove by
   justice,
And oft 'tis seen the wicked prize itself
Buys out the law: but 'tis not so above; *60*
There is no shuffling, there the action lies
In his true nature, and we ourselves com-
   pell'd

Even to the teeth and forehead of our
   faults
To give in evidence. What then? what
   rests?
Try what repentance can: what can it
   not?   *65*
Yet what can it when one can not repent?
O wretched state! O bosom black as death!
O limèd soul, that struggling to be free
Art more engaged! Help, angels! make
   assay!
Bow, stubborn knees, and, heart with
   strings of steel,   *70*
Be soft as sinews of the new-born babe!
All may be well.   (*Retires and kneels.*)
    (*Enter* HAMLET.)
    HAMLET. Now might I do it pat,
   now he is praying;
And now I'll do 't: and so he goes to
   heaven:
And so am I revenged. That would be
   scann'd;   *75*
A villain kills my father; and for that,
I, his sole son, do this same villain send
To heaven.
O, this is hire and salary, not revenge.
He took my father grossly, full of bread,
With all his crimes broad blown, as flush
   as May;   *81*
And how his audit stands who knows
   save heaven?
But in our circumstance and course of
   thought,
'Tis heavy with him: and am I then re-
   venged,
To take him in the purging of his soul,
When he is fit and season'd for his pas-
   sage?   *86*
No!
Up, sword, and know thou a more horrid
   hent:[69]
When he is drunk asleep, or in his rage,
Or, in the incestuous pleasure of his bed;
At game, a-swearing, or about some act
That has no relish of salvation in 't; *92*
Then trip him, that his heels may kick at
   heaven

[69] time to be grasped

And that his soul may be as damn'd and
  black
As hell, whereto it goes. My mother
  stays: *95*
This physic but prolongs thy sickly days.
                                                    (*Exit.*)
KING (*rising*).   My words fly up, my
  thoughts remain below:
Words without thoughts never to heaven
  go.   (*Exit.*)

SCENE 4

(*The* QUEEN'S *closet.*)
(*Enter* QUEEN *and* POLONIUS.)

POLONIUS.   He will come straight.
  Look you lay home to him:
Tell him his pranks have been too broad
  to bear with,
And that your grace hath screen'd and
  stood between
Much heat and him. I'll sconce me even
  here.
Pray you, be round with him.   *5*
HAMLET (*within*).   Mother, mother,
  mother!
QUEEN.   I'll warrant you;
Fear me not. Withdraw; I hear him
  coming.
        (POLONIUS *hides behind the arras.*)
(*Enter* HAMLET.)
HAMLET.   Now, mother, what's the
  matter?
QUEEN.   Hamlet, thou hast thy father
  much offended.
HAMLET.   Mother, you have my
  father much offended.   *10*
QUEEN.   Come, come, you answer
  with an idle tongue.
HAMLET.   Go, go, you question with
  a wicked tongue.
QUEEN.   Why, how now, Hamlet!
HAMLET.   What's the matter now?
QUEEN.   Have you forgot me?
HAMLET.   No, by the rood, not so:
You are the queen, your husband's
  brother's wife;   *15*
And—would it were not so!—you are
  my mother.

QUEEN.   Nay, then, I'll set those to
  you that can speak.
HAMLET.   Come, come, and sit you
  down; you shall not budge;
You go not till I set you up a glass
Where you may see the inmost part of
  you.   *20*
QUEEN.   What wilt thou do? thou
  wilt not murder me?
Help, help, ho!
POLONIUS (*behind*).   What, ho! help,
  help, help!
HAMLET (*drawing*).   How now! a rat?
  Dead, for a ducat, dead!
        (*Makes a pass through the arras.*)
POLONIUS (*behind*).   O, I am slain!
                                    (*Falls and dies.*)
QUEEN.   O me, what hast thou
  done?
HAMLET.   Nay, I know not: is it the
  king?   *26*
QUEEN.   O, what a rash and bloody
  deed is this!
HAMLET.   A bloody deed! almost as
  bad, good mother,
As kill a king and marry with his brother.
QUEEN.   As kill a king!
HAMLET.   Aye, lady, 'twas my
  word.
(*Lifts up the arras and discovers* PO-
LONIUS.)
Thou wretched, rash, intruding fool, fare-
  well!   *31*
I took thee for thy better: take thy for-
  tune;
Thou find'st to be too busy is some
  danger.
Leave wringing of your hands: peace!
  sit you down,
And let me wring your heart: for so I
  shall,   *35*
If it be made of penetrable stuff;
If damnèd custom have not brass'd it so,
That it be proof and bulwark against
  sense.
QUEEN.   What have I done, that thou
  darest wag thy tongue
In noise so rude against me?
HAMLET.   Such an act   *40*

That blurs the grace and blush of mod-
esty,
Calls virtue hypocrite, takes off the rose
From the fair forehead of an innocent
love,
And sets a blister there; makes marriage
vows   *44*
As false as dicers' oaths: O, such a deed
As from the body of contraction plucks
The very soul, and sweet religion makes
A rhapsody of words: heaven's face doth
glow;
Yea, this solidity and compound mass,
With tristful[70] visage, as against the
doom,   *50*
Is thought-sick at the act.
    QUEEN.   Aye me, what act,
That roars so loud and thunders in the
index?
    HAMLET.   Look here, upon this pic-
ture, and on this,
The counterfeit presentment of two
brothers.   *54*
See what a grace was seated on this brow;
Hyperion's curls, the front of Jove him-
self.
An eye like Mars, to threaten and com-
mand;
A station like the herald Mercury
New-lighted on a heaven-kissing hill;
A combination and a form indeed,   *60*
Where every god did seem to set his seal
To give the world assurance of a man:
This was your husband. Look you now,
what follows:
Here is your husband; like a mildew'd
ear,
Blasting his wholesome brother. Have
you eyes?   *65*
Could you on this fair mountain leave to
feed,
And batten on this moor? Ha! have you
eyes?
You cannot call it love, for at your age
The hey-day in the blood is tame, it's
humble,
And waits upon the judgment: and what
judgment   *70*

Would step from this to this? Sense sure
you have,
Else could you not have motion: but sure
that sense
Is apoplex'd: for madness would not err,
Nor sense to ecstasy was ne'er so thrall'd
But it reserved some quantity of choice,
To serve in such a difference. What devil
was't   *76*
That thus hath cozen'd[71] you at hoodman-
blind?
Eyes without feeling, feeling without
sight,
Ears without hands or eyes, smelling
sans[72] all,
Or but a sickly part of one true sense   *80*
Could not so mope.
O shame! where is thy blush? Rebellious
hell,
If thou canst mutine in a matron's bones,
To flaming youth let virtue be as wax
And melt in her own fire: proclaim no
shame   *85*
When the compulsive ardor gives the
charge,
Since frost itself as actively doth burn,
And reason panders will.
    QUEEN.   O Hamlet, speak no more:
Thou turn'st mine eyes into my very soul,
And there I see such black and grainèd
spots   *90*
As will not leave their tint.
    HAMLET.   Nay, but to live
In the rank sweat of an enseamèd bed,
Stew'd in corruption, honeying and mak-
ing love
Over the nasty sty,—
    QUEEN.   O, speak to me no more;
These words like daggers enter in mine
ears;   *95*
No more, sweet Hamlet!
    HAMLET.   A murderer and a villain;
A slave that is not twentieth part the
tithe
Of your precedent lord; a vice of kings;
A cutpurse of the empire and the rule,

[70] sad
[71] cheated
[72] without

That from a shelf the precious diadem
stole   *100*
And put it in his pocket!
    QUEEN.   No more!
    HAMLET. A king of shreds and
    patches—
(*Enter* GHOST.)
Save me, and hover o'er me with your
wings,
You heavenly guards! What would your
gracious figure?
    QUEEN. Alas, he's mad!   *105*
    HAMLET. Do you not come your
    tardy son to chide,
That, lapsed in time and passion, lets go
by
The important acting of your dread com-
mand?
O, say!   *109*
    GHOST. Do not forget: this visitation
Is but to whet thy almost blunted purpose.
But look, amazement on thy mother sits:
O, step between her and her fighting soul:
Conceit[73] in weakest bodies strongest
works: *114*
Speak to her, Hamlet.
    HAMLET.   How is it with you, lady?
    QUEEN. Alas, how is 't with you,
That you do bend your eye on vacancy
And with the incorporal air do hold dis-
course?
Forth at your eyes your spirits wildly
peep;   *119*
And, as the sleeping soldiers in the alarm,
Your bedded hairs, like life in excre-
ments,
Start up and stand on end. O gentle son,
Upon the heat and flame of thy distemper
Sprinkle cool patience. Whereon do you
look?
    HAMLET. On him, on him! Look you
how pale he glares!   *125*
His form and cause conjoin'd, preaching
to stones,
Would make them capable. Do not look
upon me,
Lest with this piteous action you convert
My stern effects: then what I have to do

Will want true color; tears perchance for
blood.   *130*
    QUEEN. To whom do you speak this?
    HAMLET. Do you see nothing
there?
    QUEEN. Nothing at all; yet all that
is I see.
    HAMLET. Nor did you nothing hear?
    QUEEN. No, nothing but ourselves.
    HAMLET. Why, look you there! look,
how it steals away!
My father, in his habit as he lived!   *135*
Look, where he goes, even now, out at
the portal!
                (*Exit* GHOST.)
    QUEEN. This is the very coinage of
your brain:
This bodiless creation ecstasy
Is very cunning in.
    HAMLET.   Ecstasy!
My pulse, as yours, doth temperately
keep time,   *140*
And makes as healthful music: it is not
madness
That I have utter'd: bring me to the test,
And I the matter will re-word, which
madness
Would gambol from. Mother, for love of
grace,
Lay not that flattering unction to your
soul,   *145*
That not your trespass but my madness
speaks:
It will but skin and film the ulcerous
place,
Whiles rank corruption, mining all
within,
Infects unseen. Confess yourself to
heaven;
Repent what's past, avoid what is to
come,   *150*
And do not spread the compost on the
weeds,
To make them ranker. Forgive me this
my virtue,
For in the fatness of these pursy times
Virtue itself of vice must pardon beg,
Yea, curb and woo for leave to do him
good.   *155*

---

[73] imagination

QUEEN. O Hamlet, thou hast cleft my heart in twain.

HAMLET. O, throw away the worser part of it,
And live the purer with the other half.
Good night: but go not to my uncle's bed;
Assume a virtue, if you have it not.   *160*
That monster, custom, who all sense doth eat,
Of habits devil, is angel yet in this,
That to the use of actions fair and good
He likewise gives a frock or livery,   *164*
That aptly is put on. Refrain to-night,
And that shall lend a kind of easiness
To the next abstinence; the next more easy;
For use almost can change the stamp of nature,
And either curb the devil, or throw him out
With wondrous potency. Once more, good night: *170*
And when you are desirous to be bless'd,
I'll blessing beg of you. For this same lord,

(*Pointing to* POLONIUS.)

I do repent: but heaven hath pleased it so,
To punish me with this, and this with me,
That I must be their scourge and minister.   *175*
I will bestow him, and will answer well
The death I gave him. So, again, good night.
I must be cruel, only to be kind:
Thus bad begins, and worse remains behind.
One word more, good lady.

QUEEN.   What shall I do?

HAMLET. Not this, by no means, that I bid you do: *181*
Let the bloat king tempt you again to bed;
Pinch wanton on your cheek, call you his mouse;
And let him, for a pair of reechy kisses,
Or paddling in your neck with his damn'd fingers,   *185*

Make you to ravel all this matter out,
That I essentially am not in madness,
But mad in craft. 'Twere good you let him know;
For who, that's but a queen, fair, sober, wise,
Would from a paddock,[74] from a bat, a gib,[75]   *190*
Such dear concernings hide? who would do so?
No, in despite of sense and secrecy,
Unpeg the basket on the house's top,
Let the birds fly, and like the famous ape,
To try conclusions, in the basket creep
And break your own neck down.   *196*

QUEEN. Be thou assured, if words be made of breath
And breath of life, I have no life to breathe
What thou hast said to me.

HAMLET. I must to England; you know that?

QUEEN.   Alack,   *200*
I had forgot: 'tis so concluded on.

HAMLET. There's letters seal'd: and my two schoolfellows,
Whom I will trust as I will adders fang'd,
They bear the mandate; they must sweep my way,   *204*
And marshal me to knavery. Let it work;
For 'tis the sport to have the enginer
Hoist with his own petar:[76] and 't shall go hard
But I will delve one yard below their mines,
And blow them at the moon: O, 'tis most sweet
When in one line two crafts directly meet.   *210*
This man shall set me packing:
I'll lug the guts into the neighbor room.
Mother, good night. Indeed this counselor
Is now most still, most secret and most grave,

[74] toad
[75] tom-cat
[76] a small bomb

Who was in life a foolish prating
    knave.   *215*
Come, sir, to draw toward an end with
    you.
Good night, mother.

(*Exeunt severally;* HAMLET *dragging
in* POLONIUS.)

Act IV

SCENE 1

(*A room in the castle.*)
(*Enter* KING, QUEEN, ROSENCRANTZ,
and GUILDENSTERN.)

    KING.   There's matter in these sighs,
    these profound heaves:
You must translate: 'tis fit we under-
    stand them.
Where is your son?
    QUEEN.   Bestow this place on us a
    little while.

(*Exeunt* ROSENCRANTZ *and* GUILDEN-
STERN.)

Ah, mine own lord, what have I seen
    tonight!   *5*
    KING.   What, Gertrude? How does
    Hamlet?
    QUEEN.   Mad as the sea and wind,
    when both contend
Which is the mightier: in his lawless fit,
Behind the arras hearing something stir,
Whips out his rapier, cries "A rat, a rat!"
And in this brainish apprehension
    kills   *11*
The unseen good old man.
    KING.   O heavy deed!
It had been so with us, had we been
    there:
His liberty is full of threats to all,
To you yourself, to us, to every one.   *15*
Alas, how shall this bloody deed be
    answer'd?
It will be laid to us, whose providence
Should have kept short, restrain'd and
    out of haunt,

This mad young man: but so much was
    our love,
We would not understand what was most
    fit,   *20*
But like the owner of a foul disease,
To keep it from divulging, let it feed
Even on the pith of life. Where is he
    gone?
    QUEEN.   To draw apart the body he
    hath kill'd:
O'er whom his very madness, like some
    ore   *25*
Among a mineral of metals base,
Shows itself pure; he weeps for what is
    done.
    KING.   O Gertrude, come away!
The sun no sooner shall the mountains
    touch,
But we will ship him hence: and this vile
    deed   *30*
We must, with all our majesty and skill,
Both countenance and excuse. Ho, Guild-
    enstern!

(*Re-enter* ROSENCRANTZ *and* GUILD-
ENSTERN.)

Friends both, go join you with some
    further aid:
Hamlet in madness hath Polonius slain,
And from his mother's closet he dragg'd
    him: *35*
Go seek him out; speak fair, and bring
    the body
Into the chapel. I pray you, haste in
    this.

(*Exeunt* ROSENCRANTZ *and* GUILDEN-
STERN.)

Come, Gertrude, we'll call up our wisest
    friends;
And let them know, both what we mean
    to do,
And what's untimely done; so, haply,
    slander,   *40*
Whose whisper o'er the world's diameter
As level as the cannon to his blank
Transports his poison'd shot, may miss
    our name
And hit the woundless air. O, come
    away!

My soul is full of discord and dismay.   (*Exeunt.*)   *45*

SCENE 2

(*Another room in the castle.*)
(*Enter* HAMLET.)

HAMLET.   Safely stowed.
ROSENCRANTZ ⎫ (*Within*).   Hamlet!
GUILDENSTERN ⎭   Lord Hamlet!
HAMLET.   But soft, what noise? who
calls on Hamlet? O, here they come.
(*Enter* ROSENCRANTZ *and* GUILDEN-
STERN.)
ROSENCRANTZ.   What have you done,
my lord, with the dead body?   *5*
HAMLET.   Compounded it with dust,
whereto 'tis kin.
ROSENCRANTZ.   Tell us where 'tis,
that we may take it thence and bear it to
the chapel.
HAMLET.   Do not believe it.
ROSENCRANTZ.   Believe what?   *10*
HAMLET.   That I can keep your
counsel and not mine own. Besides, to
be demanded of a sponge! what replica-
tion should be made by the son of a
king?   *14*
ROSENCRANTZ.   Take you me for a
sponge, my lord?
HAMLET.   Aye, sir; that soaks up the
king's countenance, his rewards, his
authorities. But such officers do the king
best service in the end: he keeps them,
like an ape, in the corner of his jaw;
first mouthed, to be last swallowed: when
he needs what you have gleaned, it is
but squeezing you, and, sponge, you
shall be dry again.   *23*
ROSENCRANTZ.   I understand you not,
my lord.
HAMLET.   I am glad of it: a knavish
speech sleeps in a foolish ear.
ROSENCRANTZ.   My lord, you must
tell us where the body is, and go with
us to the king.   *28*
HAMLET.   The body is with the king,
but the king is not with the body. The
king is a thing—   *30*

GUILDENSTERN.   A thing, my lord?
HAMLET.   Of nothing: bring me to
him. Hide fox, and all after.
                            (*Exeunt.*)

SCENE 3

(*Another room in the castle.*)
(*Enter* KING, *attended.*)

KING.   I have sent to seek him, and
to find the body.
How dangerous is it that this man goes
loose!
Yet must not we put the strong law on
him:
He's loved of the distracted multitude,
Who like not in their judgment, but their
eyes;   *5*
And where 'tis so, the offender's scourge
is weigh'd,
But never the offense. To bear all smooth
and even,
This sudden sending away must seem
Deliberate pause: diseases desperate
grown
By desperate appliance are relieved, *10*
Or not at all.
(*Enter* ROSENCRANTZ.)
            How now! what hath befall'n?
ROSENCRANTZ.   Where the dead body
is bestow'd, my lord,
We cannot get from him.
KING.   But where is he?
ROSENCRANTZ.   Without,   my   lord;
guarded, to know your pleasure.
KING.   Bring him before us.   *15*
ROSENCRANTZ.   Ho,   Guildenstern!
bring in my lord.
(*Enter* HAMLET *and* GUILDENSTERN.)
KING.   Now,   Hamlet,   where's
Polonius?
HAMLET.   At supper.
KING.   At supper! where?   *19*
HAMLET.   Not where he eats, but
where he is eaten: a certain convocation
of politic worms are e'en at him. Your
worm is your only emperor for diet:
we fat all creatures else to fat us, and we
fat ourselves for maggots: your fat king

and your lean beggar is but variable
service, two dishes, but to one table:
that's the end.   *26*

KING. Alas, alas!

HAMLET. A man may fish with the
worm that hath eat of a king, and eat of
the fish that hath fed of that worm. *30*

KING. What dost thou mean by this?

HAMLET. Nothing but to show you
how a king may go a progress through
the guts of a beggar.

KING. Where is Polonius?

HAMLET. In heaven; send thither to
see: if your messenger find him not there,
seek him i' the other place yourself. But
indeed, if you find him not within this
month, you shall nose him as you go up
the stairs into the lobby.

KING. Go seek him there.   *40*
       (*To some* ATTENDANTS.)

HAMLET. He will stay till you come.
       (*Exeunt* ATTENDANTS.)

KING. Hamlet, this deed, for thine
     especial safety,
Which we do tender, as we dearly grieve
For that which thou hast done, must
     send thee hence
With fiery quickness: therefore prepare
     thyself;   *45*
The bark is ready and the wind at help,
The associates tend, and every thing is
     bent
For England.

HAMLET. For England?

KING.   Aye, Hamlet.

HAMLET.   Good.

KING. So is it, if thou knew'st our
     purposes.

HAMLET. I see a cherub that sees
them. But, come; for England! Farewell,
dear mother.   *51*

KING. Thy loving father, Hamlet.

HAMLET. My mother: father and
mother is man and wife; man and wife
is one flesh, and so, my mother. Come,
for England!   (*Exit.*)

KING. Follow him at foot; tempt him
     with speed aboard;
Delay it not; I'll have him hence to-night:

Away! for every thing is seal'd and done
That else leans on the affair: pray you,
     make haste.
     (*Exeunt* ROSENCRANTZ *and* GUILDEN-
STERN.)

And, England, if my love thou hold'st at
     aught—   *60*
As my great power thereof may give thee
     sense,
Since yet thy cicatrice looks raw and red
After the Danish sword, and thy free awe
Pays homage to us—thou mayst not
     coldly set
Our sovereign process; which imports at
     full,   *65*
By letters congruing to that effect,
The present death of Hamlet. Do it,
     England;
For like the hectic in my blood he rages,
And thou must cure me; till I know 'tis
     done,
Howe'er my haps, my joys were ne'er
     begun.   (*Exit.*) *70*

SCENE 4

(*A plain in Denmark.*)
(*Enter* FORTINBRAS, *a* CAPTAIN *and*
SOLDIERS, *marching.*)

FORTINBRAS. Go, captain, from me
     greet the Danish king;
Tell him that by his license Fortinbras
Craves the conveyance of a promised
     march
Over his kingdom. You know the ren-
     dezvous.
If that his majesty would aught with
     us,   *5*
We shall express our duty in his eye;
And let him know so.

CAPTAIN.   I will do 't, my lord.

FORTINBRAS. Go softly on.
(*Exeunt* FORTINBRAS *and* SOLDIERS.)
(*Enter* HAMLET, ROSENCRANTZ,
GUILDENSTERN, *and others.*)

HAMLET. Good sir, whose powers
     are these?   *9*

CAPTAIN. They are of Norway, sir.

HAMLET. How purposed, sir, I pray you?

CAPTAIN. Against some part of Poland.

HAMLET. Who commands them, sir?

CAPTAIN. The nephew to Old Norway, Fortinbras.

HAMLET. Goes it against the main
of Poland, sir,   15
Or for some frontier?

CAPTAIN. Truly to speak, and with
no addition,
We go to gain a little patch of ground
That hath in it no profit but the name.
To pay five ducats, five, I would not
farm it;   20
Nor will it yield to Norway or the Pole
A ranker rate, should it be sold in fee.

HAMLET. Why, then the Polack
never will defend it.

CAPTAIN. Yes, it is already garrison'd.

HAMLET. Two thousand souls and
twenty thousand ducats   25
Will not debate the question of this
straw:
This is the imposthume[77] of much wealth
and peace,
That inward breaks, and shows no cause
without
Why the man dies. I humbly thank you,
sir.

CAPTAIN. God be wi' you, sir. (*Exit.*)

ROSENCRANTZ.   Will 't please you
go, my lord?   30

HAMLET. I'll be with you straight.
Go a little before.

               (*Exeunt all but* HAMLET.)

How all occasions do inform against me,
And spur my dull revenge! What is a
man,
If his chief good and market of his time
Be but to sleep and feed? a beast, no
more.   35
Sure, he that made us with such large
discourse,
Looking before and after, gave us not
That capability and god-like reason

To fust[78] in us unused. Now, whether it
be   39
Bestial oblivion, or some craven scruple
Of thinking too precisely on the event,—
A thought which, quarter'd, hath but
one part wisdom
And ever three parts coward,—I do not
know
Why yet I live to say "this thing's to do,"
Sith I have cause, and will, and strength,
and means,   45
To do 't. Examples gross as earth exhort
me:
Witness this army, of such mass and
charge,
Led by a delicate and tender prince,
Whose spirit with divine ambition puff'd
Makes mouths at the invisible event,   50
Exposing what is mortal and unsure
To all that fortune, death and danger
dare,
Even for an egg-shell. Rightly to be great
Is not to stir without great argument,
But greatly to find quarrel in a straw
When honor's at the stake. How stand I
then,   56
That have a father kill'd, a mother
stain'd,
Excitements of my reason and my blood,
And let all sleep, while to my shame I see
The imminent death of twenty thousand
men,   60
That for a fantasy and trick of fame
Go to their graves like beds, fight for a
plot
Whereon the numbers cannot try the
cause,
Which is not tomb enough and continent
To hide the slain? O, from this time
forth,   65
My thoughts be bloody, or be nothing
worth!   (*Exit.*)

SCENE 5

(ELSINORE. *A room in the castle.*)
(*Enter* QUEEN, HORATIO, *and a*
GENTLEMAN.)

---

[77] abscess

[78] grow musty

QUEEN.   I will not speak with her.

GENTLEMAN.   She is importunate, indeed distract:
Her mood will needs be pitied.

QUEEN.   What would she have?

GENTLEMAN.   She speaks much of her father, says she hears
There's tricks i' the world, and hems and beats her heart,   5
Spurns enviously at straws; speaks things in doubt,
That carry but half sense: her speech is nothing,
Yet the unshaped use of it doth move
The hearers to collection; they aim at it,
And botch the words up fit to their own thoughts;   10
Which, as her winks and nods and gestures yield them,
Indeed would make one think there might be thought,
Though nothing sure, yet much unhappily.

HORATIO.   'Twere good she were spoken with, for she may strew
Dangerous conjectures in ill-breeding minds.   15

QUEEN.   Let her come in.

(*Exit* HORATIO.)

(*Aside.*) To my sick soul, as sin's true nature is,
Each toy seems prologue to some great amiss:
So full of artless jealousy is guilt,
It spills itself in fearing to be spilt.   20

(*Re-enter* HORATIO, *with* OPHELIA.)

OPHELIA.   Where is the beauteous majesty of Denmark?

QUEEN.   How now, Ophelia!

OPHELIA (*sings*).

How should I your true love know
    From another one?
By his cockle hat and staff   25
    And his sandal shoon.

QUEEN.   Alas, sweet lady, what imports this song?

OPHELIA.   Say you? nay, pray you, mark.

(*Sings.*)

He is dead and gone, lady,
    He is dead and gone;   30
At his head a grass-green turf,
    At his heels a stone.

QUEEN.   Nay, but Ophelia,—

OPHELIA.   Pray you, mark.

(*Sings.*)

White his shroud as the mountain snow,   35

(*Enter* KING.)

QUEEN.   Alas, look here, my lord.

OPHELIA (*sings*).

    Larded with sweet flowers;
Which bewept to the grave did go
    With true-love showers.

KING.   How do you, pretty lady?   40

OPHELIA.   Well, God 'ild[79] you! They say the owl was a baker's daughter. Lord, we know what we are, but know not what we may be. God be at your table!

KING.   Conceit upon her father.   45

OPHELIA.   Pray you, let's have no words of this; but when they ask you what it means, say you this:
(*Sings.*)

To-morrow is Saint Valentine's day
    All in the morning betime,
And I a maid at your window,   50
    To be your Valentine.
Then up he rose, and donn'd his clothes,
    And dupp'd the chamber-door,
Let in the maid, that out a maid
    Never departed more.   55

KING.   Pretty Ophelia!

OPHELIA.   Indeed, la, without an oath, I'll make an end on 't:
(*Sings.*)

By Gis and by Saint Charity,
    Alack, and fie for shame!   60
Young men will do 't, if they come to 't;
    By cock, they are to blame.
Quoth she, before you tumbled me,
    You promised me to wed.

He answers:

So would I ha' done, by yonder sun,   65
    An thou hadst not come to my bed.

[79] reward

KING. How long hath she been thus?

OPHELIA. I hope all will be well. We must be patient: but I cannot choose but weep, to think they should lay him i' the cold ground. My brother shall know of it: and so I thank you for your good counsel. Come, my coach! Good night, ladies; good night, sweet ladies; good night, good night.

(*Exit.*)

KING. Follow her close; give her good watch, I pray you.   75

(*Exit* HORATIO.)

O, this is the poison of deep grief; it springs

All from her father's death. O Gertrude, Gertrude,

When sorrows come, they come not single spies,

But in battalions! First, her father slain:

Next, your son gone; and he most violent author   80

Of his own just remove: the people muddied,

Thick and unwholesome in their thoughts and whispers,

For good Polonius' death; and we have done but greenly,

In hugger-mugger[80] to inter him: poor Ophelia

Divided from herself and her fair judgment,   85

Without the which we are pictures, or mere beasts:

Last, and as much containing as all these,

Her brother is in secret come from France,

Feeds on his wonder, keeps himself in clouds,

And wants not buzzers to infect his ear   90

With pestilent speeches of his father's death;

Wherein necessity, of matter beggar'd,

Will nothing stick our person to arraign

In ear and ear. O my dear Gertrude, this,

Like to a murdering-piece, in many places   95

Gives me superfluous death.

(*A noise within.*)

QUEEN.   Alack, what noise is this?

KING. Where are my Switzers? Let them guard the door.

(*Enter another* GENTLEMAN.)

What is the matter?

GENTLEMAN.   Save yourself, my lord:

The ocean, overpeering of his list,[81]

Eats not the flats with more impetuous haste   100

Than young Laertes, in a riotous head,

O'erbears your officers. The rabble call him lord;

And, as the world were now but to begin,

Antiquity forgot, custom not known,

The ratifiers and props of every word,

They cry "Choose we; Laertes shall be king!"   106

Caps, hands and tongues applaud it to the clouds,

"Laertes shall be king, Laertes king!"

QUEEN. How cheerfully on the false trail they cry!

O, this is counter, you false Danish dogs!

(*Noise within.*)   110

KING. The doors are broke.

(*Enter* LAERTES, *armed;* DANES *following.*)

LAERTES. Where is this king? Sirs, stand you all without.

DANES. No, let's come in.

LAERTES. I pray you, give me leave.

DANES. We will, we will.

(*They retire within the door.*)

LAERTES. I thank you: keep the door. O thou vile king,   115

Give me my father!

QUEEN.   Calmly, good Laertes.

LAERTES. That drop of blood that's calm proclaims me bastard;

Cries cuckold to my father; brands the harlot

---

[80] haste   [81] shore

Even here, between the chaste un-
    smirchèd brows   *119*
Of my true mother.
    KING.   What is the cause, Laertes,
That thy rebellion looks so giant-like?
Let him go, Gertrude; do not fear our
    person:
There's such divinity doth hedge a king,
That treason can but peep to what it
    would,   *124*
Acts little of his will. Tell me, Laertes,
Why thou art thus incensed: let him go,
    Gertrude:
Speak, man.
    LAERTES.   Where is my father?
    KING.   Dead.
    QUEEN.   But not by him.
    KING.   Let him demand his fill.
    LAERTES.   How came he dead? I'll
    not be juggled with: *130*
To hell, allegiance! vows, to the blackest
    devil!
Conscience and grace, to the profoundest
    pit!
I dare damnation: to this point I stand,
That both the worlds I give to negligence,
Let come what comes; only I'll be re-
    venged   *135*
Most throughly for my father.
    KING.   Who shall stay you?
    LAERTES.   My will, not all the world:
And for my means, I'll husband them so
    well,
They shall go far with little.
    KING.   Good Laertes,
If you desire to know the certainty   *140*
Of your dear father's death, is 't writ in
    your revenge
That, swoopstake, you will draw both
    friend and foe,
Winner and loser?
    LAERTES.   None but his enemies.
    KING.   Will you know them then?
    LAERTES.   To his good friends thus
    wide I'll ope my arms;   *145*
And, like the kind life-rendering pelican,
Repast them with my blood.
    KING.   Why, now you speak
Like a good child and a true gentleman.

That I am guiltless of your father's
    death,   *149*
And am most sensibly in grief for it,
It shall as level to your judgment pierce
As day does to your eye.
    DANES (*within*).   Let her come in.
    LAERTES.   How now! what noise is
    that?
(*Re-enter* OPHELIA.)
O heat, dry up my brains! tears seven
    times salt,
Burn out the sense and virtue of mine
    eye!   *155*
By heaven, thy madness shall be paid
    with weight,
Till our scale turn the beam. O rose of
    May!
Dear maid, kind sister, sweet Ophelia!
O heavens! is 't possible a young maid's
    wits
Should be as mortal as an old man's
    life?   *160*
Nature is fine in love, and where 'tis fine
It sends some precious instance of itself
After the thing it loves.
    OPHELIA (*sings*).

    They bore him barefaced on the bier:
    Hey non nonny, nonny, hey nonny: *165*
    And in his grave rain'd many a tear,—

Fare you well, my dove!
    LAERTES.   Hadst thou thy wits, and
    didst persuade revenge,
It could not move thus.
    OPHELIA (*sings*).

    You must sing a-down a-down,   *170*
    An you call him a-down-a.

O, how the wheel becomes it! It is the
false steward, that stole his master's
daughter.
    LAERTES.   This nothing's more than
matter.
    OPHELIA.   There's rosemary, that's
for remembrance: pray you, love, remember: and there is pansies, that's for
thoughts.
    LAERTES.   A document in madness;
thoughts and remembrance fitted.   *179*

OPHELIA.   There's fennel for you, and columbines: there's rue for you: and here's some for me: we may call it herb-grace o' Sundays: O, you must wear your rue with a difference. There's a daisy: I would give you some violets, but they withered all when my father died: they say he made a good end,—   *186*
(*Sings.*)

For bonnie sweet Robin is all my joy.

LAERTES.   Thought   and   affliction, passion, hell itself,
She turns to favor and to prettiness.
OPHELIA (*sings*).

And will he not come again?   *190*
And will he not come again?
No, no, he is dead,
Go to thy death-bed,
He never will come again.
His beard was as white as snow,   *195*
All flaxen was his poll:
He is gone, he is gone,
And we cast away moan:
God ha' mercy on his soul!

And of all Christian souls, I pray God.
God be wi' you.   *200*
(*Exit.*)
LAERTES.   Do you see this, O God?
KING.   Laertes, I must commune with your grief,
Or you deny me right. Go but apart,
Make choice of whom your wisest friends you will,
And they shall hear and judge 'twixt you and me: *205*
If by direct or by collateral hand
They find us touched, we will our king-dom give,
Our crown, our life, and all that we call ours,
To you in satisfaction; but if not,
Be you content to lend your patience to us,   *210*
And we shall jointly labor with your soul
To give it due content.
LAERTES.   Let this be so;
His means of death, his obscure funeral,

No trophy, sword, nor hatchment o'er his bones,   *214*
No noble rite nor formal ostentation,
Cry to be heard, as 'twere from heaven to earth,
That I must call 't in question.
KING.   So you shall;
And where the offense is let the great axe fall.
I pray you, go with me.   (*Exeunt.*)

SCENE 6

(*Another room in the castle.*)
(*Enter* HORATIO *and a* SERVANT.)

HORATIO.   What are they that would speak with me?
SERVANT.   Sailors, sir: they say they have letters for you.
HORATIO.   Let them come in.
(*Exit* SERVANT.)
I do not know from what part of the world
I should be greeted, if not from Lord Hamlet.
(*Enter* SAILORS.)
FIRST SAILOR.   God bless you, sir.
HORATIO.   Let him bless thee too.
FIRST SAILOR.   He shall, sir, an't please him.
There's a letter for you, sir; it comes from the ambassador that was bound for England; if your name be Horatio, as I am let to know it is.   *11*
HORATIO (*reads*).   "Horatio, when thou shalt have overlooked this, give these fellows some means to the king: they have letters for him. Ere we were two days old at sea, a pirate of very warlike appointment gave us chase. Find-ing ourselves too slow of sail, we put on a compelled valor, and in the grapple I boarded them: on the instant they got clear of our ship; so I alone became their prisoner. They have dealt with me like thieves of mercy: but they knew what they did; I am to do a good turn for them. Let the king have the letters I have

sent; and repair thou to me with as much speed as thou wouldst fly death. I have words to speak in thine ear will make thee dumb; yet are they much too light for the bore of the matter. These good fellows will bring thee where I am. Rosencrantz and Guildenstern hold their course for England: of them I have much to tell you. Farewell.

"He that thou knowest thine,

HAMLET"

Come, I will make you way for these your letters;
And do't the speedier, that you may direct me
To him from whom you brought them.
(*Exeunt.*) 34

SCENE 7

(*Another room in the castle.*)
(*Enter* KING *and* LAERTES.)

KING. Now must your conscience my acquittance seal,
And you must put me in your heart for friend,
Sith you have heard, and with a knowing ear,
That he which hath your noble father slain
Pursued my life. 4
LAERTES. It well appears: but tell me
Why you proceeded not against these feats,
So crimeful and so capital in nature,
As by your safety, wisdom, all things else,
You mainly were stirr'd up.
KING. O, for two special reasons,
Which may to you perhaps seem much unsinew'd, 10
But yet to me they are strong. The queen his mother
Lives almost by his looks; and for my-self—
My virtue or my plague, be it either which—
She's so conjunctive to my life and soul,

That, as the star moves not but in his sphere, 15
I could not but by her. The other motive,
Why to a public count I might not go,
Is the great love the general gender bear him;
Who, dipping all his faults in their af-fection,
Would, like the spring that turneth wood to stone, 20
Convert his gyves[82] to graces; so that my arrows,
Too slightly timber'd for so loud a wind,
Would have reverted to my bow again
And not where I had aim'd them.
LAERTES. And so have I a noble father lost; 25
A sister driven into desperate terms,
Whose worth, if praises may go back again,
Stood challenger on mount of all the age
For her perfections: but my revenge will come.
KING. Break not your sleep for that: you must not think 30
That we are made of stuff so flat and dull
That we can let our beard be shook with danger
And think it pastime. You shortly shall hear more:
I loved your father, and we love ourself;
And that, I hope, will teach you to imagine— 35
(*Enter a* MESSENGER, *with letters.*)
How now! what news?
MESSENGER. Letters, my lord, from Hamlet:
This to your majesty; this to the queen.
KING. From Hamlet! who brought them?
MESSENGER. Sailors, my lord, they say; I saw them not:
They were given me by Claudio; he re-ceived them 40
Of him that brought them.
KING. Laertes, you shall hear them.
Leave us. (*Exit* MESSENGER.)

82 shackles

(*Reads.*) "High and mighty, you shall know I am set naked on your kingdom. To-morrow shall I beg leave to see your kingly eyes: when I shall, first asking your pardon thereunto, recount the occasion of my sudden and more strange return.   HAMLET."
What should this mean? Are all the rest
   come back?   49
Or is it some abuse, and no such thing?
   LAERTES. Know you the hand?
   KING.   'Tis   Hamlet's   character.
   "Naked"!
And in a postscript here, he says "alone."
Can you advise me?
   LAERTES. I'm lost in it, my lord. But
   let him come;   55
It warms the very sickness in my heart,
That I shall live and tell him to his teeth,
"Thus diddest thou."
   KING.   If it be so, Laertes,—
As how should it be so? how otherwise?—
Will you be ruled by me?
   LAERTES: Aye, my lord; 60
So you will not o'errule me to a peace.
   KING. To thine own peace. If he be
   now return'd,
As checking at his voyage, and that he
   means
No more to undertake it, I will work him
To an exploit now ripe in my de-
   vice,   65
Under the which he shall not choose but
   fall:
And for his death no wind of blame shall
   breathe,
But even his mother shall unchange the
   practice,
And call it accident.
   LAERTES.   My lord, I will be ruled;
The rather, if you could devise it so 70
That I might be the organ.
   KING.   It falls right.
You have been talk'd of since your travel
   much,
And that in Hamlet's hearing, for a
   quality
Wherein, they say, you shine; your sum
   of parts

Did not together pluck such envy from
   him,   75
As did that one, and that, in my regard,
Of the unworthiest siege.
   LAERTES.   What part is that, my lord?
   KING. A very riband in the cap of
   youth,
Yet needful too; for youth no less be-
   comes
The light and careless livery that it
   wears   80
Than settled age his sables and his weeds,
Importing health and graveness. Two
   months since,
Here was a gentleman of Normandy:—
I've seen myself, and served against, the
   French,
And they can well on horseback: but
   this gallant   85
Had witchcraft in 't; he grew unto his
   seat,
And to such wondrous doing brought
   this horse
As had he been incorpsed[83] and demi-
   natured
With the brave beast: so far he topp'd
   my thought   89
That I, in forgery of shapes and tricks,
Come short of what he did.
   LAERTES.   A Norman was 't?
   KING. A Norman.
   LAERTES. Upon my life, Lamond.
   KING.   The very same.
   LAERTES. I know him well: he is the
   brooch indeed
And gem of all the nation.   95
   KING. He made confession of you,
And gave you such a masterly report,
For art and exercise in your defense,
And for your rapier most especial,
That he cried out, 'twould be a sight in-
   deed   100
If one could match you: the scrimers[84]
   of their nation,
He swore, had neither motion, guard,
   nor eye,

[83] united
[84] fencers

If you opposed them. Sir, this report
of his
Did Hamlet so envenom with his envy
That he could nothing do but wish and
beg   105
Your sudden coming o'er, to play with
him.
Now, out of this—
    LAERTES.   What out of this, my lord?
    KING.   Laertes, was your father dear
    to you?
Or are you like the painting of a sorrow,
A face without a heart?
    LAERTES.   Why ask you this? *110*
    KING.   Not that I think you did not
    love your father,
But that I know love is begun by time,
And that I see, in passages of proof,
Time qualifies the spark and fire of it.
There lives within the very flame of
love   115
A kind of wick or snuff that will abate it;
And nothing is at a like goodness still,
For goodness, growing to a plurisy,[85]
Dies in his own too much: that we
would do
We should do when we would; for this
"would" changes   *120*
And hath abatements and delays as many
As there are tongues, are hands, are ac-
cidents,
And then this "should" is like a spend-
thrift sigh,
That hurts by easing. But, to the quick
o' the ulcer:
Hamlet comes back: what would you
undertake,   *125*
To show yourself your father's son in deed
More than in words?
    LAERTES.   To cut his throat i' the
    church.
    KING.   No place indeed should mur-
    der sanctuarize;
Revenge should have no bounds. But,
good Laertes,
Will you do this, keep close within your
chamber.   *130*

Hamlet return'd shall know you are come
home:
We'll put on those shall praise your
excellence
And set a double varnish on the fame
The Frenchman gave you; bring you in
fine together
And wager on your heads: he, being
remiss,   *135*
Most generous and free from all con-
triving,
Will not peruse the foils, so that with
ease,
Or with a little shuffling, you may choose
A sword unbated,[86] and in a pass of
practice
Requite him for your father.
    LAERTES.   I will do 't. *140*
And for that purpose I'll anoint my
sword.
I bought an unction of a mountebank,
So mortal that but dip a knife in it,
Where it draws blood no cataplasm[87] so
rare,
Collected from all simples that have
virtue   *145*
Under the moon, can save the thing
from death
That is but scratch'd withal: I'll touch
my point
With this contagion, that, if I gall him
slightly,
It may be death.
    KING.   Let's further think of this,
Weigh what convenience both of time
and means   *150*
May fit us to our shape: if this should
fail,
And that our drift look through our bad
performance,
'Twere better not assay'd: therefore this
project
Should have a back or second, that
might hold
If this did blast in proof. Soft! let me
see: *155*

[85] an excess

[86] lacking a button to blunt the tip
[87] poultice

We'll make a solemn wager on your
cunnings:
I ha 't:
When in your motion you are hot and
dry—
As make your bouts more violent to
that end—
And that he calls for drink, I'll have
prepared him   *160*
A chalice for the nonce; whereon but
sipping,
If he by chance escape your venom'd
stuck,
Our purpose may hold there. But stay,
what noise?
(*Enter* QUEEN.)
How now, sweet queen!
    QUEEN. One woe doth tread upon
another's heel,
So fast they follow: your sister's drown'd,
Laertes.   *165*
    LAERTES. Drown'd! O, where?
    QUEEN. There is a willow grows
aslant a brook,
That shows his hoar leaves in the glassy
stream;
There with fantastic garlands did she
come
Of crow-flowers, nettles, daisies, and long
purples,   *170*
That liberal shepherds give a grosser
name,
But our cold maids do dead men's fingers
call them:
There, on the pendent boughs her coro-
net weeds
Clambering to hang, an envious sliver
broke;
When down her weedy trophies and her-
self   *175*
Fell in the weeping brook. Her clothes
spread wide,
And mermaid-like a while they bore
her up:
Which time she chanted snatches of old
tunes,
As one incapable of her own distress,
Or like a creature native and indued   *180*

Unto that element: but long it could
not be
Till that her garments, heavy with their
drink,
Pull'd the poor wretch from her melo-
dious lay
To muddy death.
    LAERTES. Alas, then she is drown'd!
    QUEEN. Drown'd, drown'd.   *185*
    LAERTES. Too much of water hast
thou, poor Ophelia,
And therefore I forbid my tears: but yet
It is our trick; nature her custom holds,
Let shame say what it will: when these
are gone,   *189*
The woman will be out. Adieu, my lord:
I have a speech of fire that fain would
blaze,
But that this folly douts[88] it.   (*Exit.*)
    KING.   Let's follow, Gertrude:
How much I had to do to calm his rage!
Now fear I this will give it start again;
Therefore let's follow. (*Exeunt.*)   *195*

Act V

SCENE 1

(*A churchyard.*)
(*Enter two* CLOWNS, *with spades, &c.*)

FIRST CLOWN. Is she to be buried
in Christian burial that willfully seeks
her own salvation?
SECOND CLOWN. I tell thee she is;
and therefore make her grave straight:
the crowner[89] hath sat on her, and finds
it Christian burial.
FIRST CLOWN. How can that be, unless she drowned herself in her own
defense?   7
SECOND CLOWN. Why, 'tis found so.
FIRST CLOWN. It must be "se of-
fendendo";[90] it cannot be else. For here

---

[88] extinguishes
[89] coroner
[90] the clown's error for *se defendendo,* in
self-defense

lies the point: if I drown myself wittingly, it argues an act: and an act hath three branches; it is, to act, to do, and to perform: argal,[91] she drowned herself wittingly.   *14*

SECOND CLOWN.   Nay, but hear you, goodman delver.

FIRST CLOWN.   Give me leave. Here lies the water; good: here stands the man; good: if the man go to this water and drown himself, it is, will he, nill he, he goes; mark you that; but if the water come to him and drown him, he drowns not himself: argal, he that is not guilty of his own death shortens not his own life.   *22*

SECOND CLOWN.   But is this law?

FIRST CLOWN.   Aye, marry, is 't; crowner's quest law.

SECOND CLOWN.   Will you ha' the truth on 't? If this had not been a gentlewoman, she should have been buried out o' Christian burial.   *28*

FIRST CLOWN.   Why, there thou say'st: and the more pity that great folk should have countenance in this world to drown or hang themselves, more than their even Christian. Come, my spade. There is no ancient gentlemen but gardeners, ditchers and grave-makers: they hold up Adam's profession.   *35*

SECOND CLOWN.   Was he a gentleman?

FIRST CLOWN.   A' was the first that ever bore arms.   *38*

SECOND CLOWN.   Why, he had none.

FIRST CLOWN.   What, art a heathen? How dost thou understand the Scripture? The Scripture says Adam digged: could he dig without arms? I'll put another question to thee: if thou answerest me not to the purpose, confess thyself— *44*

SECOND CLOWN.   Go to.

FIRST CLOWN.   What is he that builds stronger than either the mason, the shipwright, or the carpenter?

SECOND CLOWN.   The gallows-maker;

for that frame outlives a thousand tenants.   *50*

FIRST CLOWN.   I like thy wit well, in good faith: the gallows does well; but how does it well? it does well to those that do ill: now, thou dost ill to say the gallows is built stronger than the church: argal, the gallows may do well to thee. To 't again, come.

SECOND CLOWN.   "Who builds stronger than a mason, a shipwright, or a carpenter?"

FIRST CLOWN.   Aye, tell me that, and unyoke.

SECOND CLOWN.   Marry, now I can tell.   *60*

FIRST CLOWN.   To 't.

SECOND CLOWN.   Mass, I cannot tell.

(*Enter* HAMLET *and* HORATIO, *at a distance.*)

FIRST CLOWN.   Cudgel thy brains no more about it, for your dull ass will not mend his pace with beating, and when you are asked this question next, say "a grave-maker": the houses that he makes last till doomsday. Go, get thee to Yaughan; fetch me a stoup of liquor.

(*Exit* SECOND CLOWN.)
(FIRST CLOWN *digs and sings.*)

In youth when I did love, did love,
  Methought it was very sweet,   *70*
To contract, O, the time, for, ah, my behove,
  O, methought, there was nothing meet.

HAMLET.   Has this fellow no feeling of his business that he sings at grave-making?

HORATIO.   Custom hath made it in him a property of easiness.   *76*

HAMLET.   'Tis e'en so: the hand of little employment hath the daintier sense.

FIRST CLOWN (*sings*).

  But age, with his stealing steps,
    Hath claw'd me in his clutch,   *80*
  And hath shipped me intil the land,
    As if I had never been such.

(*Throws up a skull.*)

HAMLET.   That skull had a tongue

---

[91] *ergo:* therefore

in it, and could sing once: how the knave jowls[92] it to the ground, as if it were Cain's jaw-bone, that did the first murder! It might be the pate of a politician, which this ass now o'er-reaches; one that would circumvent God, might it not?

HORATIO.   It might, my lord.   89

HAMLET.   Or of a courtier, which could say, "Good morrow, sweet lord! How dost thou, good lord?" This might be my lord such-a-one, that praised my lord such-a-one's horse, when he meant to beg it; might it not?

HORATIO.   Aye, my lord.   95

HAMLET.   Why, e'en so: and now my Lady Worm's; chapless,[93] and knocked about the mazzard[94] with a sexton's spade: here's fine revolution, an we had the trick to see 't. Did these bones cost no more the breeding, but to play at loggats[95] with 'em? mine ache to think on 't.   101

FIRST CLOWN (sings).

A pick-axe, and a spade, a spade,
    For a shrouding sheet:
O, a pit of clay for to be made
    For such a guest is meet.   105

(Throws up another skull.)

HAMLET.   There's another: why may not that be the skull of a lawyer? Where be his quiddities now, his quillets,[96] his cases, his tenures, and his tricks? why does he suffer this rude knave now to knock him about the sconce with a dirty shovel, and will not tell him of his action of battery? Hum! This fellow might be in 's time a great buyer of land, with his statutes, his recognizances, his fines, his double vouchers, his recoveries: is this the fine of his fines and the recovery of his recoveries, to have his fine pate full

of fine dirt? will his vouchers vouch him no more of his purchases, and double ones too, than the length and breadth of a pair of indentures? The very conveyances of his lands will hardly lie in this box; and must the inheritor himself have no more, ha?   121

HORATIO.   Not a jot more, my lord.

HAMLET.   Is not parchment made of sheep-skins?

HORATIO.   Aye, my lord, and of calfskins too.   124

HAMLET.   They are sheep and calves which seek out assurance in that. I will speak to this fellow. Whose grave's this, sirrah?

FIRST CLOWN.   Mine, sir.

(Sings)

O, a pit of clay for to be made
    For such a guest is meet.   130

HAMLET.   I think it be thine indeed, for thou liest in 't.

FIRST CLOWN.   You lie out on 't, sir, and therefore it is not yours: for my part, I do not lie in 't, and yet it is mine.

HAMLET.   Thou dost lie in 't, to be in 't and say it is thine; 'tis for the dead, not for the quick; therefore thou liest.

FIRST CLOWN.   'Tis a quick lie, sir; 'twill away again, from me to you.   140

Hamlet.   What man dost thou dig it for?

FIRST CLOWN.   For no man, sir.

HAMLET.   What woman then?

FIRST CLOWN.   For none neither.

HAMLET.   Who is to be buried in 't?

FIRST CLOWN.   One that was a woman, sir; but, rest her soul, she's dead.   147

HAMLET.   How absolute the knave is! we must speak by the card, or equivocation will undo us. By the Lord, Horatio, these three years I have taken note of it; the age is grown so picked that the toe of the peasant comes so near the heel of the courtier, he galls his kibe.[97] How long hast thou been a grave-maker?

92 knocks
93 lacking jaws; here, lacking the lower jaw
94 head
95 a game played with small logs
96 subtle, legalistic distinctions and arguments

97 hurts his chilblains

FIRST CLOWN. Of all the days i' the year, I came to 't that day that our last King Hamlet o'ercame Fortinbras. *157*

HAMLET. How long is that since?

FIRST CLOWN. Cannot you tell that? every fool can tell that: it was that very day that young Hamlet was born: he that is mad, and sent into England.

HAMLET. Aye, marry, why was he sent into England?

FIRST CLOWN. Why, because he was mad; he shall recover his wits there: or, if he do not, 'tis no great matter there.

HAMLET. Why?

FIRST CLOWN. 'Twill not be seen in him there; there the men are as mad as he. *170*

HAMLET. How came he mad?

FIRST CLOWN. Very strangely, they say.

HAMLET. How "strangely"?

FIRST CLOWN. Faith, e'en with losing his wits.

HAMLET. Upon what ground?

FIRST CLOWN. Why, here in Denmark: I have been sexton here, man and boy, thirty years.

HAMLET. How long will a man lie i' the earth ere he rot? *179*

FIRST CLOWN. I' faith, if he be not rotten before he die—as we have many pocky corses now-a-days, that will scarce hold the laying in—he will last you some eight year or nine year: a tanner will last you nine year. *184*

HAMLET. Why he more than another?

FIRST CLOWN. Why, sir, his hide is so tanned with his trade that he will keep out water a great while; and your water is a sore decayer of your whoreson dead body. Here's a skull now: this skull has lain in the earth three and twenty years.

HAMLET. Whose was it? *192*

FIRST CLOWN. A whoreson mad fellow's it was: whose do you think it was?

HAMLET. Nay, I know not.

FIRST CLOWN. A pestilence on him for a mad rogue! a' poured a flagon of Rhenish on my head once. This same skull, sir, was Yorick's skull, the king's jester.

HAMLET. This?

FIRST CLOWN. E'en that. *201*

HAMLET. Let me see. (*Takes the skull.*) Alas, poor Yorick! I knew him, Horatio: a fellow of infinite jest, of most excellent fancy: he hath borne me on his back a thousand times; and now how abhorred in my imagination it is! my gorge rises at it. Here hung those lips that I have kissed I know not how oft. Where be your gibes now? your gambols? your songs? your flashes of merriment, that were wont to set the table on a roar? Not one now, to mock your own grinning? quite chap-fallen? Now get you to my lady's chamber, and tell her, let her paint an inch thick, to this favor she must come; make her laugh at that. Prithee, Horatio, tell me one thing.

HORATIO. What's that, my lord?

HAMLET. Dost thou think Alexander looked o' this fashion i' the earth?

HORATIO. E'en so. *220*

HAMLET. And smelt so? pah!

(*Puts down the skull.*)

HORATIO. E'en so, my lord.

HAMLET. To what base uses we may return, Horatio! Why may not imagination trace the noble dust of Alexander, till he find it stopping a bung-hole? *226*

HORATIO. 'Twere to consider too curiously, to consider so.

HAMLET. No, faith, not a jot; but to follow him thither with modesty enough and likelihood to lead it: as thus: Alexander died, Alexander was buried, Alexander returneth into dust; the dust is earth; of earth we make loam; and why of that loam, whereto he was converted, might they not stop a beer-barrel? *235*

Imperious Cæsar, dead and turn'd to clay,
Might stop a hole to keep the wind away:
O, that that earth, which kept the world in
    awe,

Should patch a wall to expel the winter's
   flaw!

But soft! but soft! aside: here comes the
   king.   240
(*Enter* PRIESTS *&c, in procession; the*
Corpse of Ophelia, LAERTES *and* MOURN-
ERS *following;* KING, QUEEN, *their trains,*
&c.)
The queen, the courtiers: who is this
   they follow?
And with such maimèd rites? This doth
   betoken
The corse they follow did with desperate
   hand
Fordo its own life: 'twas of some estate.
Couch we awhile, and mark.   245
              (*Retiring with* HORATIO.)
LAERTES. What ceremony else?
HAMLET. That is Laertes, a very
   noble youth: mark.
LAERTES. What ceremony else?
FIRST PRIEST. Her obsequies have
   been as far enlarged
As we have warranty: her death was
   doubtful;   250
And, but that great command o'ersways
   the order
She should in ground unsanctified have
   lodged
Till the last trumpet; for charitable
   prayers,
Shards, flints and pebbles should be
   thrown on her: 254
Yet here she is allow'd her virgin crants,[98]
Her maiden strewments[99] and the bring-
   ing home
Of bell and burial.
LAERTES. Must there no more be
   done?
FIRST PRIEST.   No more be done:
We should profane the service of the
   dead
To sing a requiem and such rest to her
As to peace-parted souls.   261
LAERTES.   Lay her i' the earth:
And from her fair and unpolluted flesh

[98] garlands
[99] strewing of flowers

May violets spring! I tell thee, churlish
   priest,
A ministering angel shall my sister be,
When thou liest howling.
   HAMLET.   What, the fair Ophelia!
QUEEN (*scattering flowers*). Sweets to
   the sweet: farewell!   266
I hoped thou shouldst have been my
   Hamlet's wife;
I thought thy bride-bed to have deck'd,
   sweet maid,
And not have strew'd thy grave.
   LAERTES.   O, treble woe
Fall ten times treble on that cursèd head
Whose wicked deed thy most ingenious
   sense   271
Deprived thee of! Hold off the earth a
   while,
Till I have caught her once more in mine
   arms.
                (*Leaps into the grave.*)
Now pile your dust upon the quick and
   dead,   274
Till of this flat a mountain you have made
To o'ertop old Pelion or the skyish head
Of blue Olympus.[100]
   HAMLET (*advancing*). What is he
   whose grief
Bears such an emphasis? whose phrase
   of sorrow
Conjures the wandering stars and makes
   them stand
Like wonder-wounded hearers? This is I,
Hamlet the Dane.   281
                (*Leaps into the grave.*)
   LAERTES. The devil take thy soul!
                (*Grappling with him.*)
   HAMLET.   Thou pray'st not well.
I prithee, take thy fingers from my throat;
For, though I am not splenitive[101] and
   rash,
Yet have I in me something dangerous,
Which let thy wiseness fear. Hold off thy
   hand.   286

[100] Greek mountain ranges said in mythology to have been piled up with Ossa (see
note 103) by giants in an attempt to reach
heaven
[101] easily angered

KING.   Pluck them asunder.

QUEEN.   Hamlet, Hamlet!

ALL.   Gentlemen,—

HORATIO.   Good my lord, be quiet.

(*The* ATTENDANTS *part them, and
they come out of the grave.*)

HAMLET.   Why, I will fight with him
    upon this theme

Until my eyelids will no longer wag.   *290*

QUEEN.   O my son, what theme?

HAMLET.   I loved Ophelia: forty thou-
    sand brothers

Could not, with all their quantity of love,

Make up my sum. What wilt thou do for
    her?

KING.   O, he is mad, Laertes.   *295*

QUEEN.   For love of God, forbear
    him.

HAMLET.   'Swounds, show me what
    thou 'lt do:

Woo't weep? woo't fight? woo't fast?
    woo't tear thyself?   *298*

Woo't drink up eisel?[102] eat a crocodile?

I'll do't. Dost thou come here to whine?

To outface me with leaping in her grave?

Be buried quick with her, and so will I:

And, if thou prate of mountains, let them
    throw

Millions of acres on us, till our ground,

Singeing his pate against the burning
    zone,   *305*

Make Ossa[103] like a wart! Nay, an thou
    'lt mouth,

I'll rant as well as thou.

QUEEN.   This is mere madness:

And thus a while the fit will work on
    him;

Anon, as patient as the female dove

When that her golden couplets are dis-
    closed,   *310*

His silence will sit drooping,

HAMLET.   Hear you, sir;

What is the reason that you use me thus?

I loved you ever: but it is no matter;

Let Hercules himself do what he may,

The cat will mew, and dog will have his
    day.   *315*

(*Exit.*)

KING.   I pray thee, good Horatio,
    wait upon him.

(*Exit* HORATIO.)

(*To* LAERTES.) Strengthen your pa-
    tience in our last night's speech;

We'll put the matter to the present push.

Good Gertrude, set some watch over
    your son.   *319*

This grave shall have a living monument:

An hour of quiet shortly shall we see;

Till then, in patience our proceeding be.

(*Exeunt.*)

SCENE 2

(*A hall in the castle.*)

(*Enter* HAMLET *and* HORATIO.)

HAMLET.   So much for this, sir: now
    shall you see the other;

You do remember all the circumstance?

HORATIO.   Remember it, my lord?

HAMLET.   Sir, in my heart there was
    a kind of fighting,

That would not let me sleep: methought
    I lay   *5*

Worse than the mutines in the bilboes.[104]
    Rashly,

And praised be rashness for it, let us
    know,

Our indiscretion sometimes serves us well

When our deep plots do pall; and that
    should teach us

There's a divinity that shapes our ends,

Rough-hew them how we will.   *11*

HORATIO.   That is most certain.

HAMLET.   Up from my cabin,

My sea-gown scarf'd about me, in the
    dark

Groped I to find out them; had my desire,

Finger'd their packet, and in fine with-
    drew   *15*

To mine own room again; making so
    bold,

My fears forgetting manners, to unseal

---

[102] vinegar

[103] In his reference to Ossa, Hamlet "rants
as well" as Laertes by citing the same myth.

[104] mutineers in fetters

Their grand commission; where I found,
    Horatio,—
O royal knavery!—an exact command,
Larded with many several sorts of rea-
    sons,   20
Importing Denmark's health and Eng-
    land's too,
With, ho! such bugs and goblins in my
    life,
That, on the supervise, no leisure bated,
No, not to stay the grinding of the axe,
My head should be struck off.
    HORATIO.   Is't possible? 25
    HAMLET. Here's the commission: read
    it at more leisure,
But wilt thou hear now how I did pro-
    ceed?
    HORATIO. I beseech you.
    HAMLET. Being thus be-netted round
    with villainies,—
Ere I could make a prologue to my
    brains,   30
They had begun the play,—I sat me
    down;
Devised a new commission; wrote it fair:
I once did hold it, as our statists do,
A baseness to write fair, and labor'd
    much
How to forget that learning; but, sir,
    now   35
It did me yeoman's service: wilt thou
    know
The effect of what I wrote?
    HORATIO.   Aye, good my lord.
    HAMLET. An earnest conjuration from
    the king,
As England was his faithful tributary,
As love between them like the palm
    might flourish,   40
As peace should still her wheaten garland
    wear
And stand a comma 'tween their amities,
And many such-like "As"es of great
    charge,
That, on the view and knowing of these
    contents,
Without debatement further, more or
    less,   45

He should the bearers put to sudden
    death,
Not shriving-time allow'd.
    HORATIO.   How was this seal'd?
    HAMLET. Why, even in that was
    heaven ordinant.
I had my father's signet in my purse,
Which was the model of that Danish
    seal: 50
Folded the writ up in the form of the
    other;
Subscribed it; gave 't the impression;
    placed it safely,
The changeling never known. Now, the
    next day
Was our sea-fight; and what to this was
    sequent
Thou know'st already.   55
    HORATIO. So Guildenstern and Ro-
    sencrantz go to 't.
    HAMLET. Why, man, they did make
    love to this employment;
They are not near my conscience; their
    defeat
Does by their own insinuation grow:
'Tis dangerous when the baser nature
    comes   60
Between the pass and fell-incensèd points
Of mighty opposites.
    HORATIO.   Why, what a king is this!
    HAMLET. Does it not, think'st thee,
    stand me now upon—
He that hath kill'd my king, and whored
    my mother;
Popp'd in between the election and my
    hopes;   65
Thrown out his angle for my proper life,
And with such cozenage—is't not per-
    fect conscience,
To quit him with this arm? and is't not
    to be damn'd,
To let this canker of our nature come
In further evil?   70
    HORATIO. It must be shortly known
    to him from England
What is the issue of the business there.
    HAMLET. It will be short: the interim
    is mine;

And a man's life's no more than to say
"One."
But I am very sorry, good Horatio, 75
That to Laertes I forgot myself;
For, by the image of my cause, I see
The portraiture of his: I'll court his
favors:
But, sure, the bravery of his grief did
put me
Into a towering passion. 80
HORATIO. Peace! who comes here?
(*Enter* OSRIC.)
OSRIC. Your lordship is right wel-
come back to Denmark.
HAMLET. I humbly thank you, sir.
Dost know this waterfly?
HORATIO. No, my good lord. 85
HAMLET. Thy state is the more gra-
cious, for 'tis a vice to know him. He
hath much land, and fertile: let a beast
be lord of beasts, and his crib shall stand
at the king's mess: 'tis a chough,[105] but,
as I say, spacious in the possession of
dirt. 90
OSRIC. Sweet lord, if your lordship
were at leisure, I should impart a thing
to you from his majesty.
HAMLET. I will receive it, sir, with
all diligence of spirit. Put your bonnet
to his right use; 'tis for the head. 95
OSRIC. I thank your lordship, it is
very hot.
HAMLET. No, believe me, 'tis very
cold; the wind is northerly.
OSRIC. It is indifferent cold, my lord,
indeed. 100
HAMLET. But yet methinks it is very
sultry and hot for my complexion—
OSRIC. Exceedingly, my lord; it is
very sultry, as 'twere,—I cannot tell how.
But, my lord, his majesty bade me signify
to you that he has laid a great wager on
your head: sir, this is the matter—
HAMLET. I beseech you, remember— 108
(HAMLET *moves him to put on his
hat.*)

105 a crow; figuratively, a moneyed boor

OSRIC. Nay, good my lord; for mine
ease, in good faith. Sir, here is newly
come to court Laertes; believe me, an
absolute gentleman, full of most excellent differences, of very soft society and
great showing: indeed, to speak feelingly
of him, he is the card or calendar of
gentry, for you shall find in him the
continent of what part a gentleman would
see. 116
HAMLET. Sir, his definement suffers
no perdition in you; though, I know, to
divide him inventorially would dizzy the
arithmetic of memory, and yet but yaw
neither, in respect of his quick sail. But
in the verity of extolment, I take him to
be a soul of great article, and his infusion
of such dearth and rareness, as, to make
true diction of him, his semblable is his
mirror, and who else would trace him,
his umbrage, nothing more. 126
OSRIC. Your lordship speaks most
infallibly of him.
HAMLET. The concernancy, sir? why
do we wrap the gentleman in our more
rawer breath?
OSRIC. Sir? 130
HORATIO. Is 't not possible to understand in another tongue? You will do 't,
sir, really.
HAMLET. What imports the nomination of this gentleman?
OSRIC. Of Laertes? 135
HORATIO. His purse is empty already;
all's golden words are spent.
HAMLET. Of him, sir.
OSRIC. I know you are not ignorant— 139
HAMLET. I would you did, sir; yet,
in faith, if you did, it would not much
approve me. Well, sir?
OSRIC. You are not ignorant of what
excellence Laertes is— 144
HAMLET. I dare not confess that, lest
I should compare with him in excellence;
but, to know a man well, were to know
himself.
OSRIC. I mean, sir, for his weapon;
but in the imputation laid on him by

them, in his meed[106] he's unfellowed. *150*

HAMLET. What's his weapon?

OSRIC. Rapier and dagger.

HAMLET. That's two of his weapons: but, well.

OSRIC. The king, sir, hath wagered with him six Barbary horses: against the which he has imponed,[107] as I take it, six French rapiers and poniards, with their assigns, as girdle, hanger, and so: three of the carriages, in faith, are very dear to fancy, very responsive to the hilts, most delicate carriages, and of very liberal conceit. *160*

HAMLET. What call you the carriages?

HORATIO. I knew you must be edified by the margent ere you had done.

OSRIC. The carriages, sir, are the hangers.

HAMLET. The phrase would be more germane to the matter if we could carry a cannon by our sides: I would it might be hangers till then. But, on: six Barbary horses against six French swords, their assigns, and three liberal-conceited carriages; that's the French bet against the Danish. Why is this "imponed," as you call it? *171*

OSRIC. The king, sir, hath laid, sir, that in a dozen passes between yourself and him, he shall not exceed you three hits: he hath laid on twelve for nine; and it would come to immediate trial, if your lordship would vouchsafe the answer.

HAMLET. How if I answer "no"?

OSRIC. I mean, my lord, the opposition of your person in trial. *179*

HAMLET. Sir, I will walk here in the hall: if it please his majesty, it is the breathing time of day with me; let the foils be brought, the gentleman willing, and the king hold his purpose, I will win for him an I can; if not, I will gain nothing but my shame and the odd hits. *185*

OSRIC. Shall I redeliver you e'en so?

HAMLET. To this effect, sir, after what flourish your nature will.

OSRIC. I commend my duty to your lordship.

HAMLET. Yours, yours. (*Exit* OSRIC.) He does well to commend it himself; there are no tongues else for's turn.

HORATIO. This lapwing[108] runs away with the shell on his head. *194*

HAMLET. He did comply with his dug before he sucked it. Thus has he— and many more of the same breed that I know the drossy age dotes on—only got the tune of the time and outward habit of encounter; a kind of yesty[109] collection, which carries them through and through the most fond and winnowed opinions; and do but blow them to their trial, the bubbles are out. *202*

(*Enter a* LORD.)

LORD. My lord, his majesty commended him to you by young Osric, who brings back to him, that you attend him in the hall: he sends to know if your pleasure hold to play with Laertes, or that you will take longer time.

HAMLET. I am constant to my purposes; they follow the king's pleasure: if his fitness speaks, mine is ready; now or whensoever, provided I be so able as now. *211*

LORD. The king and queen and all are coming down.

HAMLET. In happy time.

LORD. The queen desires you to use some gentle entertainment to Laertes before you fall to play.

HAMLET. She well instructs me.

(*Exit* LORD.)

HORATIO. You will lose this wager, my lord. *219*

HAMLET. I do not think so; since he went into France, I have been in continual practice; I shall win at the odds. But thou wouldst not think how ill all's here about my heart: but it is no matter.

---

[106] merit
[107] staked
[108] a shore bird of awkward flight and shrill, wailing cries
[109] frothy

HORATIO. Nay, good my lord,— *224*

HAMLET. It is but foolery; but it is such a kind of gaingiving as would perhaps trouble a woman.

HORATIO. If your mind dislike anything, obey it. I will forestall their repair hither, and say you are not fit. *229*

HAMLET. Not a whit; we defy augury: there is special providence in the fall of a sparrow. If it be now, 'tis not to come; if it be not to come, it will be now; if it be not now, yet it will come: the readiness is all; since no man has aught of what he leaves, what is't to leave betimes? Let be. *235*

(*Enter* KING, QUEEN, LAERTES, *and* LORDS, OSRIC *and other* ATTENDANTS *with foils and gauntlets; a table and flagons of wine on it.*)

KING. Come, Hamlet, come, and take this hand from me.

(*The* KING *puts* LAERTES' *hand into* HAMLET'S.)

HAMLET. Give me your pardon, sir: I've done you wrong;

But pardon't, as you are a gentleman.

This presence knows,

And you must needs have heard, how I am punish'd *240*

With sore distraction. What I have done,

That might your nature, honor and exception

Roughly awake, I here proclaim was madness.

Was't Hamlet wrong'd Laertes? Never Hamlet:

If Hamlet from himself be ta'en away,

And when he's not himself does wrong Laertes, *246*

Then Hamlet does it not, Hamlet denies it.

Who does it then? His madness: if't be so,

Hamlet is of the faction that is wrong'd;

His madness is poor Hamlet's enemy.

Sir, in this audience, *251*

Let my disclaiming from a purposed evil

Free me so far in your most generous thoughts,

That I have shot mine arrow o'er the house,

And hurt my brother.

LAERTES.   I am satisfied in nature,

Whose motive, in this case, should stir me most *256*

To my revenge: but in my terms of honor

I stand aloof, and will no reconcilement,

Till by some elder masters of known honor

I have a voice and precedent of peace,

To keep my name ungored. But till that time *261*

I do receive your offer'd love like love

And will not wrong it.

HAMLET.   I embrace it freely,

And will this brother's wager frankly play.

Give us the foils. Come on.

LAERTES.   Come, one for me.

HAMLET. I'll be your foil, Laertes: in mine ignorance *266*

Your skill shall, like a star i' the darkest night,

Stick fiery off indeed.

LAERTES.   You mock me, sir.

HAMLET. No, by this hand.

KING. Give them the foils, young Osric. Cousin Hamlet, *270*

You know the wager?

HAMLET.   Very well, my lord;

Your grace has laid the odds o' the weaker side.

KING. I do not fear it; I have seen you both:

But since he is better'd, we have therefore odds.

LAERTES. This is too heavy; let me see another. *275*

HAMLET. This likes me well. These foils have all a length?

(*They prepare to play.*)

OSRIC. Aye, my good lord.

KING. Set me the stoups[110] of wine upon that table.

If Hamlet give the first or second hit,

Or quit in answer to the third exchange,

[110] drinking cups

Let all the battlements their ordnance
    fire;   *281*
The king shall drink to Hamlet's better
    breath;
And in the cup an union[111] shall he
    throw,
Richer than that which four successive
    kings
In Denmark's crown have worn. Give
    me the cups;   *285*
And let the kettle to the trumpet speak,
The trumpet to the cannoneer without,
The cannons to the heavens, the heavens
    to earth,
"Now the king drinks to Hamlet." Come,
    begin;
And you, the judges, bear a wary eye.
    HAMLET.   Come on, sir.   *291*
    LAERTES.   Come, my lord.
    (*They play.*)
    HAMLET.   One.
    LAERTES.   No.
    HAMLET.   Judgment.
    OSRIC.   A hit, a very palpable hit.
    LAERTES.   Well; again.
    KING.   Stay; give me drink. Hamlet,
    this pearl is thine;
Here's to thy health.
    (*Trumpets sound, and cannon shot off
within.*)
               Give him the cup.
    HAMLET.   I'll play this bout first; set
    it by awhile.   *295*
Come. (*They play.*) Another hit; what
    say you?
    LAERTES.   A touch, a touch, I do con-
    fess.
    KING.   Our son shall win.
    QUEEN.   He's fat[112] and scant of
    breath.
Here, Hamlet, take my napkin, rub thy
    brows:
The queen carouses to thy fortune, Ham-
    let.   *300*
    HAMLET.   Good madam!
    KING.   Gertrude, do not drink.

[111] pearl
[112] sweaty

    QUEEN.   I will, my lord; I pray you,
    pardon me.
    KING (*aside*).   It is the poison'd cup;
    it is too late.
    HAMLET.   I dare not drink yet,
    madam; by and by.   *304*
    QUEEN.   Come, let me wipe thy face.
    LAERTES.   My lord, I'll hit him now.
    KING.   I do not think't.
    LAERTES (*aside*).   And yet it is al-
    most against my conscience.
    HAMLET.   Come, for the third,
    Laertes; you but dally;
I pray you, pass with your best violence;
I am afeard you make a wanton of me.
    LAERTES.   Say you so? come on.   *311*
                  (*They play.*)
    OSRIC.   Nothing, neither way.
    LAERTES.   Have at you now!
    (LAERTES *wounds* HAMLET; *then, in
scuffling, they change rapiers, and* HAM-
LET *wounds* LAERTES.)
    KING.   Part them; they are in-
    censed.
    HAMLET.   Nay, come, again.
                (*The* QUEEN *falls.*)
    OSRIC.   Look to the queen there, ho!
    HORATIO.   They bleed on both sides.
    How is it, my lord?   *315*
    OSRIC.   How is't, Laertes?
    LAERTES.   Why, as a woodcock to
    mine own springe, Osric;
I am justly kill'd with mine own treachery.
    HAMLET.   How does the queen?
    KING.   She swounds to see them
    bleed.
    QUEEN.   No, no, the drink, the drink,
    —O my dear Hamlet,—   *320*
The drink, the drink! I am poison'd.
                  (*Dies.*)
    HAMLET.   O villainy! Ho! let the door
    be lock'd:
Treachery! seek it out.
               (LAERTES *falls.*)
    LAERTES.   It is here, Hamlet: Hamlet,
    thou art slain;
No medicine in the world can do thee
    good,   *325*
In thee there is not half an hour of life;

The treacherous instrument is in thy hand,
Unbated and envenom'd: the foul prac-
   tice
Hath turn'd itself on me; lo, here I lie,
Never to rise again: thy mother's poi-
   son'd: 330
I can no more: the king, the king's to
   blame.
HAMLET. The point envenom'd too!
Then, venom, to thy work.
               (*Stabs the* KING.)
ALL. Treason! treason!
KING. O, yet defend me, friends; I
   am but hurt. 335
HAMLET. Here, thou incestuous, mur-
   derous, damnèd Dane,
Drink off this potion: is thy union here?
Follow my mother. (KING *dies.*)
   LAERTES. He is justly served;
It is a poison temper'd by himself.
Exchange forgiveness with me, noble
   Hamlet: 340
Mine and my father's death come not
   upon thee,
Nor thine on me! (*Dies.*)
   HAMLET. Heaven make thee free of
   it! I follow thee.
I am dead, Horatio. Wretched queen,
   adieu!
You that look pale and tremble at this
   chance, 345
That are but mutes or audience to this
   act,
Had I but time—as this fell sergeant,
   death,
Is strict in his arrest—O, I could tell
   you—
But let it be. Horatio, I am dead;
Thou livest; report me and my cause
   aright 350
To the unsatisfied.
   HORATIO. Never believe it:
I am more an antique Roman than a
   Dane:
Here's yet some liquor left.
   HAMLET. As thou'rt a man,
Give me the cup: let go; by heaven, I'll
   have 't.
O good Horatio, what a wounded name,

Things standing thus unknown, shall live
   behind me! 356
If thou didst ever hold me in thy heart,
Absent thee from felicity a while,
And in this harsh world draw thy breath
   in pain,
To tell my story.
       (*March afar off, shot within.*)
     What warlike noise is this? 360
   OSRIC. Young Fortinbras, with con-
   quest come from Poland,
To the ambassadors of England gives
This warlike volley.
   HAMLET. O, I die, Horatio;
The potent poison quite o'er-crows my
   spirit:
I cannot live to hear the news from Eng-
   land; 365
But I do prophesy the election lights
On Fortinbras: he has my dying voice;
So tell him, with the occurrents, more
   and less,
Which have solicited. The rest is silence.
                   (*Dies.*)
   HORATIO. Now cracks a noble heart.
   Good night sweet prince, 370
And flights of angels sing thee to thy rest!
             (*March within.*)
Why does the drum come hither?
(*Enter* FORTINBRAS, *and the* ENGLISH
AMBASSADORS, *with drum, colors, and*
ATTENDANTS.)
   FORTINBRAS. Where is this sight?
   HORATIO. What is it you would see?
If aught of woe or wonder, cease your
   search.
   FORTINBRAS. This quarry cries on
   havoc. O proud death, 375
What feast is toward in thine eternal
   cell,
That thou so many princes at a shot
So bloodily hast struck?
   FIRST AMBASSADOR. The sight is
   dismal;
And our affairs from England come too
   late:
The ears are senseless that should give
   us hearing, 380
To tell him his commandment is fulfill'd,

That Rosencrantz and Guildenstern are
  dead:
Where should we have our thanks?
    HORATIO.   Not from his mouth
Had it the ability of life to thank you:
He never gave commandment for their
  death.   *385*
But since, so jump upon this bloody ques-
  tion,
You from the Polack wars, and you from
  England,
Are here arrived, give order that these
  bodies
High on a stage be placed to the view;
And let me speak to the yet unknowing
  world   *390*
How these things came about: so shall
  you hear
Of carnal, bloody and unnatural acts,
Of accidental judgments, casual slaugh-
  ters,
Of deaths put on by cunning and forced
  cause,
And, in this upshot, purposes mistook
Fall'n on the inventors' heads: all this
  can I   *396*
Truly deliver.
    FORTINBRAS.   Let us haste to hear it,
And call the noblest to the audience.

For me, with sorrow I embrace my for-
  tune:
I have some rights of memory in this
  kingdom,   *400*
Which now to claim my vantage doth
  invite me.
    HORATIO.   Of that I shall have also
  cause to speak,
And from his mouth whose voice will
  draw on more:
But let this same be presently perform'd,
Even while men's minds are wild; lest
  more mischance   *405*
On plots and errors happen.
    FORTINBRAS.   Let four captains
Bear Hamlet, like a soldier, to the stage;
For he was likely, had he been put on,
To have proved most royally: and, for
  his passage,
The soldiers' music and the rites of war
Speak loudly for him.   *411*
Take up the bodies: such a sight as
  this
Becomes the field, but here shows much
  amiss.
Go, bid the soldiers shoot.

    (*A dead march. Exeunt, bearing off
the bodies: after which a peal of ordnance is shot off.*)

MOLIÈRE / 1622–1673

Jean Baptiste Poquelin, the son of an upholsterer, attended a Jesuit college in Paris whose curriculum included rhetoric, declamation, Roman comedy, and the performance of plays in Latin. At twenty-one he joined a theatrical company in Paris which went on tour in the provinces. Molière was familiar with the farces of Plautus and Terence, which are complete playscripts; he had also encountered a kind of Italian comedy, made up of pantomime, impromptu "gags," and improvised dialogue, performed by stock types descended from the *commedia dell' arte*.

Molière was actor, manager, and finally playwright for his company. His own plays, chiefly farces and farcical comedies, blend the traditional Latin and Italian comic modes, but add a distinct satirical point, and involve recognizable social men and manners. They progress to high comedy or comedy of manners, retaining farcical elements.

After twelve years, Molière's troupe settled near Paris and won the favor of King Louis XIV. Molière's plays became the subject of attention and controversy in the fashionable world. French society was a formal, rigid, class-stratified one, with types clearly defined and norms of behavior shared and approved. Departures from the prescribed code, either from an immoderate or ungovernable bent in an individual, or from affectation, hypocrisy, or false pretenses, were fair game for ridicule in the society and in its theatre.

The laughter of derision at something abnormal, incongruous, or defective, evoked from an audience rejoicing at its freedom from such blemishes, is sometimes thought to be the true domain of comedy. According to Bergson, "In laughter we always find an avowed intention to humiliate, and consequently to correct our neighbor." According to Hobbes, "Laughter is caused . . . by apprehension of some deformed thing in another, by comparison whereof they suddenly applaud themselves." There are other kinds of comic laughter and of humor, but Molière's age was ripe for the purging of satirical laughter. Molière satirized medical mumbo jumbo in *Love's the Best Doctor* (*L'Amour médecin*), long-winded enthusiasts in *The Bores* (*Les Fâcheux*). He laughed out of fashion the affected preciosities of the salon ladies in *The Affected Ladies* (*Les Précieuses ridicules*). Avarice is his target in *The Miser* (*L'Avare*), hypochondria in *The Imaginary Invalid* (*Le Malade imaginaire*), an extreme devotion to the role of honest, plain-speaking man in *The Misanthrope*. His structure often involves a contrast between characters of two extremes, with a moderate and reasonable man between them.

Not all of Molière's comedies were rollicking or discerning enough to soften the wrath of the true or supposed targets of the satire. In *Tartuffe,* for example, he ridiculed a hypocrite feigning piety; hypocrisy is a perennially acceptable target for satire, but piety is not, and the pious took themselves to be the victims of the laughter. It took some revising and a king-flattering *deus ex machina* ending to clear *Tartuffe* for production.

Molière's influence on comedy is widespread; the eighteenth century English stage translated and adapted him, and in a somewhat similarly rigid and self-conscious society the great comic dramatists of England also reached high comedy.

The Misanthrope*

IN A TRANSLATION BY RICHARD WILBUR

CHARACTERS

ALCESTE, *in love with Célimène.*
PHILINTE, *Alceste's friend.*
ORONTE, *in love with Célimène.*
CÉLIMÈNE, *Alceste's beloved.*
ELIANTE, *Célimène's cousin.*
ARSINOÉ, *a friend of Célimène's.*
ACASTE
CLITANDRE } *marquesses.*
BASQUE, *Célimène's servant.*
A GUARD *of the Marshalsea.*
DUBOIS, *Alceste's valet.*

SCENE: *The scene throughout is in Célimène's house at Paris.*

Act I

SCENE 1

(PHILINTE, ALCESTE.)

PHILINTE. Now, what's got into you?
ALCESTE (*seated*).   Kindly
  leave me alone.
PHIL. Come, come, what is it? This
  lugubrious tone . . .
ALC. Leave me, I said; you spoil my
  solitude.
PHIL. Oh, listen to me, now, and
  don't be rude.
ALC. I choose to be rude, Sir, and
  to be hard of hearing.   5

* In *The Misanthrope* we have numbered verse every five lines. A continued line of verse, regardless of a change of speakers mid-line or regardless of a break midline, still counts as one line. The prose at the end of the play has been numbered every five lines typographically set. When the width of a line has not permitted the inclusion of a line number, either the previous line or the following line has been numbered.

166

PHIL. These ugly moods of yours
  are not endearing;
Friends though we are, I really must
  insist . . .
    ALC. (*abruptly rising*). Friends?
      Friends, you say? Well, cross me
      off your list.
I've been your friend till now, as you
  well know;
But after what I saw a moment ago   10
I tell you flatly that our ways must part.
I wish no place in a dishonest heart.
    PHIL. Why, what have I done,
      Alceste? Is this quite just?
    ALC. My God, you ought to die of
      self-disgust.
I call your conduct inexcusable, Sir,   15
And every man of honor will concur.
I see you almost hug a man to death,
Exclaim for joy until you're out of
  breath,
And supplement these loving demonstrations
With endless offers, vows, and protestations;   20
Then when I ask you "Who was that?",
  I find
That you can barely bring his name to
  mind!
Once the man's back is turned, you cease
  to love him,
And speak with absolute indifference of
  him!   24
By God, I say it's base and scandalous
To falsify the heart's affections thus;
If I caught myself behaving in such a
  way,
I'd hang myself for shame, without delay.
    PHIL. It hardly seems a hanging
      matter to me;   29
I hope that you will take it graciously

If I extend myself a slight reprieve,
And live a little longer, by your leave.
   ALC. How dare you joke about a
    crime so grave?
   PHIL. What crime? How else are
    people to behave?
   ALC. I'd have them be sincere, and
    never part   35
With any word that isn't from the heart.
   PHIL. When someone greets us with
    a show of pleasure
It's but polite to give him equal measure,
Return his love the best that we know
   how,
And trade him offer for offer, vow for
   vow.   40
   ALC. No, no, this formula you'd
    have me follow,
However fashionable, is false and hollow,
And I despise the frenzied operations
Of all these barterers of protestations,
These lavishers of meaningless embraces,
These utterers of obliging common-
   places,   46
Who court and flatter everyone on earth
And praise the fool no less than the man
   of worth.
Should you rejoice that someone fondles
   you,
Offers his love and service, swears to be
   true,   50
And fills your ears with praises of your
   name,
When to the first damned fop he'll say
   the same?
No, no: no self-respecting heart would
   dream
Of prizing so promiscuous an esteem;
However high the praise, there's nothing
   worse   55
Than sharing honors with the universe.
Esteem is founded on comparison:
To honor all men is to honor none.
Since you embrace this indiscriminate
   vice,
Your friendship comes at far too cheap
   a price;   60
I spurn the easy tribute of a heart
Which will not set the worthy man apart:

I choose, Sir, to be chosen; and in fine,
The friend of mankind is no friend of
   mine.
   PHIL. But in polite society, custom
   decrees   65
That we show certain outward cour-
   tesies. . . .
   ALC. Ah, no! we should condemn
    with all our force
Such false and artificial intercourse.
Let men behave like men; let them dis-
   play
Their inmost hearts in everything they
   say;   70
Let the heart speak, and let our senti-
   ments
Not mask themselves in silly compli-
   ments.
   PHIL. In certain cases it would be
   uncouth
And most absurd to speak the naked
   truth;   74
With all respect for your exalted notions,
It's often best to veil one's true emotions.
Wouldn't the social fabric come undone
If we were wholly frank with everyone?
Suppose you met with someone you
   couldn't bear;
Would you inform him of it then and
   there?   80
   ALC. Yes.
   PHIL.   Then you'd tell old Emilie
   it's pathetic
The way she daubs her features with
   cosmetic
And plays the gay coquette at sixty-four?
   ALC. I would.
   PHIL.   And you'd call Dorilas
   a bore,   85
And tell him every ear at court is lame
From hearing him brag about his noble
   name?
   ALC. Precisely.
   PHIL.   Ah, you're joking.
   ALC.   *Au contraire:*
In this regard there's none I'd choose to
   spare.
All are corrupt; there's nothing to be
   seen

In court or town but aggravates my
    spleen.   90
I fall into deep gloom and melancholy
When I survey the scene of human folly,
Finding on every hand base flattery,
Injustice, fraud, self-interest, treach-
    ery. . . .
Ah, it's too much; mankind has grown
    so base,   95
I mean to break with the whole human
    race.
    PHIL. This philosophic rage is a bit
    extreme;
You've no idea how comical you seem;
Indeed, we're like those brothers in the
    play
Called *School for Husbands,* one of
    whom was prey . . .   100
    ALC. Enough, now! None of your
    stupid similes.
    PHIL. Then let's have no more
    tirades, if you please.
The world won't change, whatever you
    say or do;
And since plain speaking means so much
    to you,   104
I'll tell you plainly that by being frank
You've earned the reputation of a crank,
And that you're thought ridiculous when
    you rage
And rant against the manners of the age.
    ALC. So much the better; just what
    I wish to hear.
No news could be more grateful to my
    ear.   110
All men are so detestable in my eyes,
I should be sorry if they thought me
    wise.
    PHIL. Your hatred's very sweeping,
    is it not?
    ALC. Quite right: I hate the whole
    degraded lot.
    PHIL. Must all poor human creatures
    be embraced,   115
Without distinction, by your vast distaste?
Even in these bad times, there are surely
    a few . . .
    ALC. No, I include all men in one
    dim view:

Some men I hate for being rogues; the
    others
I hate because they treat the rogues like
    brothers,   120
And, lacking a virtuous scorn for what
    is vile,
Receive the villain with a complaisant
    smile.
Notice how tolerant people choose to be
Toward that bold rascal who's at law
    with me.
His social polish can't conceal his na-
    ture;   125
One sees at once that he's a treacherous
    creature;
No one could possibly be taken in
By those soft speeches and that sugary
    grin.
The whole world knows the shady means
    by which
The low-brow's grown so powerful and
    rich,   130
And risen to a rank so bright and high
That virtue can but blush, and merit
    sigh.
Whenever his name comes up in con-
    versation,
None will defend his wretched reputa-
    tion;
Call him knave, liar, scoundrel, and all
    the rest,   135
Each head will nod, and no one will
    protest.
And yet his smirk is seen in every house,
He's greeted everywhere with smiles and
    bows,
And when there's any honor that can be
    got
By pulling strings, he'll get it, like as
    not.   140
My God! It chills my heart to see the
    ways
Men come to terms with evil nowadays;
Sometimes, I swear, I'm moved to flee
    and find
Some desert land unfouled by human-
    kind.
    PHIL. Come, let's forget the follies
    of the times   145

And pardon mankind for its petty crimes;
Let's have an end of rantings and of
   railings,
And show some leniency toward human
   failings.
This world requires a pliant rectitude;
Too stern a virtue makes one stiff and
   rude;   *150*
Good sense views all extremes with
   detestation,
And bids us to be noble in moderation.
The rigid virtues of the ancient days
Are not for us; they jar with all our
   ways   *154*
And ask of us too lofty a perfection.
And there's no greater folly, if you ask
   me,
Than trying to reform society.
Like you, I see each day a hundred and
   one
Unhandsome deeds that might be better
   done,   *160*
But still, for all the faults that meet my
   view,
I'm never known to storm and rave like
   you.
I take men as they are, or let them be,
And teach my soul to bear their frailty;
And whether in court or town, whatever
   the scene,   *165*
My phlegm's as philosophic as your
   spleen.
   ALC. This phlegm which you so
      eloquently commend,
Does nothing ever rile it up, my friend?
Suppose some man you trust should
   treacherously   *169*
Conspire to rob you of your property,
And do his best to wreck your reputa-
   tion?
Wouldn't you feel a certain indignation?
   PHIL. Why, no. These faults of which
      you so complain
Are part of human nature, I maintain,
And it's no more a matter for disgust
That men are knavish, selfish and un-
   just,   *176*
Than that the vulture dines upon the
   dead,

And wolves are furious, and apes ill-bred.
   ALC. Shall I see myself betrayed,
      robbed, torn to bits,
And not . . . Oh, let's be still and rest
   our wits.   *180*
Enough of reasoning, now. I've had my
   fill.
   PHIL. Indeed, you would do well, Sir,
      to be still.
Rage less at your opponent, and give
   some thought
To how you'll win this lawsuit that he's
   brought.
   ALC. I assure you I'll do nothing of
      the sort.   *185*
   PHIL. Then who will plead your case
      before the court?
   ALC. Reason and right and justice
      will plead for me.
   PHIL. Oh, Lord. What judges do you
      plan to see?
   ALC. Why, none. The justice of my
      cause is clear.
   PHIL. Of course, man; but there's
      politics to fear. . . .   *190*
   ALC. No, I refuse to lift a hand.
      That's flat.
I'm either right, or wrong.
   PHIL.   Don't count on that.
   ALC. No, I'll do nothing.
   PHIL.   Your enemy's influence
Is great, you know . . .
   ALC.   That makes no difference.
   PHIL. It will; you'll see.   *194*
   ALC.   Must honor bow to guile?
If so, I shall be proud to lose the trial.
   PHIL. Oh, really . . .
   ALC.   I'll discover by this case
Whether or not men are sufficiently base
And impudent and villainous and per-
   verse   *199*
To do me wrong before the universe.
   PHIL. What a man!
   ALC. Oh, I could wish, whatever the
      cost,
Just for the beauty of it, that my trial
   were lost.
   PHIL. If people heard you talking
      so, Alceste,

They'd split their sides. Your name
   would be a jest.
   ALC.   So much the worse for jesters.
   PHIL.   May I enquire *205*
Whether this rectitude you so admire,
And these hard virtues you're enamored
   of
Are qualities of the lady whom you love?
It much surprises me that you, who seem
To view mankind with furious disesteem,
Have yet found something to enchant
   your eyes   *211*
Amidst a species which you so despise.
And what is more amazing, I'm afraid,
Is the most curious choice your heart
   has made.
The honest Eliante is fond of you, *215*
Arsinoé, the prude, admires you too;
And yet your spirit's been perversely led
To choose the flighty Célimène instead,
Whose brittle malice and coquettish ways
So typify the manners of our days. *220*
How is it that the traits you most abhor
Are bearable in this lady you adore?
Are you so blind with love that you can't
   find them?
Or do you contrive, in her case, not to
   mind them?
   ALC.   My love for that young widow's
   not the kind   *225*
That can't perceive defects; no, I'm not
   blind.
I see her faults, despite my ardent love,
And all I see I fervently reprove.
And yet I'm weak; for all her falsity,
That woman knows the art of pleasing
   me,   *230*
And though I never cease complaining
   of her,
I swear I cannot manage not to love her.
Her charm outweighs her faults; I can
   but aim
To cleanse her spirit in my love's pure
   flame.
   PHIL.   That's no small task; I wish
   you all success.   *235*
You think then that she loves you?
   ALC.   Heavens, yes!
I wouldn't love her did she not love me.

   PHIL.   Well, if her taste for you is
   plain to see,
Why do these rivals cause you such
   despair?
   ALC.   True love, Sir, is possessive,
   and cannot bear   *240*
To share with all the world. I'm here
   today
To tell her she must send that mob
   away.
   PHIL.   If I were you, and had your
   choice to make,
Eliante, her cousin, would be the one
   I'd take;
That honest heart, which cares for you
   alone,   *245*
Would harmonize far better with your
   own.
   ALC.   True, true: each day my reason
   tells me so;
But reason doesn't rule in love, you
   know.
   PHIL.   I fear some bitter sorrow is in
   store;
This love . . .

                 SCENE 2

   (ORONTE, ALCESTE, PHILINTE.)

ORONTE (*to* ALCESTE).   The servants
   told me at the door   *250*
That Eliante and Célimène were out,
But when I heard, dear Sir, that you were
   about,
I came to say, without exaggeration,
That I hold you in the vastest admira-
   tion,
And that it's always been my dearest
   desire   *255*
To be the friend of one I so admire.
I hope to see my love of merit requited,
And you and I in friendship's bond
   united.
I'm sure you won't refuse—if I may be
   frank—   *259*
A friend of my devotedness—and rank.
   (*During this speech of* ORONTE's,
ALCESTE *is abstracted, and seems un-
aware that he is being spoken to. He only*

breaks off his reverie when ORONTE *says:*)

It was for you, if you please, that my
   words were intended.
  ALC. For me, Sir?
  OR. Yes, for you. You're not of-
  fended?
  ALC. By no means. But this much
  surprises me. . . .
The honor comes most unexpectedly. . . .
  OR. My high regard should not
  astonish you;   *265*
The whole world feels the same. It is
  your due.
  ALC. Sir . . .
  OR. Why, in all the State there
  isn't one
Can match your merits; they shine, Sir,
  like the sun.
  ALC. Sir . . .
  OR. You are higher in my estima-
  tion
Than all that's most illustrious in the
  nation.   *270*
  ALC. Sir . . .
  OR. If I lie, may heaven strike me
  dead!
To show you that I mean what I have
  said,
Permit me, Sir, to embrace you most
  sincerely,
And swear that I will prize our friend-
  ship dearly.
Give me your hand. And now, Sir, if you
  choose,   *275*
We'll make our vows.
  ALC.   Sir . . .
  OR.   What! You refuse?
  ALC. Sir, it's a very great honor you
  extend:
But friendship is a sacred thing, my
  friend;
It would be profanation to bestow
The name of friend on one you hardly
  know.   *280*
All parts are better played when well-
  rehearsed;
Let's put off friendship, and get ac-
  quainted first.

We may discover it would be unwise
To try to make our natures harmonize.
  OR. By heaven! You're sagacious to
  the core;   *285*
This speech has made me admire you
  even more.
Let time, then, bring us closer day by
  day;
Meanwhile, I shall be yours in every
  way.
If, for example, there should be any-
  thing
You wish at court, I'll mention it to the
  King.   *290*
I have his ear, of course; it's quite well
  known
That I am much in favor with the throne.
In short, I am your servant. And now,
  dear friend,
Since you have such fine judgment, I
  intend
To please you, if I can, with a small
  sonnet   *295*
I wrote not long ago. Please comment on
  it,
And tell me whether I ought to publish
  it.
  ALC. You must excuse me, Sir; I'm
  hardly fit
To judge such matters.
  OR.   Why not?
  ALC.   I am, I fear,   *299*
Inclined to be unfashionably sincere.
  OR. Just what I ask; I'd take no
  satisfaction
In anything but your sincere reaction.
I beg you not to dream of being kind.
  ALC. Since you desire it, Sir, I'll
  speak my mind.
  OR. *Sonnet.* It's a sonnet. . . . *Hope*
  . . . The poem's addressed   *305*
To a lady who wakened hopes within my
  breast.
Hope . . . this is not the pompous sort
  of thing,
Just modest little verses, with a tender
  ring.
  ALC. Well, we shall see.
  OR. *Hope* . . . I'm anxious to hear

Whether the style seems properly smooth
   and clear,   310
And whether the choice of words is good
   or bad.
  ALC. We'll see, we'll see.
  OR.   Perhaps I ought to add
That it took me only a quarter-hour to
   write it.
  ALC. The   time's   irrelevant,   Sir:
   kindly recite it.
  OR. (*reading*)

Hope comforts us awhile, 'tis true,   315
Lulling our cares with careless laughter,
And yet such joy is full of rue,
My Phyllis, if nothing follows after.

  PHIL. I'm charmed by this already;
   the style's delightful.
  ALC. (*sotto voce, to* PHILINTE). How
   can you say that? Why, the thing is
   frightful.   320
  OR.

Your fair face smiled on me awhile,
But was it kindness so to enchant me?
'Twould have been fairer not to smile,
If hope was all you meant to grant me.

  PHIL. What a clever thought! How
   handsomely you phrase it!   325
  ALC. (*sotto voce, to* PHILINTE). You
   know the thing is trash. How dare
   you praise it?
  OR.

If it's to be my passion's fate
Thus everlastingly to wait,
Then death will come to set me free:
For death is fairer than the fair;   330
Phyllis, to hope is to despair
When one must hope eternally.

  PHIL. The close is exquisite—full of
   feeling and grace.
  ALC. (*sotto voce, aside*). Oh, blast
   the close; you'd better close your
   face   334
Before you send your lying soul to hell.
  PHIL. I can't remember a poem I've
   liked so well.
  ALC. (*sotto voce, aside*). Good Lord!

  OR. (*to* PHILINTE).   I fear you're
   flattering me a bit.
  PHIL. Oh, no!
  ALC. (*sotto voce, aside*). What else
   d'you call it, you hypocrite?
  OR. (*to* ALCESTE). But you, Sir,
   keep your promise now: don't
   shrink
From telling me sincerely what you
   think.   340
  ALC. Sir, these are delicate matters;
   we all desire
To be told that we've the true poetic fire.
But once, to one whose name I shall not
   mention,
I said, regarding some verse of his inven-
   tion,
That gentlemen should rigorously con-
   trol   345
That itch to write which often afflicts the
   soul;
That one should curb the heady inclina-
   tion
To publicize one's little avocation;
And that in showing off one's works of
   art   349
One often plays a very clownish part.
  OR. Are you suggesting in a devious
   way
That I ought not . . .
    ALC.   Oh, that I do not say.
Further, I told him that no fault is worse
Than that of writing frigid, lifeless
   verse,
And that the merest whisper of such a
   shame   355
Suffices to destroy a man's good name.
  OR. D'you mean to say my sonnet's
   dull and trite?
  ALC. I don't say that. But I went on
   to cite
Numerous cases of once-respected men
Who came to grief by taking up the
   pen.   360
  OR. And am I like them? Do I write
   so poorly?
  ALC. I don't say that. But I told this
   person, "Surely
You're under no necessity to compose;

Why you should wish to publish, heaven
  knows.
There's no excuse for printing tedious
  rot   365
Unless one writes for bread, as you do
  not.
Resist temptation, then, I beg of you;
Conceal your pastimes from the public
  view;
And don't give up, on any provocation,
Your present high and courtly reputa-
  tion,   370
To purchase at a greedy printer's shop
The name of silly author and scribbling
  fop."
These were the points I tried to make
  him see.
   OR.   I sense that they are also aimed
  at me;
But now—about my sonnet—I'd like to
  be told . . .   375
   ALC.   Frankly, that sonnet should be
  pigeonholed.
You've chosen the worst models to
  imitate.
The style's unnatural. Let me illustrate:
   For example, *Your fair face smiled
   on me awhile,*
   Followed by, *'Twould have been fairer
   not to smile!*   380
   Or this: *such joy is full of rue;*
   Or this: *For death is fairer than the
   fair;*
   Or, *Phyllis, to hope is to despair
       When one must hope eternally!*
This artificial style, that's all the fash-
  ion,   385
Has neither taste, nor honesty, nor pas-
  sion;
It's nothing but a sort of wordy play,
And nature never spoke in such a way.
What, in this shallow age, is not de-
  based?
Our fathers, though less refined, had
  better taste;   390
I'd barter all that men admire today
For one old love-song I shall try to say:

   *If the King had given me for my own
   Paris, his citadel,*

   And I for that must leave alone   395
   Her whom I love so well,
   I'd say then to the Crown,
   Take back your glittering town;
   My darling is more fair, I swear,
   My darling is more fair.   400

The rhyme's not rich, the style is rough
  and old,
But don't you see it's the purest gold
Beside the tinsel nonsense now preferred,
And that there's passion in its every
  word?

   If the King had given me my own   405
   Paris, his citadel,
   And I for that must leave alone
   Her whom I love so well,
   I'd say then to the Crown,
   Take back your glittering town;   410
   My darling is more fair, I swear,
   My darling is more fair.

There speaks a loving heart. (*To* PHI-
  LINTE.) You're laughing, eh?
Laugh on, my precious wit. Whatever
  you say,   414
I hold that song's worth all the bibelots
That people hail today with ah's and
  oh's.
   OR.   And I maintain my sonnet's very
  good.
   ALC.   It's not at all surprising that
  you should.
You have your reasons; permit me to
  have mine
For thinking that you cannot write a
  line.   420
   OR.   Others have praised my sonnet
  to the skies.
   ALC.   I lack their art of telling pleasant lies.
   OR.   You seem to think you've got
  no end of wit.
   ALC.   To praise your verse, I'd need
  still more of it.
   OR.   I'm not in need of your approval, Sir.   425
   ALC.   That's good; you couldn't have
  it if you were.
   OR.   Come now, I'll lend you the
  subject of my sonnet;

I'd like to see you try to improve upon it.

ALC. I might, by chance, write
something just as shoddy;

But then I wouldn't show it to everybody.   *430*

OR. You're most opinionated and
conceited.

ALC. Go find your flatterers, and be
better treated.

OR. Look here, my little fellow, pray
watch your tone.

ALC. My great big fellow, you'd better watch your own.

PHIL. (*stepping between them*). Oh,
please, please, gentlemen! This will
never do.   *435*

OR. The fault is mine, and I leave
the field to you.

I am your servant, Sir, in every way.

ALC. And I, Sir, am your most abject valet.

SCENE 3

(PHILINTE, ALCESTE.)

PHIL. Well, as you see, sincerity in
excess   *439*

Can get you into a very pretty mess;

Oronte was hungry for appreciation. . . .

ALC. Don't speak to me.

PHIL.   What?

ALC.   No more conversation.

PHIL. Really, now . . .

ALC.   Leave me alone.

PHIL.   If I . . .

ALC.   Out
of my sight!

PHIL. But what . . .

ALC.   I won't listen.

PHIL.   But . . .

ALC.   Silence!

PHIL.   Now, is it
polite . . .

ALC. By heaven, I've had enough.
Don't follow me.   *445*

PHIL. Ah, you're just joking. I'll keep
you company.

Act II

SCENE 1

(ALCESTE, CÉLIMÈNE.)

ALC. Shall I speak plainly, Madam?
I confess

Your conduct gives me infinite distress,

And my resentment's grown too hot to
smother.

Soon, I foresee, we'll break with one
another.

If I said otherwise, I should deceive
you;   *5*

Sooner or later, I shall be forced to leave
you,

And if I swore that we shall never part,

I should misread the omens of my
heart.

CÉLIMÈNE. You kindly saw me
home, it would appear,

So as to pour invectives in my ear. *10*

ALC. I've no desire to quarrel. But
I deplore

Your inability to shut the door

On all these suitors who beset you so.

There's what annoys me, if you care to
know.

CEL. Is it my fault that all these men
pursue me?   *15*

Am I to blame if they're attracted to me?

And when they gently beg an audience,

Ought I to take a stick and drive them
hence?

ALC. Madam, there's no necessity
for a stick;

A less responsive heart would do the
trick.   *20*

Of your attractiveness I don't complain;

But those your charms attract, you then
detain

By a most melting and receptive manner,

And so enlist their hearts beneath your
banner.   *24*

It's the agreeable hopes which you excite

That keep these lovers round you day
and night;

Were they less liberally smiled upon,
That sighing troop would very soon be
    gone.
But tell me, Madam, why it is that lately
This man Clitandre interests you so
    greatly?   30
Because of what high merits do you deem
Him worthy of the honor of your esteem?
Is it that your admiring glances linger
On the splendidly long nail of his little
    finger?
Or do you share the general deep re-
    spect   35
For the blond wig he chooses to affect?
Are you in love with his embroidered
    hose?
Do you adore his ribbons and his bows?
Or is it that this paragon bewitches
Your tasteful eye with his vast German
    breeches?   40
Perhaps his giggle, or his falsetto voice,
Makes him the latest gallant of your
    choice?
    CEL. You're much mistaken to re-
sent him so.
Why I put up with him you surely know:
My lawsuit's very shortly to be tried,   45
And I must have his influence on my
    side.
    ALC. Then lose your lawsuit, Madam,
or let it drop;
Don't torture me by humoring such a
    fop.
    CEL. You're jealous of the whole
    world, Sir.
    ALC.   That's true
Since the whole world is well-received
    by you.   50
    CEL. That my good nature is so un-
    confined
Should serve to pacify your jealous mind;
Were I to smile on one, and scorn the
    rest,
Then you might have some cause to be
    distressed.
    ALC. Well, if I mustn't be jealous,
    tell me, then,   55
Just how I'm better treated than other
    men.

    CEL. You know you have my love.
    Will that not do?
    ALC. What proof have I that what
    you say is true?
    CEL. I would expect, Sir, that my
    having said it
Might give the statement a sufficient
    credit.   60
    ALC. But how can I be sure that you
    don't tell
The selfsame thing to other men as well?
    CEL. What a gallant speech! How
    flattering to me!
What a sweet creature you make me
    out to be!
Well then, to save you from the pangs of
    doubt,   65
All that I've said I hereby cancel out;
Now, none but yourself shall make a
    monkey of you:
Are you content?
    ALC.   Why, why am I doomed to
    love you?
I swear that I shall bless the blissful hour
When this poor heart's no longer in your
    power!   70
I make no secret of it; I've done my
    best
To exorcise this passion from my breast;
But thus far all in vain; it will not go;
It's for my sins that I must love you so.
    CEL. Your love for me is matchless,
    Sir; that's clear.   75
    ALC. Indeed, in all the world it has
    no peer;
Words can't describe the nature of my
    passion,
And no man ever loved in such a fash-
    ion.
    CEL. Yes, it's a brand-new fashion,
    I agree: 79
You show your love by castigating me,
And all your speeches are enraged and
    rude.
I've never been so furiously wooed.
    ALC. Yet you could calm that fury,
    if you chose.
Come, shall we bring our quarrels to a
    close?

Let's speak with open hearts, then, and
   begin . . .   85

SCENE 2

(CÉLIMÈNE, ALCESTE, BASQUE.)

CEL.   What is it?
BASQUE.   Acaste is here.
CEL.   Well, send him in.

SCENE 3

(CÉLIMÈNE, ALCESTE.)

ALC.   What! Shall we never be alone
   at all?
You're always ready to receive a call,
And you can't bear, for ten ticks of the
   clock,
Not to keep open house for all who
   knock.   90
CEL.   I couldn't refuse him: he'd be
   most put out.
ALC.   Surely that's not worth worry-
   ing about.
CEL.   Acaste would never forgive me
   if he guessed
That I consider him a dreadful pest.
ALC.   If he's a pest, why bother with
   him then?   95
CEL.   Heavens! One can't antagonize
   such men;
Why, they're the chartered gossips of the
   court,
And have a say in things of every sort.
One must receive them, and be full of
   charm;
They're no great help, but they can do
   you harm,   100
And though your influence be ever so
   great,
They're hardly the best people to alien-
   ate.
ALC.   I see, dear lady, that you could
   make a case
For putting up with the whole human
   race;

These friendships that you calculate so
   nicely . . .   105

SCENE 4

(ALCESTE, CÉLIMÈNE, BASQUE.)

BAS.   Madam, Clitandre is here as
   well.
ALC.   Precisely.
CEL.   Where are you going?
ALC.   Elsewhere.
CEL.   Stay.
ALC.   No, no.
CEL.   Stay, Sir.
ALC.   I can't.
CEL.   I wish it.
ALC.   No, I must go.
I beg you, Madam, not to press the mat-
   ter;
You know I have no taste for idle chat-
   ter.   110
CEL.   Stay: I command you.
ALC.   No, I cannot stay.
CEL.   Very well; you have my leave
   to go away.

SCENE 5

(ELIANTE, PHILINTE, ACASTE, CLIT-
ANDRE, ALCESTE, CÉLIMÈNE, BASQUE.)

ELIANTE (to CÉLIMÈNE).   The Mar-
   quesses have kindly come to call.
Were they announced?
CEL.   Yes. Basque, bring chairs for
   all.
(BASQUE provides the chairs, and exits.)
(To ALCESTE.)   You haven't gone?
ALC.   No; and I shan't depart
Till you decide who's foremost in your
   heart.   115
CEL.   Oh, hush.
ALC.   It's time to choose; take
   them, or me.
CEL.   You're mad.
ALC.   I'm not, as you shall shortly
   see.
CEL.   Oh?
ALC.   You'll decide.

CEL. You're joking now, dear friend.

ALC. No, no; you'll choose; my patience is at an end.   *120*

CLITANDRE. Madam, I come from court, where poor Cléonte

Behaved like a perfect fool, as is his wont.

Has he no friend to counsel him, I wonder,

And teach him less unerringly to blunder?

CEL. It's true, the man's a most accomplished dunce;   *125*

His gauche behavior strikes the eye at once;

And every time one sees him, on my word,

His manner's grown a trifle more absurd.

ACASTE. Speaking of dunces, I've just now conversed

With old Damon, who's one of the very worst;   *130*

I stood a lifetime in the broiling sun

Before his dreary monologue was done.

CEL. Oh, he's a wondrous talker, and has the power

To tell you nothing hour after hour:

If, by mistake, he ever came to the point,   *135*

The shock would put his jawbone out of joint.

EL. (*To* PHILINTE). The conversation takes its usual turn,

And all our dear friends' ears will shortly burn.

CLIT. Timante's a character, Madam.

CEL.   Isn't he, though?

A man of mystery from top to toe,   *140*

Who moves about in a romantic mist

On secret missions which do not exist.

His talk is full of eyebrows and grimaces;

How tired one gets of his momentous faces;

He's always whispering something confidential   *145*

Which turns out to be quite inconsequential;

Nothing's too slight for him to mystify;

He even whispers when he says "goodby."

ACAS. Tell us about Géralde.

CEL.   That tiresome ass.

He mixes only with the titled class,   *150*

And fawns on dukes and princes, and is bored

With anyone who's not at least a lord.

The man's obsessed with rank, and his discourses

Are all of hounds and carriages and horses;

He uses Christian names with all the great,   *155*

And the word Milord, with him, is out of date.

CLIT. He's very taken with Bélise, I hear.

CEL. She is the dreariest company, poor dear.

Whenever she comes to call, I grope about

To find some topic which will draw her out,   *160*

But, owing to her dry and faint replies,

The conversation wilts, and droops, and dies.

In vain one hopes to animate her face

By mentioning the ultimate commonplace;   *164*

But sun or shower, even hail or frost

Are matters she can instantly exhaust.

Meanwhile her visit, painful though it is,

Drags on and on through mute eternities,

And though you ask the time, and yawn, and yawn,

She sits there like a stone and won't be gone.   *170*

ACAS. Now for Adraste.

CEL.   Oh, that conceited elf

Has a gigantic passion for himself;

He rails against the court, and cannot bear it

That none will recognize his hidden merit;   *174*

All honors given to others give offense

To his imaginary exellence.

CLIT. What about young Cléon? His house, they say,

Is full of the best society, night and day.
  CEL. His cook has made him popu-
    lar, not he:
It's Cléon's table that people come to
    see   *180*
  EL. He gives a spendid dinner, you
    must admit.
  CEL. But must he serve himself along
    with it?
For my taste, he's a most insipid dish
Whose presence sours the wine and
    spoils the fish.
  PHIL. Damis, his uncle, is admired
    no end.   *185*
What's your opinion, Madam?
  CEL.   Why, he's my friend.
  PHIL. He seems a decent fellow, and
    rather clever.
  CEL. He works too hard at clever-
    ness, however.
I hate to see him sweat and struggle so
To fill his conversation with bons
    mots.   *190*
Since he's decided to become a wit
His taste's so pure that nothing pleases it;
He scolds at all the latest books and
    plays,
Thinking that wit must never stoop to
    praise,
That finding fault's a sign of intel-
    lect,   *195*
That all appreciation is abject,
And that by damning everything in
    sight
One shows oneself in a distinguished
    light.
He's scornful even of our conversations:
Their trivial nature sorely tries his pa-
    tience;   *200*
He folds his arms, and stands above the
    battle,
And listens sadly to our childish prattle.
  ACAS. Wonderful, Madam! You've
    hit him off precisely.
  CLIT. No one can sketch a character
    so nicely.
  ALC. How bravely, Sirs, you cut and
    thrust at all   *205*
These absent fools, till one by one they
    fall:

But let one come in sight, and you'll at
    once
Embrace the man you lately called a
    dunce,
Telling him in a tone sincere and fervent
How proud you are to be his humble
    servant.   *210*
  CLIT. Why pick on us? Madame's
    been speaking, Sir,
And you should quarrel, if you must,
    with her.
  ALC. No, no, by God, the fault is
    yours, because
You lead her on with laughter and ap-
    plause,
And make her think that she's the more
    delightful   *215*
The more her talk is scandalous and
    spiteful.
Oh, she would stoop to malice far, far
    less
If no such claque approved her clever-
    ness.
It's flatterers like you whose foolish praise
Nourishes all the vices of these days.   *220*
  PHIL. But why protest when someone
    ridicules
Those you'd condemn, yourself, as knaves
    or fools?
  CEL. Why, Sir? Because he loves to
    make a fuss.   *223*
You don't expect him to agree with us,
When there's an opportunity to express
His heaven-sent spirit of contrariness?
What other people think, he can't abide;
Whatever they say, he's on the other side;
He lives in deadly terror of agreeing;
'Twould make him seem an ordinary
    being.   *230*
Indeed, he's so in love with contradiction,
He'll turn against his most profound con-
    viction
And with a furious eloquence deplore it,
If only someone else is speaking for it.
  ALC. Go on; dear lady, mock me as
    you please;   *235*
You have your audience in ecstasies.
  PHIL. But what she says is true: you
    have a way
Of bridling at whatever people say;

Whether they praise or blame, your
  angry spirit
Is equally unsatisfied to hear it.   *240*
  ALC. Men, Sir, are always wrong,
  and that's the reason
That righteous anger's never out of sea-
  son;
All that I hear in all their conversation
Is flattering praise or reckless condemna-
  tion.
  CEL. But . . .
  ALC.   No, no, Madam, I am
  forced to state   *245*
That you have pleasures which I depre-
  cate,
And that these others, here, are much to
  blame
For nourishing the faults which are your
  shame.
  CLIT. I shan't defend myself, Sir;
  but I vow
I'd thought this lady faultless until now.
  ACAS. I see her charms and graces,
  which are many;   *251*
But as for faults, I've never noticed any.
  ALC. I see them, Sir; and rather than
  ignore them,
I strenuously criticize her for them.
The more one loves, the more one should
  object   *255*
To every blemish, every least defect.
Were I this lady, I would soon get rid
Of lovers who approved of all I did,
And by their slack indulgence and ap-
  plause
Endorsed my follies and excused my
  flaws.   *260*
  CEL. If all hearts beat according to
  your measure,
The dawn of love would be the end of
  pleasure;
And love would find its perfect consum-
  mation
In ecstasies of rage and reprobation
  EL. Love, as a rule, affects men
  otherwise,   *265*
And lovers rarely love to criticize.
They see their lady as a charming blur,
And find all things commendable in her.
If she has any blemish, fault, or shame,

They will redeem it by a pleasing name.
The pale-faced lady's lily-white, perforce;
The swarthy one's a sweet brunette, of
  course;   *272*
The spindly lady has a slender grace;
The fat one has a most majestic pace;
The plain one, with her dress in disarray,
They classify as *beauté négligée;*   *276*
The hulking one's a goddess in their eyes,
The dwarf, a concentrate of Paradise;
The haughty lady has a noble mind;
The mean one's witty, and the dull one's
  kind;   *280*
The chatterbox has liveliness and verve,
The mute one has a virtuous reserve.
So lovers manage, in their passion's
  cause,
To love their ladies even for their flaws.
  ALC. But I still say . . .
  CEL.   I think it would
  be nice   *285*
To stroll around the gallery once or twice.
What! You're not going, Sirs?
  CLIT. and ACAS.   No, Madam, no.
  ALC. You seem to be in terror lest
  they go.
Do what you will, Sirs; leave, or linger
  on,
But I shan't go till after you are gone.
  ACAS. I'm free to linger, unless I
  should perceive   *291*
Madame is tired, and wishes me to leave.
  CLIT. And as for me, I needn't go
  today
Until the hour of the King's *coucher.*
  CEL. (*to* ALCESTE). You're joking,
  surely?
  ALC.   Not in the least; we'll see
Whether you'd rather part with them, or
  me.   *296*

SCENE 6

(ALCESTE, CÉLIMÈNE, ELIANTE,
ACASTE, PHILINTE, CLITANDRE, BASQUE.)

  BAS. (*to* ALCESTE). Sir, there's a
  fellow here who bids me state
That he must see you, and that it can't
  wait.

ALC. Tell him that I have no such
pressing affairs.
BAS. It's a long tailcoat that this fel-
low wears,   *300*
With gold all over.
CEL. (*to* ALCESTE). You'd best go
down and see.
Or—have him enter.

SCENE 7

(ALCESTE, CÉLIMÈNE, ELIANTE,
ACASTE, PHILINTE, CLITANDRE, A GUARD
of the Marshalsea.)

ALC. (*confronting the* GUARD). Well,
what do you want with me?
Come in, Sir.
GUARD. I've a word, Sir, for your ear.
ALC. Speak it aloud, Sir; I shall
strive to hear.
GUARD. The Marshals have instructed
me to say   *305*
You must report to them without delay.
ALC. Who? Me, Sir?
GUARD.   Yes, Sir; you.
ALC.   But what do
they want?
PHIL. (*to* ALCESTE). To scotch your
silly quarrel with Oronte.
CEL. (*to* PHILINTE). What quarrel?
PHIL.   Oronte and
he have fallen out
Over some verse he spoke his mind
about;   *310*
The Marshals wish to arbitrate the mat-
ter.
ALC. Never shall I equivocate or
flatter!
PHIL. You'd best obey their sum-
mons; come, let's go.
ALC. How can they mend our quar-
rel, I'd like to know?   *314*
Am I to make a cowardly retraction,
And praise those jingles to his satisfac-
tion?
I'll not recant; I've judged that sonnet
rightly.
It's bad.

PHIL. But you might say so more
politely. . . .
ALC. I'll not back down; his verses
make me sick.
PHIL. If only you could be more
politic!   *320*
But come, let's go.
ALC.   I'll go, but I won't unsay
A single word.
PHIL.   Well, let's be on our way.
ALC. Till I am ordered by my lord
the King
To praise that poem, I shall say the thing
Is scandalous, by God, and that the
poet   *325*
Ought to be hanged for having the nerve
to show it. (*To* CLITANDRE *and*
ACASTE, *who are laughing.*)
By heaven, Sirs, I really didn't know
That I was being humorous.
CEL.   Go, Sir, go;
Settle your business.
ALC.   I shall, and when I'm
through,   *329*
I shall return to settle things with you.

Act III

SCENE 1

(CLITANDRE, ACASTE.)

CLIT. Dear Marquess, how contented
you appear;
All things delight you, nothing mars your
cheer.
Can you, in perfect honesty, declare
That you've a right to be so debonair?
ACAS. By Jove, when I survey myself,
I find   *5*
No cause whatever for distress of mind.
I'm young and rich; I can in modesty
Lay claim to an exalted pedigree;
And owing to my name and my condi-
tion
I shall not want for honors and position.
Then as to courage, that most precious
trait,   *11*

I seem to have it, as was proved of late
Upon the field of honor, where my bear-
    ing,
They say, was very cool and rather
    daring.
I've wit, of course; and taste in such
    perfection   15
That I can judge without the least re-
    flection,
And at the theater, which is my delight,
Can make or break a play on opening
    night,
And lead the crowd in hisses or bravos,
And generally be known as one who
    knows.   20
I'm clever, handsome, gracefully polite;
My waist is small, my teeth are strong
    and white;
As for my dress, the world's astonished
    eyes
Assure me that I bear away the prize.
I find myself in favor everywhere,   25
Honored by men, and worshiped by the
    fair;
And since these things are so, it seems to
    me
I'm justified in my complacency.
    CLIT. Well, if so many ladies hold
    you dear,
Why do you press a hopeless courtship
    here?   30
    ACAS. Hopeless, you say? I'm not the
    sort of fool
That likes his ladies difficult and cool.
Men who are awkward, shy, and peas-
    antish
May pine for heartless beauties, if they
    wish,   34
Grovel before them, bear their cruelties,
Woo them with tears and sighs and
    bended knees,
And hope by dogged faithfulness to gain
What their poor merits never could ob-
    tain.
For men like me, however, it makes no
    sense
To love on trust, and foot the whole ex-
    pense.   40
Whatever any lady's merits be,

I think, thank God, that I'm as choice as
    she;
That if my heart is kind enough to burn
For her, she owes me something in re-
    turn;
And that in any proper love affair   45
The partners must invest an equal share.
    CLIT. You think, then, that our host-
    ess favors you?
    ACAS. I've reason to believe that that
    is true.
    CLIT. How did you come to such a
    mad conclusion?
You're blind, dear fellow. This is sheer
    delusion.   50
    ACAS. All right, then: I'm deluded
    and I'm blind.
    CLIT. Whatever put the notion in
    your mind?
    ACAS. Delusion.
    CLIT. What persuades you that you're
    right?
    ACAS. I'm blind.
    CLIT.   But have you any
    proofs to cite?
    ACAS. I tell you I'm deluded.
    CLIT.   Have you, then,   55
Received some secret pledge from Céli-
    mène?
    ACAS. Oh, no: she scorns me.
    CLIT.   Tell me the truth, I beg.
    ACAS. She just can't bear me.
    CLIT.   Ah, don't pull my leg.
Tell me what hope she's given you, I pray.
    ACAS. I'm hopeless, and it's you who
    win the day.   60
She hates me thoroughly, and I'm so
    vexed
I mean to hang myself on Tuesday next.
    CLIT. Dear Marquess, let us have an
    armistice
And make a treaty. What do you say to
    this?
If ever one of us can plainly prove   65
That Célimène encourages his love,
The other must abandon hope, and yield,
And leave him in possession of the field.
    ACAS. Now, there's a bargain that
    appeals to me;

With all my heart, dear Marquess, I agree.
But hush.

SCENE 2

(CÉLIMÈNE, ACASTE, CLITANDRE.)

CEL.   Still here?
CLIT.   'Twas love that stayed
our feet.   71
CEL.   I think I heard a carriage in
the street.
Whose is it? D'you know?

SCENE 3

(CÉLIMÈNE, ACASTE, CLITANDRE,
BASQUE.)

BAS.   Arsinoé is here,
Madame.
CEL.   Arsinoé, you say? Oh, dear.
BAS.   Eliante is entertaining her be-
low.   75
CEL.   What brings the creature here,
I'd like to know?
ACAS.   They say she's dreadfully prud-
ish, but in fact
I think her piety . . .
CEL.   It's all an act.
At heart she's worldly, and her poor
success
In snaring men explains her prudishness.
It breaks her heart to see the beaux and
gallants   81
Engrossed by other women's charms and
talents,
And so she's always in a jealous rage
Against the faulty standards of the age.
She lets the world believe that she's a
prude   85
To justify her loveless solitude,
And strives to put a brand of moral
shame
On all the graces that she cannot claim.
But still she'd love a lover; and Alceste
Appears to be the one she'd love the
best.   90
His visits here are poison to her pride;

She seems to think I've lured him from
her side;
And everywhere, at court or in the town,
The spiteful, envious woman runs me
down.   94
In short, she's just as stupid as can be,
Vicious and arrogant in the last degree,
And . . .

SCENE 4

(ARSINOÉ, CÉLIMÈNE, CLITANDRE,
ACASTE.)

CEL.   Ah! What happy chance has
brought you here?
I've thought about you ever so much,
my dear.
ARSINOÉ.   I've come to tell you something you should know.
CEL.   How good of you to think of
doing so!   100
(CLITANDRE and ACASTE go out, laugh-
ing.)

SCENE 5

(ARSINOÉ, CÉLIMÈNE.)

ARSIN.   It's just as well those gentle-
men didn't tarry.
CEL.   Shall we sit down?
ARSIN.   That won't be necessary.
Madam, the flame of friendship ought to
burn
Brightest in matters of the most concern,
And as there's nothing which concerns
us more   105
Than honor, I have hastened to your
door
To bring you, as your friend, some in-
formation
About the status of your reputation.
I visited, last night, some virtuous folk,
And, quite by chance, it was of you they
spoke;   110
There was, I fear, no tendency to praise
Your light behavior and your dashing
ways.

The quantity of gentlemen you see
And your by now notorious coquetry
Were both so vehemently criticized   *115*
By everyone, that I was much surprised.
Of course, I needn't tell you where I
stood;
I came to your defense as best I could,
Assured them you were harmless, and
declared
Your soul was absolutely unimpaired.
But there are some things, you must
realize,   *121*
One can't excuse, however hard one tries,
And I was forced at last into conceding
That your behavior, Madam, is mislead-
ing,
That it makes a bad impression, giving
rise   *125*
To ugly gossip and obscene surmise,
And that if you were more *overtly* good,
You wouldn't be so much misunderstood.
Not that I think you've been unchaste—
no! no!
The saints preserve me from a thought
so low!   *130*
But mere good conscience never did
suffice:
One must avoid the outward show of
vice.
Madam, you're too intelligent, I'm sure,
To think my motives anything but pure
In offering you this counsel—which I do
Out of a zealous interest in you.   *136*
    CEL.   Madam, I haven't taken you
amiss;
I'm very much obliged to you for this;
And I'll at once discharge the obligation
By telling you about *your* reputation.   *140*
You've been so friendly as to let me
know
What certain people say of me, and so
I mean to follow your benign example
By offering you a somewhat similar
sample.
The other day, I went to an affair   *145*
And found some most distinguished peo-
ple there
Discussing piety, both false and true.

The conversation soon came round to
you.
Alas! Your prudery and bustling zeal   *149*
Appeared to have a very slight appeal.
Your affectation of a grave demeanor,
Your endless talk of virtue and of honor,
The aptitude of your suspicious mind
For finding sin where there is none to
find,
Your towering self-esteem, that pitying
face   *155*
With which you contemplate the human
race,
Your sermonizings and your sharp asper-
sions
On people's pure and innocent diver-
sions—
All these were mentioned, Madam, and,
in fact,
Were roundly and concertedly attacked.
"What good," they said, "are all these
outward shows,   *161*
When everything belies her pious pose?
She prays incessantly; but then, they say,
She beats her maids and cheats them of
their pay;
She shows her zeal in every holy place,
But still she's vain enough to paint her
face;   *166*
She holds that naked statues are immoral,
But with a naked *man* she'd have no
quarrel."
Of course, I said to everybody there
That they were being viciously unfair;
But still they were disposed to criticize
you,   *171*
And all agreed that someone should ad-
vise you
To leave the morals of the world alone,
And worry rather more about your own.
They felt that one's self-knowledge should
be great   *175*
Before one thinks of setting others
straight;
That one should learn the art of living
well
Before one threatens other men with
hell,

And that the Church is best equipped,
   no doubt,
To guide our souls and root our vices
   out.   *180*
Madam, you're too intelligent, I'm sure,
To think my motives anything but pure
In offering you this counsel—which I do
Out of a zealous interest in you.
   ARSIN.   I dared not hope for grati-
      tude, but I   *185*
Did not expect so acid a reply;
I judge, since you've been so extremely
   tart,
That my good counsel pierced you to the
   heart.
   CEL.   Far from it, Madam. Indeed, it
      seems to me   *189*
We ought to trade advice more fre-
   quently.
One's vision of oneself is so defective
That it would be an excellent corrective.
If you are willing, Madam, let's arrange
Shortly to have another frank exchange
In which we'll tell each other, *entre nous,*
What you've heard tell of me, and I of
   you.   *196*
   ARSIN.   Oh, people never censure
      you, my dear;
It's me they criticize. Or so I hear.
   CEL.   Madam, I think we either
      blame or praise
According to our taste and length of
   days.   *200*
There is a time of life for coquetry,
And there's a season, too, for prudery.
When all one's charms are gone, it is,
   I'm sure,
Good strategy to be devout and pure:
It makes one seem a little less forsaken.
Some day, perhaps, I'll take the road
   you've taken: *206*
Time brings all things. But I have time
   aplenty,
And see no cause to be a prude at twenty.
   ARSIN.   You give your age in such a
      gloating tone
That one would think I was an ancient
      crone;   *210*
We're not so far apart, in sober truth,

That you can mock me with a boast of
   youth!
Madam, you baffle me. I wish I knew
What moves you to provoke me as you
   do.
   CEL.   For my part, Madam, I should
      like to know   *215*
Why you abuse me everywhere you go.
Is it my fault, dear lady, that your hand
Is not, alas, in very great demand?
If men admire me, if they pay me court
And daily make me offers of the sort
You'd dearly love to have them make to
   you,   *221*
How can I help it? What would you have
   me do?
If what you want is lovers, please feel
   free
To take as many as you can from me.
   ARSIN.   Oh, come. D'you think the
      world is losing sleep   *225*
Over that flock of lovers which you keep,
Or that we find it difficult to guess
What price you pay for their devoted-
   ness?
Surely you don't expect us to suppose
Mere merit could attract so many beaux?
It's not your virtue that they're dazzled
   by;   *231*
Nor is it virtuous love for which they
   sigh.
You're fooling no one, Madam; the
   world's not blind;
There's many a lady heaven has designed
To call men's noblest, tenderest feeling
   out,   *235*
Who has no lovers dogging her about;
From which it's plain that lovers nowa-
   days
Must be acquired in bold and shameless
   ways,
And only pay one court for such reward
As modesty and virtue can't afford.   *240*
Then don't be quite so puffed up, if you
   please,
About your tawdry little victories;
Try, if you can, to be a shade less vain,
And treat the world with somewhat less
   disdain.

If one were envious of your amours,
One soon could have a following like
    yours;   *246*
Lovers are no great trouble to collect
If one prefers them to one's self-respect.
    CEL.   Collect them then, my dear; I'd
    love to see
You demonstrate that charming theory;
Who knows, you might . . .
    ARSIN.   Now, Madam, that
    will do,   *251*
It's time to end this trying interview.
My coach is late in coming to your door,
Or I'd have taken leave of you before.
    CEL.   Oh, please don't feel that you
    must rush away;   *255*
I'd be delighted, Madam, if you'd stay.
However, lest my conversation bore you,
Let me provide some better company
    for you;
This gentleman, who comes most
    apropos,
Will please you more than I could do, I
    know.   *260*

SCENE 6

(ALCESTE, CÉLIMÈNE, ARSINOÉ.)

    CEL.   Alceste, I have a little note to
    write
Which simply must go out before tonight;
Please entertain *Madame;* I'm sure that
    she
Will overlook my incivility.

SCENE 7

(ALCESTE, ARSINOÉ.)

    ARSIN.   Well, Sir, our hostess gra-
    ciously contrives   *265*
For us to chat until my coach arrives;
And I shall be forever in her debt.
For granting me this little tête-à-tête.
We women very rightly give our
    hearts   *269*
To men of noble character and parts,
And your especial merits, dear Alceste,

Have roused the deepest sympathy in my
    breast.
Oh, how I wish they had sufficient sense
At court, to recognize your excellence!
They wrong you generally, Sir. How it
    must hurt you   *275*
Never to be rewarded for your virtue!
    ALC.   Why, Madam, what cause have
    I to feel aggrieved?
What great and brilliant thing have I
    achieved?
What service have I rendered to the
    King   *279*
That I should look to him for anything?
    ARSIN.   Not everyone who's honored
    by the State
Has done great services. A man must
    wait
Till time and fortune offer him the
    chance.
Your merit, Sir, is obvious at a glance,
And . . .
    ALC.   Ah, forget my merit; I'm not
    neglected.   *285*
The court, I think, can hardly be ex-
    pected
To mine men's souls for merit, and un-
    earth
Our hidden virtues and our secret worth.
    ARSIN.   *Some* virtues, though, are far
    too bright to hide;
Yours are acknowledged, Sir, on every
    side.   *290*
Indeed, I've heard you warmly praised
    of late
By persons of considerable weight.
    ALC.   This fawning age has praise for
    everyone,
And all distinctions, Madam, are un-
    done.
All things have equal honor nowadays,
And no one should be gratified by
    praise.   *296*
To be admired, one only need exist,
And every lackey's on the honors list.
    ARSIN.   I only wish, Sir, that you had
    your eye
On some position at court, however
    high;   *300*

You'd only have to hint at such a notion
For me to set the proper wheels in
    motion;
I've certain friendships I'd be glad to use
To get you any office you might choose.
   ALC. Madame, I fear that any such
    ambition   305
Is wholly foreign to my disposition.
The soul God gave me isn't of the sort
That prospers in the weather of a court.
It's all too obvious that I don't possess
The virtues necessary for success.   310
My one great talent is for speaking plain;
I've never learned to flatter or to feign;
And anyone so stupidly sincere
Had best not seek a courtier's career.
Outside the court, I know, one must
    dispense   315
With honors, privilege, and influence;
But still one gains the right, foregoing
    these,
Not to be tortured by the wish to please.
One needn't live in dread of snubs and
    slights,
Nor praise the verse that every idiot
    writes,   320
Nor humor silly Marquesses, nor bestow
Politic sighs on Madam So-and-So.
   ARSIN. Forget the court, then; let the
    matter rest.
But I've another cause to be distressed
About your present situation, Sir.   325
It's to your love affair that I refer.
She whom you love, and who pretends to
    love you,
Is, I regret to say, unworthy of you.
   ALC. Why, Madam! Can you seri-
    ously intend
To make so grave a charge against your
    friend?   330
   ARSIN. Alas, I must. I've stood aside
    too long
And let that lady do you grievous wrong;
But now my debt to conscience shall be
    paid:
I tell you that your love has been be-
    trayed.
   ALC. I thank you. Madam; you're
    extremely kind.   335

Such words are soothing to a lover's
    mind.
   ARSIN. Yes, though she *is* my friend,
    I say again
You're very much too good for Céli-
    mène.
She's wantonly misled you from the start.
   ALC. You may be right; who knows
    another's heart?   340
But ask yourself if it's the part of charity
To shake my soul with doubts of her
    sincerity.
   ARSIN. Well, if you'd rather be a
    dupe than doubt her,
That's your affair. I'll say no more about
    her.
   ALC. Madam, you know that doubt
    and vague suspicion   345
Are painful to a man in my position;
It's most unkind to worry me this way
Unless you've some real proof of what
    you say.
   ARSIN. Sir, say no more: all doubt
    shall be removed,
And all that I've been saying shall be
    proved.   350
You've only to escort me home, and there
We'll look into the heart of this affair.
I've ocular evidence which will persuade
    you
Beyond a doubt, that Célimène's betrayed
    you.
Then, if you're saddened by that revela-
    tion,   355
Perhaps I can provide some consolation.

Act IV

SCENE 1

(ELIANTE, PHILINTE.)

   PHIL. Madam, he acted like a stub-
    born child;
I thought they never would be reconciled;
In vain we reasoned, threatened, and
    appealed;
He stood his ground and simply would
    not yield.

The Marshals, I feel sure, have never
   heard   5
An argument so splendidly absurd.
"No, gentlemen," said he, "I'll not re-
   tract.
His verse is bad: extremely bad, in fact.
Surely it does the man no harm to know
   it.
Does it disgrace him, not to be a
   poet?   10
A gentleman may be respected still,
Whether he writes a sonnet well or ill.
That I dislike his verse should not offend
   him;
In all that touches honor, I commend
   him;
He's noble, brave, and virtuous—but I
   fear   15
He can't in truth be called a sonneteer.
I'll gladly praise his wardrobe; I'll en-
   dorse
His dancing, or the way he sits a horse;
But, gentlemen, I cannot praise his
   rhyme.
In fact, it ought to be a capital crime   20
For anyone so sadly unendowed
To write a sonnet, and read the thing
   aloud."
At length he fell into a gentler mood
And, striking a concessive attitude,
He paid Oronte the following courtesies:
"Sir, I regret that I'm so hard to
   please,   26
And I'm profoundly sorry that your
   lyric
Failed to provoke me to a panegyric."
After these curious words, the two em-
   braced,
And then the hearing was adjourned—
   in haste.   30
   EL. His conduct has been very singu-
   lar lately;
Still, I confess that I respect him greatly.
The honesty in which he takes such
   pride
Has—to my mind—its noble, heroic
   side.
In this false age, such candor seems
   outrageous;   35

But I could wish that it were more con-
   tagious.
   PHIL. What most intrigues me in our
   friend Alceste
Is the grand passion that rages in his
   breast.
The sullen humors he's compounded of
Should not, I think, dispose his heart
   to love;   40
But since they do, it puzzles me still more
That he should choose your cousin to
   adore.
   EL. It does, indeed, belie the theory
That love is born of gentle sympathy,
And that the tender passion must be
   based   45
On sweet accords of temper and of taste.
   PHIL. Does she return his love, do
   you suppose?
   EL. Ah, that's a difficult question,
   Sir. Who knows?
How can we judge the truth of her de-
   votion?
Her heart's a stranger to its own emo-
   tion.   50
Sometimes it thinks it loves, when no
   love's there;
At other times it loves quite unaware.
   PHIL. I rather think Alceste is in for
   more
Distress and sorrow than he's bargained
   for;
Were he of my mind, Madam, his
   affection   55
Would turn in quite a different direction,
And we would see him more responsive
   to
The kind regard which he receives from
   you.
   EL. Sir, I believe in frankness, and
   I'm inclined,
In matters of the heart, to speak my
   mind.   60
I don't oppose his love for her; indeed,
I hope with all my heart that he'll suc-
   ceed,
And were it in my power, I'd rejoice
In giving him the lady of his choice.
But if, as happens frequently enough   65

In love affairs, he meets with a rebuff—
If Célimène should grant some rival's
   suit—
I'd gladly play the role of substitute;
Nor would his tender speeches please me
   less
Because they'd once been made without
   success.   70
   PHIL. Well, Madam, as for me, I
   don't oppose
Your hopes in this affair; and heaven
   knows
That in my conversations with the man
I plead your cause as often as I can.
But if those two should marry, and so
   remove   75
All chance that he will offer you his love,
Then I'll declare my own, and hope to
   see
Your gracious favor pass from him to
   me.
In short, should you be cheated of
   Alceste,
I'd be most happy to be second best.   80
   EL. Philinte, you're teasing.
   PHIL.   Ah, Madam, never fear;
No words of mine were ever so sincere,
And I shall live in fretful expectation
Till I can make a fuller declaration.

SCENE 2

(ALCESTE, ELIANTE, PHILINTE.)

   ALC. Avenge me, Madam! I must
   have satisfaction,   85
Or this great wrong will drive me to dis-
   traction!
   EL. Why, what's the matter? What's
   upset you so?
   ALC. Madam, I've had a mortal,
   mortal blow.
If Chaos repossessed the universe,
I swear I'd not be shaken any worse.   90
I'm ruined. . . . I can say no more. . . .
   My soul . . .
   EL. Do try, Sir, to regain your self-
   control.

   ALC. Just heaven! Why were so
   much beauty and grace
Bestowed on one so vicious and so base?
   EL. Once more, Sir, tell us. . . .
   ALC. My world has gone to
   wrack;
I'm—I'm betrayed; she's stabbed me in
   the back: 96
Yes, Célimène (who would have thought
   it of her?)
Is false to me, and has another lover.
   EL. Are you quite certain? Can you
   prove these things?
   PHIL. Lovers are prey to wild imagi-
   nings   100
And jealous fancies. No doubt there's
   some mistake. . . .
   ALC. Mind your own business, Sir,
   for heaven's sake.
   (To ELIANTE.) Madam, I have the
   proof that you demand
Here in my pocket, penned by her own
   hand.
Yes, all the shameful evidence one
   could want   105
Lies in this letter written to Oronte—
Oronte! whom I felt sure she couldn't
   love.
And hardly bothered to be jealous of.
   PHIL. Still, in a letter, appearances
   may deceive;
This may not be so bad as you be-
   lieve.   110
   ALC. Once more I beg you, Sir, to let
   me be;
Tend to your own affairs; leave mine to
   me.
   EL. Compose yourself; this anguish
   that you feel . . .
   ALC. Is something, Madam, you
   alone can heal.
My outraged heart, beside itself with
   grief,   115
Appeals to you for comfort and relief.
Avenge me on your cousin, whose unjust
And faithless nature has deceived my
   trust;
Avenge a crime your pure soul must
   detest.

EL.   But how, Sir?

ALC.   Madam, this heart within my
breast   *120*

Is yours; pray take it; redeem my heart
from her,

And so avenge me on my torturer.

Let her be punished by the fond emotion,

The ardent love, the bottomless devotion,

The faithful worship which this heart of
mine   *125*

Will offer up to yours as to a shrine.

EL.   You have my sympathy, Sir, in
all you suffer;

Nor do I scorn the noble heart you offer;

But I suspect you'll soon be mollified,

And this desire for vengeance will sub-
side.   *130*

When some beloved hand has done us
wrong

We thirst for retribution—but not for
long;

However dark the deed that she's committed,

A lovely culprit's very soon acquitted.

Nothing's so stormy as an injured lover,

And yet no storm so quickly passes
over.   *136*

ALC.   No, Madam, no—this is no
lovers' spat;

I'll not forgive her; it's gone too far for
that;

My mind's made up; I'll kill myself be-
fore   *139*

I waste my hopes upon her any more.

Ah, here she is. My wrath intensifies.

I shall confront her with her tricks and
lies,

And crush her utterly, and bring you then

A heart no longer slave to Célimène.

SCENE 3

(CÉLIMÈNE, ALCESTE.)

ALC. (*aside*).   Sweet heaven, help me
to control my passion.   *145*

CEL. (*aside*).   Oh, Lord. (*To* AL-
CESTE.)

Why stand there staring in that
fashion?

And what d'you mean by those dramatic
sighs,

And that malignant glitter in your eyes?

ALC.   I mean that sins which cause
the blood to freeze   *149*

Look innocent beside your treacheries;

That nothing Hell's or Heaven's wrath
could do

Ever produced so bad a thing as you.

CEL.   Your compliments were always sweet and pretty.

ALC.   Madam, it's not the moment
to be witty.

No, blush and hang your head; you've
ample reason,   *155*

Since I've the fullest evidence of your
treason.

Ah, this is what my sad heart prophesied;

Now all my anxious fears are verified;

My dark suspicion and my gloomy doubt

Divined the truth, and now the truth is
out.   *160*

For all your trickery, I was not deceived;

It was my bitter stars that I believed.

But don't imagine that you'll go scot-free;

You shan't misuse me with impunity.

I know that love's irrational and blind;

I know the heart's not subject to the
mind,   *166*

And can't be reasoned into beating
faster;

I know each soul is free to choose its
master;

Therefore had you but spoken from the
heart,   *169*

Rejecting my attentions from the start,

I'd have no grievance, or at any rate

I could complain of nothing but my fate.

Ah, but so falsely to encourage me—

That was a treason and a treachery

For which you cannot suffer too severely,

And you shall pay for that behavior
dearly.   *176*

Yes, now I have no pity, not a shred;

My temper's out of hand; I've lost my
head;

Shocked by the knowledge of your
double-dealings,

My reason can't restrain my savage feel-
    ings;   *180*
A righteous wrath deprives me of my
    senses,
And I won't answer for the consequences.
  CEL. What does this outburst mean?
    Will you please explain?
Have you, by any chance, gone quite
    insane?
  ALC. Yes, yes, I went insane the
    day I fell   *185*
A victim to your black and fatal spell,
Thinking to meet with some sincerity
Among the treacherous charms that
    beckoned me.
  CEL. Pooh. Of what treachery can
    you complain?
  ALC. How sly you are, how cleverly
    you feign!   *190*
But you'll not victimize me any more.
Look: here's a document you've seen
    before.
This evidence, which I acquired today,
Leaves you, I think, without a thing to
    say.
  CEL. Is this what sent you into such
    a fit?   *195*
  ALC. You should be blushing at the
    sight of it.
  CEL. Ought I to blush? I truly don't
    see why.
  ALC. Ah, now you're being bold as
    well as sly;
Since there's no signature, perhaps you'll
    claim . . .
  CEL. I wrote it, whether or not it
    bears my name.   *200*
  ALC. And you can view with equa-
    nimity
This proof of your disloyalty to me!
  CEL. Oh, don't be so outrageous and
    extreme.
  ALC. You take this matter lightly, it
    would seem.
Was it no wrong to me, no shame to
    you,   *205*
That you should send Oronte this billet-
    doux?

  CEL. Oronte! Who said it was for
    him?
  ALC.   Why, those
Who brought me this example of your
    prose.
But what's the difference? If you wrote
    the letter   *209*
To someone else, it pleases me no better.
My grievance and your guilt remain the
    same.
  CEL. But need you rage, and need
    I blush for shame,
If this was written to a *woman* friend?
  ALC. Ah! Most ingenious. I'm im-
    pressed no end;
And after that incredible evasion   *215*
Your guilt is clear. I need no more per-
    suasion.
How dare you try so clumsy a deception?
D'you think I'm wholly wanting in per-
    ception?
Come, come, let's see how brazenly
    you'll try
To bolster up so palpable a lie: *220*
Kindly construe this ardent closing
    section
As nothing more than sisterly affection!
Here, let me read it. Tell me, if you
    dare to,
That this is for a woman . . .
  CEL.   I don't care to.
What right have you to badger and
    berate me,   *225*
And so highhandedly interrogate me?
  ALC. Now, don't be angry; all I ask
    of you
Is that you justify a phrase or two . . .
  CEL. No, I shall not. I utterly re-
    fuse,
And you may take those phrases as you
    choose.   *230*
  ALC. Just show me how this letter
    could be meant
For a woman's eyes, and I shall be con-
    tent.
  CEL. No, no, it's for Oronte; you're
    perfectly right.
I welcome his attentions with delight,

I prize his character and his intel-
lect,   *235*
And everything is just as you suspect.
Come, do your worst now; give your
    rage free rein;
But kindly cease to bicker and complain.
    ALC. (*aside*). Good God! Could
    anything be more inhuman?
Was ever a heart so mangled by a
    woman?   *240*
When I complain of how she has be-
trayed me,
She bridles, and commences to upbraid
    me!
She tries my tortured patience to the
    limit;
She won't deny her guilt; she glories
    in it!
And yet my heart's too faint and cow-
ardly   *245*
To break these chains of passion, and
    be free,
To scorn her as it should, and rise above
This unrewarded, mad, and bitter love.
(*To* CÉLIMÈNE.) Ah, traitress, in how
    confident a fashion
You take advantage of my helpless pas-
sion,   *250*
And use my weakness for your faithless
    charms
To make me once again throw down my
    arms!
But do at least deny this black trans-
gression;
Take back that mocking and perverse
    confession;   *254*
Defend this letter and your innocence,
And I, poor fool, will aid in your de-
fense.
Pretend, pretend, that you are just and
    true,
And I shall make myself believe in you.
    CEL. Oh, stop it. Don't be such a
    jealous dunce,   *259*
Or I shall leave off loving you at once.
Just why should I *pretend?* What could
    impel me
To stoop so low as that? And kindly
    tell me

Why, if I loved another, I shouldn't
    merely
Inform you of it, simply and sincerely!
I've told you where you stand, and that
    admission   *265*
Should altogether clear me of suspicion;
After so generous a guarantee,
What right have you to harbor doubts
    of me?
Since women are (from natural reti-
cence)   *269*
Reluctant to declare their sentiments,
And since the honor of our sex requires
That we conceal our amorous desires,
Ought any man for whom such laws are
    broken
To question what the oracle has spoken?
Should he not rather feel an obliga-
tion   *275*
To trust that most obliging declaration?
Enough, now. Your suspicions quite
    disgust me;
Why should I love a man who doesn't
    trust me?
I cannot understand why I continue,
Fool that I am, to take an interest in
    you.   *280*
I ought to choose a man less prone to
    doubt,
And give you something to be vexed
    about.
    ALC. Ah, what a poor enchanted fool
    I am;
These gentle words, no doubt, were all
    a sham;
But destiny requires me to entrust   *285*
My happiness to you, and so I must.
I'll love you to the bitter end, and see
How false and treacherous you dare
    to be.
    CEL. No, you don't really love me as
    you ought.
    ALC. I love you more than can be
    said or thought;   *290*
Indeed, I wish you were in such distress
That I might show my deep devotedness.
Yes, I could wish that you were wretch-
edly poor,
Unloved, uncherished, utterly obscure;

That fate had set you down upon the
    earth   *295*
Without possessions, rank, or gentle
    birth;
Then, by the offer of my heart, I might
Repair the great injustice of your plight;
I'd raise you from the dust, and proudly
    prove
The purity and vastness of my love. *300*
    CEL. This is a strange benevolence
    indeed!
God grant that I may never be in
    need. . . .
Ah, here's Monsieur Dubois, in quaint
    disguise.

SCENE 4

(CÉLIMÈNE, ALCESTE, DUBOIS.)

    ALC. Well, why this costume? Why
    those frightened eyes?
What ails you?
    DUBOIS.   Well, Sir, things are most
    mysterious.   *305*
    ALC. What do you mean?
    DUB.   I fear they're very serious.
    ALC. What?
    DUB.   Shall I speak more loudly?
    ALC.   Yes; speak out.
    DUB. Isn't there someone here, Sir?
    ALC.   Speak, you lout!
Stop wasting time.
    DUB.   Sir, we must slip away.
    ALC. How's that?
    DUB.   We must decamp without
    delay.   *310*
    ALC. Explain yourself.
    DUB.   I tell you we must fly.
    ALC. What for?
    DUB.   We mustn't pause to say
    good-by.
    ALC. Now what d'you mean by all
    of this, you clown?
    DUB. I mean, Sir, that we've got to
    leave this town.
    ALC. I'll tear you limb from limb
    and joint from joint   *315*
If you don't come more quickly to the
    point.

    DUB. Well, Sir, today a man in a
    black suit,
Who wore a black and ugly scowl to
    boot,
Left us a document scrawled in such a
    hand
As even Satan couldn't understand. *320*
It bears upon your lawsuit, I don't
    doubt;
But all hell's devils couldn't make it out.
    ALC. Well, well, go on. What then?
    I fail to see
How this event obliges us to flee.
    DUB. Well, Sir: an hour later, hardly
    more,   *325*
A gentleman who's often called before
Came looking for you in an anxious way.
Not finding you, he asked me to convey
(Knowing I could be trusted with the
    same)
The following message. . . . Now, what
    was his name?   *330*
    ALC. Forget his name, you idiot.
    What did he say?
    DUB. Well, it was one of your
    friends, Sir, anyway.
He warned you to begone, and he sug-
    gested
That if you stay, you may well be ar-
    rested.
    ALC. What? Nothing more specific?
    Think, man, think!   *335*
    DUB. No, Sir. He had me bring him
    pen and ink,
And dashed you off a letter which, I'm
    sure,
Will render things distinctly less ob-
    scure.
    ALC. Well—let me have it!
    CEL.   What *is* this all about?
    ALC. God knows; but I have hopes
    of finding out.   *340*
How long am I to wait, you blitherer?
    DUB. (*after a protracted search for
    the letter*). I must have left it on
    your table, Sir.
    ALC. I ought to . . .
    CEL.   No, no, keep your self-
    control;
Go find out what's behind his rigmarole.

ALC. It seems that fate, no matter
    what I do,   *345*
Has sworn that I may not converse with
    you;
But, Madam, pray permit your faithful
    lover
To try once more before the day is over.

Act V

SCENE 1

(ALCESTE, PHILINTE.)

ALC. No, it's too much. My mind's
    made up, I tell you.
PHIL. Why should this blow, how-
    ever hard, compel you . . .
ALC. No, no, don't waste your
    breath in argument;
Nothing you say will alter my intent;
This age is vile, and I've made up my
    mind   *5*
To have no further commerce with man-
    kind.
Did not truth, honor, decency, and the
    laws
Oppose my enemy and approve my
    cause?
My claims were justified in all men's
    sight;
I put my trust in equity and right;   *10*
Yet, to my horror and the world's dis-
    grace,
Justice is mocked, and I have lost my
    case!
A scoundrel whose dishonesty is notori-
    ous
Emerges from another lie victorious!
Honor and right condone his brazen
    fraud,   *15*
While rectitude and decency applaud!
Before his smirking face, the truth stands
    charmed,
And virtue conquered, and the law dis-
    armed!
His crime is sanctioned by a court de-
    cree!
And not content with what he's done
    to me,   *20*

The dog now seeks to ruin me by stating
That I composed a book now circulating,
A book so wholly criminal and vicious
That even to speak its title is seditious!
Meanwhile Oronte, my rival, lends his
    credit   *25*
To the same libelous tale, and helps to
    spread it!
Oronte! a man of honor and of rank,
With whom I've been entirely fair and
    frank;
Who sought me out and forced me,
    willy-nilly,
To judge some verse I found extremely
    silly;   *30*
And who, because I properly refused
To flatter him, or see the truth abused,
Abets my enemy in a rotten slander!
There's the reward of honesty and can-
    dor!
The man will hate me to the end of
    time   *35*
For failing to commend his wretched
    rhyme!
And not this man alone, but all human-
    ity
Do what they do from interest and
    vanity;
They prate of honor, truth, and right-
    eousness,   *39*
But lie, betray, and swindle nonetheless.
Come then: man's villainy is too much
    to bear;
Let's leave this jungle and this jackal's
    lair.
Yes! treacherous and savage race of men,
You shall not look upon my face again.
    PHIL. Oh, don't rush into exile pre-
    maturely;   *45*
Things aren't as dreadful as you make
    them, surely.
It's rather obvious, since you're still at
    large,
That people don't believe your enemy's
    charge,
Indeed, his tale's so patently untrue
That it may do more harm to him than
    you.   *50*
    ALC. Nothing could do that scoundrel
    any harm:

His frank corruption is his greatest
    charm,
And, far from hurting him, a further
    shame
Would only serve to magnify his name.
   PHIL.   In any case, his bald prevari-
    cation   55
Has done no injury to your reputation,
And you may feel secure in that regard.
As for your lawsuit, it should not be
    hard
To have the case reopened, and contest
This judgment . . .   59
   ALC.   No, no, let the verdict rest.
Whatever cruel penalty it may bring,
I wouldn't have it changed for anything.
It shows the time's injustice with clarity
That I shall pass it down to our posterity
As a great proof and signal demonstra-
    tion   65
Of the black wickedness of this genera-
    tion.
It may cost twenty thousand francs;
    but I
Shall pay their twenty thousand, and gain
    thereby
The right to storm and rage at human
    evil,
And send the race of mankind to the
    devil.   70
   PHIL.   Listen to me. . . .
   ALC.   Why? What can you
    possibly say?
Don't argue, Sir; your labor's thrown
    away.
Do you propose to offer lame excuses
For men's behavior and the time's
    abuses?
   PHIL.   No, all you say I'll readily
    concede: 75
This is a low, conniving age indeed;
Nothing but trickery prospers nowadays,
And people ought to mend their shabby
    ways.
Yes, man's a beastly creature; but must
    we then
Abandon the society of men?   80
Here in the world, each human frailty
Provides occasion for philosophy,

And that is virtue's noblest exercise;
If honesty shone forth from all men's
    eyes,
If every heart were frank and kind and
    just,   85
What could our virtues do but gather
    dust
(Since their employment is to help us
    bear
The villainies of men without despair)?
A heart well-armed with virtue can en-
    dure. . . .
   ALC.   Sir, you're a matchless rea-
    soner, to be sure;   90
Your words are fine and full of cogency;
But don't waste time and eloquence
    on me.
My reason bids me go, for my own good.
My tongue won't lie and flatter as it
    should;
God knows what frankness it might next
    commit,   95
And what I'd suffer on account of it.
Pray let me wait for Célimène's return
In peace and quiet. I shall shortly learn,
By her response to what I have in view,
Whether her love for me is feigned or
    true.   100
   PHIL.   Till then, let's visit Eliante up-
    stairs.
   ALC.   No, I am too weighed down
    with somber cares.
Go to her, do; and leave me with my
    gloom
Here in the darkened corner of this
    room.
   PHIL.   Why, that's no sort of com-
    pany, my friend;   105
I'll see if Eliante will not descend.

SCENE 2

(CÉLIMÈNE, ORONTE, ALCESTE.)

   OR.   Yes, Madam, if you wish me to
    remain
Your true and ardent lover, you must
    deign

To give me some more positive assur-
ance.
All this suspense is quite beyond en-
durance.   *110*
If your heart shares the sweet desires of
mine,
Show me as much by some convincing
sign;
And here's the sign I urgently suggest:
That you no longer tolerate Alceste,
But sacrifice him to my love, and
sever   *115*
All your relations with the man forever.
  CEL. Why do you suddenly dislike
him so?
You praised him to the skies not long
ago.
  OR. Madam, that's not the point. I'm
here to find
Which way your tender feelings are in-
clined.   *120*
Choose, if you please, between Alceste
and me,
And I shall stay or go accordingly.
  ALC. (*emerging from the corner*).
Yes, Madam, choose; this gentle-
man's demand
Is wholly just, and I support his stand.
I too am true and ardent; I too am
here   *125*
To ask you that you make your feelings
clear.
No more delays, now; no equivocation;
The time has come to make your declara-
tion.
  OR. Sir, I've no wish in any way to be
An obstacle to your felicity.   *130*
  ALC. Sir, I've no wish to share her
heart with you;
That may sound jealous, but at least it's
true.
  OR. If, weighing us, she leans in
your direction . . .
  ALC. If she regards you with the
least affection . . .
  OR. I swear I'll yield her to you
there and then.   *135*
  ALC. I swear I'll never see her face
again.

  OR. Now, Madam, tell us what we've
come to hear.
  ALC. Madam, speak openly and
have no fear.
  OR. Just say which one is to remain
your lover.
  ALC. Just name one name, and it
will all be over.   *140*
  OR. What! Is it possible that you're
undecided?
  ALC. What! Can your feelings pos-
sibly be divided?
  CEL. Enough: this inquisition's gone
too far:
How utterly unreasonable you are!
Not that I couldn't make the choice with
ease;   *145*
My heart has no conflicting sympathies;
I know full well which one of you I
favor,
And you'd not see me hesitate or waver.
But how can you expect me to reveal
So cruelly and bluntly what I feel? *150*
I think it altogether too unpleasant
To choose between two men when both
are present;
One's heart has means more subtle and
more kind
Of letting its affections be divined,
Nor need one be uncharitably plain *155*
To let a lover know he loves in vain.
  OR. No, no, speak plainly; I for one
can stand it.
I beg you to be frank.
  ALC.   And I demand it.
The simple truth is what I wish to know,
And there's no need for softening the
blow.   *160*
You've made an art of pleasing every-
one,
But now your days of coquetry are
done:
You have no choice now, Madam, but
to choose,
For I'll know what to think if you re-
fuse;
I'll take your silence for a clear admis-
sion   *165*
That I'm entitled to my worst suspicion.

OR. I thank you for this ultimatum,
Sir,
And I may say I heartily concur.
   CEL. Really, this foolishness is very
   wearing:
Must you be so unjust and overbear-
ing?   170
Haven't I told you why I must demur?
Ah, here's Eliante; I'll put the case to
her.

SCENE 3

(ELIANTE, PHILINTE, CÉLIMÈNE, OR-
ONTE, ALCESTE.)

   CEL. Cousin, I'm being persecuted
   here
By these two person, who, it would ap-
pear,
Will not be satisfied till I confess 175
Which one I love the more, and which
the less,
And tell the latter to his face that he
Is henceforth banished from my com-
pany.
Tell me, has ever such a thing been done?
   EL. You'd best not turn to me; I'm
   not the one   180
To back you in a matter of this kind.
I'm all for those who frankly speak
their mind.
   OR. Madam, you'll search in vain
   for a defender.
   ALC. You're beaten, Madam, and
   may as well surrender.
   OR. Speak, speak, you must; and
   end this awful strain.   185
   ALC. Or don't, and your position will
   be plain.
   OR. A single word will close this
   painful scene.
   ALC. But if you're silent, I'll know
   what you mean.

SCENE 4

(ARSINOÉ, CÉLIMÈNE, ELIANTE, AL-
CESTE, PHILINTE, ACASTE, CLITANDRE,
ORONTE.)

   ACAS. (to CÉLIMÈNE). Madam, with
   all due deference, we two
Have come to pick a little bone with
you.   190
   CLIT. (to ORONTE and ALCESTE). I'm
   glad you're present, Sirs; as you'll
   soon learn,
Our business here is also your concern.
   ARSIN. (to CÉLIMÈNE). Madam, I
   visit you so soon again
Only because of these two gentlemen,
Who came to me indignant and ag-
grieved   195
About a crime too base to be believed.
Knowing your virtue, having such con-
fidence in it,
I couldn't think you guilty for a minute,
In spite of all their telling evidence; 199
And, rising above our little difference,
I've hastened here in friendship's name
to see
You clear yourself of this great calumny.
   ACAS. Yes, Madam, let us see with
   what composure
You'll manage to respond to this dis-
closure.
You lately sent Clitandre this tender
note.   205
   CLIT. And this one, for Acaste, you
   also wrote.
   ACAS. (to ORONTE and ALCESTE).
   You'll recognize this writing, Sirs, I
   think;
The lady is so free with pen and ink
That you must know it all too well, I
fear.
But listen: this is something you should
hear.   210
"How absurd you are to condemn my
lightheartedness in society, and to accuse
me of being happiest in the company of
others. Nothing could be more unjust;
and if you do not come to me 215
instantly and beg pardon for saying such
a thing, I shall never forgive you as long
as I live. Our big bumbling friend the
Viscount . . ."
What a shame that he's not here.   220

"Our big bumbling friend the Viscount, whose name stands first in your
complaint, is hardly a man to my taste;
and ever since the day I watched him
spend three-quarters of an hour *225*
spitting into a well, so as to make circles
in the water, I have been unable to think
highly of him. As for the little Mar-
quess . . ."   *229*
In all modesty, gentlemen, that is I.

"As for the little Marquess, who sat
squeezing my hand for such a long while
yesterday, I find him in all respects the
most trifling creature alive; and the only
things of value about him are his *235*
cape and his sword. As for the man with
the green ribbons . . ."
(*To* ALCESTE.) It's your turn now, Sir.

"As for the man with the green ribbons, he amuses me now and then *240*
with his bluntness and his bearish ill-
humor; but there are many times indeed
when I think him the greatest bore in the
world. And as for the sonneteer . . ."
(*To* ORONTE.) Here's your helping.

"And as for the sonneteer, who *246*
has taken it into his head to be witty,
and insists on being an author in the
teeth of opinion, I simply cannot be
bothered to listen to him, and his prose
wearies me quite as much as his *251*
poetry. Be assured that I am not always
so well-entertained as you suppose; that
I long for your company, more than I
dare to say, at all these entertainments
to which people drag me; and that *256*
the presence of those one loves is the
true and perfect seasoning to all one's
pleasures."

CLIT.   And now for me.

"Clitandre, whom you mention, *261*
and who so pesters me with his saccha-
rine speeches, is the last man on earth
for whom I could feel any affection. He
is quite mad to suppose that I love him,
and so are you, to doubt that you *266*
are loved. Do come to your senses; exchange your suppositions for his; and
visit me as often as possible, to help me

bear the annoyance of his unwelcome
attentions."   *271*
It's a sweet character that these letters
show,
And what to call it, Madam, you well
know.
Enough. We're off to make the world
acquainted
With this sublime self-portrait that you've
painted.   *275*
ACAS.   Madam, I'll make you no fare-
well oration;
No, you're not worthy of my indignation.
Far choicer hearts than yours, as you'll
discover,
Would like this little Marquess for a
lover.

SCENE 5

(CÉLIMÈNE, ELIANTE, ARSINOÉ, AL-
CESTE, ORONTE, PHILINTE.)

OR.   So! After all those loving letters
you wrote,   *280*
You turn on me like this, and cut my
throat!
And your dissembling, faithless heart, I
find,
Has pledged itself by turns to all man-
kind!
How blind I've been! But now I clearly
see;
I thank you, Madam, for enlightening me.
My heart is mine once more, and I'm
content;   *286*
The loss of it shall be your punishment.
(*To* ALCESTE.) Sir, she is yours; I'll seek
no more to stand
Between your wishes and this lady's hand.

SCENE 6

(CÉLIMÈNE, ELIANE, ARSINOÉ, AL-
CESTE, PHILINTE)

ARSÌN. (*to* CÉLIMÈNE).   Madam, I'm
forced to speak. I'm far too stirred
To keep my counsel, after what I've
heard.   *291*

I'm shocked and staggered by your want
   of morals.
It's not my way to mix in others' quar-
   rels;
But really, when this fine and noble spirit,
This man of honor and surpassing merit,
Laid down the offering of his heart be-
   fore you,   *296*
How *could* you . . .
    ALC.   Madam, permit me, I
   implore you,
To represent myself in this debate.
Don't bother, please, to be my advocate.
My heart, in any case, could not afford
To give your services their due reward;
And if I chose, for consolation's
   sake,   *302*
Some other lady, 'twould not be you I'd
   take.
    ARSIN. What makes you think you
   could, Sir? And how dare you
Imply that I've been trying to ensnare
   you?   *305*
If you can for a moment entertain
Such flattering fancies, you're extremely
   vain.
I'm not so interested as you suppose
In Célimène's discarded gigolos.
Get rid of that absurd illusion, do.
Women like me are not for such as you.
Stay with this creature, to whom you're
   so attached;   *312*
I've never seen two people better matched.

SCENE 7

(CÉLIMÈNE, ELIANTE, ALCESTE, PHI-
LINTE.)

    ALC. (*to* CÉLIMÈNE). Well, I've been
   still throughout this exposé,
Till everyone but me has said his say.
Come, have I shown sufficient self-
   restraint?   *316*
And may I now . . .
    CEL.   Yes, make your just
   complaint.
Reproach me freely, call me what you
   will;

You've every right to say I've used you
   ill.
I've wronged you, I confess it; and in my
   shame   *320*
I'll make no effort to escape the blame.
The anger of those others I could despise;
My guilt toward you I sadly recognize.
Your wrath is wholly justified, I fear;
I know how culpable I must appear, *325*
I know all things bespeak my treachery,
And that, in short, you've grounds for
   hating me.
Do so; I give you leave.
    ALC.   Ah, traitress—how,
How should I cease to love you, even
   now?
Though mind and will were passionately
   bent   *330*
On hating you, my heart would not con-
   sent.
(*To* ELIANTE *and* PHILINTE.) Be wit-
   ness to my madness, both of you;
See what infatuation drives one to;
But wait; my folly's only just begun,
And I shall prove to you before I'm done
How strange the human heart is, and
   how far   *336*
From rational we sorry creatures are.
(*To* CÉLIMÈNE.) Woman, I'm willing
   to forget your shame
And clothe your treacheries in a sweeter
   name;
I'll call them youthful errors, instead of
   crimes,   *340*
And lay the blame on these corrupting
   times.
My one condition is that you agree
To share my chosen fate, and fly with me
To that wild, trackless, solitary place
In which I shall forget the human race.
Only by such a course can you atone *346*
For those atrocious letters; by that alone
Can you remove my present horror of
   you,
And make it possible for me to love you.
    CEL. What! *I* renounce the world at
   my young age,   *350*
And die of boredom in some hermitage?

ALC. Ah, if you really loved me as
you ought,
You wouldn't give the world a moment's
thought;
Must you have me, and all the world
beside?
CEL. Alas, at twenty one is terrified
Of solitude. I fear I lack the force　*356*
And depth of soul to take so stern a
course.
But if my hand in marriage will content
you,
Why, there's a plan which I might well
consent to,
And . . .
ALC. No, I detest you now. I
could excuse　*360*
Everything else, but since you thus re-
fuse
To love me wholly, as a wife should do,
And see the world in me, as I in you,
Go! I reject your hand, and disenthrall
My heart from your enchantments, once
for all.　*365*

SCENE 8

(ELIANTE, ALCESTE, PHILINTE.)

ALC. (*to* ELIANTE). Madam, your
virtuous beauty has no peer;
Of all this world, you only are sincere;
I've long esteemed you highly, as you
know;
Permit me ever to esteem you so,
And if I do not now request your hand,
Forgive me, Madam, and try to under-
stand.　*371*
I feel unworthy of it; I sense that fate
Does not intend me for the married state,
That I should do you wrong by offering
you
My shattered heart's unhappy residue,
And that in short . . .
EL.　Your argument's well
taken:　*376*
Nor need you fear that I shall feel for-
saken.
Were I to offer him this hand of mine,
Your friend Philinte, I think, would not
decline.
PHIL. Ah, Madam, that's my heart's
most cherished goal,　*380*
For which I'd gladly give my life and
soul.
ALC. (*to* ELIANTE *and* PHILINTE).
May you be true to all you now
profess,
And so deserve unending happiness.
Meanwhile, betrayed and wronged in
everything,
I'll flee this bitter world where vice is
king,　*385*
And seek some spot unpeopled and apart
Where I'll be free to have an honest
heart.
PHIL. Come, Madam, let's do every-
thing we can
To change the mind of this unhappy man.

RICHARD BRINSLEY SHERIDAN / 1751–1816

Richard Brinsley Sheridan, son of an actor father and a playwright mother, became part owner and manager of the Drury Lane Theatre in London in 1776, the year of the American Revolution. His two best plays, *The Rivals* and *The School for Scandal*, were produced before he was twenty-seven. He had already rescued a beautiful young singer from an obnoxious suitor, fought a duel over her, married her, and "taken the town." Both *The Rivals* and *The School for Scandal* are perennially playable and readable; both have furnished phrases, allusions, and characters to the common stock of English culture. *The Rivals* is memorable for Mrs. Malaprop, who misuses words fearsomely and fearlessly; *The School for Scandal* for its entire and indivisible self. The materials of *The School for Scandal* were not new in 1777—old husbands with young wives, scheming hypocrites, love intrigues, lovable spendthrifts. Scandal, which saturates the play, was no new thing either. But the interweaving of scandal and story, characters and wit, is a triumph of precise dramaturgy. The auction scene and the screen scene are both celebrated moments of comic totality—the screen scene more so, because it forces in one instant the final exposure of all schemes. Tradition has it that passers-by were impressed with the storm of applause which shook Drury Lane when the scene reached its climax.

The School for Scandal says little, but says a great many good things, all within a laugh-provoking world of good sense and good humor, spiced lightly with satire of sentiment and scandal. It has been called "the best comedy of manners in our language, and the best play of any kind since Shakespeare."

The School for Scandal

CHARACTERS

SIR PETER TEAZLE.
SIR OLIVER SURFACE.
JOSEPH SURFACE.
CHARLES SURFACE.
CRABTREE.
SIR BENJAMIN BACKBITE.
ROWLEY.
MOSES.
TRIP.
SNAKE.
CARELESS.
SIR HARRY BUMPER.
LADY TEAZLE.
MARIA.
LADY SNEERWELL.
MRS. CANDOUR.
GENTLEMEN, MAID, *and* SERVANTS.

SCENE: *London.*
TIME: *Contemporary.*

A PORTRAIT

ADDRESSED TO MRS. CREWE, WITH THE
COMEDY OF THE SCHOOL FOR SCANDAL

BY R. B. SHERIDAN, ESQ.

Tell me, ye prim adepts in Scandal's
    school,
Who rail by precept and detract by rule,
Lives there no character so tried, so
    known,
So decked with grace, and so unlike your
    own,
That even you assist her fame to raise,
Approve by envy, and by silence praise!

Attend!—a model shall attract your view—
Daughters of calumny, I summon you!
You shall decide if this a portrait prove,
Or fond creation of the Muse and Love.
Attend, ye virgin critics, shrewd and sage,
Ye matron censors of this childish age,
Whose peering eye and wrinkled front declare
A fixed antipathy to young and fair;
By cunning, cautious; or by nature, cold,
In maiden madness, virulently bold!—
Attend, ye skilled to coin the precious tale,
Creating proof, where innuendoes fail!
Whose practised memories, cruelly exact,
Omit no circumstance, except the fact!—
Attend, all ye who boast—or old or young—
The living libel of a slanderous tongue!
So shall my theme as far contrasted be
As saints by fiends, or hymns by calumny.
Come, gentle Amoret (for 'neath that name
In worthier verse is sung thy beauty's fame);
Come—for but thee who seeks the Muse?—and while
Celestial blushes check thy conscious smile,
With timid grace and hesitating eye,
The perfect model, which I boast, supply:
Vain Muse! couldst thou the humblest sketch create
Of her, or slightest charm couldst imitate—
Could thy blest strain in kindred colors trace
The faintest wonder of her form and face—
Poets would study the immortal line,
And Reynolds own *his* art subdued by thine;
That art, which well might added lustre give
To Nature's best, and Heaven's superlative:

On Granby's cheek might bid new glories rise,
Or point a purer beam from Devon's eyes!
Hard is the task to shape that beauty's praise,
Whose judgment scorns the homage flattery pays!
But praising Amoret we cannot err,
No tongue o'ervalues Heaven or flatters her!
Yet she by Fate's perverseness—she alone—
Would doubt our truth, nor deem such praise her own.
Adorning fashion, unadorned by dress,
Simple from taste, and not from carelessness;
Discreet in gesture, in deportment mild,
Not stiff with prudence, nor uncouthly wild:
No state has Amoret; no studied mien;
She frowns no *goddess,* and she moves no *queen.*
The softer charm that in her manner lies
Is framed to captivate, yet not surprise;
It justly suits the expression of her face;
'Tis less than dignity and more than grace!
On her pure cheek the native hue is such
That, formed by Heaven to be admired so much,
The hand divine, with a less partial care,
Might well have fixed a fainter crimson there
And bade the gentle inmate of her breast—
Inshrinèd Modesty—supply the rest.
But who the peril of her lips shall paint?
Strip them of smiles—still, still all words are faint,
But moving Love himself appears to teach
Their action, though denied to rule her speech;
And thou who seest her speak and dost not hear,
Mourn not her distant accents 'scape thine ear;

Viewing those lips, thou still may'st make pretence
To judge of what she says and swear 'tis sense:
Clothed with such grace, with such expression fraught,
They move in meaning and they pause in thought!
But dost thou farther watch, with charmed surprise,
The mild irresolution of her eyes,
Curious to mark how frequent they repose
In brief eclipse and momentary close—
Ah! seest thou not an ambushed Cupid there,
Too tim'rous of his charge, with jealous care
Veils and unveils those beams of heav'nly light,
Too full, too fatal else, for mortal sight?
Nor yet, such pleasing vengeance fond to meet,
In pard'ning dimples hope a safe retreat.
What though her peaceful breast should ne'er allow
Subduing frowns to arm her altered brow,
By Love, I swear, and by his gentle wiles,
More fatal still the mercy of her smiles!
Thus lovely, thus adorned, possessing all
Of bright or fair that can to woman fall,
The height of vanity might well be thought
Prerogative in her, and Nature's fault.
Yet gentle Amoret, in mind supreme
As well as charms, rejects the vainer theme;
And, half mistrustful of her beauty's store,
She barbs with wit those darts too keen before:—
Read in all knowledge that her sex should reach,
Though Greville, or the Muse, should deign to teach,
Fond to improve, nor timorous to discern
How far it is a woman's grace to learn;
In Millar's dialect she would not prove
Apollo's priestess, but Apollo's love;

Graced by those signs which truth delights to own—
The timid blush and mild submitted tone:
Whate'er she says, though sense appear throughout,
Displays the tender hue of female doubt;
Decked with that charm, how lovely wit appears,
How graceful science when that robe she wears!
Such too her talents and her bent of mind,
As speak a sprightly heart by thought refined;
A taste for mirth, by contemplation schooled,
A turn for ridicule, by candor ruled,
A scorn of folly, which she tries to hide,
An awe of talent, which she owns with pride!

Peace, idle Muse! no more thy strain prolong,
But yield a theme thy warmest praises wrong;
Just to her merit, though thou canst not raise
Thy feeble verse, behold th' acknowledged praise
Has spread conviction through the envious train,
And cast a fatal gloom o'er Scandal's reign!
And lo! each pallid hag, with blistered tongue,
Mutters assent to all thy zeal has sung—
Owns all the colors just—the outline true,
Thee my inspirer and my model—
CREWE!

PROLOGUE

WRITTEN BY MR. GARRICK

A School for Scandal! tell me, I beseech you,
Needs there a school this modish art to teach you?

No need of lessons now, the knowing
  think;
We might as well be taught to eat and
  drink.
Caused by a dearth of scandal, should
  the vapors
Distress our fair ones—let them read the
  papers;
Their powerful mixtures such disorders
  hit,
Crave what you will—there's *quantum
sufficit.*
"Lord!" cries my Lady Wormwood (who
  loves tattle,
And puts much salt and pepper in her
  prattle),
Just ris'n at noon, all night at cards when
  threshing
Strong tea and scandal—"Bless me, how
  refreshing!
Give me the papers, Lisp—how bold and
  free! (*Sips.*)
*Last night Lord L. (sips) was caught
with Lady D.*
For aching heads what charming sal
  volatile! (*Sips.*)
If Mrs. B. will still continue flirting,
We hope she'll DRAW, *or we'll* UNDRAW
the curtain.
Fine satire, poz—in public all abuse it,
But by ourselves (*sips*), our praise we
  can't refuse it.
Now, Lisp, read you—there, at that dash
  and star."
"Yes, ma'am: *A certain lord had best
beware,*
*Who lives not twenty miles from Gros-
venor Square;*
For, should he Lady W. find willing,
Wormwood is bitter"—"Oh! that's me!
  the villain!
Throw it behind the fire, and never more
Let that vile paper come within my
  door."
Thus at our friends we laugh, who feel
  the dart;
To reach our feelings, we ourselves must
  smart.

Is our young bard so young, to think
  that he
Can stop the full spring-tide of calumny?
Knows he the world so little, and its
  trade?
Alas! the devil's sooner raised than laid.
So strong, so swift, the monster there's
  no gagging:
Cut Scandal's head off, still the tongue
  is wagging.
Proud of your smiles once lavishly be-
  stowed,
Again our young Don Quixote takes the
  road;
To show his gratitude he draws his pen,
And seeks this hydra, Scandal, in his den.
For your applause all perils he would
  through—
He'll fight—that's write—a cavalliero
  true,
Till every drop of blood—that's ink—is
  spilt for you.

Act I

SCENE 1

(LADY SNEERWELL'S *house.*)
(*Discovered,* LADY SNEERWELL *at her
dressing-table;* SNAKE *drinking chocolate.*)

LADY S.   The paragraphs, you say,
Mr. Snake, were all inserted?

SNAKE.   They were, madam; and, as
I copied them myself in a feigned hand,
there can be no suspicion whence they
came.

LADY S.   Did you circulate the report
of Lady Brittle's intrigue with Captain
Boastall?

SNAKE.   That's in as fine a train as
your ladyship could wish. In the common course of things, I think it must
reach Mrs. Clackitt's ears within four-
and-twenty hours; and then, you know,
the business is as good as done.

LADY S.   Why, truly, Mrs. Clackitt

has a very pretty talent, and a great deal of industry.

SNAKE. True, madam, and has been tolerably successful in her day. To my knowledge, she has been the cause of six matches being broken off and three sons disinherited, of four forced elopements and as many close confinements, nine separate maintenances and two divorces. Nay, I have more than once traced her causing a tête-à-tête in the *Town and Country Magazine,* when the parties, perhaps, had never seen each other's face before in the course of their lives.

LADY S. She certainly has talents, but her manner is gross.

SNAKE. 'Tis very true. She generally designs well, has a free tongue and a bold invention; but her coloring is too dark and her outlines often extravagant. She wants that delicacy of tint and mellowness of sneer which distinguish your ladyship's scandal.

LADY S. You are partial, Snake.

SNAKE. Not in the least; everybody allows that Lady Sneerwell can do more with a word or look than many can with the most labored detail, even when they happen to have a little truth on their side to support it.

LADY S. Yes, my dear Snake; and I am no hypocrite to deny the satisfaction I reap from the success of my efforts. Wounded myself, in the early part of my life, by the envenomed tongue of slander, I confess I have since known no pleasure equal to the reducing others to the level of my own injured reputation.

SNAKE. Nothing can be more natural. But, Lady Sneerwell, there is one affair in which you have lately employed me, wherein, I confess, I am at a loss to guess your motives.

LADY S. I conceive you mean with respect to my neighbor, Sir Peter Teazle, and his family?

SNAKE. I do. Here are two young men to whom Sir Peter has acted as a kind of guardian since their father's death—the eldest possessing the most amiable character and universally well spoken of; the youngest, the most dissipated and extravagant young fellow in the kingdom, without friends or character: the former an avowed admirer of your ladyship, and apparently your favorite; the latter attached to Maria, Sir Peter's ward, and confessedly beloved by her. Now, on the face of these circumstances, it is utterly unaccountable to me why you, the widow of a city knight, with a good jointure, should not close with the passion of a man of such character and expectations as Mr. Surface; and more so, why you should be so uncommonly earnest to destroy the mutual attachment subsisting between his brother Charles and Maria.

LADY S. Then, at once to unravel this mystery, I must inform you that love has no share whatever in the intercourse between Mr. Surface and me.

SNAKE. No!

LADY S. His real attachment is to Maria, or her fortune; but, finding in his brother a favored rival, he has been obliged to mask his pretensions and profit by my assistance.

SNAKE. Yet still I am more puzzled why you should interest yourself in his success.

LADY S. How dull you are! Cannot you surmise the weakness which I hitherto, through shame, have concealed even from you? Must I confess that Charles—that libertine, that extravagant, that bankrupt in fortune and reputation —that he it is for whom I'm thus anxious and malicious, and to gain whom I would sacrifice everything?

SNAKE. Now, indeed, your conduct appears consistent; but how came you and Mr. Surface so confidential?

LADY S. For our mutual interest. I have found him out a long time since. I know him to be artful, selfish, and malicious—in short, a sentimental knave

—while with Sir Peter, and indeed with all his acquaintance, he passes for a youthful miracle of prudence, good sense, and benevolence.

SNAKE. Yes; yet Sir Peter vows he has not his equal in England, and, above all, he praises him as a man of sentiment.

LADY S. True; and with the assistance of his sentiment and hypocrisy he has brought Sir Peter entirely into his interest with regard to Maria, while poor Charles has no friend in the house— though, I fear, he has a powerful one in Maria's heart, against whom we must direct our schemes.

(*Enter* SERVANT.)

SERV. Mr. Surface.

LADY S. Show him up.

(*Exit* SERVANT.)

(*Enter* JOSEPH SURFACE.)

JOSEPH. My dear Lady Sneerwell, how do you do to-day? Mr. Snake, your most obedient.

LADY S. Snake has just been rallying me on our mutual attachment, but I have informed him of our real views. You know how useful he has been to us, and, believe me, the confidence is not ill placed.

JOSEPH. Madam, it is impossible for me to suspect a man of Mr. Snake's sensibility and discernment.

LADY S. Well, well, no compliments now; but tell me when you saw your mistress, Maria—or, what is more material to me, your brother.

JOSEPH. I have not seen either since I left you, but I can inform you that they never meet. Some of your stories have taken a good effect on Maria.

LADY S. Ah, my dear Snake! the merit of this belongs to you. But do your brother's distresses increase?

JOSEPH. Every hour. I am told he has had another execution in the house yesterday. In short, his dissipation and extravagance exceed anything I have ever heard of.

LADY S. Poor Charles!

JOSEPH. True, madam; notwithstanding his vices, one can't help feeling for him. Poor Charles! I'm sure I wish it were in my power to be of any essential service to him; for the man who does not share in the distresses of a brother, even though merited by his own misconduct, deserves—

LADY S. O lud! you are going to be moral, and forget that you are among friends.

JOSEPH. Egad, that's true! I'll keep that sentiment till I see Sir Peter. However, it is certainly a charity to rescue Maria from such a libertine, who, if he is to be reclaimed, can be so only by a person of your ladyship's superior accomplishments and understanding.

SNAKE. I believe, Lady Sneerwell, here's company coming. I'll go and copy the letter I mentioned to you. Mr. Surface, your most obedient.

JOSEPH. Sir, your very devoted.

(*Exit* SNAKE.)

—Lady Sneerwell, I am very sorry you have put any farther confidence in that fellow.

LADY S. Why so?

JOSEPH. I have lately detected him in frequent conference with old Rowley, who was formerly my father's steward, and has never, you know, been a friend of mine.

LADY S. And do you think he would betray us?

JOSEPH. Nothing more likely. Take my word for't, Lady Sneerwell, that fellow hasn't virtue enough to be faithful even to his own villainy.—Ah, Maria!

(*Enter* MARIA.)

LADY S. Maria, my dear, how do you do? What's the matter?

MARIA. Oh! there's that disagreeable lover of mine, Sir Benjamin Backbite, has just called at my guardian's with his odious uncle, Crabtree; so I slipped out and ran hither to avoid them.

LADY S. Is that all?

JOSEPH. If my brother Charles had

been of the party, madam, perhaps you would not have been so much alarmed.

LADY S. Nay, now you are severe, for I dare swear the truth of the matter is, Maria heard *you* were here.—But, my dear, what has Sir Benjamin done, that you would avoid him so?

MARIA. Oh, he has done nothing— but 'tis for what he has said; his conversation is a perpetual libel on all his acquaintance.

JOSEPH. Aye, and the worst of it is, there is no advantage in not knowing him; for he'll abuse a stranger just as soon as his best friend, and his uncle's as bad.

LADY S. Nay, but we should make allowance; Sir Benjamin is a wit and a poet.

MARIA. For my part, I confess, madam, wit loses its respect with me when I see it in company with malice. What do you think, Mr. Surface?

JOSEPH. Certainly, madam; to smile at the jest which plants a thorn in another's breast is to become a principal in the mischief.

LADY S. Pshaw! there's no possibility of being witty without a little ill nature. The malice of a good thing is the barb that makes it stick. What's your opinion, Mr. Surface?

JOSEPH. To be sure, madam; that conversation where the spirit of raillery is suppressed, will ever appear tedious and insipid.

MARIA. Well, I'll not debate how far scandal may be allowable, but in a man, I am sure, it is always contemptible. We have pride, envy, rivalship, and a thousand motives to depreciate each other, but the male slanderer must have the cowardice of a woman before he can traduce one.

(*Re-enter* SERVANT.)

SERV. Madam, Mrs. Candour is below, and if your ladyship's at leisure, will leave her carriage.

LADY S. Beg her to walk in.

(*Exit* SERVANT.)

—Now, Maria, here is a character to your taste, for though Mrs. Candour is a little talkative, everybody allows her to be the best-natured and best sort of woman.

MARIA. Yes, with a very gross affectation of good nature and benevolence, she does more mischief than the direct malice of old Crabtree.

JOSEPH. I'faith that's true, Lady Sneerwell; whenever I hear the current running against the characters of my friends, I never think them in such danger as when Candour undertakes their defence.

LADY S. Hush!—here she is!

(*Enter* MRS. CANDOUR.)

MRS. CAN. My dear Lady Sneerwell, how have you been this century?—Mr. Surface, what news do you hear?— though indeed it is no matter, for I think one hears nothing else but scandal.

JOSEPH. Just so, indeed, ma'am.

MRS. CAN. Oh, Maria! child—what, is the whole affair off between you and Charles? His extravagance, I presume— the town talks of nothing else.

MARIA. Indeed! I am very sorry, ma'am, the town is not better employed.

MRS. CAN. True, true, child, but there's no stopping people's tongues. I own I was hurt to hear it, as I indeed was to learn from the same quarter that your guardian, Sir Peter, and Lady Teazle have not agreed lately as well as could be wished.

MARIA. 'Tis strangely impertinent for people to busy themselves so.

MRS. CAN. Very true, child, but what's to be done? People will talk— there's no preventing it. Why, it was but yesterday I was told that Miss Gadabout had eloped with Sir Filigree Flirt. But, Lord! there's no minding what one hears —though, to be sure, I had this from very good authority.

MARIA. Such reports are highly scandalous.

MRS. CAN. So they are, child—shameful, shameful! But the world is so censorious, no character escapes. Lord, now who would have suspected your friend, Miss Prim, of an indiscretion? Yet such is the ill-nature of people, that they say her uncle stopped her last week, just as she was stepping into the York diligence with her dancing-master.

MARIA. I'll answer for't there are no grounds for that report.

MRS. CAN. Ah, no foundation in the world, I dare swear; no more, probably, than for the story circulated last month of Mrs. Festino's affair with Colonel Cassino—though, to be sure, that matter was never rightly cleared up.

JOSEPH. The license of invention some people take is monstrous, indeed.

MARIA. 'Tis so; but in my opinion those who report such things are equally culpable.

MRS. CAN. To be sure they are; tale-bearers are as bad as the tale-makers—'tis an old observation, and a very true one: but what's to be done, as I said before? How will you prevent people from talking? To-day, Mrs. Clackitt assured me, Mr. and Mrs. Honeymoon were at last become mere man and wife, like the rest of their acquaintance. She likewise hinted that a certain widow, in the next street, had got rid of her dropsy and recovered her shape in a most surprising manner. And at the same time Miss Tattle, who was by, affirmed that Lord Buffalo had discovered his lady at a house of no extraordinary fame; and that Sir H. Bouquet and Tom Saunter were to measure swords on a similar provocation.—But Lord, do you think I would report these things! No, no! tale-bearers, as I said before, are just as bad as the tale-makers.

JOSEPH. Ah! Mrs. Candour, if everybody had your forbearance and good nature!

MRS. CAN. I confess, Mr. Surface, I cannot bear to hear people attacked behind their backs; and when ugly circumstances come out against our acquaintance, I own I always love to think the best. By-the-by, I hope 'tis not true that your brother is absolutely ruined?

JOSEPH. I am afraid his circumstances are very bad indeed, ma'am.

MRS. CAN. Ah! I heard so—but you must tell him to keep up his spirits: everybody almost is in the same way—Lord Spindle, Sir Thomas Splint, Captain Quinze, and Mr. Nickitt—all up, I hear, within this week; so, if Charles is undone, he'll find half his acquaintance ruined too, and that, you know, is a consolation.

JOSEPH. Doubtless, ma'am—a very great one.

(*Re-enter* SERVANT.)

SERV. Mr. Crabtree and Sir Benjamin Backbite. (*Exit* SERVANT.)

LADY S. So, Maria, you see your lover pursues you: positively, you sha'n't escape.

(*Enter* CRABTREE *and* SIR BENJAMIN BACKBITE.)

CRAB. Lady Sneerwell, I kiss your hand. Mrs. Candour, I don't believe you are acquainted with my nephew, Sir Benjamin Backbite? Egad, ma'am, he has a pretty wit, and is a pretty poet too; isn't he, Lady Sneerwell?

SIR BEN. Oh, fie, uncle!

CRAB. Nay, egad, it's true; I back him at a rebus or a charade against the best rhymer in the kingdom. Has your ladyship heard the epigram he wrote last week on Lady Frizzle's feather catching fire?—Do, Benjamin, repeat it, or the charade you made last night extempore at Mrs. Drowzie's conversazione. Come now; your first is the name of a fish, your second a great naval commander, and—

SIR BEN. Uncle, now—prithee—

CRAB. I'faith, ma'am, 'twould surprise you to hear how ready he is at all these fine sort of things.

LADY S. I wonder, Sir Benjamin, you never publish anything.

SIR BEN. To say truth, ma'am, 'tis very vulgar to print; and as my little productions are mostly satires and lampoons on particular people, I find they circulate more by giving copies in confidence to the friends of the parties. However, I have some love elegies which, when favored with this lady's smiles, I mean to give the public. (*Turning to* MARIA.)

CRAB. (*to* MARIA). 'Fore Heaven, ma'am, they'll immortalise you!—you will be handed down to posterity, like Petrarch's Laura, or Waller's Sacharissa.

SIR BEN. Yes, madam, I think you will like them when you shall see them on a beautiful quarto page where a neat rivulet of text shall meander through a meadow of margin. 'Fore Gad, they will be the most elegant things of their kind!

CRAB. But, ladies, that's true—have you heard the news?

MRS. CAN. What, sir, do you mean the report of—

CRAB. No, ma'am, that's not it.— Miss Nicely is going to be married to her own footman.

MRS. CAN. Impossible!

CRAB. Ask Sir Benjamin.

SIR BEN. 'Tis very true, ma'am; everything is fixed and the wedding liveries bespoke.

CRAB. Yes—and they do say there were pressing reasons for it.

LADY S. Why, I have heard something of this before.

MRS. CAN. It can't be—and I wonder anyone should believe such a story of so prudent a lady as Miss Nicely.

Sir BEN. O lud! ma'am, that's the very reason 'twas believed at once. She has always been so cautious and so reserved that everybody was sure there was some reason for it at bottom.

MRS. CAN. Why, to be sure, a tale of scandal is as fatal to the credit of a prudent lady of her stamp as a fever is generally to those of the strongest constitutions. But there is a sort of puny, sickly reputation that is always ailing, yet will outlive the robuster characters of a hundred prudes.

SIR. BEN. True, madam, there are valetudinarians in reputation as well as constitution, who, being conscious of their weak part, avoid the least breath of air and supply their want of stamina by care and circumspection.

MRS. CAN. Well, but this may be all a mistake. You know, Sir Benjamin, very trifling circumstances often give rise to the most injurious tales.

CRAB. That they do, I'll be sworn, ma'am. Did you ever hear how Miss Piper came to lose her lover and her character last summer at Tunbridge?— Sir Benjamin, you remember it?

SIR BEN. Oh, to be sure!—the most whimsical circumstance.

LADY S. How was it, pray?

CRAB. Why, one evening, at Mrs. Ponto's assembly, the conversation happened to turn on the difficulty of breeding Nova Scotia sheep in this country. Says a young lady in company, "I have known instances of it; for Miss Letitia Piper, a first cousin of mine, had a Nova Scotia sheep that produced her twins." "What!" cries the Lady Dowager Dundizzy (who you know is as deaf as a post), "has Miss Piper had twins?" This mistake, as you may imagine, threw the whole company into a fit of laughter. However, 'twas the next morning everywhere reported and in a few days believed by the whole town, that Miss Letitia Piper had actually been brought to bed of a fine boy and girl; and in less than a week there were some people who could name the father and the farm-house where the babies were put to nurse.

LADY S. Strange, indeed!

CRAB. Matter of fact, I assure you. O lud; Mr. Surface, pray, is it true that your uncle, Sir Oliver, is coming home?

JOSEPH. Not that I know of, indeed, sir.

CRAB. He has been in the East Indies

a long time. You can scarcely remember him, I believe. Sad comfort, whenever he returns, to hear how your brother has gone on!

JOSEPH. Charles has been imprudent, sir, to be sure, but I hope no busy people have already prejudiced Sir Oliver against him. He may reform.

SIR BEN. To be sure he may. For my part, I never believed him to be so utterly void of principle as people say, and, though he has lost all his friends, I am told nobody is better spoken of by the Jews.

CRAB. That's true, egad, nephew. If the Old Jewry was a ward, I believe Charles would be an alderman; no man more popular there, 'fore Gad! I hear he pays as many annuities as the Irish tontine, and that, whenever he is sick, they have prayers for the recovery of his health in all the synagogues.

SIR BEN. Yet no man lives in greater splendor. They tell me, when he entertains his friends he will sit down to dinner with a dozen of his own securities, have a score of tradesmen waiting in the ante-chamber, and an officer behind every guest's chair.

JOSEPH. This may be entertainment to you, gentlemen, but you pay very little regard to the feelings of a brother.

MARIA (*aside*). Their malice is intolerable!—(*Aloud.*) Lady Sneerwell, I must wish you a good morning; I'm not very well. (*Exit* MARIA.)

MRS. CAN. Oh, dear! she changes color very much.

LADY S. Do, Mrs. Candour, follow her; she may want your assistance.

MRS. CAN. That I will, with all my soul, ma'am.—Poor dear girl, who knows what her situation may be! (*Exit* MRS. CANDOUR.)

LADY S. 'Twas nothing but that she could not bear to hear Charles reflected on, notwithstanding their difference.

SIR BEN. The young lady's *penchant* is obvious.

CRAB. But, Benjamin, you must not give up the pursuit for that; follow her and put her into good humor. Repeat her some of your own verses. Come, I'll assist you.

SIR BEN. Mr. Surface, I did not mean to hurt you, but depend on't, your brother is utterly undone.

CRAB. O lud, aye; undone as ever man was!—can't raise a guinea.

SIR BEN. And everything sold, I'm told, that was movable.

CRAB. I have seen one that was at his house.—Not a thing left but some empty bottles that were overlooked, and the family pictures, which I believe are framed in the wainscots.

SIR BEN. (*going*). And I'm very sorry also to hear some bad stories against him.

CRAB. Oh, he has done many mean things, that's certain.

SIR BEN. (*going*). But, however, as he's your brother—

CRAB. We'll tell you all another opportunity. (*Exeunt* CRABTREE *and* SIR BENJAMIN.)

LADY S. Ha! ha! 'tis very hard for them to leave a subject they have not quite run down.

JOSEPH. And I believe the abuse was no more acceptable to your ladyship than Maria.

LADY S. I doubt[1] her affections are farther engaged than we imagine. But the family are to be here this evening, so you may as well dine where you are and we shall have an opportunity of observing farther; in the meantime, I'll go and plot mischief and you shall study sentiment. (*Exeunt.*)

SCENE 2

(*A room in* SIR PETER TEAZLE's *house.*)

(*Enter* SIR PETER.)

[1] fear; suspect

SIR PET. When an old bachelor marries a young wife, what is he to expect? 'Tis now six months since Lady Teazle made me the happiest of men—and I have been the most miserable dog ever since. We tiffed a little going to church, and fairly quarrelled before the bells had done ringing. I was more than once nearly choked with gall during the honeymoon, and had lost all comfort in life before my friends had done wishing me joy. Yet I chose with caution—a girl bred wholly in the country, who never knew luxury beyond one silk gown nor dissipation above the annual gala of a race ball. Yet she now plays her part in all the extravagant fopperies of the fashion and the town with as ready a grace as if she never had seen a bush or a grass-plot out of Grosvenor Square! I am sneered at by all my acquaintance and paragraphed in the newspapers. She dissipates my fortune and contradicts all my humors; yet the worst of it is, I doubt I love her, or I should never bear all this. However, I'll never be weak enough to own it.

(*Enter* ROWLEY.)

Row. Oh! Sir Peter, your servant; how is it with you, sir?

SIR PET. Very bad, Master Rowley, very bad. I meet with nothing but crosses and vexations.

Row. What can have happened to trouble you since yesterday?

SIR PET. A good question to a married man!

Row. Nay, I'm sure your lady, Sir Peter, can't be the cause of your uneasiness.

SIR PET. Why, has anybody told you she was dead?

Row. Come, come, Sir Peter, you love her, notwithstanding your tempers don't exactly agree.

SIR PET. But the fault is entirely hers, Master Rowley. I am, myself, the sweetest-tempered man alive, and hate a teasing temper; and so I tell her a hundred times a day.

Row. Indeed!

SIR PET. Aye; and what is very extraordinary, in all our disputes she is always in the wrong. But Lady Sneerwell and the set she meets at her house encourage the perverseness of her disposition. Then, to complete my vexation, Maria, my ward, whom I ought to have the power of a father over, is determined to turn rebel too, and absolutely refuses the man whom I have long resolved on for her husband—meaning, I suppose, to bestow herself on his profligate brother.

Row. You know, Sir Peter, I have always taken the liberty to differ with you on the subject of these two young gentlemen. I only wish you may not be deceived in your opinion of the elder. For Charles, my life on't! he will retrieve his errors yet. Their worthy father, once my honored master, was, at his years, nearly as wild a spark; yet when he died, he did not leave a more benevolent heart to lament his loss.

SIR PET. You are wrong, Master Rowley. On their father's death, you know, I acted as a kind of guardian to them both till their uncle Sir Oliver's liberality gave them an early independence; of course, no person could have more opportunities of judging of their hearts, and I was never mistaken in my life. Joseph is indeed a model for the young men of the age. He is a man of sentiment and acts up to the *sentiments* he professes; but for the other, take my word for't, if he had any grain of virtue by descent, he has dissipated it with the rest of his inheritance. Ah! my old friend, Sir Oliver, will be deeply mortified when he finds how part of his bounty has been misapplied.

Row. I am sorry to find you so violent against the young man, because this may be the most critical period of his fortune. I came hither with news that will surprise you.

SIR PET. What! let me hear.

Row. Sir Oliver *is* arrived and at this moment in town.

Sir Pet. How! you astonish me! I thought you did not expect him this month.

Row. I did not, but his passage has been remarkably quick.

Sir Pet. Egad, I shall rejoice to see my old friend. 'Tis fifteen years since we met. We have had many a day together. But does he still enjoin us not to inform his nephews of his arrival?

Row. Most strictly. He means before it is known to make some trial of their dispositions.

Sir Pet. Ah! there needs no art to discover their merits—he shall have his way; but pray, does he know I am married?

Row. Yes, and will soon wish you joy.

Sir Pet. What, as we drink health to a friend in a consumption! Ah! Oliver will laugh at me. We used to rail at matrimony together, but he has been steady to his text. Well, he must be soon at my house, though—I'll instantly give orders for his reception. But, Master Rowley, don't drop a word that Lady Teazle and I ever disagree.

Row. By no means.

Sir Pet. For I should never be able to stand Noll's jokes; so I'd have him think, Lord forgive me! that we are a very happy couple.

Row. I understand you; but then you must be very careful not to differ while he is in the house with you.

Sir Pet. Egad, and so we must— and that's impossible. Ah! Master Rowley, when an old bachelor marries a young wife, he deserves—no—the crime carries its punishment along with it. (*Exeunt.*)

Act II

SCENE 1

(*A room in* Sir Peter Teazle's *house.*)

(*Enter* Sir Peter *and* Lady Teazle.)

Sir Pet. Lady Teazle, Lady Teazle, I'll not bear it!

Lady T. Sir Peter, Sir Peter, you may bear it or not, as you please; but I ought to have my own way in everything— and what's more I will, too. What! though I was educated in the country, I know very well that women of fashion in London are accountable to nobody after they are married.

Sir Pet. Very well, ma'am, very well; so a husband is to have no influence, no authority?

Lady T. Authority! No, to be sure. If you wanted authority over me, you should have adopted me, and not married me; I am sure you were old enough.

Sir Pet. Old enough!—aye, there it is. Well, well, Lady Teazle, though my life may be made unhappy by your temper, I'll not be ruined by your extravagance!

Lady T. My extravagance! I'm sure I'm not more extravagant than a woman of fashion ought to be.

Sir Pet. No, no, madam, you shall throw away no more sums on such unmeaning luxury. 'Slife! to spend as much to furnish your dressing-room with flowers in winter as would suffice to turn the Pantheon into a greenhouse, and give a *fête champêtre* at Christmas.

Lady T. And am I to blame, Sir Peter, because flowers are dear in cold weather? You should find fault with the climate, and not with me. For my part, I'm sure I wish it was spring all the year round and that roses grew under our feet.

Sir Pet. Oons! madam—if you had been born to this, I shouldn't wonder at your talking thus; but you forget what your situation was when I married you.

Lady T. No, no, I don't; 'twas a very disagreeable one, or I should never have married you.

Sir Pet. Yes, yes, madam, you were then in somewhat a humbler style—the daughter of a plain country squire. Recollect, Lady Teazle, when I saw you first sitting at your tambour, in a pretty figured linen gown, with a bunch of keys at your side, your hair combed smooth over a roll, and your apartment hung round with fruits in worsted of your own working.

LADY T.   Oh, yes! I remember it very well, and a curious life I led—my daily occupation to inspect the dairy, superintend the poultry, make extracts from the family receipt-book, and comb my aunt Deborah's lapdog.

SIR PET.   Yes, yes, ma'am, 'twas so indeed.

LADY T.   And then, you know, my evening amusements!—to draw patterns for ruffles, which I had not materials to make up; to play Pope Joan with the curate; to read a sermon to my aunt; or to be stuck down to an old spinet to strum my father to sleep after a fox-chase.

SIR PET.   I am glad you have so good a memory. Yes, madam, these were the recreations I took you from; but now you must have your coach—vis-à-vis—and three powdered footmen before your chair; and, in the summer, a pair of white cats to draw you to Kensington Gardens. No recollection, I suppose, when you were content to ride double, behind the butler, on a docked coach-horse.

LADY T.   No—I swear I never did that. I deny the butler and the coach-horse.

SIR PET.   This, madam, was your situation and what have I done for you? I have made you a woman of fashion, of fortune, of rank—in short, I have made you my wife.

LADY T.   Well, then, and there is but one thing more you can make me to add to the obligation, and that is—

SIR PET.   My widow, I suppose?

LADY T.   Hem! hem!

SIR PET.   I thank you, madam—but don't flatter yourself; for, though your ill conduct may disturb my peace, it shall

never break my heart, I promise you: however, I am equally obliged to you for the hint.

LADY T.   Then why will you endeavor to make yourself so disagreeable to me and thwart me in every little elegant expense?

SIR PET.   'Slife, madam, I say, had you any of these little elegant expenses when you married me?

LADY T.   Lud, Sir Peter! would you have me be out of the fashion?

SIR PET.   The fashion, indeed! what had you to do with the fashion before you married me?

LADY T.   For my part, I should think you would like to have your wife thought a woman of taste.

SIR PET.   Aye—there again—taste! Zounds! madam, you had no taste when you married me!

LADY T.   That's very true, indeed, Sir Peter; and, after having married you, I should never pretend to taste again, I allow. But now, Sir Peter, if we have finished our daily jangle, I presume I may go to my engagement at Lady Sneerwell's.

SIR PET.   Aye, there's another precious circumstance—a charming set of acquaintance you have made there!

LADY T.   Nay, Sir Peter, they are all people of rank and fortune, and remarkably tenacious of reputation.

SIR PET.   Yes, egad, they are tenacious of reputation with a vengeance, for they don't choose anybody should have a character but themselves! Such a crew! Ah! many a wretch has rid on a hurdle who has done less mischief than these utterers of forged tales, coiners of scandal, and clippers of reputation.

LADY T.   What, would you restrain the freedom of speech?

SIR PET.   Ah! they have made you just as bad as any one of the society.

LADY T.   Why, I believe I do bear a part with a tolerable grace. But I vow, I bear no malice against the people I abuse; when I say an ill-natured, thing, 'tis out of pure good humor, and I take it for granted they deal exactly in the same manner with me. But Sir Peter, you know you promised to come to Lady Sneerwell's too.

SIR PET.   Well, well, I'll call in, just to look after my own character.

LADY T.   Then, indeed, you must make haste after me, or you'll be too late. So good-bye to ye.

(*Exit* LADY TEAZLE.)

SIR PET.   So—I have gained much by my intended expostulation! Yet with what a charming air she contradicts everything I say, and how pleasingly she shows her contempt for my authority! Well, though I can't make her love me, there is great satisfaction in quarrelling with her, and I think she never appears to such advantage as when she is doing everything in her power to plague me.

(*Exit.*)

SCENE 2

(*A room at* LADY SNEERWELL'S *house.*)

(*Enter* LADY SNEERWELL, MRS. CANDOUR, CRABTREE, SIR BENJAMIN BACKBITE, *and* JOSEPH SURFACE.)

LADY S.   Nay, positively, we will hear it.

JOSEPH.   Yes, yes, the epigram, by all means.

SIR BEN.   Oh, plague on't, uncle! 'tis mere nonsense.

CRAB.   No, no; 'fore Gad, very clever for an extempore!

SIR BEN.   But ladies, you should be acquainted with the circumstance. You must know that one day last week, as Lady Betty Curricle was taking the dust in Hyde Park, in a sort of duodecimo phaeton, she desired me to write some verses on her ponies; upon which, I took out my pocketbook, and in one moment produced the following:

Sure never were seen two such beautiful ponies;

Other horses are clowns, but these macaronies:
To give them this title I'm sure can't be wrong,
Their legs are so slim, and their tails are so long.

CRAB.   There, ladies, done in the smack of a whip, and on horseback too.

JOSEPH.   A very Phœbus, mounted—indeed, Sir Benjamin!

SIR BEN.   Oh! dear, sir! trifles—trifles.

(*Enter* LADY TEAZLE *and* MARIA.)

MRS. CAN.   I must have a copy.

LADY S.   Lady Teazle, I hope we shall see Sir Peter?

LADY T.   I believe he'll wait on your ladyship presently.

LADY S.   Maria, my love, you look grave. Come, you shall sit down to piquet with Mr. Surface.

MARIA.   I take very little pleasure in cards—however, I'll do as you please.

LADY T. (*aside*).   I am surprised Mr. Surface should sit down with her; I thought he would have embraced this opportunity of speaking to me before Sir Peter came.

MRS. CAN.   Now, I'll die, but you are so scandalous, I'll forswear your society.

LADY T.   What's the matter, Mrs. Candour?

MRS. CAN.   They'll not allow our friend Miss Vermilion to be handsome.

LADY S.   Oh, surely she is a pretty woman.

CRAB.   I am very glad you think so, ma'am.

MRS. CAN.   She has a charming fresh color.

LADY T.   Yes, when it is fresh put on.

MRS. CAN.   Oh, fie! I'll swear her color is natural; I have seen it come and go.

LADY T.   I dare swear you have, ma'am; it goes off at night and comes again in the morning.

SIR BEN.   True, ma'am; it not only

comes and goes, but what's more, egad, her maid can fetch and carry it!

MRS. CAN. Ha! ha! ha! how I hate to hear you talk so! But surely, now, her sister *is*, or *was*, very handsome.

CRAB. Who? Mrs. Evergreen? O Lord! she's six-and-fifty if she's an hour!

MRS. CAN. Now positively you wrong her; fifty-two or fifty-three is the utmost—and I don't think she looks more.

SIR BEN. Ah! there's no judging by her looks unless one could see her face.

LADY S. Well, well, if Mrs. Evergreen *does* take some pains to repair the ravages of time, you must allow she effects it with great ingenuity; and surely that's better than the careless manner in which the widow Ochre chalks her wrinkles.

SIR BEN. Nay now, Lady Sneerwell, you are severe upon the widow. Come, come, 'tis not that she paints so ill— but when she has finished her face, she joins it on so badly to her neck that she looks like a mended statue, in which the connoisseur may see at once that the head is modern, though the trunk's antique.

CRAB. Ha! ha! ha! Well said, nephew!

MRS. CAN. Ha! ha! ha! Well, you make me laugh; but I vow I hate you for it. What do you think of Miss Simper?

SIR BEN. Why, she has very pretty teeth.

LADY T. Yes, and on that account, when she is neither speaking nor laughing (which very seldom happens), she never absolutely shuts her mouth, but leaves it always on ajar, as it were— thus.

(*Shows her teeth.*)

MRS. CAN. How can you be so ill-natured?

LADY T. Nay, I allow even that's better than the pains Mrs. Prim takes to conceal her losses in front. She draws her mouth till it positively resembles the aperture of a poor's-box, and all her

words appear to slide out edgewise as it were—thus: "How do you do, madam? Yes, madam."

LADY S. Very well, Lady Teazle; I see you can be a little severe.

LADY T. In defense of a friend, it is but justice.—But here comes Sir Peter to spoil our pleasantry.

(*Enter* SIR PETER TEAZLE.)

SIR PET. Ladies, your most obedient. —(*Aside.*) Mercy on me, here is the whole set! a character dead at every word, I suppose.

MRS. CAN. I am rejoiced you are come, Sir Peter. They have been so censorious—and Lady Teazle as bad as anyone.

SIR PET. That must be very distressing to *you*, Mrs. Candour, I dare swear.

MRS. CAN. Oh, they will allow good qualities to nobody—not even good nature to our friend Mrs. Pursy.

LADY T. What, the fat dowager who was at Mrs. Quadrille's last night?

MRS. CAN. Nay, her bulk is her misfortune; and, when she takes so much pains to get rid of it, you ought not to reflect on her.

LADY S. That's very true, indeed.

LADY T. Yes, I know she almost lives on acids and small whey; laces herself by pulleys; and often, in the hottest noon in summer, you may see her on a little squat pony, with her hair plaited up behind like a drummer's and puffing round the Ring on a full trot.

MRS. CAN. I thank you, Lady Teazle, for defending her.

SIR PET. Yes, a good defence, truly.

MRS. CAN. Truly, Lady Teazle is as censorious as Miss Sallow.

CRAB. Yes, and she is a curious being to pretend to be censorious—an awkward gawky, without any one good point under heaven.

MRS. CAN. Positively you shall not be so very severe. Miss Sallow is a near relation of mine by marriage, and as for her person great allowance is to be made;

for let me tell you, a woman labors under many disadvantages who tries to pass for a girl at six-and-thirty.

LADY S. Though surely, she is handsome still—and for the weakness in her eyes, considering how much she reads by candlelight, it is not to be wondered at.

MRS. CAN. True, and then as to her manner: upon my word, I think it is particularly graceful, considering she never had the least education; for you know her mother was a Welsh milliner, and her father a sugar-baker at Bristol.

SIR BEN. Ah! you are both of you too good-natured!

SIR PET. (*aside*). Yes, damned good-natured! This their own relation! mercy on me!

MRS. CAN. For my part, I own I cannot bear to hear a friend ill spoken of.

SIR PET. No, to be sure!

SIR BEN. Oh! you are of a moral turn. Mrs. Candour and I can sit for an hour and hear Lady Stucco talk sentiment.

LADY T. Nay, I vow Lady Stucco is very well with the dessert after dinner, for she's just like the French fruit one cracks for mottoes—made up of paint and proverb.

MRS. CAN. Well, I will never join in ridiculing a friend, and so I constantly tell my cousin Ogle—and you all know what pretensions she has to be critical on beauty.

CRAB. Oh, to be sure! she has herself the oddest countenance that ever was seen: 'tis a collection of features from all the different countries of the globe.

SIR BEN. So she has, indeed—an Irish front—

CRAB. Caledonian locks—

SIR BEN. Dutch nose—

CRAB. Austrian lips—

SIR BEN. Complexion of a Spaniard—

CRAB. And teeth *à la Chinoise*—

SIR BEN. In short, her face resembles a table d'hôte at Spa, where no two guests are of a nation—

CRAB. Or a congress at the close of a general war—wherein all the members, even to her eyes, appear to have a different interest, and her nose and chin are the only parties likely to join issue.

MRS. CAN. Ha! ha! ha!

SIR PET. (*aside*). Mercy on my life! —a person they dine with twice a week!

LADY S. Go, go, you are a couple of provoking toads.

MRS. CAN. Nay, but I vow you shall not carry the laugh off so—for give me leave to say that Mrs. Ogle—

SIR PET. Madam, madam, I beg your pardon—there's no stopping these good gentlemen's tongues. But when I tell you, Mrs. Candour, that the lady they are abusing is a particular friend of mine, I hope you'll not take her part.

LADY S. Ha! ha! ha! well said, Sir Peter! but you are a cruel creature—too phlegmatic yourself for a jest and too peevish to allow wit in others.

SIR PET. Ah, madam, true wit is more nearly allied to good nature than your ladyship is aware of.

LADY T. True, Sir Peter, I believe they are so near akin that they can never be united.

SIR BEN. Or rather, madam, suppose them to be man and wife, because one seldom sees them together.

LADY T. But Sir Peter is such an enemy to scandal, I believe he would have it put down by Parliament.

SIR PET. 'Fore Heaven, madam, if they were to consider the sporting with reputation of as much importance as poaching on manors, and pass an act for the preservation of fame as well as game, I believe many would thank them for the bill.

LADY S. O lud! Sir Peter; would you deprive us of our privileges?

SIR PET. Aye, madam, and then no person should be permitted to kill character and run down reputations but qualified old maids and disappointed widows.

LADY S. Go, you monster!

MRS. CAN. But surely you would not be quite so severe on those who only report what they hear?

SIR PET. Yes, madam, I would have law merchant for them too; and in all cases of slander currency, whenever the drawer of the lie was not to be found, the injured parties should have a right to come on any of the indorsers.

CRAB. Well, for my part, I believe there never was a scandalous tale without some foundation.

SIR PET. Oh, nine out of ten of the malicious inventions are founded on some ridiculous misrepresentation.

LADY S. Come, ladies, shall we sit down to cards in the next room?

(*Enter* SERVANT, *who whispers to* SIR PETER.)

SIR PET. I'll be with them directly.

(*Exit* SERVANT.)

(*Aside.*) I'll get away unperceived.

LADY S. Sir Peter, you are not going to leave us?

SIR PET. Your ladyship must excuse me; I'm called away by particular business. But I leave my character behind me.

(*Exit* SIR PETER.)

SIR BEN. Well—certainly, Lady Teazle, that lord of yours is a strange being. I could tell you some stories of him would make you laugh heartily if he were not your husband.

LADY T. Oh, pray don't mind that; come, do let's hear them. (*Joins the rest of the company going into the next room.*)

JOSEPH. Maria, I see you have no satisfaction in this society.

MARIA. How is it possible I should? If to raise malicious smiles at the infirmities or misfortunes of those who have never injured us be the province of wit or humor, Heaven grant me a double portion of dulness!

JOSEPH. Yet they appear more ill-natured than they are; they have no malice at heart.

MARIA. Then is their conduct still more contemptible, for in my opinion nothing could excuse the interference of their tongues but a natural and uncontrollable bitterness of mind.

JOSEPH. Undoubtedly, madam, and it has always been a sentiment of mine that to propagate a malicious truth wantonly is more despicable than to falsify from revenge. But can you, Maria, feel thus for others and be unkind to me alone? Is hope to be denied the tenderest passion?

MARIA. Why will you distress me by renewing this subject?

JOSEPH. Ah, Maria! you would not treat me thus and oppose your guardian Sir Peter's will but that I see that profligate Charles is still a favored rival.

MARIA. Ungenerously urged! But whatever my sentiments are for that unfortunate young man, be assured I shall not feel more bound to give him up because his distresses have lost him the regard even of a brother.

JOSEPH. Nay, but, Maria, do not leave me with a frown; by all that's honest, I swear—

(*Re-enter* LADY TEAZLE *behind.*)

—(*Aside.*) Gad's life, here's Lady Teazle.

—(*Aloud to* MARIA.) You must not— no, you shall not—for though I have the greatest regard for Lady Teazle—

MARIA. Lady Teazle!

JOSEPH. Yet were Sir Peter to suspect—

(*Enter* LADY TEAZLE *and comes forward.*)

LADY T. What is this, pray? Do you take her for me?—Child, you are wanted in the next room.

(*Exit* MARIA.)

—What is all this, pray?

JOSEPH. Oh, the most unlucky circumstance in nature! Maria has somehow suspected the tender concern I have for your happiness and threatened to acquaint Sir Peter with her suspicions, and I was just endeavoring to reason with her when you came in.

LADY T. Indeed! but you seemed to adopt a very tender mode of reasoning— do you usually argue on your knees?

JOSEPH. Oh, she's a child, and I thought a little bombast—but, Lady Teazle, when are you to give me your judgment on my library, as you promised?

LADY T. No, no! I begin to think it would be imprudent, and you know I admit you as a lover no farther than fashion requires.

JOSEPH. True—a mere Platonic cicisbeo[2]—what every wife is entitled to.

LADY T. Certainly, one must not be out of the fashion. However, I have so much of my country prejudices left that though Sir Peter's ill humor may vex me ever so, it never shall provoke me to—

JOSEPH. The only revenge in your power. Well, I applaud your moderation.

LADY T. Go—you are an insinuating wretch! But we shall be missed—let us join the company.

JOSEPH. But we had best not return together.

LADY T. Well, don't stay; for Maria sha'n't come to hear any more of your reasoning, I promise you. (*Exit* LADY TEAZLE.)

JOSEPH. A curious dilemma my politics have run me into! I wanted, at first, only to ingratiate myself with Lady Teazle, that she might not be my enemy with Maria; and I have, I don't know how, become her serious lover. Sincerely I begin to wish I had never made such a point of gaining so very good a character, for it has led me into so many cursed rogueries that I doubt I shall be exposed at last. (*Exit.*)

SCENE 3

(*A room in* SIR PETER TEAZLE'S *house.*)

2 a recognized lover of a married woman

(*Enter* ROWLEY *and* SIR OLIVER SURFACE.)

SIR O. Ha! ha! ha! so my old friend is married, hey?—a young wife out of the country. Ha! ha! ha! that he should have stood bluff to old bachelor so long and sink into a husband at last!

ROW. But you must not rally him on the subject, Sir Oliver; 'tis a tender point, I assure you, though he has been married only seven months.

SIR O. Then he has been just half a year on the stool of repentance!—Poor Peter! But you say he has entirely given up Charles—never sees him, hey?

ROW. His prejudice against him is astonishing, and I am sure greatly increased by a jealousy of him with Lady Teazle, which he has industriously been led into by a scandalous society in the neighborhood, who have contributed not a little to Charles's ill name. Whereas the truth is, I believe, if the lady is partial to either of them, his brother is the favorite.

SIR O. Aye, I know there are a set of malicious, prating, prudent gossips, both male and female, who murder characters to kill time and will rob a young fellow of his good name before he has years to know the value of it. But I am not to be prejudiced against my nephew by such, I promise you! No, no; if Charles has done nothing false or mean, I shall compound for his extravagance.

ROW. Then, my life on't, you will reclaim him. Ah, sir, it gives me new life to find that *your* heart is not turned against him, and that the son of my good old master has one friend, however, left.

SIR O. What! shall I forget, Master Rowley, when I was at his years myself? Egad, my brother and I were neither of us very prudent youths, and yet, I believe, you have not seen many better men than your old master was.

ROW. Sir, 'tis this reflection gives me assurance that Charles may yet be a credit to his family. But here comes Sir Peter.

SIR O. Egad, so he does! Mercy on me! he's greatly altered, and seems to have a settled married look! One may read "husband" in his face at this distance.

(*Enter* SIR PETER TEAZLE.)

SIR PET. Ha! Sir Oliver—my old friend! Welcome to England a thousand times!

SIR O. Thank you, thank you, Sir Peter! and i'faith, I am glad to find you well, believe me!

SIR PET. Oh! 'tis a long time since we met—fifteen years, I doubt, Sir Oliver, and many a cross accident in the time.

SIR O. Aye, I have had my share. But, what! I find you are married—hey? Well, well, it can't be helped, and so— I wish you joy with all my heart!

SIR PET. Thank you, thank you, Sir Oliver.—Yes, I have entered into—the happy state; but we'll not talk of that now.

SIR O. True, true, Sir Peter; old friends should not begin on grievances at first meeting—no, no, no.

ROW. (*aside to* SIR OLIVER). Take care, pray, sir.

SIR O. Well, so one of my nephews is a wild fellow, hey?

SIR PET. Wild! Ah! my old friend, I grieve for your disappointment there; he's a lost young man, indeed. However, his brother will make you amends; Joseph is, indeed, what a youth should be. Everybody in the world speaks well of him.

SIR O. I am sorry to hear it; he has too good a character to be an honest fellow.—Everybody speaks well of him! Pshaw! then he has bowed as low to knaves and fools as to the honest dignity of genius and virtue.

SIR PET. What, Sir Oliver! do you blame him for not making enemies?

SIR O. Yes, if he has merit enough to deserve them.

SIR PET. Well, well—you'll be convinced when you know him. 'Tis edification to hear him converse; he professes the noblest sentiments.

SIR O. Oh, plague of his sentiments! If he salutes me with a scrap of morality in his mouth, I shall be sick directly. But, however, don't mistake me, Sir Peter; I don't mean to defend Charles's errors, but before I form my judgment of either of them, I intend to make a trial of their hearts, and my friend Rowley and I have planned something for the purpose.

ROW. And Sir Peter shall own for once he has been mistaken.

SIR PET. Oh, my life on Joseph's honor!

SIR O. Well—come, give us a bottle of good wine, and we'll drink the lads' health and tell you our scheme.

SIR PET. *Allons,* then!

SIR O. And don't, Sir Peter, be so severe against your old friend's son. Odds my life! I am not sorry that he has run out of the course a little. For my part, I hate to see prudence clinging to the green suckers of youth; 'tis like ivy round a sapling, and spoils the growth of the tree. (*Exeunt.*)

Act III

SCENE 1

(*A room in* SIR PETER TEAZLE'S *house.*)

(*Enter* SIR PETER TEAZLE, SIR OLIVER SURFACE, *and* ROWLEY.)

SIR PET. Well then, we will see this fellow first and have our wine afterwards. But how is this, Master Rowley? I don't see the jet[3] of your scheme.

ROW. Why, sir, this Mr. Stanley, who I was speaking of, is nearly related to them by their mother. He was once a merchant in Dublin, but has been

---

[3] point

ruined by a series of undeserved misfortunes. He has applied, by letter, to Mr. Surface and Charles. From the former he has received nothing but evasive promises of future service, while Charles has done all that his extravagance has left him power to do; and he is, at this time, endeavoring to raise a sum of money, part of which, in the midst of his own distresses, I know he intends for the service of poor Stanley.

Sir O.   Ah! he is my brother's son.

Sir Pet.   Well, but how is Sir Oliver personally to—

Row.   Why, sir, I will inform Charles and his brother that Stanley has obtained permission to apply personally to his friends; and as they have neither of them ever seen him, let Sir Oliver assume his character and he will have a fair opportunity of judging, at least of the benevolence of their dispositions. And believe me, sir, you will find in the youngest brother one who, in the midst of folly and dissipation, has still, as our immortal bard expresses it,

> a heart to pity, and a hand
> Open as day for melting charity.

Sir Pet.   Pshaw! What signifies his having an open hand or purse either when he has nothing left to give? Well, well—make the trial if you please. But where is the fellow whom you brought for Sir Oliver to examine relative to Charles's affairs?

Row.   Below, waiting his commands, and no one can give him better intelligence.—This, Sir Oliver, is a friendly Jew, who, to do him justice, has done everything in his power to bring your nephew to a proper sense of his extravagance.

Sir Pet.   Pray, let us have him in.

Row.   (*apart to* Servant).   Desire Mr. Moses to walk up stairs.

Sir Pet.   But pray, why should you suppose he will speak the truth?

Row.   Oh, I have convinced him that he has no chance of recovering certain sums advanced to Charles but through the bounty of Sir Oliver, who he knows is arrived; so that you may depend on his fidelity to his own interests. I have also another evidence in my power, one Snake, whom I have detected in a matter little short of forgery, and shall shortly produce him to remove some of your prejudices.

Sir Pet.   I have heard too much on that subject.

Row.   Here comes the honest Israelite.

(*Enter* Moses.)

—This is Sir Oliver.

Sir O.   Sir, I understand you have lately had great dealings with my nephew Charles.

Moses.   Yes, Sir Oliver, I have done all I could for him, but he was ruined before he came to me for assistance.

Sir O.   That was unlucky, truly, for you have had no opportunity of showing your talents.

Moses.   None at all; I hadn't the pleasure of knowing his distresses till he was some thousands worse than nothing.

Sir O.   Unfortunate, indeed; But I suppose you have done all in your power for him, honest Moses?

Moses.   Yes, he knows that. This very evening I was to have brought him a gentleman from the city, who does not know him and will, I believe, advance him some money.

Sir Pet.   What, one Charles has never had money from before?

Moses.   Yes—Mr. Premium of Crutched Friars, formerly a broker.

Sir Pet.   Egad, Sir Oliver, a thought strikes me!—Charles, you say, does not know Mr. Premium?

Moses.   Not at all.

Sir Pet.   Now then, Sir Oliver, you may have a better opportunity of satisfying yourself than by an old romancing tale of a poor relation; go with my friend Moses and represent Premium, and then, I'll answer for it, you'll see your nephew in all his glory.

SIR O. Egad, I like this idea better than the other, and I may visit Joseph afterwards as old Stanley.

SIR PET. True, so you may.

ROW. Well, this is taking Charles rather at a disadvantage, to be sure. However, Moses, you understand Sir Peter and will be faithful?

MOSES. You may depend upon me. —This is near the time I was to have gone.

SIR O. I'll accompany you as soon as you please, Moses—But hold! I have forgot one thing; how the plague shall I be able to pass for a Jew?

MOSES. There's no need—the principal is Christian.

SIR O. Is he? I'm very sorry to hear it. But then again, an't I rather too smartly dressed to look like a money-lender?

SIR PET. Not at all; 'twould not be out of character if you went in your own carriage—would it, Moses?

MOSES. Not in the least.

SIR O. Well, but how must I talk? there's certainly some cant of usury and mode of treating that I ought to know.

SIR PET. Oh, there's not much to learn. The great point, as I take it, is to be exorbitant enough in your demands. Hey, Moses?

MOSES. Yes, that's a very great point.

SIR O. I'll answer for't I'll not be wanting in that. I'll ask him eight or ten per cent on the loan, at least.

MOSES. If you ask him no more than that you'll be discovered immediately.

SIR O. Hey! what, the plague! how much then?

MOSES. That depends upon the circumstances. If he appears not very anxious for the supply, you should require only forty or fifty per cent; but if you find him in great distress and want the moneys very bad, you may ask double.

SIR PET. A good honest trade you're learning, Sir Oliver.

SIR O. Truly, I think so—and not unprofitable.

MOSES. Then, you know, you haven't the moneys yourself, but are forced to borrow them for him of a friend.

SIR O. Oh! I borrow it of a friend, do I?

MOSES. And your friend is an unconscionable dog, but you can't help that.

SIR O. My friend an unconscionable dog, is he?

MOSES. Yes, and he himself has not the moneys by him, but is forced to sell stock at a great loss.

SIR O. He is forced to sell stock at a great loss, is he? Well, that's very kind of him.

SIR PET. I'faith, Sir Oliver—Mr. Premium, I mean—you'll soon be master of the trade. But, Moses, would not you have him run out a little against the Annuity Bill? That would be in character, I should think.

MOSES. Very much.

ROW. And lament that a young man now must be at years of discretion before he is suffered to ruin himself?

MOSES. Aye, great pity!

SIR PET. And abuse the public for allowing merit to an act whose only object is to snatch misfortune and imprudence from the rapacious gripe of usury, and give the minor a chance of inheriting his estate without being undone by coming into possession.

SIR O. So, so—Moses shall give me farther instructions as we go together.

SIR PET. You will not have much time, for your nephew lives hard by.

SIR O. Oh, never fear! my tutor appears so able that though Charles lived in the next street, it must be my own fault if I am not a complete rogue before I turn the corner. (*Exit* SIR OLIVER SURFACE *and* MOSES.)

SIR PET. So, now, I think Sir Oliver will be convinced. You are partial, Rowley, and would have prepared Charles for the other plot.

Row. No, upon my word, Sir Peter.

Sir Pet. Well, go bring me this Snake, and I'll hear what he has to say presently. I see Maria, and want to speak with her. (*Exit* Rowley.) I should be glad to be convinced my suspicions of Lady Teazle and Charles were unjust. I have never yet opened my mind on this subject to my friend Joseph—I am determined I will do it; he will give me his opinion sincerely.

(*Enter* Maria.)

—So, child, has Mr. Surface returned with you?

Maria. No, sir; he was engaged.

Sir Pet. Well, Maria, do you not reflect, the more you converse with that amiable young man, what return his partiality for you deserves?

Maria. Indeed, Sir Peter, your frequent importunity on this subject distresses me extremely. You compel me to declare that I know no man who has ever paid me a particular attention whom I would not prefer to Mr. Surface.

Sir Pet. So—here's perverseness!—No, no, Maria, 'tis Charles only whom you would prefer. 'Tis evident his vices and follies have won your heart.

Maria. This is unkind, sir. You know I have obeyed you in neither seeing nor corresponding with him; I have heard enough to convince me that he is unworthy my regard. Yet I cannot think it culpable if, while my understanding severely condemns his vices, my heart suggests some pity for his distresses.

Sir Pet. Well, well, pity him as much as you please, but give your heart and hand to a worthier object.

Maria. Never to his brother!

Sir Pet. Go, perverse and obstinate! But take care, madam: you have never yet known what the authority of a guardian is; don't compel me to inform you of it.

Maria. I can only say, you shall not have just reason. 'Tis true, by my father's will I am for a short period bound to regard you as his substitute, but must cease to think you so when you would compel me to be miserable. (*Exit* Maria.)

Sir Pet. Was ever man so crossed as I am! everything conspiring to fret me! I had not been involved in matrimony a fortnight before her father, a hale and hearty man, died on purpose, I believe, for the pleasure of plaguing me with the care of his daughter.—But here comes my helpmate! She appears in great good humor. How happy I should be if I could tease her into loving me, though but a little!

(*Enter* Lady Teazle.)

Lady T. Lud! Sir Peter, I hope you haven't been quarrelling with Maria? It is not using me well to be ill-humored when I am not by.

Sir Pet. Ah, Lady Teazle, you might have the power to make me good-humored at all times.

Lady T. I am sure I wish I had, for I want you to be in a charming sweet temper at this moment. Do be good-humored now and let me have two hundred pounds, will you?

Sir Pet. Two hundred pounds! what, ain't I to be in a good humor without paying for it? But speak to me thus and, i'faith, there's nothing I could refuse you. You shall have it, but seal me a bond for the repayment.

Lady T. (*offering her hand*). Oh, no —there—my note of hand will do as well.

Sir Pet. And you shall no longer reproach me with not giving you an independent settlement; I mean shortly to surprise you. But shall we always live thus, hey?

Lady T. If you please. I'm sure I don't care how soon we leave off quarrelling, provided you'll own you were tired first.

Sir Pet. Well—then let our future contest be, who shall be most obliging.

Lady T. I assure you, Sir Peter, good nature becomes you. You look now as you did before we were married, when you used to walk with me under the elms and tell me stories of what a gallant you were in your youth; and chuck me under the chin, you would, and ask me if I thought I could love an old fellow who would deny me nothing—didn't you?

SIR PET. Yes, yes, and you were as kind and attentive—

LADY T. Aye, so I was, and would always take your part when my acquaintance used to abuse you and turn you into ridicule.

SIR PET. Indeed!

LADY T. Aye, and when my cousin Sophy has called you a stiff, peevish old bachelor, and laughed at me for thinking of marrying one who might be my father, I have always defended you and said I didn't think you so ugly by any means and I dared say you'd make a very good sort of a husband.

SIR PET. And you prophesied right; and we shall now be the happiest couple—

LADY T. And never differ again?

SIR PET. No, never!—though at the same time, indeed, my dear Lady Teazle, you must watch your temper very seriously; for in all our little quarrels, my dear, if you recollect, my love, you always began first.

LADY T. I beg your pardon, my dear Sir Peter; indeed, you always gave the provocation.

SIR PET. Now see, my angel! take care—contradicting isn't the way to keep friends.

LADY T. Then don't you begin it, my love!

SIR PET. There now! you—you are going on. You don't perceive, my life, that you are just doing the very thing which you know always makes me angry.

LADY T. Nay, you know if you will be angry without any reason, my dear—

SIR PET. There! now you want to quarrel again.

LADY T. No, I'm sure I don't, but if you will be so peevish—

SIR PET. There now! who begins first?

LADY T. Why, you, to be sure. I said nothing—but there's no bearing your temper.

SIR PET. No, no, madam, the fault's in your own temper.

LADY T. Aye, you are just what my cousin Sophy said you would be.

SIR PET. Your cousin Sophy is a forward, impertinent gipsy.

LADY T. You are a great bear, I'm sure, to abuse my relations.

SIR PET. Now may all the plagues of marriage be doubled on me if ever I try to be friends with you any more!

LADY T. So much the better.

SIR PET. No, no, madam: 'tis evident you never cared a pin for me, and I was a madman to marry you—a pert, rural coquette that had refused half the honest 'squires in the neighborhood.

LADY T. And I am sure I was a fool to marry you—an old dangling bachelor who was single at fifty only because he never could meet with anyone who would have him.

SIR PET. Aye, aye, madam, but you were pleased enough to listen to me; you never had such an offer before.

LADY T. No! didn't I refuse Sir Tivy Terrier, who everybody said would have been a better match? for his estate is just as good as yours, and he has broke his neck since we have been married.

SIR PET. I have done with you, madam! You are an unfeeling, ungrateful—but there's an end of everything. I believe you capable of everything that is bad. Yes, madam, I now believe the reports relative to you and Charles, madam. Yes, madam, *you* and Charles are, not without grounds—

LADY T. Take care, Sir Peter! you had better not insinuate any such thing! I'll not be suspected without cause, I promise you.

SIR PET. Very well, madam! very well! A separate maintenance as soon as you please.—Yes, madam, or a divorce! I'll make an example of myself for the benefit of all old bachelors. Let us separate, madam!

LADY T. Agreed, agreed! And now, my dear Sir Peter, we are of a mind once more, we may be the happiest couple and never differ again, you know —ha! ha! ha! Well, you are going to be in a passion, I see, and I shall only interrupt you—so, bye! bye! (*Exit.*)

SIR PET. Plagues and tortures! can't I make her angry either! Oh, I am the most miserable fellow! But I'll not bear her presuming to keep her temper—no! she may break my heart, but she shan't keep her temper. (*Exit.*)

SCENE 2

(*A room in* CHARLES SURFACE'S *house.*)

(*Enter* TRIP, MOSES, *and* SIR OLIVER SURFACE.)

TRIP. Here, Master Moses! if you'll stay a moment, I'll try whether—what's the gentleman's name?

SIR O. (*aside*). Mr. Moses, what is my name?

MOSES. Mr. Premium.

TRIP. Premium—very well. (*Exit* TRIP, *taking snuff.*)

SIR O. To judge by the servants, one wouldn't believe the master was ruined. But what!—sure, this was my brother's house?

MOSES. Yes, sir; Mr. Charles bought it of Mr. Joseph, with the furniture, pictures, etc., just as the old gentleman left it. Sir Peter thought it a piece of extravagance in him.

SIR O. In my mind, the other's economy in selling it to him was more reprehensible by half.

(*Re-enter* TRIP.)

TRIP. My master says you must wait, gentlemen; he has company and can't speak with you yet.

SIR O. If he knew who it was wanted to see him, perhaps he would not send such a message.

TRIP. Yes, yes, sir; he knows you are here—I did not forget little Premium. No, no, no!

SIR O. Very well; and I pray, sir, what may be your name?

TRIP. Trip, sir; my name is Trip, at your service.

SIR O. Well, then, Mr. Trip, you have a pleasant sort of place here, I guess?

TRIP. Why, yes—here are three or four of us pass our time agreeably enough; but then our wages are sometimes a little in arrear—and not very great either—but fifty pounds a year, and find our own bags and bouquets.

SIR O. (*aside*). Bags and bouquets? halters and bastinadoes!

TRIP. And à propos, Moses, have you been able to get me that little bill discounted?

SIR O. (*aside*). Wants to raise money too—mercy on me! Has his distresses too, I warrant, like a lord, and affects creditors and duns.

MOSES. 'Twas not to be done, indeed, Mr. Trip.

TRIP. Good lack, you surprise me! My friend Brush has indorsed it, and I thought when he put his name at the back of a bill 'twas the same as cash.

MOSES. No, 'twouldn't do.

TRIP. A small sum—but twenty pounds. Hark'ee, Moses, do you think you couldn't get it me by way of annuity?

SIR O. (*aside*). An annuity! ha! ha! a footman raise money by way of annuity! Well done, luxury, egad!

MOSES. Well, but you must insure your place.

TRIP. Oh, with all my heart! I'll insure my place, and my life too, if you please.

SIR O. (*aside*). It's more than I would your neck.

MOSES. But is there nothing you could deposit?

TRIP. Why, nothing capital of my master's wardrobe has dropped lately, but I could give you a mortgage on some of his winter clothes, with equity of redemption before November—or you shall have the reversion of the French velvet, or a post-obit on the blue and silver;—these, I should think, Moses, with a few pair of point ruffles as a collateral security—hey, my little fellow?

MOSES. Well, well. (*Bell rings.*)

TRIP. Egad, I heard the bell! I believe, gentlemen, I can now introduce you. Don't forget the annuity, little Moses!—This way, gentlemen.—I'll insure my place, you know.

SIR O. (*aside*). If the man be a shadow of the master, this is the temple of dissipation indeed! (*Exeunt.*)

SCENE 3

(*Another room in the same.*)

(CHARLES SURFACE *and his friends at a table with wine, etc.*)

CHARLES. Fore Heaven, 'tis true!—there's the great degeneracy of the age. Many of our acquaintance have taste, spirit, and politeness, but, plague on't, they won't drink.

CARE. It is so indeed, Charles! they give in to all the substantial luxuries of the table, and abstain from nothing but wine and wit. Oh, certainly society suffers by it intolerably! for now, instead of the social spirit of raillery that used to mantle over a glass of bright Burgundy, their conversation is become just like the Spa water they drink, which has all the pertness and flatulence of champagne without the spirit or flavor.

1ST GENT. But what are they to do who love play better than wine?

CARE. True! there's Sir Harry diets himself for gaming, and is now under a hazard regimen.

CHARLES. Then he'll have the worst of it. What! you wouldn't train a horse for the course by keeping him from corn? For my part, egad, I am never so successful as when I am a little merry; let me throw on a bottle of champagne, and I never lose—at least I never feel my losses, which is exactly the same thing.

2D GENT. Aye, that I believe.

CHARLES. And then, what man can pretend to be a believer in love who is an abjurer of wine? 'Tis the test by which the lover knows his own heart. Fill a dozen bumpers to a dozen beauties, and she that floats a-top is the maid that has bewitched you.

CARE. Now then, Charles, be honest and give us your real favorite.

CHARLES. Why, I have withheld her only in compassion to you. If I toast her, you must give a round of her peers, which is impossible—on earth.

CARE. Oh! then we'll find some canonised vestals or heathen goddesses that will do, I warrant!

CHARLES. Here then, bumpers, you rogues! bumpers! Maria! Maria!—

SIR H. Maria who?

CHARLES. Oh, damn the surname!—'tis too formal to be registered in Love's calendar.—But now, Sir Harry, beware, we must have beauty superlative.

CARE. Nay, never study, Sir Harry; we'll stand to the toast though your mistress should want an eye, and you know you have a song will excuse you.

SIR H. Egad, so I have! and I'll give him the song instead of the lady. (*Sings.*)

SONG

Here's to the maiden of bashful fifteen;
　　Here's to the widow of fifty;
Here's to the flaunting extravagant quean,
　　And here's to the housewife that's thrifty.
CHORUS.
　　　　Let the toast pass,—
　　　　Drink to the lass,

I'll warrant she'll prove an excuse for the
glass.
Here's to the charmer whose dimples we
prize;
Now to the maid who has none, sir;
Here's to the girl with a pair of blue eyes,
And here's to the nymph with but one,
sir.

CHORUS.
Let the toast pass, etc.
Here's to the maid with a bosom of snow;
Now to her that's as brown as a berry;
Here's to the wife with a face full of
woe,
And now to the damsel that's merry.

CHORUS.
Let the toast pass, etc.
For let 'em be clumsy, or let 'em be slim,
Young or ancient, I care not a feather;
So fill a pint bumper quite up to the brim,
So fill up your glasses—nay, fill to the
brim—.
And let us e'en toast them together.

CHORUS.
Let the toast pass, etc.

ALL. Bravo! bravo!
(*Enter* TRIP *and whispers to* CHARLES
SURFACE.)
CHARLES. Gentlemen, you must excuse me a little.—Careless, take the
chair, will you?
CARE. Nay, prithee, Charles, what
now? This is one of your peerless
beauties, I suppose, has dropped in by
chance?
CHARLES. No, faith! To tell you the
truth, 'tis a Jew and a broker, who are
come by appointment.
CARE. Oh, damn it! let's have the
Jew in.
1ST GENT. Aye, and the broker too,
by all means.
2D GENT. Yes, yes, the Jew and the
broker.
CHARLES. Egad, with all my heart!
—Trip, bid the gentlemen walk in.
(*Exit* TRIP.)
—Though there's one of them a stranger,
I can tell you.

CARE. Charles, let us give them some
generous Burgundy, and perhaps they'll
grow conscientious.
CHARLES. Oh, hang 'em, no! wine
does but draw forth a man's natural
qualities, and to make them drink would
only be to whet their knavery.
(*Re-enter* TRIP, *with* SIR OLIVER SUR-
FACE *and* MOSES.)
CHARLES. So, honest Moses, walk in;
walk in, pray, Mr. Premium—that's the
gentleman's name, isn't it, Moses?
MOSES. Yes, sir.
CHARLES. Set chairs, Trip.—Sit
down, Mr. Premium.—Glasses, Trip.
(TRIP *gives chairs and glasses, and
exit.*)
—Sit down, Moses.—Come, Mr. Pre-
mium, I'll give you a sentiment; here's
Success to usury!—Moses, fill the gentleman a bumper.
MOSES. Success to usury! (*Drinks.*)
CARE. Right, Moses—usury is pru-
dence and industry, and deserves to suc-
ceed.
SIR O. Then—here's all the success
it deserves! (*Drinks.*)
CARE. No, no, that won't do! Mr.
Premium, you have demurred at the
toast and must drink it in a pint bumper.
1ST GENT. A pint bumper, at least.
MOSES. Oh, pray, sir, consider—Mr.
Premium's a gentleman.
CARE. And therefore loves good
wine.
2D GENT. Give Moses a quart glass
—this is mutiny, and a high contempt
for the chair.
CARE. Here, now for't! I'll see justice done, to the last drop of my bottle.
SIR O. Nay, pray, gentlemen—I did
not expect this usage.
CHARLES. No, hang it, you shan't;
Mr. Premium's a stranger.
SIR O. (*aside*). Odd! I wish I was
well out of their company.
CARE. Plague on 'em then! if they
won't drink, we'll not sit down with
them. Come, Harry, the dice are in the

next room.—Charles, you'll join us when you have finished your business with the gentlemen?

CHARLES. I will! I will! (*Exeunt* SIR HARRY BUMPER *and* GENTLEMEN, CARELESS *following.*)—Careless!

CARE. (*returning*). Well!

CHARLES. Perhaps I may want you.

CARE. Oh, you know I am always ready; word, note, or bond, 'tis all the same to me. (*Exit.*)

MOSES. Sir, this is Mr. Premium, a gentleman of the strictest honor and secrecy, and always performs what he undertakes. Mr. Premium, this is—

CHARLES. Pshaw! have done. Sir, my friend Moses is a very honest fellow, but a little slow at expression; he'll be an hour giving us our titles. Mr. Premium, the plain state of the matter is this: I am an extravagant young fellow who wants to borrow money; you I take to be a prudent old fellow who have got money to lend. I am blockhead enough to give fifty per cent sooner than not have it; and you, I presume, are rogue enough to take a hundred if you can get it. Now, sir, you see we are acquainted at once, and may proceed to business without farther ceremony.

SIR. O. Exceeding frank, upon my word. I see, sir, you are not a man of many compliments.

CHARLES. Oh, no, sir! plain dealing in business I always think best.

SIR O. Sir, I like you the better for it. However, you are mistaken in one thing; I have no money to lend, but I believe I could procure some of a friend —but then, he's an unconscionable dog. Isn't he, Moses?

MOSES. But you can't help that.

SIR O. And must sell stock to accommodate you—mustn't he, Moses?

MOSES. Yes, indeed! You know I always speak the truth and scorn to tell a lie.

CHARLES. Right. People that speak truth generally do. But these are trifles,

Mr. Premium. What! I know money isn't to be bought without paying for't.

SIR O. Well, but what security could you give? You have no land, I suppose?

CHARLES. Not a mole-hill nor a twig but what's in the bough-pots out of the window.

SIR O. Nor any stock, I presume?

CHARLES. Nothing but live stock— and that only a few pointers and ponies. But pray, Mr. Premium, are you acquainted at all with any of my connections?

SIR O. Why, to say truth, I am.

CHARLES. Then you must know that I have a dev'lish rich uncle in the East Indies, Sir Oliver Surface, from whom I have the greatest expectations?

SIR O. That you have a wealthy uncle, I have heard, but how your expectations will turn out is more, I believe, than you can tell.

CHARLES. Oh, no!—there can be no doubt. They tell me I'm a prodigious favorite, and that he talks of leaving me everything.

SIR O. Indeed! this is the first I've heard of it.

CHARLES. Yes, yes, 'tis just so. Moses knows 'tis true; don't you, Moses?

MOSES. Oh, yes! I'll swear to't.

SIR O. (*aside*). Egad, they'll persuade me presently I'm at Bengal.

CHARLES. Now I propose, Mr. Premium, if it's agreeable to you, a post-obit on Sir Oliver's life—though at the same time the old fellow has been so liberal to me that I give you my word, I should be very sorry to hear that anything had happened to him.

SIR O. Not more than I should, I assure you. But the bond you mention happens to be just the worst security you could offer me—for I might live to a hundred and never see the principal.

CHARLES. Oh, yes, you would! the moment Sir Oliver dies, you know, you would come on me for the money.

SIR O. Then I believe I should be

the most unwelcome dun you ever had in your life.

CHARLES. What! I suppose you're afraid that Sir Oliver is too good a life?

SIR O. No, indeed I am not—though I have heard he is as hale and healthy as any man of his years in christendom.

CHARLES. There again, now, you are misinformed. No, no, the climate has hurt him considerably, poor Uncle Oliver. Yes, yes, he breaks apace, I'm told—and is so much altered lately that his nearest relations don't know him.

SIR O. No! Ha! ha! ha! so much altered lately that his nearest relations would not know him! Ha! ha! ha! egad —ha! ha! ha!

CHARLES. Ha! ha!—you're glad to hear that, little Premium?

SIR O. No, no, I'm not.

CHARLES. Yes, yes, you are—ha! ha! ha!—you know that mends your chance.

SIR O. But I'm told Sir Oliver is coming over; nay, some say he is actually arrived.

CHARLES. Pshaw! sure I must know better than you whether he's come or not. No, no, rely on't he's at this moment at Calcutta. Isn't he, Moses?

MOSES. Oh, yes, certainly.

SIR O. Very true, as you say, you must know better than I, though I have it from pretty good authority—haven't I, Moses?

MOSES. Yes, most undoubted!

SIR O. But, sir, as I understand you want a few hundreds immediately, is there nothing you could dispose of?

CHARLES. How do you mean?

SIR O. For instance, now, I have heard that your father left behind him a great quantity of massy old plate.

CHARLES. O lud! that's gone long ago. Moses can tell you how better than I can.

SIR O. (*aside*). Good lack! all the family race-cups and corporation-bowls! —(*Aloud.*) Then it was also supposed that his library was one of the most valuable and compact—

CHARLES. Yes, yes, so it was—vastly too much so for a private gentleman. For my part, I was always of a communicative disposition; so I thought it a shame to keep so much knowledge to myself.

SIR O. (*aside*). Mercy upon me! learning that had run in the family like an heirloom!—(*Aloud.*) Pray, what are become of the books?

CHARLES. You must inquire of the auctioneer, Master Premium, for I don't believe even Moses can direct you.

MOSES. I know nothing of books.

SIR O. So, so, nothing of the family property left, I suppose?

CHARLES. Not much, indeed, unless you have a mind to the family pictures. I have got a room full of ancestors above, and if you have a taste for old paintings, egad, you shall have 'em a bargain.

SIR O. Hey! what the devil! sure, you wouldn't sell your forefathers, would you?

CHARLES. Every man of them, to the best bidder.

SIR O. What! your great-uncles and aunts?

CHARLES. Aye, and my great-grand-fathers and grandmothers too.

SIR O. (*aside*). Now I give him up! —(*Aloud.*) What the plague, have you no bowels for your own kindred? Odds life! do you take me for Shylock in the play, that you would raise money of me on your own flesh and blood?

CHARLES. Nay, my little broker, don't be angry; what need you care, if you have your money's worth?

SIR O. Well, I'll be the purchaser; I think I can dispose of the family canvas. —(*Aside.*) Oh, I'll never forgive him this!—never!

(*Re-enter* CARELESS.)

CARE. Come, Charles, what keeps you?

CHARLES. I can't come yet. I'faith, we are going to have a sale above stairs; here's little Premium will buy all my ancestors!

CARE. Oh, burn your ancestors!

CHARLES. No, he may do that afterwards if he pleases. Stay, Careless, we want you: egad, you shall be auctioneer —so come along with us.

CARE. Oh, have with you, if that's the case.—[I can] handle a hammer as well as a dice-box!

SIR O. (aside). Oh, the profligates!

CHARLES. Come, Moses, you shall be appraiser if we want one. Gad's life, little Premium, you don't seem to like the business?

SIR O. Oh, yes, I do, vastly! Ha! ha! ha! yes, yes, I think it a rare joke to sell one's family by auction—ha! ha!— (Aside.) Oh, the prodigal!

CHARLES. To be sure! when a man wants money, where the plague should he get assistance if he can't make free with his own relations? (Exeunt.)

Act IV

SCENE 1

(Picture room at CHARLES SURFACE'S house.)

(Enter CHARLES SURFACE, SIR OLIVER SURFACE, MOSES, and CARELESS.)

CHARLES. Walk in, gentlemen, pray walk in; here they are, the family of the Surfaces up to the Conquest.

SIR O. And in my opinion a goodly collection.

CHARLES. Aye, aye, these are done in the true spirit of portrait-painting; no volontaire grâce or expression. Not like the works of your modern Raphaels, who give you the strongest resemblance, yet contrive to make your portrait independent of you, so that you may sink the original and not hurt the picture. No, no; the merit of these is the inveter-

ate likeness—all stiff and awkward as the originals, and like nothing in human nature besides.

SIR O. Ah! we shall never see such figures of men again.

CHARLES. I hope not. Well, you see, Master Premium, what a domestic character I am; here I sit of an evening surrounded by my family.—But come, get to your pulpit, Mr. Auctioneer; here's an old gouty chair of my grandfather's will answer the purpose.

CARE. Aye, aye, this will do. But, Charles, I haven't a hammer; and what's an auctioneer without his hammer?

CHARLES. Egad, that's true. What parchment have we here? Oh, our genealogy in full. Here, Careless, you shall have no common bit of mahogany; here's the family tree for you, you rogue! This shall be your hammer, and now you may knock down my ancestors with their own pedigree.

SIR O. (aside). What an unnatural rogue!—an ex post facto parricide!

CARE. Yes, yes, here's a list of your generation, indeed;—faith, Charles, this is the most convenient thing you could have found for the business, for 'twill not only serve as a hammer but a catalogue into the bargain. Come, begin— A-going, a-going, a-going!

CHARLES. Bravo! Careless! Well, here's my great-uncle, Sir Richard Raveline, a marvellous good general in his day, I assure you. He served in all the Duke of Marlborough's wars and got that cut over his eye at the battle of Malplaquet. What say you, Mr. Premium? look at him—there's a hero! not cut out of his feathers, as your modern clipped captains are, but enveloped in wig and regimentals, as a general should be. What do you bid?

MOSES. Mr. Premium would have you speak.

CHARLES. Why, then, he shall have him for ten pounds, and I'm sure that's not dear for a staff officer.

SIR O. (*aside*). Heaven deliver me! his famous uncle Richard for ten pounds! —Very well, sir, I take him at that.

CHARLES. Careless, knock down my uncle Richard.—Here, now, is a maiden sister of his, my great-aunt Deborah, done by Kneller, thought to be in his best manner and esteemed a very formidable likeness. There she is, you see, a shepherdess feeding her flock. You shall have her for five pounds ten—the sheep are worth the money.

SIR O. (*aside*). Ah! poor Deborah! —a woman who set such a value on herself!—Five pounds ten—she's mine.

CHARLES. Knock down my aunt Deborah! Here, now, are two that were a sort of cousins of theirs.—You see, Moses, these pictures were done some time ago, when beaux wore wigs and the ladies their own hair.

SIR O. Yes, truly, head-dresses appear to have been a little lower in those days.

CHARLES. Well, take that couple for the same.

MOSES. 'Tis [a] good bargain.

CHARLES. Careless!—This, now, is a grandfather of my mother's, a learned judge, well known on the western circuit. —What do you rate him at, Moses?

MOSES. Four guineas.

CHARLES. Four guineas! Gad's life, you don't bid me the price of his wig. —Mr. Premium, you have more respect for the woolsack; do let us knock his lordship down at fifteen.

SIR O. By all means.

CARE. Gone!

CHARLES. And there are two brothers of his, William and Walter Blunt, Esquires, both members of Parliament and noted speakers; and, what's very extraordinary, I believe, this is the first time they were ever bought or sold.

SIR O. That is very extraordinary, indeed! I'll take them at your own price, for the honor of Parliament.

CARE. Well said, little Premium! I'll knock them down at forty.

CHARLES. Here's a jolly fellow—I don't know what relation, but he was mayor of Manchester: take him at eight pounds.

SIR O. No, no; six will do for the mayor.

CHARLES. Come, make it guineas, and I'll throw you the two aldermen there into the bargain.

SIR O. They're mine.

CHARLES. Careless, knock down the mayor and aldermen. But, plague on't! we shall be all day retailing in this manner; do let us deal wholesale. What say you, little Premium? Give me three hundred pounds for the rest of the family in the lump.

CARE. Aye, aye, that will be the best way.

SIR O. Well, well, anything to accommodate you; they are mine. But there is one portrait which you have always passed over.

CARE. What, that ill-looking little fellow over the settee?

SIR O. Yes sir, I mean that—though I don't think him so ill-looking a little fellow, by any means.

CHARLES. What, that?—Oh, that's my uncle Oliver! 'twas done before he went to India.

CARE. Your uncle Oliver! Gad, then you'll never be friends, Charles. That, now, to me, is as stern a looking rogue as ever I saw—an unforgiving eye, and a damned disinheriting countenance!— an inveterate knave, depend on't. Don't you think so, little Premium?

SIR O. Upon my soul, sir, I do not; I think it is as honest a looking face as any in the room, dead or alive. But I suppose uncle Oliver goes with the rest of the lumber?

CHARLES. No, hang it; I'll not part with poor Noll. The old fellow has been very good to me and, egad, I'll keep his picture while I've a room to put it in.

Sir O. (*aside*). The rogue's my nephew after all!—But, sir, I have somehow taken a fancy to that picture.

Charles. I'm sorry for't, for you certainly will not have it. Oons, haven't you got enough of them?

Sir O. (*aside*). I forgive him everything!—But, sir, when I take a whim in my head, I don't value money. I'll give you as much for that as for all the rest.

Charles. Don't tease me, master broker; I tell you I'll not part with it, and there's an end of it.

Sir O. (*aside*). How like his father the dog is!—Well, well, I have done.—(*Aside*.) I did not perceive it before, but I think I never saw such a striking resemblance.—Here is a draft for your sum.

Charles. Why, 'tis for eight hundred pounds!

Sir O. You will not let Sir Oliver go?

Charles. Zounds! no! I tell you once more.

Sir O. Then never mind the difference; we'll balance that another time. But give me your hand on the bargain. You are an honest fellow, Charles—I beg pardon, sir, for being so free.—Come, Moses.

Charles. Egad, this is a whimsical old fellow!—But hark'ee, Premium, you'll prepare lodgings for these gentlemen.

Sir O. Yes, yes, I'll send for them in a day or two.

Charles. But hold; do now send a genteel conveyance for them, for I assure you, they were most of them used to ride in their own carriages.

Sir O. I will, I will—for all but Oliver.

Charles. Aye, all but the little nabob.

Sir O. You're fixed on that?

Charles. Peremptorily.

Sir O. (*aside*). A dear extravagant rogue!—Good day!—Come, Moses.—(*Aside*.) Let me hear now who dares

call him profligate! (*Exeunt* Sir Oliver Surface *and* Moses.)

Care. Why, this is the oddest genius of the sort I ever saw!

Charles. Egad, he's the prince of brokers, I think. I wonder how Moses got acquainted with so honest a fellow.—Hah, here's Rowley.—Do, Careless, say I'll join the company in a few moments.

Care. I will—but don't let that old blockhead persuade you to squander any of that money on old musty debts, or any such nonsense; for tradesmen, Charles, are the most exorbitant fellows.

Charles. Very true, and paying them is only encouraging them.

Care. Nothing else.

Charles. Aye, aye, never fear.

(*Exit* Careless.)

—So! this was an odd old fellow, indeed. Let me see, two-thirds of this is mine by right—five hundred and thirty odd pounds. 'Fore Heaven! I find one's ancestors are more valuable relations than I took them for!—Ladies and gentlemen, your most obedient and very grateful servant. (*Bows.*)

(*Enter* Rowley.)

—Ha! old Rowley! egad, you are just come in time to take leave of your old acquaintance.

Row. Yes, I heard they were a-going. But I wonder you can have such spirits under so many distresses.

Charles. Why, there's the point! my distresses are so many that I can't afford to part with my spirits; but I shall be rich and splenetic, all in good time. However, I suppose you are surprised that I am not more sorrowful at parting with so many near relations. To be sure, 'tis very affecting; but you see they never move a muscle; so why should I?

Row. There's no making you serious a moment.

Charles. Yes, faith, I am so now. Here, my honest Rowley—here, get me this changed directly, and take a hundred pounds of it immediately to old Stanley.

Row.   A hundred pounds! Consider only—

CHARLES.   Gad's life, don't talk about it! poor Stanley's wants are pressing, and if you don't make haste we shall have someone call that has a better right to the money.

Row.   Ah! there's the point! I never will cease dunning you with the old proverb—

CHARLES.   "Be just before you're generous."—Why, so I would if I could, but Justice is an old, hobbling beldame, and I can't get her to keep pace with Generosity, for the soul of me.

Row.   Yet, Charles, believe me, one hour's reflection—

CHARLES.   Aye, aye, it's all very true; but, hark'ee, Rowley, while I have, by Heaven, I'll give; so, damn your economy—and now for hazard. (*Exeunt.*)

SCENE 2

(*The parlor.*)

(*Enter* SIR OLIVER SURFACE *and* MOSES.)

MOSES.   Well, sir, I think, as Sir Peter said, you have seen Mr. Charles in high glory; 'tis great pity he's so extravagant.

SIR O.   True, but he would not sell my picture.

MOSES.   And loves wine and women so much.

SIR O.   But he would not sell my picture.

MOSES.   And games so deep.

SIR O.   But he would not sell my picture!—Oh, here's Rowley.

(*Enter* ROWLEY.)

Row.   So, Sir Oliver, I find you have made a purchase—

SIR O.   Yes, yes, our young rake has parted with his ancestors like old tapestry.

Row.   And here has he commissioned me to re-deliver you part of the purchase money—I mean, though, in your necessitous character of old Stanley.

MOSES.   Ah! there is the pity of it all; he is so damned charitable.

Row.   And I left a hosier and two tailors in the hall, who, I'm sure, won't be paid, and this hundred would satisfy them.

SIR O.   Well, well, I'll pay his debts and his benevolence too. But now I am no more a broker, and you shall introduce me to the elder brother as old Stanley.

Row.   Not yet awhile; Sir Peter, I know, means to call there about this time.

(*Enter* TRIP.)

TRIP.   Oh, gentlemen, I beg pardon for not showing you out; this way— Moses, a word. (*Exeunt* TRIP *and* MOSES.)

SIR O.   There's a fellow for you! Would you believe it, that puppy intercepted the Jew on our coming and wanted to raise money before he got to his master!

Row.   Indeed!

SIR O.   Yes; they are now planning an annuity business. Ah, Master Rowley, in my days servants were content with the follies of their masters when they were worn a little threadbare; but now they have their vices, like their birthday clothes, with the gloss on. (*Exeunt.*)

SCENE 3

(*A library in* JOSEPH SURFACE'S *house.*)
(*Enter* JOSEPH SURFACE *and* SERVANT.)

JOSEPH.   No letter from Lady Teazle?
SERV.   No, sir.

JOSEPH (*aside*).   I am surprised she has not sent if she is prevented from coming. Sir Peter certainly does not suspect me. Yet I wish I may not lose the heiress through the scrape I have drawn myself into with the wife; however, Charles's imprudence and bad character are great points in my favor.

(*Knocking without.*)

SERV. Sir, I believe that must be Lady Teazle.

JOSEPH. Hold! See whether it is or not before you go to the door. I have a particular message for you if it should be my brother.

SERV. 'Tis her ladyship, sir; she always leaves her chair at the milliner's in the next street.

JOSEPH. Stay, stay; draw that screen before the window—that will do. My opposite neighbor is a maiden lady of so curious a temper.

(SERVANT *draws the screen, and exit.*) I have a difficult hand to play in this affair. Lady Teazle has lately suspected my views on Maria, but she must by no means be let into that secret—at least till I have her more in my power.

(*Enter* LADY TEAZLE.)

LADY T. What, sentiment in soliloquy now? Have you been very impatient? O lud! don't pretend to look grave. I vow I couldn't come before.

JOSEPH. O madam, punctuality is a species of constancy very unfashionable in a lady of quality.

LADY T. Upon my word, you ought to pity me. Do you know Sir Peter is grown so ill-natured to me of late, and so jealous of Charles, too—that's the best of the story, isn't it?

JOSEPH (*aside*). I am glad my scandalous friends keep that up.

LADY T. I am sure I wish he would let Maria marry him, and then perhaps he would be convinced; don't you, Mr. Surface?

JOSEPH (*aside*). Indeed I do not.— Oh, certainly I do! for then my dear Lady Teazle would also be convinced how wrong her suspicions were of my having any design on the silly girl.

LADY T. Well, well, I'm inclined to believe you. But isn't it provoking to have the most ill-natured things said of one? And there's my friend Lady Sneerwell has circulated I don't know how many scandalous tales of me, and all without any foundation too; that's what vexes me.

JOSEPH. Aye, madam, to be sure, that is the provoking circumstance— without foundation; yes, yes, there's the mortification, indeed, for when a scandalous story is believed against one, there certainly is no comfort like the consciousness of having deserved it.

LADY T. No, to be sure; then I'd forgive their malice. But to attack me, who am really so innocent, and who never say an ill-natured thing of anybody—that is, of any friend; and then Sir Peter, too, to have him so peevish, and so suspicious, when I know the integrity of my own heart—indeed, 'tis monstrous!

JOSEPH. But, my dear Lady Teazle, 'tis your own fault if you suffer it. When a husband entertains a groundless suspicion of his wife and withdraws his confidence from her, the original compact is broken and she owes it to the honor of her sex to outwit him.

LADY T. Indeed! so that if he suspects me without cause, it follows that the best way of curing his jealousy is to give him reason for't?

JOSEPH. Undoubtedly—for your husband should never be deceived in you, and in that case it becomes you to be frail in compliment to his discernment.

LADY T. To be sure, what you say is very reasonable, and when the consciousness of my innocence—

JOSEPH. Ah, my dear madam, there is the great mistake! 'tis this very conscious innocence that is of the greatest prejudice to you. What is it makes you negligent of forms and careless of the world's opinion? why, the consciousness of your own innocence. What makes you thoughtless in your conduct and apt to run into a thousand little imprudences?

why, the consciousness of your own innocence. What makes you impatient of
Sir Peter's temper and outrageous at his
suspicions? why, the consciousness of
your innocence.

LADY T. 'Tis very true!

JOSEPH. Now, my dear Lady Teazle,
if you would but once make a trifling
faux pas, you can't conceive how cautious you would grow, and how ready to
humor and agree with your husband.

LADY T. Do you think so?

JOSEPH. Oh, I am sure on't; and then
you would find all scandal would cease
at once, for—in short, your character at
present is like a person in a plethora,
absolutely dying from too much health.

LADY T. So, so; then I perceive your
prescription is that I must sin in my own
defence and part with my virtue to preserve my reputation?

JOSEPH. Exactly so, upon my credit,
ma'am.

LADY T. Well, certainly this is the
oddest doctrine and the newest receipt
for avoiding calumny!

JOSEPH. An infallible one, believe
me. Prudence, like experience, must be
paid for.

LADY T. Why, if my understanding
were once convinced—

JOSEPH. Oh, certainly, madam, your
understanding should be convinced. Yes,
yes—Heaven forbid I should persuade
you to do anything you thought wrong.
No, no, I have too much honor to desire it.

LADY T. Don't you think we may as
well leave honor out of the argument?

JOSEPH. Ah, the ill effects of your
country education, I see, still remain
with you.

LADY T. I doubt they do, indeed;
and I will fairly own to you that if I
could be persuaded to do wrong, it
would be by Sir Peter's ill usage sooner
than your *honorable logic,* after all.

JOSEPH (*taking her hand*). Then, by
this hand, which he is unworthy of—

(*Re-enter* SERVANT.)

—'Sdeath, you blockhead—what do you
want?

SERV. I beg your pardon, sir, but I
thought you would not choose Sir Peter
to come up without announcing him.

JOSEPH. Sir Peter!—Oons—the devil!

LADY T. Sir Peter! O lud!—I'm
ruined! I'm ruined!

SERV. Sir, 'twasn't I let him in.

LADY T. Oh! I'm quite undone!
What will become of me? Now, Mr.
Logic—Oh! mercy, sir, he's on the stairs
—I'll get behind here—and if ever I'm
so imprudent again—(*Goes behind the
screen.*)

JOSEPH. Give me that book. (*Sits
down.* SERVANT *pretends to adjust his
chair.*)

(*Enter* SIR PETER.)

SIR PET. Aye, ever improving himself—Mr. Surface, Mr. Surface—

JOSEPH. Oh, my dear Sir Peter, I beg
your pardon—(*gaping, throws away the
book*). I have been dozing over a stupid
book. Well, I am much obliged to you
for this call. You haven't been here, I believe, since I fitted up this room. Books,
you know, are the only things in which
I am a coxcomb.

SIR PET. 'Tis very neat, indeed. Well,
well, that's proper; and you can make
even your screen a source of knowledge
—hung, I perceive, with maps.

JOSEPH. Oh, yes, I find great use in
that screen.

SIR PET. I dare say you must, certainly, when you want to find anything
in a hurry.

JOSEPH (*aside*). Aye, or to hide anything in a hurry either.

SIR PET. Well, I have a little private
business—

JOSEPH (*to the* SERVANT). You need
not stay.

SERV. No, sir. (*Exit.*)

JOSEPH. Here's a chair, Sir Peter—
I beg—

SIR PET. Well, now we are alone,

there is a subject, my dear friend, on which I wish to unburden my mind to you—a point of the greatest moment to my peace; in short, my good friend, Lady Teazle's conduct of late has made me very unhappy.

JOSEPH. Indeed! I am very sorry to hear it.

SIR PET. Yes, 'tis but too plain she has not the least regard for me; but what's worse I have pretty good authority to suppose she has formed an attachment to another.

JOSEPH. Indeed! you astonish me!

SIR PET. Yes! and, between ourselves, I think I've discovered the person.

JOSEPH. How! you alarm me exceedingly.

SIR PET. Aye, my dear friend, I knew you would sympathise with me!

JOSEPH. Yes—believe me, Sir Peter, such a discovery would hurt me just as much as it would you.

SIR PET. I am convinced of it. Ah! it is a happiness to have a friend whom one can trust even with one's family secrets. But have you no guess who I mean?

JOSEPH. I haven't the most distant idea. It can't be Sir Benjamin Backbite!

SIR PET. Oh, no! What say you to Charles?

JOSEPH. My brother!—impossible!

SIR PET. Oh, my dear friend, the goodness of your own heart misleads you. You judge of others by yourself.

JOSEPH. Certainly, Sir Peter, the heart that is conscious of its own integrity is ever slow to credit another's treachery.

SIR PET. True, but your brother has no sentiment—you never hear him talk so.

JOSEPH. Yet I can't but think Lady Teazle herself has too much principle.

SIR PET. Aye, but what is principle against the flattery of a handsome, lively young fellow?

JOSEPH. That's very true.

SIR PET. And there's, you know, the difference of our ages makes it very improbable that she should have any great affection for me; and if she were to be frail and I were to make it public, why, the town would only laugh at me—the foolish old bachelor who had married a girl.

JOSEPH. That's true, to be sure—they would laugh.

SIR PET. Laugh! aye, and make ballads, and paragraphs, and the devil knows what of me.

JOSEPH. No, you must never make it public.

SIR PET. But then again—that the nephew of my old friend, Sir Oliver, should be the person to attempt such a wrong, hurts me more nearly.

JOSEPH. Aye, there's the point. When ingratitude barbs the dart of injury, the wound has double danger in it.

SIR PET. Aye—I, that was, in a manner, left his guardian; in whose house he had been so often entertained; who never in my life denied him—my advice.

JOSEPH. Oh, 'tis not to be credited! There may be a man capable of such baseness, to be sure; but for my part till you can give me positive proofs, I cannot but doubt it. However, if it should be proved on him, he is no longer a brother of mine—I disclaim kindred with him; for the man who can break the laws of hospitality and tempt the wife of his friend, deserves to be branded as the pest of society.

SIR PET. What a difference there is between you! What noble sentiments!

JOSEPH. Yet I cannot suspect Lady Teazle's honor.

SIR PET. I am sure I wish to think well of her and to remove all ground of quarrel between us. She has lately reproached me more than once with having made no settlement on her, and in our last quarrel she almost hinted that she should not break her heart if I was dead. Now, as we seem to differ in our ideas of expense, I have resolved she shall have her own way and be her own mistress in that respect for the future; and if I were to die, she will find I have not been inattentive to her interest while living. Here, my friend, are the drafts of two deeds, which I wish to have your opinion on. By one she will enjoy eight hundred a year independent while I live, and by the other the bulk of my fortune at my death.

JOSEPH. This conduct, Sir Peter, is indeed truly generous.—(*Aside.*) I wish it may not corrupt my pupil.

SIR PET. Yes, I am determined she shall have no cause to complain, though I would not have her acquainted with the latter instance of my affection yet awhile.

JOSEPH (*aside*). Nor I, if I could help it.

SIR PET. And now, my dear friend, if you please, we will talk over the situation of your hopes with Maria.

JOSEPH (*softly*). Oh, no, Sir Peter; another time, if you please.

SIR PET. I am sensibly chagrined at the little progress you seem to make in her affections.

JOSEPH (*softly*). I beg you will not mention it. What are my disappointments when your happiness is in debate! —(*Aside.*) 'Sdeath, I shall be ruined every way!

SIR PET. And though you are so averse to my acquainting Lady Teazle with your passion for Maria, I'm sure she's not your enemy in the affair.

JOSEPH. Pray, Sir Peter, now oblige me. I am really too much affected by the subject we have been speaking of, to bestow a thought on my own concerns. The man who is entrusted with his friend's distresses can never—

(*Re-enter* SERVANT.)

—Well, sir?

SERV. Your brother, sir, is speaking to a gentleman in the street, and says he knows you are within.

JOSEPH. 'Sdeath, blockhead, I'm not within.—I'm out for the day.

SIR PET. Stay—hold—a thought has struck me;—you shall be at home.

JOSEPH. Well, well, let him up.— (*Exit* SERVANT.)

(*Aside.*) He'll interrupt Sir Peter, however.

SIR PET. Now, my good friend, oblige me, I entreat you. Before Charles comes, let me conceal myself somewhere; then do you tax him on the point we have been talking, and his answer may satisfy me at once.

JOSEPH. Oh, fie, Sir Peter! would you have me join in so mean a trick—to trepan my brother too?

SIR PET. Nay, you tell me you are sure he is innocent; if so, you do him the greatest service by giving him an opportunity to clear himself, and you will set my heart at rest. Come, you shall not refuse me; here, behind the screen will be—Hey! what the devil! There seems to be one listener here already.—I'll swear, I saw a petticoat!

JOSEPH. Ha! ha! ha! Well, this is ridiculous enough. I'll tell you, Sir Peter, though I hold a man of intrigue to be a most despicable character, yet, you know, it does not follow that one is to be an absolute Joseph either! Hark'ee, 'tis a little French milliner, a silly rogue that plagues me; and having some character to lose, on your coming, sir, she ran behind the screen.

SIR PET. Ah, you rogue!—But, egad, she has overheard all I have been saying of my wife.

JOSEPH. Oh, 'twill never go any farther, you may depend upon it!

SIR PET. No? then, faith, let her hear it out.—Here's a closet will do as well.

JOSEPH. Well, go in there.

SIR PET. (*going into the closet*). Sly rogue! sly rogue!

JOSEPH. A narrow escape, indeed!

and a curious situation I'm in, to part man and wife in this manner.

LADY T. (*peeping*). Couldn't I steal off?

JOSEPH. Keep close, my angel!

SIR PET. (*peeping*). Joseph, tax him home.

JOSEPH. Back, my dear friend!

LADY T. (*peeping*). Couldn't you lock Sir Peter in?

JOSEPH. Be still, my life!

SIR PET. (*peeping*). You're sure the little milliner won't blab?

JOSEPH. In, in, my dear Sir Peter! —'Fore Gad, I wish I had a key to the door.

(*Enter* CHARLES SURFACE.)

CHARLES. Holla! brother, what has been the matter? Your fellow would not let me up at first. What! have you had a Jew or a wench with you?

JOSEPH. Neither, brother, I assure you.

CHARLES. But what has made Sir Peter steal off? I thought he had been with you.

JOSEPH. He *was,* brother; but hearing you were coming, he did not choose to stay.

CHARLES. What! was the old gentleman afraid I wanted to borrow money of him?

JOSEPH. No, sir; but I am sorry to find, Charles, you have lately given that worthy man grounds for great uneasiness.

CHARLES. Yes, they tell me I do that to a great many worthy men.—But how so, pray?

JOSEPH. To be plain with you, brother, he thinks you are endeavoring to gain Lady Teazle's affection from him.

CHARLES. Who, I? O lud! not I, upon my word.—Ha! ha! ha! ha! So the old fellow has found out that he has got a young wife, has he?—or, what is worse, Lady Teazle has found out she has an old husband?

JOSEPH. This is no subject to jest on, brother. He who can laugh—

CHARLES. True, true, as you were going to say—then, seriously, I never had the least idea of what you charge me with, upon my honor.

JOSEPH (*loudly*). Well, it will give Sir Peter great satisfaction to hear this.

CHARLES. To be sure, I once thought the lady seemed to have taken a fancy to me, but upon my soul I never gave her the least encouragement. Besides, you know my attachment to Maria.

JOSEPH. But sure, brother, even if Lady Teazle had betrayed the fondest partiality for you—

CHARLES. Why, look'ee, Joseph, I hope I shall never deliberately do a dishonorable action, but if a pretty woman was purposely to throw herself in my way—and that pretty woman married to a man old enough to be her father—

JOSEPH. Well—

CHARLES. Why, I believe I should be obliged to borrow a little of your morality, that's all. But brother, do you know now that you surprise me exceedingly, by naming *me* with Lady Teazle; for, i'faith, I always understood you were her favorite.

JOSEPH. Oh, for shame, Charles! This retort is foolish.

CHARLES. Nay, I swear I have seen you exchange such significant glances—

JOSEPH. Nay, nay, sir, this is no jest.

CHARLES. Egad, I'm serious! Don't you remember one day when I called here—

JOSEPH. Nay, prithee, Charles—

CHARLES. And found you together—

JOSEPH. Zounds, sir, I insist—

CHARLES. And another time when your servant—

JOSEPH. Brother, brother, a word with you!—(*Aside.*) Gad, I must stop him.

CHARLES. Informed, I say that—

JOSEPH. Hush! I beg your pardon, but Sir Peter has overheard all we have been saying. I knew you would clear yourself, or I should not have consented.

CHARLES. How, Sir Peter! Where is he?

JOSEPH (*points to the closet*). Softly! —there!

CHARLES. Oh, 'fore Heaven, I'll have him out—Sir Peter, come forth!

JOSEPH. No, no—

CHARLES. I say, Sir Peter, come into court.—(*Pulls in* SIR PETER.) What! my old guardian!—What! turn inquisitor and take evidence incog?

SIR PET. Give me your hand, Charles —I believe I have suspected you wrongfully; but you mustn't be angry with Joseph—'twas my plan!

CHARLES. Indeed!

SIR PET. But I acquit you. I promise you I don't think near so ill of you as I did; what I have heard has given me great satisfaction.

CHARLES. Egad, then, 'twas lucky you didn't hear any more, (*apart to* JOSEPH) wasn't it, Joseph?

SIR PET. Ah! you would have retorted on him.

CHARLES. Ah, aye, that was a joke.

SIR PET. Yes, yes, I know his honor too well.

CHARLES. But you might as well have suspected *him* as *me* in this matter, for all that, (*apart to* JOSEPH) mightn't he, Joseph?

SIR PET. Well, well, I believe you.

JOSEPH (*aside*). Would they were both out of the room!

SIR PET. And in future, perhaps, we may not be such strangers.

(*Re-enter* SERVANT, *and whispers to* JOSEPH SURFACE.)

SERV. Lady Sneerwell is below, and says she will come up. (*Exit* SERVANT.)

JOSEPH. Gentlemen, I beg pardon— I must wait on you downstairs; here is a person come on particular business.

CHARLES. Well, you can see him in another room. Sir Peter and I have not met a long time, and I have something to say to him.

JOSEPH (*aside*). They must not be left together—I'll send this man away, and return directly.—(*Apart to* SIR PETER.) Sir Peter, not a word of the French milliner.

SIR PET. (*apart to* JOSEPH). I! not for the world! (*Exit* JOSEPH SURFACE.) —Ah, Charles, if you associated more with your brother, one might indeed hope for your reformation. He is a man of sentiment.—Well, there is nothing in the world so noble as a man of sentiment.

CHARLES. Pshaw! he is too moral by half; and so apprehensive of his "good name," as he calls it, that I suppose he would as soon let a priest into his house as a girl.

SIR PET. No, no—come, come—you wrong him. No, no! Joseph is no rake, but he is no such saint either, in that respect.—(*Aside.*) I have a great mind to tell him—we should have a laugh at Joseph.

CHARLES. Oh, hang him! he's a very anchorite—a young hermit!

SIR PET. Hark'ee—you must not abuse him; he may chance to hear of it again, I promise you.

CHARLES. Why, you won't tell him?

SIR PET. No—but—this way.— (*Aside.*) Egad, I'll tell him.—Hark'ee— have you a mind to have a good laugh at Joseph?

CHARLES. I should like it of all things.

SIR PET. Then, i'faith, we will! I'll be quit with him for discovering me. He had a girl with him when I called.

CHARLES. What! Joseph? you jest.

SIR PET. Hush!—a little French milliner; and the best of the jest is— she's in the room now.

CHARLES. The devil she is!

SIR PET. Hush! I tell you. (*Points.*)

CHARLES. Behind the screen! 'Slife, let's unveil her!

SIR PET. No, no, he's coming—you sha'n't, indeed!

CHARLES. Oh, egad, we'll have a peep at the little milliner!

SIR PET. Not for the world!—Joseph will never forgive me.

CHARLES. I'll stand by you—

SIR PET. Odds, here he is!

(JOSEPH SURFACE *enters just as* CHARLES SURFACE *throws down the screen.*)

CHARLES. Lady Teazle, by all that's wonderful!

SIR PET. Lady Teazle, by all that's damnable!

CHARLES. Sir Peter, this is one of the smartest French milliners I ever saw. Egad, you seem all to have been diverting yourselves here at hide and seek, and I don't see who is out of the secret. Shall I beg your ladyship to inform me? Not a word!—Brother, will you be pleased to explain this matter? What! is Morality dumb too?—Sir Peter, though I found you in the dark, perhaps you are not so now! All mute!—Well—though I can make nothing of the affair, I suppose you perfectly understand one another; so I'll leave you to yourselves.—(*Going.*) Brother, I'm sorry to find you have given that worthy man grounds for so much uneasiness.—Sir Peter! "there's nothing in the world so noble as a man of sentiment!" (*Exit* CHARLES.)

(*They stand for some time looking at each other.*)

JOSEPH. Sir Peter—notwithstanding—I confess—that appearances are against me—if you will afford me your patience—I make no doubt—but I shall explain everything to your satisfaction.

SIR PET. If you please, sir.

JOSEPH. The fact is, sir, that Lady Teazle, knowing my pretensions to your ward Maria—I say, sir, Lady Teazle, being apprehensive of the jealousy of your temper—and knowing my friendship to the family—she, sir, I say—called here—in order that—I might explain these pretensions—but on your coming—being apprehensive—as I said

—of your jealousy—she withdrew—and this, you may depend on it, is the whole truth of the matter.

SIR PET. A very clear account, upon my word, and I dare swear the lady will vouch for every article of it.

LADY T. For not one word of it, Sir Peter.

SIR PET. How! don't you think it worth while to agree in the lie?

LADY T. There is not one syllable of truth in what that gentleman has told you.

SIR PET. I believe you, upon my soul, ma'am!

JOSEPH (*aside*). 'Sdeath, madam, will you betray me?

LADY T. Good Mr. Hypocrite, by your leave, I'll speak for myself.

SIR PET. Aye, let her alone, sir; you'll find she'll make out a better story than you, without prompting.

LADY T. Hear me, Sir Peter!—I came here on no matter relating to your ward, and even ignorant of this gentleman's pretensions to her. But I came, seduced by his insidious arguments, at least to listen to his pretended passion, if not to sacrifice your honor to his baseness.

SIR PET. Now, I believe, the truth is coming, indeed!

JOSEPH. The woman's mad!

LADY T. No, sir; she has recovered her senses, and your own arts have furnished her with the means—Sir Peter, I do not expect you to credit me—but the tenderness you expressed for me when I am sure you could not think I was a witness to it, has so penetrated to my heart that had I left the place without the shame of this discovery, my future life should have spoken the sincerity of my gratitude. As for that smooth-tongued hypocrite, who would have seduced the wife of his too credulous friend while he affected honorable addresses to his ward—I behold him now in a light so truly despicable that I shall never again respect myself for having listened to him.

(*Exit* LADY TEAZLE.)

JOSEPH. Notwithstanding all this, Sir Peter, Heaven knows—

SIR PET. That you are a villain and so I leave you to your conscience.

JOSEPH. You are too rash, Sir Peter; you shall hear me. The man who shuts out conviction by refusing to—(*Exeunt* SIR PETER *and* JOSEPH SURFACE *talking*.)

Act V

SCENE 1

(*The library in* JOSEPH SURFACE's *house*.)

(*Enter* JOSEPH SURFACE *and* SERVANT.)

JOSEPH. Mr. Stanley! and why should you think I would see him? You must know he comes to ask something.

SERV. Sir, I should not have let him in, but that Mr. Rowley came to the door with him.

JOSEPH. Pshaw! blockhead! to suppose that I should now be in a temper to receive visits from poor relations!— Well, why don't you show the fellow up?

SERV. I will, sir—Why, sir, it was not my fault that Sir Peter discovered my lady—

JOSEPH. Go, fool! (*Exit* SERVANT.) —Sure, Fortune never played a man of my policy such a trick before!—my character with Sir Peter, my hopes with Maria, destroyed in a moment! I'm in a rare humor to listen to other people's distresses! I sha'nt be able to bestow even a benevolent sentiment on Stanley. —So! here he comes, and Rowley with him. I must try to recover myself and put a little charity into my face, however. (*Exit*.)

(*Enter* SIR OLIVER SURFACE *and* ROWLEY.)

SIR O. What! does he avoid us? That was he, was it not?

ROW. It was, sir. But I doubt you are come a little too abruptly. His nerves are so weak that the sight of a poor relation may be too much for him. I should have gone first to break it to him.

SIR O. Oh, plague of his nerves! Yet this is he whom Sir Peter extols as a man of the most benevolent way of thinking!

ROW. As to his way of thinking, I cannot pretend to decide; for to do him justice he appears to have as much speculative benevolence as any private gentleman in the kingdom, though he is seldom so sensual as to indulge himself in the exercise of it.

SIR O. Yet he has a string of charitable sentiments at his fingers' ends.

ROW. Or rather, at his tongue's end, Sir Oliver; for I believe there is no sentiment he has such faith in as that "charity begins at home."

SIR O. And his, I presume, is of that domestic sort which never stirs abroad at all.

ROW. I doubt you'll find it so;—but he's coming. I mustn't seem to interrupt you; and you know, immediately as you leave him, I come in to announce your arrival in your real character.

SIR O. True; and afterwards you'll meet me at Sir Peter's.

ROW. Without losing a moment. (*Exit*.)

SIR O. I don't like the complaisance of his features.

(*Re-enter* JOSEPH SURFACE.)

JOSEPH. Sir, I beg you ten thousand pardons for keeping you a moment waiting.—Mr. Stanley, I presume.

SIR O. At your service.

JOSEPH. Sir, I beg you will do me the honor to sit down—I entreat you, sir.

SIR O. Dear sir—there's no occasion. —(*Aside*.) Too civil by half!

JOSEPH. I have not the pleasure of

knowing you, Mr. Stanley, but I am extremely happy to see you look so well. You were nearly related to my mother, I think, Mr. Stanley?

SIR O. I was sir—so nearly that my present poverty, I fear, may do discredit to her wealthy children, else I should not have presumed to trouble you.

JOSEPH. Dear sir, there needs no apology; he that is in distress, though a stranger, has a right to claim kindred with the wealthy. I am sure I wish I was one of that class, and had it in my power to offer you even a small relief.

SIR O. If your uncle, Sir Oliver, were here, I should have a friend.

JOSEPH. I wish he was, sir, with all my heart; you should not want an advocate with him, believe me, sir.

SIR O. I should not need one—my distresses would recommend me. But I imagined his bounty would enable you to become the agent of his charity.

JOSEPH. My dear sir, you were strangely misinformed. Sir Oliver is a worthy man—a very worthy man; but avarice, Mr. Stanley, is the vice of age. I will tell you, my good sir, in confidence, what he has done for me has been a mere nothing—though people, I know, have thought otherwise, and for my part I never chose to contradict the report.

SIR O. What! has he never transmitted you bullion—rupees—pagodas?

JOSEPH. Oh, dear sir, nothing of the kind! No, no; a few presents now and then—china, shawls, congou tea, avadavats, and Indian crackers—little more, believe me.

SIR O. (aside). Here's gratitude for twelve thousand pounds!—avadavats and Indian crackers!

JOSEPH. Then, my dear sir, you have heard, I doubt not, of the extravagance of my brother. There are very few would credit what I have done for that unfortunate young man.

SIR O. (aside). Not I, for one!

JOSEPH. The sums I have lent him!

Indeed I have been exceedingly to blame —it was an amiable weakness; however, I don't pretend to defend it—and now I feel it doubly culpable since it has deprived me of the pleasure of serving you, Mr. Stanley, as my heart dictates.

SIR O. (aside). Dissembler!—Then, sir, you can't assist me?

JOSEPH. At present, it grieves me to say, I cannot; but whenever I have the ability, you may depend upon hearing from me.

SIR O. I am extremely sorry—

JOSEPH. Not more than I, believe me; to pity, without the power to relieve, is still more painful than to ask and be denied.

SIR O. Kind sir, your modest obedient humble servant.

JOSEPH. You leave me deeply affected, Mr. Stanley.—(Calls to SERVANT.) William, be ready to open the door.

SIR O. Oh, dear sir, no ceremony.

JOSEPH. Your very obedient.

SIR O. Your most obsequious.

JOSEPH. You may depend upon hearing from me whenever I can be of service.

SIR O. Sweet sir, you are too good!

JOSEPH. In the meantime I wish you health and spirits.

SIR O. Your ever grateful and perpetual humble servant.

JOSEPH. Sir, yours as sincerely.

SIR O. (aside). Charles, you are my heir! (Exit.)

JOSEPH. This is one bad effect of a good character; it invites application from the unfortunate, and there needs no small degree of address to gain the reputation of benevolence without incurring the expense. The silver ore of pure charity is an expensive article in the catalogue of a man's good qualities; whereas the sentimental French plate I use instead of it makes just as good a show and pays no tax.

(Re-enter ROWLEY.)

Row. Mr. Surface, your servant. I was apprehensive of interrupting you, though my business demands immediate attention, as this note will inform you.

JOSEPH. Always happy to see Mr. Rowley. (*Reads the letter.*) Sir Oliver Surface!—My uncle arrived!

Row. He is, indeed; we have just parted—quite well, after a speedy voyage, and impatient to embrace his worthy nephew.

JOSEPH. I am astonished!—William! stop Mr. Stanley if he's not gone.

Row. Oh! he's out of reach, I believe.

JOSEPH. Why did you not let me know this when you came in together?

Row. I thought you had particular business. But I must be gone to inform your brother and appoint him here to meet your uncle. He will be with you in a quarter of an hour.

JOSEPH. So he says. Well, I am strangely overjoyed at his coming.— (*Aside.*) Never, to be sure, was anything so damned unlucky!

Row. You will be delighted to see how well he looks.

JOSEPH. Oh! I'm overjoyed to hear it.—(*Aside.*) Just at this time!

Row. I'll tell him how impatiently you expect him.

JOSEPH. Do, do; pray, give my best duty and affection. Indeed, I cannot express the sensations I feel at the thought of seeing him.

(*Exit* ROWLEY.)

—Certainly his coming just at this time is the cruellest piece of ill-fortune. (*Exit.*)

SCENE 2

(*A room in* SIR PETER TEAZLE's *house.*)

(*Enter* MRS. CANDOUR *and* MAID.)

MAID. Indeed, ma'am, my lady will see nobody at present.

MRS. CAN. Did you tell her it was her friend Mrs. Candour?

MAID. Yes, ma'am, but she begs you will excuse her.

MRS. CAN. Do go again; I shall be glad to see her, if it be only for a moment, for I am sure she must be in great distress.

(*Exit* MAID.)

—Dear heart, how provoking! I'm not mistress of half the circumstances! We shall have the whole affair in the newspapers, with the names of the parties at length, before I have dropped the story at a dozen houses.

(*Enter* SIR BENJAMIN BACKBITE.)

—Oh, dear Sir Benjamin! you have heard, I suppose—

SIR BEN. Of Lady Teazle and Mr. Surface—

MRS. CAN. And Sir Peter's discovery—

SIR BEN. Oh, the strangest piece of business, to be sure!

MRS. CAN. Well, I never was so surprised in my life. I am so sorry for all parties, indeed.

SIR BEN. Now, I don't pity Sir Peter at all; he was so extravagantly partial to Mr. Surface.

MRS. CAN. Mr. Surface! Why, 'twas with Charles Lady Teazle was detected.

SIR BEN. No, no, I tell you—Mr. Surface is the gallant.

MRS. CAN. No such thing! Charles is the man. 'Twas Mr. Surface brought Sir Peter on purpose to discover them.

SIR BEN. I tell you I had it from one—

MRS. CAN. And I have it from one—

SIR BEN. Who had it from one who had it—

MRS. CAN. From one immediately— But here comes Lady Sneerwell; perhaps she knows the whole affair.

(*Enter* LADY SNEERWELL.)

LADY S. So, my dear Mrs. Candour, here's a sad affair of our friend Lady Teazle!

MRS. CAN. Aye, my dear friend, who would have thought—

LADY S. Well, there is no trusting appearances—though, indeed, she was always too lively for me.

MRS. CAN. To be sure her manners were a little too free; but then, she was so young!

LADY S. And had, indeed, some good qualities.

MRS. CAN. So she had, indeed. But have you heard the particulars?

LADY S. No, but everybody says that Mr. Surface—

SIR BEN. Aye, there! I told you Mr. Surface was the man.

MRS. CAN. No, no! indeed, the assignation was with Charles.

LADY S. With Charles! You alarm me, Mrs. Candour!

MRS. CAN. Yes, yes; he was the lover. Mr. Surface, to do him justice, was only the informer.

SIR BEN. Well, I'll not dispute with you, Mrs. Candour, but be it which it may, I hope that Sir Peter's wound will not—

MRS. CAN. Sir Peter's wound! Oh, mercy! I don't hear a word of their fighting.

LADY S. Nor I, a syllable.

SIR BEN. No! what, no mention of the duel?

MRS. CAN. Not a word.

SIR BEN. Oh, yes! they fought before they left the room.

LADY S. Pray, let us hear!

MRS. CAN. Aye, do oblige us with the duel!

SIR BEN. "Sir," says Sir Peter, immediately after the discovery, "you are a most ungrateful fellow."

MRS. CAN. Aye to Charles—

SIR BEN. No, no—to Mr. Surface— "a most ungrateful fellow; and old as I am, sir," says he, "I insist on immediate satisfaction."

MRS. CAN. Aye, that must have been

to Charles, for 'tis very unlikely Mr. Surface should fight in his own house.

SIR BEN. Gad's life, ma'am, not at all—"giving me immediate satisfaction." —On this, ma'am, Lady Teazle, seeing Sir Peter in such danger, ran out of the room in strong hysterics, and Charles after her, calling out for hartshorn and water; then, madam, they began to fight with swords—

(*Enter* CRABTREE.)

CRAB. With pistols, nephew—pistols! I have it from undoubted authority.

MRS. CAN. Oh, Mr. Crabtree, then it is all true!

CRAB. Too true, indeed, madam, and Sir Peter is dangerously wounded—

SIR BEN. By a thrust in second quite through his left side—

CRAB. By a bullet lodged in the thorax.

MRS. CAN. Mercy on me! Poor Sir Peter!

CRAB. Yes, madam—though Charles would have avoided the matter if he could.

MRS. CAN. I knew Charles was the person.

SIR BEN. My uncle, I see, knows nothing of the matter.

CRAB. But Sir Peter taxed him with the basest ingratitude—

SIR BEN. That I told you, you know—

CRAB. Do, nephew, let me speak!— and insisted on immediate—

SIR BEN. Just as I said—

CRAB. Odds life, nephew, allow others to know something too! A pair of pistols lay on the bureau (for Mr. Surface, it seems, had come home the night before late from Salthill, where he had been to see the Montem with a friend who has a son at Eton), so, unluckily, the pistols were left charged.

SIR BEN. I heard nothing of this.

CRAB. Sir Peter forced Charles to take one, and they fired, it seems pretty nearly together. Charles's shot took effect, as I tell you, and Sir Peter's missed; but what is very extraordinary, the ball struck against a little bronze Shakespeare that stood over the fireplace, grazed out of the window at a right angle, and wounded the postman, who was just coming to the door with a double letter from Northamptonshire.

SIR BEN. My uncle's account is more circumstantial, I confess; but I believe mine is the true one, for all that.

LADY S. (*aside*). I am more interested in this affair than they imagine, and must have better information.

(*Exit* LADY SNEERWELL.)

SIR BEN. Ah! Lady Sneerwell's alarm is very easily accounted for.

CRAB. Yes, yes, they certainly do say —but that's neither here nor there.

MRS. CAN. But pray, where is Sir Peter at present?

CRAB. Oh! they brought him home, and he is now in the house, though the servants are ordered to deny him.

MRS. CAN. I believe so; and Lady Teazle, I suppose, attending him.

CRAB. Yes, yes; and I saw one of the faculty enter just before me.

SIR BEN. Hey! who comes here?

CRAB. Oh, this is he—the physician, depend on't.

MRS. CAN. Oh, certainly! it must be the physician; and now we shall know.

(*Enter* SIR OLIVER SURFACE.)

CRAB. Well, doctor, what hopes?

MRS. CAN. Aye, doctor, how's your patient?

SIR BEN. Now, doctor, isn't it a wound with a small-sword?

CRAB. A bullet lodged in the thorax, for a hundred!

SIR O. Doctor!—a wound with a small-sword! and a bullet in the thorax! —Oons! are you mad, good people?

SIR BEN. Perhaps, sir, you are not a doctor?

SIR O. Truly, I am to thank you for my degree if I am.

CRAB. Only a friend of Sir Peter's then, I presume. But sir, you must have heard of his accident?

SIR O. Not a word!

CRAB. Not of his being dangerously wounded?

SIR O. The devil he is!

SIR BEN. Run through the body—

CRAB. Shot in the breast—

SIR BEN. By one Mr. Surface—

CRAB. Aye, the younger.

SIR O. Hey! what the plague! you seem to differ strangely in your accounts; however, you agree that Sir Peter is dangerously wounded.

SIR BEN. Oh, yes, we agree in that.

CRAB. Yes, yes, I believe there can be no doubt of that.

SIR O. Then, upon my word, for a person in that situation, he is the most imprudent man alive; for here he comes, walking as if nothing at all was the matter.

(*Enter* SIR PETER TEAZLE.)

—Odds heart, Sir Peter, you are come in good time, I promise you, for we had just given you over!

SIR BEN. (*aside to* CRABTREE). Egad, uncle, this is the most sudden recovery!

SIR O. Why, man! what do you out of bed with a small-sword through your body and a bullet lodged in your thorax?

SIR PET. A small-sword and a bullet!

SIR O. Aye; these gentlemen would have killed you without law or physic, and wanted to dub me a doctor to make me an accomplice.

SIR PET. Why, what is all this?

SIR BEN. We rejoice, Sir Peter, that the story of the duel is not true, and are sincerely sorry for your other misfortune.

SIR PET. (*aside*). So, so—all over the town already!

CRAB. Though, Sir Peter, you were certainly vastly to blame to marry at your years.

SIR PET. Sir, what business is that of yours?

MRS. CAN.—Though, indeed, as Sir Peter made so good a husband, he's very much to be pitied.

SIR PET. Plague on your pity, ma'am! I desire none of it.

SIR BEN. However, Sir Peter, you must not mind the laughing and jests you will meet with on the occasion.

SIR PET. Sir, sir! I desire to be master in my own house.

CRAB. 'Tis no uncommon case, that's one comfort.

SIR PET. I insist on being left to myself—without ceremony, I insist on your leaving my house directly!

MRS. CAN. Well, well, we are going; and depend on't, we'll make the best report of it we can. (*Exit.*)

SIR PET. Leave my house!

CRAB.—And tell how hardly you've been treated. (*Exit.*)

SIR PET. Leave my house!

SIR BEN.—And how patiently you bear it. (*Exit.*)

SIR PET. Friends! vipers! furies! Oh! that their own venom would choke them!

SIR O. They are very provoking indeed, Sir Peter.

(*Enter* ROWLEY.)

ROW. I heard high words; what has ruffled you, sir?

SIR PET. Pshaw! what signifies asking? Do I ever pass a day without my vexations?

ROW. Well, I'm not inquisitive.

SIR O. Well, Sir Peter, I have seen both my nephews in the manner we proposed.

SIR PET. A precious couple they are!

ROW. Yes, and Sir Oliver is convinced that your judgment was right, Sir Peter.

SIR O. Yes, I find Joseph is indeed the man, after all.

ROW. Aye, as Sir Peter says, he is a man of sentiment.

SIR O. And acts up to the sentiments he professes.

ROW. It certainly is edification to hear him talk.

SIR O. Oh, he's a model for the young men of the age!— But how's this, Sir Peter? you don't join us in your friend Joseph's praise as I expected.

SIR PET. Sir Oliver, we live in a damned wicked world, and the fewer we praise the better.

ROW. What! do you say so, Sir Peter, who were never mistaken in your life?

SIR PET. Pshaw! plague on you both! I see by your sneering you have heard the whole affair. I shall go mad among you!

ROW. Then, to fret you no longer, Sir Peter, we are indeed acquainted with it all. I met Lady Teazle coming from Mr. Surface's so humbled that she deigned to request me to be her advocate with you.

SIR PET. And does Sir Oliver know all this?

SIR O. Every circumstance.

SIR PET. What—of the closet and the screen, hey?

SIR O. Yes, yes, and the little French milliner. Oh, I have been vastly diverted with the story! ha! ha! ha!

SIR PET. 'Twas very pleasant.

SIR O. I never laughed more in my life, I assure you—ha! ha! ha!

SIR PET. Oh, vastly diverting!—ha! ha! ha!

ROW. To be sure, Joseph with his sentiments! ha! ha! ha!

SIR PET. Yes, yes, his sentiments! ha ha! ha—Hypocritical villain!

SIR O. Aye, and that rogue Charles to pull Sir Peter out of the closet: ha! ha! ha!

SIR PET. Ha! ha! 'twas devilish entertaining, to be sure

SIR O. Ha! ha! ha! Egad, Sir Peter, I should like to have seen your face when the screen was thrown down—ha! ha!

SIR PET. Yes, yes, my face when the screen was thrown down—ha! ha! ha! Oh, I must never show my head again!

SIR O. But come, come, it isn't fair to laugh at you neither, my old friend—though, upon my soul, I can't help it.

SIR PET. Oh, pray, don't restrain your mirth on my account; it does not hurt me at all. I laugh at the whole affair myself. Yes, yes, I think being a standing jest for all one's acquaintance a very happy situation. Oh, yes, and then of a morning to read the paragraphs about Mr. S——, Lady T——, and Sir P——, will be so entertaining!

ROW. Without affectation, Sir Peter, you may despise the ridicule of fools. But I see Lady Teazle going towards the next room; I am sure you must desire a reconciliation as earnestly as she does.

SIR O. Perhaps my being here prevents her coming to you. Well, I'll leave honest Rowley to mediate between you; but he must bring you all presently to Mr. Surface's, where I am now returning, if not to reclaim a libertine at least to expose hypocrisy.

SIR PET. Ah, I'll be present at your discovering yourself there with all my heart, though 'tis a vile unlucky place for discoveries.

ROW. We'll follow.

(*Exit* SIR OLIVER SURFACE.)

SIR PET. She is not coming here, you see, Rowley.

ROW. No, but she has left the door of that room open, you perceive. See, she is in tears.

SIR PET. Certainly a little mortification appears very becoming in a wife. Don't you think it will do her good to let her pine a little?

ROW. Oh, this is ungenerous in you!

SIR PET. Well, I know not what to think. You remember the letter I found of hers evidently intended for Charles?

ROW. A mere forgery, Sir Peter!—laid in your way on purpose. This is one of the points which I intend Snake shall give you conviction of.

SIR PET. I wish I were once satisfied of that. She looks this way. What a remarkably elegant turn of the head she has! Rowley, I'll go to her.

ROW. Certainly.

SIR PET. Though when it is known that we are reconciled, people will laugh at me ten times more.

ROW. Let them laugh, and retort their malice only by showing them you are happy in spite of it.

SIR PET. I'faith, so I will; and, if I'm not mistaken, we may yet be the happiest couple in the country.

ROW. Nay, Sir Peter, he who once lays aside suspicion—

SIR PET. Hold, Master Rowley! if you have any regard for me, never let me hear you utter anything like a sentiment; I have had enough of them to serve me the rest of my life. (*Exeunt.*)

SCENE 3

(*The library in* JOSEPH SURFACE'S *house.*)

(*Enter* JOSEPH SURFACE *and* LADY SNEERWELL.)

LADY S. Impossible! Will not Sir Peter immediately be reconciled to Charles, and of course no longer oppose his union with Maria? The thought is distraction to me.

JOSEPH. Can passion furnish a remedy?

LADY S. No, nor cunning neither. Oh, I was a fool, an idiot, to league with such a blunderer!

JOSEPH. Sure, Lady Sneerwell, I am the greatest sufferer; yet you see I bear the accident with calmness.

LADY S. Because the disappointment doesn't reach your heart; your interest only attached you to Maria. Had you felt for her what I have for that ungrateful libertine, neither your temper nor hypocrisy could prevent your showing the sharpness of your vexation.

JOSEPH. But why should your reproaches fall on me for this disappointment?

LADY S. Are you not the cause of it? Had you not a sufficient field for your roguery in imposing upon Sir Peter and supplanting your brother, but you must endeavor to seduce his wife? I hate such an avarice of crimes; 'tis an unfair monopoly, and never prospers.

JOSEPH. Well, I admit I have been to blame. I confess I deviated from the direct road of wrong, but I don't think we're so totally defeated neither.

LADY S. No!

JOSEPH. You tell me you have made a trial of Snake since we met, and that you still believe him faithful to us?

LADY S. I do believe so.

JOSEPH. And that he has undertaken, should it be necessary, to swear and prove that Charles is at this time contracted by vows and honor to your ladyship, which some of his former letters to you will serve to support.

LADY S. This, indeed, might have assisted.

JOSEPH. Come, come; it is not too late yet.—(*Knocking at the door.*) But hark! this is probably my uncle, Sir Oliver. Retire to that room; we'll consult farther when he is gone.

LADY S. Well, but if *he* should find you out too?

JOSEPH. Oh, I have no fear of that. Sir Peter will hold his tongue for his own credit's sake—and you may depend on it, I shall soon discover Sir Oliver's weak side!

LADY S. I have no diffidence of your abilities, only be constant to one roguery at a time.

JOSEPH. I will, I will!

(*Exit* LADY SNEERWELL.)

—So! 'tis confounded hard, after such bad fortune, to be baited by one's confederate in evil. Well, at all events my character is so much better than Charles's that I certainly—hey!—what—this is not Sir Oliver, but old Stanley again. Plague on't that he should return to tease me just now! I shall have Sir Oliver come and find him here—and—

(*Enter* SIR OLIVER SURFACE.)

—Gad's life, Mr. Stanley, why have you come back to plague me at this time? You must not stay now, upon my word.

SIR O. Sir, I hear your uncle Oliver is expected here, and though he has been so penurious to you, I'll try what he'll do for me.

JOSEPH. Sir, 'tis impossible for you to stay now; so I must beg—Come any other time, and I promise you, you shall be assisted.

SIR O. No; Sir Oliver and I must be acquainted.

JOSEPH. Zounds, sir! then I insist on your quitting the room directly.

SIR O. Nay, sir—

JOSEPH. Sir, I insist on't!—Here, William! show this gentleman out. Since you compel me, sir, not one moment—this is such insolence. (*Going to push him out.*)

(*Enter* CHARLES SURFACE.)

CHARLES. Heyday! what's the matter now? What the devil, have you got hold of my little broker here? Zounds, brother, don't hurt little Premium. What's the matter, my little fellow?

JOSEPH. So! he has been with you, too, has he?

CHARLES. To be sure, he has. Why, he's as honest a little—But sure, Joseph, you have not been borrowing money too, have you?

JOSEPH. Borrowing! no! But brother, you know we expect Sir Oliver here every—

CHARLES. O Gad, that's true! Noll mustn't find the little broker here, to be sure.

JOSEPH. Yet, Mr. Stanley insists—

CHARLES. Stanley! why, his name's Premium.

JOSEPH. No, sir, Stanley.

CHARLES. No, no, Premium.

JOSEPH. Well, no matter which—but—

CHARLES. Aye, aye, Stanley or Premium, 'tis the same thing, as you say; for I suppose he goes by half a hundred names, besides "A. B." at the coffeehouse. (*Knocking.*)

JOSEPH. 'Sdeath! here's Sir Oliver at the door. Now, I beg, Mr. Stanley—

CHARLES. Aye, aye, and I beg, Mr. Premium—

SIR O. Gentlemen—

JOSEPH. Sir, by Heaven, you shall go!

CHARLES. Aye, out with him, certainly!

SIR O. This violence—

JOSEPH. Sir, 'tis your own fault.

CHARLES. Out with him, to be sure! (*Both forcing* SIR OLIVER *out.*)

(*Enter* SIR PETER *and* LADY TEAZLE, MARIA, *and* ROWLEY.)

SIR PET. My old friend, Sir Oliver—Hey! what in the name of wonder—here are dutiful nephews—assault their uncle at a first visit!

LADY T. Indeed, Sir Oliver, 'twas well we came to rescue you.

ROW. Truly it was; for I perceive, Sir Oliver, the character of old Stanley was no protection to you.

SIR O. Nor of Premium either; the necessities of the former could not extort a shilling from that benevolent gentleman, and now, egad, with the other I stood a chance of faring worse than my ancestors, and being knocked down without being bid for.

JOSEPH. Charles!

CHARLES. Joseph!

JOSEPH. 'Tis now complete!

CHARLES. Very!

SIR O. Sir Peter, my friend, and Rowley too—look on that elder nephew of mine. You know what he has already received from my bounty, and you also know how gladly I would have regarded half my fortune as held in trust for him; judge, then, my disappointment in discovering him to be destitute of faith, charity, and gratitude!

SIR PET. Sir Oliver, I should be more surprised at this declaration if I had not myself found him to be mean, treacherous, and hypocritical.

LADY T. And if the gentleman pleads not guilty to these, pray let him call *me* to his character.

SIR PET. Then I believe we need add no more. If he knows himself, he will consider it as the most perfect punishment, that he is known to the world.

CHARLES (*aside*). If they talk this way to Honesty, what will they say to me by and by?

SIR O. As for that prodigal, his brother, there—

CHARLES (*aside*). Aye, now comes my turn: the damned family pictures will ruin me!

JOSEPH. Sir Oliver—uncle, will you honor me with a hearing?

CHARLES (*aside*). Now, if Joseph would make one of his long speeches, I might recollect myself a little.

SIR O. (*to* JOSEPH). I suppose you would undertake to justify yourself entirely?

JOSEPH. I trust I could.

SIR O. (*to* CHARLES). Well, sir!—and you could justify yourself too, I suppose?

CHARLES. Not that I know of, Sir Oliver.

SIR O. What!—Little Premium has been let too much into the secret, I suppose?

CHARLES. True, sir; but they were *family* secrets, and should not be mentioned again, you know.

ROW. Come, Sir Oliver, I know you cannot speak of Charles's follies with anger.

SIR O. Odds heart, no more I can, nor with gravity either. Sir Peter, do you know the rogue bargained with me for all his ancestors—sold me judges and generals by the foot, and maiden aunts as cheap as broken china.

CHARLES. To be sure, Sir Oliver, I did make a little free with the family canvas, that's the truth on't. My ancestors may rise in judgment against me, there's no denying it; but believe me sincere when I tell you—and upon my soul I would not say so if I was not—that if I do not appear mortified at the exposure of my follies, it is because I feel at this moment the warmest satisfaction in seeing you, my liberal benefactor.

SIR O. Charles, I believe you. Give me your hand again. The ill-looking little fellow over the settee has made your peace.

CHARLES. Then, sir, my gratitude to the original is still increased.

LADY T. Yet, I believe, Sir Oliver, here is one whom Charles is still more anxious to be reconciled to.

SIR O. Oh, I have heard of his attachment there; and, with the young lady's pardon, if I construe right—that blush—

SIR PET. Well, child, speak your sentiments!

MARIA. Sir, I have little to say, but that I shall rejoice to hear that he is happy; for me, whatever claim I had to his attention, I willingly resign to one who has a better title.

CHARLES. How, Maria!

SIR PET. Heyday! what's the mystery now? While he appeared an incorrigible rake, you would give your hand to no one else; and now that he is likely to reform, I'll warrant you won't have him!

MARIA. His own heart and Lady Sneerwell know the cause.

CHARLES. Lady Sneerwell!

JOSEPH. Brother, it is with great concern I am obliged to speak on this point, but my regard to justice compels me and Lady Sneerwell's injuries can no longer be concealed. (*Opens the door.*)

(*Enter* LADY SNEERWELL.)

SIR PET. So! another French milliner! Egad, he has one in every room in the house, I suppose!

LADY S. Ungrateful Charles! Well may you be surprised, and feel for the indelicate situation your perfidy has forced me into.

CHARLES. Pray, uncle, is this another plot of yours? For, as I have life, I don't understand it.

JOSEPH. I believe, sir, there is but the evidence of one person more necessary to make it extremely clear.

SIR PET. And that person, I imagine, is Mr. Snake.—Rowley, you were perfectly right to bring him with us, and pray let him appear.

ROW. Walk in, Mr. Snake.

(*Enter* SNAKE.)

I thought his testimony might be wanted; however, it happens unluckily that he comes to confront Lady Sneerwell, not to support her.

LADY S. A villain! Treacherous to me at last! Speak, fellow; have you too conspired against me?

SNAKE. I beg your ladyship ten thousand pardons: you paid me extremely liberally for the lie in question, but I unfortunately have been offered double to speak the truth.

SIR PET. Plot and counter-plot, egad!

LADY S. (*going*). The torments of shame and disappointment on you all!

LADY T. Hold, Lady Sneerwell—before you go, let me thank you for the trouble you and that gentleman have taken, in writing letters from me to Charles and answering them yourself; and let me also request you to make my respects to the scandalous college of which you are president, and inform them that Lady Teazle, licentiate, begs leave to return the diploma they granted her, as she leaves off practice and kills characters no longer.

LADY S. You, too, madam!—provoking—insolent! May your husband live these fifty years! (*Exit.*)

SIR PET. Oons! what a fury! ·

LADY T. A malicious creature, indeed!

SIR PET. What!—not for her last wish!

LADY T. Oh, no!

SIR O. Well, sir, and what have you to say now?

JOSEPH. Sir, I am so confounded to find that Lady Sneerwell could be guilty of suborning Mr. Snake in this manner to impose on us all, that I know not what to say; however, lest her revengeful spirit should prompt her to injure my brother, I had certainly better follow her directly. (*Exit.*)

SIR PET. Moral to the last drop!

SIR O. Aye, and marry her, Joseph, if you can. Oil and vinegar, egad! you'll do very well together.

Row. I believe we have no more occasion for Mr. Snake at present?

SNAKE. Before I go, I beg pardon once for all for whatever uneasiness I have been the humble instrument of causing to the parties present.

SIR PET. Well, well, you have made atonement by a good deed at last.

SNAKE. But I must request of the company that it shall never be known.

SIR PET. Hey! what the plague! are you ashamed of having done a right thing once in your life?

SNAKE. Ah, sir, consider—I live by the badness of my character; I have nothing but my infamy to depend on, and if it were once known that I had been betrayed into an honest action, I should lose every friend I have in the world.

SIR O. Well, well, we'll not traduce you by saying anything in your praise; never fear.

(*Exit* SNAKE.)

SIR PET. There's a precious rogue!

LADY T. See, Sir Oliver, there needs no persuasion now to reconcile your nephew and Maria.

SIR O. Aye, aye, that's as it should be, and, egad, we'll have the wedding to-morrow morning.

CHARLES. Thank you, dear uncle.

SIR PET. What, you rogue! don't you ask the girl's consent first?

CHARLES. Oh, I have done that a long time—a minute ago—and she has looked yes.

MARIA. For shame, Charles!—I protest, Sir Peter, there has not been a word.

SIR O. Well, then, the fewer the better; may your love for each other never know abatement!

SIR PET. And may you live as happily together as Lady Teazle and I intend to do!

CHARLES. Rowley, my old friend, I am sure you congratulate me; and I suspect that I owe you much.

SIR O. You do, indeed, Charles.

Row. If my efforts to serve you had not succeeded, you would have been in my debt for the attempt; but deserve to be happy, and you overpay me.

SIR PET. Aye, honest Rowley always said you would reform.

CHARLES. Why, as to reforming, Sir Peter, I'll make no promises, and that I take to be a proof that I intend to set about it. But here shall be my monitor— my gentle guide.—Ah! can I leave the virtuous path those eyes illumine?

Though thou, dear maid, shouldst waive
    thy beauty's sway,
Thou still must rule, because I will obey:
An humble fugitive from Folly, view;
No sanctuary near but Love and you.
(*To the audience.*)
You can, indeed, each anxious fear re-
    move,
For even Scandal dies if you approve.
(*Exeunt omnes.*)

EPILOGUE

BY MR. COLMAN
SPOKEN BY LADY TEAZLE

I, who was late so volatile and gay,

Like a trade-wind must now blow all one
    way,
Bend all my cares, my studies, and my
    vows,
To one dull rusty weathercock—my
    spouse!
So wills our virtuous bard—the motley
    Bayes
Of crying epilogues and laughing plays!
Old bachelors who marry smart young
    wives,
Learn from our play to regulate their
    lives;
Each bring his dear to town, all faults
    upon her—
London will prove the very source of
    honor.
Plunged fairly in, like a cold bath it
    serves,
When principles relax, to brace the
    nerves.
Such is my case; and yet I must deplore
That the gay dream of dissipation's o'er.
And say, ye fair! was ever lively wife,
Born with a genius for the highest life,
Like me, untimely blasted in her bloom,
Like me condemned to such a dismal
    doom?
Save money—when I just knew how to
    waste it!
Leave London—just as I began to taste
    it!
Must I then watch the early crowing
    cock,
The melancholy ticking of a clock,
In a lone rustic hall forever pounded,
With dogs, cats, rats, and squalling brats
    surrounded?
With humble curate can I now retire
(While good Sir Peter boozes with the
    squire),

And at backgammon mortify my soul
That pants for loo, or flutters at a vole?
"Seven's the main!" Dear sound that
    must expire,
Lost at hot cockles round a Christmas
    fire!
The transient hour of fashion too soon
    spent,
Farewell the tranquil mind, farewell con-
    tent!
Farewell the plumèd head, the cushioned
    tête,
That takes the cushion from its proper
    seat!
That spirit-stirring drum!—card drums I
    mean,
Spadille—odd trick—pam—basto—king
    and queen!
And you, ye knockers, that, with brazen
    throat,
The welcome visitors' approach denote;
Farewell all quality of high renown,
Pride, pomp, and circumstance of glori-
    ous town!
Farewell! your revels I partake no more,
And Lady Teazle's occupation's o'er!
All this I told our bard; he smiled, and
    said 'twas clear,
I ought to play deep tragedy next
    year.
Meanwhile he drew wise morals from
    his play,
And in these solemn periods stalked
    away:
"Bless'd were the fair like you; her faults
    who stopped
And closed her follies when the curtain
    dropped!
No more in vice or error to engage,
Or play the fool at large on life's great
    stage."

HENRIK IBSEN / 1828–1906

Henrik Johan Ibsen, a Norwegian, was taken from school and apprenticed to an apothecary at sixteen, learned playwriting without instruction, and in 1851, with only a little success to his credit, became theater poet in Bergen, and in 1857 took the same position in Christiania. He left Norway in 1864, officially for a period of study, but actually embittered by the reception of his plays, which had been chiefly romantic treatments of Norwegian ballad, saga, and historical material.

Ibsen then changed his dramatic manner to the realistic, and his external subject matter to the political, social, and psychological problems of contemporary life, in a series of plays which made him a world figure. *A Doll's House* (1879), *Ghosts* (1881), *The Wild Duck* (1884), *Rosmersholm* (1886), *Hedda Gabler* (1890), and *The Master Builder* (1896) were powerful contributions to the new use of the theater as a social instrument on the side of the new realistic and scientific approach to human problems.

The "problem play," a serious drama concentrated on a particular weakness or evil, presumably remediable if attacked from a new direction, brought the theater into the arena of social reform. Because problem plays are pointed at existing problems which may in time be alleviated if the action they call for is taken, they sometimes seem dated by the problem, or limited to a sociological meaning only. The best of them, however, outlive the problem because it was only an external means for exhibiting universal human nature under tragic forces. Ibsen's plays, which served as powerful arguments both for realistic drama and realistic thought, have passed the "time test" and emerged as dateless serious dramas or tragedies.

Ghosts (1881) uses marriage and moral codes as its subject matter, but the truths discovered by Mrs. Alving too late to save herself by them apply to many experiences other than middle-class Norwegian marriage. *Ghosts* has often been called a true tragedy, Greek or Sophoclean in its structure and irony.

Ghosts

A FAMILY DRAMA IN THREE ACTS
TRANSLATED BY WILLIAM ARCHER

CHARACTERS

MRS. HELEN ALVING, *widow of Captain Alving, late Chamberlain to the King.*
OSWALD ALVING, *her son, a painter.*
PASTOR MANDERS.
JACOB ENGSTRAND, *a carpenter.*
REGINA ENGSTRAND, *Mrs. Alving's maid.*

SCENE: *The action takes place at Mrs. Alving's country house, beside one of the large fjords in Western Norway.*

Act I

(*A spacious garden-room, with one door to the left, and two doors to the*

*right. In the middle of the room a round
table, with chairs about it. On the table
lie books, periodicals, and newspapers.
In the foreground to the left a window,
and by it a small sofa, with a work table
in front of it. In the background, the
room is continued into a somewhat nar-
rower conservatory, the walls of which
are formed by large panes of glass. In the
right-hand wall of the conservatory is a
door leading down into the garden.
Through the glass wall a gloomy fjord-
landscape is faintly visible, veiled by
steady rain.)*

(ENGSTRAND, *the carpenter, stands by
the garden door. His left leg is somewhat
bent; he has a clump of wood under the
sole of his boot.* REGINA, *with an empty
garden syringe in her hand, hinders him
from advancing.)*

REGINA (*in a low voice*). What do
you want? Stop where you are. You're
positively dripping.

ENGSTRAND. It's the Lord's own rain,
my girl.

REGINA. It's the devil's rain, *I* say.

ENGSTRAND. Lord, how you talk,
Regina. (*Limps a step or two forward
into the room.*) It's just this as I wanted
to say—

REGINA. Don't clatter so with that
foot of yours, I tell you! The young
master's asleep upstairs.

ENGSTRAND. Asleep? In the middle
of the day?

REGINA. It's no business of yours.

ENGSTRAND. I was out on the loose
last night—

REGINA. I can quite believe that.

ENGSTRAND. Yes, we're weak vessels,
we poor mortals, my girl—

REGINA. So it seems.

ENGSTRAND. —and temptations are
manifold in this world, you see. But all
the same, I was hard at work, God
knows, at half-past five this morning.

REGINA. Very well; only be off now.
I won't stop here and have *rendezvous's*
with you.

ENGSTRAND. What do you say you
won't have?

REGINA. I won't have any one find
you here; so just you go about your business.

ENGSTRAND (*advances a step or two*).
Blest if I go before I've had a talk with
you. This afternoon I shall have finished
my work at the school-house, and then
I shall take to-night's boat and be off
home to the town.

REGINA (*mutters*). Pleasant journey
to you!

ENGSTRAND. Thank you, my child.
To-morrow the Orphanage is to be
opened, and then there'll be fine doings,
no doubt, and plenty of intoxicating
drink going, you know. And nobody
shall say of Jacob Engstrand that he
can't keep out of temptation's way.

REGINA. Oh!

ENGSTRAND. You see, there's to be
heaps of grand folks here to-morrow.
Pastor Manders is expected from town,
too.

REGINA. He's coming to-day.

ENGSTRAND. There, you see! And I
should be cursedly sorry if he found out
anything against me, don't you understand?

REGINA. Oho! is that your game?

ENGSTRAND. Is what my game?

REGINA (*looking hard at him*). What
are you going to fool Pastor Manders
into doing, this time?

ENGSTRAND. Sh! sh! Are you crazy?
Do *I* want to fool Pastor Manders? Oh
no! Pastor Manders has been far too
good a friend to me for that. But I just
wanted to say, you know—that I mean
to be off home again to-night.

REGINA. The sooner the better, say I.

ENGSTRAND. Yes, but I want you
with me, Regina.

REGINA (*open-mouthed*). You want
me—? What are you talking about?

ENGSTRAND. I want you to come
home with me, I say.

REGINA (*scornfully*). Never in this
world shall you get me home with you.

ENGSTRAND. Oh, we'll see about that.

REGINA. Yes, you may be sure we'll see about it! Me, that have been brought up by a lady like Mrs. Alving! Me, that am treated almost as a daughter here! Is it me you want to go home with you? —to a house like yours? For shame?

ENGSTRAND. What the devil do you mean? Do you set yourself up against your father, you hussy?

REGINA (*mutters without looking at him*). You've said often enough I was no concern of yours.

ENGSTRAND. Pooh! Why should you bother about that—

REGINA. Haven't you many a time sworn at me and called me a—? *Fi donc!*

ENGSTRAND. Curse me, now, if ever I used such an ugly word.

REGINA. Oh, I remember very well what word you used.

ENGSTRAND. Well, but that was only when I was a bit on, don't you know? Temptations are manifold in this world, Regina.

REGINA. Ugh!

ENGSTRAND. And besides, it was when your mother was that aggravating —I had to find something to twit her with, my child. She was always setting up for a fine lady. (*Mimics.*) "Let me go, Engstrand; let me be. Remember I was three years in Chamberlain Alving's family at Rosenvold." (*Laughs.*) Mercy on us! She could never forget that the Captain was made a Chamberlain while she was in service here.

REGINA. Poor mother! you very soon tormented her into her grave.

ENGSTRAND (*with a twist of his shoulders*). Oh, of course! I'm to have the blame for everything.

REGINA (*turns away; half aloud*). Ugh—! And that leg too!

ENGSTRAND. What do you say, my child?

REGINA. *Pied de mouton.*

ENGSTRAND. Is that English, eh?

REGINA. Yes.

ENGSTRAND. Ay, ay; you've picked up some learning out here; and that may come in useful now, Regina.

REGINA (*after a short silence*). What do you want with me in town?

ENGSTRAND. Can you ask what a father wants with his only child? A'n't I a lonely, forlorn widower?

REGINA. Oh, don't try on any nonsense like that with me! Why do you want me?

ENGSTRAND. Well, let me tell you, I've been thinking of setting up in a new line of business.

REGINA (*contemptuously*). You've tried that often enough, and much good you've done with it.

ENGSTRAND. Yes, but this time you shall see, Regina! Devil take me—

REGINA (*stamps*). Stop your swearing!

ENGSTRAND. Hush, hush; you're right enough there, my girl. What I wanted to say was just this—I've laid by a very tidy pile from this Orphanage job.

REGINA. Have you? That's a good thing for you.

ENGSTRAND. What can a man spend his ha'pence on here in this country hole?

REGINA. Well, what then?

ENGSTRAND. Why, you see, I thought of putting the money into some paying speculation. I thought of a sort of a sailors' tavern—

REGINA. Pah!

ENGSTRAND. A regular high-class affair, of course; not any sort of pig-sty for common sailors. No! damn it! it would be for captains and mates, and— and—regular swells, you know.

REGINA. And I was to—?

ENGSTRAND. You were to help, to be sure. Only for the look of the thing, you understand. Devil a bit of hard work shall you have, my girl. You shall do exactly what you like.

REGINA. Oh, indeed!

ENGSTRAND. But there must be a petticoat in the house; that's as clear as daylight. For I want to have it a bit lively-like in the evenings, with singing

and dancing, and so on. You must remember they're weary wanderers on the
ocean of life. (*Nearer.*) Now don't be a
fool and stand in your own light, Regina.
What's to become of you out here? Your
mistress has given you a lot of learning;
but what good is that to you? You're to
look after the children at the new Orphanage, I hear. Is that the sort of thing
for you, eh? Are you so dead set on
wearing your life out for a pack of dirty
brats?

REGINA. No; if things go as I want
them to— Well there's no saying—there's
no saying.

ENGSTRAND. What do you mean by
"there's no saying"?

REGINA. Never you mind.—How
much money have you saved?

ENGSTRAND. What with one thing
and another, a matter of seven or eight
hundred crowns.

REGINA. That's not so bad.

ENGSTRAND. It's enough to make a
start with, my girl.

REGINA. Aren't you thinking of giving me any?

ENGSTRAND. No, I'm blest if I am!

REGINA. Not even of sending me a
scrap of stuff for a new dress?

ENGSTRAND. Come to town with me,
my lass, and you'll soon get dresses
enough.

REGINA. Pooh! I can do that on my
own account, if I want to.

ENGSTRAND. No, a father's guiding
hand is what you want, Regina. Now,
I've got my eye on a capital house in
Little Harbour Street. They don't want
much ready-money; and it could be a
sort of a Sailors' Home, you know.

REGINA. But I will not live with you!
I have nothing whatever to do with you.
Be off!

ENGSTRAND. You wouldn't stop long
with me, my girl. No such luck! If you
knew how to play your cards, such a fine
figure of a girl as you've grown in the
last year or two—

REGINA. Well?

ENGSTRAND. You'd soon get hold of
some mate—or maybe even a captain—

REGINA. I won't marry any one of
that sort. Sailors have no *savoir vivre*.

ENGSTRAND. What's that they haven't
got?

REGINA. I know what sailors are, I
tell you. They're not the sort of people
to marry.

ENGSTRAND. Then never mind about
marrying them. You can make it pay all
the same. (*More confidentially.*) He—
the Englishman—the man with the
yacht—he came down with three hundred dollars, he did; and she wasn't a bit
handsomer than you.

REGINA (*making for him*). Out you
go!

ENGSTRAND (*falling back*). Come,
come! You're not going to hit me, I
hope.

REGINA. Yes, if you begin talking
about mother I shall hit you. Get away
with you, I say! (*Drives him back towards the garden door.*) And don't slam
the doors. Young Mr. Alving—

ENGSTRAND. He's asleep; I know.
You're mighty taken up about young
Mr. Alving— (*More softly.*) Oho! you
don't mean to say it's him as—?

REGINA. Be off this minute! You're
crazy, I tell you! No, not that way. There
comes Pastor Manders. Down the kitchen
stairs with you.

ENGSTRAND (*towards the right*). Yes,
yes, I'm going. But just you talk to him
as is coming there. He's the man to tell
you what a child owes its father. For I
am your father all the same, you know.
I can prove it from the church register.

(*He goes out through the second door
to the right, which* REGINA *has opened,
and closes again after him.* REGINA
*glances hastily at herself in the mirror,
dusts herself with her pocket handkerchief, and settles her necktie; then she
busies herself with the flowers.*)

(PASTOR MANDERS, *wearing an over-*

coat, carrying an umbrella, and with a small travelling-bag on a strap over his shoulder, comes through the garden door into the conservatory.)

MANDERS. Good-morning, Miss Engstrand.

REGINA (*turning round, surprised and pleased*). No, really! Good-morning, Pastor Manders. Is the steamer in already?

MANDERS. It is just in. (*Enters the sitting-room.*) Terrible weather we have been having lately.

REGINA (*follows him*). It's such blessed weather for the country, sir.

MANDERS. No doubt; you are quite right. We townspeople give too little thought to that. (*He begins to take off his overcoat.*)

REGINA. Oh, mayn't I help you?—There! Why, how wet it is! I'll just hang it up in the hall. And your umbrella, too—I'll open it and let it dry.

(*She goes out with the things through the second door on the right.* PASTOR MANDERS *takes off his travelling-bag and lays it and his hat on a chair. Meanwhile* REGINA *comes in again.*)

MANDERS. Ah, it's a comfort to get safe under cover. I hope everything is going on well here?

REGINA. Yes, thank you, sir.

MANDERS. You have your hands full, I suppose, in preparation for to-morrow?

REGINA. Yes, there's plenty to do, of course.

MANDERS. And Mrs. Alving is at home, I trust?

REGINA. Oh dear, yes. She's just upstairs, looking after the young master's chocolate.

MANDERS. Yes, by-the-bye—I heard down at the pier that Oswald had arrived.

REGINA. Yes, he came the day before yesterday. We didn't expect him before to-day.

MANDERS. Quite strong and well, I hope?

REGINA. Yes, thank you, quite; but dreadfully tired with the journey. He has made one rush right through from Paris—the whole way in one train, I believe. He's sleeping a little now, I think; so perhaps we'd better talk a little quietly.

MANDERS. Sh!—as quietly as you please.

REGINA (*arranging an arm-chair beside the table*). Now, do sit down, Pastor Manders, and make yourself comfortable. (*He sits down; she places a footstool under his feet.*) There! Are you comfortable now, sir?

MANDERS. Thanks, thanks, extremely so. (*Looks at her.*) Do you know, Miss Engstrand, I positively believe you have grown since I last saw you.

REGINA. Do you think so, sir? Mrs. Alving says I've filled out too.

MANDERS. Filled out? Well, perhaps a little; just enough.

(*Short pause.*)

REGINA. Shall I tell Mrs. Alving you are here?

MANDERS. Thanks, thanks, there is no hurry, my dear child.—By-the-bye, Regina, my good girl, tell me: how is your father getting on out here?

REGINA. Oh, thank you, sir, he's getting on well enough.

MANDERS. He called upon me last time he was in town.

REGINA. Did he, indeed? He's always so glad of a chance of talking to you, sir.

MANDERS. And you often look in upon him at his work, I daresay?

REGINA. I? Oh, of course, when I have time, I—

MANDERS. Your father is not a man of strong character, Miss Engstrand. He stands terribly in need of a guiding hand.

REGINA. Oh, yes; I daresay he does.

MANDERS. He requires some one near him whom he cares for, and whose judgment he respects. He frankly admitted as much when he last came to see me.

REGINA. Yes, he mentioned something of the sort to me. But I don't know whether Mrs. Alving can spare me; especially now that we've got the new Orphanage to attend to. And then I should be so sorry to leave Mrs. Alving; she has always been so kind to me.

MANDERS. But a daughter's duty, my good girl— Of course, we should first have to get your mistress's consent.

REGINA. But I don't know whether it would be quite proper for me, at my age, to keep house for a single man.

MANDERS. What! My dear Miss Engstrand! When the man is your own father!

REGINA. Yes, that may be; but all the same— Now, if it were in a thoroughly nice house, and with a real gentleman—

MANDERS. Why, my dear Regina—

REGINA. —one I could love and respect, and be a daughter to—

MANDERS. Yes, but my dear, good child—

REGINA. Then I should be glad to go to town. It's very lonely out here; you know yourself, sir, what it is to be alone in the world. And I can assure you I'm both quick and willing. Don't you know of any such place for me, sir?

MANDERS. I? No, certainly not.

REGINA. But, dear, dear sir, do remember me if—

MANDERS (rising). Yes, yes, certainly, Miss Engstrand.

REGINA. For if I—

MANDERS. Will you be so good as to tell your mistress I am here?

REGINA. I will, at once, sir. (She goes out to the left.)

MANDERS (paces the room two or three times, stands a moment in the background with his hands behind his back, and looks out over the garden. Then he returns to the table, takes up a book, and looks at the title-page; starts, and looks at several books). Ha—indeed!

(MRS. ALVING enters by the door on the left; she is followed by REGINA, who immediately goes out by the first door on the right.)

MRS. ALVING (holds out her hand). Welcome, my dear Pastor.

MANDERS. How do you do, Mrs. Alving? Here I am as I promised.

MRS. ALVING. Always punctual to the minute.

MANDERS. You may believe it was not easy for me to get away. With all the Boards and Committees I belong to—

MRS. ALVING. That makes it all the kinder of you to come so early. Now we can get through our business before dinner. But where is your portmanteau?

MANDERS (quickly). I left it down at the inn. I shall sleep there to-night.

MRS. ALVING (suppressing a smile). Are you really not to be persuaded, even now, to pass the night under my roof?

MANDERS. No, no, Mrs. Alving; many thanks. I shall stay at the inn, as usual. It is so conveniently near the landing-stage.

MRS. ALVING. Well, you must have your own way. But I really should have thought we two old people—

MANDERS. Now you are making fun of me. Ah, you're naturally in great spirits to-day—what with to-morrow's festival and Oswald's return.

MRS. ALVING. Yes; you can think what a delight it is to me! It's more than two years since he was home last. And now he has promised to stay with me all the winter.

MANDERS. Has he really? That is very nice and dutiful of him. For I can well believe that life in Rome and Paris has very different attractions from any we can offer here.

MRS. ALVING. Ah, but here he has his mother, you see. My own darling boy—he hasn't forgotten his old mother!

MANDERS. It would be grievous indeed, if absence and absorption in art and that sort of thing were to blunt his natural feelings.

MRS. ALVING. Yes, you may well say

so. But there's nothing of that sort to fear with him. I'm quite curious to see whether you know him again. He'll be down presently; he's upstairs just now, resting a little on the sofa. But do sit down, my dear Pastor.

MANDERS. Thank you. Are you quite at liberty—?

MRS. ALVING. Certainly. (*She sits by the table.*)

MANDERS. Very well. Then let me show you— (*He goes to the chair where his travelling-bag lies, takes out a packet of papers, sits down on the opposite side of the table, and tries to find a clear space for the papers.*) Now, to begin with, here is— (*Breaking off.*) Tell me, Mrs. Alving, how do these books come to be here?

MRS. ALVING. These books? They are books I am reading.

MANDERS. Do you read this sort of literature?

MRS. ALVING. Certainly I do.

MANDERS. Do you feel better or happier for such reading?

MRS. ALVING. I feel, so to speak, more secure.

MANDERS. That is strange. How do you mean?

MRS. ALVING. Well, I seem to find explanation and confirmation of all sorts of things I myself have been thinking. For that is the wonderful part of it, Pastor Manders—there is really nothing new in these books, nothing but what most people think and believe. Only most people either don't formulate it to themselves, or else keep quiet about it.

MANDERS. Great heavens! Do you really believe that most people—?

MRS. ALVING. I do, indeed.

MANDERS. But surely not in this country? Not here among us?

MRS. ALVING. Yes, certainly; here as elsewhere.

MANDERS. Well, I really must say—!

MRS. ALVING. For the rest, what do you object to in these books?

MANDERS. Object to in them? You surely do not suppose that I have nothing better to do than to study such publications as these?

MRS. ALVING. That is to say, you know nothing of what you are condemning?

MANDERS. I have read enough about these writings to disapprove of them.

MRS. ALVING. Yes; but your own judgment—

MANDERS. My dear Mrs. Alving, there are many occasions in life when one must rely upon others. Things are so ordered in this world; and it is well that they are. Otherwise, what would become of society?

MRS. ALVING. Well, well, I daresay you're right there.

MANDERS. Besides, I of course do not deny that there may be much that is attractive in such books. Nor can I blame you for wishing to keep up with the intellectual movements that are said to be going on in the great world—where you have let your son pass so much of his life. But—

MRS. ALVING. But?

MANDERS (*lowering his voice*). But one should not talk about it, Mrs. Alving. One is certainly not bound to account to everybody for what one reads and thinks within one's own four walls.

MRS. ALVING. Of course not; I quite agree with you.

MANDERS. Only think, now, how you are bound to consider the interests of this Orphanage, which you decided on founding at a time when—if I understand you rightly—you thought very differently on spiritual matters.

MRS. ALVING. Oh, yes; I quite admit that. But it was about the Orphanage—

MANDERS. It was about the Orphanage we were to speak; yes. All I say is: prudence, my dear lady! And now let us get to business. (*Opens the packet, and takes out a number of papers.*) Do you see these?

MRS. ALVING. The documents?

MANDERS. All—and in perfect order.

I can tell you it was hard work to get them in time. I had to put on strong pressure. The authorities are almost morbidly scrupulous when there is any decisive step to be taken. But here they are at last. (*Looks through the bundle.*) See! here is the formal deed of gift of the parcel of ground known as Solvik in the Manor of Rosenvold, with all the newly constructed buildings, schoolrooms, master's house, and chapel. And here is the legal fiat for the endowment and for the Bye-laws of the Institution. Will you look at them? (*Reads.*) "Byelaws for the Children's Home to be known as 'Captain Alving's Foundation.' "

MRS. ALVING (*looks long at the paper*). So there it is.

MANDERS. I have chosen the designation "Captain" rather than "Chamberlain." "Captain" looks less pretentious.

MRS. ALVING. Oh, yes; just as you think best.

MANDERS. And here you have the Bank Account of the capital lying at interest to cover the current expenses of the Orphanage.

MRS. ALVING. Thank you; but please keep it—it will be more convenient.

MANDERS. With pleasure. I think we will leave the money in the Bank for the present. The interest is certainly not what we could wish—four per cent and six months' notice of withdrawal. If a good mortgage could be found later on —of course it must be a first mortgage and an unimpeachable security—then we could consider the matter.

MRS. ALVING. Certainly, my dear Pastor Manders. You are the best judge in these things.

MANDERS. I will keep my eyes open at any rate.—But now there is one thing more which I have several times been intending to ask you.

MRS. ALVING. And what is that?

MANDERS. Shall the Orphanage buildings be insured or not?

MRS. ALVING. Of course they must be insured.

MANDERS. Well, wait a moment, Mrs. Alving. Let us look into the matter a little more closely.

MRS. ALVING. I have everything insured; buildings and movables and stock and crops.

MANDERS. Of course you have—on your own estate. And so have I—of course. But here, you see, it is quite another matter. The Orphanage is to be consecrated, as it were, to a higher purpose.

MRS. ALVING. Yes, but that's no reason—

MANDERS. For my own part, I should certainly not see the smallest impropriety in guarding against all contingencies—

MRS. ALVING. No, I should think not.

MANDERS. But what is the general feeling in the neighbourhood? You, of course, know better than I.

MRS. ALVING. Well—the general feeling—

MANDERS. Is there any considerable number of people—really responsible people—who might be scandalised?

MRS. ALVING. What do you mean by "really responsible people"?

MANDERS. Well, I mean people in such independent and influential positions that one cannot help attaching some weight to their opinions.

MRS. ALVING. There are several people of that sort here, who would very likely be shocked if—

MANDERS. There, you see! In town we have many such people. Think of all my colleague's adherents! People would be only too ready to interpret our action as a sign that neither you nor I had the right faith in a Higher Providence.

MRS. ALVING. But for your own part, my dear Pastor, you can at least tell yourself that—

MANDERS. Yes, I know—I know; my conscience would be quite easy, that is true enough. But nevertheless we should not escape grave misinterpretation; and that might very likely react unfavourably upon the Orphanage.

MRS. ALVING. Well, in that case—

MANDERS. Nor can I entirely lose sight of the difficult—may even say painful—position in which *I* might perhaps be placed. In the leading circles of the town, people take a lively interest in this Orphanage. It is, of course, founded partly for the benefit of the town, as well; and it is to be hoped it will, to a considerable extent, result in lightening our Poor Rates. Now, as I have been your adviser, and have had the business arrangements in my hands, I cannot but fear that I may have to bear the brunt of fanaticism—

MRS. ALVING. Oh, you mustn't run the risk of that.

MANDERS. To say nothing of the attacks that would assuredly be made upon me in certain papers and periodicals, which—

MRS. ALVING. Enough, my dear Pastor Manders. That consideration is quite decisive.

MANDERS. Then you do not wish the Orphanage to be insured?

MRS. ALVING. No. We will let it alone.

MANDERS (*leaning back in his chair*). But if, now, a disaster were to happen? One can never tell— Should you be able to make good the damage?

MRS. ALVING. No; I tell you plainly I should do nothing of the kind.

MANDERS. Then I must tell you, Mrs. Alving—we are taking no small responsibility upon ourselves.

MRS. ALVING. Do you think we can do otherwise?

MANDERS. No, that is just the point; we really cannot do otherwise. We ought not to expose ourselves to misinterpretation; and we have no right whatever to give offence to the weaker brethren.

MRS. ALVING. You, as a clergyman, certainly should not.

MANDERS. I really think, too, we may trust that such an institution has fortune on its side; in fact, that it stands under a special providence.

MRS. ALVING. Let us hope so, Pastor Manders.

MANDERS. Then we will let it take its chance?

MRS. ALVING. Yes, certainly.

MANDERS. Very well. So be it. (*Makes a note.*) Then—no insurance.

MRS. ALVING. It's odd that you should just happen to mention the matter to-day—

MANDERS. I have often thought of asking you about it—

MRS. ALVING. —for we very nearly had a fire down there yesterday.

MANDERS. You don't say so!

MRS. ALVING. Oh, it was a trifling matter. A heap of shavings had caught fire in the carpenter's workshop.

MANDERS. Where Engstrand works?

MRS. ALVING. Yes. They say he's often very careless with matches.

MANDERS. He has so much on his mind, that man—so many things to fight against. Thank God, he is now striving to lead a decent life, I hear.

MRS. ALVING. Indeed! Who says so?

MANDERS. He himself assures me of it. And he is certainly a capital workman.

MRS. ALVING. Oh, yes; so long as he's sober—

MANDERS. Ah, that melancholy weakness! But he is often driven to it by his injured leg, he says. Last time he was in town I was really touched by him. He came and thanked me so warmly for having got him work here, so that he might be near Regina.

MRS. ALVING. He doesn't see much of her.

MANDERS. Oh, yes; he has a talk with her every day. He told me so himself.

MRS. ALVING. Well, it may be so.

MANDERS. He feels so acutely that he needs some one to keep a firm hold on him when temptation comes. That is what I cannot help liking about Jacob Engstrand: he comes to you so helplessly, accusing himself and confessing his own weakness. The last time he was talking to me— Believe me, Mrs. Alving, supposing it were a real necessity for him to have Regina home again—

MRS. ALVING (*rising hastily*). Regina!

MANDERS. —you must not set yourself against it.

MRS. ALVING. Indeed I shall set myself against it. And besides—Regina is to have a position in the Orphanage.

MANDERS. But, after all, remember he is her father—

MRS. ALVING. Oh, I know very well what sort of a father he has been to her. No! She shall never go to him with my goodwill.

MANDERS (*rising*). My dear lady, don't take the matter so warmly. You sadly misjudge poor Engstrand. You seem to be quite terrified—

MRS. ALVING (*more quietly*). It makes no difference. I have taken Regina into my house, and there she shall stay. (*Listens.*) Hush, my dear Mr. Manders; say no more about it. (*Her face lights up with gladness.*) Listen! there is Oswald coming downstairs. Now we'll think of no one but him.

(OSWALD ALVING, *in a light overcoat, hat in hand, and smoking a large meerschaum, enters by the door on the left; he stops in the doorway.*)

OSWALD. Oh, I beg your pardon; I thought you were in the study. (*Comes forward.*) Good-morning, Pastor Manders.

MANDERS (*staring*). Ah— How strange—!

MRS. ALVING. Well now, what do you think of him, Mr. Manders?

MANDERS. I—I—can it really be—?

OSWALD. Yes, it's really the Prodigal Son, sir.

MANDERS (*protesting*). My dear young friend—

OSWALD. Well, then, the Lost Sheep Found.

MRS. ALVING. Oswald is thinking of the time when you were so much opposed to his becoming a painter.

MANDERS. To our human eyes many a step seems dubious, which afterwards proves— (*Wrings his hand.*) But first of all, welcome, welcome home! Do not think, my dear Oswald—I suppose I may call you by your Christian name?

OSWALD. What else should you call me?

MANDERS. Very good. What I wanted to say was this, my dear Oswald —you must not think that I utterly condemn the artist's calling. I have no doubt there are many who can keep their inner self unharmed in that profession, as in any other.

OSWALD. Let us hope so.

MRS. ALVING (*beaming with delight*). I know one who has kept both his inner and his outer self unharmed. Just look at him, Mr. Manders.

OSWALD (*moves restlessly about the room*). Yes, yes, my dear mother; let's say no more about it.

MANDERS. Why, certainly—that is undeniable. And you have begun to make a name for yourself already. The newspapers have often spoken of you, most favourably. Just lately, by-the-bye, I fancy I haven't seen your name quite so often.

OSWALD (*up in the conservatory*). I haven't been able to paint so much lately.

MRS. ALVING. Even a painter needs a little rest now and then.

MANDERS. No doubt, no doubt. And meanwhile he can be preparing himself and mustering his forces for some great work.

OSWALD. Yes.—Mother, will dinner soon be ready?

MRS. ALVING. In less than half an hour. He has a capital appetite, thank God.

MANDERS. And a taste for tobacco, too.

OSWALD. I found my father's pipe in my room—

MANDERS. Aha—then that accounts for it!

MRS. ALVING. For what?

MANDERS. When Oswald appeared there, in the doorway, with the pipe in his mouth, I could have sworn I saw his father, large as life.

OSWALD. No, really?

MRS. ALVING. Oh, how can you say so? Oswald takes after me.

MANDERS. Yes, but there is an expression about the corners of the mouth —something about the lips—that reminds one exactly of Alving: at any rate, now that he is smoking.

MRS. ALVING. Not in the least. Oswald has rather a clerical curve about his mouth, I think.

MANDERS. Yes, yes; some of my colleagues have much the same expression.

MRS. ALVING. But put your pipe away, my dear boy; I won't have smoking in here.

OSWALD (*does so*). By all means. I only wanted to try it; for I once smoked it when I was a child.

MRS. ALVING. You?

OSWALD. Yes. I was quite small at the time. I recollect I came up to father's room one evening when he was in great spirits.

MRS. ALVING. Oh, you can't recollect anything of those times.

OSWALD. Yes, I recollect it distinctly. He took me on his knee, and gave me the pipe. "Smoke, boy," he said; "smoke away, boy!" And I smoked as hard as I could, until I felt I was growing quite pale, and the perspiration stood in great drops on my forehead. Then he burst out laughing heartily—

MANDERS. That was most extraordinary.

MRS. ALVING. My dear friend, it's only something Oswald has dreamt.

OSWALD. No, mother, I assure you I didn't dream it. For—don't you remember this?—you came and carried me out into the nursery. Then I was sick, and I saw that you were crying.— Did father often play such practical jokes?

MANDERS. In his youth he overflowed with the joy of life—

OSWALD. And yet he managed to do so much in the world; so much that was good and useful; although he died so early.

MANDERS. Yes, you have inherited the name of an energetic and admirable man, my dear Oswald Alving. No doubt it will be an incentive to you—

OSWALD. It ought to, indeed.

MANDERS. It was good of you to come home for the ceremony in his honour.

OSWALD. I could do no less for my father.

MRS. ALVING. And I am to keep him so long! That is the best of all.

MANDERS. You are going to pass the winter at home, I hear.

OSWALD. My stay is indefinite, sir.— But, ah! it is good to be at home!

MRS. ALVING (*beaming*). Yes, isn't it, dear?

MANDERS (*looking sympathetically at him*). You went out into the world early, my dear Oswald.

OSWALD. I did. I sometimes wonder whether it wasn't too early.

MRS. ALVING. Oh, not at all. A healthy lad is all the better for it; especially when he's an only child. He oughtn't to hang on at home with his mother and father, and get spoilt.

MANDERS. That is a very disputable point, Mrs. Alving. A child's proper place is, and must be, the home of his fathers.

OSWALD. There I quite agree with you, Pastor Manders.

MANDERS. Only look at your own son—there is no reason why we should not say it in his presence—what has the consequence been for him? He is six or seven and twenty, and has never had the opportunity of learning what a well-ordered home really is.

OSWALD. I beg your pardon, Pastor; there you're quite mistaken.

MANDERS. Indeed? I thought you had lived almost exclusively in artistic circles.

OSWALD. So I have.

MANDERS. And chiefly among the younger artists?

OSWALD. Yes, certainly.

MANDERS. But I thought few of those young fellows could afford to set up house and support a family.

OSWALD. There are many who cannot afford to marry, sir.

MANDERS. Yes, that is just what I say.

OSWALD. But they may have a home for all that. And several of them have, as a matter of fact; and very pleasant, well-ordered homes they are, too.

(MRS. ALVING *follows with breathless interest; nods, but says nothing.*)

MANDERS. But I'm not talking of bachelors' quarters. By a "home" I understand the home of a family, where a man lives with his wife and children.

OSWALD. Yes; or with his children and his children's mother.

MANDERS (*starts; claps his hands*). But, good heavens—

OSWALD. Well?

MANDERS. Lives with—his children's mother!

OSWALD. Yes. Would you have him turn his children's mother out of doors?

MANDERS. Then it is illicit relations you are talking of! Irregular marriages, as people call them!

OSWALD. I have never noticed anything particularly irregular about the life these people lead.

MANDERS. But how is it possible that a—a young man or young woman with any decency of feeling can endure to live in that way?—in the eyes of all the world!

OSWALD. What are they to do? A poor young artist—a poor girl—marriage costs a great deal! What are they to do?

MANDERS. What are they to do? Let me tell you, Mr. Alving, what they ought to do. They ought to exercise self-restraint from the first; that is what they ought to do.

OSWALD. That doctrine will scarcely go down with warm-blooded young people who love each other.

MRS. ALVING. No, scarcely!

MANDERS (*continuing*). How can the authorities tolerate such things! Allow them to go on in the light of day! (*Confronting* MRS. ALVING.) Had I not cause to be deeply concerned about your son? In circles where open immorality prevails, and has even a sort of recognised position—!

OSWALD. Let me tell you, sir, that I have been in the habit of spending nearly all my Sundays in one or two such irregular homes—

MANDERS. Sunday of all days!

OSWALD. Isn't that the day to enjoy one's self? Well, never have I heard an offensive word, and still less have I witnessed anything that could be called immoral. No; do you know when and where I have come across immorality in artistic circles?

MANDERS. No, thank heaven, I don't!

OSWALD. Well, then, allow me to inform you. I have met with it when one or other of our pattern husbands and fathers has come to Paris to have a look round on his own account, and has done the artists the honour of visiting their humble haunts. They knew what was what. These gentlemen could tell us all about places and things we had never dreamt of.

MANDERS. What! Do you mean to say that respectable men from home here would—?

OSWALD. Have you never heard these respectable men, when they got home again, talking about the way in which immorality runs rampant abroad?

MANDERS. Yes, no doubt—

MRS. ALVING. I have too.

OSWALD. Well, you may take their word for it. They know what they are talking about! (*Presses his hands to his head.*) Oh! that that great, free, glorious life out there should be defiled in such a way!

MRS. ALVING. You mustn't get excited, Oswald. It's not good for you.

OSWALD. Yes; you're quite right, mother. It's bad for me, I know. You see, I'm wretchedly worn out. I shall go for a little turn before dinner. Excuse me, Pastor: I know you can't take my point of view; but I couldn't help speaking out. (*He goes out by the second door to the right.*)

MRS. ALVING. My poor boy!

MANDERS. You may well say so. Then this is what he has come to!

(MRS. ALVING *looks at him silently.*)

MANDERS (*walking up and down*). He called himself the Prodigal Son. Alas! alas!

(MRS. ALVING *continues looking at him.*)

MANDERS. And what do you say to all this?

MRS. ALVING. I say that Oswald was right in every word.

MANDERS (*stands still*). Right? Right! In such principles?

MRS. ALVING. Here, in my loneliness, I have come to the same way of thinking, Pastor Manders. But I have never dared to say anything. Well! now my boy shall speak for me.

MANDERS. You are greatly to be pitied, Mrs. Alving. But now I must

speak seriously to you. And now it is no longer your business manager and adviser, your own and your husband's early friend, who stands before you. It is the priest—the priest who stood before you in the moment of your life when you had gone farthest astray.

MRS. ALVING. And what has the priest to say to me?

MANDERS. I will first stir up your memory a little. The moment is well chosen. To-morrow will be the tenth anniversary of your husband's death. To-morrow the memorial in his honour will be unveiled. To-morrow I shall have to speak to the whole assembled multitude. But to-day I will speak to you alone.

MRS. ALVING. Very well, Pastor Manders. Speak.

MANDERS. Do you remember that after less than a year of married life you stood on the verge of an abyss? That you forsook your house and home? That you fled from your husband? Yes, Mrs. Alving—fled, fled, and refused to return to him, however much he begged and prayed you?

MRS. ALVING. Have you forgotten how infinitely miserable I was in that first year?

MANDERS. It is the very mark of the spirit of rebellion to crave for happiness in this life. What right have we human beings to happiness? We have simply to do our duty, Mrs. Alving! And your duty was to hold firmly to the man you had once chosen, and to whom you were bound by the holiest ties.

MRS. ALVING. You know very well what sort of life Alving was leading— what excesses he was guilty of.

MANDERS. I know very well what rumours there were about him; and I am the last to approve the life he led in his young days, if report did not wrong him. But a wife is not appointed to be her husband's judge. It was your duty to bear with humility the cross which a Higher Power had, in its wisdom, laid upon you.

But instead of that you rebelliously throw away the cross, desert the backslider whom you should have supported, go and risk your good name and reputation, and—nearly succeed in ruining other people's reputation into the bargain.

MRS. ALVING. Other people's? One other person's, you mean.

MANDERS. It was incredibly reckless of you to seek refuge with me.

MRS. ALVING. With our clergyman? With our intimate friend?

MANDERS. Just on that account. Yes, you may thank God that I possessed the necessary firmness; that I succeeded in dissuading you from your wild designs; and that it was vouchsafed me to lead you back to the path of duty, and home to your lawful husband.

MRS. ALVING. Yes, Pastor Manders, that was certainly your work.

MANDERS. I was but a poor instrument in a Higher Hand. And what a blessing has it not proved to you, all the days of your life, that I induced you to resume the yoke of duty and obedience! Did not everything happen as I foretold? Did not Alving turn his back on his errors, as a man should? Did he not live with you from that time, lovingly and blamelessly, all his days? Did he not become a benefactor to the whole district? And did he not help you to rise to his own level, so that you, little by little, became his assistant in all his undertakings? And a capital assistant, too —oh, I know, Mrs. Alving, that praise is due to you.—But now I come to the next great error in your life.

MRS. ALVING. What do you mean?

MANDERS. Just as you once disowned a wife's duty, so you have since disowned a mother's.

MRS. ALVING. Ah—!

MANDERS. You have been all your life under the dominion of a pestilent spirit of self-will. The whole bias of your mind has been towards insubordination and lawlessness. You have never known how to endure any bond. Everything that

has weighed upon you in life you have cast away without care or conscience, like a burden you were free to throw off at will. It did not please you to be a wife any longer, and you left your husband. You found it troublesome to be a mother, and you sent your child forth among strangers.

MRS. ALVING. Yes, that is true. I did so.

MANDERS. And thus you have become a stranger to him.

MRS. ALVING. No! no! I am not.

MANDERS. Yes, you are; you must be. And in what state of mind has he returned to you? Bethink yourself well, Mrs. Alving. You sinned greatly against your husband;—that you recognise by raising yonder memorial to him. Recognise now, also, how you have sinned against your son—there may yet be time to lead him back from the paths of error. Turn back yourself, and save what may yet be saved in him. For (*with uplifted forefinger*) verily, Mrs. Alving, you are a guilt-laden mother!—This I have thought it my duty to say to you.

(*Silence.*)

MRS. ALVING (*slowly and with self-control*). You have now spoken out, Pastor Manders; and to-morrow you are to speak publicly in memory of my husband. I shall not speak to-morrow. But now I will speak frankly to you, as you have spoken to me.

MANDERS. To be sure; you will plead excuses for your conduct—

MRS. ALVING. No. I will only tell you a story.

MANDERS. Well—?

MRS. ALVING. All that you have just said about my husband and me, and our life after you had brought me back to the path of duty—as you called it— about all that you know nothing from personal observation. From that moment you, who had been our intimate friend, never set foot in our house again.

MANDERS. You and your husband left the town immediately after.

MRS. ALVING. Yes; and in my husband's lifetime you never came to sée us. It was business that forced you to visit me when you undertook the affairs of the Orphanage.

MANDERS (*softly and hesitatingly*). Helen—if that is meant as a reproach, I would beg you to bear in mind—

MRS. ALVING. —the regard you owed to your position, yes; and that I was a runaway wife. One can never be too cautious with such unprincipled creatures.

MANDERS. My dear—Mrs. Alving, you know that is an absurd exaggeration—

MRS. ALVING. Well well, suppose it is. My point is that your judgment as to my married life is founded upon nothing but common knowledge and report.

MANDERS. I admit that. What then?

MRS. ALVING. Well, then, Pastor Manders—I will tell you the truth. I have sworn to myself that one day you should know it—you alone!

MANDERS. What is the truth, then?

MRS. ALVING. The truth is that my husband died just as dissolute as he had lived all his days.

MANDERS (*feeling after a chair*). What do you say?

MRS. ALVING. After nineteen years of marriage, as dissolute—in his desires at any rate—as he was before you married us.

MANDERS. And those—those wild oats—those irregularities—those excesses, if you like—you call "a dissolute life"?

MRS. ALVING. Our doctor used the expression.

MANDERS. I do not understand you.

MRS. ALVING. You need not.

MANDERS. It almost makes me dizzy. Your whole married life, the seeming union of all these years, was nothing more than a hidden abyss!

MRS. ALVING. Neither more nor less. Now you know it.

MANDERS. This is—this is inconceivable to me. I cannot grasp it! I cannot realise it! But how was it possible to—? How could such a state of things be kept secret?

MRS. ALVING. That has been my ceaseless struggle, day after day. After Oswald's birth, I thought Alving seemed to be a little better. But it did not last long. And then I had to struggle twice as hard, fighting as though for life or death, so that nobody should know what sort of man my child's father was. And you know what power Alving had of winning people's hearts. Nobody seemed able to believe anything but good of him. He was one of those people whose life does not bite upon their reputation. But at last, Mr. Manders—for you must know the whole story—the most repulsive thing of all happened.

MANDERS. More repulsive than what you have told me!

MRS. ALVING. I had gone on bearing with him, although I knew very well the secrets of his life out of doors. But when he brought the scandal within our own walls—

MANDERS. Impossible! Here!

MRS. ALVING. Yes; here in our own home. It was there (*pointing towards the first door on the right*), in the dining-room, that I first came to know of it. I was busy with something in there, and the door was standing ajar. I heard our housemaid come up from the garden, with water for those flowers.

MANDERS. Well—?

MRS. ALVING. Soon after, I heard Alving come in too. I heard him say something softly to her. And then I heard—(*with a short laugh*)—oh! it still sounds in my ears, so hateful and yet so ludicrous—I heard my own servant-maid whisper, "Let me go, Mr. Alving! Let me be!"

MANDERS. What unseemly levity on his part! But it cannot have been more than levity, Mrs. Alving; believe me, it cannot.

MRS. ALVING. I soon knew what to believe. Mr. Alving had his way with the girl; and that connection had consequences, Mr. Manders.

MANDERS (*as though petrified*). Such things in this house! in this house!

MRS. ALVING. I had borne a great deal in this house. To keep him at home in the evenings, and at night, I had to make myself his boon companion in his secret orgies up in his room. There I have had to sit alone with him, to clink glasses and drink with him, and to listen to his ribald, silly talk. I have had to fight with him to get him dragged to bed—

MANDERS (*moved*). And you were able to bear all this!

MRS. ALVING. I had to bear it for my little boy's sake. But when the last insult was added; when my own servant maid—; then I swore to myself: This shall come to an end! And so I took the reins into my own hand—the whole control—over him and everything else. For now I had a weapon against him, you see; he dared not oppose me. It was then I sent Oswald away from home. He was nearly seven years old, and was beginning to observe and ask questions, as children do. That I could not bear. It seemed to me the child must be poisoned by merely breathing the air of this polluted home. That was why I sent him away. And now you can see, too, why he was never allowed to set foot inside his home so long as his father lived. No one knows what that cost me.

MANDERS. You have indeed had a life of trial.

MRS. ALVING. I could never have borne it if I had not had my work. For I may truly say that I have worked! All the additions to the estate—all the improvements—all the labour-saving appliances, that Alving was so much praised for having introduced—do you suppose he had energy for anything of the sort? —he, who lay all day on the sofa, reading an old Court Guide! No; but I may tell you this too: when he had his better intervals, it was I who urged him on; it was I who had to drag the whole load when he relapsed into his evil ways, or sank into querulous wretchedness.

MANDERS. And it is to this man that you raise a memorial?

MRS. ALVING. There you see the power of an evil conscience.

MANDERS. Evil—? What do you mean?

MRS. ALVING. It always seemed to me impossible but that the truth must come out and be believed. So the Orphanage was to deaden all rumours and set every doubt at rest.

MANDERS. In that you have certainly not missed your aim, Mrs. Alving.

MRS. ALVING. And besides, I had one other reason. I was determined that Oswald, my own boy, should inherit nothing whatever from his father.

MANDERS. Then it is Alving's fortune that—?

MRS. ALVING. Yes. The sums I have spent upon the Orphanage, year by year, make up the amount—I have reckoned it up precisely—the amount which made Lieutenant Alving "a good match" in his day.

MANDERS. I don't understand—

MRS. ALVING. It was my purchase-money. I do not choose that that money should pass into Oswald's hands. My son shall have everything from me—everything.

(OSWALD ALVING *enters through the second door to the right; he has taken off his hat and overcoat in the hall.*)

MRS. ALVING (*going towards him*). Are you back again already? My dear, dear boy!

OSWALD. Yes. What can a fellow do out of doors in this eternal rain? But I hear dinner is ready. That's capital!

REGINA (*with a parcel, from the dining-room*). A parcel has come for you, Mrs. Alving. (*Hands it to her.*)

MRS. ALVING (*with a glance at* MR. MANDERS). No doubt copies of the ode for to-morrow's ceremony.

MANDERS. H'm—

REGINA. And dinner is ready.

MRS. ALVING. Very well. We will come directly. I will just— (*Begins to open the parcel.*)

REGINA (*to* OSWALD). Would Mr. Alving like red or white wine?

OSWALD. Both, if you please.

REGINA. *Bien.* Very well, sir. (*She goes into the dining-room.*)

OSWALD. I may as well help to un-cork it. (*He also goes into the dining room, the door of which swings half open behind him.*)

MRS. ALVING (*who has opened the parcel*). Yes, I thought so. Here is the Ceremonial Ode, Pastor Manders.

MANDERS (*with folded hands*). With what countenance I am to deliver my discourse to-morrow—!

MRS. ALVING. Oh, you will get through it somehow.

MANDERS (*softly, so as not to be heard in the dining-room*). Yes, it would not do to provoke scandal.

MRS. ALVING (*under her breath, but firmly*). No. But then this long, hate-ful comedy will be ended. From the day after to-morrow, I shall act in every way as though he who is dead had never lived in this house. There shall be no one here but my boy and his mother.

(*From the dining-room comes the noise of a chair overturned, and at the same moment is heard*)

REGINA (*sharply, but in a whisper*). Oswald! take care! are you mad? Let me go!

MRS. ALVING (*starts in terror*). Ah—!

(*She stares wildly towards the half-open door.* OSWALD *is heard laughing and humming. A bottle is uncorked.*)

MANDERS (*agitated*). What can be the matter? What is it, Mrs. Alving?

MRS. ALVING (*hoarsely*). Ghosts!

The couple from the conservatory—risen again!

MANDERS. Is it possible! Regina—? Is she—?

MRS. ALVING. Yes. Come. Not a word—!

(*She seizes* PASTOR MANDERS *by the arm, and walks unsteadily towards the dining-room.*)

Act II

(*The same room. The mist still lies heavy over the landscape.*)

(MANDERS *and* MRS. ALVING *enter from the dining-room.*)

MRS. ALVING (*still in the doorway*). *Velbekomme,* Mr. Manders. (*Turns back towards the dining-room.*) Aren't you coming too, Oswald?

OSWALD (*from within*). No, thank you. I think I shall go out a little.

MRS. ALVING. Yes, do. The weather seems a little brighter now. (*She shuts the dining-room door, goes to the hall door, and calls:*) Regina!

REGINA (*outside*). Yes, Mrs. Alving?

MRS. ALVING. Go down to the laun-dry, and help with the garlands.

REGINA. Yes, Mrs. Alving.

(MRS. ALVING *assures herself that* REGINA *goes; then shuts the door.*)

MANDERS. I suppose he cannot over-hear us in there?

MRS. ALVING. Not when the door is shut. Besides, he's just going out.

MANDERS. I am still quite upset. I don't know how I could swallow a mor-sel of dinner.

MRS. ALVING (*controlling her nervous-ness, walks up and down*). Nor I. But what is to be done now?

MANDERS. Yes, what is to be done? I am really quite at a loss. I am so utterly without experience in matters of this sort.

MRS. ALVING. I feel sure that, so far, no mischief has been done.

MANDERS. No; heaven forbid! But it is an unseemly state of things, nevertheless.

MRS. ALVING. It is only an idle fancy on Oswald's part; you may be sure of that.

MANDERS. Well, as I say, I am not accustomed to affairs of this kind. But I should certainly think—

MRS. ALVING. Out of the house she must go, and that immediately. That is as clear as daylight—

MANDERS. Yes, of course she must.

MRS. ALVING. But where to? It would not be right to—

MANDERS. Where to? Home to her father, of course.

MRS. ALVING. To whom did you say?

MANDERS. To her— But then, Engstrand is not—? Good God, Mrs. Alving, it's impossible! You must be mistaken after all.

MR. ALVING. Unfortunately there is no possibility of mistake. Johanna confessed everything to me; and Alving could not deny it. So there was nothing to be done but to get the matter hushed up.

MANDERS. No, you could do nothing else.

MRS. ALVING. The girl left our service at once, and got a good sum of money to hold her tongue for the time. The rest she managed for herself when she got to town. She renewed her old acquaintance with Engstrand, no doubt let him see that she had money in her purse, and told him some tale about a foreigner who put in here with a yacht that summer. So she and Engstrand got married in hot haste. Why, you married them yourself.

MANDERS. But then how to account for—? I recollect distinctly Engstrand coming to give notice of the marriage. He was quite overwhelmed with contrition, and bitterly reproached himself for the misbehavior he and his sweetheart had been guilty of.

MRS. ALVING. Yes; of course he had to take the blame upon himself.

MANDERS. But such a piece of duplicity on his part! And towards me too! I never could have believed it of Jacob Engstrand. I shall not fail to take him seriously to task; he may be sure of that. —And then the immorality of such a connection! For money—! How much did the girl receive?

MRS. ALVING. Three hundred dollars.

MANDERS. Just think of it—for a miserable three hundred dollars, to go and marry a fallen woman!

MRS. ALVING. Then what have you to say of me? I went and married a fallen man.

MANDERS. Why—good heavens!—what are you talking about! A fallen man!

MRS. ALVING. Do you think Alving was any purer when I went with him to the altar than Johanna was when Engstrand married her?

MANDERS. Well, but there is a world of difference between the two cases—

MRS. ALVING. Not so much difference after all—except in the price:—a miserable three hundred dollars and a whole fortune.

MANDERS. How can you compare such absolutely dissimilar cases? You had taken counsel with your own heart and with your natural advisers.

MRS. ALVING (without looking at him). I thought you understood where what you call my heart had strayed to at the time.

MANDERS (distantly). Had I understood anything of the kind, I should not have been a daily guest in your husband's house.

MRS. ALVING. At any rate, the fact remains that with myself I took no counsel whatever.

MANDERS. Well then, with your nearest relatives—as your duty bade you —with your mother and your two aunts.

MRS. ALVING. Yes, that is true.

Those three cast up the account for me.
Oh, it's marvelous how clearly they
made out that it would be downright
madness to refuse such an offer. If
mother could only see me now, and
know what all that grandeur has come
to!

MANDERS. Nobody can be held responsible for the result. This, at least,
remains clear: your marriage was in full
accordance with law and order.

MRS. ALVING (*at the window*). Oh,
that perpetual law and order! I often
think that is what does all the mischief
in this world of ours.

MANDERS. Mrs. Alving, that is a sinful way of talking.

MRS. ALVING. Well, I can't help it;
I must have done with all this constraint
and insincerity. I can endure it no longer.
I must work my way out to freedom.

MANDERS. What do you mean by
that?

MRS. ALVING (*drumming on the win-
dow-frame*). I ought never to have concealed the facts of Alving's life. But at
that time I dared not do anything else—
I was afraid, partly on my own account.
I was such a coward.

MANDERS. A coward?

MRS. ALVING. If people had come to
know anything, they would have said—
"Poor man! with a runaway wife, no
wonder he kicks over the traces."

MANDERS. Such remarks might have
been made with a certain show of right.

MRS. ALVING (*looking steadily at
him*). If I were what I ought to be,
I should go to Oswald and say, "Listen,
my boy: your father led a vicious life—"

MANDERS. Merciful heavens—!

MRS. ALVING. —and then I should
tell him all I have told you—every word
of it.

MANDERS. You shock me unspeakably, Mrs. Alving.

MRS. ALVING. Yes; I know that. I
know that very well. I myself am shocked
at the idea. (*Goes away from the window.*) I am such a coward.

MANDERS. You call it "cowardice" to
do your plain duty? Have you forgotten
that a son ought to love and honour his
father and mother?

MRS. ALVING. Do not let us talk in
such general terms. Let us ask: Ought
Oswald to love and honour Chamberlain
Alving?

MANDERS. Is there no voice in your
mother's heart that forbids you to destroy your son's ideals?

MRS. ALVING. But what about the
truth?

MANDERS. But what about the ideals?

MRS. ALVING. Oh—ideals, ideals! If
only I were not such a coward!

MANDERS. Do not despise ideals,
Mrs. Alving; they will avenge themselves cruelly. Take Oswald's case: he,
unfortunately, seems to have few enough
ideals as it is; but I can see that his father
stands before him as an ideal.

MRS. ALVING. Yes, that is true.

MANDERS. And this habit of mind
you have yourself implanted and fostered
by your letters.

MRS. ALVING. Yes; in my superstitious awe for duty and the proprieties, I
lied to my boy, year after year. Oh, what
a coward—what a coward I have been!

MANDERS. You have established a
happy illusion in your son's heart, Mrs.
Alving; and assuredly you ought not to
undervalue it.

MRS. ALVING. H'm, who knows
whether it is so happy after all—? But,
at any rate, I will not have any tamper-
ing with Regina. He shall not go and
wreck the poor girl's life.

MANDERS. No; good God—that
would be terrible!

MRS. ALVING. If I knew he was in
earnest, and that it would be for his
happiness—

MANDERS. What? What then?

MRS. ALVING. But it couldn't be; for
unfortunately Regina is not the right
sort of woman.

MANDERS. Well, what then? What
do you mean?

MRS. ALVING. If I weren't such a pitiful coward, I should say to him, "Marry her, or make what arrangement you please, only let us have nothing underhand about it."

MANDERS. Merciful heavens, would you let them marry? Anything so dreadful—! so unheard of—

MRS. ALVING. Do you really mean "unheard of"? Frankly, Pastor Manders, do you suppose that throughout the country there are not plenty of married couples as closely akin as they?

MANDERS. I don't in the least understand you.

MRS. ALVING. Oh yes, indeed you do.

MANDERS. Ah, you are thinking of the possibility that—Alas! yes, family life is certainly not always so pure as it ought to be. But in such a case as you point to, one can never know—at least with any certainty. Here, on the other hand—that you, a mother, can think of letting your son—!

MRS. ALVING. But I cannot—I wouldn't for anything in the world; that is precisely what I am saying.

MANDERS. No, because you are a "coward," as you put it. But if you were not a "coward," then—? Good God! a connection so shocking!

MRS. ALVING. So far as that goes, they say we are all sprung from connections of that sort. And who is it that arranged the world so, Pastor Manders?

MANDERS. Questions of that kind I must decline to discuss with you, Mrs. Alving; you are far from being in the right frame of mind for them. But that you dare to call your scruples "cowardly"—!

MRS. ALVING. Let me tell you what I mean. I am timid and faint-hearted because of the ghosts that hang about me, and that I can never quite shake off.

MANDERS. What do you say hangs about you?

MRS. ALVING. Ghosts! When I heard Regina and Oswald in there, it was as though ghosts rose up before me. But I almost think we are all of us ghosts, Pastor Manders. It is not only what we have inherited from our father and mother that "walks" in us. It is all sorts of dead ideas, and lifeless old beliefs, and so forth. They have no vitality, but they cling to us all the same, and we cannot shake them off. Whenever I take up a newspaper, I seem to see ghosts gliding between the lines. There must be ghosts all the country over, as thick as the sands of the sea. And then we are, one and all, so pitifully afraid of the light.

MANDERS. Aha—here we have the fruits of your reading. And pretty fruits they are, upon my word! Oh, those horrible, revolutionary, freethinking books!

MRS. ALVING. You are mistaken, my dear Pastor. It was you yourself who set me thinking, and I thank you for it with all my heart.

MANDERS. I!

MRS. ALVING. Yes—when you forced me under the yoke of what you called duty and obligation; when you lauded as right and proper what my whole soul rebelled against as something loathsome. It was then that I began to look into the seams of your doctrines. I wanted only to pick at a single knot; but when I had got that undone, the whole thing ravelled out. And then I understood that it was all machine-sewn.

MANDERS (softly, with emotion). And was that the upshot of my life's hardest battle?

MRS. ALVING. Call it rather your most pitiful defeat.

MANDERS. It was my greatest victory, Helen—the victory over myself.

MRS. ALVING. It was a crime against us both.

MANDERS. When you went astray, and came to me crying, "Here I am; take me!" I commanded you, saying, "Woman, go home to your lawful husband." Was that a crime?

MRS. ALVING. Yes, I think so.

MANDERS. We two do not understand each other.

MRS. ALVING. Not now, at any rate.

MANDERS. Never—never in my most secret thoughts have I regarded you otherwise than as another's wife.

MRS. ALVING. Oh—indeed?

MANDERS. Helen—!

MRS. ALVING. People so easily forget their past selves.

MANDERS. I do not. I am what I always was.

MRS. ALVING (*changing the subject*). Well well well; don't let us talk of old times any longer. You are now over head and ears in Boards and Committees, and I am fighting my battle with ghosts, both within me and without.

MANDERS. Those without I shall help you to lay. After all the terrible things I have heard from you to-day, I cannot in conscience permit an unprotected girl to remain in your house.

MRS. ALVING. Don't you think the best plan would be to get her provided for?—I mean, by a good marriage.

MANDERS. No doubt. I think it would be desirable for her in every respect. Regina is now at the age when— Of course I don't know much about these things, but—

MRS. ALVING. Regina matured very early.

MANDERS. Yes, I thought so. I have an impression that she was remarkably well developed, physically, when I prepared her for confirmation. But in the meantime, she ought to be at home, under her father's eye—Ah! but Engstrand is not— That he—that he—could so hide the truth from me!

(*A knock at the door into the hall.*)

MRS. ALVING. Who can this be? Come in!

ENGSTRAND (*in his Sunday clothes, in the doorway*). I humbly beg your pardon, but—

MANDERS. Aha! H'm—

MRS. ALVING. Is that you, Engstrand?

ENGSTRAND. —there was none of the servants about, so I took the great liberty of just knocking.

MRS. ALVING. Oh, very well. Come in. Do you want to speak to me?

ENGSTRAND (*comes in*). No, I'm obliged to you, ma'am; it was with his Reverence I wanted to have a word or two.

MANDERS (*walking up and down the room*). Ah—indeed! You want to speak to me, do you?

ENGSTRAND. Yes, I'd like so terrible much to—

MANDERS (*stops in front of him*). Well; may I ask what you want?

ENGSTRAND. Well, it was just this, your Reverence: we've been paid off down yonder—my grateful thanks to you, ma'am—and now everything's finished, I've been thinking it would be but right and proper if we, that have been working so honestly together all this time—well, I was thinking we ought to end up with a little prayer-meeting to-night.

MANDERS. A prayer-meeting? Down at the Orphanage?

ENGSTRAND. Oh, if your Reverence doesn't think it proper—

MANDERS. Oh yes, I do; but—h'm—

ENGSTRAND. I've been in the habit of offering up a little prayer in the evenings, myself—

MRS. ALVING. Have you?

ENGSTRAND. Yes, every now and then—just a little edification, in a manner of speaking. But I'm a poor, common man, and have little enough gift, God help me!—and so I thought, as the Reverend Mr. Manders happened to be here, I'd—

MANDERS. Well, you see, Engstrand, I have a question to put to you first. Are you in the right frame of mind for such a meeting? Do you feel your conscience clear and at ease?

ENGSTRAND. Oh, God help us, your Reverence! we'd better not talk about conscience.

MANDERS. Yes, that is just what we must talk about. What have you to answer?

ENGSTRAND. Why—a man's conscience—it can be bad enough now and then.

MANDERS. Ah, you admit that. Then perhaps you will make a clean breast of it, and tell me—the real truth about Regina?

MRS. ALVING (*quickly*). Mr. Manders!

MANDERS (*reassuringly*). Please allow me—

ENGSTRAND. About Regina! Lord, what a turn you gave me! (*Looks at* MRS. ALVING.) There's nothing wrong about Regina, is there?

MANDERS. We will hope not. But I mean, what is the truth about you and Regina? You pass for her father, eh?

ENGSTRAND (*uncertain*). Well—h'm —your Reverence knows all about me and poor Johanna.

MANDERS. Come now, no more prevarication! Your wife told Mrs. Alving the whole story before quitting her service.

ENGSTRAND. Well, then, may—! Now, did she really?

MANDERS. You see we know you now, Engstrand.

ENGSTRAND. And she swore and took her Bible oath—

MANDERS. Did she take her Bible oath?

ENGSTRAND. No; she only swore; but she did it that solemn-like.

MANDERS. And you have hidden the truth from me all these years? Hidden it from me, who have trusted you without reserve, in everything.

ENGSTRAND. Well, I can't deny it.

MANDERS. Have I deserved this of you, Engstrand? Have I not always been ready to help you in word and deed, so far as it lay in my power? Answer me. Have I not?

ENGSTRAND. It would have been a poor look-out for me many a time but for the Reverend Mr. Manders.

MANDERS. And this is how you reward me! You cause me to enter falsehoods in the Church Register, and you withhold from me, year after year, the explanations you owed alike to me and to the truth. Your conduct has been wholly inexcusable, Engstrand; and from this time forward I have done with you!

ENGSTRAND (*with a sigh*). Yes! I suppose there's no help for it.

MANDERS. How can you possibly justify yourself?

ENGSTRAND. Who could ever have thought she'd have gone and made bad worse by talking about it? Will your Reverence just fancy yourself in the same trouble as poor Johanna—

MANDERS. I!

ENGSTRAND. Lord bless you, I don't mean just exactly the same. But I mean, if your Reverence had anything to be ashamed of in the eyes of the world, as the saying goes. We menfolk oughtn't to judge a poor woman too hardly, your Reverence.

MANDERS. I am not doing so. It is you I am reproaching.

ENGSTRAND. Might I make so bold as to ask your Reverence a bit of a question?

MANDERS. Yes, if you want to.

ENGSTRAND. Isn't it right and proper for a man to raise up the fallen?

MANDERS. Most certainly it is.

ENGSTRAND. And isn't a man bound to keep his sacred word?

MANDERS. Why, of course he is; but—

ENGSTRAND. When Johanna had got into trouble through that Englishman— or it might have been an American or a Russian, as they call them—well, you see, she came down into the town. Poor thing, she'd sent me about my business once or twice before: for she couldn't bear the sight of anything as wasn't handsome; and I'd got this damaged leg of mine. Your Reverence recollects how I ventured up into a dancing saloon, where seafaring men was carrying on with drink and devilry, as the saying goes. And then, when I was for giving them a bit of an admonition to lead a new life—

MRS. ALVING (*at the window*). H'm—

MANDERS. I know all about that, Engstrand; the ruffians threw you downstairs. You have told me of the affair already. Your infirmity is an honour to you.

ENGSTRAND. I'm not puffed up about it, your Reverence. But what I wanted to say was, that when she came and confessed all to me, with weeping and gnashing of teeth, I can tell your Reverence I was sore at heart to hear it.

MANDERS. Were you indeed, Engstrand? Well, go on.

ENGSTRAND. So I says to her, "The American, he's sailing about on the boundless sea. And as for you, Johanna," says I, "you've committed a grievous sin, and you're a fallen creature. But Jacob Engstrand," says I, "he's got two good legs to stand upon, he has—" You see, your Reverence, I was speaking figurative-like.

MANDERS. I understand quite well. Go on.

ENGSTRAND. Well, that was how I raised her up and made an honest woman of her, so as folks shouldn't get to know how as she'd gone astray with foreigners.

MANDERS. In all that you acted very well. Only I cannot approve of your stooping to take money—

ENGSTRAND. Money? I? Not a farthing!

MANDERS (*inquiringly to* MRS. ALVING). But—

ENGSTRAND. Oh, wait a minute!—now I recollect. Johanna did have a trifle

of money. But I would have nothing to do with that. "No," says I, "that's mammon; that's the wages of sin. This dirty gold—or notes, or whatever it was—we'll just fling that back in the American's face," says I. But he was off and away, over the stormy sea, your Reverence.

MANDERS. Was he really, my good fellow?

ENGSTRAND. He was indeed, sir. So Johanna and I, we agreed that the money should go to the child's education; and so it did, and I can account for every blessed farthing of it.

MANDERS. Why, this alters the case considerably.

ENGSTRAND. That's just how it stands, your Reverence. And I make so bold as to say as I've been an honest father to Regina, so far as my poor strength went; for I'm but a weak vessel, worse luck!

MANDERS. Well, well, my good fellow—

ENGSTRAND. All the same, I bear myself witness as I've brought up the child, and lived kindly with poor Johanna, and ruled over my own house, as the Scripture has it. But it couldn't never enter my head to go to your Reverence and puff myself up and boast because even the likes of me had done some good in the world. No, sir; when anything of that sort happens to Jacob Engstrand, he holds his tongue about it. It don't happen so terrible often, I daresay. And when I do come to see your Reverence, I find a mortal deal that's wicked and weak to talk about. For I said it before, and I says it again—a man's conscience isn't always as clean as it might be.

MANDERS. Give me your hand, Jacob Engstrand.

ENGSTRAND. Oh, Lord! your Reverence—

MANDERS. Come, no nonsense. (*Wrings his hand.*) There we are!

ENGSTRAND. And if I might humbly beg your Reverence's pardon—

MANDERS. You? On the contrary, it is I who ought to beg your pardon—

ENGSTRAND. Lord, no, sir!

MANDERS. Yes, assuredly. And I do it with all my heart. Forgive me for misunderstanding you. I only wish I could give you some proof of my hearty regret, and of my good-will towards you—

ENGSTRAND. Would your Reverence do it?

MANDERS. With the greatest pleasure.

ENGSTRAND. Well then, here's the very chance. With the bit of money I've saved here, I was thinking I might set up a Sailors' Home down in the town.

MRS. ALVING. You?

ENGSTRAND. Yes; it might be a sort of Orphanage, too, in a manner of speaking. There's such a many temptations for seafaring folk ashore. But in this Home of mine, a man might feel like as he was under a father's eye, I was thinking.

MANDERS. What do you say to this, Mrs. Alving?

ENGSTRAND. It isn't much as I've got to start with, Lord help me! But if I could only find a helping hand, why—

MANDERS. Yes, yes; we will look into the matter more closely. I entirely approve of your plan. But now, go before me and make everything ready, and get the candles lighted, so as to give the place an air of festivity. And then we will pass an edifying hour together, my good fellow; for now I quite believe you are in the right frame of mind.

ENGSTRAND. Yes, I trust I am. And so I'll say good-bye, ma'am, and thank you kindly; and take good care of Regina for me—(*wipes a tear from his eye*)—poor Johanna's child. Well, it's a queer thing, now; but it's just like as if she'd growed into the very apple of my eye. It is, indeed. (*He bows and goes out through the hall.*)

MANDERS. Well, what do you say of that man now, Mrs. Alving? That was a very different account of matters, was it not?

MRS. ALVING. Yes, it certainly was.

MANDERS. It only shows how excessively careful one ought to be in judging one's fellow creatures. But what a heartfelt joy it is to ascertain that one has been mistaken! Don't you think so?

MRS. ALVING. I think you are, and will always be, a great baby, Manders.

MANDERS. I?

MRS. ALVING (*laying her two hands upon his shoulders*). And I say that I have half a mind to put my arms round your neck, and kiss you.

MANDERS (*stepping hastily back*). No, no! God bless me! What an idea!

MRS. ALVING (*with a smile*). Oh, you needn't be afraid of me.

MANDERS (*by the table*). You have sometimes such an exaggerated way of expressing yourself. Now, let me just collect all the documents, and put them in my bag. (*He does so.*) There, that's all right. And now, good-bye for the present. Keep your eyes open when Oswald comes back. I shall look in again later. (*He takes his hat and goes out through the hall door.*)

MRS. ALVING (*sighs, looks for a moment out of the window, sets the room in order a little, and is about to go into the dining-room, but stops at the door with a half-suppressed cry*). Oswald, are you still at table?

OSWALD (*in the dining-room*). I'm only finishing my cigar.

MRS. ALVING. I thought you had gone for a little walk.

OSWALD. In such weather as this?

(*A glass clinks. MRS. ALVING leaves the door open, and sits down with her knitting on the sofa by the window.*)

OSWALD. Wasn't that Pastor Manders that went out just now?

MRS. ALVING. Yes; he went down to the Orphanage.

OSWALD. H'm. (*The glass and decanter clink again.*)

MRS. ALVING (*with a troubled glance*). Dear Oswald, you should take care of that liqueur. It is strong.

OSWALD. It keeps out the damp.

MRS. ALVING. Wouldn't you rather come in here, to me?

OSWALD. I mayn't smoke in there.

MRS. ALVING. You know quite well you may smoke cigars.

OSWALD. Oh, all right then; I'll come in. Just a tiny drop more first.—There! (*He comes into the room with his cigar, and shuts the door after him. A short silence.*) Where has the pastor gone to?

MRS. ALVING. I have just told you; he went down to the Orphanage.

OSWALD. Oh, yes; so you did.

MRS. ALVING. You shouldn't sit so long at table, Oswald.

OSWALD (*holding his cigar behind him*). But I find it so pleasant, mother. (*Strokes and caresses her.*) Just think what it is for me to come home and sit at mother's own table, in mother's room, and eat mother's delicious dishes.

MRS. ALVING. My dear, dear boy!

OSWALD (*somewhat impatiently, walks about and smokes*). And what else can I do with myself here? I can't set to work at anything.

MRS. ALVING. Why can't you?

OSWALD. In such weather as this? Without a single ray of sunshine the whole day? (*Walks up the room.*) Oh, not to be able to work—!

MRS. ALVING. Perhaps it was not quite wise of you to come home?

OSWALD. Oh, yes, mother; I had to.

MRS. ALVING. You know I would ten times rather forego the joy of having you here, than let you—

OSWALD (*stops beside the table*). Now just tell me, mother: does it really make you so very happy to have me home again?

MRS. ALVING. Does it make me happy!

OSWALD (*crumpling up a newspaper*). I should have thought it must be pretty much the same to you whether I was in existence or not.

MRS. ALVING. Have you the heart to say that to your mother, Oswald?

OSWALD. But you've got on very well without me all this time.

MRS. ALVING. Yes; I have got on without you. That is true.

(*A silence. Twilight slowly begins to fall.* OSWALD *paces to and fro across the room. He has laid his cigar down.*)

OSWALD (*stops beside* MRS. ALVING). Mother, may I sit on the sofa beside you?

MRS. ALVING (*makes room for him*). Yes, do, my dear boy.

OSWALD (*sits down*). There is something I must tell you, mother.

MRS. ALVING (*anxiously*). Well?

OSWALD (*looks fixedly before him*). For I can't go on hiding it any longer.

MRS. ALVING. Hiding what? What is it?

OSWALD (*as before*). I could never bring myself to write to you about it; and since I've come home—

MRS. ALVING (*seizes him by the arm*). Oswald, what is the matter?

OSWALD. Both yesterday and to-day I have tried to put the thoughts away from me—to cast them off; but it's no use.

MRS. ALVING (*rising*). Now you must tell me everything, Oswald!

OSWALD (*draws her down to the sofa again*). Sit still; and then I will try to tell you.—I complained of fatigue after my journey—

MRS. ALVING. Well? What then?

OSWALD. But it isn't that that is the matter with me; not any ordinary fatigue—

MRS. ALVING (*tries to jump up*). You are not ill, Oswald?

OSWALD (*draws her down again*). Sit still, mother. Do take it quietly. I'm not downright ill, either; not what is commonly called "ill." (*Clasps his hands above his head.*) Mother, my mind is broken down—ruined—I shall never be able to work again! (*With his hands before his face, he buries his head in her lap, and breaks into bitter sobbing.*)

MRS. ALVING (*white and trembling*).

Oswald! Look at me! No, no; it's not true.

OSWALD (*looks up with despair in his eyes*). Never to be able to work again! Never!—never! A living death! Mother, can you imagine anything so horrible?

MRS. ALVING. My poor boy! How has this horrible thing come upon you?

OSWALD (*sitting upright again*). That's just what I cannot possibly grasp or understand. I have never led a dissipated life—never, in any respect. You mustn't believe that of me, mother! I've never done that.

MRS. ALVING. I am sure you haven't, Oswald.

OSWALD. And yet this has come upon me just the same—this awful misfortune!

MRS. ALVING. Oh, but it will pass over, my dear, blessed boy. It's nothing but over-work. Trust me, I am right.

OSWALD (*sadly*). I thought so too, at first; but it isn't so.

MRS. ALVING. Tell me everything, from beginning to end.

OSWALD. Yes, I will.

MRS. ALVING. When did you first notice it?

OSWALD. It was directly after I had been home last time, and had got back to Paris again. I began to feel the most violent pains in my head—chiefly in the back of my head, they seemed to come. It was as though a tight iron ring was being screwed round my neck and upwards.

MRS. ALVING. Well, and then?

OSWALD. At first I thought it was nothing but the ordinary headache I had been so plagued with while I was growing up—

MRS. ALVING. Yes, yes—

OSWALD. But it wasn't that. I soon found that out. I couldn't work any more. I wanted to begin upon a big new picture, but my powers seemed to fail me; all my strength was crippled; I could form no definite images; everything swam

before me—whirling round and round. Oh, it was an awful state! At last I sent for a doctor—and from him I learned the truth.

MRS. ALVING. How do you mean?

OSWALD. He was one of the first doctors in Paris. I told him my symptoms; and then he set to work asking me a string of questions which I thought had nothing to do with the matter. I couldn't imagine what the man was after—

MRS. ALVING. Well?

OSWALD. At last he said: "There has been something worm-eaten in you from your birth." He used that very word—*vermoulu.*

MRS. ALVING (*breathlessly*). What did he mean by that?

OSWALD. I didn't understand either, and begged him to explain himself more clearly. And then the old cynic said— (*Clenching his fist.*) Oh—!

MRS. ALVING. What did he say?

OSWALD. He said, "The sins of the fathers are visited upon the children."

MRS. ALVING (*rising slowly*). The sins of the fathers—!

OSWALD. I very nearly struck him in the face—

MRS. ALVING (*walks away across the room*). The sins of the fathers—

OSWALD (*smiles sadly*). Yes; what do you think of that? Of course I assured him that such a thing was out of the question. But do you think he gave in? No, he stuck to it; and it was only when I produced your letters and translated the passages relating to father—

MRS. ALVING. But then—?

OSWALD. Then of course he had to admit that he was on the wrong track; and so I learned the truth—the incomprehensible truth! I ought not to have taken part with my comrades in that lighthearted, glorious life of theirs. It had been too much for my strength. So I had brought it upon myself!

MRS. ALVING. Oswald! No, no; do not believe it!

OSWALD. No other explanation was possible, he said. That's the awful part of it. Incurably ruined for life—by my own heedlessness! All that I meant to have done in the world—I never dare think of it again—I'm not able to think of it. Oh! if I could only live over again, and undo all I have done! (*He buries his face in the sofa.*)

(MRS. ALVING *wrings her hands and walks, in silent struggle, backwards and forwards.*)

OSWALD (*after a while, looks up and remains resting upon his elbow*). If it had only been something inherited—something one wasn't responsible for! But this! To have thrown away so shamefully, thoughtlessly, recklessly, one's own happiness, one's own health, everything in the world—one's future, one's very life—!

MRS. ALVING. No, no, my dear, darling boy; this is impossible! (*Bends over him.*) Things are not so desperate as you think.

OSWALD. Oh, you don't know—(*Springs up.*) And then, mother, to cause you all this sorrow! Many a time I have almost wished and hoped that at bottom you didn't care so very much about me.

MRS. ALVING. I, Oswald? My only boy! You are all I have in the world! The only thing I care about!

OSWALD (*seizes both her hands and kisses them*). Yes, yes, I see it. When I'm at home, I see it, of course; and that's almost the hardest part for me.—But now you know the whole story; and now we won't talk any more about it to-day. I daren't think of it for long together. (*Goes up the room.*) Get me something to drink, mother.

MRS. ALVING. To drink? What do you want to drink now?

OSWALD. Oh, anything you like. You have some cold punch in the house.

MRS. ALVING. Yes, but my dear Oswald—

OSWALD. Don't refuse me, mother.

Do be kind, now! I must have something to wash down all these gnawing thoughts. (*Goes into the conservatory.*) And then —it's so dark here! (MRS. ALVING *pulls a bell-rope on the right.*) And this ceaseless rain! It may go on week after week, for months together. Never to get a glimpse of the sun! I can't recollect ever having seen the sun shine all the times I've been at home.

MRS. ALVING. Oswald—you are thinking of going away from me.

OSWALD. H'm—(*Drawing a heavy breath.*)—I'm not thinking of anything. I cannot think of anything. (*In a low voice.*) I let thinking alone.

REGINA (*from the dining-room*). Did you ring, ma'am?

MRS. ALVING. Yes; let us have the lamp in.

REGINA. Yes, ma'am. It's ready lighted. (*Goes out.*)

MRS. ALVING (*goes across to* OSWALD). Oswald, be frank with me.

OSWALD. Well, so I am, mother. (*Goes to the table.*) I think I have told you enough.

(REGINA *brings the lamp and sets it upon the table.*)

MRS. ALVING. Regina, you may bring us a small bottle of champagne.

REGINA. Very well, ma'am. (*Goes out.*)

OSWALD (*puts his arm round* MRS. ALVING'S *neck*). That's just what I wanted. I knew mother wouldn't let her boy go thirsty.

MRS. ALVING. My own, poor, darling Oswald; how could I deny you anything now?

OSWALD (*eagerly*). Is that true, mother? Do you mean it?

MRS. ALVING. How? what?

OSWALD. That you couldn't deny me anything.

MRS. ALVING. My dear Oswald—

OSWALD. Hush!

REGINA (*brings a tray with a half-bottle*

of champagne and two glasses, which she sets on the table). Shall I open it?

OSWALD. No, thanks. I will do it myself.

(REGINA *goes out again.*)

MRS. ALVING (*sits down by the table.*) What was it you meant—that I mustn't deny you?

OSWALD (*busy opening the bottle*). First let us have a glass—or two. (*The cork pops; he pours wine into one glass, and is about to pour it into the other.*)

MRS. ALVING (*holding her hand over it*). Thanks; not for me.

OSWALD. Oh! won't you? Then I will! (*He empties the glass, fills, and empties it again; then he sits down by the table.*)

MRS. ALVING (*in expectancy*). Well?

OSWALD (*without looking at her*). Tell me—I thought you and Pastor Manders seemed so odd—so quiet—at dinner to-day.

MRS. ALVING. Did you notice it?

OSWALD. Yes. H'm— (*After a short silence.*) Tell me: what do you think of Regina?

MRS. ALVING. What do I think?

OSWALD. Yes; isn't she splendid?

MRS. ALVING. My dear Oswald, you don't know her as I do—

OSWALD. Well?

MRS. ALVING. Regina, unfortunately, was allowed to stay at home too long. I ought to have taken her earlier into my house.

OSWALD. Yes, but isn't she splendid to look at, mother? (*He fills his glass.*)

MRS. ALVING. Regina has many serious faults—

OSWALD. Oh, what does that matter? (*He drinks again.*)

MRS. ALVING. But I am fond of her, nevertheless, and I am responsible for her. I wouldn't for all the world have any harm happen to her.

OSWALD (*springs up*). Mother, Regina is my only salvation!

MRS. ALVING (*rising*). What do you mean by that?

OSWALD. I cannot go on bearing all this anguish of soul alone.

MRS. ALVING. Have you not your mother to share it with you?

OSWALD. Yes; that's what I thought; and so I came home to you. But that will not do. I see it won't do. I cannot endure my life here.

MRS. ALVING. Oswald!

OSWALD. I must live differently, mother. That is why I must leave you. I will not have you looking on at it.

MRS. ALVING. My unhappy boy! But, Oswald, while you are so ill as this—

OSWALD. If it were only the illness, I should stay with you, mother, you may be sure; for you are the best friend I have in the world.

MRS. ALVING. Yes, indeed I am, Oswald; am I not?

OSWALD (*wanders restlessly about*). But it's all the torment, the gnawing remorse—and then, the great, killing dread. Oh—that awful dread!

MRS. ALVING (*walking after him*). Dread? What dread? What do you mean?

OSWALD. Oh, you mustn't ask me any more. I don't know. I can't describe it.

MRS. ALVING (*goes over to the right and pulls the bell.*)

OSWALD. What is it you want?

MRS. ALVING. I want my boy to be happy—that is what I want. He sha'n't go on brooding over things. (*To* REGINA, *who appears at the door:*) More champagne—a large bottle.

(REGINA *goes.*)

OSWALD. Mother!

MRS. ALVING. Do you think we don't know how to live here at home?

OSWALD. Isn't she splendid to look at? How beautifully she's built! And so thoroughly healthy!

MRS. ALVING (*sits by the table*). Sit down, Oswald; let us talk quietly together.

OSWALD (*sits*). I daresay you don't know, mother, that I owe Regina· some reparation.

MRS. ALVING. You!

OSWALD. For a bit of thoughtlessness, or whatever you like to call it—very innocent, at any rate. When I was home last time—

MRS. ALVING. Well?

OSWALD. She used often to ask me about Paris, and I used to tell her one thing and another. Then I recollect I happened to say to her one day, "Shouldn't you like to go there yourself?"

MRS. ALVING. Well?

OSWALD. I saw her face flush, and then she said, "Yes, I should like it of all things." "Ah, well," I replied, "it might perhaps be managed"—or something like that.

MRS. ALVING. And then?

OSWALD. Of course I had forgotten all about it; but the day before yesterday I happened to ask her whether she was glad I was to stay at home so long—

MRS. ALVING. Yes?

OSWALD. And then she gave me such· a strange look, and asked, "But what's to become of my trip to Paris?"

MRS. ALVING. Her trip!

OSWALD. And so it came out that she had taken the thing seriously; that she had been thinking of me the whole time, and had set to work to learn French—

MRS. ALVING. So that was why—!

OSWALD. Mother—when I saw that fresh, lovely, splendid girl standing there, before me—till then I had hardly noticed her—but when she stood there, as though with open arms ready to receive me—

MRS. ALVING. Oswald!

OSWALD. —then it flashed upon me that in her lay my salvation; for I saw that she was full of the joy of life.

MRS. ALVING (*starts*). The joy of life—? Can there be salvation in that?

REGINA (*from the dining-room, with a bottle of champagne*). I'm sorry to have been so long, but I had to go to the cellar. (*Places the bottle on the table.*)

OSWALD. And now bring another glass.

REGINA (*looks at him in surprise*). There is Mrs. Alving's glass, Mr. Alving.

OSWALD. Yes, but bring one for yourself, Regina. (REGINA *starts and gives a lightning-like side glance at* MRS. ALVING). Why do you wait?

REGINA (*softly and hesitatingly*). Is it Mrs. Alving's wish?

MRS. ALVING. Bring the glass, Regina. (REGINA *goes out into the dining-room.*)

OSWALD (*follows her with his eyes*). Have you noticed how she walks?—so firmly and lightly!

MRS. ALVING. This can never be, Oswald!

OSWALD. It's a settled thing. Can't you see that? It's no use saying anything against it.

(REGINA *enters with an empty glass, which she keeps in her hand.*)

OSWALD. Sit down, Regina.

(REGINA *looks inquiringly at* MRS. ALVING.)

MRS. ALVING. Sit down. (REGINA *sits on a chair by the dining-room door, still holding the empty glass in her hand.*) Oswald—what were you saying about the joy of life?

OSWALD. Ah, the joy of life, mother—that's a thing you don't know much about in these parts. I have never felt it here.

MRS. ALVING. Not when you are with me?

OSWALD. Not when I'm at home. But you don't understand that.

MRS. ALVING. Yes, yes; I think I almost understand it—now.

OSWALD. And then, too, the joy of work! At bottom, it's the same thing. But that, too, you know nothing about.

MRS. ALVING. Perhaps you are right. Tell me more about it, Oswald.

OSWALD. I only mean that here people are brought up to believe that work is a curse and a punishment for sin, and that life is something miserable, something it would be best to have done with, the sooner the better.

MRS. ALVING. "A vale of tears," yes; and we certainly do our best to make it one.

OSWALD. But in the great world people won't hear of such things. There, nobody really believes such doctrines any longer. There, you feel it a positive bliss and ecstasy merely to draw the breath of life. Mother, have you noticed that everything I have painted has turned upon the joy of life?—always, always upon the joy of life?—light and sunshine and glorious air—and faces radiant with happiness. That is why I'm afraid of remaining at home with you.

MRS. ALVING. Afraid? What are you afraid of here, with me?

OSWALD. I'm afraid lest all my instincts should be warped into ugliness.

MRS. ALVING (*looks steadily at him*). Do you think that is what would happen?

OSWALD. I know it. You may live the same life here as there, and yet it won't be the same life.

MRS. ALVING (*who has been listening eagerly, rises, her eyes big with thought, and says:*) Now I see the sequence of things.

OSWALD. What is it you see?

MRS. ALVING. I see it now for the first time. And now I can speak.

OSWALD (*rising*). Mother, I don't understand you.

REGINA (*who has also risen*). Perhaps I ought to go?

MRS. ALVING. No. Stay here. Now I can speak. Now, my boy, you shall know the whole truth. And then you can choose. Oswald! Regina!

OSWALD. Hush! The Pastor——

MANDERS (*enters by the hall door*).

There! We have had a most edifying time down there.

OSWALD. So have we.

MANDERS. We must stand by Engstrand and his Sailors' Home. Regina must go to him and help him—

REGINA. No thank you, sir.

MANDERS (*noticing her for the first time*). What—? You here? And with a glass in your hand!

REGINA (*hastily putting the glass down*). *Pardon!*

OSWALD. Regina is going with me, Mr. Manders.

MANDERS. Going! With you!

OSWALD. Yes; as my wife—if she wishes it.

MANDERS. But, merciful God—!

REGINA. I can't help it, sir.

OSWALD. Or she'll stay here, if I stay.

REGINA (*involuntarily*). Here!

MANDERS. I am thunderstruck at your conduct, Mrs. Alving.

MRS. ALVING. They will do neither one thing nor the other; for now I can speak out plainly.

MANDERS. You surely will not do that! No, no, no!

MRS. ALVING. Yes, I can speak and I will. And no ideals shall suffer after all.

OSWALD. Mother—what is it you are hiding from me?

REGINA (*listening*). Oh, ma'am, listen! Don't you hear shouts outside. (*She goes into the conservatory and looks out.*)

OSWALD (*at the window on the left*). What's going on? Where does that light come from?

REGINA (*cries out*). The Orphanage is on fire!

MRS. ALVING (*rushing to the window*). On fire!

MANDERS. On fire! Impossible! I've just come from there.

OSWALD. Where's my hat? Oh, never mind it—Father's Orphanage—! (*He rushes out through the garden door.*)

MRS. ALVING. My shawl, Regina! The whole place is in a blaze!

MANDERS. Terrible! Mrs. Alving, it is a judgment upon this abode of lawlessness.

MRS. ALVING. Yes, of course. Come, Regina.

(*She and* REGINA *hasten out through the hall.*)

MANDERS (*clasps his hands together*). And we left it uninsured! (*He goes out the same way.*)

Act III

(*The room as before. All the doors stand open. The lamp is still burning on the table. It is dark out of doors; there is only a faint glow from the conflagration in the background to the left.*)

(MRS. ALVING, *with a shawl over her head, stands in the conservatory, looking out.* REGINA, *also with a shawl on, stands a little behind her.*)

MRS. ALVING. The whole thing burnt!—burnt to the ground!

REGINA. The basement is still burning.

MRS. ALVING. How is it Oswald doesn't come home? There's nothing to be saved.

REGINA. Should you like me to take down his hat to him?

MRS. ALVING. Has he not even got his hat on?

REGINA (*pointing to the hall*). No; there it hangs.

MRS. ALVING. Let it be. He must come up now. I shall go and look for him myself. (*She goes out through the garden door.*)

MANDERS (*comes in from the hall*). Is not Mrs. Alving here?

REGINA. She has just gone down the garden.

MANDERS. This is the most terrible night I ever went through.

REGINA. Yes; isn't it a dreadful misfortune, sir?

MANDERS. Oh, don't talk about it! I can hardly bear to think of it.

REGINA. How can it have happened—?

MANDERS. Don't ask me, Miss Engstrand! How should *I* know? Do you, too—? Is it not enough that your father—?

REGINA. What about him?

MANDERS. Oh, he has driven me distracted—

ENGSTRAND (*enters through the hall*). Your Reverence—

MANDERS (*turns round in terror*). Are you after me here, too?

ENGSTRAND. Yes, strike me dead, but I must—! Oh, Lord! what am I saying? But this is a terrible ugly business, your Reverence.

MANDERS (*walks to and fro*). Alas! alas!

REGINA. What's the matter?

ENGSTRAND. Why, it all came of this here prayer-meeting, you see. (*Softly.*) The bird's limed, my girl. (*Aloud.*) And to think it should be my doing that such a thing should be his Reverence's doing!

MANDERS. But I assure you, Engstrand—

ENGSTRAND. There wasn't another soul except your Reverence as ever laid a finger on the candles down there.

MANDERS (*stops*). So you declare. But I certainly cannot recollect that I ever had a candle in my hand.

ENGSTRAND. And I saw as clear as daylight how your Reverence took the candle and snuffed it with your fingers, and threw away the snuff among the shavings.

MANDERS. And you stood and looked on?

ENGSTRAND. Yes; I saw it as plain as a pike-staff, I did.

MANDERS. It's quite beyond my comprehension. Besides, it has never been my habit to snuff candles with my fingers.

ENGSTRAND. And terrible risky it looked, too, that it did! But is there such a deal of harm done after all, your Reverence?

MANDERS (*walks restlessly to and fro*). Oh, don't ask me!

ENGSTRAND (*walks with him*). And your Reverence hadn't insured it, neither?

MANDERS. (*continuing to walk up and down*). No, no, no; I have told you so.

ENGSTRAND (*following him*). Not insured! And then to go straight away down and set light to the whole thing! Lord, Lord, what a misfortune!

MANDERS (*wipes the sweat from his forehead*). Ay, you may well say that, Engstrand.

ENGSTRAND. And to think that such a thing should happen to a benevolent Institution, that was to have been a blessing both to town and country, as the saying goes! The newspapers won't be for handling your Reverence very gently, I expect.

MANDERS. No; that is just what I am thinking of. That is almost the worst of the whole matter. All the malignant attacks and imputations—! Oh, it makes me shudder to think of it!

MRS. ALVING (*comes in from the garden*). He is not to be persuaded to leave the fire.

MANDERS. Ah, there you are, Mrs. Alving.

MRS. ALVING. So you have escaped your Inaugural Address, Pastor Manders.

MANDERS. Oh, I should so gladly—

MRS. ALVING (*in an undertone*). It is all for the best. That Orphanage would have done no one any good.

MANDERS. Do you think not?

MRS. ALVING. Do you think it would?

MANDERS. It is a terrible misfortune, all the same.

MRS. ALVING. Let us speak of it plainly, as a matter of business—Are you waiting for Mr. Manders, Engstrand?

ENGSTRAND (*at the hall door*). That's just what I'm a'doing of, ma'am.

MRS. ALVING. Then sit down meanwhile.

ENGSTRAND. Thank you, ma'am; I'd as soon stand.

MRS. ALVING (*to* MANDERS). I suppose you are going by the steamer?

MANDERS. Yes; it starts in an hour.

MRS. ALVING. Then be so good as to take all the papers with you. I won't hear another word about this affair. I have other things to think of—

MANDERS. Mrs. Alving—

MRS. ALVING. Later on I shall send you a Power of Attorney to settle everything as you please.

MANDERS. That I will very readily undertake. The original destination of the endowment must now be completely changed, alas!

MRS. ALVING. Of course it must.

MANDERS. I think, first of all, I shall arrange that the Solvik property shall pass to the parish. The land is by no means without value. It can always be turned to account for some purpose or other. And the interest of the money in the Bank I could, perhaps, best apply for the benefit of some undertaking of acknowledged value to the town.

MRS. ALVING. Do just as you please. The whole matter is now completely indifferent to me.

ENGSTRAND. Give a thought to my Sailors' Home, your Reverence.

MANDERS. Upon my word, that is not a bad suggestion. That must be considered.

ENGSTRAND. Oh, devil take considering—Lord forgive me!

MANDERS (*with a sigh*). And unfortunately I cannot tell how long I shall be able to retain control of these things—whether public opinion may not compel me to retire. It entirely depends upon the result of the official inquiry into the fire—

MRS. ALVING. What are you talking about?

MANDERS. And the result can by no means be foretold.

ENGSTRAND (*comes close to him*). Ay, but it can though. For here stands old Jacob Engstrand.

MANDERS. Well well, but—?

ENGSTRAND (*more softly*). And Jacob Engstrand isn't the man to desert a noble benefactor in the hour of need, as the saying goes.

MANDERS. Yes, but my good fellow —how—?

ENGSTRAND. Jacob Engstrand may be likened to a sort of a guardian angel, he may, your Reverence.

MANDERS. No, no; I really cannot accept that.

ENGSTRAND. Oh, that'll be the way of it, all the same. I know a man as has taken others' sins upon himself before now, I do.

MANDERS Jacob! (*Wrings his hand.*) Yours is a rare nature. Well, you shall be helped with your Sailors' Home. That you may rely upon.

(ENGSTRAND *tries to thank him, but cannot for emotion.*)

MANDERS (*hangs his travelling-bag over his shoulders*). And now let us set out. We two will go together.

ENGSTRAND (*at the dining-room door, softly to* REGINA). You come along too, my lass. You shall live as snug as the yolk in an egg.

REGINA (*tosses her head*). *Merci!* (*She goes out into the hall and fetches* MANDERS' *overcoat.*)

MANDERS. Good-bye, Mrs. Alving! and may the spirit of Law and Order descend upon this house, and that quickly.

MRS. ALVING. Good-bye, Pastor Manders. (*She goes up towards the conservatory, as she sees* OSWALD *coming in through the garden door.*)

ENGSTRAND (*while he and* REGINA *help* MANDERS *to get his coat on*). Good-bye, my child. And if any trouble should come to you, you know where Jacob Engstrand is to be found. (*Softly.*) Little Harbour Street, h'm—! (*To* MRS. ALVING *and* OSWALD.) And the refuge for wandering mariners shall be called "Chamberlain Alving's Home," that it shall! And if so be as I'm spared to carry on that house in my own way, I make so bold as to promise that it shall be worthy of the Chamberlain's memory.

MANDERS (*in the doorway*). H'm— h'm!—Come along, my dear Engstrand. Good-bye! Good-bye! (*He and* ENGSTRAND *go out through the hall.*)

OSWALD (*goes towards the table*). What house was he talking about?

MRS. ALVING. Oh, a kind of Home that he and Pastor Manders want to set up.

OSWALD. It will burn down like the other.

MRS. ALVING. What makes you think so?

OSWALD. Everything will burn. All that recalls father's memory is doomed. Here am I, too, burning down.

(REGINA *starts and looks at him.*)

MRS. ALVING. Oswald! You oughtn't to have remained so long down there, my poor boy.

OSWALD (*sits down by the table*). I almost think you are right.

MRS. ALVING. Let me dry your face, Oswald; you are quite wet. (*She dries his face with her pocket-handkerchief.*)

OSWALD (*stares indifferently in front of him*). Thanks, mother.

MRS. ALVING. Are you not tired, Oswald? Should you like to sleep?

OSWALD (*nervously*). No, no—not to sleep! I never sleep. I only pretend to. (*Sadly.*) That will come soon enough.

MRS. ALVING (*looking sorrowfully at him*). Yes, you really are ill, my blessed boy.

REGINA (*eagerly*). Is Mr. Alving ill?

OSWALD (*impatiently*). Oh, do shut all the doors! This killing dread—

MRS. ALVING. Close the doors, Regina.

(REGINA *shuts them and remains standing by the hall door.* MRS. ALVING *takes her shawl off.* REGINA *does the same.* MRS. ALVING *draws a chair across to* OSWALD's, *and sits by him.*)

MRS. ALVING. There now! I am going to sit beside you—

OSWALD. Yes, do. And Regina shall stay here too. Regina shall be with me always. You will come to the rescue, Regina, won't you?

REGINA. I don't understand—

MRS. ALVING. To the rescue?

OSWALD. Yes—when the need comes.

MRS. ALVING. Oswald, have you not your mother to come to the rescue?

OSWALD. You? (*Smiles.*) No, mother; that rescue you will never bring me. (*Laughs sadly.*) You! ha ha! (*Looks earnestly at her.*) Though, after all, who ought to do it if not you? (*Impetuously.*) Why can't you say "thou" to me, Regina? Why don't you call me "Oswald"?

REGINA (*softly*). I don't think Mrs. Alving would like it.

MRS. ALVING. You shall have leave to, presently. And meanwhile sit over here beside us.

(REGINA *seats herself demurely and hesitatingly at the other side of the table.*)

MRS. ALVING. And now, my poor suffering boy, I am going to take the burden off your mind—

OSWALD. You, mother?

MRS. ALVING. —all the gnawing remorse and self-reproach you speak of.

OSWALD. And you think you can do that?

MRS. ALVING. Yes, now I can, Oswald. A little while ago you spoke of the joy of life; and at that word a new light burst for me over my life and everything connected with it.

OSWALD (*shakes his head*). I don't understand you.

MRS. ALVING. You ought to have known your father when he was a young

lieutenant. He was brimming over with the joy of life!

OSWALD. Yes, I know he was.

MRS. ALVING. It was like a breezy day only to look at him. And what exuberant strength and vitality there was in him!

OSWALD. Well—?

MRS. ALVING. Well then, child of joy as he was—for he was like a child in those days—he had to live at home here in a half-grown town, which had no joys to offer him—only dissipations. He had no object in life—only an official position. He had no work into which he could throw himself heart and soul; he had only business. He had not a single comrade that could realise what the joy of life meant—only loungers and booncompanions—

OSWALD. Mother—!

MRS. ALVING. So the inevitable happened.

OSWALD. The inevitable?

MRS. ALVING. You told me yourself, this evening, what would become of you if you stayed at home.

OSWALD. Do you mean to say that father—?

MRS. ALVING. Your poor father found no outlet for the overpowering joy of life that was in him. And I brought no brightness into his home.

OSWALD. Not even you?

MRS. ALVING. They had taught me a great deal about duties and so forth, which I went on obstinately believing in. Everything was marked out into duties—into my duties, and his duties, and—I am afraid I made his home intolerable for your poor father, Oswald.

OSWALD. Why have you never spoken of this in writing to me?

MRS. ALVING. I have never before seen it in such a light that I could speak of it to you, his son.

OSWALD. In what light did you see it, then?

MRS. ALVING (*slowly*). I saw only this one thing: that your father was a broken-down man before you were born.

OSWALD (*softly*). Ah—! (*He rises and walks away to the window.*)

MRS. ALVING. And then, day after day, I dwelt on the one thought that by rights Regina should be at home in this house—just like my own boy.

OSWALD (*turning round quickly*). Regina—!

REGINA (*springs up and asks, with bated breath*). I—?

MRS. ALVING. Yes, now you know it, both of you.

OSWALD. Regina!

REGINA (*to herself*). So mother was that kind of woman.

MRS. ALVING. Your mother had many good qualities, Regina.

REGINA. Yes, but she was one of that sort, all the same. Oh, I've often suspected it; but—And now, if you please, ma'am, may I be allowed to go away at once?

MRS. ALVING. Do you really wish it, Regina?

REGINA. Yes, indeed I do.

MRS. ALVING. Of course you can do as you like; but—

OSWALD (*goes towards* REGINA). Go away now? Your place is here.

REGINA. *Merci*, Mr. Alving!—or now, I suppose, I may say Oswald. But I can tell you this wasn't at all what I expected.

MRS. ALVING. Regina, I have not been frank with you—

REGINA. No, that you haven't indeed. If I'd known that Oswald was an invalid, why—And now, too, that it can never come to anything serious between us—I really can't stop out here in the country and wear myself out nursing sick people.

OSWALD. Not even one who is so near to you?

REGINA. No, that I can't. A poor girl must make the best of her young days, or she'll be left out in the cold before she knows where she is. And I, too, have the joy of life in me, Mrs. Alving!

MRS. ALVING. Unfortunately, you have. But don't throw yourself away, Regina.

REGINA. Oh, what must be, must be. If Oswald takes after his father, I take after my mother, I dare say.—May I ask, ma'am, if Pastor Manders knows all this about me?

MRS. ALVING. Pastor Manders knows all about it.

REGINA (*busied in putting on her shawl*). Well then, I'd better make haste and get away by this steamer. The Pastor is such a nice man to deal with; and I certainly think I've as much right to a little of that money as he has—that brute of a carpenter.

MRS. ALVING. You are heartily welcome to it, Regina.

REGINA (*looks hard at her*). I think you might have brought me up as a gentleman's daughter, ma'am; it would have suited me better. (*Tosses her head.*) But pooh—what does it matter! (*With a bitter side glance at the corked bottle.*) I may come to drink champagne with gentlefolks yet.

MRS. ALVING. And if you ever need a home, Regina, come to me.

REGINA. No, thank you, ma'am. Pastor Manders will look after me, I know. And if the worst comes to the worst, I know of one house where I've every right to a place.

MRS. ALVING. Where is that?

REGINA. "Chamberlain Alving's Home."

MRS. ALVING. Regina—now I see it —you are going to your ruin.

REGINA. Oh, stuff! Good-bye. (*She nods and goes out through the hall.*)

OSWALD (*stands at the window and looks out*). Is she gone?

MRS. ALVING. Yes.

OSWALD (*murmuring aside to himself*). I think it was a mistake, this.

MRS. ALVING (*goes up behind him and lays her hands on his shoulders*). Oswald, my dear boy—has it shaken you very much?

OSWALD (*turns his face towards her*). All that about father, do you mean?

MRS. ALVING. Yes, about your unhappy father. I am so afraid it may have been too much for you.

OSWALD. Why should you fancy that? Of course it came upon me as a great surprise; but it can make no real difference to me.

MRS. ALVING (*draws her hands away*). No difference! That your father was so infinitely unhappy!

OSWALD. Of course I can pity him, as I would anybody else; but—

MRS. ALVING. Nothing more! Your own father!

OSWALD (*impatiently*). Oh, "father," —"father"! I never knew anything of father. I remember nothing about him, except that he once made me sick.

MRS. ALVING. This is terrible to think of! Ought not a son to love his father, whatever happens?

OSWALD. When a son has nothing to thank his father for? has never known him? Do you really cling to that old superstition?—you who are so enlightened in other ways?

MRS. ALVING. Can it be only a superstition—?

OSWALD. Yes; surely you can see that, mother. It's one of those notions that are current in the world, and so—

MRS. ALVING (*deeply moved*). Ghosts!

OSWALD (*crossing the room*). Yes; you may call them ghosts.

MRS. ALVING (*wildly*). Oswald— then you don't love me, either!

OSWALD. You I know, at any rate—

MRS. ALVING. Yes, you know me; but is that all!

OSWALD. And, of course, I know how fond you are of me, and I can't but be grateful to you. And then you can be so useful to me, now that I am ill.

MRS. ALVING. Yes, cannot I, Oswald? Oh, I could almost bless the illness that has driven you home to me. For I see very plainly that you are not mine: I have to win you.

OSWALD (*impatiently*). Yes yes yes; all these are just so many phrases. You must remember that I am a sick man, mother. I can't be much taken up with other people; I have enough to do thinking about myself.

MRS. ALVING (*in a low voice*). I shall be patient and easily satisfied.

OSWALD. And cheerful too, mother!

MRS. ALVING. Yes, my dear boy, you are quite right. (*Goes towards him.*) Have I relieved you of all remorse and self-reproach now?

OSWALD. Yes, you have. But now who will relieve me of the dread?

MRS. ALVING. The dread?

OSWALD (*walks across the room*). Regina could have been got to do it.

MRS. ALVING. I don't understand you. What is this about dread—and Regina?

OSWALD. Is it very late, mother?

MRS. ALVING. It is early morning. (*She looks out through the conservatory.*) The day is dawning over the mountains. And the weather is clearing, Oswald. In a little while you shall see the sun.

OSWALD. I'm glad of that. Oh, I may still have much to rejoice in and live for—

MRS. ALVING. I should think so, indeed!

OSWALD. Even if I can't work—

MRS. ALVING. Oh, you'll soon be able to work again, my dear boy—now that you haven't got all those gnawing and depressing thoughts to brood over any longer.

OSWALD. Yes, I'm glad you were able to rid me of all those fancies. And when

I've got over this one thing more—(*Sits on the sofa.*) Now we will have a little talk, mother—

MRS. ALVING. Yes, let us. (*She pushes an arm-chair towards the sofa, and sits down close to him.*)

OSWALD. And meantime the sun will be rising. And then you will know all. And then I shall not feel this dread any longer.

MRS. ALVING. What is it that I am to know?

OSWALD (*not listening to her*). Mother, did you not say a little while ago, that there was nothing in the world you would not do for me, if I asked you?

MRS. ALVING. Yes, indeed I said so!

OSWALD. And you'll stick to it, mother?

MRS. ALVING. You may rely on that, my dear and only boy! I have nothing in the world to live for but you alone.

OSWALD. Very well, then; now you shall hear—Mother, you have a strong, steadfast mind, I know. Now you're to sit quite still when you hear it.

MRS. ALVING. What dreadful thing can it be—?

OSWALD. You're not to scream out. Do you hear? Do you promise me that? We will sit and talk about it quietly. Do you promise me, mother?

MRS. ALVING. Yes, yes; I promise. Only speak!

OSWALD. Well, you must know that all this fatigue—and my inability to think of work—all that is not the illness itself—

MRS. ALVING. Then what is the illness itself?

OSWALD. The disease I have as my birthright—(*he points to his forehead and adds very softly*)—is seated here.

MRS. ALVING (*almost voiceless*). Oswald! No—no!

OSWALD. Don't scream. I can't bear it. Yes, mother, it is seated here—waiting. And it may break out any day—at any moment.

MRS. ALVING. Oh, what horror—!

OSWALD. Now, quiet, quiet. That is how it stands with me—

MRS. ALVING (*springs up*). It's not true, Oswald! It's impossible! It cannot be so!

OSWALD. I have had one attack down there already. It was soon over. But when I came to know the state I had been in, then the dread descended upon me, raging and ravening; and so I set off home to you as fast as I could.

MRS. ALVING. Then this is the dread—!

OSWALD. Yes—it's so indescribably loathsome, you know. Oh, if it had only been an ordinary mortal disease—! For I'm not so afraid of death—though I should like to live as long as I can.

MRS. ALVING. Yes, yes, Oswald, you must!

OSWALD. But this is so unutterably loathsome. To become a little baby again! To have to be fed! To have to—Oh, it's not to be spoken of!

MRS. ALVING. The child has his mother to nurse him.

OSWALD (*springs up*). No, never that! That is just what I will not have. I can't endure to think that perhaps I should lie in that state for many years—and get old and grey. And in the meantime you might die and leave me. (*Sits in* MRS. ALVING's *chair.*) For the doctor said it wouldn't necessarily prove fatal at once. He called it a sort of softening of the brain—or something like that. (*Smiles sadly.*) I think that expression sounds so nice. It always sets me thinking of cherry-colored velvet—something soft and delicate to stroke.

MRS. ALVING (*shrieks*). Oswald!

OSWALD (*springs up and paces the room*). And now you have taken Regina from me. If I could only have had her! She would have come to the rescue, I know.

MRS. ALVING (*goes to him*). What do you mean by that, my darling boy?

Is there any help in the world that I would not give you?

OSWALD. When I got over my attack in Paris, the doctor told me that when it comes again—and it will come—there will be no more hope.

MRS. ALVING. He was heartless enough to—

OSWALD. I demanded it of him. I told him I had preparations to make—(*He smiles cunningly.*) And so I had. (*He takes a little box from his inner breast pocket and opens it.*) Mother, do you see this?

MRS. ALVING. What is it?

OSWALD. Morphia.

MRS. ALVING (*looks at him horror-struck*). Oswald—my boy.

OSWALD. I've scraped together twelve pilules—

MRS. ALVING (*snatches at it*). Give me the box, Oswald.

OSWALD. Not yet, mother. (*He hides the box again in his pocket.*)

MRS. ALVING. I shall never survive this!

OSWALD. It must be survived. Now if I'd had Regina here, I should have told her how things stood with me—and begged her to come to the rescue at the last. She would have done it. I know she would.

MRS. ALVING. Never!

OSWALD. When the horror had come upon me, and she saw me lying there helpless, like a little new-born baby, impotent, lost, hopeless—past all saving—

MRS. ALVING. Never in all the world would Regina have done this!

OSWALD. Regina would have done it. Regina was so splendidly light-hearted. And she would soon have wearied of nursing an invalid like me.

MRS. ALVING. Then heaven be praised that Regina is not here.

OSWALD. Well then, it is you that must come to the rescue, mother.

MRS. ALVING (*shrieks aloud*). I!

OSWALD. Who should do it if not you?

MRS. ALVING. I! your mother!

OSWALD. For that very reason.

MRS. ALVING. I, who gave you life!

OSWALD. I never asked you for life. And what sort of a life have you given me? I will not have it! You shall take it back again!

MRS. ALVING. Help! Help! (*She runs out into the hall.*)

OSWALD (*going after her*). Do not leave me! Where are you going?

MRS. ALVING (*in the hall*). To fetch the doctor, Oswald! Let me pass!

OSWALD (*also outside*). You shall not go out. And no one shall come in. (*The locking of a door is heard.*)

MRS. ALVING (*comes in again*). Oswald! Oswald—my child!

OSWALD (*follows her*). Have you a mother's heart for me—and yet can see me suffer from this unutterable dread?

MRS. ALVING (*after a moment's silence, commands herself, and says:*) Here is my hand upon it.

OSWALD. Will you—?

MRS. ALVING. If it should ever be necessary. But it will never be necessary. No, no; it is impossible.

OSWALD. Well, let us hope so. And let us live together as long as we can. Thank you, mother. (*He seats himself in the arm-chair which* MRS. ALVING *has moved to the sofa. Day is breaking. The lamp is still burning on the table.*)

MRS. ALVING (*drawing near cautiously*). Do you feel calm now?

OSWALD. Yes.

MRS. ALVING (*bending over him*). It has been a dreadful fancy of yours, Oswald—nothing but a fancy. All this excitement has been too much for you. But now you shall have a long rest; at home with your mother, my own blessed boy. Everything you point to you shall have, just as when you were a little child.—There now. The crisis is over. You see how easily it passed! Oh, I was sure it would.—And do you see, Oswald, what a lovely day we are going to have? Brilliant sunshine! Now you can really see your home. (*She goes to the table and puts out the lamp. Sunrise. The glacier and the snow-peaks in the background glow in the morning light.*)

OSWALD (*sits in the arm-chair with his back towards the landscape, without moving. Suddenly he says:*) Mother, give me the sun.

MRS. ALVING (*by the table, starts and looks at him*). What do you say?

OSWALD (*repeats, in a dull, toneless voice*). The sun. The sun.

MRS. ALVING (*goes to him*). Oswald, what is the matter with you?

(OSWALD *seems to shrink together in the chair; all his muscles relax; his face is expressionless, his eyes have a glassy stare.*)

MRS. ALVING (*quivering with terror*). What is this? (*Shrieks.*) Oswald! what is the matter with you? (*Falls on her knees beside him and shakes him.*) Oswald! Oswald! Look at me! Don't you know me?

OSWALD (*tonelessly as before*). The sun.—The sun.

MRS. ALVING (*springs up in despair, entwines her hands in her hair and shrieks*). I cannot bear it! (*Whispers, as though petrified.*) I cannot bear it! Never! (*Suddenly.*) Where has he got them? (*Fumbles hastily in his breast.*) Here! (*Shrinks back a few steps and screams:*) No; no; no!—Yes!—No; no! (*She stands a few steps away from him with her hands twisted in her hair, and stares at him in speechless horror.*)

OSWALD (*sits motionless as before and says:*) The sun.—The sun.

GEORGE BERNARD SHAW / 1856–1950

George Bernard Shaw, though Irish by birth, was of English Protestant ancestry and, after a childhood in Dublin, left his native land for London while still a young man. In England he quickly became immersed in the intellectual and literary life of the capital, where he made the beginnings of several careers which were not so much preludes to his dramatist's career as parallels to it. He maintained throughout his long life a remarkable number of interests and supported a great variety of causes apparently diverse, but actually united by their common source in Shaw's militant rationality. He was a vegetarian, abstainer from tobacco and alcohol, reformer of spelling, and socialist.

His literary work began with five novels, of which perhaps two retain any interest today. His political life began with involvement in the Fabian Society, which was, during Shaw's early life, the principal organization of English socialists. With this group he gained experience as a debater and speaker and as a writer of polemical essays. For a time Shaw was a music critic and for a time a drama critic. In these roles he strove to reform the tastes of his contemporaries, in drama particularly by combatting the sentimentality and false hero-worship of an earlier time still persisting into the last decades of the Victorian era. He admired the work of Ibsen, and in his little book of 1891, *The Quintessence of Ibsenism,* he argued the case for a rational reform of human affairs and for the role of modern literature as an inspiration and guide in that enterprise.

Yet in Shaw's career as playwright the propagandist is submerged in the dramatist. While all of the plays are pervaded by a spirit of rationality and a yearning for justice, they do not beat drums for specific causes; Shaw's ridicule of folly and deceit may as readily be turned against the zealot for good causes as against the entrenched reactionary. If Shaw was a direct heir of Ibsen's dramatic legacy, he was his own man as well. Though he shared Ibsen's concern with the effects of social evil and hypocrisy on individual lives, there is little of Ibsen's somber tones in the lighting of Shaw's stage. Ibsen's low-keyed yet intense dialogue is replaced here by a flashing wit which is so uniquely Shaw's that it has come to be called "Shavian." But if there is levity there is little light-mindedness, and Shaw combines with consummate skill the entertaining and the instructive.

Of Shaw's nearly forty plays, a remarkable number seem likely to survive. Among the more impressive are *Candida* (1897), *Caesar and Cleopatra* (1899), *Man and Superman* (1902), *Major Barbara* (1905), *Androcles and the Lion* (1912), *Pygmalion* (1913), *Heartbreak House* (1919), *Back to Methuselah* (1921), and *Saint Joan* (1923). The play offered here is one of a group published in 1898 as *Plays: Pleasant and Unpleasant.* Though a minor work, *The Man of Destiny* (1897) exhibits the characteristic features of Shaw's plays. Its construction and reliance on such time-worn devices as disguise and mistaken identity show an early phase of Shaw's transition from the well-made play of an earlier generation to a skillful though essentially conventional stage craftsmanship of his own. The expanded stage directions foreshadow Shaw's habit of writing long prefaces providing witty dissertations on the problems dramatized in the plays. The dialogue combines a sense of realistic speech with a quite implausible polish of phrasing involving wit, paradox, and an aphoristic tone. And, finally, the attitudes informing the play are quite frankly anti-romantic.

The Man of Destiny

CAST OF CHARACTERS

GIUSEPPE GRANDI, *innkeeper in Tavazzano.*
GENERAL NAPOLEON BONAPARTE.
THE STRANGE LADY
THE LIEUTENANT.

(The twelfth of May, 1796, in north Italy, at Tavazzano, on the road from Lodi to Milan. The afternoon sun is blazing serenely over the plains of Lombardy, treating the Alps with respect and the anthills with indulgence, not incommoded by the basking of the swine and oxen in the villages nor hurt by its cool reception in the churches, but fiercely disdainful of two hordes of mischievous insects which are the French and Austrian armies. Two days before, at Lodi, the Austrians tried to prevent the French from crossing the river by the narrow bridge there; but the French, commanded by a general aged 26, NAPOLEON BONAPARTE, who does not understand the art of war, rushed the fireswept bridge, supported by a tremendous cannonade in which the young general assisted with his own hands. Cannonading is his technical specialty; he has been trained in the artillery under the old régime, and made perfect in the military arts of shirking his duties, swindling the paymaster over travelling expenses, and dignifying war with the noise and smoke of cannon, as depicted in all military portraits. He is, however, an original observer, and has perceived, for the first time since the invention of gunpowder, that a cannon ball, if it strikes a man, will kill him. To a thorough grasp of this remarkable dis-
covery, he adds a highly evolved faculty for physical geography and for the calculation of times and distances. He has prodigious powers of work, and a clear, realistic knowledge of human nature in public affairs, having seen it exhaustively tested in that department during the French Revolution. He is imaginative without illusions, and creative without religion, loyalty, patriotism or any of the common ideals. Not that he is incapable of these ideals: on the contrary, he has swallowed them all in his boyhood, and now, having a keen dramatic faculty, is extremely clever at playing upon them by the arts of the actor and stage manager. Withal, he is no spoiled child. Poverty, ill-luck, the shifts of impecunious shabby-gentility, repeated failure as a would-be author, humiliation as a rebuffed time server, reproof and punishment as an incompetent and dishonest officer, an escape from dismissal from the service so narrow that if the emigration of the nobles had not raised the value of even the most rascally lieutenant to the famine price of a general he would have been swept contemptuously from the army: these trials have ground the conceit out of him, and forced him to be self-sufficient and to understand that to such men as he is the world will give nothing that he cannot take from it by force. In this the world is not free from cowardice and folly; for NAPOLEON, as a merciless cannonader of political rubbish, is making himself useful: indeed, it is even now impossible to live in England without sometimes feeling how much that country lost in not being conquered by him as well as by Julius Caesar.

However, on this May afternoon in 1796, it is early days with him. He is only 26, and has but recently become a general, partly by using his wife to seduce the Directory (then governing France), partly by the scarcity of officers caused by the emigration as aforesaid; partly by his faculty of knowing a country, with all its roads, rivers, hills and valleys, as he knows the palm of his hand; and largely by that new faith of his in the efficacy of firing cannons at people. His army is, as to discipline, in a state which has so greatly shocked some modern writers before whom the following story has been enacted, that they, impressed with the later glory of "L'Empereur," have altogether refused to credit it. But NAPOLEON *is not "L'Empereur" yet: he has only just been dubbed "Le Petit Caporal," and is in the stage of gaining influence over his men by displays of pluck. He is not in a position to force his will on them, in orthodox military fashion, by the cat o' nine tails. The French Revolution, which has escaped suppression solely through the monarchy's habit of being at least four years in arrears with its soldiers in the matter of pay, has substituted for that habit, as far as possible, the habit of not paying at all, except in promises and patriotic flatteries which are not compatible with martial law of the Prussian type.* NAPOLEON *has therefore approached the Alps in command of men without money, in rags, and consequently indisposed to stand much discipline, especially from upstart generals. This circumstance, which would have embarrassed an idealist soldier, has been worth a thousand cannon to* NAPOLEON. *He has said to his army, "You have patriotism and courage; but you have no money, no clothes, and deplorably indifferent food. In Italy there are all these things, and glory as well, to be gained by a devoted army led by a general who regards loot as the natural right of the*

soldier. I am such a general. En avant, mes enfants!" The result has entirely justified him. The army conquers Italy as the locusts conquered Cyprus. They fight all day and march all night, covering impossible distances and appearing in incredible places, not because every soldier carries a field marshal's baton in his knapsack, but because he hopes to carry at least half a dozen silver forks there next day.

It must be understood, by the way, that the French army does not make war on the Italians. It is there to rescue them from the tyranny of their Austrian conquerors, and confer republican institutions on them; so that in incidentally looting them, it merely makes free with the property of its friends, who ought to be grateful to it, and perhaps would be if ingratitude were not the proverbial failing of their country. The Austrians, whom it fights, are a thoroughly respectable regular army, well disciplined, commanded by gentlemen trained and versed in the art of war: at the head of them Beaulieu, practising the classic art of war under orders from Vienna, and getting horribly beaten by NAPOLEON, *who acts on his own responsibility in defiance of professional precedents or orders from Paris. Even when the Austrians win a battle, all that is necessary is to wait until their routine obliges them to return to their quarters for afternoon tea, so to speak, and win it back again from them: a course pursued later on with brilliant success at Marengo. On the whole, with his foe handicapped by Austrian statesmanship, classic generalship, and the exigencies of the aristocratic social structure of Viennese society,* NAPOLEON *finds it possible to be irresistible without working heroic miracles. The world, however, likes miracles and heroes, and is quite incapable of conceiving the action of such forces as academic militarism or Viennese drawing-roomism. Hence it has already begun to manufacture "L'Em-*

pereur," and thus to make it difficult for the romanticists of a hundred years later to credit the little scene now in question at Tavazzano as aforesaid.

The best quarters at Tavazzano are at a little inn, the first house reached by travellers passing through the place from Milan to Lodi. It stands in a vineyard; and its principal room, a pleasant refuge from the summer heat, is open so widely at the back to this vineyard that it is almost a large veranda. The bolder children, much excited by the alarums and excursions of the past few days, and by an irruption of French troops at six o'clock, know that the French commander has quartered himself in this room, and are divided between a craving to peep in the front windows, and a mortal terror of the sentinel, a young gentleman-soldier, who, having no natural moustache, has had a most ferocious one painted on his face with boot blacking by his sergeant. As his heavy uniform, like all the uniforms of that day, is designed for parade without the least reference to his health or comfort, he perspires profusely in the sun; and his painted moustache has run in little streaks down his chin and round his neck except where it has dried in stiff japanned flakes, and had its sweeping outline chipped off in grotesque little bays and headlands, making him unspeakably ridiculous in the eye of History a hundred years later, but monstrous and horrible to the contemporary north Italian infant, to whom nothing would seem more natural than that he should relieve the monotony of his guard by pitchforking a stray child up on his bayonet, and eating it uncooked. Nevertheless one girl of bad character, in whom an instinct of privilege with soldiers is already dawning, does peep in at the safest window for a moment, before a glance and a clink from the sentinel sends her flying. Most of what she sees she has seen before: the vineyard at the

back, with the old winepress and a cart among the vines; the door close down on her right leading to the inn entry; the landlord's best sideboard, now in full action for dinner, further back on the same side; the fireplace on the other side, with a couch near it, and another door, leading to the inner rooms, between it and the vineyard; and the table in the middle with its repast of Milanese risotto, cheese, grapes, bread, olives, and a big wickered flask of red wine.

The landlord, GIUSEPPE GRANDI, is also no novelty. He is a swarthy, vivacious, shrewdly cheerful, black-curled, bullet-headed, grinning little man of 40. Naturally an excellent host, he is in quite special spirits this evening at his good fortune in having the French commander as his guest to protect him against the license of the troops, and actually sports a pair of gold earrings which he would otherwise have hidden carefully under the winepress with his little equipment of silver plate.

NAPOLEON, sitting facing her on the further side of the table, and NAPOLEON'S hat, sword and riding whip lying on the couch, she sees for the first time. He is working hard, partly at his meal, which he has discovered how to dispatch, by attacking all the courses simultaneously, in ten minutes (this practice is the beginning of his downfall), and partly at a map which he is correcting from memory, occasionally marking the position of the forces by taking a grapeskin from his mouth and planting it on the map with his thumb like a wafer. He has a supply of writing materials before him mixed up in disorder with the dishes and cruets; and his long hair gets sometimes into the risotto gravy and sometimes into the ink.)

GIUSEPPE.   Will your excellency—
NAPOLEON (*intent on his map, but cramming himself mechanically with his left hand*).   Don't talk. I'm busy.

GIUS. (*with perfect goodhumor*). Excellency: I obey.

NAP. Some red ink.

GIUS. Alas! excellency, there is none.

NAP. (*with Corsican facetiousness*). Kill something and bring me its blood.

GIUS. (*grinning*). There is nothing but your excellency's horse, the sentinel, the lady upstairs, and my wife.

NAP. Kill your wife.

GIUS. Willingly, your excellency; but unhappily I am not strong enough. She would kill me.

NAP. That will do equally well.

GIUS. Your excellency does me too much honor. (*Stretching his hand toward the flask.*) Perhaps some wine will answer your excellency's purpose.

NAP. (*hastily protecting the flask, and becoming quite serious*). Wine! No: that would be waste. You are all the same: waste! waste! waste! (*He marks the map with gravy, using his fork as a pen.*) Clear away. (*He finishes his wine; pushes back his chair; and uses his napkin, stretching his legs and leaning back, but still frowning and thinking.*)

GIUS. (*clearing the table and removing the things to a tray on the sideboard*). Every man to his trade, excellency. We innkeepers have plenty of cheap wine: we think nothing of spilling it. You great generals have plenty of cheap blood: you think nothing of spilling it. Is it not so, excellency?

NAP. Blood costs nothing: wine costs money. (*He rises and goes to the fireplace.*)

GIUS. They say you are careful of everything except human life, excellency.

NAP. Human life, my friend, is the only thing that takes care of itself. (*He throws himself at his ease on the couch.*)

GIUS. (*admiring him*). Ah, excellency, what fools we all are beside you! If I could only find out the secret of your success!

NAP. You would make yourself Emperor of Italy, eh?

GIUS. Too troublesome, excellency:

I leave all that to you. Besides, what would become of my inn if I were Emperor? See how you enjoy looking on at me whilst I keep the inn for you and wait on you! Well, I shall enjoy looking on at you whilst you become Emperor of Europe, and govern the country for me. (*Whilst he chatters, he takes the cloth off without removing the map and inkstand, and takes the corners in his hands and the middle of the edge in his mouth, to fold it up.*)

NAP. Emperor of Europe, eh? Why only Europe?

GIUS. Why, indeed? Emperor of the world, excellency! Why not? (*He folds and rolls up the cloth, emphasizing his phrases by the steps of the process.*) One man is like another (*Fold.*): one country is like another (*Fold.*): one battle is like another. (*At the last fold, he slaps the cloth on the table and deftly rolls it up, adding, by way of peroration.*) Conquer one: conquer all. (*He takes the cloth to the sideboard, and puts it in a drawer.*)

NAP. And govern for all; fight for all; be everybody's servant under cover of being everybody's master. Giuseppe.

GIUS. (*at the sideboard*). Excellency.

NAP. I forbid you to talk to me about myself.

GIUS. (*coming to the foot of the couch*). Pardon. Your excellency is so unlike other great men. It is the subject they like best.

NAP. Well, talk to me about the subject they like next best, whatever that may be.

GIUS. (*unabashed*). Willingly, your excellency. Has your excellency by any chance caught a glimpse of the lady upstairs? (*NAPOLEON promptly sits up and looks at him with an interest which entirely justifies the implied epigram.*)

NAP. How old is she?

GIUS. The right age, excellency.

NAP. Do you mean seventeen or thirty?

GIUS. Thirty, excellency.

NAP. Goodlooking?

GIUS. I cannot see with your excellency's eyes: every man must judge that for himself. In my opinion, excellency, a fine figure of a lady. (*Slyly.*) Shall I lay the table for her collation here?

NAP. (*brusquely, rising*). No: lay nothing here until the officer for whom I am waiting comes back. (*He looks at his watch, and takes to walking to and fro between the fireplace and the vineyard.*)

GIUS. (*with conviction*). Excellency: believe me, he has been captured by the accursed Austrians. He dare not keep you waiting if he were at liberty.

NAP. (*turning at the edge of the shadow of the veranda*). Giuseppe: if that turns out to be true, it will put me into such a temper that nothing short of hanging you and your whole household, including the lady upstairs, will satisfy me.

GIUS. We are all cheerfully at your excellency's disposal, except the lady. I cannot answer for her; but no lady could resist you, General.

NAP. (*sourly, resuming his march*). Hm! You will never be hanged. There is no satisfaction in hanging a man who does not object to it.

GIUS. (*sympathetically*). Not the least in the world, excellency: is there? (NAPOLEON *again looks at his watch, evidently growing anxious.*) Ah, one can see that you are a great man, General: you know how to wait. If it were a corporal now, or a sub-lieutenant, at the end of three minutes he would be swearing, fuming, threatening, pulling the house about our ears.

NAP. Giuseppe: your flatteries are insufferable. Go and talk outside. (*He sits down again at the table, with his jaws in his hands, and his elbows propped on the map, poring over it with a troubled expression.*)

GIUS. Willingly, your excellency. You shall not be disturbed. (*He takes up the tray and prepares to withdraw.*)

NAP. The moment he comes back, send him to me.

GIUS. Instantaneously, your excellency.

A LADY'S VOICE (*calling from some distant part of the inn*). Giusep-pe! (*The voice is very musical, and the two final notes make an ascending interval.*)

NAP. (*startled*). What's that? What's that?

GIUS. (*resting the end of his tray on the table and leaning over to speak the more confidentially*). The lady, excellency.

NAP. (*absently*). Yes. What lady? Whose lady?

GIUS. The strange lady, excellency.

NAP. What strange lady?

GIUS. (*with a shrug*). Who knows? She arrived here half an hour before you in a hired carriage belonging to the Golden Eagle at Borghetto. Actually by herself, excellency. No servants. A dressing bag and a trunk: that is all. The postillion says she left a horse—a charger, with military trappings, at the Golden Eagle.

NAP. A woman with a charger! That's extraordinary.

THE LADY'S VOICE (*the two final notes now making a peremptory descending interval*). Giuseppe!

NAP. (*rising to listen*). That's an interesting voice.

GIUS. (*pleadingly*). Let me go, excellency. (*Calling.*) Coming, lady, coming. (*He makes for the inner door.*)

NAP. (*arresting him with a strong hand on his shoulder*). Stop. Let her come.

VOICE. Giuseppe!! (*Impatiently.*)

GIUS. (*pleadingly*). Let me go, excellency. It is my point of honor as an innkeeper to come when I am called. I appeal to you as a soldier.

A MAN'S VOICE (*outside, at the inn door, shouting*). Here, someone. Hollo! Landlord. Where are you? (*Somebody raps vigorously with a whip handle on a bench in the passage.*)

NAP. (*suddenly becoming the com-

manding officer again and throwing GIUSEPPE *off*). There he is at last. (*Pointing to the inner door.*) Go. Attend to your business: the lady is calling you. (*He goes to the fireplace and stands with his back to it with a determined military air.*)

GIUS. (*with bated breath, snatching up his tray*). Certainly, excellency. (*He hurries out by the inner door.*)

THE MAN'S VOICE (*impatiently*). Are you all asleep here?

(*The door opposite the fireplace is kicked rudely open; and a dusty sub-lieutenant bursts into the room. He is a chuckleheaded young man of 24, with the fair, delicate, clear skin of a man of rank, and a self-assurance on that ground which the French Revolution has failed to shake in the smallest degree. He has a thick silly lip, an eager credulous eye, an obstinate nose, and a loud confident voice. A young man without fear, without reverence, without imagination, without sense, hopelessly insusceptible to the Napoleonic or any other idea, stupendously egotistical, eminently qualified to rush in where angels fear to tread, yet of a vigorous babbling vitality which bustles him into the thick of things. He is just now boiling with vexation, attributable by a superficial observer to his impatience at not being promptly attended to by the staff of the inn, but in which a more discerning eye can perceive a certain moral depth, indicating a more permanent and momentous grievance. On seeing* NAPOLEON, *he is sufficiently taken aback to check himself and salute; but he does not betray by his manner any of that prophetic consciousness of Marengo and Austerlitz, Waterloo and St. Helena, or the Napoleonic pictures of Delaroche and Meissonier, which modern culture will instinctively expect from him.*)

NAP. (*sharply*). Well, sir, here you are at last. Your instructions were that I should arrive here at six, and that I

was to find you waiting for me with my mail from Paris and with despatches. It is now twenty minutes to eight. You were sent on this service as a hard rider with the fastest horse in the camp. You arrive a hundred minutes late, on foot. Where is your horse!

LIEUTENANT (*moodily pulling off his gloves and dashing them with his cap and whip on the table*). Ah! where indeed? That's just what I should like to know, General. (*With emotion.*) You don't know how fond I was of that horse.

NAP. (*angrily sarcastic*). Indeed! (*With sudden misgiving.*) Where are the letters and despatches?

LIEUT. (*importantly, rather pleased than otherwise at having some remarkable news*). I don't know.

NAP. (*unable to believe his ears*). You don't know!

LIEUT. No more than you do, General. Now I suppose I shall be court-martialled. Well, I don't mind being court-martialled; but (*with solemn determination*) I tell you, General, If ever I catch that innocent looking youth, I'll spoil his beauty, the slimy little liar! I'll make a picture of him. I'll——

NAP. (*advancing from the hearth to the table*). What innocent looking youth? Pull yourself together, sir, will you; and give an account of yourself.

LIEUT. (*facing him at the opposite side of the table, leaning on it with his fists*). Oh, I'm all right, General: I'm perfectly ready to give an account of myself. I shall make the court-martial thoroughly understand that the fault was not mine. Advantage has been taken of the better side of my nature; and I'm not ashamed of it. But with all respect to you as my commanding officer, General, I say again that if ever I set eyes on that son of Satan, I'll——

NAP. (*angrily*). So you said before.

LIEUT. (*drawing himself upright*). I say it again. Just wait until I catch him. Just wait: that's all. (*He folds his arms* resolutely, and breathes hard, with compressed lips.)

NAP. I am waiting, sir—for your explanation.

LIEUT. (confidently). You'll change your tone, General, when you hear what has happened to me.

NAP. Nothing has happened to you, sir: you are alive and not disabled. Where are the papers entrusted to you?

LIEUT. Nothing! Nothing! Oho! Well, we'll see. (Posing himself to overwhelm NAPOLEON with his news.) He swore eternal brotherhood with me. Was that nothing? He said my eyes reminded him of his sister's eyes. Was that nothing? He cried—actually cried—over the story of my separation from Angelica. Was that nothing? He paid for both bottles of wine, though he only ate bread and grapes himself. Perhaps you call that nothing! He gave me his pistols and his horse and his despatches—most important despatches—and let me go away with them. (Triumphantly, seeing that he has reduced NAPOLEON to blank stupefaction.) Was that nothing?

NAP. (enfeebled by astonishment). What did he do that for?

LIEUT. (as if the reason were obvious). To shew his confidence in me. (NAPOLEON'S jaw does not exactly drop; but its hinges become nerveless. The LIEUTENANT proceeds with honest indignation.) And I was worthy of his confidence: I brought them all back honorably. But would you believe it?—when I trusted him with my pistols, and my horse, and my despatches—

NAP. (enraged). What the devil did you do that for?

LIEUT. Why, to shew my confidence in him, of course. And he betrayed it—abused it—never came back. The thief! the swindler! the heartless, treacherous little blackguard! You call that nothing, I suppose. But look here, General: (again resorting to the table with his fist for greater emphasis) you may put up with this outrage from the Austrians if you like; but speaking for myself personally, I tell you that if ever I catch—

NAP. (turning on his heel in disgust and irritably resuming his march to and fro). Yes: you have said that more than once already.

LIEUT. (excitedly). More than once! I'll say it fifty times; and what's more, I'll do it. You'll see, General. I'll shew my confidence in him, so I will. I'll—

NAP. Yes, yes, sir: no doubt you will. What kind of man was he?

LIEUT. Well, I should think you ought to be able to tell from his conduct the sort of man he was.

NAP. Psh! What was he like?

LIEUT. Like! He's like—well, you ought to have just seen the fellow: that will give you a notion of what he was like. He won't be like it five minutes after I catch him; for I tell you that if ever—

NAP. (shouting furiously for the innkeeper). Giuseppe! (To the LIEUTENANT, out of all patience.) Hold your tongue, sir, if you can.

LIEUT. I warn you it's no use to try to put the blame on me. (Plaintively.) How was I to know the sort of fellow he was? (He takes a chair from between the sideboard and the outer door; places it near the table; and sits down.) If you only knew how hungry and tired I am, you'd have more consideration.

GIUS. (returning). What is it, excellency?

NAP. (struggling with his temper). Take this—this officer. Feed him; and put him to bed, if necessary. When he is in his right mind again, find out what has happened to him and bring me word. (To the LIEUTENANT.) Consider yourself under arrest, sir.

LIEUT. (with sulky stiffness). I was prepared for that. It takes a gentleman to understand a gentleman. (He throws his sword on the table. GIUSEPPE takes it up and politely offers it to NAPOLEON, *who throws it violently on the couch.*)

GIUS. (*with sympathetic concern*). Have you been attacked by the Austrians, lieutenant? Dear, dear, dear!

LIEUT. (*contemptuously*). Attacked! I could have broken his back between my finger and thumb. I wish I had, now. No: it was by appealing to the better side of my nature: that's what I can't get over. He said he'd never met a man he liked so much as me. He put his handkerchief round my neck because a gnat bit me, and my stock was chafing it. Look! (*He pulls a handkerchief from his stock. GIUSEPPE takes it and examines it.*)

GIUS. (*to NAPOLEON*). A lady's handkerchief, excellency. (*He smells it.*) Perfumed!

NAP. Eh? (*He takes it and looks at it attentively.*) Hm! (*He smells it.*) Ha! (*He walks thoughtfully across the room, looking at the handkerchief, which he finally sticks in the breast of his coat.*)

LIEUT. Good enough for him, anyhow. I noticed that he had a woman's hands when he touched my neck, with his coaxing, fawning ways, the mean, effeminate little hound. (*Lowering his voice with thrilling intensity.*) But mark my words, General. If ever—

THE LADY'S VOICE (*outside, as before*). Giuseppe!

LIEUT. (*petrified*). What was that?

GIUS. Only a lady upstairs, lieutenant, calling me.

LIEUT. Lady!

VOICE. Giuseppe, Giuseppe: where are you?

LIEUT. (*murderously*). Give me that sword. (*He strides to the couch; snatches the sword; and draws it.*)

GIUS. (*Rushing forward and seizing his right arm.*) What are you thinking of, lieutenant? It's a lady: don't you hear that it's a woman's voice?

LIEUT. It's his voice, I tell you. Let me go.

(*He breaks away, and rushes to the inner door. It opens in his face; and the STRANGE LADY steps in. She is a very attractive lady, tall and extraordinarily graceful, with a delicately intelligent, apprehensive, questioning face—perception in the brow, sensitiveness in the nostrils, character in the chin: all keen, refined, and original. She is very feminine, but by no means weak: the lithe, tender figure is hung on a strong frame: the hands and feet, neck and shoulders, are no fragile ornaments, but of full size in proportion to her stature, which considerably exceeds that of NAPOLEON and the innkeeper, and leaves her at no disadvantage with the lieutenant. Only her elegance and radiant charm keep the secret of her size and strength. She is not, judging by her dress, an admirer of the latest fashions of the Directory; or perhaps she uses up her old dresses for travelling. At all events she wears no jacket with extravagant lapels, no Greco-Tallien sham chiton, nothing, indeed, that the Princesse de Lamballe might not have worn. Her dress of flowered silk is long waisted, with a Watteau pleat behind, but with the paniers reduced to mere rudiments, as she is too tall for them. It is cut low in the neck, where it is eked out by a creamy fichu. She is fair, with golden brown hair and grey eyes.*

She enters with the self-possession of a woman accustomed to the privileges of rank and beauty. The innkeeper, who has excellent natural manners, is highly appreciative of her. NAPOLEON, on whom her eyes first fall, is instantly smitten self-conscious. His color deepens: he becomes stiffer and less at ease than before. She perceives this instantly, and, not to embarrass him, turns in an infinitely well bred manner to pay the respect of a glance to the other gentleman, who is staring at her dress, as at the earth's final masterpiece of treacherous dissimulation, with feelings altogether inexpressible and indescribable. As she looks at him, she becomes deadly pale. There is no mistaking her expression: a revelation of some fatal error, utterly unexpected, has suddenly appalled her in the midst of tranquillity, security and victory. The next moment a wave of color rushes up from beneath the creamy fichu and drowns her whole face. One can see that she is blushing all over her body. Even the LIEUTENANT, *ordinarily incapable of observation, and just now lost in the tumult of his wrath, can see a thing when it is painted red for him. Interpreting the blush as the involuntary confession of black deceit confronted with its victim, he points to it with a loud crow of retributive triumph, and then, seizing her by the wrist, pulls her past him into the room as he claps the door to, and plants himself with his back to it.)*

LIEUT. So I've got you, my lad. So you've disguised yourself, have you? (*In a voice of thunder.*) Take off that skirt.

GIUS. (*remonstrating*). Oh, lieutenant!

LADY (*affrighted, but highly indignant at his having dared to touch her*). Gentlemen: I appeal to you. Giuseppe. (*Making a movement as if to run to* GIUSEPPE.)

LIEUT. (*interposing, sword in hand*). No you don't.

LADY (*taking refuge with* NAPOLEON). Oh, sir, you are an officer—a general. You will protect me, will you not?

LIEUT. Never you mind him, General. Leave me to deal with him.

NAP. With him! With whom, sir? Why do you treat this lady in such a fashion?

LIEUT. Lady! He's a man! the man I shewed my confidence in. (*Advancing threateningly.*) Here you—

LADY (*running behind* NAPOLEON *and in her agitation embracing the arm which he instinctively extends before her as a fortification*). Oh, thank you, General. Keep him away.

NAP. Nonsense, sir. This is certainly a lady (*she suddenly drops his arm and blushes again*); and you are under arrest. Put down your sword, sir, instantly.

LIEUT. General: I tell you he's an Austrian spy. He passed himself off on me as one of General Masséna's staff this afternoon; and now he's passing himself off on you as a woman. Am I to believe my own eyes or not?

LADY. General: it must be my brother. He is on General Masséna's staff. He is very like me.

LIEUT. (*his mind giving way*). Do you mean to say that you're not your brother, but your sister?—the sister who was so like me?—who had my beautiful blue eyes? It was a lie: your eyes are not like mine: they're exactly like your own. What perfidy!

NAP. Lieutenant: will you obey my orders and leave the room, since you are convinced at last that this is no gentleman?

LIEUT. Gentleman! I should think not. No gentleman would have abused my confi-

NAP. (*out of all patience*). Enough, sir, enough. Will you leave the room. I order you to leave the room.

LADY. Oh, pray let me go instead.

NAP. (*drily*). Excuse me, madame. With all respect to your brother, I do not yet understand what an officer on General Masséna's staff wants with my letters. I have some questions to put to you.

GIUS. (*discreetly*). Come, lieutenant. (*He opens the door.*)

LIEUT. I'm off. General: take warning by me: be on your guard against the better side of your nature. (*To the* LADY.) Madame: my apologies. I thought you were the same person, only of the opposite sex; and that naturally misled me.

LADY (*sweetly*). It was not your fault, was it? I'm so glad you're not angry with me any longer, lieutenant. (*She offers her hand.*)

LIEUT. (*bending gallantly to kiss it*). Oh, madam, not the lea—(*Checking himself and looking at it.*) You have your brother's hand. And the same sort of ring.

LADY (*sweetly*). We are twins.

LIEUT. That accounts for it. (*He kisses her hand.*) A thousand pardons. I didn't mind about the despatches at all: that's more the General's affair than mine: it was the abuse of my confidence through the better side of my nature. (*Taking his cap, gloves, and whip from the table and going.*) You'll excuse my leaving you, General, I hope. Very sorry, I'm sure. (*He talks himself out of the room.* GIUSEPPE *follows him and shuts the door.*)

NAP. (*looking after them with concentrated irritation*). Idiot! (*The* STRANGE LADY *smiles sympathetically. He comes frowning down the room between the table and the fireplace, all his awkwardness gone now that he is alone with her.*)

LADY. How can I thank you, General, for your protection?

NAP. (*turning on her suddenly*). My despatches: come! (*He puts out his hand for them.*)

LADY. General! (*She involuntarily puts her hands on her fichu as if to protect something there.*)

NAP. You tricked that blockhead out of them. You disguised yourself as a man. I want my despatches. They are there in the bosom of your dress, under your hands.

LADY (*quickly removing her hands*). Oh, how unkindly you are speaking to me! (*She takes her handkerchief from her fichu.*) You frighten me. (*She touches her eyes as if to wipe away a tear.*)

NAP. I see you don't know me, madam, or you would save yourself the trouble of pretending to cry.

LADY (*producing an effect of smiling through her tears*). Yes, I do know

you. You are the famous General Buonaparte. (*She gives the name a marked Italian pronunciation— Bwaw-na-parr-te.*)

NAP. (*angrily, with the French pronunciation*). Bonaparte, madame, Bonaparte. The papers, if you please.

LADY. But I assure you—(*He snatches the handkerchief rudely from her.*) General! (*Indignantly.*)

NAP. (*taking the other handkerchief from his breast*). You were good enough to lend one of your handkerchiefs to my lieutenant when you robbed him. (*He looks at the two handkerchiefs.*) They match one another. (*He. smells them.*) The same scent. (*He flings them down on the table.*) I am waiting for the despatches. I shall take them, if necessary, with as little ceremony as the handkerchief. (*This historical incident was used eighty years later, by M. Victorien Sardou, in his drama entitled "Dora."*)

LADY (*in dignified reproof*). General: do you threaten women?

NAP. (*bluntly*). Yes.

LADY (*disconcerted, trying to gain time*). But I don't understand. I—

NAP. You understand perfectly. You came here because your Austrian employers calculated that I was six leagues away. I am always to be found where my enemies don't expect me. You have walked into the lion's den. Come: you are a brave woman. Be a sensible one: I have no time to waste. The papers. (*He advances a step ominously.*)

LADY (*breaking down in the childish rage of impotence, and throwing herself in tears on the chair left beside the table by the* LIEUTENANT.) I brave! How little you know! I have spent the day in an agony of fear. I have a pain here from the tightening of my heart at every suspicious look, every threatening movement. Do you think every one is as brave as you? Oh, why will not you brave people do the brave things? Why do you leave them to us, who have no courage at all? I'm not brave: I shrink from violence: danger makes me miserable.

NAP. (*interested*). Then why have you thrust yourself into danger?

LADY. Because there is no other way: I can trust nobody else. And now it is all useless—all because of you, who have no fear, because you have no heart, no feeling, no—(*She breaks off, and throws herself on her knees.*) Ah, General, let me go: let me go without asking any questions. You shall have your despatches and letters: I swear it.

NAP. (*holding out his hand*). Yes: I am waiting for them. (*She gasps, daunted by his ruthless promptitude into despair of moving him by cajolery; but as she looks up perplexedly at him, it is plain that she is racking her brains for some device to outwit him. He meets her regard inflexibly.*)

LADY (*rising at last with a quiet little sigh*). I will get them for you. They are in my room. (*She turns to the door.*)

NAP. I shall accompany you, madame.

LADY (*drawing herself up with a noble air of offended delicacy*). I cannot permit you, General, to enter my chamber.

NAP. Then you shall stay here, madame, whilst I have your chamber searched for my papers.

LADY (*spitefully, openly giving up her plan*). You may save yourself the trouble. They are not there.

NAP. No: I have already told you where they are. (*Pointing to her breast.*)

LADY (*with pretty piteousness*). General: I only want to keep one little private letter. Only one. Let me have it.

NAP. (*cold and stern*). Is that a reasonable demand, madam?

LADY (*encouraged by his not refusing point blank*). No; but that is why you must grant it. Are your own demands reasonable? thousands of lives for the sake of your victories, your ambitions, your destiny! And what I ask is such a little thing. And I am only a weak woman, and you are a brave man. (*She looks at him with her eyes full of tender pleading and is about to kneel to him again.*)

NAP. (*brusquely*). Get up, get up. (*He turns moodily away and takes a turn across the room, pausing for a moment to say, over his shoulder.*) You're talking nonsense; and you know it. (*She gets up and sits down in almost listless despair on the couch. When he turns and sees her there, he feels that his victory is complete, and that he may now indulge in a little play with his victim. He comes back and sits beside her. She looks alarmed and moves a little away from him; but a ray of rallying hope beams from her eye. He begins like a man enjoying some secret joke.*) How do you know I am a brave man?

LADY (*amazed*). You! General Buonaparte. (*Italian pronunciation.*)

NAP. Yes, I, General Bonaparte. (*Emphasizing the French pronunciation.*)

LADY. Oh, how can you ask such a question? you! who stood only two days ago at the bridge at Lodi, with the air full of death, fighting a duel with cannons across the river! (*Shuddering.*) Oh, you do brave things.

NAP. So do you.

LADY. I! (*With a sudden odd thought.*) Oh! Are you a coward?

NAP. (*Laughing grimly and pinching her cheek.*) That is the one question you must never ask a soldier. The sergeant asks after the recruit's height, his age, his wind, his limb, but never after his courage. (*He gets up and walks about with his hands behind him and his head bowed, chuckling to himself.*)

LADY (*as if she had found it no laughing matter*). Ah, you can laugh at fear. Then you don't know what fear is.

NAP. (*Coming behind the couch*).

Tell me this. Suppose you could have got that letter by coming to me over the bridge at Lodi the day before yesterday! Suppose there had been no other way, and that this was a sure way—if only you escaped the cannon! (*She shudders and covers her eyes for a moment with her hands.*) Would you have been afraid?

LADY. Oh, horribly afraid, agonizingly afraid. (*She presses her hands on her heart.*) It hurts only to imagine it.

NAP. (*inflexibly*). Would you have come for the despatches?

LADY (*overcome by the imagined horror*). Don't ask me. I must have come.

NAP. Why?

LADY. Because I must. Because there would have been no other way.

NAP. (*with conviction*). Because you would have wanted my letter enough to bear your fear. There is only one universal passion: fear. Of all the thousand qualities a man may have, the only one you will find as certainly in the youngest drummer boy in my army as in me, is fear. It is fear that makes men fight: it is indifference that makes them run away: fear is the mainspring of war. Fear!—I know fear well, better than you, better than any woman. I once saw a regiment of good Swiss soldiers massacred by a mob in Paris because I was afraid to interfere: I felt myself a coward to the tips of my toes as I looked on at it. Seven months ago I revenged my shame by pounding that mob to death with cannon balls. Well, what of that? Has fear ever held a man back from anything he really wanted—or a woman either? Never. Come with me; and I will shew you twenty thousand cowards who will risk death every day for the price of a glass of brandy. And do you think there are no women in the army, braver than the men, because their lives are worth less? Psha! I think nothing of your fear or your bravery. If you had had to come across to me at Lodi, you

would not have been afraid; once on the bridge, every other feeling would have gone down before the necessity— the necessity—for making your way to my side and getting what you wanted.

And now, suppose you had done all this—suppose you had come safely out with that letter in your hand, knowing that when the hour came, your fear had tightened, not your heart, but your grip of your own purpose—that it had ceased to be fear, and had become strength, penetration, vigilance, iron resolution— how would you answer then if you were asked whether you were a coward?

LADY (*rising*). Ah, you are a hero, a real hero.

NAP. Pooh! there's no such thing as a real hero. (*He strolls down the room, making light of her enthusiasm, but by no means displeased with himself for having evoked it.*)

LADY. Ah, yes, there is. There is a difference between what you call my bravery and yours. You wanted to win the battle of Lodi for yourself and not for anyone else, didn't you?

NAP. Of course. (*Suddenly recollecting himself.*) Stop: no. (*He pulls himself piously together, and says, like a man conducting a religious service.*) I am only the servant of the French republic, following humbly in the footsteps of the heroes of classical antiquity. I win battles for humanity—for my country, not for myself.

LADY (*disappointed*). Oh, then you are only a womanish hero, after all. (*She sits down again, all her enthusiasm gone, her elbow on the end of the couch, and her cheek propped on her hand.*)

NAP. (*greatly astonished*). Womanish!

LADY (*listlessly*). Yes, like me. (*With deep melancholy.*) Do you think that if I only wanted those despatches for myself, I dare venture into a battle for them? No: if that were all, I should not have the courage to ask to see you at your hotel, even. My courage is mere slavishness: it is of no use to me for my own purpose. It is only through love, through pity, through the instinct to save and protect someone else, that I can do the things that terrify me.

NAP. (*contemptuously*). Pshaw! (*He turns slightly away from her.*)

LADY. Aha! now you see that I'm not really brave. (*Relapsing into petulant listlessness.*) But what right have you to despise me if you only win your battles for others? for your country! through patriotism! That is what I call woman-ish: it is so like a Frenchman!

NAP. (*furiously*). I am no French-man.

LADY (*innocently*). I thought you said you won the battle of Lodi for your country, General Bu—shall I pronounce it in Italian or French?

NAP. You are presuming on my patience, madam. I was born a French subject, but not in France.

LADY (*folding her arms on the end of the couch, and leaning on them with a marked access of interest in him*). You were not born a subject at all, I think.

NAP. (*greatly pleased, starting on a fresh march*). Eh? Eh? You think not.

LADY. I am sure of it.

NAP. Well, well, perhaps not. (*The self-complacency of his assent catches his own ear. He stops short, reddening. Then, composing himself into a solemn attitude, modelled on the heroes of classi-cal antiquity, he takes a high moral tone.*) But we must not live for our-selves alone, little one. Never forget that we should always think of others, and work for others, and lead and govern them for their own good. Self-sacrifice is the foundation of all true nobility of character.

LADY (*again relaxing her attitude with a sigh*). Ah, it is easy to see that you have never tried it, General.

NAP. (*indignantly, forgetting all about Brutus and Scipio*). What do you mean by that speech, madam?

LADY. Haven't you noticed that people always exaggerate the value of the things they haven't got? The poor think they only need riches to be quite happy and good. Everybody worships truth, purity, unselfishness, for the same reason—because they have no experience of them. Oh, if they only knew!

NAP. (*with angry derision*). If they only knew! Pray, do you know?

LADY (*with her arms stretched down and her hands clasped on her knees, looking straight before her*). Yes. I had the misfortune to be born good. (*Glancing up at him for a moment.*) And it is a misfortune, I can tell you, General. I really am truthful and un-selfish and all the rest of it; and it's nothing but cowardice; want of char-acter; want of being really, strongly, positively oneself.

NAP. Ha? (*Turning to her quickly with a flash of strong interest.*)

LADY (*earnestly, with rising enthusi-asm*). What is the secret of your power? Only that you believe in your-self. You can fight and conquer for your-self and for nobody else. You are not afraid of your own destiny. You teach us what we all might be if we had the will and courage; and that (*suddenly sinking on her knees before him*) is why we all begin to worship you. (*She kisses his hands.*)

NAP. (*embarrassed*). Tut, tut! Pray rise, madam.

LADY. Do not refuse my homage: it's your right. You will be emperor of France—

NAP. (*hurriedly*). Take care. Trea-son!

LADY (*insisting*). Yes, emperor of France; then of Europe; perhaps of the world. I am only the first subject to swear allegiance. (*Again kissing his hand.*) My Emperor!

NAP. (*overcome, raising her*). Pray, pray. No, no, little one: this is folly. Come: be calm, be calm. (*Petting her.*) There, there, my girl.

LADY (*struggling with happy tears*). Yes, I know it is an impertinence in me to tell you what you must know far better than I do. But you are not angry with me, are you?

NAP. Angry! No, no: not a bit, not a bit. Come: you are a very clever and sensible and interesting little woman. (*He pats her on the cheek.*) Shall we be friends?

LADY (*enraptured*). Your friend! You will let me be your friend! Oh! (*She offers him both her hands with a radiant smile.*) You see: I shew my confidence in you.

NAP. (*with a yell of rage, his eyes flashing*). What!

LADY. What's the matter?

NAP. Shew your confidence in me! So that I may shew my confidence in you in return by letting you give me the slip with the despatches, eh? Ah, Dalila, Dalila, you have been trying your tricks on me; and I have been as great a gull as my jackass of a lieutenant. (*He advances threateningly on her.*) Come: the despatches. Quick: I am not to be trifled with now.

LADY (*flying round the couch*). General—

NAP. Quick, I tell you. (*He passes swiftly up the middle of the room and intercepts her as she makes for the vineyard.*)

LADY (*at bay, confronting him*). You dare address me in that tone.

NAP. Dare!

LADY. Yes, dare. Who are you that you should presume to speak to me in that coarse way? Oh, the vile, vulgar Corsican adventurer comes out in you very easily.

NAP (*beside himself*). You she devil! (*Savagely.*) Once more, and only once, will you give me those papers or shall I tear them from you—by force?

LADY (*letting her hands fall*). Tear them from me—by force! (*As he glares at her like a tiger about to spring, she crosses her arms on her breast in the attitude of a martyr. The gesture and pose instantly awaken his theatrical instinct: he forgets his rage in the desire to shew her that in acting, too, she has met her match. He keeps her a moment in suspense; then suddenly clears up his countenance; puts his hands behind him with provoking coolness; looks at her up and down a couple of times; takes a pinch of snuff; wipes his fingers carefully and puts up his handkerchief, her heroic pose becoming more and more ridiculous all the time.*)

NAP. (*at last*). Well?

LADY (*disconcerted, but with her arms still crossed devotedly*). Well: what are you going to do?

NAP. Spoil your attitude.

LADY. You brute! (*Abandoning the attitude, she comes to the end of the couch, where she turns with her back to it, leaning against it and facing him with her hands behind her.*)

NAP. Ah, that's better. Now listen to me. I like you. What's more, I value your respect.

LADY. You value what you have not got, then.

NAP. I shall have it presently. Now attend to me. Suppose I were to allow myself to be abashed by the respect due to your sex, your beauty, your heroism and all the rest of it? Suppose I, with nothing but such sentimental stuff to stand between these muscles of mine and those papers which you have about you, and which I want and mean to have: suppose I, with the prize within my grasp, were to falter and sneak away with my hands empty; or, what would be worse, cover up my weakness by playing the magnanimous hero, and sparing you the violence I dared not use, would you not despise me from the depths of your woman's soul? Would any woman be such a fool? Well, Bonaparte can rise to the situation and act like a woman when it is necessary. Do you understand?

(*The* LADY, *without speaking, stands upright, and takes a packet of papers from her bosom. For a moment she has an intense impulse to dash them in his face. But her good breeding cuts her off from any vulgar method of relief. She hands them to him politely, only averting her head. The moment he takes them, she hurries across to the other side of the room; covers her face with her hands; and sits down, with her body turned away to the back of the chair.*)

NAP. (*gloating over the papers*). Aha! That's right. That's right. (*Before opening them he looks at her and says.*) Excuse me. (*He sees that she is hiding her face.*) Very angry with me, eh? (*He unties the packet, the seal of which is already broken, and puts it on the table to examine its contents.*)

LADY (*quietly, taking down her hands and shewing that she is not crying, but only thinking*). No. You were right. But I am sorry for you.

NAP. (*pausing in the act of taking the uppermost paper from the packet*). Sorry for me! Why?

LADY. I am going to see you lose your honor.

NAP. Hm! Nothing worse than that? (*He takes up the paper.*)

LADY. And your happiness.

NAP. Happiness, little woman, is the most tedious thing in the world to me. Should I be what I am if I cared for happiness? Anything else?

LADY. Nothing—(*He interrupts her with an exclamation of satisfaction. She proceeds quietly.*) except that you will cut a very foolish figure in the eyes of France.

NAP. (*quickly*). What? (*The hand holding the paper involuntarily drops. The Lady looks at him enigmatically in tranquil silence. He throws the letter down and breaks out into a torrent of scolding.*) What do you mean? Eh? Are

you at your tricks again? Do you think I don't know what these papers contain? I'll tell you. First, my information as to Beaulieu's retreat. There are only two things he can do—leather-brained idiot that he is!—shut himself up in Mantua or violate the neutrality of Venice by taking Peschiera. You are one of old Leather-brain's spies: he has discovered that he has been betrayed, and has sent you to intercept the information at all hazards—as if that could save him from me, the old fool! The other papers are only my usual correspondence from Paris, of which you know nothing.

LADY (*prompt and businesslike*). General: let us make a fair division. Take the information your spies have sent you about the Austrian army; and give me the Paris correspondence. That will content me.

NAP. (*his breath taken away by the coolness of the proposal*). A fair di— (*He gasps.*) It seems to me, madame, that you have come to regard my letters as your own property, of which I am trying to rob you.

LADY (*earnestly*). No: on my honor I ask you for no letter of yours—not a word that has been written by you or to you. That packet contains a stolen letter: a letter written by a woman to a man—a man not her husband—a letter that means disgrace, infamy—

NAP. A love letter?

LADY (*bitter-sweetly*). What else but a love letter could stir up so much hate?

NAP. Why is it sent to me? To put the husband in my power, eh?

LADY. No, no: it can be of no use to you: I swear that it will cost you nothing to give it to me. It has been sent to you out of sheer malice—solely to injure the woman who wrote it.

NAP. Then why not send it to her husband instead of to me?

LADY (*completely taken aback*). Oh! (*Sinking back into the chair.*) I—I don't know. (*She breaks down.*)

NAP. Aha! I thought so: a little

romance to get the papers back. (*He throws the packet on the table and confronts her with cynical goodhumor.*) Per Bacco, little woman, I can't help admiring you. If I could lie like that, it would save me a great deal of trouble.

LADY (*wringing her hands*). Oh, how I wish I really had told you some lie! You would have believed me then. The truth is the one thing that nobody will believe.

NAP. (*with coarse familiarity, treating her as if she were a vivandière*). Capital! Capital! (*He puts his hands behind him on the table, and lifts himself on to it, sitting with his arms akimbo and his legs wide apart.*) Come: I am a true Corsican in my love for stories. But I could tell them better than you if I set my mind to it. Next time you are asked why a letter compromising a wife should not be sent to her husband, answer simply that the husband would not read it. Do you suppose, little innocent, that a man wants to be compelled by public opinion to make a scene, to fight a duel, to break up his household, to injure his career by a scandal, when he can avoid it all by taking care not to know?

LADY (*revolted*). Suppose that packet contained a letter about your own wife?

NAP. (*offended, coming off the table*). You are impertinent, madame.

LADY (*humbly*). I beg your pardon. Caesar's wife is above suspicion.

NAP. (*with a deliberate assumption of superiority*). You have committed an indiscretion. I pardon you. In future, do not permit yourself to introduce real persons in your romances.

LADY (*politely ignoring a speech which is to her only a breach of good manners, and rising to move towards the table*). General: there really is a woman's letter there. (*Pointing to the packet.*) Give it to me.

NAP. (*with brute conciseness, moving so as to prevent her getting too near the letters*). Why?

LADY. She is an old friend: we were at school together. She has written to me imploring me to prevent the letter falling into your hands.

NAP. Why has it been sent to me?

LADY. Because it compromises the director Barras.

NAP. (*frowning, evidently startled*). Barras! (*Haughtily.*) Take care, madame. The director Barras is my attached personal friend.

LADY (*nodding placidly*). Yes. You became friends through your wife.

NAP. Again! Have I not forbidden you to speak of my wife? (*She keeps looking curiously at him, taking no account of the rebuke. More and more irritated, he drops his haughty manner, of which he is himself somewhat impatient, and says suspiciously, lowering his voice.*) Who is this woman with whom you sympathize so deeply?

LADY. Oh, General! How could I tell you that?

NAP. (*ill-humoredly, beginning to walk about again in angry perplexity*). Ay, ay: stand by one another. You are all the same, you women.

LADY (*indignantly*). We are not all the same, any more than you are. Do you think that if *I* loved another man, I should pretend to go on loving my husband, or be afraid to tell him or all the world? But this woman is not made that way. She governs men by cheating them; and (*with disdain*) they like it, and let her govern them. (*She sits down again, with her back to him.*)

NAP. (*not attending to her*). Barras, Barras! (*Turning very threateningly to her, his face darkening.*) Take care, take care: do you hear? You may go too far.

LADY (*innocently turning her face to him*). What's the matter?

NAP. What are you hinting at? Who is this woman?

LADY (*meeting his angry searching gaze with tranquil indifference as she sits looking up at him with her right arm resting lightly along the back of her chair, and one knee crossed over the other.*) A vain, silly, extravagant creature, with a very able and ambitious husband who knows her through and through—knows that she has lied to him about her age, her income, her social position, about everything that silly women lie about—knows that she is incapable of fidelity to any principle or any person; and yet could not help loving her—could not help his man's instinct to make use of her for his own advancement with Barras.

NAP. (*in a stealthy, coldly furious whisper*). This is your revenge, you she cat, for having had to give me the letters.

LADY. Nonsense! Or do you mean that you are that sort of man?

NAP. (*exasperated, clasps his hands behind him, his fingers twitching, and says, as he walks irritably away from her to the fireplace*). This woman will drive me out of my senses. (*To her.*) Begone.

LADY (*seated immovably*). Not without that letter.

NAP. Begone, I tell you. (*Walking from the fireplace to the vineyard and back to the table.*) You shall have no letter. I don't like you. You're a detestable woman, and as ugly as Satan. I don't choose to be pestered by strange women. Be off. (*He turns his back on her. In quiet amusement, she leans her cheek on her hand and laughs at him. He turns again, angrily mocking her.*) Ha! ha! ha! What are you laughing at?

LADY. At you, General. I have often seen persons of your sex getting into a pet and behaving like children; but I never saw a really great man do it before.

NAP. (*brutally, flinging the words in her face*). Pooh: flattery! flattery! coarse, impudent flattery!

LADY (*springing up with a bright flush in her cheeks*). Oh, you are too bad. Keep your letters. Read the story of

your own dishonor in them; and much good may they do you. Good-bye. (*She goes indignantly towards the inner door.*)

NAP. My own—! Stop. Come back. Come back, I order you. (*She proudly disregards his savagely peremptory tone and continues on her way to the door. He rushes at her; seizes her by the wrist; and drags her back.*) Now, what do you mean? Explain. Explain, I tell you, or—(*Threatening her. She looks at him with unflinching defiance.*) Rrrr! you obstinate devil, you. Why can't you answer a civil question?

LADY (*deeply offended by his violence*). Why do you ask me? You have the explanation.

NAP. Where?

LADY (*pointing to the letters on the table*). There. You have only to read it. (*He snatches the packet up; hesitates; looks at her suspiciously; and throws it down again.*)

NAP. You seem to have forgotten your solicitude for the honor of your old friend.

LADY. She runs no risk now: she does not quite understand her husband.

NAP. I am to read the letter, then? (*He stretches out his hand as if to take up the packet again, with his eye on her.*)

LADY. I do not see how you can very well avoid doing so now. (*He instantly withdraws his hand.*) Oh, don't be afraid. You will find many interesting things in it.

NAP. For instance?

LADY. For instance, a duel—with Barras, a domestic scene, a broken household, a public scandal, a checked career, all sorts of things.

NAP. Hm! (*He looks at her; takes up the packet and looks at it, pursing his lips and balancing it in his hand; looks at her again; passes the packet into his left hand and puts it behind his back, raising his right to scratch the back of his head as he turns and goes up to the edge of the vineyard, where he stands for a moment looking out into the vines, deep in thought. The* LADY *watches him in silence, somewhat slightingly. Suddenly he turns and comes back again, full of force and decision.*) I grant your request, madame. Your courage and resolution deserve to succeed. Take the letters for which you have fought so well; and remember henceforth that you found the vile, vulgar Corsican adventurer as generous to the vanquished after the battle as he was resolute in the face of the enemy before it. (*He offers her the packet.*)

LADY (*without taking it, looking hard at him*). What are you at now, I wonder? (*He dashes the packet furiously to the floor.*) Aha! I've spoiled that attitude, I think. (*She makes him a pretty mocking curtsey.*)

NAP. (*snatching it up again*). Will you take the letters and begone (*advancing and thrusting them upon her*)?

LADY (*escaping round the table*). No: I don't want your letters.

NAP. Ten minutes ago, nothing else would satisfy you.

LADY (*keeping the table carefully between them*). ·Ten minutes ago you had not insulted me past all bearing.

NAP. I—(*swallowing his spleen*) I apologize.

LADY (*coolly*). Thanks. (*With forced politeness he offers her the packet across the table. She retreats a step out of its reach and says*) But don't you want to know whether the Austrians are at Mantua or Peschiera?

NAP. I have already told you that I can conquer my enemies without the aid of spies, madame.

LADY. And the letter! don't you want to read that?

NAP. You have said that it is not addressed to me. I am not in the habit of reading other people's letters. (*He again offers the packet.*)

LADY. In that case there can be no objection to your keeping it. All I wanted

was to prevent your reading it. (*Cheerfully.*) Good afternoon, General. (*She turns coolly towards the inner door.*)

NAP. (*furiously flinging the packet on the couch*). Heaven grant me patience! (*He goes up determinedly and places himself before the door.*) Have you any sense of personal danger? Or are you one of those women who like to be beaten black and blue?

LADY. Thank you, General: I have no doubt the sensation is very voluptuous; but I had rather not. I simply want to go home: that's all. I was wicked enough to steal your despatches; but you have got them back; and you have forgiven me, because (*Delicately reproducing his rhetorical cadence.*) you are as generous to the vanquished after the battle as you are resolute in the face of the enemy before it. Won't you say good-bye to me? (*She offers her hand sweetly.*)

NAP. (*repulsing the advance with a gesture of concentrated rage, and opening the door to call fiercely*). Giuseppe! (*Louder.*) Giuseppe! (*He bangs the door to, and comes to the middle of the room. The lady goes a little way into the vineyard to avoid him.*)

GIUS. (*appearing at the door*). Excellency?

NAP. Where is that fool?

GIUS. He has had a good dinner, according to your instructions, excellency, and is now doing me the honor to gamble with me to pass the time.

NAP. Send him here. Bring him here. Come with him. (GIUSEPPE, *with unruffled readiness, hurries off.* NAPOLEON *turns curtly to the lady, saying*) I must trouble you to remain some moments longer, madame. (*He comes to the couch. She comes from the vineyard down the opposite side of the room to the sideboard, and posts herself there, leaning against it, watching him. He takes the packet from the couch and deliberately buttons it carefully into his breast pocket, looking at her meanwhile with an expression which suggests that she will soon find out the meaning of his proceedings, and will not like it. Nothing more is said until the* LIEUTENANT *arrives followed by* GIUSEPPE, *who stands modestly in attendance at the table. The* LIEUTENANT, *without cap, sword or gloves, and much improved in temper and spirits by his meal, chooses the* LADY's *side of the room, and waits, much at his ease, for* NAPOLEON *to begin.*)

NAP. Lieutenant.

LIEUT. (*encouragingly*). General.

NAP. I cannot persuade this lady to give me much information; but there can be no doubt that the man who tricked you out of your charge was, as she admitted to you, her brother.

LIEUT. (*triumphantly*). What did I tell you, General! What did I tell you!

NAP. You must find that man. Your honor is at stake; and the fate of the campaign, the destiny of France, of Europe, of humanity, perhaps, may depend on the information those despatches contain.

LIEUT. Yes, I suppose they really are rather serious (*as if this had hardly occurred to him before*).

NAP. (*energetically*). They are so serious, sir, that if you do not recover them, you will be degraded in the presence of your regiment.

LIEUT. Whew! The regiment won't like that, I can tell you.

NAP. Personally, I am sorry for you. I would willingly conceal the affair if it were possible. But I shall be called to account for not acting on the despatches. I shall have to prove to all the world that I never received them, no matter what the consequences may be to you. I am sorry; but you see that I cannot help myself.

LIEUT. (*goodnaturedly*). Oh, don't take it to heart, General: it's really very good of you. Never mind what happens to me: I shall scrape through somehow; and we'll beat the Austrians for you, despatches or no despatches. I hope you won't insist on my starting off on a wild goose chase after the fellow now. I haven't a notion where to look for him.

GIUS. (*deferentially*). You forget, Lieutenant: he has your horse.

LIEUT. (*starting*). I forgot that. (*Resolutely.*) I'll go after him, General: I'll find that horse if it's alive anywhere in Italy. And I shan't forget the despatches: never fear. Giuseppe: go and saddle one of those mangy old posthorses of yours, while I get my cap and sword and things. Quick march. Off with you (*bustling him*).

GIUS. Instantly, Lieutenant, instantly. (*He disappears in the vineyard, where the light is now reddening with the sunset.*)

LIEUT. (*looking about him on his way to the inner door*). By the way, General, did I give you my sword or did I not? Oh, I remember now. (*Fretfully.*) It's all that nonsense about putting a man under arrest: one never knows where to find—(*Talks himself out of the room.*)

LADY (*still at the sideboard*). What does all this mean, General?

NAP. He will not find your brother.

LADY. Of course not. There's no such person.

NAP. The despatches will be irrecoverably lost.

LADY. Nonsense! They are inside your coat.

NAP. You will find it hard, I think, to prove that wild statement. (*The Lady starts. He adds, with clinching emphasis.*) Those papers are lost.

LADY (*anxiously, advancing to the corner of the table*). And that unfortunate young man's career will be sacrificed.

NAP. His career! The fellow is not worth the gunpowder it would cost to have him shot. (*He turns contemptu-*

*ously and goes to the hearth, where he
stands with his back to her.*)

LADY (*wistfully*). You are very
hard. Men and women are nothing to
you but things to be used, even if they
are broken in the use.

NAP. (*turning on her*). Which of us
has broken this fellow—I or you? Who
tricked him out of the despatches? Did
you think of his career then?

LADY (*naively concerned about him*).
Oh, I never thought of that. It was
brutal of me; but I couldn't help it,
could I? How else could I have got the
papers? (*Supplicating.*) General: you
will save him from disgrace.

NAP. (*laughing sourly*). Save him
yourself, since you are so clever: it was
you who ruined him. (*With savage intensity.*) I hate a bad soldier.

(*He goes out determinedly through
the vineyard. She follows him a few
steps with an appealing gesture, but is
interrupted by the return of the* LIEU-
TENANT, *gloved and capped, with his
sword on, ready for the road. He is
crossing to the outer door when she intercepts him.*)

LIEUT. (*importantly*). You mustn't
delay me, you know. Duty, madame,
duty.

LADY (*imploringly*). Oh, sir, what
are you going to do to my poor brother?

LIEUT. Are you very fond of him?

LADY. I should die if anything happened to him. You must spare him.
(*The* LIEUTENANT *shakes his head gloomily.*) Yes, yes: you must: you shall: he
is not fit to die. Listen to me. If I tell
you where to find him—if I undertake
to place him in your hands a prisoner,
to be delivered up by you to General
Bonaparte—will you promise me on
your honor as an officer and a gentleman
not to fight with him or treat him unkindly in any way?

LIEUT. But suppose he attacks me.
He has my pistols.

LADY. He is too great a coward.

LIEUT. I don't feel so sure about
that. He's capable of anything.

LADY. If he attacks you, or resists
you in any way, I release you from your
promise.

LIEUT. My promise! I didn't mean
to promise. Look here: you're as bad
as he is: you've taken an advantage of
me through the better side of my nature.
What about my horse?

LADY. It is part of the bargain that
you are to have your horse and pistols
back.

LIEUT. Honor bright?

LADY. Honor bright. (*She offers her
hand.*)

LIEUT. (*taking it and holding it*).
All right: I'll be as gentle as a lamb
with him. His sister's a very pretty
woman. (*He attempts to kiss her.*)

LADY (*slipping away from him*).
Oh, Lieutenant! You forget: your career
is at stake—the destiny of Europe—of
humanity.

LIEUT. Oh, bother the destiny of
humanity. (*Making for her.*) Only a
kiss.

LADY (*retreating round the table*).
Not until you have regained your honor
as an officer. Remember: you have not
captured my brother yet.

LIEUT. (*seductively*). You'll tell me
where he is, won't you?

LADY. I have only to send him a
certain signal; and he will be here in
quarter of an hour.

LIEUT. He's not far off, then.

LADY. No: quite close. Wait here
for him: when he gets my message he
will come here at once and surrender
himself to you. You understand?

LIEUT. (*intellectually overtaxed*).
Well, it's a little complicated; but I daresay it will be all right.

LADY. And now, whilst you're waiting, don't you think you had better make
terms with the General?

LIEUT. Oh, look here, this is getting
frightfully complicated. What terms?

LADY. Make him promise that if you catch my brother he will consider that you have cleared your character as a soldier. He will promise anything you ask on that condition.

LIEUT. That's not a bad idea. Thank you: I think I'll try it.

LADY. Do. And mind, above all things, don't let him see how clever you are.

LIEUT. I understand. He'd be jealous.

LADY. Don't tell him anything except that you are resolved to capture my brother or perish in the attempt. He won't believe you. Then you will produce my brother—

LIEUT. (*interrupting as he masters the plot*). And have the laugh at him! I say: what a clever little woman you are! (*Shouting.*) Giuseppe!

LADY. Sh! Not a word to Giuseppe about me.

(*She puts her finger on her lips. He does the same. They look at one another warningly. Then, with a ravishing smile, she changes the gesture into wafting him a kiss, and runs out through the inner door. Electrified, he bursts into a volley of chuckles. GIUSEPPE comes back by the outer.*)

GIUS. The horse is ready, Lieutenant.

LIEUT. I'm not going just yet. Go and find the General, and tell him I want to speak to him.

GIUS. (*shaking his head*). That will never do, Lieutenant.

LIEUT. Why not?

GIUS. In this wicked world a general may send for a lieutenant; but a lieutenant must not send for a general.

LIEUT. Oh, you think he wouldn't like it. Well, perhaps you're right: one has to be awfully particular about that sort of thing now we've got a republic.

(*NAPOLEON reappears, advancing from the vineyard, buttoning the breast of his coat, pale and full of gnawing thoughts.*)

GIUS. (*unconscious of* NAPOLEON'S *approach*). Quite true, Lieutenant, quite true. You are all like innkeepers now in France: you have to be polite to everybody.

NAP. (*putting his hand on* GIUSEPPE'S *shoulder*). And that destroys the whole value of politeness, eh?

LIEUT. The very man I wanted! See here, General: suppose I catch that fellow for you!

NAP. (*with ironical gravity*). You will not catch him, my friend.

LIEUT. Aha! you think so; but you'll see. Just wait. Only, if I do catch him and hand him over to you, will you cry quits? Will you drop all this about degrading me in the presence of my regiment? Not that *I* mind, you know; but still no regiment likes to have all the other regiments laughing at it.

NAP. (*a cold ray of humor striking pallidly across his gloom*). What shall we do with this officer, Giuseppe? Everything he says is wrong.

GIUS. (*promptly*). Make him a general, excellency; and then everything he says will be right.

LIEUT. (*crowing*). How-aw! (*He throws himself ecstatically on the couch to enjoy the joke.*)

NAPOLEON (*laughing and pinching* GIUSEPPE'S *ear*). You are thrown away in this inn, Giuseppe. (*He sits down and places* GIUSEPPE *before him like a schoolmaster with a pupil.*) Shall I take you away with me and make a man of you?

GIUS. (*shaking his head rapidly and repeatedly*). No, thank you, General. All my life long people have wanted to make a man of me. When I was a boy, our good priest wanted to make a man of me by teaching me to read and write. Then the organist at Melegnano wanted to make a man of me by teaching me to read music. The recruiting sergeant would have made a man of me if I had been a few inches taller. But it always meant making me work; and I am too lazy for that, thank Heaven! So I taught myself to cook and became an innkeeper; and now I keep servants to do the work, and have nothing to do myself except talk, which suits me perfectly.

NAP. (*looking at him thoughtfully*). You are satisfied?

GIUS. (*with cheerful conviction*). Quite, excellency.

NAP. And you have no devouring devil inside you who must be fed with action and victory—gorged with them night and day—who makes you pay, with the sweat of your brain and body, weeks of Herculean toil for ten minutes of enjoyment—who is at once your slave and your tyrant, your genius and your doom—who brings you a crown in one hand and the oar of a galley slave in the other—who shews you all the kingdoms of the earth and offers to make you their master on condition that you become their servant!—have you nothing of that in you?

GIUS. Nothing of it! Oh, I assure you, excellency, my devouring devil is far worse than that. He offers me no crowns and kingdoms: he expects to get everything for nothing—sausages, omelettes, grapes, cheese, polenta, wine—three times a day, excellency; nothing less will content him.

LIEUT. Come, drop it, Giuseppe: you're making me feel hungry again.

(GIUSEPPE, *with an apologetic shrug, retires from the conversation, and busies himself at the table, dusting it, setting the map straight, and replacing* NAPOLEON's *chair, which the* LADY *has pushed back.*)

NAP. (*turning to the* LIEUTENANT *with sardonic ceremony*). I hope I have not been making you feel ambitious.

LIEUT. Not at all: I don't fly so high. Besides: I'm better as I am: men like me are wanted in the army just now. The fact is, the Revolution was all very

well for civilians; but it won't work in the army. You know what soldiers are, General: they will have men of family for their officers. A subaltern must be a gentleman, because he's so much in contact with the men. But a general, or even a colonel, may be any sort of riff-raff if he understands the shop well enough. A lieutenant is a gentleman: all the rest is chance. Why, who do you suppose won the battle of Lodi? I'll tell you. My horse did.

NAP. (*rising*). Your folly is carrying you too far, sir. Take care.

LIEUT. Not a bit of it. You remember all that red-hot cannonade across the river: the Austrians blazing away at you to keep you from crossing, and you blazing away at them to keep them from setting the bridge on fire? Did you notice where I was then?

NAP. (*with menacing politeness*). I am sorry. I am afraid I was rather occupied at the moment.

GIUS. (*with eager admiration*). They say you jumped off your horse and worked the big guns with your own hands, General.

LIEUT. That was a mistake: an officer should never let himself down to the level of his men. (NAPOLEON *looks at him dangerously, and begins to walk tigerishly to and fro.*) But you might have been firing away at the Austrians still, if we cavalry fellows hadn't found the ford and got across and turned old Beaulieu's flank for you. You know you daren't have given the order to charge the bridge if you hadn't seen us on the other side. Consequently, I say that whoever found that ford won the battle of Lodi. Well, who found it? I was the first man to cross: and I know. It was my horse that found it. (*With conviction, as he rises from the couch.*) That horse is the true conqueror of the Austrians.

NAP. (*passionately*). You idiot: I'll have you shot for losing those despatches: I'll have you blown from the mouth of a cannon: nothing less could make any impression on you. (*Baying at him.*) Do you hear? Do you understand?

(*A* FRENCH OFFICER *enters unobserved, carrying his sheathed sabre in his hand.*)

LIEUT. (*unabashed*). If I don't capture him, General. Remember the if.

NAP. If! If! Ass: there is no such man.

OFFICER (*suddenly stepping between them and speaking in the unmistakable voice of the* STRANGE LADY). Lieutenant: I am your prisoner. (*She offers him her sabre. They are amazed.* NAPOLEON *gazes at her for a moment thunderstruck; then seizes her by the wrist and drags her roughly to him, looking closely and fiercely at her to satisfy himself as to her identity; for it now begins to darken rapidly into night, the red glow over the vineyard giving way to clear starlight.*)

NAP. Pah! (*He flings her hand away with an exclamation of disgust, and turns his back on her with his hand in his breast and his brow lowering.*)

LIEUT. (*triumphantly, taking the sabre*). No such man: eh, General? (*To the* LADY.) I say: where's my horse?

LADY. Safe at Borghetto, waiting for you, Lieutenant.

NAP. (*turning on them*). Where are the despatches?

LADY. You would never guess. They are in the most unlikely place in the world. Did you meet my sister here, any of you?

LIEUT. Yes. Very nice woman. She's wonderfully like you; but of course she's better looking.

LADY (*mysteriously*). Well, do you know that she is a witch?

GIUS. (*running down to them in terror, crossing himself*). Oh, no, no, no. It is not safe to jest about such things. I cannot have it in my house, excellency.

LIEUT. Yes, drop it. You're my prisoner, you know. Of course I don't

believe in any such rubbish; but still it's not a proper subject for joking.

LADY. But this is very serious. My sister has bewitched the General. (GIUSEPPE *and the* LIEUTENANT *recoil from* NAPOLEON.) General: open your coat: you will find the despatches in the breast of it. (*She puts her hand quickly on his breast.*) Yes: there they are: I can feel them. Eh? (*She looks up into his face half coaxingly, half mockingly.*) Will you allow me, General? (*She takes a button as if to unbutton his coat, and pauses for permission.*)

NAP. (*inscrutably*). If you dare.

LADY. Thank you. (*She opens his coat and takes out the despatches.*) There! (*To* GIUSEPPE, *shewing him the despatches.*) See!

GIUS. (*flying to the outer door*). No, in heaven's name! They're bewitched.

LADY (*turning to the* LIEUTENANT). Here, Lieutenant: you're not afraid of them.

LIEUT. (*retreating*). Keep off. (*Seizing the hilt of the sabre.*) Keep off, I tell you.

LADY (*to* NAPOLEON). They belong to you, General. Take them.

GIUS. Don't touch them, excellency. Have nothing to do with them.

LIEUTENANT. Be careful, General: be careful.

GIUS. Burn them. And burn the witch, too.

LADY (*to* NAPOLEON). Shall I burn them?

NAP. (*thoughtfully*). Yes, burn them. Giuseppe: go and fetch a light.

GIUS. (*trembling and stammering*). Do you mean go alone—in the dark—with a witch in the house?

NAP. Psha! You're a poltroon. (*To the* LIEUTENANT.) Oblige me by going, Lieutenant.

LIEUT. (*remonstrating*). Oh, I say, General! No, look here, you know: nobody can say I'm a coward after Lodi. But to ask me to go into the dark by myself without a candle after such an awful conversation is a little too much. How would you like to do it yourself?

NAP. (*irritably*). You refuse to obey my order?

LIEUT. (*resolutely*). Yes, I do. It's not reasonable. But I'll tell you what I'll do. If Giuseppe goes, I'll go with him and protect him.

NAP. (*to* GIUSEPPE). There! will that satisfy you? Be off, both of you.

GIUS. (*humbly, his lips trembling*). W-willingly, your excellency. (*He goes reluctantly towards the inner door.*) Heaven protect me! (*To the* LIEUTENANT.) After you, Lieutenant.

LIEUT. You'd better go first: I don't know the way.

GIUS. You can't miss it. Besides (*Imploringly, laying his hand on his sleeve.*), I am only a poor innkeeper; and you are a man of family.

LIEUT. There's something in that. Here: you needn't be in such a fright. Take my arm. (GIUSEPPE *does so.*) That's the way. (*They go out, arm in arm. It is now starry night. The* LADY *throws the packet on the table and seats herself at her ease on the couch enjoying the sensation of freedom from petticoats.*)

LADY. Well, General: I've beaten you.

NAP. (*walking about*). You have been guilty of indelicacy—of unwomanliness. Do you consider that costume a proper one to wear?

LADY. It seems to me much the same as yours.

NAP. Psha! I blush for you.

LADY (*naively*). Yes: soldiers blush so easily! (*He growls and turns away. She looks mischievously at him, balancing the despatches in her hand.*) Wouldn't you like to read these before they're burnt, General? You must be dying with curiosity. Take a peep. (*She throws the packet on the table, and turns her face away from it.*) I won't look.

NAP. I have no curiosity whatever, madame. But since you are evidently burning to read them, I give you leave to do so.

LADY. Oh, I've read them already.

NAP. (*starting*). What!

LADY. I read them the first thing after I rode away on that poor lieutenant's horse. So you see I know what's in them; and you don't.

NAP. Excuse me: I read them when I was out there in the vineyard ten minutes ago.

LADY. Oh! (*Jumping up.*) Oh, General: I've not beaten you. I do admire you so. (*He laughs and pats her cheek.*) This time really and truly without shamming, I do you homage. (*Kissing his hand.*)

NAP. (*quickly withdrawing it*). Brr! Don't do that. No more witchcraft.

LADY. I want to say something to you—only you would misunderstand it.

NAP. Need that stop you?

LADY. Well, it is this. I adore a man who is not afraid to be mean and selfish.

NAP. (*indignantly*). I am neither mean nor selfish.

LADY. Oh, you don't appreciate yourself. Besides, I don't really mean meanness and selfishness.

NAP. Thank you. I thought perhaps you did.

LADY. Well, of course I do. But what I mean is a certain strong simplicity about you.

NAP. That's better.

LADY. You didn't want to read the letters; but you were curious about what was in them. So you went into the garden and read them when no one was looking, and then came back and pretended you hadn't. That's the meanest thing I ever knew any man do; but it exactly fulfilled your purpose; and so you weren't a bit afraid or ashamed to do it.

NAP. (*abruptly*). Where did you pick up all these vulgar scruples—this (*with contemptuous emphasis*) conscience of yours? I took you for a lady—an aristocrat. Was your grandfather a shopkeeper, pray?

LADY. No: he was an Englishman.

NAP. That accounts for it. The English are a nation of shopkeepers. Now I understand why you've beaten me.

LADY. Oh, I haven't beaten you. And I'm not English.

NAP. Yes, you are—English to the backbone. Listen to me: I will explain the English to you.

LADY (*eagerly*). Do. (*With a lively air of anticipating an intellectual treat, she sits down on the couch and composes herself to listen to him. Secure of his audience, he at once nerves himself for a performance. He considers a little before he begins; so as to fix her attention by a moment of suspense. His style is at first modelled on Talma's in Corneille's "Cinna"; but it is somewhat lost in the darkness, and Talma presently gives way to Napoleon, the voice coming through the gloom with startling intensity.*)

NAP. There are three sorts of people in the world, the low people, the middle people, and the high people. The low people and the high people are alike in one thing: they have no scruples, no morality. The low are beneath morality, the high above it. I am not afraid of either of them: for the low are unscrupulous without knowledge, so that they make an idol of me; whilst the high are unscrupulous without purpose, so that they go down before my will. Look you: I shall go over all the mobs and all the courts of Europe as a plough goes over a field. It is the middle people who are dangerous: they have both knowledge and purpose. But they, too, have their weak point. They are full of scruples—chained hand and foot by their morality and respectability.

LADY. Then you will beat the English; for all shopkeepers are middle people.

NAP. No, because the English are a race apart. No Englishman is too low to have scruples: no Englishman is high enough to be free from their tyranny. But every Englishman is born with a certain miraculous power that makes him master of the world. When he wants a thing, he never tells himself that he wants it. He waits patiently until there comes into his mind, no one knows how, a burning conviction that it is his moral and religious duty to conquer those who have got the thing he wants. Then he becomes irresistible. Like the aristocrat, he does what pleases him and grabs what he wants: like the shopkeeper, he pursues his purpose with the industry and steadfastness that come from strong religious conviction and deep sense of moral responsibility. He is never at a loss for an effective moral attitude. As the great champion of freedom and national independence, he conquers and annexes half the world, and calls it Colonization. When he wants a new market for his adulterated Manchester goods, he sends a missionary to teach the natives the gospel of peace. The natives kill the missionary: he flies to arms in defence of Christianity; fights for it; conquers for it; and takes the market as a reward from heaven. In defence of his island shores, he puts a chaplain on board his ship; nails a flag with a cross on it to his top-gallant mast; and sails to the ends of the earth, sinking, burning and destroying all who dispute the empire of the seas with him. He boasts that a slave is free the moment his foot touches British soil; and he sells the children of his poor at six years of age to work under the lash in his factories for sixteen hours a day. He makes two revolutions, and then declares war on our one in the name of law and order. There is nothing so bad or so good that you will not find

Englishmen doing it; but you will never find an Englishman in the wrong. He does everything on principle. He fights you on patriotic principles; he robs you on business principles; he enslaves you on imperial principles; he bullies you on manly principles; he supports his king on loyal principles, and cuts off his king's head on republican principles. His watchword is always duty; and he never forgets that the nation which lets its duty get on the opposition side to its interest is lost. He—

LADY. W-w-w-w-w-wh! Do stop a moment. I want to know how you make me out to be English at this rate.

NAP. (*dropping his rhetorical style*). It's plain enough. You wanted some letters that belonged to me. You have spent the morning in stealing them— yes, stealing them, by highway robbery. And you have spent the afternoon in putting me in the wrong about them— in assuming that it was *I* who wanted to steal your letters—in explaining that it all came about through my meanness and selfishness, and your goodness, your devotion, your self-sacrifice. That's English.

LADY. Nonsense. I am sure I am not a bit English. The English are a very stupid people.

NAP. Yes, too stupid sometimes to know when they're beaten. But I grant that your brains are not English. You see, though your grandfather was an Englishman, your grandmother was— what? A Frenchwoman?

LADY. Oh, no. An Irishwoman.

NAP. (*quickly*). Irish! (*Thoughtfully.*) Yes: I forgot the Irish. An English army led by an Irish general: that might be a match for a French army led by an Italian general. (*He pauses, and adds, half jestingly, half moodily.*) At all events, you have beaten me; and what beats a man first will beat him last. (*He goes meditatively into the moonlit*

vineyard and looks up. She steals out after him. She ventures to rest her hand on his shoulder, overcome by the beauty of the night and emboldened by its obscurity.*)

LADY (*softly*). What are you looking at?

NAP. (*pointing up*). My star.

LADY. You believe in that?

NAP. I do. (*They look at it for a moment, she leaning a little on his shoulder.*)

LADY. Do you know that the English say that a man's star is not complete without a woman's garter?

NAP. (*scandalized—abruptly shaking her off and coming back into the room*). Pah! The hypocrites! If the French said that, how they would hold up their hands in pious horror! (*He goes to the inner door and holds it open, shouting.*) Hallo! Giuseppe. Where's that light, man. (*He comes between the table and the sideboard, and moves the chair to the table, beside his own.*) We have still to burn the letter. (*He takes up the packet. GIUSEPPE comes back, pale and still trembling, carrying a branched candlestick with a couple of candles alight, in one hand, and a broad snuffers tray in the other.*)

GIUS. (*piteously, as he places the light on the table*). Excellency: what were you looking up at just now—out there? (*He points across his shoulder to the vineyard, but is afraid to look round.*)

NAP. (*unfolding the packet*). What is that to you?

GIUS. (*stammering*). Because the witch is gone—vanished; and no one saw her go out.

LADY (*coming behind him from the vineyard*). We were watching her riding up to the moon on your broomstick, Giuseppe. You will never see her again.

GIUS. Gesu Maria! (*He crosses himself and hurries out.*)

NAP. (*throwing down the letters in a*

heap on the table). Now. (*He sits down at the table in the chair which he has just placed.*)

LADY. Yes; but you know you have the letter in your pocket. (*He smiles; takes a letter from his pocket; and tosses it on the top of the heap. She holds it up and looks at him, saying.*) About Caesar's wife.

NAP. Caesar's wife is above suspicion. Burn it.

LADY (*taking up the snuffers and holding the letter to the candle flame with it*). I wonder would Caesar's wife be above suspicion if she saw us here together!

NAP. (*echoing her, with his elbows on the table and his cheeks on his hands, looking at the letter*). I wonder! (*The* STRANGE LADY *puts the letter down alight on the snuffers tray, and sits down beside* NAPOLEON, *in the same attitude, elbows on table, cheeks on hands, watching it burn. When it is burnt, they simultaneously turn their eyes and look at one another. The curtain steals down and hides them.*)

ANTON CHEKHOV / 1860–1904

Anton Chekhov was born in the south of Russia, into a family of limited means, but he entered the University of Moscow as a medical student in 1879. He wrote constantly throughout his college years and while he was a practising physician, turning out almost four hundred short stories and several short farces. In 1896, the failure of his second play, *The Sea Gull,* in St. Petersburg, sent him back to short stories for some years. In 1899 the same play succeeded brilliantly at the Moscow Art Theater under the direction of Stanislavsky. The Moscow Art Theater was one of the galvanizing new centers of dramatic experiment and experience in Europe, dedicated to a new realism in both staging and acting. Chekhov continued to write plays for it for the remaining six years of his tuberculosis-shortened life. The association was mutually stimulating and helpful—the director and company understood the Chekhovian effects, and Chekhov's plays gave vitality and originality to the repertoire. *The Sea Gull, Uncle Vanya, The Three Sisters,* and his masterpiece *The Cherry Orchard* are the finest of his long plays; *The Boor* and *The Proposal* are two of his best short farces.

Chekhov lived in an unhappy but awakening period in Russia, a period still withered under the repressions of the old regime, but, in literature and the arts, coming to the "study of life" and throwing off traditional shackles as energetically as possible. Chekhov was a selfless humanitarian, doctoring the poor without charge, serving in epidemics, asking nothing and understanding much. Gorky said, "All his life Chekhov lived in his own soul; he was always himself, inwardly free."

A Chekhov play or story is harder to explain than to experience. It seems tentative, impressionistic, fragile, insubstantial. Something real but not visible is happening, or suddenly *has happened.* No structure is apparent, but out of a *non sequitur* stream of babble and inconsequence, certain repetitions, relationships, or clusterings of impressions make a comment, an insight, an anticipation.

The Cherry Orchard presents a group of people incapable not only of halting the passing of their order, but even of trying to halt it. The reason it must pass is in themselves. The sound of the breaking string and of the blows of the axe, old Firs crossing to the locked door, his "Life's gone on as if I'd never lived"—these things count as much as dialogue, and more than action. And yet a whole social order does pass, and another begins.

318

The Cherry Orchard

A COMEDY IN FOUR ACTS
TRANSLATED BY CONSTANCE GARNETT

CHARACTERS

MADAME RANEVSKY (LYUBOV ANDRE-
YEVNA), *the owner of the Cherry
Orchard.*
ANYA, *her daughter, aged 17.*
VARYA, *her adopted daughter, aged 24.*
GAEV (LEONID ANDREYEVITCH), *brother
of Madame Ranevsky.*
LOPAHIN (YERMOLAY ALEXEYEVITCH),
a merchant.
TROFIMOV (PYOTR SERGEYEVITCH), *a
student.*
SEMYONOV-PISHTCHIK, *a landowner.*
CHARLOTTA IVANOVNA, *a governess.*
EPIHODOV (SEMYON PANTALEYEVITCH),
a clerk.
DUNYASHA, *a maid.*
FIRS, *an old valet, aged 87.*
YASHA, *a young valet.*
A VAGRANT.
THE STATION MASTER.
A POST-OFFICE CLERK.
VISITORS, SERVANTS.

SCENE: *The estate of* MADAME RANEV-
SKY.

Characters: Russians have three
names: a given name (Lyubov), a patronymic (Andreyevna = daughter of
Andrey), and a surname (Ranevsky). In
the Russia of Chekhov's day, decorum
prescribed title and surname (Madame
Ranevsky) for formal relationships; given
name and patronymic (Lyubov Andreyevna) for relationships somewhat less
formal; given name alone for familiarity;
and a diminutive of the given name
(Lyuba for Lyubov) to indicate affection
or condescension.

Act I

(*A room, which has always been called
the nursery. One of the doors leads into*
ANYA'S *room. Dawn, sun rises during
the scene. May, the cherry trees in
flower, but it is cold in the garden with
the frost of early morning. Windows
closed.*)

(*Enter* DUNYASHA *with a candle and*
LOPAHIN *with a book in his hand.*)

LOPAHIN. The train's in, thank God.
What time is it?
DUNYASHA. Nearly two o'clock.
(*Puts out the candle.*) It's daylight
already.
LOPAHIN. The train's late! Two
hours, at least. (*Yawns and stretches.*)
I'm a pretty one; what a fool I've been.
Came here on purpose to meet them at
the station and dropped asleep. . . .
Dozed off as I sat in the chair. It's annoying. . . . You might have waked me.
DUNYASHA. I thought you had gone.
(*Listens.*) There, I do believe they're
coming!
LOPAHIN (*listens*). No, what with
the luggage and one thing and another.
(*A pause.*) Lyubov Andreyevna has been
abroad five years; I don't know what
she is like now. . . . She's a splendid
woman. A good-natured, kind-hearted
woman. I remember when I was a lad
of fifteen, my poor father—he used to
keep a little shop here in the village in
those days—gave me a punch in the
face with his fist and made my nose
bleed. We were in the yard here, I forget what we'd come about—he had had

319

a drop. Lyubov Andreyevna—I can see her now—she was a slim young girl then—took me to wash my face, and then brought me into this very room, into the nursery. "Don't cry, little peasant," says she, "it will be well in time for your wedding day." . . . (*A pause.*) Little peasant. . . . My father was a peasant, it's true, but here am I in a white waistcoat and brown shoes, like a pig in a bun shop. Yes, I'm a rich man, but for all my money, come to think, a peasant I was, and a peasant I am. (*Turns over the pages of the book.*) I've been reading this book and I can't make head or tail of it. I fell asleep over it. (*A pause.*)

DUNYASHA. The dogs have been awake all night, they feel that the mistress is coming.

LOPAHIN. Why, what's the matter with you, Dunyasha?

DUNYASHA. My hands are all of a tremble. I feel as though I should faint.

LOPAHIN. You're a spoilt soft creature, Dunyasha. And dressed like a lady too, and your hair done up. That's not the thing. One must know one's place.

(*Enter* EPIHODOV *with a nosegay; he wears a pea-jacket and highly polished creaking topboots; he drops the nosegay as he comes in.*)

EPIHODOV (*picking up the nosegay*). Here! the gardener's sent this, says you're to put it in the dining-room. (*Gives* DUNYASHA *the nosegay.*)

LOPAHIN. And bring me some kvass.

DUNYASHA. I will. (*Goes out.*)

EPIHODOV. It's chilly this morning, three degrees of frost, though the cherries are all in flower. I can't say much for our climate (*sighs*). I can't. Our climate is not often propitious to the occasion. Yermolay Alexeyevitch, permit me to call your attention to the fact that I purchased myself a pair of boots the day before yesterday, and they creak, I venture to assure you, so that there's no tolerating them. What ought I to grease them with?

LOPAHIN. Oh, shut up! Don't bother me.

EPIHODOV. Every day some misfortune befalls me. I don't complain, I'm used to it, and I wear a smiling face.

(DUNYASHA *comes in, hands* LOPAHIN *the kvass.*)

EPIHODOV. I am going. (*Stumbles against a chair, which falls over.*) There! (*As though triumphant.*) There you see now, excuse the expression, an accident like that among others. . . . It's positively remarkable. (*Goes out.*)

DUNYASHA. Do you know, Yermolay Alexeyevitch, I must confess, Epihodov has made me a proposal.

LOPAHIN. Ah!

DUNYASHA. I'm sure I don't know. . . . He's a harmless fellow, but sometimes when he begins talking, there's no making anything of it. It's all very fine and expressive, only there's no understanding it. I've a sort of liking for him too. He loves me to distraction. He's an unfortunate man; every day there's something. They tease him about it—two and twenty misfortunes they call him.

LOPAHIN (*listening*). There! I do believe they're coming.

DUNYASHA. They are coming! What's the matter with me? . . . I'm cold all over.

LOPAHIN. They really are coming. Let's go and meet them. Will she know me? It's five years since I saw her.

DUNYASHA (*in a flutter*). I shall drop this very minute. . . . Ah, I shall drop.

(*There is a sound of two carriages driving up to the house.* LOPAHIN *and* DUNYASHA *go out quickly. The stage is left empty. A noise is heard in the adjoining rooms.* FIRS, *who has driven to meet* MADAME RANEVSKY, *crosses the stage hurriedly leaning on a stick. He is wearing old-fashioned livery and a high hat. He says something to himself, but not a word can be distinguished. The noise behind the scenes goes on increasing. A voice:* "Come, let's go in here."

Enter LYUBOV ANDREYEVNA, ANYA, *and* CHARLOTTA IVANOVNA *with a pet dog on a chain, all in travelling dresses,* VARYA *in an out-door coat with a kerchief over her head,* GAEV, SEMYONOV-PISHTCHIK, LOPAHIN, DUNYASHA *with bag and parasol, servants with other articles. All walk across the room.*)

ANYA. Let's come in here. Do you remember what room this is, mamma?

LYUBOV (*joyfully, through her tears*). The nursery!

VARYA. How cold it is, my hands are numb. (*To* LYUBOV ANDREYEVNA.) Your rooms, the white room and the lavender one, are just the same as ever, mamma.

LYUBOV. My nursery, dear delightful room. . . . I used to sleep here when I was little. . . . (*Cries.*) And here I am, like a little child. . . . (*Kisses her brother and* VARYA, *and then her brother again.*) Varya's just the same as ever, like a nun. And I knew Dunyasha. (*Kisses* DUNYASHA.)

GAEV. The train was two hours late. What do you think of that? Is that the way to do things?

CHARLOTTA (*to* PISHTCHIK). My dog eats nuts, too.

PISHTCHIK (*wonderingly*). Fancy that!

(*They all go out except* ANYA *and* DUNYASHA.)

DUNYASHA. We've been expecting you so long. (*Takes* ANYA's *hat and coat.*)

ANYA. I haven't slept for four nights on the journey. I feel dreadfully cold.

DUNYASHA. You set out in Lent, there was snow and frost, and now? My darling! (*Laughs and kisses her.*) I *have* missed you, my precious, my joy. I must tell you . . . I can't put it off a minute. . . .

ANYA (*wearily*). What now?

DUNYASHA. Epihodov, the clerk, made me a proposal just after Easter.

ANYA. It's always the same thing with you. . . . (*Straightening her hair.*) I've lost all my hairpins. . . . (*She is staggering from exhaustion.*)

DUNYASHA. I don't know what to think, really. He does love me, he does love me so!

ANYA (*looking towards her door, tenderly*). My own room, my windows just as though I had never gone away. I'm home! Tomorrow morning I shall get up and run into the garden. . . . Oh, if I could get to sleep! I haven't slept all the journey, I was so anxious and worried.

DUNYASHA. Pyotr Sergeyevitch came the day before yesterday.

ANYA (*joyfully*). Petya!

DUNYASHA. He's asleep in the bath house, he has settled in there. I'm afraid of being in their way, says he. (*Glancing at her watch.*) I was to have waked him, but Varvara Mihalovna told me not to. Don't you wake him, says she.

(*Enter* VARYA *with a bunch of keys at her waist.*)

VARYA. Dunyasha, coffee and make haste. . . . Mamma's asking for coffee.

DUNYASHA. This very minute. (*Goes out.*)

VARYA. Well, thank God, you've come. You're home again. (*Petting her.*) My little darling has come back! My precious beauty has come back again!

ANYA. I have had a time of it!

VARYA. I can fancy.

ANYA. We set off in Holy Week—it was so cold then, and all the way Charlotta would talk and show off her tricks. What did you want to burden me with Charlotta for?

VARYA. You couldn't have travelled all alone, darling. At seventeen!

ANYA. We got to Paris at last, it was cold there—snow. I speak French shockingly. Mamma lives on the fifth floor. I went up to her and there were a lot of French people, ladies, an old priest with a book. The place smelt of tobacco and so comfortless. I felt sorry, oh! so sorry for mamma all at once, I put my arms round her neck, and hugged her and wouldn't let her go. Mamma was as kind as she could be, and she cried. . . .

VARYA (*through her tears*). Don't speak of it, don't speak of it!

ANYA. She had sold her villa at Mentone, she had nothing left, nothing. I hadn't a farthing left either, we only just had enough to get here. And mamma doesn't understand! When we had dinner at the stations, she always ordered the most expensive things and gave the waiters a whole rouble. Charlotta's just the same. Yasha too must have the same as we do; it's simply awful. You know Yasha is mamma's valet now, we brought him here with us.

VARYA. Yes, I've seen the young rascal.

ANYA. Well, tell me—have you paid the arrears on the mortgage?

VARYA. How could we get the money?

ANYA. Oh, dear! Oh, dear!

VARYA. In August the place will be sold.

ANYA. My goodness!

LOPAHIN (*peeps in at the door and moos like a cow*). Moo! (*Disappears.*)

VARYA (*weeping*). There, that's what I could do to him. (*Shakes her fist.*)

ANYA (*embracing* VARYA, *softly*). Varya, has he made you an offer? (VARYA *shakes her head.*) Why, but he loves you. Why is it you don't come to an understanding? What are you waiting for?

VARYA. I believe that there never will be anything between us. He has a lot to do, he has no time for me . . . and takes no notice of me. Bless the man, it makes me miserable to see him. . . . Everyone's talking of our being married, everyone's congratulating me, and all the while there's really nothing in it; it's all like a dream! (*In another tone.*) You have a new brooch like a bee.

ANYA (*mournfully*). Mamma bought it. (*Goes into her own room and in a light-hearted childish tone:*) And you

know, in Paris I went up in a balloon!

VARYA. My darling's home again! My pretty is home again!

(DUNYASHA *returns with the coffee-pot and is making the coffee.*)

VARYA (*standing at the door*). All day long, darling, as I go about looking after the house, I keep dreaming all the time. If only we could marry you to a rich man, then I should feel more at rest. Then I would go off by myself on a pilgrimage to Kiev, to Moscow . . . and so I would spend my life going from one place to another. . . . I would go on and on. . . . What bliss!

ANYA. The birds are singing in the garden. What time is it?

VARYA. It must be nearly three. It's time you were asleep, darling. (*Going into* ANYA's *room.*) What bliss!

(YASHA *enters with a rug and a travelling bag.*)

YASHA (*crosses the stage, mincingly*). May one come in here, pray?

DUNYASHA. I shouldn't have known you, Yasha. How you have changed abroad.

YASHA. H'm! . . . And who are you?

DUNYASHA. When you went away, I was that high. (*Shows distance from floor.*) Dunyasha, Fyodor's daughter. . . . You don't remember me!

YASHA. H'm! . . . You're a peach! (*Looks round and embraces her: she shrieks and drops a saucer.* YASHA *goes out hastily.*)

VARYA (*in the doorway, in a tone of vexation*). What now?

DUNYASHA (*through her tears*). I have broken a saucer.

VARYA. Well, that brings good luck.

ANYA (*coming out of her room*). We ought to prepare mamma: Petya is here.

VARYA. I told them not to wake him.

ANYA (*dreamily*). It's six years since father died. Then only a month later little brother Grisha was drowned in the river, such a pretty boy he was, only seven. It was more than mamma could bear, so she went away, went away without looking back. (*Shuddering.*) . . . How well I understand her, if only she knew! (*A pause.*) And Petya Trofimov was Grisha's tutor, he may remind her.

(*Enter* FIRS: *he is wearing a pea-jacket and a white waistcoat.*)

FIRS (*goes up to the coffee-pot, anxiously*). The mistress will be served here. (*Puts on white gloves.*) Is the coffee ready? (*Sternly to* DUNYASHA.) Girl! Where's the cream?

DUNYASHA. Ah, mercy on us! (*Goes out quickly.*)

FIRS (*fussing round the coffee-pot*). Ech! you good-for-nothing! (*Muttering to himself.*) Come back from Paris. And the old master used to go to Paris too . . . horses all the way. (*Laughs.*)

VARYA. What is it, Firs?

FIRS. What is your pleasure? (*Gleefully.*) My lady has come home! I have lived to see her again! Now I can die. (*Weeps with joy.*)

(*Enter* LYUBOV ANDREYEVNA, GAEV *and* SEMYONOV-PISHTCHIK; *the latter is in a short-waisted full coat of fine cloth, and full trousers.* GAEV, *as he comes in, makes a gesture with his arms and his whole body, as though he were playing billiards.*)

LYUBOV. How does it go? Let me remember. Cannon off the red!

GAEV. That's it—in off the white! Why, once, sister, we used to sleep together in this very room, and now I'm fifty-one, strange as it seems.

LOPAHIN. Yes, time flies.

GAEV. What do you say?

LOPAHIN. Time, I say, flies.

GAEV. What a smell of patchouli!

ANYA. I'm going to bed. Good-night, mamma. (*Kisses her mother.*)

LYUBOV. My precious darling. (*Kisses her hands.*) Are you glad to be home? I can't believe it.

ANYA. Good-night, uncle.

GAEV (*kissing her face and hands*). God bless you! How like you are to your mother! (*To his sister.*) At her age you were just the same, Lyuba.

(ANYA *shakes hands with* LOPAHIN *and* PISHTCHIK, *then goes out, shutting the door after her.*)

LYUBOV. She's quite worn out.

PISHTCHIK. Aye, it's a long journey, to be sure.

VARYA (*to* LOPAHIN *and* PISHTCHIK). Well, gentlemen? It's three o'clock and time to say good-bye.

LYUBOV (*laughs*). You're just the same as ever, Varya. (*Draws her to her and kisses her.*) I'll just drink my coffee and then we will all go and rest. (FIRS *puts a cushion under her feet.*) Thanks, friend. I am so fond of coffee, I drink it day and night. Thanks, dear old man. (*Kisses* FIRS.)

VARYA. I'll just see whether all the things have been brought in. (*Goes out.*)

LYUBOV. Can it really be me sitting here? (*Laughs.*) I want to dance about and clap my hands. (*Covers her face with her hands.*) And I could drop asleep in a moment! God knows I love my country, I love it tenderly; I couldn't look out of the window in the train, I kept crying so. (*Through her tears.*) But I must drink my coffee, though. Thank you, Firs, thanks, dear old man. I'm so glad to find you still alive.

FIRS. The day before yesterday.

GAEV. He's rather deaf.

LOPAHIN. I have to set off for Harkov directly, at five o'clock. . . . It is annoying! I wanted to have a look at you, and a little talk. . . . You are just as splendid as ever.

PISHTCHIK (*breathing heavily*). Handsomer, indeed. . . . Dressed in Parisian style . . . completely bowled me over.

LOPAHIN. Your brother, Leonid Andreyevitch here, is always saying that I'm a low-born knave, that I'm a money-grubber, but I don't care one straw for that. Let him talk. Only I do want you to believe in me as you used to. I do want your wonderful tender eyes to look at me as they used to in the old days. Merciful God! My father was a serf of your father and of your grandfather, but you—you—did so much for me once, that I've forgotten all that; I love you as though you were my kin . . . more than my kin.

LYUBOV. I can't sit still, I simply can't. . . (*Jumps up and walks about in violent agitation.*) This happiness is too much for me. . . . You may laugh at me, I know I'm silly. . . . My own book-case. (*Kisses the bookcase.*) My little table.

GAEV. Nurse died while you were away.

LYUBOV (*sits down and drinks coffee*). Yes, the Kingdom of Heaven be hers! You wrote me of her death.

GAEV. And Anastasy is dead. Squinting Petruchka has left me and is in service now with the police captain in the town. (*Takes a box of caramels out of his pocket and sucks one.*)

PISHTCHIK. My daughter, Dashenka, wishes to be remembered to you.

LOPAHIN. I want to tell you something very pleasant and cheering. (*Glancing at his watch.*) I'm going directly . . . there's no time to say much . . . well, I can say it in a couple of words. I needn't tell you your cherry orchard is to be sold to pay your debts; the 22nd of August is the date fixed for the sale; but don't you worry, dearest lady, you may sleep in peace, there is a way of saving it. . . . This is what I propose. I beg your attention! Your estate is not twenty miles from the town, the railway runs close by it, and if the cherry orchard and the land along the river bank were cut up into building plots and then let on lease for summer villas, you would make an income of at least 25,000 roubles a year out of it.

GAEV. That's all rot, if you'll excuse me.

LYUBOV. I don't quite understand you, Yermolay Alexeyevitch.

LOPAHIN. You will get a rent of at least 25 roubles a year for a three-acre plot from summer visitors, and if you say the word now, I'll bet you what you like there won't be one square foot of ground vacant by the autumn, all the plots will be taken up. I congratulate you; in fact, you are saved. It's a perfect situation with that deep river. Only, of course, it must be cleared—all the old buildings, for example, must be removed, this house too, which is really good for nothing, and the old cherry orchard must be cut down.

LYUBOV. Cut down? My dear fellow, forgive me, but you don't know what you are talking about. If there is one thing interesting—remarkable indeed—in the whole province, it's just our cherry orchard.

LOPAHIN. The only thing remarkable about the orchard is that it's a very large one. There's a crop of cherries every alternate year, and then there's nothing to be done with them, no one buys them.

GAEV. This orchard is mentioned in the "Encyclopædia."

LOPAHIN (*glancing at his watch*). If we don't decide on something and don't take some steps, on the 22nd of August the cherry orchard and the whole estate too will be sold by auction. Make up your minds! There is no other way of saving it, I'll take my oath on that. No, No!

FIRS. In the old days, forty or fifty years ago, they used to dry the cherries, soak them, pickle them, make jam too, and they used . . .

GAEV. Be quiet, Firs.

FIRS. And they used to send the preserved cherries to Moscow and to Harkov by the wagon-load. That brought the money in! And the preserved cherries in those days were soft and juicy, sweet and fragrant. . . . They knew the way to do them then. . . .

LYUBOV. And where is the recipe now?

FIRS. It's forgotten. Nobody remembers it.

PISHTCHIK (*to* LYUBOV ANDREYEVNA). What's it like in Paris? Did you eat frogs there?

LYUBOV. Oh, I ate crocodiles.

PISHTCHIK. Fancy that now!

LOPAHIN. There used to be only the gentlefolks and the peasants in the country, but now there are these summer visitors. All the towns, even the small ones, are surrounded nowadays by these summer villas. And one may say for sure, that in another twenty years there'll be many more of these people and that they'll be everywhere. At present the summer visitor only drinks tea in his verandah, but maybe he'll take to working his bit of land too, and then your cherry orchard would become happy, rich and prosperous. . . .

GAEV (*indignant*). What rot!

(*Enter* VARYA *and* YASHA.)

VARYA. There are two telegrams for you, mamma. (*Takes out keys and opens an old-fashioned bookcase with a loud crack.*) Here they are.

LYUBOV. From Paris. (*Tears the telegrams, without reading them.*) I have done with Paris.

GAEV. Do you know, Lyuba, how old that bookcase is? Last week I pulled out the bottom drawer and there I found the date branded on it. The bookcase was made just a hundred years ago. What do you say to that? We might have celebrated its jubilee. Though it's an inanimate object, still it is a *book* case.

PISHTCHIK (*amazed*). A hundred years! Fancy that now.

GAEV. Yes. . . . It is a thing . . . (*feeling the bookcase*). Dear, honoured bookcase! Hail to thee who for more than a hundred years hast served the pure ideals of good and justice; thy silent call to fruitful labour has never flagged in those hundred years, maintaining (*in tears*) in the generations of man, courage and faith in a brighter future and fostering in us ideals of good and social consciousness. (*A pause.*)

LOPAHIN. Yes. . . .

LYUBOV. You are just the same as ever, Leonid.

GAEV (*a little embarrassed*). Cannon off the right into the pocket!

LOPAHIN (*looking at his watch*). Well, it's time I was off.

YASHA (*handing* LYUBOV ANDREYEVNA *medicine*). Perhaps you will take your pills now.

PISHTCHIK. You shouldn't take medicines, my dear madam . . . they do no harm and no good. Give them here . . . honoured lady. (*Takes the pill-box, pours the pills into the hollow of his hand, blows on them, puts them in his mouth and drinks off some kvass.*) There!

LYUBOV (*in alarm*). Why, you must be out of your mind!

PISHTCHIK. I have taken all the pills.

LOPAHIN. What a glutton! (*All laugh.*)

FIRS. His honour stayed with us in Easter week, ate a gallon and a half of cucumbers . . . (*Mutters.*)

LYUBOV. What is he saying?

VARYA. He has taken to muttering like that for the last three years. We are used to it.

YASHA. His declining years!

(CHARLOTTA IVANOVNA, *a very thin, lanky figure in a white dress with a lorgnette in her belt, walks across the stage.*)

LOPAHIN. I beg your pardon. Charlotta Ivanovna, I have not had time to greet you. (*Tries to kiss her hand.*)

CHARLOTTA (*pulling away her hand*). If I let you kiss my hand, you'll be wanting to kiss my elbow, and then my shoulder.

LOPAHIN. I've no luck today! (*All laugh.*) Charlotta Ivanovna, show us some tricks!

LYUBOV. Charlotta, do show us some tricks!

CHARLOTTA. I don't want to. I'm sleepy. (*Goes out.*)

LOPAHIN. In three weeks' time we shall meet again. (*Kisses* LYUBOV ANDREYEVNA'S *hand.*) Good-bye till then—

I must go. (*To* GAEV.) Good-bye. (*Kisses* PISHTCHIK.) Good-bye. (*Gives his hand to* VARYA, *then to* FIRS *and* YASHA.) I don't want to go. (*To* LYUBOV ANDREYEVNA.) If you think over my plan for the villas and make up your mind, then let me know; I will lend you 50,000 roubles. Think of it seriously.

VARYA (*angrily*). Well, do go, for goodness' sake.

LOPAHIN. I'm going, I'm going. (*Goes out.*)

GAEV. Low-born knave! I beg pardon, though . . . Varya is going to marry him, he's Varya's fiancé.

VARYA. Don't talk nonsense, uncle.

LYUBOV. Well, Varya, I shall be delighted. He's a good man.

PISHTCHIK. He is, one must acknowledge, a most worthy man. And my Dashenka . . . says too that . . . she says . . . various things. (*Snores, but at once wakes up.*) But all the same, honoured lady, could you oblige me . . . with a loan of 240 roubles . . . to pay the interest on my mortgage tomorrow?

VARYA (*dismayed*). No, no.

LYUBOV. I really haven't any money.

PISHTCHIK. It will turn up. (*Laughs.*) I never lose hope. I thought everything was over, I was a ruined man, and lo and behold—the railway passed through my land and . . . they paid me for it. And something else will turn up again, if not today, then tomorrow . . . Dashenka'll win two hundred thousand . . . she's got a lottery ticket.

LYUBOV. Well, we've finished our coffee, we can go to bed.

FIRS (*brushes* GAEV, *reprovingly*). You have got on the wrong trousers again! What am I to do with you?

VARYA (*softly*). Anya's asleep. (*Softly opens the window.*) Now the sun's risen, it's not a bit cold. Look, mamma, what exquisite trees! My goodness! And the air! The starlings are singing!

GAEV (*opens another window*). The orchard is all white. You've not forgotten it, Lyuba? That long avenue that runs straight, straight as an arrow, how it shines on a moonlight night. You remember? You've not forgotten?

LYUBOV (*looking out of the window into the garden*). Oh, my childhood, my innocence! It was in this nursery I used to sleep, from here I looked out into the orchard, happiness waked with me every morning and in those days the orchard was just the same, nothing has changed. (*Laughs with delight.*) All, all white! Oh, my orchard! After the dark gloomy autumn, and the cold winter; you are young again, and full of happiness, the heavenly angels have never left you. . . . If I could cast off the burden that weighs on my heart, if I could forget the past!

GAEV. H'm! and the orchard will be sold to pay our debts; it seems strange. . . .

LYUBOV. See, our mother walking . . . all in white, down the avenue! (*Laughs with delight.*) It is she!

GAEV. Where?

VARYA. Oh, don't, mamma!

LYUBOV. There is no one. It was my fancy. On the right there, by the path to the arbour, there is a white tree bending like a woman. . . .

(*Enter* TROFIMOV *wearing a shabby student's uniform and spectacles.*)

LYUBOV. What a ravishing orchard! White masses of blossoms, blue sky. . . .

TROFIMOV. Lyubov Andreyevna! (*She looks round at him.*) I will just pay my respects to you and then leave you at once. (*Kisses her hand warmly.*) I was told to wait until morning, but I hadn't the patience to wait any longer. . . .

(LYUBOV ANDREYEVNA *looks at him in perplexity.*)

VARYA (*through her tears*). This is Petya Trofimov.

TROFIMOV. Petya Trofimov, who was your Grisha's tutor. . . . Can I have changed so much?

(LYUBOV ANDREYEVNA *embraces him and weeps quietly.*)

GAEV (*in confusion*). There, there, Lyuba.

VARYA (*crying*). I told you, Petya, to wait till tomorrow.

LYUBOV. My Grisha . . . my boy . . . Grisha . . . my son!

VARYA. We can't help it, mamma, it is God's will.

TROFIMOV (*softly through his tears*). There . . . there.

LYUBOV (*weeping quietly*). My boy was lost . . . drowned. Why? Oh, why, dear Petya? (*More quietly.*) Anya is asleep in there, and I'm talking loudly . . . making this noise. . . But, Petya? Why have you grown so ugly? Why do you look so old?

TROFIMOV. A peasant-woman in the train called me a mangy-looking gentleman.

LYUBOV. You were quite a boy then, a pretty little student, and now your hair's thin—and spectacles. Are you really a student still? (*Goes towards the door.*)

TROFIMOV. I seem likely to be a perpetual student.

LYUBOV (*kisses her brother, then* VARYA). Well, go to bed. . . . You are older too, Leonid.

PISHTCHIK (*follows her*). I suppose it's time we were asleep. . . . Ugh! my gout. I'm staying the night! Lyubov Andreyevna, my dear soul, if you could . . . tomorrow morning . . . 240 roubles.

GAEV. That's always his story.

PISHTCHIK. 240 roubles . . . to pay the interest on my mortgage.

LYUBOV. My dear man, I have no money.

PISHTCHIK. I'll pay it back, my dear . . . a trifling sum.

LYUBOV. Oh, well, Leonid will give it you. . . . You give him the money, Leonid.

GAEV. Me give it him! Let him wait till he gets it!

LYUBOV. It can't be helped, give it him. He needs it. He'll pay it back.

(LYUBOV ANDREYEVNA, TROFIMOV, PISHTCHIK *and* FIRS *go out.* GAEV, VARYA *and* YASHA *remain.*)

GAEV. Sister hasn't got out of the habit of flinging away her money. (*To* YASHA.) Get away, my good fellow, you smell of the hen-house.

YASHA (*with a grin*). And you, Leonid Andreyevitch, are just the same as ever.

GAEV. What's that? (*To* VARYA). What did he say?

VARYA (*to* YASHA). Your mother has come from the village; she has been sitting in the servants' room since yesterday, waiting to see you.

YASHA. Oh, bother her!

VARYA. For shame!

YASHA. What's the hurry? She might just as well have come tomorrow. (*Goes out.*)

VARYA. Mamma's just the same as ever, she hasn't changed a bit. If she had her own way, she'd give away everything.

GAEV. Yes. (*A pause.*) If a great many remedies are suggested for some disease, it means that the disease is incurable. I keep thinking and racking my brains; I have many schemes, a great many, and that really means none. If we could only come in for a legacy from somebody, or marry our Anya to a very rich man, or we might go to Yaroslavl and try our luck with our old aunt, the Countess. She's very, very rich, you know.

VARYA (*weeps*). If God would help us.

GAEV. Don't blubber. Aunt's very rich, but she doesn't like us. First, sister married a lawyer instead of a nobleman. . . .

(ANYA *appears in the doorway.*)

GAEV. And then her conduct, one can't call it virtuous. She is good, and kind, and nice, and I love her, but, however one allows for extenuating circumstances, there's no denying that she's an immoral woman. One feels it in her slightest gesture.

VARYA (*in a whisper*). Anya's in the doorway.

GAEV. What do you say? (*A pause.*) It's queer, there seems to be something wrong with my right eye. I don't see as well as I did. And on Thursday when I was in the district Court . . .

(*Enter* ANYA.)

VARYA. Why aren't you asleep, Anya?

ANYA. I can't get to sleep.

GAEV. My pet. (*Kisses* ANYA'S *face and hands.*) My child. (*Weeps.*) You are not my niece, you are my angel, you are everything to me. Believe me, believe . . .

ANYA. I believe you, uncle. Everyone loves you and respects you . . . but, uncle dear, you must be silent . . . simply be silent. What were you saying just now about my mother, about your own sister? What made you say that?

GAEV. Yes, yes . . . (*Puts his hand over his face.*) Really, that was awful! My God, save me! And today I made a speech to the bookcase . . . so stupid! And only when I had finished, I saw how stupid it was.

VARYA. It's true, uncle, you ought to keep quiet. Don't talk, that's all.

ANYA. If you could keep from talking it would make things easier for you, too.

GAEV. I won't speak. (*Kisses* ANYA's *and* VARYA's *hands.*) I'll be silent. Only this is about business. On Thursday I was in the district Court; well, there was a large party of us there and we began talking of one thing and another, and this and that, and do you know, I believe that it will be possible to raise a loan on an I.O.U. to pay the arrears on the mortgage.

VARYA. If the Lord would help us!

GAEV. I'm going on Tuesday; I'll talk of it again. (*To* VARYA.) Don't

blubber. (*To* ANYA.) Your mamma will talk to Lopahin; of course, he won't refuse her. And as soon as you're rested you shall go to Yaroslavl to the Countess, your great-aunt. So we shall all set to work in three directions at once, and the business is done. We shall pay off arrears, I'm convinced of it. (*Puts a caramel in his mouth.*) I swear on my honour, I swear by anything you like, the estate shan't be sold. (*Excitedly.*) By my own happiness, I swear it! Here's my hand on it, call me the basest, vilest of men, if I let it come to an auction! Upon my soul I swear it!

ANYA (*her equanimity has returned, she is quite happy*). How good you are, uncle, and how clever! (*Embraces her uncle.*) I'm at peace now! Quite at peace! I'm happy!

(*Enter* FIRS.)

FIRS (*reproachfully*). Leonid Andreyevitch have you no fear of God? When are you going to bed?

GAEV. Directly, directly. You can go, Firs. I'll . . . yes, I will undress myself. Come, children, bye-bye. We'll go into details tomorrow, but now go to bed. (*Kisses* ANYA *and* VARYA.) I'm a man of the 'eighties. They run down that period, but still I can say I have had to suffer not a little for my convictions in my life. It's not for nothing that the peasant loves me. One must know the peasant! One must know how . . .

ANYA. At it again, uncle!

VARYA. Uncle dear, you'd better be quiet!

FIRS (*angrily*). Leonid Andreyevitch!

GAEV. I'm coming. I'm coming. Go to bed. Potted the shot—there's a shot for you! A beauty! (*Goes out,* FIRS *hobbling after him.*)

ANYA. My mind's at rest now. I don't want to go to Yaroslavl, I don't like my great-aunt, but still my mind's at rest. Thanks to uncle. (*Sits down.*)

VARYA. We must go to bed. I'm going. Something unpleasant happened

while you were away. In the old servants' quarters there are only the old
servants, as you know—Efimyushka,
Polya and Yevstigney—and Karp too.
They began letting stray people in to
spend the night—I said nothing. But all
at once I heard they had been spreading
a report that I gave them nothing but
pease pudding to eat. Out of stinginess,
you know. . . . And it was all Yevstigney's doing. . . . Very well, I said to
myself. . . . If that's how it is, I thought,
wait a bit. I sent for Yevstigney. . . .
(*Yawns.*) He comes. . . . "How's this,
Yevstigney," I said, "you could be such
a fool as to? . . ." (*Looking at* ANYA.)
Anitchka! (*A pause.*) She's asleep. (*Puts
her arm round* ANYA.) Come to bed
. . . come along! (*Leads her.*) My
darling has fallen asleep! Come . . .
(*They go.*)

(*Far away beyond the orchard a shepherd plays on a pipe.* TROFIMOV *crosses
the stage and, seeing* VARYA *and* ANYA,
stands still.)

VARYA. Sh! asleep, asleep. Come, my
own.

ANYA (*softly, half asleep*). I'm so
tired. Still those bells. Uncle . . . dear
. . . mamma and uncle. . . .

VARYA. Come, my own, come along.
(*They go into* ANYA'S *room.*)

TROFIMOV (*tenderly*). My sunshine!
My spring.

Act II

(*The open country. An old shrine,
long abandoned and fallen out of the
perpendicular; near it a well, large stones
that have apparently once been tomb-
stones, and an old garden seat. The road
to* GAEV'S *house is seen. On one side
rise dark poplars; and there the cherry
orchard begins. In the distance a row
of telegraph poles and far, far away on
the horizon there is faintly outlined a
great town, only visible in very fine clear*

weather. It is near sunset. CHARLOTTA,
YASHA *and* DUNYASHA *are sitting on the
seat.* EPIHODOV *is standing near, playing
something mournful on a guitar. All sit
plunged in thought.* CHARLOTTA *wears
an old forage cap; she has taken a gun
from her shoulder and is tightening the
buckle on the strap.*)

CHARLOTTA (*musingly*). I haven't a
real passport of my own, and I don't
know how old I am, and I always feel
that I'm a young thing. When I was
a little girl, my father and mother used
to travel about to fairs and give performances—very good ones. And I used to
dance *salto-mortale* and all sorts of
things. And when papa and mamma
died, a German lady took me and had
me educated. And so I grew up and became a governess. But where I came
from, and who I am, I don't know. . . .
Who my parents were, very likely they
weren't married . . . I don't know.
(*Takes a cucumber out of her pocket
and eats.*) I know nothing at all. (*A
pause.*) One wants to talk and has no
one to talk to . . . I have nobody.

EPIHODOV (*plays on the guitar and
sings*). "What care I for the noisy
world! What care I for friends or foes!"
How agreeable it is to play on the mandolin!

DUNYASHA. That's a guitar, not a
mandolin. (*Looks in a hand-mirror and
powders herself.*)

EPIHODOV. To a man mad with love,
it's a mandolin. (*Sings.*) "Were her
heart but aglow with love's mutual
flame." (YASHA *joins in.*)

CHARLOTTA. How shockingly these
people sing! Foo! Like jackals!

DUNYASHA (*to* YASHA). What happiness, though, to visit foreign lands.

YASHA. Ah, yes! I rather agree with
you there. (*Yawns, then lights a cigar.*)

EPIHODOV. That's comprehensible. In
foreign lands everything has long since
reached full complexion.

YASHA. That's so, of course.

EPIHODOV. I'm a cultivated man, I read remarkable books of all sorts, but I can never make out the tendency I am myself precisely inclined for, whether to live or to shoot myself, speaking precisely, but nevertheless I always carry a revolver. Here it is . . . (*Shows revolver.*)

CHARLOTTA. I've had enough, and now I'm going. (*Puts on the gun.*) Epihodov, you're a very clever fellow, and a very terrible one too, all the women must be wild about you. Br-r-r! (*Goes.*) These clever fellows are all so stupid; there's not a creature for me to speak to. . . . Always alone, alone, nobody belonging to me . . . and who I am, and why I'm on earth, I don't know. (*Walks away slowly.*)

EPIHODOV. Speaking precisely, not touching upon other subjects, I'm bound to admit about myself, that destiny behaves mercilessly to me, as a storm to a little boat. If, let us suppose, I am mistaken, then why did I wake up this morning, to quote an example, and look round, and there on my chest was a spider of fearful magnitude . . . like this. (*Shows with both hands.*) And then I take up a jug of kvass, to quench my thirst, and in it there is something in the highest degree unseemly of the nature of a cockroach. (*A pause.*) Have you read Buckle? (*A pause.*) I am desirous of troubling you, Dunyasha, with a couple of words.

DUNYASHA. Well, speak.

EPIHODOV. I should be desirous to speak with you alone. (*Sighs.*)

DUNYASHA (*embarrassed*). Well— only bring me my mantle first. It's by the cupboard. It's rather damp here.

EPIHODOV. Certainly. I will fetch it. Now I know what I must do with my revolver. (*Takes guitar and goes off playing on it.*)

YASHA. Two and twenty misfortunes! Between ourselves, he's a fool. (*Yawns.*)

DUNYASHA. God grant he doesn't shoot himself! (*A pause.*) I am so nervous, I'm always in a flutter. I was a little girl when I was taken into our lady's house, and now I have quite grown out of peasant ways, and my hands are white, as white as a lady's. I'm such a delicate, sensitive creature, I'm afraid of everything. I'm so frightened. And if you deceive me, Yasha, I don't know what will become of my nerves.

YASHA (*kisses her*). You're a peach! Of course a girl must never forget herself; what I dislike more than anything is a girl being flighty in her behaviour.

DUNYASHA. I'm passionately in love with you, Yasha; you are a man of culture—you can give your opinion about anything. (*A pause.*)

YASHA (*yawns*). Yes, that's so. My opinion is this: if a girl loves anyone, that means that she has no principles. (*A pause.*) It's pleasant smoking a cigar in the open air. (*Listens.*) Someone's coming this way . . . it's the gentlefolk. (*DUNYASHA embraces him impulsively.*) Go home, as though you had been to the river to bathe; go by that path, or else they'll meet you and suppose I have made an appointment with you here. That I can't endure.

DUNYASHA (*coughing softly*). The cigar has made my head ache. . . . (*Goes off.*)

(*YASHA remains sitting near the shrine. Enter* LYUBOV ANDREYEVNA, GAEV *and* LOPAHIN.)

LOPAHIN. You must make up your mind once for all—there's no time to lose. It's quite a simple question, you know. Will you consent to letting the land for building or not? One word in answer: Yes or no? Only one word!

LYUBOV. Who is smoking such horrible cigars here? (*Sits down.*)

GAEV. Now the railway line has been brought near, it's made things very convenient. (*Sits down.*) Here we have been over and lunched in town. Cannon off the white! I should like to go home and have a game.

LYUBOV. You have plenty of time.

LOPAHIN. Only one word! (*Beseechingly.*) Give me an answer!

GAEV (*yawning*). What do you say?

LYUBOV (*looks in her purse*). I had quite a lot of money here yesterday, and there's scarcely any left today. My poor Varya feeds us all on milk soup for the sake of economy; the old folks in the kitchen get nothing but pease pudding, while I waste my money in a senseless way. (*Drops purse, scattering gold pieces.*) There, they have all fallen out! (*Annoyed.*)

YASHA. Allow me, I'll soon pick them up. (*Collects the coins.*)

LYUBOV. Pray do, Yasha. And what did I go off to the town to lunch for? Your restaurant's a wretched place with its music and the tablecloth smelling of soap. . . . Why drink so much, Leonid? And eat so much? And talk so much? Today you talked a great deal again in the restaurant, and all so inappropriately. About the era of the 'seventies, about the decadents. And to whom? Talking to waiters about decadents!

LOPAHIN. Yes.

GAEV (*waving his hand*). I'm incorrigible; that's evident. (*Irritably to* YASHA.) Why is it you keep fidgeting about in front of us!

YASHA (*laughs*). I can't help laughing when I hear your voice.

GAEV (*to his sister*). Either I or he . . .

LYUBOV. Get along! Go away, Yasha.

YASHA (*gives* LYUBOV ANDREYEVNA *her purse*). Directly. (*Hardly able to suppress his laughter.*) This minute . . . (*Goes off.*)

LOPAHIN. Deriganov, the millionaire, means to buy your estate. They say he is coming to the sale himself.

LYUBOV. Where did you hear that?

LOPAHIN. That's what they say in town.

GAEV. Our aunt in Yaroslavl has promised to send help; but when, and how much she will send, we don't know.

LOPAHIN. How much will she send? A hundred thousand? Two hundred?

LYUBOV. Oh, well . . . Ten or fifteen thousand, and we must be thankful to get that.

LOPAHIN. Forgive me, but such reckless people as you are—such queer, unbusiness-like people—I never met in my life. One tells you in plain Russian your estate is going to be sold, and you seem not to understand it.

LYUBOV. What are we to do? Tell us what to do.

LOPAHIN. I do tell you every day. Every day I say the same thing. You absolutely must let the cherry orchard and the land on building leases; and do it at once, as quick as may be—the auction's close upon us! Do understand! Once make up your mind to build villas, and you can raise as much money as you like, and then you are saved.

LYUBOV. Villas and summer visitors —forgive me saying so—it's so vulgar.

GAEV. There I perfectly agree with you.

LOPAHIN. I shall sob, or scream, or fall into a fit. I can't stand it! You drive me mad! (*To* GAEV.) You're an old woman!

GAEV. What do you say?

LOPAHIN. An old woman! (*Gets up to go.*)

LYUBOV (*in dismay*). No, don't go! Do stay, my dear friend! Perhaps we shall think of something.

LOPAHIN. What is there to think of?

LYUBOV. Don't go, I entreat you! With you here it's more cheerful, anyway. (*A pause.*) I keep expecting something, as though the house were going to fall about our ears.

GAEV (*in profound dejection*). Potted the white! It fails—a kiss.

LYUBOV. We have been great sinners. . . .

LOPAHIN. You have no sins to repent of.

GAEV (*puts a caramel in his mouth*). They say I've eaten up my property in caramels. (*Laughs.*)

LYUBOV. Oh, my sins! I've always thrown my money away recklessly like a lunatic. I married a man who made nothing but debts. My husband died of champagne—he drank dreadfully. To my misery I loved another man, and immediately—it was my first punishment!—the blow fell upon me, here, in the river . . . my boy was drowned and I went abroad—went away for ever, never to return, not to see that river again . . . I shut my eyes, and fled, distracted, and *he* after me . . . pitilessly, brutally. I bought a villa at Mentone, for *he* fell ill there, and for three years I had no rest day or night. His illness wore me out, my soul was dried up. And last year, when my villa was sold to pay my debts, I went to Paris and there he robbed me of everything and abandoned me for another woman; and I tried to poison myself. . . . So stupid, so shameful! . . . And suddenly I felt a yearning for Russia, for my country, for my little girl . . . (*Dries her tears.*) Lord, Lord, be merciful! Forgive my sins! Do not chastise me more! (*Takes a telegram out of her pocket.*) I got this today from Paris. He implores forgiveness, entreats me to return. (*Tears up the telegram.*) I fancy there is music somewhere. (*Listens.*)

GAEV. That's our famous Jewish orchestra. You remember, four violins, a flute and a double bass.

LYUBOV. That's still in existence? We ought to send for them one evening, and give a dance.

LOPAHIN (*listens*). I can't hear. . . . (*Hums softly.*) "For money the Germans will turn a Russian into a Frenchman." (*Laughs.*) I did see such a piece at the theatre yesterday! It was funny!

LYUBOV. And most likely there was nothing funny in it. You shouldn't look at plays, you should look at yourselves a little oftener. How grey your lives are! How much nonsense you talk.

LOPAHIN. That's true. One may say honestly, we live a fool's life. (*Pause.*) My father was a peasant, an idiot; he knew nothing and taught me nothing, only beat me when he was drunk, and always with his stick. In reality I am just such another blockhead and idiot. I've learnt nothing properly. I write a wretched hand. I write so that I feel ashamed before folks, like a pig.

LYUBOV. You ought to get married, my dear fellow.

LOPAHIN. Yes . . . that's true.

LYUBOV. You should marry our Varya, she's a good girl.

LOPAHIN. Yes.

LYUBOV. She's a good-natured girl, she's busy all day long, and what's more, she loves you. And you have liked her for ever so long.

LOPAHIN. Well? I'm not against it. . . . She's a good girl. (*Pause.*)

GAEV. I've been offered a place in the bank: 6,000 roubles a year. Did you know?

LYUBOV. You would never do for that! You must stay as you are.

(*Enter* FIRS *with overcoat.*)

FIRS. Put it on, sir, it's damp.

GAEV (*putting it on*). You bother me, old fellow.

FIRS. You can't go on like this. You went away in the morning without leaving word. (*Looks him over.*)

LYUBOV. You look older, Firs!

FIRS. What is your pleasure?

LOPAHIN. You look older, she said.

FIRS. I've had a long life. They were arranging my wedding before your papa was born. . . . (*Laughs.*) I was the head footman before the emancipation came. I wouldn't consent to be set free then; I stayed on with the old master. . . .

(*A pause.*) I remember what rejoicings they made and didn't know themselves what they were rejoicing over.

LOPAHIN. Those were fine old times. There was flogging anyway.

FIRS (*not hearing*). To be sure! The peasants knew their place, and the masters knew theirs; but now they're all at sixes and sevens, there's no making it out.

GAEV. Hold your tongue, Firs. I must go to town tomorrow. I have been promised an introduction to a general, who might let us have a loan.

LOPAHIN. You won't bring that off. And you won't pay your arrears, you may rest assured of that.

LYUBOV. That's all his nonsense. There is no such general!

(*Enter* TROFIMOV, ANYA *and* VARYA.)

GAEV. Here come our girls.

ANYA. There's mamma on the seat.

LYUBOV (*tenderly*). Come here, come along. My darlings! (*Embraces* ANYA *and* VARYA.) If you only knew how I love you both. Sit beside me, there, like that. (*All sit down.*)

LOPAHIN. Our perpetual student is always with the young ladies.

TROFIMOV. That's not your business.

LOPAHIN. He'll soon be fifty, and he's still a student.

TROFIMOV. Drop your idiotic jokes.

LOPAHIN. Why are you so cross, you queer fish?

TROFIMOV. Oh, don't persist!

LOPAHIN (*laughs*). Allow me to ask you what's your idea of me?

TROFIMOV. I'll tell you my idea of you, Yermolay Alexeyevitch: you are a rich man, you'll soon be a millionaire. Well, just as in the economy of nature a wild beast is of use, who devours everything that comes in his way, so you too have your use. (*All laugh.*)

VARYA. Better tell us something about the planets, Petya.

LYUBOV. No, let us go on with the conversation we had yesterday.

TROFIMOV. What was it about?

GAEV. About pride.

TROFIMOV. We had a long conversation yesterday, but we came to no conclusion. In pride, in your sense of it, there is something mystical. Perhaps you are right from your point of view; but if one looks at it simply, without subtlety, what sort of pride can there be, what sense is there in it, if man in his physiological formation is very imperfect, if in the immense majority of cases he is coarse, dull-witted, profoundly unhappy? One must give up glorification of self. One should work, and nothing else.

GAEV. One must die in any case.

TROFIMOV. Who knows? And what does it mean—dying? Perhaps man has a hundred senses, and only the five we know are lost at death, while the other ninety-five remain alive.

LYUBOV. How clever you are, Petya!

LOPAHIN (*ironically*). Fearfully clever!

TROFIMOV. Humanity progresses, perfecting its powers. Everything that is beyond its ken now will one day become familiar and comprehensive; only we must work, we must with all our powers aid the seekers after truth. Here among us in Russia the workers are few in number as yet. The vast majority of the intellectual people I know, seek nothing, do nothing, are not fit as yet for work of any kind. They call themselves intellectual, but they treat their servants as inferiors, behave to the peasants as though they were animals, learn little, read nothing seriously, do practically nothing, only talk about science and know very little about art. They are all serious people, they all have severe faces, they all talk of weighty matters and air their theories, and yet the vast majority of us—ninety-nine per cent.—live like savages, at the least thing fly to blows and abuse, eat piggishly, sleep in filth and stuffiness, bugs everywhere, stench and damp and moral impurity. And it's clear all our fine talk is only to divert our attention and other people's. Show me where to find the crèches there's so much talk about, and the reading-rooms? They only exist in novels: in real life there are none of them. There is nothing but filth and vulgarity and Asiatic apathy. I fear and dislike very serious faces. I'm afraid of serious conversations. We should do better to be silent.

LOPAHIN. You know, I get up at five o'clock in the morning, and I work from morning to night; and I've money, my own and other people's, always passing through my hands, and I see what people are made of all round me. One has only to begin to do anything to see how few honest, decent people there are. Sometimes when I lie awake at night, I think: "Oh! Lord, thou hast given us immense forests, boundless plains, the widest horizons, and living here we ourselves ought really to be giants."

LYUBOV. You ask for giants! They are no good except in storybooks; in real life they frighten us.

(EPIHODOV *advances in the background, playing on the guitar.*)

LYUBOV (*dreamily*). There goes Epihodov.

ANYA (*dreamily*). There goes Epihodov.

GAEV. The sun has set, my friends.

TROFIMOV. Yes.

GAEV (*not loudly, but, as it were, declaiming*). O nature, divine nature, thou art bright with eternal lustre, beautiful and indifferent! Thou, whom we call mother, thou dost unite within thee life and death! Thou dost give life and dost destroy!

VARYA (*in a tone of supplication*). Uncle!

ANYA. Uncle, you are at it again!

TROFIMOV. You'd much better be cannoning off the red!

GAEV. I'll hold my tongue, I will.

(*All sit plunged in thought. Perfect stillness. The only thing audible is the muttering of* FIRS. *Suddenly there is a sound in the distance, as it were from the sky—the sound of a breaking harp-string, mournfully dying away.*)

LYUBOV. What is that?

LOPAHIN. I don't know. Somewhere far away a bucket fallen and broken in the pits. But somewhere very far away.

GAEV. It might be a bird of some sort—such as a heron.

TROFIMOV. Or an owl.

LYUBOV (*shudders*). I don't know why, but it's horrid. (*A pause.*)

FIRS. It was the same before the calamity—the owl hooted and the samovar hissed all the time.

GAEV. Before what calamity?

FIRS. Before the emancipation. (*A pause.*)

LYUBOV. Come, my friends, let us be going; evening is falling. (*To* ANYA.) There are tears in your eyes. What is it, darling? (*Embraces her.*)

ANYA. Nothing, mamma; it's nothing.

TROFIMOV. There is somebody coming.

(THE WAYFARER *appears in a shabby white forage cap and an overcoat; he is slightly drunk.*)

WAYFARER. Allow me to inquire, can I get to the station this way?

GAEV. Yes. Go along that road.

WAYFARER. I thank you most feelingly. (*Coughing.*) The weather is superb. (*Declaims.*) My brother, my suffering brother! . . . Come out to the Volga! Whose groan do you hear? . . . (*To* VARYA.) Mademoiselle, vouchsafe a hungry Russian thirty kopeks.

(VARYA *utters a shriek of alarm.*)

LOPAHIN (*angrily*). There's a right and a wrong way of doing everything!

LYUBOV (*hurriedly*). Here, take this. (*Looks in her purse.*) I've no silver. No matter—here's gold for you.

WAYFARER. I thank you most feelingly! (*Goes off.*)

(*Laughter.*)

VARYA (*frightened*). I'm going home —I'm going . . . Oh, mamma, the servants have nothing to eat, and you gave him gold!

LYUBOV. There's no doing anything with me. I'm so silly! When we get home, I'll give you all I possess. Yermolay Alexeyevitch, you will lend me some more . . . !

LOPAHIN. I will.

LYUBOV. Come, friends, it's time to be going. And Varya, we have made a match of it for you. I congratulate you.

VARYA (*through her tears*). Mamma, that's not a joking matter.

LOPAHIN. "Ophelia, get thee to a nunnery!"

GAEV. My hands are trembling; it's a long while since I had a game of billiards.

LOPAHIN. "Ophelia! Nymph, in thy orisons be all my sins remember'd."

LYUBOV. Come, it will soon be supper-time.

VARYA. How he frightened me! My heart's simply throbbing.

LOPAHIN. Let me remind you, ladies and gentlemen: on the 22nd of August the cherry orchard will be sold. Think about that! Think about it! (*All go off, except* TROFIMOV *and* ANYA.)

ANYA (*laughing*). I'm grateful to the wayfarer! He frightened Varya and we are left alone.

TROFIMOV. Varya's afraid we shall fall in love with each other, and for days together she won't leave us. With her narrow brain she can't grasp that we are above love. To eliminate the petty and transitory which hinders us from being free and happy—that is the aim and meaning of our life. Forward! We go forward irresistibly towards the bright star that shines yonder in the distance. Forward! Do not lag behind, friends.

ANYA (*claps her hands*). How well you speak! (*A pause.*) It is divine here today.

TROFIMOV. Yes, it's glorious weather.

ANYA. Somehow, Petya, you've made me so that I don't love the cherry orchard as I used to. I used to love it so dearly. I used to think that there was no spot on earth like our garden.

TROFIMOV. All Russia is our garden. The earth is great and beautiful—there are many beautiful places in it. (*A pause.*) Think only, Anya, your grandfather, and great-grandfather, and all your ancestors were slave-owners—the owners of living souls—and from every cherry in the orchard, from every leaf, from every trunk there are human creatures looking at you. Cannot you hear their voices? Oh, it is awful! Your orchard is a fearful thing, and when in the evening or at night one walks about the orchard, the old bark on the trees glimmers dimly in the dusk, and the old cherry trees seem to be dreaming of centuries gone by and tortured by fearful visions. Yes! We are at least two hundred years behind, we have really gained nothing yet, we have no definite attitude to the past, we do nothing but theorise or complain of depression or drink vodka. It is clear that to begin to live in the present we must first expiate our past, we must break with it; and we can expiate it only by suffering, by extraordinary unceasing labour. Understand that, Anya.

ANYA. The house we live in has long ceased to be our own, and I shall leave it, I give you my word.

TROFIMOV. If you have the house keys, fling them into the well and go away. Be free as the wind.

ANYA (*in ecstasy*). How beautifully you said that!

TROFIMOV. Believe me, Anya, believe me! I am not thirty yet, I am young, I am still a student, but I have gone through so much already! As soon as winter comes I am hungry, sick, careworn, poor as a beggar, and what ups and downs of fortune have I not known! And my soul was always, every minute, day and night, full of inexplicable forebodings. I have a foreboding of happiness, Anya. I see glimpses of it already.

ANYA (*pensively*). The moon is rising.

(EPIHODOV *is heard playing still the same mournful song on the guitar. The moon rises. Somewhere near the poplars* VARYA *is looking for* ANYA *and calling* "Anya! Where are you?")

TROFIMOV. Yes, the moon is rising. (*A pause.*) Here is happiness—here it comes! It is coming nearer and nearer; already I can hear its footsteps. And if we never see it—if we may never know it—what does it matter? Others will see it after us.

VARYA's VOICE. Anya! Where are you?

TROFIMOV. That Varya again! (*Angrily.*) It's revolting!

ANYA. Well, let's go down to the river. It's lovely there.

TROFIMOV. Yes, let's go. (*They go.*)

VARYA's VOICE. Anya! Anya!

Act III

(*A drawing-room divided by an arch from a larger drawing-room. A chandelier burning. The Jewish orchestra, the same that was mentioned in Act II, is heard playing in the ante-room. It is evening. In the larger drawing-room they are dancing the grand chain. The voice of* SEMYONOV-PISHTCHIK: "Promenade à une paire!" *Then enter the drawing-room in couples first* PISHTCHIK *and* CHARLOTTA IVANOVNA, *then* TROFIMOV *and* LYUBOV ANDREYEVNA, *thirdly* ANYA *with the* POST-OFFICE CLERK, *fourthly* VARYA *with the* STATION MASTER, *and other guests,* VARYA *is quietly weeping and wiping away her tears as she dances. In the last couple is* DUNYASHA. *They move across the drawing-room.* PISHTCHIK *shouts:* "Grand rond, balancez!" *and* "Les Cavaliers à genou et remerciez vos dames." FIRS *in a swallow-tail coat brings in seltzer water on a tray.* PISHTCHIK *and* TROFIMOV *enter the drawing-room.*)

PISHTCHIK. I am a full-blooded man; I have already had two strokes. Dancing's hard work for me, but as they say, if you're in the pack, you must bark with the rest. I'm as strong, I may say, as a horse. My parent, who would have his joke—may the Kingdom of Heaven be his!—used to say about our origin that the ancient stock of the Semyonov-Pishtchiks was derived from the very horse that Caligula made a member of the senate. (*Sits down.*) But I've no money, that's where the mischief is. A hungry dog believes in nothing but meat. . . . (*Snores, but at once wakes up.*) That's like me . . . I can think of nothing but money.

TROFIMOV. There really is something horsy about your appearance.

PISHTCHIK. Well . . . a horse is a fine beast . . . a horse can be sold.

(*There is the sound of billiards being played in an adjoining room.* VARYA *appears in the arch leading to the larger drawing-room.*)

TROFIMOV (*teasing*). Madame Lopahin! Madame Lopahin!

VARYA (*angrily*). Mangy-looking gentleman!

TROFIMOV. Yes, I am a mangy-looking gentleman, and I'm proud of it!

VARYA (*pondering bitterly*). Here we have hired musicians and nothing to pay them! (*Goes out.*)

TROFIMOV (*to* PISHTCHIK). If the

energy you have wasted during your lifetime in trying to find the money to pay your interest, had gone to something else, you might in the end have turned the world upside down.

PISHTCHIK. Nietzsche, the philosopher, a very great and celebrated man . . . of enormous intellect . . . says in his works, that one can make forged bank-notes.

TROFIMOV. Why, have you read Nietzsche?

PISHTCHIK. What next . . . Dashenka told me. . . . And now I am in such a position, I might just as well forge bank-notes. The day after tomorrow I must pay 310 roubles—130 I have procured. (*Feels in his pockets, in alarm.*) The money's gone! I have lost my money! (*Through his tears.*) Where's the money? (*Gleefully.*) Why, here it is behind the lining. . . . It has made me hot all over.

(*Enter* LYUBOV ANDREYEVNA *and* CHARLOTTA IVANOVNA.)

LYUBOV (*hums the Lezginka*). Why is Leonid so long? What can he be doing in town? (*To* DUNYASHA.) Offer the musicians some tea.

TROFIMOV. The sale hasn't taken place, most likely.

LYUBOV. It's the wrong time to have the orchestra, and the wrong time to give a dance. Well, never mind. (*Sits down and hums softly.*)

CHARLOTTA (*gives* PISHTCHIK *a pack of cards*). Here's a pack of cards. Think of any card you like.

PISHTCHIK. I've thought of one.

CHARLOTTA. Shuffle the pack now. That's right. Give it here, my dear Mr. Pishtchik. Ein, zwei, drei—now look, it's in your breast pocket.

PISHTCHIK (*taking a card out of his breast pocket*). The eight of spades! Perfectly right! (*Wonderingly.*) Fancy that now!

CHARLOTTA (*holding pack of cards in her hands, to* TROFIMOV). Tell me quickly which is the top card.

TROFIMOV. Well, the queen of spades.

CHARLOTTA. It is! (*To* PISHTCHIK.) Well, which card is uppermost?

PISHTCHIK. The ace of hearts.

CHARLOTTA. It is! (*Claps her hands, pack of cards disappears.*) Ah! what lovely weather it is today!

(*A mysterious feminine voice which seems coming out of the floor answers her.* "Oh, yes, it's magnificent weather, madam.")

CHARLOTTA. You are my perfect ideal.

VOICE. And I greatly admire you too, madam.

STATION MASTER (*applauding*). The lady ventriloquist—bravo!

PISHTCHIK (*wonderingly*). Fancy that now! Most enchanting Charlotta Ivanovna. I'm simply in love with you.

CHARLOTTA. In love? (*Shrugging shoulders.*) What do you know of love, guter Mensch, aber schlechter Musikant.

TROFIMOV (*pats* PISHTCHIK *on the shoulder*). You dear old horse. . . .

CHARLOTTA. Attention, please! Another trick! (*Takes a travelling rug from the chair.*) Here's a very good rug; I want to sell it. (*Shaking it out.*) Doesn't anyone want to buy it?

PISHTCHIK (*wonderingly*). Fancy that!

CHARLOTTA. Ein, zwei, drei! (*Quickly picks up rug she has dropped; behind the rug stands* ANYA; *she makes a curtsey, runs to her mother, embraces her and runs back into the larger drawing-room amidst general enthusiasm.*)

LYUBOV (*applauds*). Bravo! Bravo!

CHARLOTTA. Now again! Ein, zwei, drei! (*Lifts up the rug; behind the rug stands* VARYA, *bowing.*)

PISHTCHIK (*wonderingly*). Fancy that now!

CHARLOTTA. That's the end. (*Throws the rug at* PISHTCHIK, *makes a curtsey, runs into the larger drawing-room.*)

PISHTCHIK (*hurries after her*). Mischievous creature! Fancy! (*Goes out.*)

LYUBOV. And still Leonid doesn't come. I can't understand what he's doing in the town so long! Why, everything must be over by now. The estate is sold, or the sale has not taken place. Why keep us so long in suspense?

VARYA (*trying to console her*). Uncle's bought it. I feel sure of that.

TROFIMOV (*ironically*). Oh, yes!

VARYA. Great-aunt sent him an authorisation to buy it in her name, and transfer the debt. She's doing it for Anya's sake, and I'm sure God will be merciful. Uncle will buy it.

LYUBOV. My aunt in Yaroslavl sent fifteen thousand to buy the estate in her name, she doesn't trust us—but that's not enough even to pay the arrears. (*Hides her face in her hands.*) My fate is being sealed today, my fate . . .

TROFIMOV (*teasing* VARYA). Madame Lopahin.

VARYA (*angrily*). Perpetual student! Twice already you've been sent down from the University.

LYUBOV. Why are you angry, Varya? He's teasing you about Lopahin. Well, what of that? Marry Lopahin if you like, he's a good man, and interesting; if you don't want to, don't! Nobody compels you, darling.

VARYA. I must tell you plainly, mamma, I look at the matter seriously; he's a good man, I like him.

LYUBOV. Well, marry him. I can't see what you're waiting for.

VARYA. Mamma, I can't make him an offer myself. For the last two years, everyone's been talking to me about him. Everybody talks; but he says nothing or else makes a joke. I see what it means. He's growing rich, he's absorbed in business, he has no thoughts for me. If I had money, were it ever so little, if I had only a hundred roubles, I'd throw everything up and go far away. I would go into a nunnery.

TROFIMOV. What bliss!

VARYA (*to* TROFIMOV). A student ought to have sense! (*In a soft tone with tears.*) How ugly you've grown, Petya! How old you look! (*To* LYUBOV ANDREYEVNA, *no longer crying.*) But I can't do without work, mamma; I must have something to do every minute.

(*Enter* YASHA.)

YASHA (*hardly restraining his laughter*). Epihodov has broken a billiard cue! (*Goes out.*)

VARYA. What is Epihodov doing here? Who gave him leave to play billiards? I can't make these people out. (*Goes out.*)

LYUBOV. Don't tease her, Petya. You see she has grief enough without that.

TROFIMOV. She is so very officious, meddling in what's not her business. All the summer she's given Anya and me no peace. She's afraid of a love affair between us. What's it to do with her? Besides, I have given no grounds for it. Such triviality is not in my line. We are above love!

LYUBOV. And I suppose I am beneath love. (*Very uneasily.*) Why is it Leonid's not here? If only I could know whether the estate is sold or not! It seems such an incredible calamity that I really don't know what to think. I am distracted . . . I shall scream in a minute . . . I shall do something stupid. Save me, Petya, tell me something, talk to me!

TROFIMOV. What does it matter whether the estate is sold today or not? That's all done with long ago. There's no turning back, the path is overgrown. Don't worry yourself, dear Lyubov Andreyevna. You mustn't deceive yourself; for once in your life you must face the truth!

LYUBOV. What truth? You see where the truth lies, but I seem to have lost my sight, I see nothing. You settle every great problem so boldly, but tell me, my dear boy, isn't it because you're young—because you haven't yet understood one of your problems through suffering? You look forward boldly, and isn't it that you don't see and don't expect anything dreadful because life is still hidden from your young eyes? You're bolder, more honest, deeper than we are, but think, be just a little magnanimous, have pity on me. I was born here, you know, my father and mother lived here, my grandfather lived here, I love this house. I can't conceive of life without the cherry orchard, and if it really must be sold, then sell me with the orchard. (*Embraces* TROFIMOV, *kisses him on the forehead.*) My boy was drowned here. (*Weeps.*) Pity me, my dear kind fellow.

TROFIMOV. You know I feel for you with all my heart.

LYUBOV. But that should have been said differently, so differently. (*Takes out her handkerchief, telegram falls on the floor.*) My heart is so heavy today. It's so noisy here, my soul is quivering at every sound, I'm shuddering all over, but I can't go away; I'm afraid to be quiet and alone. Don't be hard on me, Petya . . . I love you as though you were one of ourselves. I would gladly let you marry Anya—I swear I would—only, my dear boy, you must take your degree, you do nothing—you're simply tossed by fate from place to place. That's so strange. It is, isn't it? And you must do something with your beard to make it grow somehow. (*Laughs.*) You look so funny!

TROFIMOV (*picks up the telegram*). I've no wish to be a beauty.

LYUBOV. That's a telegram from Paris. I get one every day. One yesterday and one today. That savage creature is ill again, he's in trouble again. He begs forgiveness, beseeches me to go, and really I ought to go to Paris to see him. You look shocked, Petya. What am I to do, my dear, what am I to do? He is ill, he is alone and unhappy, and who'll

look after him, who'll keep him from doing the wrong thing, who'll give him his medicine at the right time? And why hide it or be silent? I love him, that's clear. I love him! I love him! He's a millstone about my neck, I'm going to the bottom with him, but I love that stone and can't live without it. (*Presses* TROFIMOV's *hand.*) Don't think ill of me, Petya, don't tell me anything, don't tell me . . .

TROFIMOV (*through his tears*). For God's sake forgive my frankness: why, he robbed you!

LYUBOV. No! No! No! You mustn't speak like that. (*Covers her ears.*)

TROFIMOV. He is a wretch! You're the only person that doesn't know it! He's a worthless creature! A despicable wretch!

LYUBOV (*getting angry, but speaking with restraint*). You're twenty-six or twenty-seven years old, but you're still a schoolboy.

TROFIMOV. Possibly.

LYUBOV. You should be a man at your age! You should understand what love means! And you ought to be in love yourself. You ought to fall in love! (*Angrily.*) Yes, yes, and it's not purity in you, you're simply a prude, a comic fool, a freak.

TROFIMOV (*in horror*). The things she's saying!

LYUBOV. I am above love! You're not above love, but simply as our Firs here says, "You are a good-for-nothing." At your age not to have a mistress!

TROFIMOV (*in horror*). This is awful! The things she is saying! (*Goes rapidly into the larger drawing-room clutching his head.*) This is awful! I can't stand it! I'm going. (*Goes off, but at once returns.*) All is over between us! (*Goes off into the ante-room.*)

LYUBOV (*shouts after him*). Petya! Wait a minute! You funny creature! I was joking! Petya! (*There is a sound of somebody running quickly downstairs*

and suddenly falling with a crash. ANYA
and VARYA *scream, but there is a sound
of laughter at once.*)

LYUBOV. What has happened?

(ANYA *runs in.*)

ANYA (*laughing*). Petya's fallen
downstairs! (*Runs out.*)

LYUBOV. What a queer fellow that
Petya is!

(*The* STATION MASTER *stands in the
middle of the larger room and reads
"The Magdalene," by Alexey Tolstoy.
They listen to him, but before he has
recited many lines strains of a waltz are
heard from the ante-room and the reading is broken off. All dance.* TROFIMOV,
ANYA, VARYA *and* LYUBOV ANDREYEVNA
come in from the ante-room.)

LYUBOV. Come, Petya—come, pure
heart! I beg your pardon. Let's have a
dance! (*Dances with* PETYA.)

(ANYA *and* VARYA *dance.* FIRS *comes
in, puts his stick down near the side
door.* YASHA *also comes into the drawing-room and looks on at the dancing.*)

YASHA. What is it, old man?

FIRS. I don't feel well. In old days
we used to have generals, barons and
admirals dancing at our balls, and now
we send for the post-office clerk and the
station master and even they're not over-
anxious to come. I am getting feeble.
The old master, the grandfather, used to
give sealing-wax for all complaints. I
have been taking sealing-wax for twenty
years or more. Perhaps that's what's
kept me alive.

YASHA. You bore me, old man!
(*Yawns.*) It's time you were done with.

FIRS. Ach, you're a good-for-nothing! (*Mutters.*)

(TROFIMOV *and* LYUBOV ANDREYEVNA
*dance in larger room and then on to the
stage.*)

LYUBOV. Merci. I'll sit down a little.
(*Sits down.*) I'm tired.

(*Enter* ANYA.)

ANYA (*excitedly*). There's a man in

the kitchen has been saying that the
cherry orchard's been sold today.

LYUBOV. Sold to whom?

ANYA. He didn't say to whom. He's
gone away.

(*She dances with* TROFIMOV, *and they
go off into the larger room.*)

YASHA. There was an old man gossiping there, a stranger.

FIRS. Leonid Andreyevitch isn't here
yet, he hasn't come back. He has his
light overcoat on, *demi-saison,* he'll catch
cold for sure. Ach! Foolish young things!

LYUBOV. I feel as though I should
die. Go, Yasha, find out to whom it has
been sold.

YASHA. But he went away long ago,
the old chap. (*Laughs.*)

LYUBOV (*with slight vexation*).
What are you laughing at? What are you
pleased at?

YASHA. Epihodov is so funny. He's
a silly fellow, two and twenty misfortunes.

LYUBOV. Firs, if the estate is sold,
where will you go?

FIRS. Where you bid me, there I'll
go.

LYUBOV. Why do you look like that?
Are you ill? You ought to be in bed.

FIRS. Yes. (*Ironically.*) Me go to
bed and who's to wait here? Who's to
see to things without me? I'm the only
one in all the house.

YASHA (*to* LYUBOV ANDREYEVNA).
Lyubov Andreyevna, permit me to make
a request of you; if you go back to Paris
again, be so kind as to take me with you.
It's positively impossible for me to stay
here. (*Looking about him; in an undertone.*) There's no need to say it, you see
for yourself—an uncivilised country, the
people have no morals, and then the dull-
ness! The food in the kitchen's abominable, and then Firs runs after one
muttering all sorts of unsuitable words.
Take me with you, please do!

(*Enter* PISHTCHIK.)

PISHTCHIK. Allow me to ask you for a waltz, my dear lady. (LYUBOV ANDREYEVNA *goes with him.*) Enchanting lady, I really must borrow of you just 180 roubles (*dances*), only 180 roubles. (*They pass into the larger room.*)

YASHA (*hums softly*). "Knowest thou my soul's emotion."

(*In the larger drawing-room, a figure in a grey top hat and in check trousers is gesticulating and jumping about. Shouts of "Bravo, Charlotta Ivanovna."*)

DUNYASHA (*she has stopped to powder herself*). My young lady tells me to dance. There are plenty of gentlemen, and too few ladies, but dancing makes me giddy and makes my heart beat. Firs, the post-office clerk said something to me just now that quite took my breath away.

(*Music becomes more subdued.*)

FIRS. What did he say to you?

DUNYASHA. He said I was like a flower.

YASHA (*yawns*). What ignorance! (*Goes out.*)

DUNYASHA. Like a flower. I am a girl of such delicate feelings. I am awfully fond of soft speeches.

FIRS. Your head's being turned.

(*Enter* EPIHODOV.)

EPIHODOV. You have no desire to see me, Dunyasha. I must be an insect. (*Sighs.*) Ah! life!

DUNYASHA. What is it you want?

EPIHODOV. Undoubtedly you may be right. (*Sighs.*) But of course, if one looks at it from that point of view, if I may so express myself, you have, excuse my plain speaking, reduced me to a complete state of mind. I know my destiny. Every day some misfortune befalls me and I have long ago grown accustomed to it, so that I look upon my fate with a smile. You gave me your word, and though I . . .

DUNYASHA. Let us have a talk later, I entreat you, but now leave me in peace, for I am lost in reverie. (*Plays with her fan.*)

EPIHODOV. I have a misfortune every day, and if I may venture to express myself, I merely smile at it, I even laugh.

(*VARYA enters from the larger drawing-room.*)

VARYA. You still have not gone, Epihodov. What a disrespectful creature you are, really! (*To* DUNYASHA.) Go along, Dunyasha! (*To* EPIHODOV.) First you play billiards and break the cue, then you go wandering about the drawing-room like a visitor!

EPIHODOV. You really cannot, if I may so express myself, call me to account like this.

VARYA. I'm not calling you to account, I'm speaking to you: You do nothing but wander from place to place and don't do your work. We keep you as a counting-house clerk, but what use you are I can't say.

EPIHODOV (*offended*). Whether I work or whether I walk, whether I eat or whether I play billiards, is a matter to be judged by persons of understanding and my elders.

VARYA. You dare to tell me that! (*Firing up.*) You dare! You mean to say I've no understanding. Begone from here! This minute!

EPIHODOV (*intimidated*). I beg you to express yourself with delicacy.

VARYA (*beside herself with anger*). This moment! get out! away! (*He goes towards the door, she following him.*) Two and twenty misfortunes! Take yourself off! Don't let me set eyes on you! (EPIHODOV *has gone out, behind the door his voice,* "I shall lodge a complaint against you.") What! You're coming back? (*Snatches up the stick* FIRS *has put down near the door.*) Come! Come! Come! I'll show you! What! you're coming? Then take that! (*She swings the stick, at the very moment that* LOPAHIN *comes in.*)

LOPAHIN. Very much obliged to you!

VARYA (*angrily and ironically*). I beg your pardon!

LOPAHIN. Not at all! I humbly thank you for your kind reception!

VARYA. No need of thanks for it. (*Moves away, then looks round and asks softly.*) I haven't hurt you?

LOPAHIN. Oh, no! Not at all! There's an immense bump coming up, though!

VOICES FROM LARGER ROOM. Lopahin has come! Yermolay Alexeyevitch!

PISHTCHIK. What do I see and hear? (*Kisses* LOPAHIN.) There's a whiff of cognac about you, my dear soul, and we're making merry here too!

(*Enter* LYUBOV ANDREYEVNA.)

LYUBOV. Is it you, Yermolay Alexeyevitch? Why have you been so long? Where's Leonid?

LOPAHIN. Leonid Andreyevitch arrived with me. He is coming.

LYUBOV (*in agitation*). Well! Well! Was there a sale? Speak!

LOPAHIN (*embarrassed, afraid of betraying his joy*). The sale was over at four o'clock. We missed our train—had to wait till half-past nine. (*Sighing heavily.*) Ugh! I feel a little giddy.

(*Enter* GAEV. *In his right hand he has purchases, with his left hand he is wiping away his tears.*)

LYUBOV. Well, Leonid? What news? (*Impatiently, with tears*). Make haste, for God's sake!

GAEV (*makes her no answer, simply waves his hand. To* FIRS, *weeping*). Here, take them; there's anchovies, Kertch herrings. I have eaten nothing all day. What I have been through! (*Door into the billiard room is open. There is heard a knocking of balls and the voice of* YASHA *saying* "Eighty-seven." GAEV's *expression changes, he leaves off weeping.*) I am fearfully tired. Firs, come and help me change my things. (*Goes to his own room across the larger drawing-room.*)

PISHTCHIK. How about the sale? Tell us, do!

LYUBOV. Is the cherry orchard sold?

LOPAHIN. It is sold.

LYUBOV. Who has bought it?

LOPAHIN. I have bought it.

(*A pause.* LYUBOV *is crushed; she would fall down if she were not standing near a chair and table.* VARYA *takes keys from her waist-band, flings them on the floor in middle of drawing-room and goes out.*)

LOPAHIN. I have bought it! Wait a bit, ladies and gentlemen, pray. My head's a bit muddled, I can't speak. (*Laughs.*) We came to the auction. Deriganov was there already. Leonid Andreyevitch only had 15,000 and Deriganov bid 30,000, besides the arrears, straight off. I saw how the land lay. I bid against him. I bid 40,000, he bid 45,000, I said 55, and so he went on, adding 5 thousand and I adding 10. Well . . . So it ended. I bid 90, and it was knocked down to me. Now the cherry orchard's mine! Mine! (*Chuckles.*) My God, the cherry orchard's mine! Tell me that I'm drunk, that I'm out of my mind, that it's all a dream. (*Stamps with his feet.*) Don't laugh at me! If my father and my grandfather could rise from their graves and see all that has happened! How their Yermolay, ignorant, beaten Yermolay, who used to run about barefoot in winter, how that very Yermolay has bought the finest estate in the world! I have bought the estate where my father and grandfather were slaves, where they weren't even admitted into the kitchen. I am asleep, I am dreaming! It is all fancy, it is the work of your imagination plunged in the darkness of ignorance. (*Picks up keys, smiling fondly.*) She threw away the keys, she means to show she's not the housewife now. (*Jingles the keys.*) Well, no matter. (*The orchestra is heard tuning up.*) Hey, musicians! Play! I want to hear you. Come, all of you, and look how Yermolay Lopahin will take the axe to the cherry orchard, how the trees will fall to the ground! We will build houses on it and our grandsons and great-grandsons will see a new life springing up there. Music! Play up!

(*Music begins to play.* LYUBOV AN-DREYEVNA *has sunk into a chair and is weeping bitterly.*)

LOPAHIN (*reproachfully*). Why, why didn't you listen to me? My poor friend! Dear lady, there's no turning back now. (*With tears.*) Oh, if all this could be over, oh, if our miserable disjointed life could somehow soon be changed!

PISHTCHIK (*takes him by the arm; in an undertone*). She's weeping, let us go and leave her alone. Come. (*Takes him by the arm and leads him into the larger drawing-room.*)

LOPAHIN. What's that? Musicians, play up! All must be as I wish it. (*With irony.*) Here comes the new master, the owner of the cherry orchard! (*Accidentally tips over a little table, almost upsetting the candelabra.*) I can pay for everything! (*Goes out with* PISHTCHIK. *No one remains on the stage or in the larger drawing-room except* LYUBOV, *who sits huddled up, weeping bitterly. The music plays softly.* ANYA *and* TRO-FIMOV *come in quickly.* ANYA *goes up to her mother and falls on her knees before her.* TROFIMOV *stands at the entrance to the larger drawing-room.*)

ANYA. Mamma! Mamma, you're crying, dear, kind, good mamma! My precious! I love you! I bless you! The cherry orchard is sold, it is gone, that's true, that's true! But don't weep, mamma! Life is still before you, you have still your good, pure heart! Let us go, let us go, darling, away from here! We will make a new garden, more splendid than this one; you will see it, you will understand. And joy, quiet, deep joy, will sink into your soul like the sun at evening!

And you will smile, mamma! Come, darling, let us go!

Act IV

(SCENE: *Same as in First Act. There are neither curtains on the windows nor pictures on the walls: only a little furniture remains piled up in a corner as if for sale. There is a sense of desolation; near the outer door and in the background of the scene are packed trunks, travelling bags, etc. On the left the door is open, and from here the voices of* VARYA *and* ANYA *are audible.* LOPAHIN *is standing waiting.* YASHA *is holding a tray with glasses full of champagne. In front of the stage* EPIHODOV *is tying up a box. In the background behind the scene a hum of talk from the peasants who have come to say good-bye. The voice of* GAEV: "Thanks, brothers, thanks!")

YASHA. The peasants have come to say good-bye. In my opinion, Yermolay Alexeyevitch, the peasants are good-natured, but they don't know much about things.

(*The hum of talk dies away. Enter across front of stage* LYUBOV ANDRE-YEVNA *and* GAEV. *She is not weeping, but is pale; her face is quivering—she cannot speak.*)

GAEV. You give them your purse, Lyuba. That won't do—that won't do!

LYUBOV. I couldn't help it! I couldn't help it! (*Both go out.*)

LOPAHIN (*in the doorway, calls after them.*) You will take a glass at parting? Please do. I didn't think to bring any from the town, and at the station I could only get one bottle. Please take a glass. (*A pause.*) What? You don't care for any? (*Comes away from the door.*) If I'd known, I wouldn't have brought it. Well, and I'm not going to drink it. (YASHA *carefully sets the tray down on a chair.*) You have a glass, Yasha, any-way.

YASHA. Good luck to the travellers, and luck to those that stay behind! (*Drinks.*) This champagne isn't the real thing, I can assure you.

LOPAHIN. It cost eight roubles the bottle. (*A pause.*) It's devilish cold here.

YASHA. They haven't heated the stove today—it's all the same since we're going. (*Laughs.*)

LOPAHIN. What are you laughing for?

YASHA. For pleasure.

LOPAHIN. Though it's October, it's as still and sunny as though it were sum-mer. It's just right for building! (*Looks at his watch; says in doorway:*) Take note, ladies and gentlemen, the train goes in forty-seven minutes; so you ought to start for the station in twenty minutes. You must hurry up!

(TROFIMOV *comes in from out of doors wearing a great-coat.*)

TROFIMOV. I think it must be time to start, the horses are ready. The devil only knows what's become of my go-loshes; they're lost. (*In the doorway.*) Anya! My goloshes aren't here. I can't find them.

LOPAHIN. And I'm getting off to Harkov. I am going in the same train with you. I'm spending all the winter at Harkov. I've been wasting all my time gossiping with you and fretting with no work to do. I can't get on without work. I don't know what to do with my hands, they flap about so queerly, as if they didn't belong to me.

TROFIMOV. Well, we're just going away, and you will take up your profit-able labours again.

LOPAHIN. Do take a glass.

TROFIMOV. No, thanks.

LOPAHIN. Then you're going to Mos-cow now?

TROFIMOV. Yes. I shall see them as far as the town, and tomorrow I shall go on to Moscow.

LOPAHIN. Yes, I daresay, the profes-sors aren't giving any lectures, they're waiting for your arrival.

TROFIMOV. That's not your business.

LOPAHIN. How many years have you been at the University?

TROFIMOV. Do think of something newer than that—that's stale and flat. (*Hunts for goloshes.*) You know we shall most likely never see each other again, so let me give you one piece of advice at parting: don't wave your arms about—get out of the habit. And another thing, building villas, reckoning up that the summer visitors will in time become independent farmers—reckoning like that, that's not the thing to do either. After all, I am fond of you: you have fine delicate fingers like an artist, you've a fine delicate soul.

LOPAHIN (*embraces him*). Good-bye, my dear fellow. Thanks for every-thing. Let me give you money for the journey, if you need it.

TROFIMOV. What for? I don't need it.

LOPAHIN. Why, you haven't got a halfpenny.

TROFIMOV. Yes, I have, thank you. I got some money for a translation. Here it is in my pocket, (*anxiously*) but where can my goloshes be!

VARYA (*from the next room*). Take the nasty things! (*Flings a pair of go-loshes onto the stage.*)

TROFIMOV. Why are you so cross, Varya? h'm! . . . but those aren't my goloshes.

LOPAHIN. I sowed three thousand acres with poppies in the spring, and now I have cleared forty thousand profit. And when my poppies were in flower, wasn't it a picture! So here, as I say, I made forty thousand, and I'm offering you a loan because I can afford to. Why turn up your nose? I am a peasant—I speak bluntly.

TROFIMOV. Your father was a peasant, mine was a chemist—and that proves absolutely nothing whatever. (LOPAHIN *takes out his pocketbook.*) Stop that—stop that. If you were to offer me two hundred thousand I wouldn't take it. I am an independent man, and everything that all of you, rich and poor alike, prize so highly and hold so dear, hasn't the slightest power over me—it's like so much fluff fluttering in the air. I can get on without you. I can pass by you. I am strong and proud. Humanity is advancing towards the highest truth, the highest happiness which is possible on earth, and I am in the front ranks.

LOPAHIN. Will you get there?

TROFIMOV. I shall get there. (*A pause.*) I shall get there, or I shall show others the way to get there.

(*In the distance is heard the stroke of an axe on a tree.*)

LOPAHIN. Good-bye, my dear fellow; it's time to be off. We turn up our noses at one another, but life is passing all the while. When I am working hard without resting, then my mind is more at ease, and it seems to me as though I too know what I exist for; but how many people there are in Russia, my dear boy, who exist, one doesn't know what for. Well, it doesn't matter. That's not what keeps things spinning. They tell me Leonid Andreyevitch has taken a situation. He is going to be a clerk at the bank—6,000 roubles a year. Only, of course, he won't stick to it—he's too lazy.

ANYA (*in doorway*). Mamma begs you not to let them chop down the orchard until she's gone.

TROFIMOV. Yes, really, you might have the tact.

(*Walks out across the front of the stage.*)

LOPAHIN. I'll see to it! I'll see to it! Stupid fellows!

(*Goes out after him.*)

ANYA. Has Firs been taken to the hospital?

YASHA. I told them this morning. No doubt they have taken him.

ANYA (*to* EPIHODOV, *who passes across the drawing-room*). Semyon Pantaleyevitch, inquire, please, if Firs has been taken to the hospital.

YASHA (*in a tone of offence*). I told Yegor this morning—why ask a dozen times?

EPIHODOV. Firs is advanced in years. It's my conclusive opinion no treatment would do him good; it's time he was gathered to his fathers. And I can only envy him. (*Puts a trunk down on a cardboard hat-box and crushes it.*) There now, of course—I knew it would be so.

YASHA (*jeeringly*). Two and twenty misfortunes!

VARYA (*through the door*). Has Firs been taken to the hospital?

ANYA. Yes.

VARYA. Why wasn't the note for the doctor taken too?

ANYA. Oh, then, we must send it after them. (*Goes out.*)

VARYA (*from the adjoining room*). Where's Yasha? Tell him his mother's come to say good-bye to him.

YASHA (*waves his hand*). They put me out of all patience!

(DUNYASHA *has all this time been busy about the luggage. Now, when* YASHA *is left alone, she goes up to him.*)

DUNYASHA. You might just give me one look, Yasha. You're going away. You're leaving me. (*Weeps and throws herself on his neck.*)

YASHA. What are you crying for? (*Drinks the champagne.*) In six days I shall be in Paris again. Tomorrow we shall get into the express train and roll away in a flash. I can scarcely believe it! *Vive la France!* It doesn't suit me here—it's not the life for me; there's no doing anything. I have seen enough of the ignorance here. I have had enough of it. (*Drinks champagne.*) What are you crying for? Behave yourself properly, and then you won't cry.

DUNYASHA (*powders her face, looking in a pocket-mirror*). Do send me a letter from Paris. You know how I loved you, Yasha—how I loved you! I am a tender creature, Yasha.

YASHA. Here they are coming! (*Busies himself about the trunks, humming softly. Enter* LYUBOV ANDREYEVNA, GAEV, ANYA *and* CHARLOTTA IVANOVNA.)

GAEV. We ought to be off. There's not much time now. (*Looking at* YASHA.) What a smell of herrings!

LYUBOV. In ten minutes we must get into the carriage. (*Casts a look about the room.*) Farewell, dear house, dear old home of our fathers! Winter will pass and spring will come, and then you will be no more; they will tear you down! How much those walls have seen! (*Kisses her daughter passionately.*) My treasure, how bright you look! Your eyes are sparkling like diamonds! Are you glad? Very glad?

ANYA. Very glad! A new life is beginning, mamma.

GAEV. Yes, really, everything is all right now. Before the cherry orchard was sold, we were all worried and wretched, but afterwards, when once the question was settled conclusively, irrevocably, we all felt calm and even cheerful! I am a bank clerk now—I am a financier—cannon off the red. And you, Lyuba, after all, you are looking better; there's no question of that.

LYUBOV. Yes. My nerves are better, that's true. (*Her hat and coat are handed to her.*) I'm sleeping well. Carry out my things, Yasha. It's time. (*To* ANYA.) My darling, we shall soon see each other again. I am going to Paris. I can live there on the money your Yaroslavl auntie sent us to buy the estate with— hurrah for auntie!—but that money won't last long.

ANYA. You'll come back soon, mamma, won't you? I'll be working up for my examination in the high school, and when I have passed that, I shall set

to work and be a help to you. We will read all sorts of things together, mamma, won't we? (*Kisses her mother's hands.*) We will read in the autumn evenings. We'll read lots of books, and a new wonderful world will open out before us. (*Dreamily.*) Mamma, come soon.

LYUBOV. I shall come, my precious treasure. (*Embraces her.*)

(*Enter* LOPAHIN. CHARLOTTA *softly hums a song.*)

GAEV. Charlotta's happy; she's singing!

CHARLOTTA (*picks up a bundle like a swaddled baby*). Bye, bye, my baby. (*A baby is heard crying: "Ooah! ooah!"*) Hush, hush, my pretty boy! (*Ooah! ooah!*) Poor little thing! (*Throws the bundle back.*) You must please find me a situation. I can't go on like this.

LOPAHIN. We'll find you one, Charlotta Ivanovna. Don't you worry yourself.

GAEV. Everyone's leaving us. Varya's going away. We have become of no use all at once.

CHARLOTTA. There's nowhere for me to be in the town. I must go away. (*Hums.*) What care I . . .

(*Enter* PISHTCHIK.)

LOPAHIN. The freak of nature!

PISHTCHIK (*gasping*). Oh! . . . let me get my breath. . . . I'm worn out . . . my most honoured . . . Give me some water.

GAEV. Want some money, I suppose? Your humble servant! I'll go out of the way of temptation. (*Goes out.*)

PISHTCHIK. It's a long while since I have been to see you . . . dearest lady. (*To* LOPAHIN.) You are here . . . glad to see you . . . a man of immense intellect . . . take . . . here (*gives* LOPAHIN) 400 roubles. That leaves me owing 840.

LOPAHIN (*shrugging his shoulders in amazement*). It's like a dream. Where did you get it?

PISHTCHIK. Wait a bit . . . I'm hot . . . a most extraordinary occurrence!

Some Englishmen came along and found in my land some sort of white clay. (*To* LYUBOV ANDREYEVNA.) And 400 for you . . . most lovely . . . wonderful. (*Gives money.*) The rest later. (*Sips water.*) A young man in the train was telling me just now that a great philosopher advises jumping off a house-top. "Jump!" says he; "the whole gist of the problem lies in that." (*Wonderingly.*) Fancy that, now! Water, please!

LOPAHIN. What Englishmen?

PISHTCHIK. I have made over to them the rights to dig the clay for twenty-four years . . . and now, excuse me . . . I can't stay . . . I must be trotting on. I'm going to Znoikovo . . . to Karadamanovo. . . . I'm in debt all round. (*Sips.*) . . . To your very good health! . . . I'll come in on Thursday.

LYUBOV. We are just off to the town, and tomorrow I start for abroad.

PISHTCHIK. What! (*In agitation.*) Why to the town? Oh, I see the furniture . . . the boxes. No matter . . . (*Through his tears.*) . . . no matter . . . men of enormous intellect . . . these Englishmen. . . . Never mind . . . be happy. God will succour you . . . no matter . . . everything in this world must have an end. (*Kisses* LYUBOV ANDREYEVNA'S *hand.*) If the rumour reaches you that my end has come, think of this . . . old horse, and say: "There once was such a man in the world . . . Semyonov-Pishtchik . . . the Kingdom of Heaven be his!" . . . most extraordinary weather . . . yes. (*Goes out in violent agitation, but at once returns and says in the doorway:*) Dashenka wishes to be remembered to you. (*Goes out.*)

LYUBOV. Now we can start. I leave with two cares in my heart. The first is leaving Firs ill. (*Looking at her watch.*) We still have five minutes.

ANYA. Mamma, Firs has been taken to the hospital! Yasha sent him off this morning.

LYUBOV. My other anxiety is Varya. She is used to getting up early and work-ing; and now, without work, she's like a fish out of water. She is thin and pale, and she's crying, poor dear! (*A pause.*) You are well aware, Yermolay Alexeyevitch, I dreamed of marrying her to you, and everything seemed to show that you would get married. (*Whispers to* ANYA *and motions to* CHARLOTTA *and both go out.*) She loves you—she suits you. And I don't know—I don't know why it is you seem, as it were, to avoid each other. I can't understand it!

LOPAHIN. I don't understand it myself, I confess. It's queer somehow, altogether. If there's still time, I'm ready now at once. Let's settle it straight off, and go ahead; but without you, I feel I shan't make her an offer.

LYUBOV. That's excellent. Why, a single moment's all that's necessary. I'll call her at once.

LOPAHIN. And there's champagne all ready too. (*Looking into the glasses.*) Empty! Someone's emptied them already. (YASHA *coughs.*) I call that greedy.

LYUBOV (*eagerly*). Capital! We will go out. Yasha, *allez!* I'll call her in. (*At the door.*) Varya, leave all that; come here. Come along! (*Goes out with* YASHA.)

LOPAHIN (*looking at his watch*). Yes.

(*A pause. Behind the door, smothered laughter and whispering, and, at last, enter* VARYA.)

VARYA (*looking a long while over the things*). It is strange, I can't find it anywhere.

LOPAHIN. What are you looking for?

VARYA. I packed it myself, and I can't remember. (*A pause.*)

LOPAHIN. Where are you going now, Varvara Mihailova?

VARYA. I? To the Ragulins. I have arranged to go to them to look after the house—as a housekeeper.

LOPAHIN. That's in Yashnovo? It'll be seventy miles away. (*A pause.*) So this is the end of life in this house!

VARYA (*looking among the things*). Where is it? Perhaps I put it in the trunk. Yes, life in this house is over—there will be no more of it.

LOPAHIN. And I'm just off to Harkov—by this next train. I've a lot of business there. I'm leaving Epihodov here, and I've taken him on.

VARYA. Really!

LOPAHIN. This time last year we had snow already, if you remember; but now it's so fine and sunny. Though it's cold, to be sure—three degrees of frost.

VARYA. I haven't looked. (*A pause.*) And besides, our thermometer's broken. (*A pause.*)

(*Voice at the door from the yard:* "Yermolay Alexeyevitch!")

LOPAHIN (*as though he had long been expecting this summons*). This minute!

(LOPAHIN *goes out quickly.* VARYA, *sitting on the floor and laying her head on a bag full of clothes, sobs quietly. The door opens.* LYUBOV ANDREYEVNA *comes in cautiously.*)

LYUBOV. Well? (*A pause.*) We must be going.

VARYA (*has wiped her eyes and is no longer crying*). Yes, mamma, it's time to start. I shall have time to get to the Ragulins today, if only you're not late for the train.

LYUBOV (*in the doorway*). Anya, put your things on.

(*Enter* ANYA, *then* GAEV *and* CHARLOTTA IVANOVNA. GAEV *has on a warm coat with a hood. Servants and cabmen come in.* EPIHODOV *bustles about the luggage.*)

LYUBOV. Now we can start on our travels.

ANYA (*joyfully*). On our travels!

GAEV. My friends—my dear, my precious friends! Leaving this house for ever, can I be silent? Can I refrain from giving utterance at leave-taking to those emotions which now flood all my being?

ANYA (*supplicatingly*). Uncle!

VARYA. Uncle, you mustn't!

GAEV (*dejectedly*). Cannon and into the pocket . . . I'll be quiet. . . .

(*Enter* TROFIMOV *and afterwards* LOPAHIN.)

TROFIMOV. Well, ladies and gentlemen, we must start.

LOPAHIN. Epihodov, my coat!

LYUBOV. I'll stay just one minute. It seems as though I have never seen before what the walls, what the ceilings in this house were like, and now I look at them with greediness, with such tender love.

GAEV. I remember when I was six years old sitting in that window on Trinity Day watching my father going to church.

LYUBOV. Have all the things been taken?

LOPAHIN. I think all. (*Putting on overcoat, to* EPIHODOV.) You, Epihodov, mind you see everything is right.

EPIHODOV (*in a husky voice*). Don't you trouble, Yermolay Alexeyevitch.

LOPAHIN. Why, what's wrong with your voice?

EPIHODOV. I've just had a drink of water, and I choked over something.

YASHA (*contemptuously*). The ignorance!

LYUBOV. We are going—and not a soul will be left here.

LOPAHIN. Not till the spring.

VARYA (*pulls a parasol out of a bundle, as though about to hit someone with it.* LOPAHIN *makes a gesture as though alarmed*). What is it? I didn't mean anything.

TROFIMOV. Ladies and gentlemen, let us get into the carriage. It's time. The train will be in directly.

VARYA. Petya, here they are, your goloshes, by that box. (*With tears.*) And what dirty old things they are!

TROFIMOV (*putting on his goloshes*). Let us go, friends!

GAEV (*greatly agitated, afraid of weeping*). The train—the station! Double baulk, ah!

LYUBOV. Let us go!

LOPAHIN. Are we all here? (*Locks the side-door on left.*) The things are all here. We must lock up. Let us go!

ANYA. Good-bye, home! Good-bye to the old life!

TROFIMOV. Welcome to the new life! (TROFIMOV *goes out with* ANYA. VARYA *looks round the room and goes out slowly.* YASHA *and* CHARLOTTA IVANOVNA, *with her dog, go out.*)

LOPAHIN. Till the spring, then! Come, friends, till we meet! (*Goes out.*)

(LYUBOV ANDREYEVNA *and* GAEV *remain alone. As though they had been waiting for this, they throw themselves on each other's necks, and break into subdued smothered sobbing, afraid of being overheard.*)

GAEV (*in despair*). Sister, my sister!

LYUBOV. Oh, my orchard!—my sweet, beautiful orchard! My life, my youth, my happiness, good-bye! good-bye!

VOICE OF ANYA (*calling gaily*). Mamma!

VOICE OF TROFIMOV (*gaily, excitedly*). Aa—oo!

LYUBOV. One last look at the walls, at the windows. My dear mother loved to walk about this room.

GAEV. Sister, sister!

VOICE OF ANYA. Mamma!

VOICE OF TROFIMOV. Aa—oo!

LYUBOV. We are coming. (*They go out.*)

(*The stage is empty. There is the sound of the doors being locked up, then of the carriages driving away. There is silence. In the stillness there is the dull stroke of an axe in a tree, clanging with a mournful lonely sound. Footsteps are heard.* FIRS *appears in the doorway on the right. He is dressed as always—in a pea-jacket and white waistcoat, with slippers on his feet. He is ill.*)

FIRS (*goes up to the doors, and tries the handles*). Locked! They have gone. . . . (*Sits down on sofa.*) They have forgotten me. . . . Never mind . . . I'll sit here a bit. . . . I'll be bound Leonid Andreyevitch hasn't put his fur coat on and has gone off in his thin overcoat. (*Sighs anxiously.*) I didn't see after him. . . . These young people . . . (*Mutters something that can't be distinguished.*) Life has slipped by as though I hadn't lived. (*Lies down.*) I'll lie down a bit. . . . There's no strength in you, nothing left you—all gone! Ech! I'm good for nothing. (*Lies motionless.*)

(*A sound is heard that seems to come from the sky, like a breaking harp-string, dying away mournfully. All is still again, and there is heard nothing but the strokes of the axe far away in the orchard.*)

LUIGI PIRANDELLO / 1867–1936

Luigi Pirandello, a Sicilian, was educated in Italy and at Bonn, Germany, and became a professor of Italian literature. His marriage to a girl whose mind became deranged but whom he refused to entrust to an institution, together with a crippling decline in his father's business fortunes, kept Pirandello under severe strain. His professorship and many short stories and novels paid for an embittered existence on his own terms.

He turned to playwriting at the age of forty-six, and became increasingly absorbed in drama and the theater as a mode of expressing himself after the success of *Six Characters in Search of an Author* in 1921.

Pirandello founded an experimental theater in Rome and became both a director and a sustaining playwright. His plays, like Chekhov's, are harder to explain than to experience; he has some affinities with intellectual comedy, some with psychological drama, some with fantasy and the grotesque. All three types are exploited to express his absorption in the invisible inner life. Pirandello's originality and intellectual subtlety in psychological analysis, exercised on exhibiting multiple personality—illusion contesting with reality, sanity contesting with insanity—won him the Nobel Prize in 1934. To project invisible, subjective states in a dramatic situation requires a break with most realistic theatrical conventions and the creation of original substitute means. The techniques of Pirandello are a current part of the drama's resources.

The mask symbol for what men are and what they seem to be, for the difference between the exposed and the hidden face, testifies to the contrast between role and identity which has fascinated many modern thinkers and artists. Actors assume roles; the stage is an illusion. Pirandello moves to the use of plays within plays and actors *vs.* their roles as external means in *Tonight We Improvize* and *Six Characters in Search of an Author*.

It Is *So!* (*If You Think So*) is a good starting point for the drama of reality *vs.* illusion, because it dramatizes the basic question—what is identity? The Italian title, *Così è (se vi pare!)*, has been translated literally and figuratively in several ways, all of which try to emphasize the relation of the title to the point of the play: *Right You Are!* (*If You Think So*); *As You Like It; There Is Nothing Right or Wrong but Thinking Makes It So; Right You Are!* (*If You Think You Are*).

It *Is* So! (If You Think So)

(*Così è, se vi pare!*)

A PARABLE IN THREE ACTS
ENGLISH VERSION BY ARTHUR LIVINGSTON

CHARACTERS

LAMBERTO LAUDISI.
SIGNORA FROLA.
PONZA, *son-in-law of Signora Frola.*
SIGNORA PONZA, *Ponza's wife.*
COMMENDATORE AGAZZI, *a provincial councillor.*
AMALIA, *his wife.*
DINA, *their daughter.*
SIRELLI.
SIGNORA SIRELLI, *his wife.*
THE PREFECT.
CENTURI, *a police commissioner.*
SIGNORA CINI.
SIGNORA NENNI.
A BUTLER.
A number of GENTLEMEN *and* LADIES.

SCENE: *Our own times, in a small Italian town, the capital of the province.*

Act I

(*The parlor in the house of* COMMENDATORE AGAZZI.)

(*A door, the general entrance, at the back; doors leading to the wings, left and right.*)

(LAUDISI *is a man nearing the forties, quick and energetic in his movements. He is smartly dressed, in good taste. At this moment he is wearing a semi-formal street suit: a sack coat, of a violet cast, with black lapels, and with black braid around the edges; trousers of a light but different color. Laudisi has a keen, analytical mind, but is impatient and irritable in argument. Nevertheless, however angry he gets momentarily, his good humor soon comes to prevail. Then he laughs and lets people have their way, enjoying, meanwhile, the spectacle of the stupidity and gullibility of others.*)

(AMALIA, *Agazzi's wife, is Laudisi's sister. She is a woman of forty-five more or less. Her hair is already quite grey. Signora Agazzi is always showing a certain sense of her own importance from the position occupied by her husband in the community; but she gives you to understand that if she had a free rein she would be quite capable of playing her own part in the world and, perhaps, do it somewhat better than Commendatore Agazzi.*)

(DINA *is the daughter of Amalia and Agazzi. She is nineteen. Her general manner is that of a young person conscious of understanding everything better than papa and mamma; but this defect must not be exaggerated to the extent of concealing her attractiveness and charm as a good-looking winsome girl.*)

(*As the curtain rises* LAUDISI *is walking briskly up and down the parlor to give vent to his irritation.*)

LAUDISI. I see, I see! So he did take the matter up with the prefect!

AMALIA. But Lamberto *dear*, please remember that the man is a subordinate of his.

LAUDISI. A subordinate of his . . . very well! But a subordinate in the office, not at home nor in society!

351

DINA. And he hired an apartment for that woman, his mother-in-law, right here in this very building, and on our floor.

LAUDISI. And why not, pray? He was looking for an apartment; the apartment was for rent, so he leased it—for his mother-in-law. You mean to say that a mother-in-law is in duty bound to make advances to the wife and daughter of the man who happens to be her son-in-law's superior on his job?

AMALIA. That is not the way it is, Lamberto. We didn't ask her to call on us. Dina and I took the first step by calling on her and—she *refused to receive us!*

LAUDISI. Well, is that any reason why your husband should go and lodge a complaint with the man's boss? Do you expect the government to order him to invite you to tea?

AMALIA. I think he deserves all he gets! That is not the way to treat two ladies. I hope he gets fired! The idea!

LAUDISI. Oh, you women! I say, making that complaint is a dirty trick. By Jove! If people see fit to keep to themselves in their own houses, haven't they a right to?

AMALIA. Yes, but you don't understand! We were trying to do her a favor. She is new in the town. We wanted to make her feel at home.

DINA. Now, now, Nunky dear, don't be so cross! Perhaps we did go there out of curiosity more than anything else; but it's all so funny, isn't it! Don't you think it was natural to feel just a little bit curious?

LAUDISI. Natural be damned! It was none of your business!

DINA. Now, see here, Nunky, let's suppose—here you are right here minding your own business and quite indifferent to what other people are doing all around you. Very well! I come into the room and right here on this table, under your very nose, and with a long face like an undertaker's, or, rather, with the long face of that jailbird you are

defending, I set down—well, what?—anything—a pair of dirty old shoes!

LAUDISI. I don't see the connection.

DINA. Wait, don't interrupt me! I said a pair of old shoes. Well, no, not a pair of old shoes—a flat iron, a rolling pin, or your shaving brush for instance—and I walk out again without saying a word to anybody! Now I leave it to you, wouldn't you feel justified in wondering just a little, little, bit as to what in the world I meant by it?

LAUDISI. Oh, you're irresistible, Dina! And you're clever, aren't you? But you're talking with old Nunky, remember! You see, you have been putting all sorts of crazy things on the table here; and you did it with the idea of making me ask what it's all about; and, of course, since you were doing all that on purpose, you can't blame me if I do ask, why those old shoes just there, on that table, dearie? But what's all that got to do with it? You'll have to show me now that this Mr. Ponza of ours, that jailbird as you say, or that rascal, that boor, as your father calls him, brought his mother-in-law to the apartment next to ours with the idea of stringing us all! You've got to show me that he did it on purpose!

DINA. I don't say that he did it on purpose—not at all! But you can't deny that this famous Mr. Ponza has come to this town and done a number of things which are unusual, to say the least; and which he must have known were likely to arouse a very natural curiosity in everybody. Look Nunky, here is a man: he comes to town to fill an important public position, and—what does he do? Where does he go to live? He hires an apartment on the *top* floor, if you please, of that dirty old tenement out there on the very outskirts of the town. Now, I ask you—did you ever see the place? Inside?

LAUDISI. I suppose you went and had a look at it?

DINA. Yes, Nunky dear, I went—

with mamma! And we weren't the only ones, you know. The whole town has been to have a look at it. It's a five story tenement with an interior court so dark at noontime you can hardly see your hand before your face. Well, there is an iron balcony built out from the fifth story around the courtyard. A basket is hanging from the railing . . . They let it up and down—on a rope!

LAUDISI. Well, what of it?

DINA (*looking at him with astonished indignation*). What of it? Well, there, if you please, is where he keeps his wife!

AMALIA. While her mother lives here next door to us!

LAUDISI. A fashionable apartment, for his mother-in-law, in the residential district!

AMALIA. Generous to the old lady, eh? But he does that to keep her from seeing her daughter!

LAUDISI. How do you know that? How do you know that the old lady, rather, does not prefer this arrangement, just to have more elbow room for herself?

DINA. No, no, Nunky, you're wrong. Everybody knows that it is he who is doing it.

AMALIA. See here, Lamberto, everybody understands, if a girl, when she marries, goes away from her mother to live with her husband in some other town. But supposing this poor mother can't stand being separated from her daughter and follows her to the place, where she herself is also a complete stranger. And supposing now she not only does not live with her daughter, but is not even allowed to see her? I leave it to you . . . is that so easy to understand?

LAUDISI. Oh say, you have about as much imagination as so many mud turtles. A mother-in-law and a son-in-law! Is it so hard to suppose that either through her fault or his fault or the fault of both, they should find it hard to get along together and should therefore consider it wiser to live apart?

DINA (*with another look of pitying astonishment at her uncle*). How stupid of you, Nunky! The trouble is not between the mother-in-law and the son-in-law, but between the mother and the daughter.

LAUDISI. How do you know that?

DINA. Because he is as thick as pudding with the old lady; because they are always together, arm in arm, and as loving as can be. Mother-in-law and son-in-law, if you please! Whoever heard the like of that?

AMALIA. And he comes here every evening to see how the old lady is getting on!

DINA. And that is not the worst of it! Sometimes he comes during the daytime, once or twice!

LAUDISI. How scandalous! Do you think he is making love to the old woman?

DINA. Now don't be improper, uncle. No, we will acquit him of that. She is a poor old lady, quite on her last legs.

AMALIA. But he never, never brings his wife! A daughter kept from seeing her mother! The idea!

LAUDISI. Perhaps the young lady is not well; perhaps she isn't able to go out.

DINA. Nonsense! The old lady goes to see *her!*

AMALIA. Exactly! And she never gets in! She can see her only from a distance. Now will you explain to me why, in the name of common sense, that poor mother should be forbidden ever to enter her daughter's house?

DINA. And if she wants to talk to her she has to shout up from the courtyard!

AMALIA. Five stories, if you please! . . . And her daughter comes out and looks down from the balcony up there. The poor old woman goes into the courtyard and pulls a string that leads up to the balcony; a bell rings; the girl comes out and her mother talks up at her, her head thrown back, just as though she were shouting from out of a well. . . .

(*There is a knock at the door and* THE BUTLER *enters.*)

BUTLER. Callers, madam!

AMALIA. Who is it, please?

BUTLER. Signor Sirelli, and the Signora with another lady, madam.

AMALIA. Very well, show them in.

(THE BUTLER *bows and withdraws.*)

(SIRELLI, SIGNORA SIRELLI, SIGNORA CINI *appear in the doorway, rear.*)

(SIRELLI, *also a man of about forty, is a bald, fat gentleman with some pretensions to stylish appearance that do not quite succeed: the overdressed provincial.*)

(SIGNORA SIRELLI, *his wife, plump, petite, a faded blonde, still young and girlishly pleasing. She, too, is somewhat overdressed with the provincial's fondness for display. She has the aggressive curiosity of the small-town gossip. She is chiefly occupied in keeping her husband in his place.*)

(SIGNORA CINI *is the old provincial lady of affected manners, who takes malicious delight in the failings of others, all the while affecting innocence and inexperience regarding the waywardness of mankind.*)

AMALIA (*as the visitors enter, and taking* SIGNORA SIRELLI'S *hands effusively*). Dearest! Dearest!

SIGNORA SIRELLI. I took the liberty of bringing my good friend, Signora Cini, along. She was so anxious to know you!

AMALIA. So good of you to come, Signora! Please make yourself at home! My daughter Dina, Signora Cini, and this is my brother, Lamberto Laudisi.

SIRELLI (*bowing to the ladies*). Signora, Signorina. (*He goes over and shakes hands with* LAUDISI.)

SIGNORA SIRELLI. Amalia dearest, we have come here as to the fountain of knowledge. We are two pilgrims athirst for the truth!

AMALIA. The truth? Truth about what?

SIGNORIA SIRELLI. Why . . . about this blessed Mr. Ponza of ours, the new secretary at the prefecture. He is the talk of the town, take my word for it, Amalia.

SIGNORA CINI. And we are all just dying to find out!

AMALIA. But we are as much in the dark as the rest of you, I assure you, madam.

SIRELLI (*to his wife*). What did I tell you? They know no more about it than I do. In fact, I think they know less about it than I do. Why is it this poor woman is not allowed to see her daughter? Do you know the reason, you people, the real reason?

AMALIA. Why, I was just discussing the matter with my brother.

LAUDISI. And my view of it is that you're all a pack of gossips!

DINA. The reason is, they say, that Ponza will not allow her to.

SIGNORA CINI. Not a sufficient reason, if I may say so, Signorina.

SIGNORA SIRELLI. Quite insufficient! There's more to it than that!

SIRELLI. I have a new item for you, fresh, right off the ice: he keeps her locked up at home!

AMALIA. His mother-in-law?

SIRELLI. No, no, his wife!

SIGNORA CINI. Under lock and key!

DINA. There, Nunky, what have you to say to that? And you've been trying to defend him all along!

SIRELLI (*staring in astonishment at* LAUDISI). Trying to defend that man? Really . . .

LAUDISI. Defending him? No! I am not defending anybody. All I'm saying, if you ladies will excuse me, is that all this gossip is not worthy of you. More than that, you are just wasting your breath; because, so far as I can see, you're not getting anywhere at all.

SIRELLI. I don't follow you, sir!

LAUDISI.   You're getting nowhere, my charming ladies!

SIGNORA CINI.   But we're trying to get somewhere—we are trying to find out!

LAUDISI.   Excuse me, what can you find out? What can we really know about other people—who they are—what they are—what they are doing, and why they are doing it?

SIGNORA SIRELLI.   How can we know? Why not? By asking, of course! You tell me what you know, and I tell you what I know.

LAUDISI.   In that case, madam, you ought to be the best informed person in the world. Why, your husband knows more about what others are doing than any other man—or woman, for that matter—in this neighborhood.

SIRELLI (*deprecatingly but pleased*). Oh I say, I say . . .

SIGNORA SIRELLI (*to her husband*). No dear, he's right, he's right. (*Then turning to* AMALIA.) The real truth, Amalia, is this: for all my husband says he knows, I never manage to keep posted on anything!

SIRELLI.   And no wonder! The trouble is—that woman never trusts me! The moment I tell her something she is convinced it is not *quite* as I say. Then, sooner or later, she claims that it *can't* be as I say. And at last she is certain it is the exact opposite of what I say!

SIGNORA SIRELLI.   Well, you ought to hear all he tells me!

LAUDISI (*laughing aloud*). Hah! Hah! Hah! Hah! Hah! Hah! May I speak, madam? Let me answer your husband. My dear Sirelli, how do you expect your wife to be satisfied with things as you explain them to her, if you, as is natural, represent them as they seem to you?

SIGNORA SIRELLI.   And that means— as they cannot possibly be!

LAUDISI.   Why no, Signora, now you are wrong. From your husband's point of view things are, I assure you, exactly as he represents them.

SIRELLI.   As they are in reality!

SIGNORA SIRELLI.   Not at all! You are always wrong.

SIRELLI.   No, not a bit of it! It is you who are always wrong. I'm always right.

LAUDISI.   The fact is that neither of you is wrong. May I explain? I will prove it to you. Now here you are, you, Sirelli, and Signora Sirelli, your wife, there; and here I am. You see me, don't you?

SIRELLI.   Well . . . er . . . yes.

LAUDISI.   Do you see me, or do you not?

SIRELLI.   Oh, I'll bite! Of course I see you.

LAUDISI.   So you see me! But that's not enough. Come here!

SIRELLI (*smiling, he obeys, but with a puzzled expression on his face as though he fails to understand what* LAUDISI *is driving at*). Well, here I am!

LAUDISI.   Yes! Now take a better look at me . . . Touch me! That's it— that's it! Now you are touching me, are you not? And you see me! You're sure you see me?

SIRELLI.   Why, I should say . . .

LAUDISI.   Yes, but the point is, you're sure! Of course you're sure! Now if you please, Signora Sirelli, you come here— or rather . . . no . . . (*gallantly*) it is my place to come to you! (*He goes over to* SIGNORA SIRELLI *and kneels chivalrously on one knee.*) You see me, do you not, madam? Now that hand of yours . . . touch me! A pretty hand, on my word! (*He pats her hand.*)

SIRELLI.   Easy! Easy!

LAUDISI.   Never mind your husband, madam! Now, you have touched me, have you not? And you see me? And you are absolutely sure about me, are you not? Well, now madam, I beg of you; do not tell your husband, nor my sister, nor my niece, nor Signora Cini here, what you think of me; because, if you were to do that, they would all tell you that you are completely wrong. But, you see, you are really right; because I am really what you take me to be; though, my dear madam, that does not prevent me from also being really what your husband, my sister, my niece, and Signora Cini take me to be—because they also are absolutely right!

SIGNORA SIRELLI. In other words you are a different person for each of us.

LAUDISI. Of course I'm a different person! And you, madam, pretty as you are, aren't you a different person, too?

SIGNORA SIRELLI (*hastily*). No siree! I assure you, as far as I'm concerned, I'm always the same always, yesterday, today, and forever!

LAUDISI. Ah, but so am I, from my point of view, believe me! And, I would say that you are all mistaken unless you see me as I see myself; but that would be an inexcusable presumption on my part—as it would be on yours, my dear madam!

SIRELLI. And what has all this rigmarole got to do with it, may I ask?

LAUDISI. What has it got to do with it? Why . . . I find all you people here at your wits' ends trying to find out who and what other people are; just as though other people had to be this, or that, and nothing else.

SIGNORA SIRELLI. All you are saying is that we can never find out the truth! A dreadful idea!

SIGNORA CINI. I give up! I give up! If we can't believe even what we see with our eyes and feel with our fingers . . .

LAUDISI. But you must understand, madam! Of course you can believe what you see with *your* eyes and feel with *your* fingers. All I'm saying is that you should show some respect for what other people see with their eyes and feel with their fingers, even though it be the exact opposite of what you see and feel.

SIGNORA SIRELLI. The way to answer

you is to refuse to talk with you. See, I turn my back on you! I am going to move my chair around and pretend you aren't in the room. Why, you're driving me crazy, crazy!

LAUDISI. Oh, I beg your pardon. Don't let me interfere with your party. Please go on! Pray continue your argument about Signora Frola and Signor Ponza—I promise not to interrupt again!

AMALIA. You're right for once, Lamberto; and I think it would be even better if you should go into the other room.

DINA. Serves you right, Nunky; into the other room with you, into the other room!

LAUDISI. No, I refuse to budge! Fact is, I enjoy hearing you gossip; but I promise not to say anything more, don't fear! At the very most, with your permission, I shall indulge in a laugh or two.

SIGNORA SIRELLI. How funny . . . and our idea in coming here was to find out . . . But really, Amalia, I thought this Ponza man was your husband's secretary at the Provincial building.

AMALIA. He is his secretary—in the office. But here at home what authority has Agazzi over the fellow?

SIGNORA SIRELLI. Of course! I understand! But may I ask . . . haven't you even tried to see Signora Frola, next door?

DINA. Tried? I should say we had! Twice, Signora!

SIGNORA CINI. Well . . . so then . . . you have probably talked to her . . .

DINA. We were not *received,* if you please!

SIGNORA SIRELLI, SIRELLI, SIGNORA CINI (*in chorus*). Not received? Why! Why! Why!

DINA. This very forenoon!

AMALIA. The first time we waited fully fifteen minutes at the door. We rang and rang and rang, and no one came. Why, we weren't even able to leave our cards! So we went back today . . .

DINA (*throwing up her hands in an expression of horror*). And *he* came to the door.

SIGNORA SIRELLI. Why yes, with that face of his . . . you can tell by just looking at the man . . . Such a face! Such a face! You can't blame people for talking! And then, with that black suit of his . . . Why, they all dress in black. Did you ever notice? Even the old lady! And the man's eyes, too! . . .

SIRELLI (*with a glance of pitying disgust at his wife*). What do you know about his eyes? You never saw his eyes! And you never saw the woman. How do you know she dresses in black? *Probably* she dresses in black . . . By the way, they come from a little town in the next county. Had you heard that? A village called Marsica!

AMALIA. Yes, the village that was destroyed a short time ago.

SIRELLI. Exactly! By an earthquake! Not a house left standing in the place.

DINA. And all their relatives were lost, I have heard. Not one of them left in the world!

SIGNORA CINI (*impatient to get on with the story*). Very well, very well, so then . . . he came to the door . . .

AMALIA. Yes . . . And the moment I saw him in front of me with that weird face of his I had hardly enough gumption left to tell him that we had just come to call on his mother-in-law, and he . . . well . . . not a word, not a word . . . not even a "thank you," if you please!

DINA. That is not quite fair, mamma: . . . he did bow!

AMALIA. Well, yes, a bow . . . if you want to call it that. Something like this! . . .

DINA. And his eyes! You ought to see his eyes—the eyes of a devil, and then some! You never saw a man with eyes like that!

SIGNORA CINI. Very well, what did he say, finally?

DINA. He seemed quite taken aback.

AMALIA. He was all confused like; he hitched about for a time; and at last he said that Signora Frola was not feeling well, but that she would appreciate our kindness in having come; and then he just stood there, and stood there, apparently waiting for us to go away.

DINA. I never was more mortified in my life!

SIRELLI. A boor, a plain boor, I say! Oh, it's his fault, I am telling you. And . . . who knows? Perhaps he has got the old lady also under lock and key.

SIGNORA SIRELLI. Well, I think something should be done about it! . . . After all, you are the wife of a superior of his. You can *refuse* to be treated like that.

AMALIA. As far as that goes, my husband did take it rather badly—as a lack of courtesy on the man's part; and he went straight to the prefect with the matter, insisting on an apology.

(SIGNOR AGAZZI, *commendatore and provincial councillor, appears in the doorway rear.*)

DINA. Oh goody, here's papa now!

(AGAZZI *is well on toward fifty. He has the harsh, authoritarian manner of the provincial of importance. Red hair and beard, rather unkempt; gold-rimmed eyeglasses.*)

AGAZZI. Oh Sirelli, glad to see you! (*He steps forward and bows to the company.*)

AGAZZI. Signora! . . . (*He shakes hands with* SIGNORA SIRELLI.)

AMALIA (*introducing* SIGNORA CINI). My husband, Signora Cini!

AGAZZI (*with a bow and taking her hand*). A great pleasure, madam! (*Then turning to his wife and daughter in a mysterious voice.*) I have come back from the office to give you some real news! Signora Frola will be here shortly.

SIGNORA SIRELLI (*clapping her hands delightedly*). Oh, the mother-in-law! She is coming? Really? Coming here?

SIRELLI (*going over to* AGAZZI *and pressing his hand warmly as an expression of admiration*). That's the talk, old man, that's the talk! What's needed here is some show of authority.

AGAZZI. Why I had to, you see, I had to! . . . I can't let a man treat my wife and daughter that way! . . .

SIRELLI. I should say not! I was just expressing myself to that effect right here.

SIGNORA SIRELLI. And it would have been entirely proper to inform the prefect also . . .

AGAZZI (anticipating) . . . of all the talk that is going around on this fine gentleman's account? Oh, leave that to me! I didn't miss the opportunity.

SIRELLI. Fine! Fine!

SIGNORA CINI. And such talk!

AMALIA. For my part, I never heard of such a thing. Why, do you know, he has them both under lock and key!

DINA. No, mamma, we are not *quite* sure of that. We are not *quite* sure about the old lady, yet.

AMALIA. Well, we know it about his wife, anyway.

SIRELLI. And what did the prefect have to say?

AGAZZI. Oh the prefect . . . well, the prefect . . . he was very much impressed, *very* much impressed, with what I had to say.

SIRELLI. I should hope so!

AGAZZI. You see, some of the talk had reached his ears already. And he agrees that it is better, as a matter of his own official prestige, for all this mystery in connection with one of his assistants to be cleared up, so that once and for all we shall know the truth.

LAUDISI. Hah, hah, hah, hah, hah, hah, hah!

AMALIA. That is Lamberto's usual contribution. He laughs!

AGAZZI. And what is there to laugh about?

SIGNORA SIRELLI. Why he says that no one can ever know the truth.

(THE BUTLER *appears at the door in back set.*)

THE BUTLER. Excuse me, Signora Frola!

SIRELLI. Ah, here she is now!

AGAZZI. Now we'll see if we can settle it!

SIGNORA SIRELLI. Splendid! Oh, I am so glad I came.

AMALIA (*rising*). Shall we have her come in?

AGAZZI. Wait, you keep your seat, Amalia! Let's have her come right in here. (*Turning to* THE BUTLER.) Show her in!

(*Exit* BUTLER.)

(*A moment later all rise as* SIGNORA FROLA *enters, and* AMALIA *steps forward, holding out her hand in greeting.*)

(SIGNORA FROLA *is a slight, modestly but neatly dressed old lady, very eager to talk and apparently fond of people. There is a world of sadness in her eyes, tempered, however, by a gentle smile that is constantly playing about her lips.*)

AMALIA. Come right in, Signora Frola! (*She takes the old lady's hand and begins the introductions.*) Mrs. Sirelli, a good friend of mine; Signora Cini; my husband; Mr. Sirelli; and this is my daughter, Dina; my brother Lamberto Laudisi. Please take a chair, Signora!

SIGNORA FROLA. Oh, I am so very, very sorry! I have come to excuse myself for having been so negligent of my social duties. You, Signora Agazzi, were so kind, so very kind, to have honored me with a first call—when it was my place to leave my card with you!

AMALIA. Oh, we are just neighbors, Signora Frola? Why stand on ceremony? I just thought that you, being new in town and all alone by yourself, would perhaps like to have a little company.

SIGNORA FROLA. Oh, how very kind of you it was!

SIGNORA SIRELLI. And you are quite alone, aren't you?

SIGNORA FROLA. Oh no! No! I have a daughter, married, though she hasn't been here very long, either.

SIRELLI. And your daughter's husband is the new secretary at the prefecture, Signor Ponza, I believe?

SIGNORA FROLA. Yes, yes, exactly! And I hope that Signor Agazzi, as his superior, will be good enough to excuse me—and him, too!

AGAZZI. I will be quite frank with you, madam! I was a bit put out.

SIGNORA FROLA (*interrupting*). And you were quite right! But I do hope you will forgive him. You see, we are still— what shall I say—still so upset by the terrible things that have happened to us . . .

AMALIA. You went through the earthquake, didn't you?

SIGNORA SIRELLI. And you lost all your relatives?

SIGNORA FROLA. Every one of them! All our family—yes, madam. And our village was left just a miserable ruin, a pile of bricks and stones and mortar.

SIRELLI. Yes, we heard about it.

SIGNORA FROLA. It wasn't so bad for me, I suppose. I had only one sister and her daughter, and my niece had no family. But my poor son-in-law had a much harder time of it. He lost his mother, two brothers, and their wives, a sister and her husband, and there were two little ones, his nephews.

SIRELLI. A massacre!

SIGNORA FROLA. Oh, one doesn't forget such things! You see, it sort of leaves you with your feet off the ground.

AMALIA. I can imagine.

SIGNORA SIRELLI. And all over-night with no warning at all! It's a wonder you didn't go mad.

SIGNORA FROLA. Well, you see, we haven't quite gotten our bearings yet; and we do things that may seem impolite, without in the least intending to. I hope you understand!

AGAZZI. Oh please, Signora Frola, of course!

AMALIA. In fact it was partly on account of your trouble that my daughter

and I thought we ought to go to see you first.

SIGNORA SIRELLI (*literally writhing with curiosity*). Yes, of course, since they saw you all alone by yourself, and yet . . . excuse me, Signora Frola . . . if the question doesn't seem impertinent . . . how is it that when you have a daughter here in town and after a disaster like the one you have been through . . . I should think you people would all stand together, that you would need one another.

SIGNORA FROLA. Whereas I am left here all by myself?

SIRELLI. Yes, exactly. It does seem strange, to tell the honest truth.

SIGNORA FROLA. Oh, I understand— of course! But you know, I have a feeling that a young man and a young woman who have married should be left a good deal to themselves.

LAUDISI. Quite so, quite so! They should be left to themselves. They are beginning a life of their own, a life different from anything they have led before. One should not interfere in these relations between a husband and a wife!

SIGNORA SIRELLI. But there are limits to everything, Laudisi, if you will excuse me! And when it comes to shutting one's own mother out of one's life . . .

LAUDISI. Who is shutting her out of the girl's life? Here, if I have understood the lady, we see a mother who understands that her daughter cannot and must not remain so closely associated with her as she was before, for now the young woman must begin a new life on her own account.

SIGNORA FROLA (*with evidence of keen gratitude and relief*). You have hit the point exactly, sir. You have said what I would like to have said. You are exactly right! Thank you!

SIGNORA CINI. But your daughter, I imagine, often comes to see you . . .

SIGNORA FROLA (*hesitating, and manifestly ill at ease*). Why yes . . . I . . .

I . . . we do see each other, of course!

SIRELLI (*quickly pressing the advantage*). But your daughter never goes out of her house! At least no one in town has ever seen her.

SIGNORA CINI. Oh, she probably has her little ones to take care of.

SIGNORA FROLA (*speaking up quickly*). No, there are no children yet, and perhaps there won't be any, now. You see, she has been married seven years. Oh, of course, she has a lot to do about the house; but that is not the reason, really. You know, we women who come from the little towns in the country—we are used to staying indoors much of the time.

AGAZZI. Even when your mothers are living in the same town, but not in your house? You prefer staying indoors to going and visiting your mothers?

AMALIA. But it's Signora Frola probably who visits her daughter.

SIGNORA FROLA (*quickly*). Of course, of course, why not! I go there once or twice a day.

SIRELLI. And once or twice a day you climb all those stairs up to the fifth story of that tenement, eh?

SIGNORA FROLA (*growing pale and trying to conceal under a laugh the torture of that cross-examination*). Why . . . er . . . to tell the truth, I don't go up. You're right, five flights would be quite too much for me. No, I don't go up. My daughter comes out on the balcony in the courtyard and . . . well . . . we see each other . . . and we talk!

SIGNORA SIRELLI. And that's all, eh? How terrible! You never see each other more intimately than that?

DINA. I have a mamma and certainly I wouldn't expect her to go up five flights of stairs to see me, either; but at the same time I could never stand talking to her that way, shouting at the top of my lungs from a balcony on the fifth story. I am sure I should want a kiss

from her occasionally, and feel her near me, at least.

SIGNORA FROLA (*with evident signs of embarrassment and confusion*). And you're right! Yes, exactly . . . quite right! I must explain. Yes . . . I hope you people are not going to think that my daughter is something she really is not. You must not suspect her of having so little regard for me and for my years, and you mustn't believe that I, her mother, am . . . well . . . five, six, even more stories to climb would never prevent a real mother, even if she were as old and infirm as I am, from going to her daughter's side and pressing her to her heart with a real mother's love . . . oh no!

SIGNORA SIRELLI (*triumphantly*). There you have it, there you have it, just as we were saying!

SIGNORA CINI. But there must be a reason, there must be a reason!

AMALIA (*pointedly to her brother*). Aha, Lamberto, now you see, there *is* a reason, after all!

SIRELLI (*insisting*). Your son-in-law, I suppose?

SIGNORA FROLA. Oh please, please, please, don't think badly of *him*. He is such a very good boy. Good is no name for it, my dear sir. You can't imagine all he does for me! Kind, attentive, solicitous for my comfort, everything! And as for my daughter—I doubt if any girl ever had a more affectionate and well-intentioned husband. No, on that point I am proud of myself! I could not have found a better man for her.

SIGNORA SIRELLI. Well then . . . What? What? *What?*

SIGNORA CINI. So your son-in-law is not the reason?

AGAZZI. I never thought it was his fault. Can you imagine a man forbidding his wife to call on her mother, or preventing the mother from paying an occasional visit to her daughter?

SIGNORA FROLA. Oh, it's not a case of forbidding! Who ever dreamed of such a thing! No, it's we, Commendatore, I and my daughter, that is. Oh, please, believe me! We refrain from visiting each other of our own accord, out of consideration for him, you understand.

AGAZZI. But excuse me . . . how in the world could he be offended by such a thing? I *don't* understand.

SIGNORA FROLA. Oh, please don't be angry, Signor Agazzi. You see it's a . . . what shall I say . . . a feeling . . . that's it, a feeling, which it would perhaps be very hard for anyone else to understand; and yet, when you do understand it, it's all so simple, I am sure . . . so simple . . . and believe me, my dear friends, it is no slight sacrifice that I am making, and that my daughter is making, too.

AGAZZI. Well, one thing you will admit, madam. This is a very, very unusual situation.

SIRELLI, Unusual, indeed! And such as to justify a curiosity even more persistent than ours.

AGAZZI. It is not only unusual, madam. I might even say it is suspicious.

SIGNORA FROLA. Suspicious? You mean you suspect Signor Ponza? Oh please, Commendatore, don't say that. What fault can you possibly find with him, Signor Agazzi?

AGAZZI. I didn't say just that . . . Please don't misunderstand! I said simply that the situation is so very strange that people might legitimately suspect . . .

SIGNORA FROLA. Oh, no, no, no! What could they suspect? We are in perfect agreement, all of us; and we are really quite happy, very happy, I might even say . . . both I and my daughter.

SIGNORA SIRELLI. Perhaps it's a case of jealousy?

SIGNORA FROLA. Jealousy of me? It would be hardly fair to say that, although . . . really . . . oh, it is so hard to explain! . . . You see, he is in love with my daughter . . . so much so that he wants her whole heart, her every thought, as it were, for himself; so much so that he insists that the affections which my daughter must have for me, her mother—he finds that love quite natural of course, why not? Of course he does!—should reach me through him—that's it, through him—don't you understand?

AGAZZI. Oh, that is going pretty strong! No, I don't understand. In fact it seems to me a case of downright cruelty!

SIGNORA FROLA. Cruelty? No, no, please don't call it cruelty, Commendatore. It is something else, believe me! You see it's so hard for me to explain the matter. Nature, perhaps . . . but no, that's hardly the word. What shall I call it? Perhaps a sort of disease. It's a fullness of love, of a love shut off from the world. There, I guess that's it . . . a fullness . . . a completeness of devotion in which his wife must live without ever departing from it, and into which no other person must ever be allowed to enter.

DINA. Not even her mother, I suppose?

SIRELLI. It is the worst case of selfishness I ever heard of, if you want my opinion!

SIGNORA FROLA. Selfishness? Perhaps! But a selfishness, after all, which offers itself wholly in sacrifice. A case where the selfish person gives all he has in the world to the one he loves. Perhaps it would be fairer to call me selfish; for selfish it surely is for me to be always trying to break into this closed world of theirs, break in by force if necessary; when I know that my daughter is really so happy, so passionately adored—you ladies understand, don't you? A true mother should be satisfied when she knows her daughter is happy, oughtn't she? Besides I'm not completely separated from my daughter, am I? I see her and I speak to her. (*She assumes a more confidential tone.*) You see, when she lets down the basket there in the courtyard I always find a letter in it—a short note, which keeps me posted on the news of the day; and I put in a little letter that I have written. That is some consolation, a great consolation indeed, and now, in course of time, I've grown used to it. I am resigned, there! Resignation, that's it! And I've ceased really to suffer from it at all.

AMALIA. Oh well then, after all, if you people are satisfied, why should . . .

SIGNORA FROLA (*rising*). Oh yes, yes! But, remember, I told you he is such a good man! Believe me, he couldn't be better, really! We all have our weaknesses in this world, haven't we! And we get along best by having a little charity, a little indulgence, for one another. (*She holds out her hand to* AMALIA.) Thank you for calling, madam. (*She bows to* SIGNORA SIRELLI, SIGNORA CINI, *and* DINA; *then turning to* AGAZZI, *she continues.*) And I do hope you have forgiven me!

AGAZZI. Oh, my dear madam, please, please! And we are extremely grateful for your having come to call on us.

SIGNORA FROLA (*offering her hand to* SIRELLI *and* LAUDISI *and again turning to* AMALIA *who has risen to show her out.*) Oh no, please, Signora Agazzi, please stay here with your friends! Don't put yourself to any trouble!

AMALIA. No, no, I will go with you; and believe me, we were very, very glad to see you!

(*Exit* SIGNORA FROLA *with* AMALIA *showing her the way.* AMALIA *returns immediately.*)

SIRELLI. Well, there you have the story, ladies and gentlemen! Are you satisfied with the explanation?

AGAZZI. An explanation, you call it? So far as I can see she has explained nothing. I tell you there is some big mystery in all this business.

SIGNORA SIRELLI. That poor woman! Who knows what torment she must be suffering?

DINA. And to think of that poor girl!

SIGNORA CINI. She could hardly keep in her tears as she talked.

AMALIA. Yes, and did you notice when I mentioned all those stairs she would have to climb before really being able to see her daughter?

LAUDISI. What impressed me was her concern, which amounted to a steadfast determination, to protect her son-in-law from the slightest suspicion.

SIGNORA SIRELLI. Not at all, not at all! What could she say for him? She couldn't really find a single word to say for him.

SIRELLI. And I would like to know how anyone could condone such violence, such downright cruelty!

THE BUTLER (*appearing again in the doorway*). Beg pardon, sir! Signor Ponza calling.

SIGNORA SIRELLI. The man himself, upon my word!

(*An animated ripple of surprise and curiosity, not to say of guilty self-consciousness, sweeps over the company.*)

AGAZZI. Did he ask to see me?

BUTLER. He asked simply if he might be received. That was all he said.

SIGNORA SIRELLI. Oh, please, Signor Agazzi, please let him come in! I am really afraid of the man; but I confess the greatest curiosity to have a close look at the monster.

AMALIA. But what in the world can he be wanting?

AGAZZI. The way to find that out is to have him come in. (*To* THE BUTLER.) Show him in, please.

(*THE BUTLER bows and goes out. A second later* PONZA *appears, aggressively, in the doorway.*)

(*PONZA is a short, thick set, dark complexioned man of a distinctly unpre-*

possessing appearance; black hair, very thick and coming down low over his forehead; a black mustache upcurling at the ends, giving his face a certain ferocity of expression. He is dressed entirely in black. From time to time he draws a black-bordered handkerchief and wipes the perspiration from his brow. When he speaks his eyes are invariably hard, fixed, sinister.)

AGAZZI. This way please, Ponza, come right in! (*Introducing him.*) Signor Ponza, our new provincial secretary; my wife; Signora Sirelli; Signora Cini; my daughter Dina. This is Signor Sirelli; and here is Laudisi, my brother-in-law. Please join our party, won't you, Ponza?

PONZA. So kind of you! You will pardon the intrusion. I shall disturb you only a moment, I hope.

AGAZZI. You had some private business to discuss with me?

PONZA. Why yes, but I could discuss it right here. In fact, perhaps as many people as possible should hear what I have to say. You see it is a declaration that I owe, in a certain sense, to the general public.

AGAZZI. Oh my dear Ponza, if it is that little matter of your mother-in-law's not calling on us, it is quite all right; because you see . . .

PONZA. No, that was not what I came for, Commendatore. It was not to apologize for her. Indeed I may say that Signora Frola, my wife's mother, would certainly have left her cards with Signora Agazzi, your wife, and Signorina Agazzi, your daughter, long before they were so kind as to honor her with their call, had I not exerted myself to the utmost to prevent her coming, since I am absolutely unable to consent to her paying or receiving visits!

AGAZZI (*drawing up into an authoritative attitude and speaking with some severity*). Why? If you will be so kind as to explain, Ponza?

PONZA (*with evidences of increasing excitement in spite of his efforts to preserve his self-control*). I suppose my mother-in-law has been talking to you people about her daughter, my wife. Am I mistaken? And I imagine she told you further that I have forbidden her entering my home and seeing her daughter intimately.

AMALIA. Oh not at all, not at all, Signor Ponza! Signora Frola had only the nicest things to say about you. She could not have spoken of you with greater respect and kindness.

DINA. She seems to be very fond of you indeed.

AGAZZI. She says that she refrains from visiting your house of her own accord, out of regard for feelings of yours which we frankly confess we are unable to understand.

SIGNORA SIRELLI. Indeed, if we were to express our honest opinion . . .

AGAZZI. Well, yes, why not be honest? We think you are extremely harsh with the woman, extremely harsh, perhaps cruel would be an exacter word.

PONZA. Yes, that is what I thought; and I came here for the express purpose of clearing the matter up. The condition this poor woman is in is a pitiable one indeed—not less pitiable than my own perhaps; because, as you see, I am compelled to come here and make apologies—a public declaration—which only such violence as has just been used upon me could ever bring me to make in the world . . . (*He stops and looks about the room. Then he says slowly with emphatic emphasis on the important syllables:*) My mother-in-law, Signora Frola, is not in her right mind! She is insane.

THE COMPANY. Insane! A lunatic! Oh my! Really! No! Impossible!

PONZA. And she has been insane for four years.

SIGNORA SIRELLI. Dear me, who would ever have suspected it! She doesn't show it in the least.

AGAZZI. Insane? Are you sure?

PONZA. She doesn't show it, does she? But she is insane, nevertheless; and her delusion consists precisely in believing that I am forbidding her to see her daughter. (*His face takes on an expression of cruel suffering mingled with a sort of ferocious excitement.*) What daughter, for God's sake? Why her daughter died four years ago. (*A general sensation.*)

EVERYONE AT ONCE. Died? She is dead? What do you mean? Oh, really? Four years ago? Why! Why!

PONZA. Four years ago! In fact it was the death of the poor girl that drove her mad.

SIRELLI. Are we to understand that the wife with whom you are now living . . .

PONZA. Exactly! She is my second wife. I married her two years ago.

AMALIA. And Signora Frola believes that her daughter is still living, that she is your wife still?

PONZA. Perhaps it was best for her that way. She was in charge of a nurse in her own room, you see. Well, when she chanced to see me passing by inadvertence on her street one day, with this woman, my second wife, she suddenly began to laugh and cry and tremble all over in an extreme of happiness. She was sure her daughter, whom she had believed dead, was alive and well; and from a condition of desperate despondency which was the first form of her mental disturbance, she entered on a second obsession, believing steadily that her daughter was not dead at all; but that I, the poor girl's husband, am so completely in love with her that I want her wholly for myself and will not allow anyone to approach her. She became otherwise quite well, you might say. Her nervousness disappeared. Her physical condition improved, and her powers of reasoning returned quite clear. Judge for yourself, ladies and gentlemen! You have

seen her and talked with her. You would never suspect in the world that she is crazy.

AMALIA. Never in the world! Never!

SIGNORA SIRELLI. And the poor woman says she is so happy, so happy!

PONZA. That is what she says to everybody; and for that matter she really has a wealth of affection and gratitude for me; because, as you may well suppose, I do my very best, in spite of the sacrifices entailed, to keep up this beneficial illusion in her. The sacrifices you can readily understand. In the first place I have to maintain two homes on my small salary. Then it is very hard on my wife, isn't it? But she, poor thing, does the very best she can to help me out! She comes to the window when the old lady appears. She talks to her from the balcony. She writes letters to her. But you people will understand that there are limits to what I can ask of my poor wife. Signora Frola, meanwhile, lives practically in confinement. We have to keep a pretty close watch on her. We have to lock her up, virtually. Otherwise, some fine day she would be walking right into my house. She is of a gentle, placid disposition fortunately; but you understand that my wife, good as she is, could never bring herself to accepting caresses intended for another woman, a dead woman! That would be a torment beyond conception.

AMALIA. Oh, of course! Poor woman! Just imagine!

SIGNORA SIRELLI. And the old lady herself consents to being locked up all the time?

PONZA. You, Commendatore, will understand that I couldn't permit her calling here except under absolute constraint.

AGAZZI. I understand perfectly, my dear Ponza, and you have my deepest sympathy.

PONZA. When a man has a misfortune like this fall upon him he must not go about in society; but of course when, by complaining to the prefect, you practically compelled me to have Signora Frola call, it was my duty to volunteer this further information; because, as a public official, and with due regard for the post of responsibility I occupy, I could not allow any discreditable suspicions to remain attached to my reputation. I could not have you good people suppose for a moment that, out of jealousy or for any other reason, I could ever prevent a poor suffering mother from seeing her own daughter. (*He rises.*) Again my apologies for having intruded my personal troubles upon your party. (*He bows.*) My compliments, Commendatore. Good afternoon, good afternoon! Thank you! (*Bowing to* LAUDISI, SIR-ELLI, *and the others in turn, he goes out through the door, rear.*)

AMALIA (*with a sigh of sympathy and astonishment*). Uhh! Crazy! What do you think of that?

SIGNORA SIRELLI. The poor old thing! But you wouldn't have believed it, would you?

DINA. I always knew there was something under it all.

SIGNORA CINI. But who could ever have guessed . . .

AGAZZI. Oh, I don't know, I don't know! You could tell from the way she talked . . .

LAUDISI. You mean to say that you thought . . . ?

AGAZZI. No, I can't say that. But at the same time, if you remember, she could never quite find her words.

SIGNORA SIRELLI. How could she, poor thing, out of her head like that?

SIRELLI. And yet, if I may raise the question, it seems strange to me that an insane person . . . oh, I admit that she couldn't really talk rationally . . . but what surprises me is her trying to find a reason to explain why her son-in-law should be keeping her away from her daughter. This effort of hers to justify it

and then to adapt herself to excuses of her own invention . . .

AGAZZI. Yes, but that is only another proof that she's insane. You see, she kept offering excuses for Ponza that really were not excuses at all.

AMALIA. Yes, that's so. She would say a thing without really saying it, taking it back almost in the next words.

AGAZZI. But there is one more thing. If she weren't a downright lunatic, how could she or any other woman ever accept such a situation from a man? How could she ever consent to talk with her own daughter only by shouting up from the bottom of a well five stories deep?

SIRELLI. But if I remember rightly she has you there! Notice, she doesn't accept the situation. She says she is resigned to it. That's different! No, I tell you, there is still something funny about this business. What do you say, Laudisi?

LAUDISI. Why, I say nothing, nothing at all!

THE BUTLER (*appearing at the door and visibly excited*). Beg pardon, Signora Frola is here again.

AMALIA (*with a start*). Oh dear me, again? Do you suppose she'll be pestering us all the time now?

SIGNORA SIRELLI. I understand how you feel now that you know she's a lunatic.

SIGNORA CINI. My, my, what do you suppose she is going to say now?

SIRELLI. For my part I'd really like to hear what she's got to say.

DINA. Oh yes, mamma, don't be afraid! Ponza said she was quite harmless. Let's have her come in.

AGAZZI. Of course, we can't send her away. Let's have her come in; and, if she makes any trouble, why . . . (*Turning to* THE BUTLER.) Show her in. (THE BUTLER *bows and withdraws.*)

AMALIA. You people stand by me, please! Why, I don't know what I am ever going to say to her now!

(SIGNORA FROLA *appears at the door.*

AMALIA *rises and steps forward to welcome her. The others look on in astonished silence.*)

SIGNORA FROLA.   May I please . . . ?

AMALIA.   Do come in. Signora Frola, do come in! You know all these ladies. They were here when you came before.

SIGNORA FROLA (*with an expression of sadness on her features, but still smiling gently*).   How you all look at me—and even you, Signora Agazzi! I am sure you think I am a lunatic, don't you!

AMALIA.   My dear Signora Frola, what in the world are you talking about?

SIGNORA FROLA.   But I am sure you will forgive me if I disturb you for a moment. (*Bitterly.*) Oh, my dear Signora Agazzi, I wish I had left things as they were. It was hard to feel that I had been impolite to you by not answering the bell when you called that first time; but I could never have supposed that you would come back and force me to call upon you. I could foresee the consequences of such a visit from the very first.

AMALIA.   Why, not at all, not at all! I don't understand. Why?

DINA.   What consequences could you foresee, madam?

SIGNORA FROLA.   Why, my son-in-law, Signor Ponza, has just been here, hasn't he?

AGAZZI.   Why, yes, he was here! He came to discuss certain office matters with me . . . just ordinary business, you understand!

SIGNORA FROLA (*visibly hurt and quite dismayed*).   Oh, I know you are saying that just to spare me, just in order not to hurt my feelings.

AGAZZI.   Not at all, not at all! That was really why he came.

SIGNORA FROLA (*with some alarm*). But he was quite calm, I hope, quite calm?

AGAZZI.   Calm? As calm as could be! Why not? Of course!

(*The members of the company all nod in confirmation.*)

SIGNORA FROLA.   Oh, my dear friends, I am sure you are trying to reassure me; but as a matter of fact I came to set you right about my son-in-law.

SIGNORA SIRELLI.   Why no, Signora, what's the trouble?

AGAZZI.   Really, it was just a matter of politics we talked about . . .

SIGNORA FROLA.   But I can tell from the way you all look at me . . . Please excuse me, but it is not a question of me at all. From the way you all look at me I can tell that he came here to prove something that I would never have confessed for all the money in the world. You will all bear me out, won't you? When I came here a few moments ago you all asked me questions that were very cruel questions to me, as I hope you will understand. And they were questions that I couldn't answer very well; but anyhow I gave an explanation of our manner of living which can be satisfactory to nobody, I am well aware. But how could I give you the real reason? How could I tell you people, as he's doing, that my daughter has been dead for four years and that I'm a poor, insane mother who believes that her daughter is still living and that her husband will not allow me to see her?

AGAZZI (*quite upset by the ring of deep sincerity he finds in Signora Frola's manner of speaking*).   What do you mean, your daughter?

SIGNORA FROLA (*hastily and with anguished dismay written on her features*). You know that's so. Why do you try to deny it? He did say that to you, didn't he?

SIRELLI (*with some hesitation and studying her features warily*).   Yes . . . in fact . . . he did say that.

SIGNORA FROLA.   I know he did; and I also know how it pained him to be obliged to say such a thing of me. It is a great pity, Commendatore! We have made continual sacrifices, involving unheard-of suffering, I assure you; and we could endure them only by living as we are living now. Unfortunately, as I well understand, it must look very strange to people, seem even scandalous, arouse no end of gossip! But after all, if he is an excellent secretary, scrupulously honest, attentive to his work, why should people complain? You have seen him in the office, haven't you? He is a good worker, isn't he?

AGAZZI.   To tell the truth, I have not watched him particularly, as yet.

SIGNORA FROLA.   Oh he really is, he really is! All the men he ever worked for say he's most reliable; and I beg of you, please don't let this other matter interfere. And why then should people go tormenting him with all this prying into his private life, laying bare once more a misfortune which he has succeeded in mastering and which, if it were widely talked about, might upset him again personally, and even hurt him in his career?

AGAZZI.   Oh no, no, Signora, no one is trying to hurt him. It is nothing to his disgrace that I can see. Nor would we hurt you either.

SIGNORA FROLA.   But my dear sir, how can you help hurting me when you force him to give almost publicly an explanation which is quite absurd—ridiculous I might even say! Surely people like you can't seriously believe what he says? You can't possibly be taking me for a lunatic? You don't really think that this woman is his second wife? And yet it is all so necessary! He needs to have it that way. It is the only way he can pull himself together; get down to his work again . . . the only way . . . the only way! Why he gets all wrought up, all excited, when he is forced to talk of this other matter; because he knows himself how hard it is for him to say certain things. You may have noticed it . . .

AGAZZI.   Yes, that is quite true. He did seem very much excited.

SIGNORA SIRELLI.   Well, well, well, so then it's he!

SIRELLI (*triumphantly*).   I always said it was he.

AGAZZI.   Oh, I say! Is that really possible? (*He motions to the company to be quiet.*)

SIGNORA FROLA (*joining her hands beseechingly*).   My dear friends, what are you really thinking? It is only on this subject that he is a little queer. The point is, you must simply not mention this particular matter to him. Why, really now, you could never suppose that I would leave my daughter shut up with him all alone like that? And yet just watch him at his work and in the office. He does everything he is expected to do and no one in the world could do it better.

AGAZZI.   But this is not enough, madam, as you will understand. Do you mean to say that Signor Ponza, your son-in-law, came here and made up a story out of whole cloth?

SIGNORA FROLA.   Yes, sir, yes sir, exactly . . . only I will explain. You must understand—you must look at things from his point of view.

AGAZZI.   What do you mean? Do you mean that your daughter is not dead?

SIGNORA FROLA.   God forbid! Of course she is not dead!

AGAZZI.   Well, then, he is the lunatic!

SIGNORA FROLA.   No, no, look, look! . . .

SIRELLI.   I always said it was he! . . .

SIGNORA FROLA.   No, look, look, not that, not that! Let me explain . . . You have noticed him, haven't you? Fine, strong looking man. Well, when he married my daughter you can imagine how fond he was of her. But alas, she fell sick with a contagious disease; and the doctors had to separate her from him.

Not only from him, of course, but from all her relatives. They're all dead now, poor things, in the earthquake, you understand. Well, he just refused to have her taken to the hospital; and he got so overwrought that they actually had to put him under restraint; and he broke down nervously as the result of it all and he was sent to a sanatorium. But my daughter got better very soon, while he got worse and worse. He had a sort of obsession that his wife had died in the hospital, that perhaps they had killed her there; and you couldn't get that idea out of his head.

Just imagine when we brought my daughter back to him quite recovered from her illness—and a pretty thing she was to look at, too—he began to scream and say, no, no, no, she wasn't his wife, his wife was dead! He looked at her: No, no, no, not at all! She wasn't the woman! Imagine my dear friends, how terrible it all was. Finally he came up close to her and for a moment it seemed that he was going to recognize her again; but once more it was "No, no, no, she is not my wife!" And do you know, to get him to accept my daughter at all again, we were obliged to pretend having a second wedding, with the collusion of his doctors and his friends, you understand!

SIGNORA SIRELLI. Ah, so that is why he says that . . .

SIGNORA FROLA. Yes, but he doesn't really believe it, you know; and he hasn't for a long time, I am sure. But he seems to feel a need for maintaining the pretense. He can't do without it. He feels surer of himself that way. He is seized with a terrible fear, from time to time, that this little wife he loves may be taken from him again. (*Smiling and in a low, confidential tone.*) So he keeps her locked up at home where he can have her all for himself. But he worships her—he worships her; and I am really quite convinced that my daughter is one of the happiest women in the world.

(*She gets up.*) And now I must be going. You see, my son-in-law is in a terrible state of mind at present. I wouldn't like to have him call, and find me not at home. (*With a sigh, and gesturing with her joined hands.*) Well, I suppose we must get along as best we can; but it is hard on my poor girl. She has to pretend all along that she is not herself; but another, his second wife; and I . . . oh, as for me, I have to pretend that I am a lunatic when he's around, my dear friends; but I'm glad to, I'm glad to, really, so long as it does him some good. (*The ladies rise as she steps nearer to the door.*) No, no, don't let me interrupt your party. I know the way out! Good afternoon! Good afternoon!

(*Bowing and smiling, she goes out through the rear door. The others stand there in silence, looking at each other with blank astonishment on their faces.*)

LAUDISI (*coming forward*). So you want the truth, eh? The truth! The truth! Hah! hah! hah! hah! hah! hah! hah!

Act II

(COUNCILLOR AGAZZI's *study in the same house. Antique furnishings with old paintings on the walls. A portière over the rear entrance and over the door to the left which opens into the drawing room shown in the first act. To the right a substantial fireplace with a big mirror above the mantel. A flat-top desk with a telephone. A sofa, armchairs, straight-back chairs, etc.*)

(*As the curtain rises* AGAZZI *is shown standing beside his desk with the telephone receiver pressed to his ear.* LAUDISI *and* SIRELLI *sit looking at him expectantly.*)

AGAZZI. Yes, I want Centuri. Hello . . . hello . . . Centuri? Yes, Agazzi speaking. That you, Centuri? It's me, Agazzi. Well? (*He listens for some time.*) What's that? Really? (*Again he listens at length.*) I understand, but you might go at the matter with a little more speed . . . (*Another long pause.*) Well, I give up! How can that possibly be? (*A pause.*) Oh, I see, I see . . . (*Another pause.*) Well, never mind, I'll look into it myself. Goodbye, Centuri, goodbye! (*He lays down the receiver and steps forward on the stage.*)

SIRELLI (*eagerly*). Well?

AGAZZI. Nothing! Absolutely nothing!

SIRELLI. Nothing at all?

AGAZZI. You see the whole blamed village was wiped out. Not a house left standing! In the collapse of the town hall, followed by a fire, all the records of the place seem to have been lost—births, deaths, marriages, everything.

SIRELLI. But not everybody was killed. They ought to be able to find somebody who knows them.

AGAZZI. Yes, but you see they didn't rebuild the place. Everybody moved away, and no record was ever kept of the people, of course. So far they have found nobody who knows the Ponzas. To be sure, if the police really went at it, they might find somebody, but it would be a tough job.

SIRELLI. So we can't get anywhere along that line! We have got to take what they say and let it go at that.

AGAZZI. That, unfortunately, is the situation.

LAUDISI (*rising*). Well, you fellows take a piece of advice from me: believe them both!

AGAZZI. What do you mean—"believe them both"? . . .

SIRELLI. But if she says one thing, and he says another . . .

LAUDISI. Well, in that case, you needn't believe either of them!

SIRELLI. Oh, you're just joking. We may not be able to verify the stories; but that doesn't prove that either one or the other may not be telling the truth. Some document or other . . .

LAUDISI. Oh, documents! Documents! Suppose you had them? What good would they do you?

AGAZZI. Oh, I say! Perhaps we can't get them now, but there were such documents once. If the old lady is the lunatic, there was, as there still may be somewhere, the death certificate of the daughter. Or look at it from the other angle: if we found all the records, and the death certificate were not there for the simple reason that it never existed, why then, it's Ponza, the son-in-law. He would be the lunatic.

SIRELLI. You mean to say you wouldn't give in if we stuck that certificate under your nose to-morrow or the next day? Would you still deny . . .

LAUDISI. Deny? Why . . . why . . . I'm not denying anything! In fact, I'm very careful not to be denying anything. You're the people who are looking up the records to be able to affirm or deny something. Personally, I don't give a rap for the documents; for the truth in my eyes is not a matter of black and white, but a matter of those two people. And into their minds I can penetrate only through what they say to me of themselves.

SIRELLI. Very well—She says he's crazy and he says she's crazy. Now one of them must be crazy. You can't get away from that. Well which is it, she or he?

AGAZZI. There, that's the way to put it!

LAUDISI. But just observe; in the first place, it isn't true that they are accusing each other of insanity. Ponza, to be sure, says his mother-in-law is insane. She denies this, not only of herself, but also of him. At the most, she says that he was a little off once, when they took her daughter from him; but that now he is quite all right.

SIRELLI. I see! So you're rather inclined, as I am, to trust what the old lady says.

AGAZZI. The fact is, indeed, that if you accept his story, all the facts in' the case are explained.

LAUDISI. But all the facts in the case are explained if you take her story, aren't they?

SIRELLI. Oh, nonsense! In that case neither of them would be crazy! Why, one of them must be, damn it all!

LAUDISI. Well, which one? You can't tell, can you? Neither can anybody else! And it is not because those documents you are looking for have been destroyed in an accident—a fire, an earthquake—what you will; but because those people have concealed those documents in themselves, in their own souls. Can't you understand that? She has created for him, or he for her, a world of fancy which has all the earmarks of reality itself. And in this fictitious reality they get along perfectly well, and in full accord with each other; and this world of fancy, this reality of theirs, no document can possibly destroy because the air they breathe is of that world. For them it is something they can see with their eyes, hear with their ears, and touch with their fingers. Oh, I grant you—if you could get a death certificate or a marriage certificate or something of the kind, you might be able to satisfy that stupid curiosity of yours. Unfortunately, you can't get it. And the result is that you are in the extraordinary fix of having before you, on the one hand, a world of fancy, and on the other, a world of reality, and you, for the life of you, are not able to distinguish one from the other.

AGAZZI. Philosophy, my dear boy, philosophy! And I have no use for philosophy. Give me facts, if you please! Facts! So, I say, keep at it; and I'll bet you we get to the bottom of it sooner or later.

SIRELLI. First we got her story and then we got his; and then we got a new one from her. Let's bring the two of them together—and you think that then we won't be able to tell the false from the true?

LAUDISI. Well, bring them together if you want to! All I ask is permission to laugh when you're through.

AGAZZI. Well, we'll let you laugh all you want. In the meantime let's see . . . (*He steps to the door at the left and calls.*) Amalia, Signora Sirelli, won't you come in here a moment?

(*The ladies enter with* DINA.)

SIGNORA SIRELLI (*catching sight of* LAUDISI *and shaking a finger at him*). But how is it a man like you, in the presence of such an extraordinary situation, can escape the curiosity we all feel to get at the bottom of this mystery? Why, I lie awake nights thinking of it!

AGAZZI. As your husband says, that man's impossible! Don't bother about him, Signora Sirelli.

LAUDISI. No, don't bother with me; you just listen to Agazzi! He'll keep you from lying awake tonight.

AGAZZI. Look here, ladies. This is what I want—I have an idea: won't you just step across the hall to Signora Frola's?

AMALIA. But will she come to the door?

AGAZZI. Oh, I imagine she will!

DINA. We're just returning the call, you see . . .

AMALIA. But didn't he ask us not to call on his mother-in-law? Hasn't he forbidden her to receive visits?

SIRELLI. No, not exactly! That's how he explained what had happened; but at that time nothing was known. Now that the old lady, through force of circumstance, has spoken, giving her version at least of her strange conduct, I should think that . . .

SIGNORA SIRELLI. I have a feeling that she'll be awfully glad to see us, if for nothing else, for the chance of talking about her daughter.

DINA. And she really is a jolly old

lady. There is no doubt in my mind, not the slightest: Ponza is the lunatic!

AGAZZI. Now, let's not go too fast. You just listen to me; (*He looks at his wife.*) don't stay too long—five or ten minutes at the outside!

SIRELLI (*to his wife*). And for heaven's sake, keep your mouth shut!

SIGNORA SIRELLI. And why such considerate advice to me?

SIRELLI. Once *you* get going . . .

DINA (*with the idea of preventing a scene*). Oh, we are not going to stay very long, ten minutes—fifteen, at the outside. I'll see that no breaks are made.

AGAZZI. And I'll just drop around to the office, and be back at eleven o'clock —ten or twenty minutes at the most.

SIRELLI. And what can I do?

AGAZZI. Wait! (*Turning to the ladies.*) Now, here's the plan! You people invent some excuse or other so as to get Signora Frola in here.

AMALIA. What? How can we possibly do that?

AGAZZI. Oh, find some excuse! You'll think of something in the course of your talk; and if you don't, there's Dina and Signora Sirelli. But when you come back, you understand, go into the drawing room. (*He steps to the door on the left, makes sure that it is wide open, and draws aside the portière.*) This door must stay open, wide open, so that we can hear you talking from in here. Now, here are some papers that I ought to take with me to the office. However, I forget them here. It is a brief that requires Ponza's immediate personal attention. So then, I forget it. And when I get to the office I have to bring him back here to find them—See?

SIRELLI. But just a moment. Where do I come in? When am I expected to appear?

AGAZZI. Oh, yes! . . . A moment or two after eleven, when the ladies are again in the drawing room, and I am back here, you just drop in—to take your wife home, see? You ring the bell and ask for me, and I'll have you brought in here. Then I'll invite the whole crowd in! That's natural enough, isn't it?—into my office? . . .

LAUDISI (*interrupting*). And we'll have the Truth, the whole Truth with a capital T!

DINA. But look, Nunky, of course we'll have the truth—once we get them together face to face—capital T and all!

AGAZZI. Don't get into an argument with that man. Besides, it's time you ladies were going. None of us has any too much leeway.

SIGNORA SIRELLI. Come, Amalia, come Dina! And as for you, sir, (*Turning to* LAUDISI.) I won't even shake hands with you.

LAUDISI. Permit me to do it for you, madam. (*He shakes one hand with the other.*) Good luck to you, my dear ladies.

(*Exit* DINA, AMALIA, SIGNORA SIRELLI).

AGAZZI (*to* SIRELLI). And now we'd better go, too. Suppose we hurry!

SIRELLI. Yes, right away. Goodbye, Lamberto!

LAUDISI. Goodbye, good luck, good luck! (AGAZZI *and* SIRELLI *leave.* LAUDISI, *left alone, walks up and down the study a number of times, nodding his head and occasionally smiling. Finally he draws up in front of the big mirror that is hanging over the mantelpiece. He sees himself in the glass, stops, and addresses his image.*)

LAUDISI. So there you are! (*He bows to himself and salutes, touching his forehead with his fingers.*) I say, old man, who is the lunatic, you or I? (*He levels a finger menacingly at his image in the glass; and, of course, the image in turn levels a finger at him. As he smiles, his image smiles.*) Of course, I understand! I say it's you, and you say it's me. You— you are the lunatic! No? It's me? Very well! It's me! Have it *your* way. Between you and me, we get along very well, don't we! But the trouble is, others don't think of you just as I do; and that being the case, old man, what a fix you're in! As for me, I say that here, right in front of you, I can see myself with my eyes and touch myself with my fingers. But what are you for other people? What are you in their eyes? An image, my dear sir, just an image in the glass! "What fools these mortals be!" as old Shakespeare said. They're all carrying just such a phantom around inside themselves, and here they are racking their brains about the phantoms in other people; and they think all that is quite another thing!

(THE BUTLER *has entered the room in time to catch* LAUDISI *gesticulating at himself in the glass. He wonders if the man is crazy. Finally he speaks up.*)

BUTLER. Ahem! . . . Signor Laudisi, if you please . . .

LAUDISI (*coming to himself*).   Uff!

BUTLER. Two ladies calling, sir! Signora Cini and another lady!

LAUDISI.   Calling to see me?

BUTLER. Really, they asked for the signora; but I said that she was out—on a call next door; and then . . .

LAUDISI.   Well, what then?

BUTLER. They looked at each other and said, "Really! Really!" and finally they asked me if anybody else was at home.

LAUDISI. And of course you said that everyone was out!

BUTLER.   I said that you were in!

LAUDISI. Why, not at all! I'm miles and miles away! Perhaps that fellow they call Laudisi is here!

BUTLER.   I don't understand, sir.

LAUDISI. Why? You think the Laudisi they know is the Laudisi I am?

BUTLER.   I don't understand, sir.

LAUDISI.   Who are you talking to?

BUTLER. Who am I talking to? I thought I was talking to you.

LAUDISI.   Are you really sure the

Laudisi you are talking to is the Laudisi the ladies want to see?

BUTLER. Why, I think so, sir. They said they were looking for the brother of Signora Agazzi.

LAUDISI. Ah, in that case you are right! (*Turning to the image in the glass.*) You are not the brother of Signora Agazzi? No, it's me! (*To* THE BUTLER.) Right you are! Tell them I am in. And show them in here, won't you?

(THE BUTLER *retires.*)

SIGNORA CINI.   May I come in?

LAUDISI. Please, please, this way, madam!

SIGNORA CINI. I was told Signora Agazzi was not at home, and I brought Signora Nenni along. Signora Nenni is a friend of mine, and she was most anxious to make the acquaintance of . . .

LAUDISI.   . . . of Signora Frola?

SIGNORA CINI. Of Signora Agazzi, your sister!

LAUDISI. Oh, she will be back very soon, and Signora Frola will be here, too.

SIGNORA CINI. Yes, we thought as much.

(SIGNORA NENNI *is an oldish woman of the type of Signora Cini, but with the mannerisms of the latter somewhat more pronounced. She, too, is a bundle of concentrated curiosity, but of the sly, cautious type, ready to find something frightful under everything.*)

LAUDISI. Well, it's all planned in advance! It will be a most interesting scene! The curtain rises at eleven, precisely!

SIGNORA CINI. Planned in advance? What is planned in advance?

LAUDISI (*mysteriously, first with a gesture of his finger and then aloud*). Why, bringing the two of them together! (*A gesture of admiration.*) Great idea, I tell you!

SIGNORA CINI. The two of them—together—who?

LAUDISI.   Why, the two of them. He

—in here! (*Pointing to the room about him.*)

SIGNORA CINI. Ponza, you mean?

LAUDISI. And she—in there! (*He points toward the drawing room.*)

SIGNORA CINI. Signora Frola?

LAUDISI. Exactly! (*With an expressive gesture of his hands and even more mysteriously.*) But afterwards, all of them—in here! Oh, a great idea, a great idea!

SIGNORA CINI. In order to get . . .

LAUDISI. The truth! Precisely: the truth!

SIGNORA CINI. But the truth is known already!

LAUDISI. Of course! The only question is stripping it bare, so that everyone can see it!

SIGNORA CINI (*with the greatest surprise*). Oh, really? So they know the truth! And which is it—He or she?

LAUDISI. Well, I'll tell you . . . you just guess! Who do you think it is?

SIGNORA CINI (*ahemming*). Well . . . I say . . . really . . . you see . . .

LAUDISI. Is it she or is it he? You don't mean to say you don't know! Come now, give a guess!

SIGNORA CINI. Why, for my part I should say . . . well, I'd say . . . it's *he*.

LAUDISI (*looks at her admiringly*). Right you are! It *is* he!

SIGNORA CINI. Really? I always thought so! Of course, it was perfectly plain all along. It had to be he!

SIGNORA NENNI. All of us women in town said it was he. We always said so!

SIGNORA CINI. But how did you get at it? I suppose Signor Agazzi ran down the documents, didn't he—the birth certificate, or something?

SIGNORA NENNI. Through the prefect, of course! There was no getting away from those people. Once the police start investigating . . . !

LAUDISI (*motions to them to come closer to him; then in a low voice and in the same mysterious manner, and stressing each syllable*). The certificate!—Of the second marriage!

SIGNORA CINI (*starting back with astonishment*). What?

SIGNORA NENNI (*likewise taken aback*). What did you say? The second marriage?

SIGNORA CINI. Well, in that case he was *right*.

LAUDISI. Oh, documents, ladies, documents! This certificate of the second marriage, so it seems, talks as plain as day.

SIGNORA NENNI. Well, then, *she* is the lunatic.

LAUDISI. Right you are! She it is!

SIGNORA CINI. But I thought you said . . .

LAUDISI. Yes, I did say . . . but this certificate of the second marriage may very well be, as Signora Frola said, a fictitious document, gotten up through the influence of Ponza's doctors and friends to pamper him in the notion that his wife was not his first wife, but another woman.

SIGNORA CINI. But it's a public document. You mean to say a public document can be a fraud?

LAUDISI. I mean to say—well, it has just the value that each of you chooses to give it. For instance, one could find somewhere, possibly, those letters that Signora Frola said she gets from her daughter, who lets them down in the basket in the courtyard. There are such letters, aren't there?

SIGNORA CINI. Yes, of course!

LAUDISI. They are documents, aren't they? Aren't letters documents? But it all depends on how you read them. Here comes Ponza, and he says they are just made up to pamper his mother-in-law in her obsession . . .

SIGNORA CINI. Oh, dear, dear, so then we're never sure about anything?

LAUDISI. Never sure about anything? Why not at all, not at all! Let's be exact. We are sure of many things, aren't we?

How many days are there in the week?
Seven—Sunday, Monday, Tuesday,
Wednesday . . . How many months in
the year are there? Twelve: January,
February, March . . .

SIGNORA CINI. Oh, I see, you're just
joking! You're just joking! (DINA *appears, breathless, in the doorway, at the
rear.*)

DINA. Oh, Nunky, won't you please
. . . (*She stops at the sight of* SIGNORA
CINI.) Oh, Signora Cini, you here?

SIGNORA CINI. Why, I just came to
make a call! . . .

LAUDISI. . . . with Signora Cenni.

SIGNORA NENNI. No, my name is
Nenni.

LAUDISI. Oh yes, pardon me! She
was anxious to make Signora Frola's acquaintance . . .

SIGNORA NENNI. Why, not at all!

SIGNORA CINI. He has just been making fun of us! You ought to see what
fools he made of us!

DINA. Oh, he's perfectly insufferable,
even with mamma and me. Will you excuse me for just a moment? No, everything is all right. I'll just run back and
tell mamma that you people are here
and I think that will be enough. Oh,
Nunky, if you had only heard her talk!
Why, she is a perfect *dear,* and what a
good, kind soul! . . . She showed us all
those letters her daughter wrote . . .

SIGNORA CINI. Yes, but as Signor
Laudisi was just saying . . .

DINA. He hasn't even seen them!

SIGNORA NENNI. You mean they are
not really fictitious?

DINA. Fictitious nothing! They talk
as plain as day. And such things! You
can't fool a mother when her own
daughter talks to her. And you know—
the letter she got yesterday! . . . (*She
stops at the sound of voices coming into
the study from the drawing room.*) Oh,
here they are, here they are, already!
(*She goes to the door and peeps into the
room.*)

SIGNORA CINI (*following her to the
door*). Is *she* there, too?

DINA. Yes, but you had better come
into the other room. All of us women
must be in the drawing room. And it is
just eleven o'clock, Nunky!

AMALIA (*entering with decision from
the door on the left*). I think this
whole business is quite unnecessary! We
have absolutely no further need of
proofs . . .

DINA. Quite so! I thought of that
myself. Why bring Ponza here?

AMALIA (*taken somewhat aback by
Signora Cini's presence*). Oh, my dear
Signora Cini! . . .

SIGNORA CINI (*introducing Signora
Nenni*). A friend of mine, Signora
Nenni! I ventured to bring her with
me . . .

AMALIA (*bowing, but somewhat
coolly, to the visitor*). A great pleasure,
Signora! (*After a pause.*) There is not
the slightest doubt in the world: . . .
it's he!

SIGNORA CINI. It's he? Are you sure
it's he?

DINA. And such a trick on the poor
old lady!

AMALIA. Trick is not the name for
it! It is downright dishonest!

LAUDISI. Oh, I agree with you: it's
outrageous! Quite! So much so, I'm
quite convinced it must be *she!*

AMALIA. She? What do you mean?
How can you say that?

LAUDISI. I say, it is *she,* it is *she,* it's
she!

AMALIA. Oh, I say! If you had heard
her talk . . . !

DINA. It is absolutely clear to us
now.

SIGNORA CINI *and* SIGNORA NENNI
(*swallowing*). Really? You are sure?

LAUDISI. Exactly! Now that you are
sure it's he, why, obviously—it must be
she.

DINA. Oh dear me, why talk to that
man? He is just impossible!

AMALIA. Well, we must go into the other room . . . This way, if you please!

(SIGNORA CINI, SIGNORA NENNI *and* AMALIA *withdraw through the door on the left.* DINA *starts to follow, when* LAUDISI *calls her back.*)

LAUDISI. Dina!

DINA. I refuse to listen to you! I refuse!

LAUDISI. I was going to suggest that, since the whole matter is closed, you might close the door also.

DINA. But papa . . . he told us to leave it open. Ponza will be here soon; and if papa finds it closed—well, you know how papa is!

LAUDISI. But you can convince him! . . . You especially. You can show him that there really was no need of going any further. You are convinced yourself, aren't you?

DINA. I am as sure of it, as I am that I'm alive!

LAUDISI (*putting her to the test with a smile*). Well, close the door then!

DINA. I see, you're trying to make me say that I'm not really sure. Well, I won't close the door, but it's just on account of papa.

LAUDISI. Shall I close it for you?

DINA. If you take the responsibility yourself! . . .

LAUDISI. But you see, *I* am sure! I *know* that Ponza is the lunatic!

DINA. The thing for you to do is to come into the other room and just hear her talk a while. Then you'll be sure, absolutely sure. Coming?

LAUDISI. Yes, I'm coming, and I'll close the door behind me—on my own responsibility, of course.

DINA. Ah, I see. So you're convinced even before you hear her talk.

LAUDISI. No, dear, it's because I'm sure that your papa, who has been with Ponza, is just as certain as you are that any further investigation is unnecessary.

DINA. How can you say that?

LAUDISI. Why, of course, if you talk with Ponza, you're sure the old lady is crazy. (*He walks resolutely to the door.*) I am going to shut this door.

DINA (*restraining him nervously, then hesitating a moment*). Well, why not . . . if you're really sure? What do you say—let's leave it open!

LAUDISI. Hah! hah! hah! hah! hah! hah! hah!

DINA. But just because papa told us to!

LAUDISI. And papa will tell you something else by and by. Say . . . let's leave it open!

(*A piano starts playing in the adjoining room—an ancient tune, full of soft and solemn melody; the "Nina" of Pergolesi.*)

DINA. Oh, there she is. She's playing! Do you hear? Actually playing the piano!

LAUDISI. The old lady?

DINA. Yes! And you know? She told us that her daughter used to play this tune, always the same tune. How well she plays! Come! Come!

(*They hurry through the door.*)

(*The stage, after the exit of* LAUDISI *and* DINA, *remains empty for a space of time while the music continues from the other room.* PONZA, *appearing at the door with* AGAZZI, *catches the concluding notes and his face changes to an expression of deep emotion—an emotion that will develop into a virtual frenzy as the scene proceeds.*)

AGAZZI (*in the doorway*). After you, after you, please! (*He takes* PONZA'S *elbow and motions him into the room. He goes over to his desk, looks about for the papers which he pretends he had forgotten, finds them eventually and says.*) Why, here they are! I was sure I had left them here. Won't you take a chair, Ponza? (*PONZA seems not to hear. He stands looking excitedly at the door into the drawing room, through which the sound of the piano is still coming.*)

AGAZZI. Yes, they are the ones! (*He*

takes the papers and steps to PONZA's *side, opening the folder.*) It is an old case, you see. Been running now for years and years! To tell you the truth I haven't made head or tail of the stuff myself. I imagine you'll find it one big mess. (*He, too, becomes aware of the music and seems somewhat irritated by it. His eyes also rest on the door to the drawing room.*) That noise, just at this moment! (*He walks with a show of anger to the door.*) Who is that at the piano anyway? (*In the doorway he stops and looks, and an expression of astonishment comes into his face.*) Ah!

PONZA (*going to the door also. On looking into the next room he can hardly restrain his emotion*). In the name of God, is *she* playing?

AGAZZI. Yes—Signora Frola! And how well she does play!

PONZA. How is this? You people have brought her in here, again! And you're letting her play!

AGAZZI. Why not? What's the harm?

PONZA. Oh, please, please, no, not that song! It is the one her daughter used to play.

AGAZZI. Oh, I see! And it hurts you?

PONZA. Oh, no, not me—but her—it hurts her—and you don't know how much! I thought I had made you and those women understand just how that poor old lady was!

AGAZZI. Yes, you did . . . quite true! But you see . . . but see here, Ponza! (*Trying to pacify the man's growing emotion.*)

PONZA (*continuing*). But you *must* leave her alone! You *must* not go to her house! She *must* not come in here! I am the only person who can deal with her. You are killing her . . . killing her!

AGAZZI. No, I don't think so. It is not so bad as that. My wife and daughter are surely tactful enough . . . (*Suddenly the music ceases. There is a burst of applause.*)

AGAZZI. There, you see. Listen! Listen!

(*From the next room the following conversation is distinctly heard.*)

DINA. Why, Signora Frola, you are perfectly *marvellous* at the piano!

SIGNORA FROLA. But you should hear how my Lena plays!

(PONZA *digs his nails into his hands.*)

AGAZZI. Her daughter, of course!

PONZA. Didn't you hear? "How my Lena plays! How my Lena *plays*"!

(*Again from the inside.*)

SIGNORA FROLA. Oh, no, not now! . . . She hasn't played for a long time— since that happened. And you know, it is what she takes hardest, poor girl!

AGAZZI. Why, that seems quite natural to me! Of course, she thinks the girl is still alive!

PONZA. But she shouldn't be allowed to say such things. She *must* not—she *must* not say such things! Didn't you hear? "She hasn't played since that happened"! She said "she *hasn't* played since that happened"! Talking of the piano, you understand! Oh, you don't understand, no, of course! My first wife had a piano and played that tune. Oh, oh, oh! You people are determined to ruin me!

(SIRELLI *appears at the back door at this moment, and hearing the concluding words of* PONZA *and noticing his extreme exasperation, stops short, uncertain as to what to do.* AGAZZI *is himself very much affected and motions to* SIRELLI *to come in.*)

AGAZZI. Why, no, my dear fellow, I don't see any reason . . . (*To* SIRELLI). Won't you just tell the ladies to come in here?

(SIRELLI, *keeping at a safe distance from* PONZA, *goes to the door at the left and calls.*)

PONZA. The ladies in here? In here with me? Oh, no, no, please, rather . . .

(*At a signal from* SIRELLI, *who stands*

in the doorway to the left, his face taut with intense emotion, the ladies enter. They all show various kinds and degrees of excitement and emotion. SIGNORA FROLA *appears, and catching sight of* PONZA *in the condition he is in, stops, quite overwhelmed. As he assails her during the lines that follow, she exchanges glances of understanding from time to time with the ladies about her. The action here is rapid, nervous, tense with excitement, and extremely violent.*)

PONZA. You? Here? How is this? You! Here! Again! What are you doing here?

SIGNORA FROLA. Why, I just came . . . don't be cross!

PONZA. You came here to tell these ladies . . . What did you tell these ladies?

SIGNORA FROLA. Nothing! I swear to God, nothing!

PONZA. Nothing? What do you mean, nothing? I heard you with my own ears, and this gentleman here heard you also. You said "she plays." Who plays? Lena plays! And you know very well that Lena has been dead—for four years!

SIGNORA FROLA. Yes, yes, I know . . . Don't get excited, my dear . . . Oh, yes, oh yes. I know . . .

PONZA. And you said "she hasn't been able to play since that happened." Of course she hasn't been able to play since that happened. How could she, if she's dead?

SIGNORA FROLA. Why, of course, certainly. Isn't that what I said? Ask these ladies. I said that she hasn't been able to play since that happened. Of course. How could she, if she's dead?

PONZA. And why were you worrying about that piano, then?

SIGNORA FROLA. No, no! I'm not worrying about any piano . . .

PONZA. I broke that piano up and destroyed it. You know that, the moment

your daughter died, to keep this second wife of mine from playing on it. For that matter you know that this second woman never plays.

SIGNORA FROLA. Why, of course, dear! Of course! She doesn't know how to play!

PONZA. And one thing more: Your daughter was Lena, wasn't she? Her name was Lena. Now, see here! You just tell these people what my second wife's name is. Speak up! You know very well what her name is! What is it? What is it?

SIGNORA FROLA. Her name is Julia! Yes, yes, of course, my dear friends, her name is Julia! (*Winks at someone in the company.*)

PONZA. Exactly! Her name is Julia, and not Lena! Who are you winking at? Don't you go trying to suggest by those winks of yours that she's not Julia!

SIGNORA FROLA. Why, what do you mean? I wasn't winking! Of course I wasn't!

PONZA. I saw you! I saw you very distinctly! You are trying to ruin me! You are trying to make these people think that I am keeping your daughter all to myself, just as though she were not dead, (*He breaks into convulsive sobbing.*) . . . just as though she were not dead!

SIGNORA FROLA (*hurrying forward and speaking with infinite kindness and sympathy*). Oh no! Come, come, my poor boy. Come! Don't take it so hard. I never said any such thing, did I, madam?

AMALIA, SIGNORA SIRELLI, DINA. Of course she never said such a thing! She always said the girl was dead! Yes! Of course! No!

SIGNORA FROLA. I did, didn't I? I said she's dead, didn't I? And that you are so very good to me. Didn't I, didn't I? I, trying to ruin you? I, trying to get you into trouble?

PONZA. And you, going into other people's houses where there are pianos, playing your daughter's tunes on them! Saying that Lena plays them that way, or even better!

SIGNORA FROLA. No, it was . . . why . . . you see . . . it was . . . well . . . just to see whether . . .

PONZA. But you *can't* . . . you *mustn't!* How could you ever dream of trying to play a tune that your dead daughter played!

SIGNORA FROLA. You are quite right! . . . Oh, yes! Poor boy! Poor boy! (*She also begins to weep.*) I'll never do it again: Never, never, never again!

PONZA (*advancing upon her threateningly*). What are you doing here? Get out of here! Go home at once! Home! Home! Go home!

SIGNORA FROLA. Yes, Yes! Home! I am going home! Oh dear, oh dear!

(*She backs out the rear door, looking beseechingly at the company, as though urging everyone to have pity on her son-in-law. She retires, sobbing. The others stand there looking at* PONZA *with pity and terror; but the moment* SIGNORA FROLA *has left the room, he regains his normal composure, an air of despairing melancholy, and he says coolly, but with profound seriousness:*)

PONZA. I hope you good people will excuse me for this scene. A scene it really was, I suppose! But how could I avoid it? I had to rave like that to repair the damage which you good people, with the best of intentions, and surely without dreaming what you are really doing, have done to this unfortunate woman.

AGAZZI (*in astonishment*). What do you mean? That you were just acting? You were pretending all that?

PONZA. Of course I was! Don't you people understand that I had to? The only way to keep her in her obsession is for me to shout the truth that way, as

though I myself had gone mad, as though I were the lunatic! Understand? But please forgive me. I must be going now. I must go in and see how she is. (*He hurries out through the rear door. The others stand where they are in blank amazement.*)

LAUDISI (*coming forward*). And there, ladies and gentlemen, you have the truth! Hah! hah! hah; hah; hah; hah! hah!

Act III

(*The same scene. As the curtain rises,* LAUDISI *is sprawling in an easy chair, reading a book. Through the door that leads into the parlor on the left comes the confused murmur of many voices.*)

(THE BUTLER *appears in the rear door, introducing* THE POLICE COMMISSIONER, CENTURI. CENTURI *is a tall, stiff, scowling official, with a decidedly professional air. He is in the neighborhood of forty.*)

THE BUTLER. This way, sir. I will call Signor Agazzi at once.

LAUDISI (*drawing himself up in his chair and looking around*). Oh, it's you, Commissioner! (*He rises hastily and recalls* THE BUTLER, *who has stepped out through the door.*) One moment, please! Wait! (*To* CENTURI.) Anything new, Commissioner?

COMMISSIONER (*stiffly*). Yes, something new!

LAUDISI. Ah! Very well. (*To* THE BUTLER.) Never mind. I'll call him myself. (*He motions with his hand toward the door on the left.* THE BUTLER *bows and withdraws.*) You have worked miracles, Commissioner! You're the savior of this town. Listen! Do you hear them? You are the lion of the place! How does it feel to be the father of your country? But say, what you've discovered is all solid fact?

COMMISSIONER. We've managed to unearth a few people.

LAUDISI. From Ponza's town? People who know all about him?

COMMISSIONER. Yes! And we have gathered from them a few facts,—not many, perhaps, but well authenticated.

LAUDISI. Ah, that's nice. Congratulations! For example . . .

COMMISSIONER. For example? Why, for instance, here . . . well, here are all the communications I have received. Read 'em yourself! (*From an inner pocket he draws a yellow envelope, opened at one end, from which he takes a document and hands it to* LAUDISI.)

LAUDISI. Interesting, I am sure. Very interesting! . . . (*He stands, reading the document carefully, commenting from time to time with exclamations in different tones. First an "ah" of satisfaction, then another "ah" which attenuates this enthusiasm very much. Finally an "eh" of disappointment, which leads to another "eh" of complete disgust.*) Why, no, what's all this amount to, Commissioner?

COMMISSIONER. Well, it's what we were able to find out.

LAUDISI. But this doesn't prove anything, you understand! It leaves everything just where it was. There's nothing of any significance whatever here. (*He looks at* THE COMMISSIONER *for a moment and then, as though suddenly making up his mind, he says:*) I wonder, Commissioner, would you like to do something really great—render a really distinguished service to this town; and meanwhile lay up a treasure in heaven?

COMMISSIONER (*looking at him in perplexity*). What are you thinking of, sir?

LAUDISI. I'll explain. Here, please, take this chair! (*He sets the chair in front of* AGAZZI's *desk.*) I advise you, Mr. Commissioner, to tear up this sheet of paper that you've brought and which

has absolutely no significance at all. But here on this other piece of paper, why don't you write down something that will be precise and clear?

COMMISSIONER. Why . . . why . . . myself? What do you mean? What should I write?

LAUDISI. Anything, anything at all! Anything that comes into your head, provided, however, it be *precise* and *clear!* Say, for instance, that Signora Frola is a lunatic, or, if you will, if you prefer, that the second marriage of Ponza's was a frame-up!

COMMISSIONER. I don't get you, Signor Laudisi. What are you driving at? I forge the document?

LAUDISI (*insisting*). Forge? Just say something—anything—that these two old acquaintances of Ponza's whom you managed to get hold of might have said. Come, Commissioner, rise to the occasion! Do something for the commonwealth! Bring this town back to normal again! Don't you see what they are after? They all want the truth—a truth, that is: Something specific; something concrete! They don't care what it is. All they want is something categorical, something that speaks plainly! Then they'll quiet down.

COMMISSIONER. *The* truth—*a* truth? Excuse me, have I understood you clearly? You were suggesting that I commit a forgery? I am astonished that you dare propose such a thing, and when I say I am astonished, I'm not saying half what I actually feel. Be so good as to tell the Commendatore that I am here!

LAUDISI (*dropping his arms dejectedly*). As you will, Commissioner!

(*He steps over to the door on the left. As he draws the portières and swings the door more widely open, the voices become louder and more confused. As he steps through, there is a sudden silence.* THE POLICE COMMISSIONER *stands waiting with a satisfied air, twirling one of the points of his*

*mustache. All of a sudden, there is com-
motion and cheering in the next room.
Cries of delight and applause, mixed
with hand-clapping.* THE POLICE COM-
MISSIONER *comes out of his reverie and
looks up with an expression of surprise
on his features, as though not understanding what it's all about. Through the
door to the left come* AGAZZI, SIRELLI,
LAUDISI, AMALIA, DINA, SIGNORA SI-
RELLI, SIGNORA CINI, SIGNORA NENNI,
and many other ladies and gentlemen.
AGAZZI *leads the procession. They are
all still talking and laughing excitedly,
clapping their hands, and crying "I told
you so! Fine! Fine! Good! How wonderful! Now we'll know!" etc.)*

AGAZZI (*stepping forward cordially*).
Ah, my dear Centuri, I was sure you
could! Nothing ever gets by *our* chief!

COMPANY. Fine! Good! What did
you find out! Have you brought something? Is it she? Is it he? Tell us?

COMMISSIONER (*who doesn't yet understand what all the excitement is
about. For him it has been a mere matter of routine*). Why, no . . . why,
Commendatore, simply . . . you understand . . .

AGAZZI. Hush! Give him a chance!
. . .

COMMISSIONER. I have done my
best. I . . . but what did Signor Laudisi
tell you?

AGAZZI. He told us that you have
brought news, real news!

SIRELLI. Specific data, clear, precise! . . .

LAUDISI (*amplifying*). . . . not many,
perhaps, but well authenticated! The
best they've managed to trace! Old
neighbors of Ponza, you see; people well
acquainted with him . . .

EVERYBODY. Ah! At last! At last!
Now we'll know! At last!

(THE COMMISSIONER *hands the document to* AGAZZI.)

COMMISSIONER. There you have it,
Commendatore!

AGAZZI (*opening the sheet, as all
crowd around him*). Let's have a look
at it!

COMMISSIONER. But you, Signor
Laudisi . . .

LAUDISI. Don't interrupt, please, the
document speaks for itself! Agazzi, you
read it.

AGAZZI (*to* LAUDISI). But give me a
chance, won't you? Please! Please! Now!
There you are!

LAUDISI. Oh, I don't care. I've read
the thing already.

EVERYBODY (*crowding round him*).
You've read it already? What did it say?
Is it he? Is it she?

LAUDISI (*speaking very formally*).
There is no doubt whatever, as a former
neighbor of Ponza's testifies, that the
woman Frola was once in a sanatorium!

THE GROUP (*cries of disappointment*).
Oh really! Too bad! Too bad!

SIGNORA SIRELLI. Signora Frola, did
you say?

DINA. Are you sure it was she?

AGAZZI. Why, no! Why, no, it
doesn't say anything of the kind! (*Coming forward and waving the document
triumphantly*.) It doesn't say anything
of the kind! (*General excitement*.)

EVERYBODY. Well, what does it say?
What does it say?

LAUDISI (*insisting*). It does too! It
says "the Frola woman"—the Frola
woman, categorically.

AGAZZI. Nothing of the kind! The
witness says that he *thinks* she was in a
sanatorium. He does not assert that she
was. Besides, there is another point. He
doesn't know whether this Frola woman
who was in a sanatorium was the mother
or the daughter, the first wife, that is.

EVERYBODY (*with relief*). Ah!

LAUDISI (*insistingly*). But I say he
does. It must be the mother! Who else
could it be?

SIRELLI. No, of course, it's the
daughter! It's the daughter!

SIGNORA SIRELLI. Just as the old
lady said herself!

AMALIA. Exactly! That time when

they took her away by force from her husband! . . .

DINA. Yes, she says that her daughter was taken to a sanatorium on account of a contagious disease.

AGAZZI. Furthermore, observe another thing. The witness does not really belong to their town. He says that he used to go there frequently, but that he does not remember particularly. He remembers that he heard something or other! . . .

SIRELLI. Ah! How can you depend on such a man's testimony? Nothing but hearsay!

LAUDISI. But, excuse me! If all you people are so sure that Signora Frola is right, what more do you want? Why do you go looking for documents? This is all nonsense!

SIRELLI. If it weren't for the fact that the prefect has accepted Ponza's side of the story, I'll tell you . . .

COMMISSIONER. Yes, that's true. The prefect said as much to me . . .

AGAZZI. Yes, but that's because the prefect has never talked with the old lady who lives next door.

SIGNORA SIRELLI. You bet he hasn't. He talked only with Ponza.

SIRELLI. But, for that matter, there are other people of the same mind as the prefect.

A GENTLEMAN. That is my situation, my situation, exactly. Yes sir! Because I know of just such a case where a mother went insane over the death of her daughter and insists that the daughter's husband will not allow her to see the girl. The same case to a T.

A SECOND GENTLEMAN. Not exactly to a T! Not exactly to a T! In the case you mention the man didn't marry again. Here, this man Ponza is living with another woman . . .

LAUDISI (*his face brightening with a new idea that has suddenly come to him*). I have it, ladies and gentlemen! Did you hear that? It's perfectly simple. Dear me, as simple as Columbus's egg!

EVERYBODY. What? What? What? What?

THE SECOND GENTLEMAN. What did I say? I didn't realize it was important.

LAUDISI. Just a moment, ladies and gentlemen! (*Turning to* AGAZZI.) Is the prefect coming here, by chance?

AGAZZI. Yes, we were expecting him. But what's the new idea?

LAUDISI. Why, you were bringing him here to talk with Signora Frola. So far, he is standing by Ponza. When he has talked with the old lady, he'll know whether to believe Ponza or her. That's *your* idea! Well, I've thought of something better that the prefect can do. Something that he only can do.

EVERYBODY. What is it? What is it? What is it?

LAUDISI (*triumphantly*). Why, this wife of Ponza's, of course . . . at least, the woman he is living with! What this gentleman said suggested the idea to me.

SIRELLI. Get the second woman to talk? Of course! Of course!

DINA. But how can we, when she is kept under lock and key?

LAUDISI. Why, the prefect can use his authority—order her to speak!

AMALIA. Certainly, she is the one who can clear up the whole mystery.

SIGNORA SIRELLI. I don't believe it. She'll say just what her husband tells her to say.

LAUDISI. Of course, if she were to speak in his presence . . . of course!

SIRELLI. She must speak with the prefect privately, all by himself.

AGAZZI. And the prefect, as the final authority over the man, will insist that the wife make a formal explicit statement before him. Of course, of course! What do you say, Commissioner?

COMMISSIONER. Why certainly, there's no doubt that if the prefect were so inclined . . .

AGAZZI. It is the only way out of it, after all. We ought to 'phone him and explain that he needn't go to the trouble of coming here. You attend to that, will you, Commissioner?

COMMISSIONER. Very glad to! My compliments, ladies! Good afternoon, gentlemen!

SIGNORA SIRELLI. A good idea for once, Laudisi.

DINA. Oh, Nunky, how clever of you! Wise old Nunky!

THE COMPANY. The only way out of it! Yes! Yes! Fine! At last!

AGAZZI. Curious none of us thought of that before!

SIRELLI. Not so curious! None of us ever set eyes on the woman. She might as well be in another world, poor girl.

LAUDISI (*as though suddenly impressed by this latter reflection*). In another world? Why yes,—are you really sure there is such a woman?

AMALIA. Oh I say! Please, please, Lamberto!

SIRELLI (*with a laugh*). You mean to say you think there is no such woman?

LAUDISI. How can you be sure there is? You can't guarantee it!

DINA. But the old lady sees her and talks with her every day.

SIGNORA SIRELLI. And Ponza says that, too. They both agree on that point!

LAUDISI. Yes, yes, I don't deny that. But just a moment! If you think of it, isn't Signora Frola right? Well, in that case who is the woman in Ponza's eyes? The phantom of a second wife, of course! Or else Ponza himself is right, and in that case you have the phantom of a daughter in the old lady's eyes! Two phantoms, in other words! Now we've got to find out, ladies and gentlemen, whether this woman, who must be a mere phantom for the one or for the other, is a person, after all, for herself. In the situation we are in, I should say there was very good ground for doubting.

AGAZZI. Oh, you make me tired! If we listen to you . . .

LAUDISI. No, ladies and gentlemen,

notice! It may be that she is nothing but a phantom in her own eyes.

SIGNORA NENNI. Why, this is getting to be almost spooky!

SIGNORA CINI. You mean to say it's a ghost, a real ghost? How can you frighten us so?

EVERYBODY. Nonsense! He's only joking! He's only joking!

LAUDISI. Not a bit of it! I'm not joking at all! Who ever saw the woman? No one ever set eyes on her. He talks of her, to be sure, and she, the old woman that is, says that she often sees her.

SIRELLI. Nonsense! Any number of people have seen her; she comes to the balcony of the courtyard.

LAUDISI. Who comes to the balcony?

SIRELLI. A woman in flesh and bones —in skirts, for that matter. People have heard her talk. For heaven's sake, man!

LAUDISI. Are you sure of that?

AGAZZI. And why not, pray? You said so yourself a moment ago!

LAUDISI. Why yes, I did say so! I did say that the prefect ought to have a talk with whatever woman is there. But notice one thing, it is certain that no ordinary woman is there. No *ordinary* woman! Of that much we can be sure! And I, for my part, have come to doubt whether she is in any sense of the term, a woman.

SIGNORA SIRELLI. Dear me, dear me! That man simply drives me crazy.

LAUDISI. Well, supposing we wait and see!

EVERYBODY. Well, who is she then? But people have seen her! His wife! On the balcony! She writes letters!

POLICE COMMISSIONER (*in the heat of the confusion comes into the room, excitedly announcing*). The prefect is coming! The prefect!

AGAZZI. What do you mean? Coming here? But you want to . . .

COMMISSIONER. Why yes, but I met

him hardly a block away. He was coming here; and Ponza is with him.

SIRELLI. Ah, Ponza!

AGAZZI. Oh, if Ponza is with him, I doubt whether he is coming here. They are probably on their way to the old lady's. Please, Centuri, you just wait on the landing there and ask him if he won't step in here as he promised?

COMMISSIONER. Very well! I'll do so! (*He withdraws hurriedly through the door in the rear.*)

AGAZZI. Won't you people just step into the other room?

SIGNORA SIRELLI. But remember now, be sure to make him see the point! It's the only way out, the only way.

AMALIA (*at the door to the left*). This way, ladies, if you please!

AGAZZI. Won't you just stay here, Sirelli; and you, too, Lamberto?

(*All the others go out through the door to the left.*)

AGAZZI (*to* LAUDISI). But let me do the talking, won't you!

LAUDISI. Oh, as for that, don't worry. In fact, if you prefer, I'll go into the other room . . .

AGAZZI. No, no, it's better for you to be here. Ah, here he is now!

(THE PREFECT *is a man of about sixty, tall, thick set, good-natured, affable.*)

PREFECT. Ah, Agazzi, glad to see you. How goes it, Sirelli? Good to see you again, Laudisi. (*He shakes hands all around.*)

AGAZZI (*motioning toward a chair*). I hope you won't mind my having asked you to come here.

PREFECT. No, I was coming, just as I promised you!

AGAZZI (*noticing* THE POLICE COMMISSIONER *at the door*). Oh, I'm sorry, Commissioner! Please come in! Here, have a chair!

PREFECT (*good-naturedly to* SIRELLI). By the way, Sirelli, they tell me that you've gone half nutty over this blessed affair of our new secretary.

SIRELLI. Oh, no, governor, believe me. I'm not the only one! The whole village is worked up.

AGAZZI. And that's putting it very mildly.

PREFECT. What's it all about? What's it all about? Good heavens!

AGAZZI. Of course, governor, you're probably not posted on the whole business. The old lady lives here next door. . . .

PREFECT. Yes, I understand so.

SIRELLI. No, one moment, please, governor. You haven't talked with the poor old lady yet.

PREFECT. I was on my way to see her. (*Turning to* AGAZZI.) I had promised you to see her here, but Ponza came and begged me, almost on my knees, to see her in her own house. His idea was to put an end to all this talk that's going around. Do you think he would have done such a thing if he weren't absolutely sure?

AGAZZI. Of course, he's sure! Because when she's talking in front of him, the poor woman . . .

SIRELLI (*suddenly getting in his oar*). She says just what he wants her to say, governor; which proves that she is far from being as insane as he claims.

AGAZZI. We had a sample of that, here, yesterday, all of us.

PREFECT. Why, I understand so. You see he's trying all the time to make her believe he's crazy. He warned me of that. And how else could he keep the poor woman in her illusion? Do you see any way? All this talk of yours is simply torture to the poor fellow! Believe me, pure torture!

SIRELLI. Very well, governor! But supposing *she* is the one who is trying to keep *him* in the idea that her daughter is dead; so as to reassure him that his wife will not be taken from him again.

In that case, you see, governor, it's the old lady who is being tortured, and not Ponza!

AGAZZI. The moment you see the possibility of that, governor . . . Well, you ought to hear her talk; but all by herself, when he's not around. Then you'd see the possibility all right . . .

SIRELLI. Just as we all see it!

PREFECT. Oh, I wonder! You don't seem to me so awfully sure; and for my part, I'm quite willing to confess that I'm not so sure myself. How about you, Laudisi?

LAUDISI. Sorry, governor, I promised Agazzi here to keep my mouth shut.

AGAZZI (protesting angrily). Nothing of the kind! How dare you say that? When the governor asks you a plain question . . . It's true I told him not to talk, but do you know why? He's been doing his best for the past two days to keep us all rattled so that we can't find out anything.

LAUDISI. Don't you believe him, governor. On the contrary. I've been doing my best to bring these people to common sense.

SIRELLI. Common sense! And do you know what he calls common sense? According to him it is not possible to discover the truth; and now he's been suggesting that Ponza is living not with a woman, but with a ghost!

PREFECT (enjoying the situation). That's a new one! Quite an idea! How do you make that out, Laudisi?

AGAZZI. Oh, I say! . . . You know how he is. There's no getting anywhere with him!

LAUDISI. I leave it to you, governor. I was the one who first suggested bringing the woman here.

PREFECT. And do you think, Laudisi, I ought to see the old lady next door?

LAUDISI. No, I advise no such thing, governor. In my judgment you are doing very well in depending on what Ponza tells you.

PREFECT. Ah, I see! Because you, too, think that Ponza . . .

LAUDISI. No, not at all . . . because I'm also satisfied to have all these people stand on what Signora Frola says, if that does them any good.

AGAZZI. So you see, eh, governor? That's what you call arguing, eh?

PREFECT. Just a moment! Let me understand! (Turning to LAUDISI.) So you say we can also trust what the old lady says?

LAUDISI. Of course you can! Implicitly! And so you can depend upon what Ponza says. Implicitly!

PREFECT. Excuse me, I don't follow you!

SIRELLI. But man alive, if they both say the exact opposite of each other! . . .

AGAZZI (angrily and with heat). Listen to me, governor, please. I am prejudiced neither in favor of the old lady nor in favor of Ponza. I recognize that he may be right and that she may be right. But we ought to settle the matter, and there is only one way to do it.

SIRELLI. The way that Laudisi here suggested.

PREFECT. He suggested it? That's interesting? What is it?

AGAZZI. Since we haven't been able to get any positive proof, there is only one thing left. You, as Ponza's final superior, as the man who can fire him if need be, can obtain a statement from his wife.

PREFECT. Make his wife talk, you mean?

SIRELLI. But not in the presence of her husband, you understand.

AGAZZI. Yes, making sure she tells the truth!

SIRELLI. . . . tell whether she's the daughter of Signora Frola, that is, as we think she must be . . .

AGAZZI. . . . or a second wife who is consenting to impersonate the daughter of Signora Frola, as Ponza claims.

PREFECT. . . . and as I believe myself, without a shadow of doubt! (*Thinking a moment.*) Why, I don't see any objection to having her talk. Who could object? Ponza? But Ponza, as I know very well, is more eager than anybody else to have this talk quieted down. He's all upset over this whole business, and said he was willing to do anything I proposed. I'm sure he will raise no objection. So if it will ease the minds of you people here . . . Say, Centuri (THE POLICE COMMISSIONER *rises*), won't you just ask Ponza to step in here a moment? He's next door with his mother-in-law.

COMMISSIONER. At once, Your Excellency! (*He bows and withdraws through the door at the rear.*)

AGAZZI. Oh well, if he consents . . .

PREFECT. He'll consent, all right. And we'll be through with it in a jiffy. We'll bring her right in here so that you people . . .

AGAZZI. Here, in my house?

SIRELLI. You think he'll let his wife come in here?

PREFECT. Just leave it to me, just leave it to me! I prefer to have her right here because otherwise, you see, you people would always suppose that I and Ponza had . . .

AGAZZI. Oh, please, governor, no! That's not fair!

SIRELLI. Oh, no, governor, we trust you implicitly!

PREFECT. Oh, I'm not offended, not at all! But you know very well that I'm on his side in this matter; and you'd always be thinking that to hush up any possible scandal in connection with a man in my office. . . . No, you see, I must insist on having the interview here. . . . Where's your wife, Agazzi?

AGAZZI. In the other room, governor, with some other ladies.

PREFECT. Other ladies? Aha, I see! (*Laughing.*) You have a regular detective bureau here, eh? (THE POLICE COMMISSIONER *enters with* PONZA.)

COMMISSIONER. May I come in? Signor Ponza is here.

PREFECT. Thanks, Centuri. This way, Ponza, come right in! (PONZA *bows.*)

AGAZZI. Have a chair, Ponza. (PONZA *bows and sits down.*)

PREFECT. I believe you know these gentlemen? (PONZA *rises and bows.*)

AGAZZI. Yes, I introduced them yesterday. And this is Laudisi, my wife's brother. (PONZA *bows.*)

PREFECT. I venture to disturb you, my dear Ponza, just to tell you that here with these friends of mine . . . (*At the first words of* THE PREFECT, PONZA *evinces the greatest nervousness and agitation.*)

PREFECT. Was there something you wanted to say, Ponza?

PONZA. Yes, there is something I want to say, governor. I want to present my resignation here and now.

PREFECT. Oh, my dear fellow, I'm so sorry! But just a few moments ago down at the office you were talking . . .

PONZA. Oh, really, this is an outrage, governor! This is just plain persecution, plain persecution!

PREFECT. Oh, now, don't take it that way, old man. See here. These good people . . .

AGAZZI. Persecution, did you say? On my part? . . .

PONZA. On the part of all of you! And I am sick and tired of it! I am going to resign, governor. I refuse to submit to this ferocious prying into my private affairs which will end by undoing a work of love that has cost me untold sacrifice these past two years. You don't know, governor! Why, I've treated that dear old lady in there just as tenderly as though she were my own mother. And yesterday I had to shout at her in the most cruel and terrible way! Why, I found her just now so worked up and excited that . . .

AGAZZI. That's queer! While she was

in here Signora Frola was quite mistress of herself. If anybody was worked up, Ponza, it was you. And even now, if I might say . . .

PONZA. But you people don't know what you're making me go through!

PREFECT. Oh, come, come, my dear fellow, don't take it so hard. After all, I'm here, am I not? And you know I've always stood by you! And I always will!

PONZA. Yes, governor, and I appreciate your kindness, really!

PREFECT. And then you say that you're as fond of this poor old lady as you would be if she were your own mother. Well, now, just remember that these good people here seem to be prying into your affairs because they, too, are fond of her! . . .

PONZA. But they're killing her, I tell you, governor! They're killing her, and I warned them in advance.

PREFECT. Very well, Ponza, very well! Now we'll get through with this matter in no time. See here, it is all very simple. There is one way that you can convince these people without the least doubt in the world. Oh, not me—I don't need convincing. I believe *you*.

PONZA. But *they* won't believe me, no matter what I say.

AGAZZI. That's not so! When you came here after your mother-in-law's first visit and told us that she was insane, all of us . . . well, we were surprised, but we believed you. (*Turning to* THE PREFECT.) But after he left, you understand, the old lady came back . . .

PREFECT. Yes, yes, I know. He told me. (*Turning to* PONZA *again*.) She came back here and said that she was trying to do with you exactly what you say you were trying to do with her. It's natural, isn't it, that people hearing both stories, should be somewhat confused. Now you see that these good people, in view of what your mother-in-law says, can't possibly be sure of what you say. So there you are. Now, such being the

case, you and your mother-in-law—why, it's perfectly simple—you two just step aside. Now you know you're telling the truth, don't you? So do I! So you can't possibly object to their hearing the testimony of the only person who does know, aside from you two.

PONZA. And who may that be, pray?

PREFECT. Why, your wife!

PONZA. My wife! (*Decisively and angrily*.) Ah, no! I refuse! Never in the world! Never!

PREFECT. And why not, old man?

PONZA. Bring my wife here to satisfy the curiosity of these strangers?

PREFECT (*sharply*). And my curiosity, too, if you don't mind! What objection can you have?

PONZA. Oh, but governor, no! My wife! Here? No! Why drag my wife in? These people ought to believe me!

PREFECT. But don't you see, my dear fellow, that the course you're taking now is just calculated to discredit what you say?

AGAZZI. His mistake in the first place, governor, was trying to prevent his mother-in-law from coming here and calling—a double discourtesy, mark you, to my wife and to my daughter!

PONZA. But what in the name of God do you people want of me? You've been nagging and nagging at that poor old woman next door; and now you want to get your clutches on my wife! No, governor! I refuse to submit to such an indignity! She owes nothing to anybody. My wife is not making visits in this town. You say you believe me, governor? That's enough for me! Here's my resignation! I'll go out and look for another job!

PREFECT. No, no, Ponza, I must speak plainly. In the first place I have always treated you on the square; and you have no right to speak in that tone of voice to me. In the second place you are beginning to make me doubt your word by refusing to furnish me—not

other people—but me, the evidence that
I have asked for in your interest, evidence, moreover, that so far as I can see,
cannot possibly do you any harm. It
seems to me that my colleague here,
Signor Agazzi, can ask a lady to come to
his house! But no, if you prefer, we'll
go and see her.

PONZA. So you really insist, governor?

PREFECT. I insist, but as I told you,
in your own interest. You realize, besides, that I might have the legal right to
question her . . .

PONZA. I see, I see! So that's it! An
official investigation! Well, why not,
after all? I will bring my wife here, just
to end the whole matter. But how can
you guarantee me that this poor old
lady next door will not catch sight of
her?

PREFECT. Why, I hadn't thought of
that! She does live right next door.

AGAZZI (*speaking up*). We are perfectly willing to go to Signor Ponza's
house.

PONZA. No, no, I was just thinking
of you people. I don't want you to play
any more tricks on me. Any mistakes
might have the most frightful consequences, set her going again!

AGAZZI. You're not very fair to us,
Ponza, it seems to me.

PREFECT. Or you might bring your
wife to my office, rather . . .

PONZA. No, no! Since you're going
to question her anyway, we might as
well get through with it. We'll bring her
here, right here. I'll keep an eye on my
mother-in-law myself. We'll have her
here right away, governor, and get an
end of this nonsense once and for all,
once and for all! (*He hurries away
through the rear exit.*)

PREFECT. I confess I was not expecting so much opposition on his part.

AGAZZI. Ah, you'll see. He'll go and
cook up with his wife just what she's to
say!

PREFECT. Oh, don't worry as to that!
I'll question the woman myself.

SIRELLI. But he's more excited than
he's ever been before.

PREFECT. Well, I confess I never saw
him just in this state of mind. Perhaps it
is the sense of outrage he feels in having
to bring his wife . . .

SIRELLI. In having to let her loose
for once, you ought to say!

PREFECT. A man isn't necessarily
crazy because he wants to keep an eye
on his wife.

AGAZZI. Of course he says it's to
protect her from the mother-in-law.

PREFECT. I wasn't thinking of just
that—he may be jealous of the woman!

SIRELLI. Jealous to the extent of refusing her a servant? For you know,
don't you, he makes his wife do all the
housework?

AGAZZI. And he does all the market-
ing himself every morning.

COMMISSIONER. That's right, governor! I've had him shadowed. An er-
rand boy from the market carries the
stuff as far as the door.

SIRELLI. But he never lets the boy
inside.

PREFECT. Dear me, dear me! He excused himself for that servant business when I took the matter up with
him.

LAUDISI. And that's information
right from the source!

PREFECT. He says he does it to save
money.

LAUDISI. He has to keep two estab-
lishments on one salary.

SIRELLI. Oh, we weren't criticising
how he runs his house; but I ask you as
a matter of common sense: he is a man
of some position, and do you think that
this second wife of his, as he calls her,
who ought to be a lady, would consent
to do all the work about the house? . . .

AGAZZI. The hardest and most disagreeable work, you understand . . .

SIRELLI. . . . just out of consideration for the mother of her husband's first wife?

AGAZZI. Oh, I say, governor, be honest now! That doesn't seem probable, does it?

PREFECT. I confess it does seem queer . . .

LAUDISI. . . . in case this second woman is an ordinary woman!

PREFECT. Yes, but let's be frank. It doesn't seem reasonable. But yet, one might say—well, you could explain it as generosity on her part, and even better, as jealousy on his part. Lunatic or no lunatic, there is no denying that he's jealous!

(*A confused clamor of voices is heard from next door.*)

AGAZZI. My, I wonder what's going on in there!

(AMALIA *enters from the door on the left in a state of great excitement.*)

AMALIA. Signora Frola is here!

AGAZZI. Impossible! How in the world did she get in? Who sent for her?

AMALIA. Nobody! She came of her own accord!

PREFECT. Oh, no, please—just a moment! No! Send her away, madam, please!

AGAZZI. We've got to get rid of her. Don't let her in here! We must absolutely keep her out!

(SIGNORA FROLA *appears at the door on the left, trembling, beseeching, weeping, a handkerchief in her hand. The people in the next room are crowding around behind her.*)

SIGNORA FROLA. Oh, please, please! You tell them, Signor Agazzi! Don't let them send me away!

AGAZZI. But you must go away, madam! We simply can't allow you to be here now!

SIGNORA FROLA (*desperately*). Why? Why? (*Turning to* AMALIA.) I appeal to you, Signora Agazzi.

AMALIA. But don't you see? The prefect is there! They're having an important meeting.

SIGNORA FROLA. Oh, the prefect! Please, governor, please! I was intending to go and see you.

PREFECT. No, I am so sorry, madam. I can't see you just now! You must go away!

SIGNORA FROLA. Yes, I am going away. I am going to leave town this very day! I am going to leave town and never come back again!

AGAZZI. Oh, we didn't mean that, my dear Signora Frola. We meant that we couldn't see you here, just now, in this room. Do me a favor, please! You can see the governor by and by.

SIGNORA FROLA. But why? I don't understand! What's happened?

AGAZZI. Why, your son-in-law will soon be here! There, now do you see?

SIGNORA FROLA. Oh, he's coming here? Oh, yes, in that case . . . Yes, yes, . . . I'll go! But there was something I wanted to say to you people. You must stop all this. You must let us alone. You think you are helping me. You are trying to do me a favor; but really, what you're doing is working me a great wrong. I've got to leave town this very day because he must not be aroused. What do you want of him anyway? What are you trying to do to him? Why are you having him come here? Oh, Mr. Governor . . .

PREFECT. Come, Signora Frola, don't worry, don't worry. I'll see you by and by and explain everything. You just step out now, won't you?

AMALIA. Please, Signora Frola . . . yes, that's right! Come with me!

SIGNORA FROLA. Oh, my dear Signora Agazzi, you are trying to rob me of the one comfort I had in life, the chance of seeing my daughter once in a while, at least from a distance! (*She begins to weep.*)

PREFECT. What in the world are you

thinking of? We are not asking you to leave town. We just want you to leave this room, for the time being. There, now do you understand?

SIGNORA FROLA. But it's on his account, governor . . . it's on his account I was coming to ask you to help him! It was on his account, not on mine!

PREFECT. There, there, everything will be all right. We'll take care of him. And we'll have this whole business settled in a jiffy.

SIGNORA FROLA. But how . . . how can I be sure? I can see that everybody here hates him. They are trying to do something to him.

PREFECT. No, no, not at all! And even if they were, I would look after him. There, there, don't worry, don't worry!

SIGNORA FROLA. Oh, so you believe him? Oh, thank you; thank you, sir! That means that at least *you* understand!

PREFECT. Yes, yes, madam, I understand, I understand! And I cautioned all these people here. It's a misfortune that came to him long, long ago. He's all right now! He's all right now!

SIGNORA FROLA. . . . Only he must not go back to all those things.

PREFECT. You're right, you're quite right, Signora Frola, but as I told you, I understand!

SIGNORA FROLA. Yes, governor, that's it! If he compels us to live this way— well, what does it matter? That doesn't do anybody any harm so long as we're satisfied, and my daughter is happy this way. That's enough for me, and for her! But you'll look after us, governor. They mustn't spoil anything. Otherwise there's nothing left for me except to leave town and never see her again—never, not even from a distance. You must not irritate him. You must leave him alone. Oh, please!

(*At this moment a wave of surprise, anxiety, dismay, sweeps over the company. Everybody falls silent and turns to*

the door. Suppressed exclamations are audible.*)

VOICES. Oh! Oh! Look! There she is! Oh! Oh!

SIGNORA FROLA (*noticing the change in people, and groaning, all of a tremble.*) What's the matter? What's the matter?

(*The company divides to either hand. A lady has appeared at the door in back. She is dressed in deep mourning and her face is concealed with a thick, black, impenetrable veil.*)

SIGNORA FROLA (*uttering a piercing shriek of joy*). Oh, Lena! Lena! Lena! Lena!

(*She dashes forward and throws her arms about the veiled woman with the passionate hysteria of a mother who has not embraced her daughter for years and years. But at the same time from beyond the door in the rear another piercing cry comes.* PONZA *dashes into the room.*)

PONZA. No! Julia! Julia! Julia!

(*At his voice* SIGNORA PONZA *draws up stiffly in the arms of* SIGNORA FROLA *who is clasping her tightly.* PONZA *notices that his mother-in-law is thus desperately entwined about his wife and he shrieks desperately.*)

PONZA. Cowards! Liars! I knew you would! I knew you would! It is just like the lot of you!

SIGNORA PONZA (*turning her veiled head with a certain austere solemnity toward her husband*). Never mind! Don't be afraid! Just take her away, just take her away! Please go away, now, both of you! Please go away!

(SIGNORA FROLA, *at these words, turns to her son-in-law and humbly, tremblingly, goes over and embraces him.*)

SIGNORA FROLA. Yes, yes, you poor boy, come with me, come with me!

(*Their arms about each other's waists, and holding each other up affectionately,* PONZA *and his mother-in-law withdraw through the rear door. They are both weeping. Profound silence in the company. All those present stand there with their eyes fixed upon the departing couple. As* SIGNORA FROLA *and* PONZA *are lost from view, all eyes turn expectantly upon the veiled lady. Some of the women are weeping.*)

SIGNORA PONZA. And what can you want of me now, after all this, ladies and gentlemen? In our lives, as you see, there is something which must remain concealed. Otherwise the remedy which our love for each other has found cannot avail.

PREFECT (*with tears in his eyes*). We surely are anxious to respect your sorrow, madam, but we must know, and we want you to tell . . .

SIGNORA PONZA. What? The truth? The truth is simply this. I am the daughter of Signora Frola, and I am the second wife of Signor Ponza. Yes, and—for myself, I am nobody, I am nobody . . .

PREFECT. Ah, but no, madam, for yourself . . . you must be . . . either the one or the other.

SIGNORA PONZA. Not at all, not at all, sir! No, for myself I am . . . whoever you choose to have me. (*Without removing her veil, she proudly casts a sweeping glance around at the company, and withdraws. They all stand looking after her. Profound silence on the stage.*)

LAUDISI. Well, and there, my friends, you have the truth! But are you satisfied? Hah! hah! hah! hah! hah! hah! hah!

JOHN MILLINGTON SYNGE / 1871–1909

John Millington Synge, an Irish æsthete and artist, left his native county Dublin for the continent after studying at Trinity College. Music (violin, piano, and flute), language, and literature were his chief interests. William Butler Yeats found Synge in Paris in 1898 and converted him to the possibilities of creative national art through the theater, making drama of the minds, hearts, and language of the common folk of Ireland. The Irish Literary Theatre opened in 1899; it became the Abbey Theatre in 1904. As playwright and manager, Yeats supported and steered the Abbey Theatre through many national and religious storms; few theaters have attempted to inspire its society more artistically or courageously. It became an active center of, and stimulus to, Irish thought, Irish arts, and Irish creativity, and the scene of many displays of Irish factional partisanship and prejudice. Yeats, Synge, Lady Gregory, Sean O'Casey, and Paul Vincent Carroll continued in turn to give individual vitality to plays which, while chiefly derived from Irish life, gave invigorating dramatic experiences to audiences through the world.

Synge, like Yeats, was more poet than dramatist, sensitive to the rhythms and phrases of folk speech, and attuned to the lyrical and inexpressible. None of his Irish plays is nationalistic, and he scorned didacticism. He lived among the fisherfolk of the Aran Islands, and later among the peasants of the mainland; mastered dramatic construction and even stagecraft sufficiently to become one of the original directors of the Abbey Theatre; and in the five years before his death produced six plays. Of these the three-act comedy *The Playboy of the Western World,* although full of whimsical drollery and burlesque, is the most substantial, *Deirdre of the Sorrows* the best folk play.

Riders to the Sea is set apart for its perfect realization of a tragic mood in a lyrical manner. The antagonistic sea is always present; its inevitable destruction of those who live by it is known. Whether *Riders to the Sea* is static, a tone poem, mood poem, chant, incantation, or tragic idyll, or whether the antagonistic sea in claiming the last of Maurya's sons is a force with which Maurya rises to a reconciliation is really not the important matter. In *Riders to the Sea* one of the cherished beliefs of Yeats and Synge, that the speech of common Irish folk far from the towns should be heard in the theater, is poetically realized in a play in which the life and the language of the Aran Islanders are one.

Riders to the Sea

CHARACTERS	SCENE: *An island off the west of Ireland.*

MAURYA, *an old woman.*
BARTLEY, *her son.*
CATHLEEN, *her daughter.*
NORA, *a younger daughter.*
MEN *and* WOMEN.

SCENE: *An island off the west of Ireland. Cottage kitchen, with nets, oil-skins, spinning-wheel, some new boards standing by the wall, etc.* CATHLEEN, *a girl of about twenty, finishes kneading cake, and puts it down in the pot-oven by the fire; then wipes her hands, and begins to spin at the wheel.* NORA, *a young girl, puts her head in at the door.*

NORA (*in a low voice*). Where is she?

CATHLEEN. She's lying down, God help her, and may be sleeping, if she's able.

(NORA *comes in softly, and takes a bundle from under her shawl.*)

CATHLEEN (*spinning the wheel rapidly*). What is it you have?

NORA. The young priest is after bringing them. It's a shirt and a plain stocking were got off a drowned man in Donegal.

(CATHLEEN *stops her wheel with a sudden movement, and leans out to listen.*)

NORA. We're to find out if it's Michael's they are, some time herself will be down looking by the sea.

CATHLEEN. How would they be Michael's, Nora? How would he go the length of that way to the far north?

NORA. The young priest says he's known the like of it. "If it's Michael's they are," says he, "you can tell herself he's got a clean burial by the grace of God, and if they're not his, let no one say a word about them, for she'll be getting her death," says he, "with crying and lamenting."

(*The door which* NORA *half closed is blown open by a gust of wind.*)

CATHLEEN (*looking out anxiously*). Did you ask him would he stop Bartley going this day with the horses to the Galway fair?

NORA. "I won't stop him," says he, "but let you not be afraid. Herself does be saying prayers half through the night, and the Almighty God won't leave her destitute," says he, "with no son living."

CATHLEEN. Is the sea bad by the white rocks, Nora?

NORA. Middling bad, God help us. There's a great roaring in the west, and it's worse it'll be getting when the tide's

turned to the wind. (*She goes over to the table with the bundle.*) Shall I open it now?

CATHLEEN. Maybe she'd wake up on us, and come in before we'd done. (*Coming to the table.*) It's a long time we'll be, and the two of us crying.

NORA (*goes to the inner door and listens*). She's moving about on the bed. She'll be coming in a minute.

CATHLEEN. Give me the ladder, and I'll put them up in the turf-loft, the way she won't know of them at all, and maybe when the tide turns she'll be going down to see would he be floating from the east.

(*They put the ladder against the gable of the chimney;* CATHLEEN *goes up a few steps and hides the bundle in the turf-loft.* MAURYA *comes from the inner room.*)

MAURYA (*looking up at* CATHLEEN *and speaking querulously*). Isn't it turf enough you have for this day and evening?

CATHLEEN. There's a cake baking at the fire for a short space (*throwing down the turf*) and Bartley will want it when the tide turns if he goes to Connemara.

(NORA *picks up the turf and puts it round the pot-oven.*)

MAURYA (*sitting down on a stool at the fire*). He won't go this day with the wind rising from the south and west. He won't go this day, for the young priest will stop him surely.

NORA. He'll not stop him, mother, and I heard Eamon Simon and Stephen Pheety and Colum Shawn saying he would go.

MAURYA. Where is he itself?

NORA. He went down to see would there be another boat sailing in the week, and I'm thinking it won't be long till he's here now, for the tide's turning at the green head, and the hooker's tacking from the east.

CATHLEEN. I hear some one passing the big stones.

NORA (*looking out*). He's coming now, and he in a hurry.

BARTLEY (*comes in and looks round the room; speaking sadly and quietly*). Where is the bit of new rope, Cathleen, which was bought in Connemara?

CATHLEEN (*coming down*). Give it to him, Nora; it's on a nail by the white boards. I hung it up this morning, for the pig with the black feet was eating it.

NORA (*giving him a rope*). Is that it, Bartley?

MAURYA. You'd do right to leave that rope, Bartley, hanging by the boards. (BARTLEY *takes the rope*.) It will be wanting in this place, I'm telling you, if Michael is washed up to-morrow morning or the next morning, or any morning in the week, for it's a deep grave we'll make him by the grace of God.

BARTLEY (*beginning to work with the rope*). I've no halter the way I can ride down on the mare, and I must go now quickly. This is the one boat going for two weeks or beyond it, and the fair will be a good fair for horses I heard them saying below.

MAURYA. It's a hard thing they'll be saying below if the body is washed up and there's no man in it to make the coffin, and I after giving a big price for the finest white boards you'd find in Connemara.

(*She looks round at the boards.*)

BARTLEY. How would it be washed up, and we after looking each day for nine days, and a strong wind blowing a while back from the west and south?

MAURYA. If it wasn't found itself, that wind is raising the sea, and there was a star up against the moon, and it rising in the night. If it was a hundred horses, or a thousand horses you had itself, what is the price of a thousand horses against a son where there is one son only?

BARTLEY (*working at the halter, to* CATHLEEN). Let you go down each day, and see the sheep aren't jumping in on the rye, and if the jobber comes you can sell the pig with the black feet if there is a good price going.

MAURYA. How would the like of her get a good price for a pig?

BARTLEY (*to* CATHLEEN). If the west wind holds with the last bit of the moon let you and Nora get up weed enough for another cock for the kelp. It's hard set we'll be from this day with no one in it but one man to work.

MAURYA. It's hard set we'll be surely the day you're drownd'd with the rest. What way will I live and the girls with me, and I an old woman looking for the grave?

(BARTLEY *lays down the halter, takes off his old coat, and puts on a newer one of the same flannel.*)

BARTLEY (*to* NORA). Is she coming to the pier?

NORA (*looking out*). She's passing the green head and letting fall her sails.

BARTLEY (*getting his purse and tobacco*). I'll have half an hour to go down, and you'll see me coming again in two days, or in three days, or maybe in four days if the wind is bad.

MAURYA (*turning round to the fire, and putting her shawl over her head*). Isn't it a hard and cruel man won't hear a word from an old woman, and she holding him from the sea?

CATHLEEN. It's the life of a young man to be going on the sea, and who would listen to an old woman with one thing and she saying it over?

BARTLEY (*taking the halter*). I must go now quickly. I'll ride down on the red mare, and the gray pony'll run behind me. . . . The blessing of God on you. (*He goes out.*)

MAURYA (*crying out as he is in the door*). He's gone now, God spare us, and we'll not see him again. He's gone now, and when the black night is falling I'll have no son left me in the world.

CATHLEEN. Why wouldn't you give him your blessing and he looking round in the door? Isn't it sorrow enough is on every one in this house without your sending him out with an unlucky word behind him, and a hard word in his ear?

(MAURYA *takes up the tongs and begins raking the fire aimlessly without looking round.*)

NORA (*turning toward her*). You're taking away the turf from the cake.

CATHLEEN (*crying out*). The Son of God forgive us, Nora, we're after forgetting his bit of bread.

(*She comes over to the fire.*)

NORA. And it's destroyed he'll be going till dark night, and he after eating nothing since the sun went up.

CATHLEEN (*turning the cake out of the oven*). It's destroyed he'll be, surely. There's no sense left on any person in a house where an old woman will be talking forever.

(MAURYA *sways herself on her stool.*)

CATHLEEN (*cutting off some of the bread and rolling it in a cloth; to* MAURYA). Let you go down now to the spring well and give him this and he passing. You'll see him then and the dark word will be broken, and you can say "God speed you," the way he'll be easy in his mind.

MAURYA (*taking the bread*). Will I be in it as soon as himself?

CATHLEEN. If you go now quickly.

MAURYA (*standing up unsteadily*). It's hard set I am to walk.

CATHLEEN (*looking at her anxiously*). Give her the stick, Nora, or maybe she'll slip on the big stones.

NORA. What stick?

CATHLEEN. The stick Michael brought from Connemara.

MAURYA (*taking a stick* NORA *gives her*). In the big world the old people do be leaving things after them for their sons and children, but in this place it is the young men do be leaving things behind for them that do be old.

(*She goes out slowly.* NORA *goes over to the ladder.*)

CATHLEEN. Wait, Nora, maybe she'd turn back quickly. She's that sorry, God help her, you wouldn't know the thing she'd do.

NORA. Is she gone round by the bush?

CATHLEEN (*looking out*). She's gone now. Throw it down quickly, for the Lord knows when she'll be out of it again.

NORA (*getting the bundle from the loft*). The young priest said he'd be passing to-morrow, and we might go down and speak to him below if it's Michael's they are surely.

CATHLEEN (*taking the bundle*). Did he say what way they were found?

NORA (*coming down*). "There were two men," says he, "and they rowing round with poteen before the cocks crowed, and the oar of one of them caught the body, and they passing the black cliffs of the north."

CATHLEEN (*trying to open the bundle*). Give me a knife, Nora, the string's perished with the salt water, and there's a black knot on it you wouldn't loosen in a week.

NORA (*giving her a knife*). I've heard tell it was a long way to Donegal.

CATHLEEN (*cutting the string*). It is surely. There was a man in here a while ago—the man sold us that knife—and he said if you set off walking from the rocks beyond, it would be seven days you'd be in Donegal.

NORA. And what time would a man take, and he floating?

(CATHLEEN *opens the bundle and takes out a bit of a stocking. They look at them eagerly.*)

CATHLEEN (*in a low voice*). The Lord spare us, Nora! isn't it a queer hard thing to say if it's his they are surely?

NORA. I'll get his shirt off the hook

the way we can put the one flannel on the other. (*She looks through some clothes hanging in the corner.*) It's not with them, Cathleen, and where will it be?

CATHLEEN. I'm thinking Bartley put it on him in the morning, for his own shirt was heavy with the salt in it. (*Pointing to the corner.*) There's a bit of a sleeve was of the same stuff. Give me that and it will do.

(NORA *brings it to her and they compare the flannel.*)

CATHLEEN. It's the same stuff, Nora; but if it is itself aren't there great rolls of it in the shops of Galway, and isn't it many another man may have a shirt of it as well as Michael himself?

NORA (*who has taken up the stocking and counted the stitches, crying out*). It's Michael, Cathleen, it's Michael; God spare his soul, and what will herself say when she hears this story, and Bartley on the sea?

CATHLEEN (*taking the stocking*). It's a plain stocking.

NORA. It's the second one of the third pair I knitted, and I put up three-score stitches, and I dropped four of them.

CATHLEEN (*counts the stitches*). It's that number is in it. (*Crying out.*) Ah, Nora, isn't it a bitter thing to think of him floating that way to the far north, and no one to keen him but the black hags that do be flying on the sea?

NORA (*swinging herself round, and throwing out her arms on the clothes*). And isn't it a pitiful thing when there is nothing left of a man who was a great rower and fisher, but a bit of an old shirt and a plain stocking?

CATHLEEN (*after an instant*). Tell me is herself coming, Nora? I hear a little sound on the path.

NORA (*looking out*). She is, Cathleen. She's coming up to the door.

CATHLEEN. Put these things away before she'll come in. Maybe it's easier she'll be after giving her blessing to

Bartley, and we won't let on we've heard anything the time he's on the sea.

NORA (*helping* CATHLEEN *to close the bundle*). We'll put them here in the corner.

(*They put them into a hole in the chimney corner.* CATHLEEN *goes back to the spinning-wheel.*)

NORA. Will she see it was crying I was?

CATHLEEN. Keep your back to the door the way the light'll not be on you.

(NORA *sits down at the chimney corner, with her back to the door.* MAURYA *comes in very slowly, without looking at the girls, and goes over to her stool at the other side of the fire. The cloth with the bread is still in her hand. The girls look at each other, and* NORA *points to the bundle of bread.*)

CATHLEEN (*after spinning for a moment*). You didn't give him his bit of bread?

(MAURYA *begins to keen softly, without turning round.*)

CATHLEEN. Did you see him riding down? (MAURYA *goes on keening.*)

CATHLEEN (*a little impatiently*). God forgive you; isn't it a better thing to raise your voice and tell what you seen, then to be making lamentation for a thing that's done? Did you see Bartley, I'm saying to you.

MAURYA (*with a weak voice*). My heart's broken from this day.

CATHLEEN (*as before*). Did you see Bartley?

MAURYA. I seen the fearfulest thing.

CATHLEEN (*leaves her wheel and looks out*). God forgive you; he's riding the mare now over the green head, and the gray pony behind him.

MAURYA (*starts, so that her shawl falls back from her head and shows her white tossed hair; with a frightened voice*). The gray pony behind him.

CATHLEEN (*coming to the fire*). What is it ails you, at all?

MAURYA (*speaking very slowly*). I've seen the fearfulest thing any person has seen, since the day Bride Dara seen the dead man with a child in his arms.

CATHLEEN AND NORA. Uah.

(*They crouch down in front of the old woman at the fire.*)

NORA. Tell us what it is you seen.

MAURYA. I went down to the spring well, and I stood there saying a prayer to myself. Then Bartley came along, and he riding on the red mare with the gray pony behind him. (*She puts up her hands, as if to hide something from her eyes.*) The Son of God spare us, Nora!

CATHLEEN. What is it you seen?

MAURYA. I seen Michael himself.

CATHLEEN (*speaking softly*). You did not, mother; it wasn't Michael you seen, for his body is after being found in the Far North, and he's got a clean burial by the grace of God.

MAURYA (*a little defiantly*). I'm after seeing him this day, and he riding and galloping. Bartley came first on the red mare; and I tried to say, "God speed you," but something choked the words in my throat. He went by quickly; and "the blessing of God on you," says he, and I could say nothing. I looked up then, and I crying, at the gray pony, and there was Michael upon it—with fine clothes on him, and new shoes on his feet.

CATHLEEN (*begins to keen*). It's destroyed we are from this day. It's destroyed, surely.

NORA. Didn't the young priest say the Almighty God wouldn't leave her destitute with no son living?

MAURYA (*in a low voice, but clearly*). It's little the like of him knows of the sea. . . . Bartley will be lost now, and let you call in Eamon and make me a good coffin out of the white boards, for I won't live after them. I've had a husband, and a husband's father, and six sons in this house—six fine men, though it was a hard birth I had with every one of them and they coming to the world—and some of them were found and some

of them were not found, but they're gone now the lot of them. . . . There were Stephen, and Shawn, were lost in the great wind, and found after in the Bay of Gregory of the Golden Mouth, and carried up the two of them on the one plank, and in by that door.

(*She pauses for a moment; the girls start as if they heard something through the door that is half open behind them.*)

NORA (*in a whisper*). Did you hear that, Cathleen? Did you hear a noise in the northeast?

CATHLEEN (*in a whisper*). There's some one after crying out by the seashore.

MAURYA (*continues without hearing anything*). There was Sheamus and his father, and his own father again, were lost in a dark night, and not a stick or sign was seen of them when the sun went up. There was Patch after was drowned out of a curagh that turned over. I was sitting here with Bartley, and he a baby, lying on my two knees, and I seen two women, and three women, and four women coming in, and they crossing themselves, and not saying a word. I looked out then, and there were men coming after them, and they holding a thing in the half of a red sail, and water dripping out of it—it was a dry day, Nora—and leaving a track to the door.

(*She pauses again with her hand stretched out toward the door. It opens softly and old women begin to come in, crossing themselves on the threshold, and kneeling down in front of the stage with red petticoats over their heads.*)

MAURYA (*half in a dream, to CATHLEEN*). Is it Patch, or Michael, or what is it at all?

CATHLEEN. Michael is after being found in the Far North, and when he is found there how could he be here in this place?

MAURYA. There does be a power of young men floating round in the sea, and what way would they know if it was Michael they had, or another man like him, for when a man is nine days in the sea, and the wind blowing, it's hard set his own mother would be to say what man was it.

CATHLEEN. It's Michael, God spare him, for they're after sending us a bit of his clothes from the Far North.

(*She reaches out and hands* MAURYA *the clothes that belonged to* MICHAEL. MAURYA *stands up slowly, and takes them in her hands.* NORA *looks out.*)

NORA. They're carrying a thing among them and there's a water dripping out of it and leaving a track by the big stones.

CATHLEEN (*in a whisper to the women who have come in*). Is it Bartley it is?

ONE OF THE WOMEN. It is surely, God rest his soul.

(*Two younger women come in and pull out the table. Then men carry in the body of* BARTLEY, *laid on a plank, with a bit of a sail over it, and lay it on the table.*)

CATHLEEN (*to the women, as they are doing so*). What way was he drowned?

ONE OF THE WOMEN. The gray pony knocked him into the sea, and he was washed out where there is a great surf on the white rocks.

(*MAURYA has gone over and knelt down at the head of the table. The women are keening softly and swaying themselves with a slow movement.* CATHLEEN *and* NORA *kneel at the other end of the table. The men kneel near the door.*)

MAURYA (*raising her head and speaking as if she did not see the people around her*). They're all gone now, and there isn't anything more the sea can do to me. . . . I'll have no call now to be up crying and praying when the wind breaks from the south, and you can hear the surf is in the east, and the surf is in the west, making a great stir with the two noises, and they hitting one on the other. I'll have no call now to be going down and getting Holy Water in the dark nights after Samhain, and I won't care what way the sea is when the other women will be keening. (*To* NORA.) Give me the Holy Water, Nora; there's a small sup still on the dresser.

(NORA *gives it to her.*)

MAURYA (*drops* MICHAEL'S *clothes across* BARTLEY'S *feet, and sprinkles the Holy Water over him*). It isn't that I haven't prayed for you, Bartley, to the Almighty God. It isn't that I haven't said prayers in the dark night till you wouldn't know what I'd be saying; but it's a great rest I'll have now, and it's time surely. It's a great rest I'll have now, and great sleeping in the long nights after Samhain, if it's only a bit of wet flour we do have to eat, and maybe a fish that would be stinking.

(*She kneels down again, crossing herself, and saying prayers under her breath.*)

CATHLEEN (*to an* OLD MAN). Maybe yourself and Eamon would make a coffin when the sun rises. We have fine white boards herself bought, God help her, thinking Michael would be found, and I have a new cake you can eat while you'll be working.

THE OLD MAN (*looking at the boards*). Are there nails with them?

CATHLEEN. There are not, Colum; we didn't think of the nails.

ANOTHER MAN. It's a great wonder she wouldn't think of the nails, and all the coffins she's seen made already.

CATHLEEN. It's getting old she is, and broken.

(MAURYA *stands up again very slowly and spreads out the pieces of* MICHAEL'S *clothes beside the body, sprinkling them with the last of the Holy Water.*)

NORA (*in a whisper to* CATHLEEN). She's quiet now and easy; but the day Michael was drowned you could hear her crying out from this to the spring well. It's fonder she was of Michael, and would any one have thought that?

CATHLEEN (*slowly and clearly*). An old woman will be soon tired with anything she will do, and isn't it nine days herself is after crying and keening, and making great sorrow in the house?

MAURYA (*puts the empty cup, mouth downwards, on the table, and lays her hands together on* BARTLEY'S *feet*). They're all together this time, and the end is come. May the Almighty God have mercy on Bartley's soul, and on Michael's soul, and on the souls of Sheamus and Patch, and Stephen and Shawn; (*bending her head*) and may He have mercy on my soul, Nora, and on the soul of every one is left living in the world.

(*She pauses, and the keen rises a little more loudly from the women, then sinks away.*)

MAURYA (*continuing*). Michael has a clean burial in the Far North, by the grace of the Almighty God. Bartley will have a fine coffin out of the white boards, and a deep grave surely. What more can we want than that? No man at all can be living forever, and we must be satisfied.

(*She kneels down again and the curtain falls slowly.*)

EUGENE O'NEILL / 1888–1953

Eugene Gladstone O'Neill was the son of an actor, James O'Neill, who took Eugene with him on some of his tours with *The Count of Monte Cristo*. But Eugene's education was conventional in other ways—preparatory school in New England, Princeton in 1906—before he took off on wanderings to Honduras, South America, and England, sometimes as a sailor. He turned to playwriting after some instruction in Professor George Pierce Baker's "Workshop 47" at Harvard, and in his ascent was a sustaining playwright in a series of experimental theater groups: The Provincetown Players, The Greenwich Village Theatre, and finally the Theatre Guild. The Nobel Prize in 1936 recognized his contribution through the American stage to international drama.

Ibsen, Shaw, and O'Neill are sometimes bracketed as the three greatest modern dramatists, but there is a difference. Some ten plays by Ibsen or by Shaw are recognizably their own; each artist has achieved a kind of play which says for him what he wants to say. O'Neill, on the other hand, is a restless, sometimes reckless, experimenter, who is always searching for a better dramatic way to present his meaning. There is no O'Neill type of play, but rather a series of powerful, direct, not-to-be-repeated creations. Generally speaking, his experiments were those stirring the world theater of his time: realism tearing off the traditional romantic veil over staged life, naturalism doing it more extremely, expressionism and symbolism revealing the psychological forces under surface behavior. Among his technical experiments were the use of masks in *The Great God Brown,* of double-dialogue or asides in *Strange Interlude,* and of tom-toms in *The Emperor Jones.*

Nor is there a single O'Neill message, platform, or body of conviction; he explores the things which people are up against, poverty, ignorance, bad environments, mental and spiritual limitations in themselves, the ghosts of dead traditions. He says some savage things about "what man has made of man," but seldom loses compassion for the human pain of experience, whatever the causes, and at intervals he reveals a comic or tender strain.

His first plays were of the sea and sailors: *Moon of the Caribbees, In the Zone,* and *The Long Voyage Home* (all collected as *S.S. Glencairn,* 1924). *Anna Christie* (1921) and *The Hairy Ape* (1922) also stay close to the waterfront. But *Mourning Becomes Electra, Desire Under the Elms, Ah! Wilderness,* and *A Touch of the Poet* treat of New England under widely differing guises. His autobiographical *Long Day's Journey Into Night* won a Pulitzer award.

Desire Under the Elms, called by John Gassner a "peasant tragedy," interweaves human and environmental limitations which rise from a niggardly soil and combine to destroy its human products at the point of their greatest effort to reach a spiritual level above their limitations. Greek in starkness and severity, carefully constructed for tragic causality, bare and powerful, *Desire Under the Elms* has provoked critical labels ranging from "melodrama" to "true tragedy."

Desire Under the Elms

A PLAY IN THREE PARTS

CHARACTERS

EPHRAIM CABOT.

SIMEON ⎫
PETER ⎬ *his sons.*
EBEN ⎭

ABBIE PUTNAM.

YOUNG GIRL, TWO FARMERS, THE FID-
DLER, A SHERIFF, *and other folk from
the neighboring farms.*

SCENE: *The action of the entire play takes
place in, and immediately outside of, the
Cabot farmhouse in New England, in
the year 1850. The south end of the
house faces front to a stone wall with
a wooden gate at center opening on a
country road. The house is in good condition but in need of paint. Its walls are
a sickly grayish, the green of the shutters
faded. Two enormous elms are on each
side of the house. They bend their trailing branches down over the roof. They
appear to protect and at the same time
subdue. There is a sinister maternity in
their aspect, a crushing, jealous absorption. They have developed from their intimate contact with the life of man in
the house an appalling humanness.
They brood oppressively over the house.
They are like exhausted women resting
their sagging breasts and hands and hair
on its roof, and when it rains their tears
trickle down monotonously and rot on
the shingles.*

*There is a path running from the gate
around the right corner of the house to
the front door. A narrow porch is on
this side. The end wall facing us has
two windows in its upper story, two
larger ones on the floor below. The two
upper are those of the father's bedroom
and that of the brothers. On the left,
ground floor, is the kitchen—on the
right, the parlor, the shades of which are
always drawn down.*

Part I

SCENE 1

(*Exterior of the farmhouse. It is sunset of a day at the beginning of summer
in the year 1850. There is no wind and
everything is still. The sky above the
roof is suffused with deep colors, the
green of the elms glows, but the house
is in shadow, seeming pale and washed
out by contrast.*

A door opens and EBEN CABOT *comes
to the end of the porch and stands looking down the road to the right. He has a
large bell in his hand and this he swings
mechanically, awakening a deafening
clangor. Then he puts his hands on his
hips and stares up at the sky. He sighs
with a puzzled awe and blurts out with
halting appreciation.*)

EBEN. God! Purty! (*His eyes fall
and he stares about him frowningly. He
is twenty-five, tall and sinewy. His face
is well-formed, good-looking, but its expression is resentful and defensive. His
defiant, dark eyes remind one of a wild
animal's in captivity. Each day is a cage
in which he finds himself trapped but
inwardly unsubdued. There is a fierce
repressed vitality about him. He has
black hair, mustache, a thin curly trace
of beard. He is dressed in rough farm
clothes.*)

(*He spits on the ground with intense disgust, turns and goes back into the house.*)

(SIMEON *and* PETER *come in from their work in the fields. They are tall men, much older than their half-brother* —SIMEON *is thirty-nine and* PETER *thirty-seven—, built on a squarer, simpler model, fleshier in body, more bovine and homelier in face, shrewder and more practical. Their shoulders stoop a bit from years of farm work. They clump heavily along in their clumsy thick-soled boots caked with earth. Their clothes, their faces, hands, bare arms and throats are earth-stained. They smell of earth. They stand together for a moment in front of the house and, as if with the one impulse, stare dumbly up at the sky, leaning on their hoes. Their faces have a compressed, unresigned expression. As they look upward, this softens.*)

SIMEON (*grudgingly*).   Purty.

PETER.   Ay-eh.

SIMEON (*suddenly*).   Eighteen year ago.

PETER.   What?

SIMEON.   Jenn. My woman. She died.

PETER.   I'd fergot.

SIMEON.   I rec'lect—now an' agin. Makes it lonesome. She'd hair long's a hoss' tail—an' yaller like gold!

PETER.   Waal—she's gone. (*This with indifferent finality—then after a pause.*) They's gold in the West, Sim.

SIMEON (*still under the influence of sunset—vaguely*).   In the sky?

PETER.   Waal—in a manner o' speakin'—thar's the promise. (*Growing excited.*) Gold in the sky—in the West —Golden Gate—Californi-a!—Goldest West!—fields o' gold!

SIMEON (*excited in his turn*).   Fortunes layin' just atop o' the ground waitin' t' be picked! Solomon's mines, they says! (*For a moment they continue looking up at the sky—then their eyes drop.*)

PETER (*with sardonic bitterness*). Here—it's stones atop o' the ground— stones atop o' stones—makin' stone walls —year atop o' year—him 'n' yew 'n' me 'n' then Eben—makin' stone walls fur him to fence us in!

SIMEON.   We've wuked. Give our strength. Give our years. Plowed 'em under in the ground—(*He stamps rebelliously.*)—rottin'—makin' soil for his crops! (*A pause.*) Waal—the farm pays good for hereabouts.

PETER.   If we plowed in Californi-a, they'd be lumps o' gold in the furrow!

SIMEON.   Californi-a's t'other side o' earth, a'most. We got t' calc'late—

PETER (*after a pause*).   'Twould be hard fur me, too, to give up what we've 'arned here by our sweat. (*A pause.* EBEN *sticks his head out of the dining-room window, listening.*)

SIMEON.   Ay-eh. (*A pause.*) Mebbe— he'll die soon.

PETER (*doubtfully*).   Mebbe.

SIMEON.   Mebbe—fur all we knows —he's dead now.

PETER.   Ye'd need proof.

SIMEON.   He's been gone two months —with no word.

PETER.   Left us in the fields an evenin' like this. Hitched up an' druv off into the West. That's plumb onnateral. He hain't never been off this farm 'ceptin' t' the village in thirty year or more, not since he married Eben's maw. (*A pause. Shrewdly.*) I calc'late we might git him declared crazy by the court.

SIMEON.   He skinned 'em too slick. He got the best o' all on 'em. They'd never b'lieve him crazy. (*A pause.*) We got t' wait—till he's under ground.

EBEN (*with a sardonic chuckle*). Honor thy father! (*They turn, startled, and stare at him. He grins, then scowls.*) I pray he's died. (*They stare at him. He continues matter-of-factly.*) Supper's ready.

SIMEON *and* PETER (*together*). Ay-eh.

EBEN (*gazing up at the sky*). Sun's downin' purty.

SIMEON *and* PETER (*together*). Ay-eh. They's gold in the West.

EBEN. Ay-eh. (*Pointing.*) Yonder atop o' the hill pasture, ye mean?

SIMEON *and* PETER (*together*). In Californi-a!

EBEN. Hunh? (*Stares at them indifferently for a second, then drawls.*) Waal—supper's gittin' cold. (*He turns back into kitchen.*)

SIMEON (*startled—smacks his lips*). I air hungry!

PETER (*sniffing*). I smells bacon!

SIMEON (*with hungry appreciation*). Bacon's good!

PETER (*in same tone*). Bacon's bacon! (*They turn, shouldering each other, their bodies bumping and rubbing together as they hurry clumsily to their food, like two friendly oxen toward their evening meal. They disappear around the right corner of house and can be heard entering the door.*)

(*The curtain falls.*)

SCENE 2

(*The color fades from the sky. Twilight begins. The interior of the kitchen is now visible. A pine table is at center, a cook-stove in the right rear corner, four rough wooden chairs, a tallow candle on the table. In the middle of the rear wall is fastened a big advertizing poster with a ship in full sail and the word "California" in big letters. Kitchen utensils hang from nails. Everything is neat and in order but the atmosphere is of a men's camp kitchen rather than that of a home.*)

(*Places for three are laid. EBEN takes boiled potatoes and bacon from the stove and puts them on the table, also a loaf of bread and a crock of water. SIMEON and PETER shoulder in, slump down in their chairs without a word. EBEN joins them. The three eat in silence for a*

moment, the two elder as naturally unrestrained as beasts of the field, EBEN picking at his food without appetite, glancing at them with a tolerant dislike.*)

SIMEON (*suddenly turns to EBEN*). Looky here! Ye'd oughtn't t' said that, Eben.

PETER. 'Twa'n't righteous.

EBEN. What?

SIMEON. Ye prayed he'd died.

EBEN. Waal—don't yew pray it? (*A pause.*)

PETER. He's our Paw.

EBEN (*violently*). Not mine!

SIMEON (*dryly*). Ye'd not let no one else say that about yer Maw! Ha! (*He gives one abrupt sardonic guffaw. PETER grins.*)

EBEN (*very pale*). I meant—I hain't his'n—I hain't like him—he hain't me!

PETER (*dryly*). Wait till ye've growed his age!

EBEN (*intensely*). I'm Maw—every drop o' blood! (*A pause. They stare at him with indifferent curiosity.*)

PETER (*reminiscently*). She was good t' Sim 'n' me. A good Step-maw's scurse.

SIMEON. She was good t' everyone.

EBEN (*greatly moved, gets to his feet and makes an awkward bow to each of them—stammering*). I be thankful t' ye. I'm her—her heir. (*He sits down in confusion.*)

PETER (*after a pause—judicially*). She was good even t' him.

EBEN (*fiercely*). An' fur thanks he killed her!

SIMEON (*after a pause*). No one never kills nobody. It's allus somethin'. That's the murderer.

EBEN. Didn't he slave Maw t' death?

PETER. He's slaved himself t' death. He's slaved Sim 'n' me 'n' yew t' death —on'y none o' us hain't died—yit.

SIMEON. It's somethin'—drivin' him —t' drive us!

EBEN (*vengefully*). Waal—I hold

him t' jedgment! (*Then scornfully.*) Somethin'! What's somethin'?

SIMEON. Dunno.

EBEN (*sardonically*). What's drivin' yew to Californi-a, mebbe? (*They look at him in surprise.*) Oh, I've heerd ye! (*Then, after a pause.*) But ye'll never go t' the gold fields!

PETER (*assertively*). Mebbe!

EBEN. Whar'll ye git the money?

PETER. We kin walk. It's an a'mighty ways—Californi-a—but if yew was t' put all the steps we've walked on this farm end t' end we'd be in the moon!

EBEN. The Injuns'll skulp ye on the plains.

SIMEON (*with grim humor*). We'll mebbe make 'em pay a hair fur a hair!

EBEN (*decisively*). But t'ain't that. Ye won't never go because ye'll wait here for yer share o' the farm, thinkin allus he'll die soon.

SIMEON (*after a pause*). We've a right.

PETER. Two-thirds belongs t'us.

EBEN (*jumping to his feet*). Ye've no right! She wa'n't yewr Maw! It was her farm! Didn't he steal it from her? She's dead. It's my farm.

SIMEON (*sardonically*). Tell that t' Paw—when he comes! I'll bet ye a dollar he'll laugh—fur once in his life. Ha! (*He laughs himself in one single mirthless bark.*)

PETER (*amused in turn, echoes his brother*). Ha!

SIMEON (*after a pause*). What've ye got held agin us, Eben? Year arter year it's skulked in yer eye—somethin'.

PETER. Ay-eh.

EBEN. Ay-eh. They's somethin'. (*Suddenly exploding.*) Why didn't ye never stand between him 'n' my Maw when he was slavin' her to her grave—t' pay her back fur the kindness she done t' yew? (*There is a long pause. They stare at him in surprise.*)

SIMEON. Waal—the stock'd got t' be watered.

PETER. 'R they was woodin' t' do.

SIMEON. 'R plowin'.

PETER. 'R hayin'.

SIMEON. 'R spreadin' manure.

PETER. 'R weedin'.

SIMEON. 'R prunin'.

PETER. 'R milkin'.

EBEN (*breaking in harshly*). An makin' walls—stone atop o' stone—makin' walls till yer heart's a stone ye heft up out o' the way o' growth onto a stone wall t' wall in yer heart!

SIMEON (*matter-of-factly*). We never had no time t' meddle.

PETER (*to* EBEN). Yew was fifteen afore yer Maw died—an' big fur yer age. Why didn't ye never do nothin'?

EBEN (*harshly*). They was chores t' do, wa'n't they? (*A pause—then slowly.*) It was on'y arter she died I come to think o' it. Me cookin'—doin' her work—that made me know her, suffer her sufferin'—she'd come back t' help—come back t' bile potatoes—come back t' fry bacon—come back t' bake biscuits—come back all cramped up t' shake the fire, an' carry ashes, her eyes weepin' an' bloody with smoke an' cinders same's they used t' be. She still comes back—stands by the stove thar in the evenin'—she can't find it nateral sleepin' an' restin' in peace. She can't git used t' bein' free—even in her grave.

SIMEON. She never complained none.

EBEN. She'd got too tired. She'd got too used t' bein' too tired. That was what he done. (*With vengeful passion.*) An' sooner'r later, I'll meddle. I'll say the thin's I didn't then t' him! I'll yell 'em at the top o' my lungs. I'll see t' it my Maw gits some rest an' sleep in her grave! (*He sits down again, relapsing into a brooding silence. They look at him with a queer indifferent curiosity.*)

PETER (*after a pause*). Whar in tarnation d'ye s'pose he went, Sim?

SIMEON. Dunno. He druv off in the buggy, all spick an' span, with the mare all breshed an' shiny, druv off clackin' his tongue an' wavin' his whip. I remember it right well. I was finishin' plowin', it was spring an' May an' sunset, an' gold in the West, an' he druv off into it. I yells "Whar ye goin', Paw?" an' he hauls up by the stone wall a jiffy. His old snake's eyes was glitterin' in the sun like he'd been drinkin' a jugful an' he says with a mule's grin: "Don't ye run away till I come back!"

PETER. Wonder if he knowed we was wantin' fur Californi-a?

SIMEON. Mebbe. I didn't say nothin' and he says, lookin' kinder queer an' sick: "I been hearin' the hens cluckin' an' the roosters crowin' all the durn day. I been listenin' t' the cows lowin' an' everythin' else kickin' up till I can't stand it no more. It's spring an' I'm feelin' damned," he says. "Damned like an old bare hickory tree fit on'y fur burnin'," he says. An' then I calc'late I must've looked a mite hopeful, fur he adds real spry and vicious: "But don't git no fool idee I'm dead. I've sworn t' live a hundred an' I'll do it, if on'y t' spite yer sinful greed! An' now I'm ridin' out t' learn God's message t' me in the spring, like the prophets done. An' yew git back t' yer plowin'," he says. An' he druv off singin' a hymn. I thought he was drunk—'r I'd stopped him goin'.

EBEN (scornfully). No, ye wouldn't! Ye're scared o' him. He's stronger—inside—than both o' ye put together!

PETER (sardonically). An' yew—be yew Samson?

EBEN. I'm gittin' stronger. I kin feel it growin' in me—growin' an' growin'—till it'll bust out—! (He gets up and puts on his coat and a hat. They watch him, gradually breaking into grins. EBEN avoids their eyes sheepishly.) I'm goin' out fur a spell—up the road.

PETER. T' the village?

SIMEON. T' see Minnie?

EBEN (defiantly). Ay-eh!

PETER (jeeringly). The Scarlet Woman!

SIMEON. Lust—that's what's growin' in ye!

EBEN. Waal—she's purty!

PETER. She's been purty fur twenty year!

SIMEON. A new coat o' paint'll make a heifer out of forty.

EBEN. She hain't forty!

PETER. If she hain't, she's teeterin' on the edge.

EBEN (desperately). What d'yew know—

PETER. All they is . . . Sim knew her—an' then me arter—

SIMEON. An' Paw kin tell you somethin' too! He was fust!

EBEN. D'ye mean t'say he . . . ?

SIMEON (with a grin). Ay-eh! We air his heirs in everythin'!

EBEN (intensely). That's more to it! That grows on it! It'll bust soon! (Then violently.) I'll go smash my fist in her face! (He pulls open the door in rear violently.)

SIMEON (with a wink at PETER—drawlingly). Mebbe—but the night's wa'm—purty—by the time ye git thar mebbe ye'll kiss her instead!

PETER. Sart'n he will! (They both roar with coarse laughter. EBEN rushes out and slams the door—then the outside front door—comes around the corner of the house and stands still by the gate, staring up at the sky.)

SIMEON (looking after him). Like his Paw.

PETER. Dead spit an' image!

SIMEON. Dog'll eat dog!

PETER. Ay-eh. (Pause. With yearning.) Mebbe a year from now we'll be in Californi-a.

SIMEON. Ay-eh. (A pause. Both yawn). Let's git t'bed. (He blows out the candle. They go out door in rear. EBEN stretches his arms up to the sky—rebelliously.)

EBEN. Waal—thar's a star, an' somewhar's they's him, an' here's me, an' thar's Min up the road—in the same night. What if I does kiss her? She's like t'night, she's soft 'n' wa'm, her eyes kin wink like a star, her mouth's wa'm, her arms're wa'm, she smells like a wa'm plowed field, she's purty . . . Ay-eh! By God A'mighty she's purty, an' I don't give a damn how many sins she's sinned afore mine or who she's sinned 'em with, my sin's as purty as any one on 'em! (*He strides off down the road to the left.*)

SCENE 3

(*It is the pitch darkness just before dawn.* EBEN *comes in from the left and goes around to the porch, feeling his way, chuckling bitterly and cursing half-aloud to himself.*)

EBEN. The cussed old miser! (*He can be heard going in the front door. There is a pause as he goes upstairs, then a loud knock on the bedroom door of the brothers.*) Wake up!

SIMEON (*startedly*). Who's thar?

EBEN (*pushing open the door and coming in, a lighted candle in his hand. The bedroom of the brothers is revealed. Its ceiling is the sloping roof. They can stand upright only close to the center dividing wall of the upstairs.* SIMEON *and* PETER *are in a double bed, front.* EBEN's *cot is to the rear.* EBEN *has a mixture of silly grin and vicious scowl on his face*). I be!

PETER (*angrily*). What in hell's-fire . . . ?

EBEN. I got news fur ye! Ha! (*He gives one abrupt sardonic guffaw.*)

SIMEON (*angrily*). Couldn't ye hold it 'til we'd got our sleep?

EBEN. It's nigh sunup. (*Then explosively.*) He's gone an' married agen!

SIMEON *and* PETER (*explosively*). Paw?

EBEN. Got himself hitched to a female 'bout thirty-five—an' purty, they says . . .

SIMEON (*aghast*). It's a durn lie!

PETER. Who says?

SIMEON. They been stringin' ye!

EBEN. Think I'm a dunce, do ye? The hull village says. The preacher from New Dover, he brung the news—told it t'our preacher—New Dover, that's whar the old loon got himself hitched—that's whar the woman lived—

PETER (*no longer doubting—stunned*). Waal . . . !

SIMEON (*the same*). Waal . . . !

EBEN (*sitting down on a bed—with vicious hatred*). Ain't he a devil out o' hell? It's jest t' spite us—the damned old mule!

PETER (*after a pause*). Everythin'll go t' her now.

SIMEON. Ay'eh. (*A pause—dully.*) Waal—if it's done—

PETER. It's done us. (*Pause—then persuasively.*) They's gold in the fields o' Californi-a, Sim. No good a-stayin' here now.

SIMEON. Jest what I was a-thinkin'. (*Then with decision.*) S'well fust's last! Let's light out and git this mornin'.

PETER. Suits me.

EBEN. Ye must like walkin'.

SIMEON (*sardonically*). If ye'd grow wings on us we'd fly thar!

EBEN. Ye'd like ridin' better—on a boat, wouldn't ye? (*Fumbles in his pocket and takes out a crumpled sheet of foolscap.*) Waal, if ye sign this ye kin ride on a boat. I've had it writ out an' ready in case ye'd ever go. It says fur three hundred dollars t' each ye agree yewr shares o' the farm is sold t' me. (*They look suspiciously at the paper. A pause.*)

SIMEON (*wonderingly*). But if he's hitched agen—

PETER. An' whar'd yew git that sum o' money, anyways?

EBEN (*cunningly*). I know whar it's hid. I been waitin'—Maw told me. She knew whar it lay fur years, but she was waitin' . . . It's her'n—the money he hoarded from her farm an' hid from Maw. It's my money by rights now.

PETER. Whar's it hid?

EBEN (*cunningly*). Whar yew won't never find it without me. Maw spied on him—'r she'd never knowed. (*A pause. They look at him suspiciously, and he at them.*) Waal, is it fa'r trade?

SIMEON. Dunno.

PETER. Dunno.

SIMEON (*looking at window*). Sky's grayin'.

PETER. Ye better start the fire, Eben.

SIMEON. An' fix some vittles.

EBEN. Ay-eh. (*Then with a forced jocular heartiness.*) I'll git ye a good one. If ye're startin' t' hoof it t' Californi-a ye'll need somethin' that'll stick t' yer ribs. (*He turns to the door, adding meaningly.*) But ye kin ride on a boat if ye'll swap. (*He stops at the door and pauses. They stare at him.*)

SIMEON (*suspiciously*). Whar was ye all night?

EBEN (*defiantly*). Up t' Min's. (*Then slowly.*) Walkin' thar, fust I felt 's if I'd kiss her; then I got a-thinkin' o' what ye'd said o' him an' her an' I says, I'll bust her nose for that! Then I got t' the village an' heerd the news an' I got madder'n hell an' run all the way t' Min's not knowin' what I'd do—(*He pauses—then sheepishly but more defiantly.*) Waal—when I seen her, I didn't hit her—nor I didn't kiss her nuther—I begun t' beller like a calf an' cuss at the same time, I was so durn mad—an' she got scared—an' I just grabbed holt an' tuk her! (*Proudly.*) Yes, sirree! I tuk her. She may've been his'n—an your'n, too—but she's mine now!

SIMEON (*dryly*). In love, air yew?

EBEN (*with lofty scorn*). Love! I don't take no stock in sech slop!

PETER (*winking at* SIMEON). Mebbe Eben's aimin' t' marry, too.

SIMEON. Min'd make a true faithful he'pmeet! (*They snicker.*)

EBEN. What do I care fur her—'ceptin' she's round an' wa'm? The p'int is she was his'n—an' now she b'longs t' me! (*He goes to the door—then turns—rebelliously.*) An' Min hain't sech a bad un. They's worse'n Min in the world, I'll bet ye! Wait'll we see this cow the Old Man's hitched t'! She'll beat Min, I got a notion! (*He starts to go out.*)

SIMEON (*suddenly*). Mebbe ye'll try t' make her your'n, too?

PETER. Ha! (*He gives a sardonic laugh of relish at this idea.*)

EBEN (*spitting with disgust*). Her—here—sleepin' with him—stealin' my Maw's farm! I'd as soon pet a skunk 'r kiss a snake! (*He goes out. The two stare after him suspiciously. A pause. They listen to his steps receding.*)

PETER. He's startin' the fire.

SIMEON. I'd like t' ride t' Californi-a —but—

PETER. Min might o' put some scheme in his head.

SIMEON. Mebbe it's all a lie 'bout Paw marryin'. We'd best wait an' see the bride.

PETER. An' don't sign nothin' till we does!

SIMEON. Nor till we've tested it's good money! (*Then with a grin.*) But if Paw's hitched we'd be sellin' Eben somethin' we'd never git nohow!

PETER. We'll wait an' see. (*Then with sudden vindictive anger.*) An' till he comes, let's yew 'n' me not wuk a lick, let Eben tend to thin's if he's a mind t', let's us jest sleep an' eat an' drink likker, an' let the hull damned farm go t'blazes!

SIMEON (*excitedly*). By God, we've 'arned a rest! We'll play rich fur a change. I hain't a-going to stir outa bed till breakfast's ready.

PETER. An' on the table!

SIMEON (*after a pause—thoughtfully*). What d'ye calc'late she'll be like—our new Maw? Like Eben thinks?

PETER. More'n likely.

SIMEON (*vindictively*). Waal—I hope

she's a she-devil that'll make him wish he was dead an' livin' in the pit o' hell fur comfort!

PETER (*fervently*).   Amen!

SIMEON (*imitating his father's voice*). "I'm ridin' out t' learn God's message t' me in the spring like the prophets done," he says. I'll bet right then an' thar he knew plumb well he was goin' whorin', the stinkin' old hypocrite!

SCENE 4

(*Same as Scene 2—shows the interior of the kitchen with a lighted candle on table. It is gray dawn outside.* SIMEON *and* PETER *are just finishing their breakfast.* EBEN *sits before his plate of untouched food, brooding frowningly.*)

PETER (*glancing at him rather irritably*).   Lookin' glum don't help none.

SIMEON (*sarcastically*).   Sorrowin' over his lust o' the flesh!

PETER (*with a grin*).   Was she yer fust?

EBEN (*angrily*).   None o' yer business. (*A pause.*) I was thinkin' o' him. I got a notion he's gittin' near—I kin feel him comin' on like yew kin feel malaria chill afore it takes ye.

PETER.   It's too early yet.

SIMEON.   Dunno. He'd like t' catch us nappin'—jest t' have somethin' t' hoss us 'round over.

PETER (*mechanically gets to his feet. *SIMEON *does the same*).   Waal—let's git t' wuk. (*They both plod mechanically toward the door before they realize. Then they stop short.*)

SIMEON (*grinning*).   Ye're a cussed fool, Pete—and I be wuss! Let him see we hain't wukin'! We don't give a durn!

PETER (*as they go back to the table*). Not a damned durn! It'll serve t' show him we're done with him. (*They sit down again.* EBEN *stares from one to the other with surprise.*)

SIMEON (*grins at him*).   We're aimin' t' start bein' lilies o' the field.

PETER.   Nary a toil 'r spin 'r lick o' wuk do we put in!

SIMEON.   Ye're sole owner—till he comes—that's what ye wanted. Waal, ye got t' be sole hand, too.

PETER.   The cows air bellerin'. Ye better hustle at the milkin'.

EBEN (*with excited joy*).   Ye mean ye'll sign the paper?

SIMEON (*dryly*).   Mebbe.

PETER.   Mebbe.

SIMEON.   We're considerin'. (*Peremptorily.*) Ye better git t' wuk.

EBEN (*wtih queer excitement*).   It's Maw's farm agen! It's my farm! Them's my cows! I'll milk my durn fingers off fur cows o' mine! (*He goes out door in rear, they stare after him indifferently.*)

SIMEON.   Like his Paw.

PETER.   Dead spit 'n' image!

SIMEON.   Waal—let dog eat dog! (EBEN *comes out of front door and around the corner of the house. The sky is beginning to grow flushed with sunrise.* EBEN *stops by the gate and stares around him with glowing possessive eyes. He takes in the whole farm with his embracing glance of desire.*)

EBEN.   It's purty! It's damned purty! It's mine! (*He suddenly throws his head back boldly and glares with hard, defiant eyes at the sky.*) Mine, d'ye hear? Mine! (*He turns and walks quickly off left, rear, toward the barn. The two brothers light their pipes.*)

SIMEON (*putting his muddy boots up on the table, tilting back his chair, and puffing defiantly*).   Waal—this air solid comfort—fur once.

PETER.   Ay-eh. (*He follows suit. A pause. Unconsciously they both sigh.*)

SIMEON (*suddenly*).   He never was much o' a hand at milkin', Eben wa'n't.

PETER (*with a snort*).   His hands air like hoofs! (*A pause.*)

SIMEON.   Reach down the jug thar! Let's take a swaller. I'm feelin' kind o' low.

PETER.   Good idee! (*He does so—*

gets two glasses—they pour out drinks of whisky.) Here's t' the gold in Cali-forni-a!

SIMEON. An' luck t' find it! (*They drink—puff resolutely—sigh—take their feet down from the table.*)

PETER. Likker don't pear t' sot right.

SIMEON. We hain't used t' it this early. (*A pause. They become very restless.*)

PETER. Gittin' close in this kitchen.

SIMEON (*with immense relief*). Let's git a breath o' air. (*They arise briskly and go out rear—appear around house and stop by the gate. They stare up at the sky with a numbed appreciation.*)

PETER. Purty!

SIMEON. Ay-eh. Gold's t' the East now.

PETER. Sun's startin' with us fur the Golden West.

SIMEON (*staring around the farm, his compressed face tightened, unable to conceal his emotion*). Waal—it's our last mornin'—mebbe.

PETER (*the same*). Ay-eh.

SIMEON (*stamps his foot on the earth and addresses it desperately*). Waal—ye've thirty year o' me buried in ye—spread out over ye—blood an' bone an' sweat—rotted away—fertilizin' ye—richin' yer soul—prime manure, by God, that's what I been t' ye!

PETER. Ay-eh! An' me!

SIMEON. An' yew, Peter. (*He sighs—then spits.*) Waal—no use'n cryin' over spilt milk.

PETER. They's gold in the West—an' freedom, mebbe. We been slaves t' stone walls here.

SIMEON (*defiantly*). We hain't no-body's slaves from this out—nor no thin's slaves nuther. (*A pause—restlessly.*) Speakin' o' milk, wonder how Eben's managin'?

PETER. I s'pose he's managin'.

SIMEON. Mebbe we'd ought t' help —this once.

PETER. Mebbe. The cows knows us.

SIMEON. An' likes us. They don't know him much.

PETER. An' the hosses, an' pigs, an' chickens. They don't know him much.

SIMEON. They knows us like brothers —an' likes us! (*Proudly.*) Hain't we raised 'em t' be fust-rate, number one prize stock?

PETER. We hain't—not no more.

SIMEON (*dully*). I was fergittin'. (*Then resignedly.*) Waal, let's go help Eben a spell an' git waked up.

PETER. Suits me. (*They are starting off down left, rear, for the barn when EBEN appears from there hurrying toward them, his face excited.*)

EBEN (*breathlessly*). Waal—har they be! The old mule an' the bride! I seen 'em from the barn down below at the turnin'.

PETER. How could ye tell that far?

EBEN. Hain't I as far-sight as he's near-sight? Don't I know the mare 'n' buggy, an' two people settin' in it? Who else. . . . ? An' I tell ye I kin feel 'em a-comin', too! (*He squirms as if he had the itch.*)

PETER (*beginning to be angry*). Waal —let him do his own unhitchin'!

SIMEON (*angry in his turn*). Let's hustle in an' git our bundles an' be a-goin' as he's a-comin'. I don't want never t' step inside the door agen arter he's back. (*They both start back around the corner of the house. EBEN follows them.*)

EBEN (*anxiously*). Will ye sign it afore ye go?

PETER. Let's see the color o' the old skinflint's money an' we'll sign. (*They disappear left. The two brothers clump upstairs to get their bundles. EBEN appears in the kitchen, runs to window, peers out, comes back and pulls up a strip of flooring in under stove, takes out a canvas bag and puts it on table, then sets the floorboard back in place. The two brothers appear a moment after. They carry old carpet bags.*)

EBEN (*puts his hand on bag guardingly*). Have ye signed?

SIMEON (*shows paper in his hand*). Ay-eh. (*Greedily.*) Be that the money?

EBEN (*opens bag and pours out pile of twenty-dollar gold pieces.*) Twenty-dollar pieces—thirty on 'em. Count 'em. (PETER *does so, arranging them in stacks of five, biting one or two to test them.*)

PETER. Six hundred. (*He puts them in bag and puts it inside his shirt carefully.*)

SIMEON (*handing paper to* EBEN). Har ye be.

EBEN (*after a glance, folds it carefully and hides it under his shirt—gratefully*). Thank yew.

PETER. Thank yew fur the ride.

SIMEON. We'll send ye a lump o' gold fur Christmas. (*A pause.* EBEN *stares at them and they at him.*)

PETER (*awkwardly*). Waal—we're a-goin'.

SIMEON. Comin' out t' the yard?

EBEN. No. I'm waitin' in here a spell. (*Another silence. The brothers edge awkwardly to door in rear—then turn and stand.*)

SIMEON. Waal—good-by.

PETER. Good-by.

EBEN. Good-by. (*They go out. He sits down at the table, faces the stove and pulls out the paper. He looks from it to the stove. His face, lighted up by the shaft of sunlight from the window, has an expression of trance. His lips move. The two brothers come out to the gate.*)

PETER (*looking off toward barn*). Thar he be—unhitchin'!

SIMEON (*with a chuckle*). I'll bet ye he's riled!

PETER. An' thar she be.

SIMEON. Let's wait 'n' see what our new Maw looks like.

PETER (*with a grin*). An' give him our partin' cuss!

SIMEON (*grinning*). I feel like raisin' fun. I feel light in my head an' feet.

PETER. Me, too. I feel like laffin' till I'd split up the middle.

SIMEON. Reckon it's the likker?

PETER. No. My feet feel itchin' t' walk an' walk—an' jump high over thin's —an'. . . .

SIMEON. Dance? (*A pause.*)

PETER (*puzzled*). It's plumb onnateral.

SIMEON (*a light coming over his face*). I calc-late it's 'cause school's out. It's holiday. Fur once we're free!

PETER (*dazedly*). Free?

SIMEON. The halter's broke—the harness is busted—the fence bars is down—the stone walls air crumblin' an' tumblin'! We'll be kickin' up an' tearin' away down the road!

PETER (*drawing a deep breath—oratorically*). Anybody that wants this stinkin' old rock-pile of a farm kin hev it. T'ain't our'n, no sirree!

SIMEON (*takes the gate off its hinges and puts it under his arm*). We harby 'bolishes shet gates, an' open gates, an' all gates, by thunder!

PETER. We'll take it with us fur luck an' let 'er sail free down some river.

SIMEON (*as a sound of voices comes from left, rear*). Har they comes! (*The two brothers congeal into two stiff, grim-visaged statues.* EPHRAIM CABOT *and* ABBIE PUTNAM *come in.* CABOT *is seventy-five, tall and gaunt, with great, wiry, concentrated power, but stoop-shouldered from toil. His face is as hard as if it were hewn out of a boulder, yet there is a weakness in it, a petty pride in its own narrow strength. His eyes are small, close together, and extremely near-sighted, blinking continually in the effort to focus on objects, their stare having a straining, ingrowing quality. He is dressed in his dismal black Sunday suit.* ABBIE *is thirty-five, boxom, full of vitality. Her round face is pretty but marred by its rather gross sensuality. There is strength and obstinacy in her jaw, a hard determination in her eyes, and about her whole personality the same unsettled, untamed, desperate quality which is so apparent in* EBEN.)

CABOT (*as they enter—a queer strangled emotion in his dry cracking voice*). Har we be t' hum, Abbie.

ABBIE (*with lust for the word*). Hum! (*Her eyes gloating on the house without seeming to see the two stiff figures at the gate.*) It's purty—purty! I can't b'lieve it's r'ally mine.

CABOT (*sharply*). Yewr'n? Mine! (*He stares at her penetratingly. She stares back. He adds relentingly.*) Our'n —mebbe! It was lonesome too long. I was growin' old in the spring. A hum's got t' hev a woman.

ABBIE (*her voice taking possession*). A woman's got t' hev a hum!

CABOT (*nodding uncertainly*). Ay-eh. (*Then irritably.*) Whar be they? Ain't thar nobody about—'r wukin'—'r nothin'?

ABBIE (*sees the brothers. She returns their stare of cold appraising contempt with interest—slowly*). Thar's two men loafin' at the gate an' starin' at me like a couple o' strayed hogs.

CABOT (*straining his eyes*). I kin see 'em—but I can't make out. . . .

SIMEON. It's Simeon.

PETER. It's Peter.

CABOT (*exploding*). Why hain't ye wukin'?

SIMEON (*dryly*). We're waitin' t' welcome ye hum—yew an' the bride!

CABOT (*confusedly*). Huh? Waal— this be yer new Maw, boys. (*She stares at them and they at her.*)

SIMEON (*turns away and spits contemptuously*). I see her!

PETER (*spits also*). An' I see her!

ABBIE (*with the conqueror's conscious superiority*). I'll go in an' look at *my* house. (*She goes slowly around to porch.*)

SIMEON (*with a snort*). *Her* house!

PETER (*calls after her*). Ye'll find

Eben inside. Ye better not tell him it's *yewr* house.

ABBIE (*mouthing the name*). Eben. (*Then quietly.*) I'll tell Eben.

CABOT (*with a contemptuous sneer*). Ye needn't heed Eben. Eben's a dumb fool—like his Maw—soft an' simple!

SIMEON (*with his sardonic burst of laughter*). Ha! Eben's a chip o' yew— spit 'n' image—hard 'n' bitter's a hickory tree! Dog'll eat dog. He'll eat ye yet, old man!

CABOT (*commandingly*). Ye git t' wuk!

SIMEON (*as* ABBIE *disappears in house —winks at* PETER *and says tauntingly*). So that thar's our new Maw, be it? Whar in hell did ye dig her up? (*He and* PETER *laugh.*)

PETER. Ha! Ye'd better turn her in the pen with the other sows. (*They laugh uproariously, slapping their thighs.*)

CABOT (*so amazed at their effrontery that he stutters in confusion*). Simeon! Peter! What's come over ye? Air ye drunk?

SIMEON. We're free, old man—free o' yew an' the hull damned farm! (*They grow more and more hilarious and excited.*)

PETER. An' we're startin' out fur the gold fields o' Californi-a!

SIMEON. Ye kin take this place an' burn it!

PETER. An' bury it—fur all we cares!

SIMEON. We're free, old man! (*He cuts a caper.*)

PETER. Free! (*He gives a kick in the air.*)

SIMEON (*in a frenzy*). Whoop!

PETER. Whoop! (*They do an absurd Indian war dance about the old man who is petrified between rage and the fear that they are insane.*)

SIMEON. We're free as Injuns! Lucky we don't skulp ye!

PETER. An' burn yer barn an' kill the stock!

SIMEON. An' rape yer new woman!

Whoop! (*He and* PETER *stop their dance, holding their sides, rocking with wild laughter.*)

CABOT (*edging away*).   Lust fur gold —fur the sinful, easy gold o' Californi-a! It's made ye mad!

SIMEON (*tauntingly*).   Wouldn't ye like us to send ye back some sinful gold, ye old sinner?

PETER.   They's gold besides what's in Californi-a! (*He retreats back beyond the vision of the old man and takes the bag of money and flaunts it in the air above his head, laughing.*)

SIMEON.   And sinfuller, too!

PETER.   We'll be voyagin' on the sea! Whoop! (*He leaps up and down*).

SIMEON.   Livin' free! Whoop! (*He leaps in turn.*)

CABOT (*suddenly roaring with rage*). My cuss on ye!

SIMEON.   Take our'n in trade for it! Whoop!

CABOT.   I'll hev ye both chained up in the asylum!

PETER.   Ye old skinflint! Good-by!

SIMEON.   Ye old blood sucker! Good-by!

CABOT.   Go afore I. . . . !

PETER.   Whoop! (*He picks a stone from the road.* SIMEON *does the same.*)

SIMEON.   Maw'll be in the parlor.

PETER.   Ay-eh! One! Two!

CABOT (*frightened*).   What air ye. . . . ?

PETER.   Three! (*They both throw, the stones hitting the parlor window with a crash of glass, tearing the shade.*)

SIMEON.   Whoop!

PETER.   Whoop!

CABOT (*in a fury now, rushing toward them*).   If I kin lay hands on ye—I'll break yer bones fur ye! (*But they beat a capering retreat before him,* SIMEON *with the gate still under his arm.* CABOT *comes back, panting with impotent rage. Their voices as they go off take up the song of the gold-seekers to the old tune of "Oh, Susannah!"*)

I jumped aboard the Liza ship,
And traveled on the sea,
And every time I thought of home
I wished it wasn't me!
Oh! Californi-a,
That's the land fur me!
I'm off to Californi-a!
With my wash bowl on my knee.

(*In the meantime, the window of the upper bedroom on right is raised and* ABBIE *sticks her head out. She looks down at* CABOT—*with a sigh of relief.*)

ABBIE.   Waal—that's the last o' them two, hain't it? (*He doesn't answer. Then in possessive tones.*) This here's a nice bedroom, Ephraim. It's a r'al nice bed. Is it my room, Ephraim?

CABOT (*grimly—without looking up*). Our'n! (*She cannot control a grimace of aversion and pulls back her head slowly and shuts the window. A sudden horrible thought seems to enter* CABOT's *head.*) They been up to somethin'! Mebbe— mebbe they've pizened the stock—'r somethin'! (*He almost runs off down toward the barn. A moment later the kitchen door is slowly pushed open and* ABBIE *enters. For a moment she stands looking at* EBEN. *He does not notice her at first. Her eyes take him in penetratingly with a calculating appraisal of his strength as against hers. But under this her desire is dimly awakened by his youth and good looks. Suddenly he becomes conscious of her presence and looks up. Their eyes meet. He leaps to his feet, glowering at her speechlessly.*)

ABBIE (*in her most seductive tones which she uses all through this scene*). Be you—Eben? I'm Abbie— (*She laughs.*) I mean, I'm yer new Maw.

EBEN (*viciously*).   No, damn ye!

ABBIE (*as if she hadn't heard—with a queer smile*).   Yer Paw's spoke a lot o' yew. . . .

EBEN.   Ha!

ABBIE.   Ye mustn't mind him. He's an old man. (*A long pause. They stare at each other.*) I don't want t' pretend playin' Maw t' ye, Eben. (*Admiringly.*) Ye're too big an' too strong for that. I want t' be frens with ye. Mebbe with me fur a fren ye'd find ye'd like livin' here better. I kin make it easy fur ye with him, mebbe. (*With a scornful sense of power.*) I calc'late I kin git him t' do most anythin' fur me.

EBEN (*with bitter scorn*). Ha! (*They stare again,* EBEN *obscurely moved, physically attracted to her—in forced stilted tones.*) Yew kin go t' the devil!

ABBIE (*calmly*). If cussin' me does ye good, cuss all ye've a mind t'. I'm all prepared t' have ye agin me—at fust. I don't blame ye nuther. I'd feel the same at any stranger comin' t' take my Maw's place. (*He shudders. She is watching him carefully.*) Yew must've cared a lot fur yewr Maw, didn't ye? My Maw died afore I'd growed. I don't remember her none. (*A pause.*) But yew won't hate me long, Eben. I'm not the wust in the world—an' yew an' me've got a lot in common. I kin tell that by lookin' at ye. Waal—I've had a hard life, too—oceans o' trouble an' nuthin' but wuk fur reward. I was a orphan early an' had t' wuk fur others in other folks' hums. Then I married an' he turned out a drunken spreer an' so he had to wuk fur others an' me too agen in other folks' hums, an' the baby died, an' my husband got sick an' died too, an' I was glad sayin' now I'm free fur once, on'y I diskivered right away all I was free fur was t' wuk agen in other folks' hums, doin' other folks' wuk till I'd most give up hope o' ever doin' my own wuk in my own hum, an' then your Paw come. . . . (CABOT *appears returning from the barn. He comes to the gate and looks down the road the brothers have gone. A faint strain of their retreating voices is heard: "Oh, Californi-a! That's the place for me." He stands glowing, his fist clenched, his face grim with rage.*)

EBEN (*fighting against his growing at-*

traction and sympathy—harshly*). An' bought yew—like a harlot! (*She is stung and flushes angrily. She has been sincerely moved by the recital of her troubles. He adds furiously.*) An' the price he's payin' ye—this farm—was my Maw's, damn ye!—an' mine now!

ABBIE (*with a cool laugh of confidence*). Yewr'n? We'll see 'bout that! (*Then strongly.*) Waal—what if I did need a hum? What else'd I marry an old man like him fur?

EBEN (*maliciously*). I'll tell him ye said that!

ABBIE (*smiling*). I'll say ye're lyin' a-purpose—an' he'll drive ye off the place!

EBEN. Ye devil!

ABBIE (*defying him*). This be my farm—this be my hum—this be my kitchen—!

EBEN (*furiously, as if he were going to attack her*). Shut up, damn ye!

ABBIE (*walks up to him—a queer coarse expression of desire in her face and body—slowly*). An' upstairs—that be my bedroom—an' my bed! (*He stares into her eyes, terribly confused and torn. She adds softly.*) I hain't bad nor mean —'ceptin' fur an enemy—but I got t' fight fur what's due me out o' life, if I ever 'spect t' git it. (*Then putting her hand on his arm—seductively.*) Let's yew 'n' me be frens, Eben.

EBEN (*stupidly—as if hypnotized*). Ay-eh. (*Then furiously flinging off her arm.*) No, ye durned old witch! I hate ye! (*He rushes out the door.*)

ABBIE (*looks after him smiling satisfiedly—then half to herself, mouthing the word*). Eben's nice. (*She looks at the table, proudly.*) I'll wash up *my* dishes now. (EBEN *appears outside, slamming the door behind him. He comes around corner, stops on seeing his father, and stands staring at him with hate.*)

CABOT (*raising his arms to heaven in*

the fury he can no longer control). Lord God o' Hosts, smite the undutiful sons with Thy wust cuss!

EBEN (*breaking in violently*). Yew 'n' yewr God! Allus cussin' folks—allus naggin' em!

CABOT (*oblivious to him—summoningly*). God o' the old! God o' the lonesome!

EBEN (*mockingly*). Naggin' His sheep t' sin! T' hell with yewr God! (CABOT *turns. He and* EBEN *glower at each other.*)

CABOT (*harshly*). So it's yew. I might've knowed it. (*Shaking his finger threateningly at him.*) Blasphemin' fool! (*Then quickly.*) Why hain't ye t' wuk?

EBEN. Why hain't yew? They've went. I can't wuk it all alone.

CABOT (*contemptuously*). Nor noways! I'm wuth ten o' ye yit, old's I be! Ye'll never be more'n half a man! (*Then, matter-of-factly.*) Waal—let's git t' the barn. (*They go. A last faint note of the "Californi-a" song is heard from the distance.* ABBIE *is washing her dishes.*)

(*The curtain falls.*)

Part II

SCENE 1

(*The exterior of the farmhouse, as in Part I—a hot Sunday afternoon two months later.* ABBIE, *dressed in her best, is discovered sitting in a rocker at the end of the porch. She rocks listlessly, enervated by the heat, staring in front of her with bored, half-closed eyes.*)

(EBEN *sticks his head out of his bedroom window. He looks around furtively and tries to see—or hear—if anyone is on the porch, but although he has been careful to make no noise,* ABBIE *has sensed his movement. She stops rocking, her face grows animated and eager, she waits attentively.* EBEN *seems to feel her presence, he scowls back his thoughts of her and spits with exaggerated disdain— then withdraws back into the room.* ABBIE *waits, holding her breath as she listens with passionate eagerness for every sound within the house.*)

(EBEN *comes out. Their eyes meet. His falter, he is confused, he turns away and slams the door resentfully. At this gesture,* ABBIE *laughs tantalizingly, amused but at the same time piqued and irritated. He scowls, strides off the porch to the path and starts to walk past her to the road with a grand swagger of ignoring her existence. He is dressed in his store suit, spruced up, his face shines from soap and water.* ABBIE *leans forward on her chair, her eyes hard and angry now, and, as he passes her, gives a sneering, taunting chuckle.*)

EBEN (*stung—turns on her furiously*). What air yew cacklin' 'bout?

ABBIE (*triumphant*). Yew!

EBEN. What about me?

ABBIE. Ye look all slicked up like a prize bull.

EBEN (*with a sneer*). Waal—ye hain't so durned purty yerself, be ye? (*They stare into each other's eyes, his held by hers in spite of himself, hers glowingly possessive. Their physical attraction becomes a palpable force quivering in the hot air.*)

ABBIE (*softly*). Ye don't mean that, Eben. Ye may think ye mean it, mebbe, but ye don't. Ye can't. It's agin nature, Eben. Ye been fightin' yer nature ever since the day I come—tryin' t' tell yerself I hain't purty t'ye. (*She laughs a low humid laugh without taking her eyes from his. A pause—her body squirms desirously—she murmurs languorously.*) Hain't the sun strong an' hot? Ye kin feel it burnin' into the earth—Nature— makin' thin's grow—bigger 'n' bigger— burnin' inside ye—makin' ye want t' grow—into somethin' else—till ye're jined with it—an' it's your'n—but it owns ye, too—an' makes ye grow bigger —like a tree—like them elums—(*She laughs again softly, holding his eyes. He take a step toward her, compelled against his will.*) Nature'll beat ye, Eben. Ye might's well own up t' it fust 's last.

EBEN (*trying to break from her spell —confusedly*). If Paw'd hear ye goin' on. . . . (*Resentfully.*) But ye've made such a damned idjit out o' the old devil. . .! (ABBIE *laughs.*)

ABBIE. Waal—hain't it easier fur yew with him changed softer?

EBEN (*defiantly*). No, I'm fightin' him—fightin' yew—fightin' fur Maw's rights t' her hum! (*This breaks her spell for him. He glowers at her.*) An' I'm onto ye. Ye hain't foolin' me a mite. Ye're aimin' t' swaller up everythin' an' make it your'n. Waal, you'll find I'm a heap sight bigger hunk nor yew kin chew! (*He turns from her with a sneer.*)

ABBIE (*trying to regain her ascendancy —seductively*). Eben!

EBEN. Leave me be! (*He starts to walk away.*)

ABBIE (*more commandingly*). Eben!

EBEN (*stops—resentfully*). What d'ye want?

ABBIE (*trying to conceal a growing excitement*). Whar air ye goin'?

EBEN (*with malicious nonchalance*). Oh—up the road a spell.

ABBIE. T' the village?

EBEN (*airily*). Mebbe.

ABBIE (*excitedly*). T' see that Min, I s'pose?

EBEN. Mebbe.

ABBIE (*weakly*). What d'ye want t' waste time on her fur?

EBEN (*revenging himself now—grinning at her*). Ye can't beat Nature, didn't ye say? (*He laughs and again starts to walk away.*)

ABBIE (*bursting out*). An ugly old hake!

EBEN (*with a tantalizing sneer*). She's purtier'n yew be!

ABBIE. That every wuthless drunk in the country has. . . .

EBEN (*tauntingly*). Mebbe—but she's better'n yew. She owns up fa'r 'n' squar' t' her doin's.

ABBIE (*furiously*). Don't ye dare compare. . . .

EBEN. She don't go sneakin' an' stealin'—what's mine.

ABBIE (*savagely seizing on his weak point*). Your'n? Yew mean—my farm?

EBEN. I mean the farm yew sold yerself fur like any other old whore—my farm!

ABBIE (*stung—fiercely*). Ye'll never live t' see the day when even a stinkin' weed on it 'll belong t' ye! (*Then in a scream.*) Git out o' my sight! Go on t' yer slut—disgracin' yer Paw 'n' me! I'll git yer Paw t' horsewhip ye off the place if I want t'! Ye're only livin' here 'cause I tolerate ye! Git along! I hate the sight o' ye! (*She stops, panting and glaring at him.*)

EBEN (*returning her glance in kind*). An' I hate the sight o' yew! (*He turns and strides off up the road. She follows his retreating figure with concentrated hate. Old* CABOT *appears coming up from the barn. The hard, grim expression of his face has changed. He seems in some queer way softened, mellowed. His eyes have taken on a strange, incongruous dreamy quality. Yet there is no hint of physical weakness about him—rather he looks more robust and younger.* ABBIE *sees him and turns away quickly with unconcealed aversion. He comes slowly up to her.*)

CABOT (*mildly*). War yew an' Eben quarrelin' agen?

ABBIE (*shortly*). No.

CABOT. Ye was talkin' a'mighty loud. (*He sits down on the edge of porch.*)

ABBIE (*snappishly*). If ye heerd us they hain't no need askin' questions.

CABOT. I didn't hear what ye said.

ABBIE (*relieved*). Waal—it wa'n't nothin' t' speak on.

CABOT (*after a pause*).   Eben's queer.

ABBIE (*bitterly*).   He's the dead spit 'n' image o' yew!

CABOT (*queerly interested*).   D'ye think so, Abbie? (*After a pause, ruminatingly.*) Me 'n' Eben's allus fit 'n' fit. I never could b'ar him noways. He's so thunderin' soft—like his Maw.

ABBIE (*scornfully*).   Ay-eh! 'Bout as soft as yew be!

CABOT (*as if he hadn't heard*). Mebbe I been too hard on him.

ABBIE (*jeeringly*).   Waal—ye're gittin' soft now—soft as slop! That's what Eben was sayin'.

CABOT (*his face instantly grim and ominous*).   Eben was sayin'? Waal, he'd best not do nothin' t' try me 'r he'll soon diskiver. . . . (*A pause. She keeps her face turned away. His gradually softens. He stares up at the sky.*) Purty, hain't it?

ABBIE (*crossly*).   I don't see nothin' purty.

CABOT.   The sky. Feels like a wa'm field up thar.

ABBIE (*sarcastically*).   Air yew aimin' t' buy up over the farm too? (*She snickers contemptuously.*)

CABOT (*strangely*).   I'd like t' own my place up thar. (*A pause.*) I'm gittin' old, Abbie. I'm gittin' ripe on the bough. (*A pause. She stares at him mystified. He goes on.*) It's allus lonesome cold in the house—even when it's bilin' hot outside. Hain't yew noticed?

ABBIE.   No.

CABOT.   It's wa'm down t' the barn —nice smellin' an warm—with the cows. (*A pause.*) Cows is queer.

ABBIE.   Like yew?

CABOT.   Like Eben. (*A pause.*) I'm gittin' t' feel resigned t' Eben—jest as I got t' feel 'bout his Maw. I'm gittin' t' learn to b'ar his softness—jest like her'n. I calc'late I c'd a'most take t' him—if he wa'n't sech a dumb fool! (*A pause.*) I s'pose it's old age a-creepin' in my bones.

ABBIE (*indifferently*).   Waal—ye hain't dead yet.

CABOT (*roused*).   No, I hain't, yew bet—not by a hell of a sight—I'm sound 'n' tough as hickory! (*Then moodily.*) But arter three score and ten the Lord warns ye t' prepare. (*A pause.*) That's why Eben's come in my head. Now that his cussed sinful brothers is gone their path t' hell, they's no one left but Eben.

ABBIE (*resentfully*).   They's me, hain't they? (*Agitatedly.*) What's all this sudden likin' ye've tuk to Eben? Why don't ye saying nothin' 'bout me? Hain't I yer lawful wife?

CABOT (*simply*).   Ay-eh. Ye be. (*A pause—he stares at her desirously—his eyes grow avid—then with a sudden movement he seizes her hands and squeezes them, declaiming in a queer camp meeting preacher's tempo.*) Yew air my Rose o' Sharon! Behold, yew air fair; yer eyes air doves; yer lips air like scarlet; yer two breasts air like two fawns; yer navel be like a round goblet; yer belly be like a heap o' wheat. . . . (*He covers her hands with kisses. She does not seem to notice. She stares before her with hard angry eyes.*)

ABBIE (*jerking her hands away— harshly*).   So ye're plannin' t' leave the farm t' Eben, air ye?

CABOT (*dazedly*).   Leave . . .? (*Then with resentful obstinacy.*) I hain't a-givin' it t' no one!

ABBIE (*remorselessly*).   Ye can't take it with ye.

CABOT (*thinks a moment—then reluctantly*).   No, I calc'late not. (*After a pause—with a strange passion.*) But if I could, I would, by the Etarnal! 'R if I could, in my dyin' hour, I'd set it afire an' watch it burn—this house an' every ear o' corn an' every tree down t' the last blade o' hay! I'd sit an' know it was all a-dying with me an' no one else'd ever own what was mine, what I'd made out o' nothin' with my own sweat 'n' blood! (*A pause—then he adds with a queer affection.*) 'Ceptin' the cows. Them I'd turn free.

ABBIE (*harshly*). An' me?

CABOT (*with a queer smile*). Ye'd be turned free, too.

ABBIE (*furiously*). So that's the thanks I git fur marryin' ye—t' have ye change kind to Eben who hates ye, an' talk o' turnin' me out in the road.

CABOT (*hastily*). Abbie! Ye know I wa'n't. . . .

ABBIE (*vengefully*). Just let me tell ye a thing or two 'bout Eben! Whar's he gone? T' see that harlot, Min! I tried fur t' stop him. Disgracin' yew an' me—on the Sabbath, too!

CABOT (*rather guiltily*). He's a sinner—nateral-born. It's lust eatin' his heart.

ABBIE (*enraged beyond endurance—wildly vindictive*). An' his lust fur me! Kin ye find excuses fur that?

CABOT (*stares at her—after a dead pause*). Lust—fur yew?

ABBIE (*defiantly*). He was tryin' t' make love t' me—when ye heerd us quarrelin'.

CABOT (*stares at her—then a terrible expression of rage comes over his face—he springs to his feet shaking all over*). By the A'mighty God—I'll end him!

ABBIE (*frightened now for* EBEN). No! Don't ye!

CABOT (*violently*). I'll git the shotgun an' blow his soft brains t' the top o' them elums!

ABBIE (*throwing her arms around him*). No, Ephraim!

CABOT (*pushing her away violently*). I will, by God!

ABBIE (*in a quieting tone*). Listen, Ephraim. 'Twa'n't nothin' bad—on'y a boy's foolin'—'twa'n't meant serious—jest jokin' an' teasin'. . . .

CABOT. Then why did ye say—lust?

ABBIE. It must hev sounded wusser'n I meant. An' I was mad at thinkin'—ye'd leave him the farm.

CABOT (*quieter but still grim and cruel*). Waal then, I'll horsewhip him off the place if that much'll content ye.

ABBIE (*reaching out and taking his hand*). No. Don't think o' me! Ye mustn't drive him off. 'Tain't sensible. Who'll ye get to help ye on the farm? They's no one hereabouts.

CABOT (*considers this—then nodding his appreciation*). Ye got a head on ye. (*Then irritably.*) Waal, let him stay. (*He sits down on the edge of the porch. She sits beside him. He murmurs contemptuously.*) I oughtn't t' git riled so —at that 'ere fool calf. (*A pause.*) But har's the p'int. What son o' mine'll keep on here t' the farm—when the Lord does call me? Simeon an' Peter air gone t' hell—an Eben's follerin' 'em.

ABBIE. They's me.

CABOT. Ye're on'y a woman.

ABBIE. I'm yewr wife.

CABOT. That hain't me. A son is me —my blood—mine. Mine ought t' git mine. An' then it's still mine—even though I be six foot under. D'ye see?

ABBIE (*giving him a look of hatred*). Ay-eh. I see. (*She becomes very thoughtful, her face growing shrewd, her eyes studying* CABOT *craftily.*)

CABOT. I'm gittin' old—ripe on the bough. (*Then with a sudden forced reassurance.*) Not but what I hain't a hard nut t' crack even yet—an' fur many a year t' come! By the Etarnal, I kin break most o' the young fellers' backs at any kind o' work any day o' the year!

ABBIE (*suddenly*). Mebbe the Lord'll give *us* a son.

CABOT (*turns and stares at her eagerly*). Ye mean—a son—t' me 'n' yew?

ABBIE (*with a cajoling smile*). Ye're a strong man yet, hain't ye? 'Tain't noways impossible, be it? We know that. Why d'ye stare so? Hain't ye never thought o' that afore? I been thinkin' o' it all along. Ay-eh—an' I been prayin' it'd happen, too.

CABOT (*his face growing full of joy-*

ous pride and a sort of religious ecstasy).
Ye been prayin', Abbie?—fur a son?—
t' us?

ABBIE. Ay-eh. (*With a grim resolution.*) I want a son now.

CABOT (*excitedly clutching both of her hands in his*). It'd be the blessin' o' God, Abbie—the blessin' o' God A'mighty on me—in my old age—in my lonesomeness! They hain't nothin' I wouldn't do fur ye then, Abbie. Ye'd hev on'y t' ask it—anythin' ye'd a mind t'!

ABBIE (*interrupting*). Would ye will the farm t' me then—t' me an' it . . .?

CABOT (*vehemently*). I'd do anythin' ye axed, I tell ye! I swar it! May I be everlastin' damned t' hell if I wouldn't! (*He sinks to his knees pulling her down with him. He trembles all over with the fervor of his hopes.*) Pray t' the Lord agen, Abbie. It's the Sabbath! I'll jine ye! Two prayers air better nor one. "An' God hearkened unto Rachel"! An' God hearkened unto Abbie! Pray, Abbie! Pray fur him to hearken! (*He bows his head, mumbling. She pretends to do likewise but gives him a side glance of scorn and triumph.*)

SCENE 2

(*About eight in the evening. The interior of the two bedrooms on the top floor is shown. EBEN is sitting on the side of his bed in the room on the left. On account of the heat he has taken off everything but his undershirt and pants. His feet are bare. He faces front, brooding moodily, his chin propped on his hands, a desperate expression on his face.*)

(*In the other room CABOT and ABBIE are sitting side by side on the edge of their bed, an old four-poster with feather mattress. He is in his night shirt, she in her nightdress. He is still in the queer, excited mood into which the notion of a son has thrown him. Both rooms are lighted dimly and flickeringly by tallow candles.*)

CABOT. The farm needs a son.

ABBIE. I need a son.

CABOT. Ay-eh. Sometimes ye air the farm an' sometimes the farm be yew. That's why I clove t' ye in my lonesomeness. (*A pause. He pounds his knee with his fist.*) Me an' the farm has got t' beget a son!

ABBIE. Ye'd best go t' sleep. Ye're gittin' thin's all mixed.

CABOT (*with an impatient gesture*). No, I hain't. My mind's clear's a well. Ye don't know me, that's it. (*He stares hopelessly at the floor.*)

ABBIE (*indifferently*). Mebbe. (*In the next room EBEN gets up and paces up and down distractedly. ABBIE hears him. Her eyes fasten on the intervening wall with concentrated attention. EBEN stops and stares. Their hot glances seem to meet through the wall. Unconsciously he stretches out his arms for her and she half rises. Then aware, he mutters a curse at himself and flings himself face downward on the bed, his clenched fists above his head, his face buried in the pillow. ABBIE relaxes with a faint sigh but her eyes remain fixed on the wall; she listens with all her attention for some movement from EBEN.*)

CABOT (*suddenly raises his head and looks at her—scornfully*). Will ye ever know me—'r will any man 'r woman? (*Shaking his head.*) No. I calc'late 't wa'n't t' be. (*He turns away. ABBIE looks at the wall. Then, evidently unable to keep silent about his thoughts, without looking at his wife, he puts out his hand and clutches her knee. She starts violently, looks at him, sees he is not watching her, concentrates again on the wall and pays no attention to what he says.*) Listen, Abbie. When I come here fifty odd year ago—I was jest twenty an' the strongest an' hardest ye ever seen—

ten times as strong an' fifty times as hard as Eben. Waal—this place was nothin' but fields o' stones. Folks laughed when I tuk it. They couldn't know what I knowed. When ye kin make corn sprout out o' stones, God's livin' in yew! They wa'n't strong enuf fur that! They reckoned God was easy. They laughed. They don't laugh no more. Some died hereabouts. Some went West an' died. They're all under ground—fur follerin' arter an easy God. God hain't easy. (*He shakes his head slowly.*) An' I growed hard. Folks kept allus sayin' he's a hard man like 'twas sinful t' be hard, so's at last I said back at 'em: Waal then, by thunder, ye'll git me hard an' see how ye like it! (*Then suddenly.*) But I give in t' weakness once. 'Twas arter I'd been here two year. I got weak—despairful— they was so many stones. They was a party leavin', givin' up, goin' West. I jined 'em. We tracked on 'n' on. We come t' broad medders, plains, whar the soil was black an' rich as gold. Nary a stone. Easy. Ye'd on'y to plow an' sow an' then set an' smoke yer pipe an' watch thin's grow. I could o' been a rich man —but somethin' in me fit me an' fit me —the voice o' God sayin': "This hain't wuth nothin' t' Me. Git ye back t' hum!" I got afeerd o' that voice an' I lit out back t' hum here, leavin' my claim an' crops t' whoever'd a mind t' take 'em. Ay-eh. I actoolly give up what was rightful mine! God's hard, not easy! God's in the stones! Build my church on a rock— out o' stones an' I'll be in them! That's what He meant t' Peter! (*He sighs heavily—a pause.*) Stones. I picked 'em up an' piled 'em into walls. Ye kin read the years o' my life in them walls, every day a hefted stone, climbin' over the hills up and down, fencin' in the fields that was mine, whar I'd made thin's grow out o' nothin'—like the will o' God, like the servant o' His hand. It wa'n't easy. It was hard an' He made me hard fur it. (*He pauses.*) All the time I kept gittin' lonesomer. I tuk a wife. She bore Simeon

an' Peter. She was a good woman. She wuked hard. We was married twenty year. She never knowed me. She helped but she never knowed what she was helpin'. I was allus lonesome. She died. After that it wa'n't so lonesome fur a spell. (*A pause.*) I lost count o' the years. I had no time t' fool away countin' 'em. Sim an' Peter helped. The farm growed. It was all mine! When I thought o' that I didn't feel lonesome. (*A pause.*) But ye can't hitch yer mind t' one thin' day an' night. I tuk another wife— Eben's Maw. Her folks was contestin' me at law over my deeds t' the farm—my farm! That's why Eben keeps a-talkin' his fool talk o' this bein' his Maw's farm. She bore Eben. She was purty—but soft. She tried t' be hard. She couldn't. She never knowed me nor nothin'. It was lonesomer 'n hell with her. After a matter o' sixteen odd years, she died. (*A pause.*) I lived with the boys. They hated me 'cause I was hard. I hated them 'cause they was soft. They coveted the farm without knowin' what it meant. It made me bitter 'n wormwood. It aged me—them coveting what I'd made fur mine. Then this spring the call come —the voice o' God cryin' in my wilderness, in my lonesomeness—t' go out an' seek an' find! (*Turning to her with strange passion.*) I sought ye an' I found ye! Yew air my Rose o' Sharon! Yer eyes air like. . . . (*She has turned a blank face, resentful eyes to his. He stares at her for a moment—then harshly.*) Air ye any the wiser fur all I've told ye?

ABBIE (*confusedly*). Mebbe.

CABOT (*pushing her away from him— angrily*). Ye don't know nothin'—nor never will. If ye don't hev a son t' redeem ye. . . . (*This in a tone of cold threat.*)

ABBIE (*resentfully*). I've prayed, hain't I?

CABOT (*bitterly*). Pray agen—fur understandin'!

ABBIE (*a veiled threat in her tone*).

Ye'll have a son out o' me, I promise ye.

CABOT. How kin ye promise?

ABBIE. I got second-sight, mebbe. I kin foretell. (*She gives a queer smile.*)

CABOT. I believe ye have. Ye give me the chills sometimes. (*He shivers.*) It's cold in this house. It's oneasy. They's thin's pokin' about in the dark—in the corners. (*He pulls on his trousers, tucking in his night shirt, and pulls on his boots.*)

ABBIE (*surprised*). Whar air ye goin'?

CABOT (*queerly*). Down whar it's restful—whar it's warm—down t' the barn. (*Bitterly.*) I kin talk t' the cows. They know. They know the farm an' me. They'll give me peace. (*He turns to go out the door.*)

ABBIE (*a bit frightenedly*). Air ye ailin' tonight, Ephraim?

CABOT. Growin'. Growin' ripe on the bough. (*He turns and goes, his boots clumping down the stairs. EBEN sits up with a start, listening. ABBIE is conscious of his movement and stares at the wall. CABOT comes out of the house around the corner and stands by the gate, blinking at the sky. He stretches up his hands in a tortured gesture.*) God A'mighty, call from the dark! (*He listens as if expecting an answer. Then his arms drop, he shakes his head and plods off toward the barn. EBEN and ABBIE stare at each other through the wall. EBEN sighs heavily and ABBIE echoes it. Both become terribly nervous, uneasy. Finally ABBIE gets up and listens, her ear to the wall. He acts as if he saw every move she was making, he becomes resolutely still. She seems driven into a decision— goes out the door in rear determinedly. His eyes follow her. Then as the door of his room is opened softly, he turns away, waits in an attitude of strained fixity. ABBIE stands for a second staring at him, her eyes burning with desire. Then with a little cry she runs over and throws her arms about his neck, she pulls his head back and covers his mouth with kisses. At first, he submits dumbly; then he puts his arms about her neck and returns her kisses, but finally, suddenly aware of his hatred, he hurls her away from him, springing to his feet. They stand speechless and breathless, panting like two animals.*)

ABBIE (*at last—painfully*). Ye shouldn't, Eben—ye shouldn't—I'd make ye happy!

EBEN (*harshly*). I don't want t' be happy—from yew!

ABBIE (*helplessly*). Ye do, Eben! Ye do! Why d'ye lie?

EBEN (*viciously*). I don't take t'ye, I tell ye! I hate the sight o'ye!

ABBIE (*with an uncertain troubled laugh*). Waal, I kissed ye anyways— an' ye kissed back—yer lips was burnin' —ye can't lie 'bout that! (*Intensely.*) If ye don't care, why did ye kiss me back —why was yer lips burnin'?

EBEN (*wiping his mouth*). It was like pizen on 'em. (*Then tauntingly.*) When I kissed ye back, mebbe I thought 'twas someone else.

ABBIE (*wildly*). Min?

EBEN. Mebbe.

ABBIE (*torturedly*). Did ye go t' see her? Did ye r'ally go? I thought ye mightn't. Is that why ye throwed me off jest now?

EBEN (*sneeringly*). What if it be?

ABBIE (*raging*). Then ye're a dog, Eben Cabot!

EBEN (*threateningly*). Ye can't talk that way t' me!

ABBIE (*with a shrill laugh*). Can't I? Did ye think I was in love with ye—a weak thin' like yew! Not much! I on'y wanted ye fur a purpose o' my own—an' I'll hev ye fur it yet 'cause I'm stronger'n yew be!

EBEN (*resentfully*). I knowed well it was on'y part o' yer plan t' swaller everythin'!

ABBIE (*tauntingly*). Mebbe!

EBEN (*furious*). Git out o' my room!

ABBIE. This air my room an' ye're on'y hired help!

EBEN (*threateningly*). Git out afore I murder ye!

ABBIE (*quite confident now*). I hain't a mit afeered. Ye want me, don't ye? Yes, ye do! An yer Paw's son'll never kill what he wants! Look at yer eyes! They's lust for me in 'em, burnin' 'em up! Look at yer lips now! They're tremblin' an' longin' t' kiss me, an' yer teeth t' bite! (*He is watching her now with a horrible fascination. She laughs a crazy triumphant laugh.*) I'm a-goin' t' make all o' this hum my hum! They's one room hain't mine yet, but it's a-goin' t' be tonight. I'm a-goin' down now an' light up! (*She makes him a mocking bow.*) Won't ye come courtin' me in the best parlor, Mister Cabot?

EBEN (*staring at her—horribly confused—dully*). Don't ye dare! It hain't been opened since Maw died an' was laid out thar! Don't ye. . . ! (*But her eyes are fixed on his so burningly that his will seems to wither before hers. He stands swaying toward her helplessly.*)

ABBIE (*holding his eyes and putting all her will into her words as she backs out the door*). I'll expect ye afore long, Eben.

EBEN (*stares after her for a while, walking toward the door. A light appears in the parlor window. He murmurs*). In the parlor? (*This seems to arouse connotations for he comes back and puts on his white shirt, collar, half ties the tie mechanically, puts on coat, takes his hat, stands barefooted looking about him in bewilderment, mutters wonderingly.*) Maw! Whar air yew? (*Then goes slowly toward the door in rear.*)

SCENE 3

(*A few minutes later. The interior of the parlor is shown. A grim, repressed room like a tomb in which the family has been interred alive. ABBIE sits on the edge of the horsehair sofa. She has lighted all the candles and the room is revealed in all its preserved ugliness. A change has come over the woman. She looks awed and frightened now, ready to run away.*)

(*The door is opened and EBEN appears. His face wears an expression of obsessed confusion. He stands staring at her, his arms hanging disjointedly from his shoulders, his feet bare, his hat in his hand.*)

ABBIE (*after a pause—with a nervous, formal politeness*). Won't ye set?

EBEN (*dully*). Ay-eh. (*Mechanically he places his hat carefully on the floor near the door and sits stiffly beside her on the edge of the sofa. A pause. They both remain rigid, looking straight ahead with eyes full of fear.*)

ABBIE. When I fust come in—in the dark—they seemed somethin' here.

EBEN (*simply*). Maw.

ABBIE. I kin still feel—somethin'. . . .

EBEN. It's Maw.

ABBIE. At first I was feered o' it. I wanted t' yell an' run. Now—since yew come—seems like it's growin' soft an' kind t' me. (*Addressing the air—queerly.*) Thank yew.

EBEN. Maw allus loved me.

ABBIE. Mebbe it knows I love yew, too. Mebbe that makes it kind t' me.

EBEN (*dully*). I dunno. I should think she'd hate ye.

ABBIE (*with certainty*). No. I kin feel it don't—not no more.

EBEN. Hate ye fur stealin' her place —here in her hum—settin' in her parlor whar she was laid—(*He suddenly stops, staring stupidly before him.*)

ABBIE. What is it, Eben?

EBEN (*in a whisper*). Seems like Maw didn't want me t' remind ye.

ABBIE (*excitedly*). I knowed, Eben! It's kind t' me! It don't b'ar me no grudges fur what I never knowed an' couldn't help!

EBEN. Maw b'ars him a grudge.

ABBIE. Waal, so does all o' us.

EBEN. Ay-eh. (*With passion.*) I does, by God!

ABBIE (*taking one of his hands in hers and patting it*). Thar! Don't git riled thinkin' o' him. Think o' yer Maw who's kind t' us. Tell me about yer Maw, Eben.

EBEN. They hain't nothin' much. She was kind. She was good.

ABBIE (*putting one arm over his shoulder. He does not seem to notice—passionately*). I'll be kind an' good t' ye!

EBEN. Sometimes she used t' sing fur me.

ABBIE. I'll sing fur ye!

EBEN. This was her hum. This was her farm.

ABBIE. This is my hum! This is my farm!

EBEN. He married her t' steal 'em. She was soft an' easy. He couldn't 'preciate her.

ABBIE. He can't 'preciate me!

EBEN. He murdered her with his hardness.

ABBIE. He's murderin' me!

EBEN. She died. (*A pause.*) Sometimes she used to sing fur me. (*He bursts into a fit of sobbing.*)

ABBIE (*both her arms around him—with wild passion*). I'll sing fur ye! I'll die fur ye! (*In spite of her overwhelming desire for him, there is a sincere maternal love in her manner and voice—a horribly frank mixture of lust and mother love.*) Don't cry, Eben! I'll take yer Maw's place! I'll be everythin' she was t' ye! Let me kiss ye, Eben! (*She pulls his head around. He makes a bewildered pretense of resistance. She is tender.*) Don't be afeered! I'll kiss ye pure, Eben—same 's if I was a Maw t' ye—an' ye kin kiss me back 's if yew was my son—my boy—sayin' good-night t' me! Kiss me, Eben.

(*They kiss in restrained fashion. Then suddenly wild passion overcomes her. She kisses him lustfully again and again*

and he flings his arms about her and returns her kisses. Suddenly, as in the bedroom, he frees himself from her violently and springs to his feet. He is trembling all over, in a strange state of terror. ABBIE strains her arms toward him with fierce pleading.*) Don't ye leave me, Eben! Can't ye see it hain't enuf—lovin' ye like a Maw—can't ye see it's got t' be that an' more—much more—a hundred times more—fur me t' be happy—fur yew t' be happy?

EBEN (*to the presence he feels in the room*). Maw! Maw! What d'ye want? What air ye tellin' me?

ABBIE. She's tellin' ye t' love me. She knows I love ye an' I'll be good t' ye. Can't ye feel it? Don't ye know? She's tellin' ye t' love me, Eben!

EBEN. Ay-eh. I feel—mebbe she—but—I can't figger out—why—when ye've stole her place—here in her hum—in the parlor whar she was—

ABBIE (*fiercely*). She knows I love ye!

EBEN (*his face suddenly lighting up with a fierce, triumphant grin*). I see it! I sees why. It's her vengeance on him—so's she kin rest quiet in her grave!

ABBIE (*wildly*). Vengeance o' God on the hull o' us! What d'we give a durn? I love ye, Eben! God knows I love ye! (*She stretches out her arms for him.*)

EBEN (*throws himself on his knees beside the sofa and grabs her in his arms—releasing all his pent-up passion*). An' I love yew, Abbie!—now I kin say it! I been dyin' fur want o' ye—every hour since ye come! I love ye! (*Their lips meet in a fierce, bruising kiss.*)

SCENE 4

(*Exterior of the farmhouse. It is just dawn. The front door at right is opened and* EBEN *comes out and walks around to the gate. He is dressed in his working clothes. He seems changed. His face wears a bold and confident expression, he is grinning to himself with evident satisfaction. As he gets near the gate, the window of the parlor is heard opening and the shutters are flung back and* ABBIE *sticks her head out. Her hair tumbles over her shoulders in disarray, her face is flushed, she looks at* EBEN *with tender, languorous eyes and calls softly.*)

ABBIE. Eben. (*As he turns—playfully.*) Jest one more kiss afore ye go. I'm goin' t' miss ye fearful all day.

EBEN. An me yew, ye kin bet! (*He goes to her. They kiss several times. He draws away, laughingly.*) Thar. That's enuf, hain't it? Ye won't hev none left for next time.

ABBIE. I got a million o' 'em left fur yew! (*Then a bit anxiously.*) D'ye r'ally love me, Eben?

EBEN (*emphatically*). I like ye better'n any gal I ever knowed! That's gospel!

ABBIE. Likin' hain't lovin'.

EBEN. Waal then—I love ye. Now air yew satisfied?

ABBIE. Ay-eh, I be. (*She smiles at him adoringly.*)

EBEN. I better git t' the barn. The old critter's liable t' suspicion an' come sneakin' up.

ABBIE (*with a confident laugh*). Let him! I kin allus pull the wool over his eyes. I'm goin' t' leave the shutters open and let in the sun 'n' air. This room's been dead long enuf. Now it's goin' t' be my room!

EBEN (*frowning*). Ay-eh.

ABBIE (*hastily*). I meant—our room.

EBEN. Ay-eh.

ABBIE. We made it our'n last night, didn't we? We give it life—our lovin' did. (*A pause.*)

EBEN (*with a strange look*). Maw's gone back t' her grave. She kin sleep now.

ABBIE. May she rest in peace! (*Then*

tenderly rebuking.) Ye oughtn't t' talk o' sad thin's—this mornin'.

EBEN. It jest come up in my mind o' itself.

ABBIE. Don't let it. (*He doesn't answer. She yawns.*) Waal, I'm a-goin' t' steal a wink o' sleep. I'll tell the Old Man I hain't feelin' pert. Let him git his own vittles.

EBEN. I see him comin' from the barn. Ye better look smart an' git upstairs.

ABBIE. Ay-eh. Good-by. Don't ferget me. (*She throws him a kiss. He grins—then squares his shoulders and awaits his father confidently.* CABOT *walks slowly up from the left, staring up at the sky with a vague face.*)

EBEN (*jovially*). Mornin', Paw. Stargazin' in daylight?

CABOT. Purty, hain't it?

EBEN (*looking around him possessively*). It's a durned purty farm.

CABOT. I mean the sky.

EBEN (*grinning*). How d'ye know? Them eyes o' your'n can't see that fur. (*This tickles his humor and he slaps his thigh and laughs.*) Ho-ho! That's a good un!

CABOT (*grimly sarcastic*). Ye're feelin' right chipper, hain't ye? Whar'd ye steal the likker?

EBEN (*good-naturedly*). 'Tain't likker. Jest life. (*Suddenly holding out his hand—soberly.*) Yew 'n' me is quits. Let's shake hands.

CABOT (*suspiciously*). What's come over ye?

EBEN. Then don't. Mebbe it's jest as well. (*A moment's pause.*) What's come over me? (*Queerly.*) Didn't ye feel her passin'—goin' back t' her grave?

CABOT (*dully*). Who?

EBEN. Maw. She kin rest now an' sleep content. She's quits with ye.

CABOT (*confusedly*). I rested. I slept good—down with the cows. They know how t' sleep. They're teachin' me.

EBEN (*suddenly jovial again*). Good

fur the cows! Waal—ye better git t' work.

CABOT (*grimly amused*). Air yew bossin' me, ye calf?

EBEN (*beginning to laugh*). Ay-eh! I'm bossin' yew! Ha-ha-ha! See how ye like it! Ha-ha-ha! I'm the prize rooster o' this roost. Ha-ha-ha! (*He goes off toward the barn laughing.*)

CABOT (*looks after him with scornful pity*). Soft-headed. Like his Maw. Dead spit 'n' image. No hope in him! (*He spits with contemptuous disgust.*) A born fool! (*Then matter-of-factly.*) Waal—I'm gittin' peckish. (*He goes toward door.*)

(*The curtain falls.*)

Part III

SCENE 1

(*A night in late spring the following year. The kitchen and the two bedrooms upstairs are shown. The two bedrooms are dimly lighted by a tallow candle in each.* EBEN *is sitting on the side of the bed in his room, his chin propped on his fists, his face a study of the struggle he is making to understand his conflicting emotions. The noisy laughter and music from below where a kitchen dance is in progress annoy and distract him. He scowls at the floor.*)

(*In the next room a cradle stands beside the double bed.*)

(*In the kitchen all is festivity. The stove has been taken down to give more room to the dancers. The chairs, with wooden benches added, have been pushed back against the walls. On these are seated, squeezed in tight against one another, farmers and their wives and their young folks of both sexes from the neighboring farms. They are all chattering and laughing loudly. They evidently have some secret joke in common. There is no end of winking, of nudging, of meaning nods of the head toward* CABOT *who, in a state of extreme hilarious excitement increased by the amount he has drunk, is standing near the rear door where there is a small keg of whisky and serving drinks to all the men. In the left corner, front, dividing the attention with her husband,* ABBIE *is sitting in a rocking chair, a shawl wrapped about her shoulders. She is very pale, her face is thin and drawn, her eyes are fixed anxiously on the open door in rear as if waiting for someone.*)

(*The* MUSICIAN *is tuning up his fiddle, seated in the far right corner. He is a lanky young fellow with a long, weak face. His pale eyes blink incessantly and he grins about him slyly with a greedy malice.*)

ABBIE (*suddenly turning to a* YOUNG GIRL *on her right*). Whar's Eben?

YOUNG GIRL (*eyeing her scornfully*). I dunno, Mrs. Cabot. I hain't seen Eben in ages. (*Meaningly.*) Seems like he's spent most o' his time t' hum since yew come.

ABBIE (*vaguely*). I tuk his Maw's place.

YOUNG GIRL. Ay-eh. So I've heerd. (*She turns away to retail this bit of gossip to her mother sitting next to her.* ABBIE *turns to her left to a big stoutish middle-aged* MAN *whose flushed face and starting eyes show the amount of "likker" he has consumed.*)

ABBIE. Ye hain't seen Eben, hev ye?

MAN. No, I hain't. (*Then he adds with a wink.*) If yew hain't, who would?

ABBIE. He's the best dancer in the county. He'd ought t' come an' dance.

MAN (*with a wink*). Mebbe he's doin' the dutiful an' walkin' the kid t' sleep. It's a boy, hain't it?

ABBIE (*nodding vaguely*). Ay-eh— born two weeks back—purty's a picter.

MAN. They all is—t' their Maws. (*Then in a whisper, with a nudge and a leer.*) Listen, Abbie—if ye ever git tired o' Eben, remember me! Don't fergit now! (*He looks at her uncomprehending face for a second—then grunts disgustedly.*) Waal—guess I'll likker agin. (*He goes over and joins* CABOT *who is arguing noisily with an old farmer over cows. They all drink.*)

ABBIE (*this time appealing to nobody in particular*). Wonder what Eben's a-doin'? (*Her remark is repeated down the line with many a guffaw and titter until it reaches the* FIDDLER. *He fastens his blinking eyes on* ABBIE.)

FIDDLER (*raising his voice*). Bet I kin tell ye, Abbie, what Eben's doin'! He's down t' the church offerin' up prayers o' thanksgivin'. (*They all titter expectantly.*)

A MAN. What fur? (*Another titter.*)

FIDDLER. 'Cause unto him a—(*he hesitates just long enough*) brother is born! (*A roar of laughter. They all look from* ABBIE *to* CABOT. *She is oblivious, staring at the door.* CABOT, *although he hasn't heard the words, is irritated by the laughter and steps forward, glaring about him. There is an immediate silence.*)

CABOT. What're ye all bleatin' about —like a flock o' goats? Why don't ye dance, damn ye? I axed ye here t' dance —t' eat, drink an' be merry—an' thar ye set cacklin' like a lot o' wet hens with the pip! Ye've swilled my likker an' guzzled my vittles like hogs, hain't ye? Then dance fur me, can't ye? That's fa'r an' squar', hain't it? (*A grumble of resentment goes around but they are all evidently in too much awe of him to express it openly.*)

FIDDLER (*slyly*). We're waitin' fur Eben. (*A suppressed laugh.*)

CABOT (*with a fierce exultation*). T'hell with Eben! Eben's done fur now! I got a new son! (*His mood switching with drunken suddenness.*) But ye needn't t' laugh at Eben, none o' ye! He's my blood, if he be a dumb fool. He's better nor any o' yew! He kin do a day's work a'most up t' what I kin—an'

that'd put any o' yew pore critters t' shame!

FIDDLER. An' he kin do a good night's work, too! (*A roar of laughter.*)

CABOT. Laugh, ye damn fools! Ye're right jist the same, Fiddler. He kin work day an' night too, like I kin, if need be!

OLD FARMER (*from behind the keg where he is weaving drunkenly back and forth—with great simplicity*). They hain't many t' touch ye, Ephraim—a son at seventy-six. That's a hard man fur ye! I be on'y sixty-eight an' I couldn't do it. (*A roar of laughter in which* CABOT *joins uproariously.*)

CABOT (*slapping him on the back*). I'm sorry fur ye, Hi. I'd never suspicion sech weakness from a boy like yew!

OLD FARMER. An' I never reckoned yew had it in ye nuther, Ephraim. (*There is another laugh.*)

CABOT (*suddenly grim*). I got a lot in me—a hell of a lot—folks don't know on. (*Turning to the* FIDDLER.) Fiddle 'er up, durn ye! Give 'em somethin' t' dance t'! What air ye, an ornament? Hain't this a celebration? Then grease yer elbow an' go it!

FIDDLER (*seizes a drink which the* OLD FARMER *holds out to him and downs it*). Here goes! (*He starts to fiddle "Lady of the Lake." Four young fellows and four girls form in two lines and dance a square dance. The* FIDDLER *shouts directions for the different movements, keeping his words in the rhythm of the music and interspersing them with jocular personal remarks to the dancers themselves. The people seated along the walls stamp their feet and clap their hands in unison.* CABOT *is especially active in this respect. Only* ABBIE *remains apathetic, staring at the door as if she were alone in a silent room.*)

FIDDLER. Swing your partner t' the right! That's it, Jim! Give her a b'ar hug! Her Maw hain't lookin'. (*Laughter.*) Change partners! That suits ye, don't it, Essie, now ye got Reub afore ye? Look at her redden up, will ye? Waal, life is short an' so's love, as the feller says. (*Laughter.*)

CABOT (*excitedly, stamping his foot*). Go it, boys! Go it, gals!

FIDDLER (*with a wink at the others*). Ye're the spryest seventy-six ever I sees, Ephraim! Now if ye'd on'y good eyesight . . . ! (*Suppressed laughter. He gives* CABOT *no chance to retort but roars.*) Promenade! Ye're walkin' like a bride down the aisle, Sarah! Waal, while they's life they's allus hope, I've heerd tell. Swing your partner to the left! Gosh A'mighty, look at Johnny Cook highsteppin'! They hain't goin' t'be much strength left fur howin' in the corn lot t'morrow. (*Laughter.*)

CABOT. Go it! Go it! (*Then suddenly, unable to restrain himself any longer, he prances into the midst of the dancers, scattering them, waving his arms about wildly.*) Ye're all hoofs! Git out o' my road! Give me room! I'll show ye dancin'. Ye're all too soft! (*He pushes them roughly away. They crowd back toward the walls, muttering, looking at him resentfully.*)

FIDDLER (*jeeringly*). Go it, Ephraim! Go it! (*He starts "Pop, Goes the Weasel," increasing the tempo with every verse until at the end he is fiddling crazily as fast as he can go.*)

CABOT (*starts to dance, which he does very well and with tremendous vigor. Then he begins to improvise, cuts incredibly grotesque capers, leaping up and cracking his heels together, prancing around in a circle with body bent in an Indian war dance, then suddenly straightening up and kicking as high as he can with both legs. He is like a monkey on a string. And all the while he intersperses his antics with shouts and derisive comments*). Whoop! Here's dancin' fur ye! Whoop! See that! Seventy-six, if I'm a day! Hard as iron yet! Beatin' the young 'uns like I allus done! Look at me! I'd invite ye t' dance on my hundredth birth-day on'y ye'll all be dead by then. Ye're a sickly generation! Yer hearts air pink, not red! Yer veins is full o' mud an' water! I be the on'y man in the county! Whoop! See that! I'm a Injun! I've killed Injuns in the West afore ye was born—an' skulped 'em too! They's a arrer wound on my backside I c'd show ye! The hull tribe chased me. I outrun 'em all—with the arrer stuck in me! An' I tuk vengeance on 'em. Ten eyes fur an eye, that was my motter! Whoop! Look at me! I kin kick the ceilin' off the room! Whoop!

FIDDLER (*stops playing—exhaustedly*). God A'mighty, I got enuf. Ye got the devil's strength in ye.

CABOT (*delightedly*). Did I beat yew, too? Waal, ye played smart. Hev a swig. (*He pours whisky for himself and* FIDDLER. *They drink. The others watch* CABOT *silently with cold, hostile eyes. There is a dead pause. The* FIDDLER *rests.* CABOT *leans against the keg, panting, glaring around him confusedly. In the room above,* EBEN *gets to his feet and tiptoes out the door in rear, appearing a moment later in the other bedroom. He moves silently, even frightenedly, toward the cradle and stands there looking down at the baby. His face is as vague as his reactions are confused, but there is a trace of tenderness, of interested discovery. At the same moment that he reaches the cradle,* ABBIE *seems to sense something. She gets up weakly and goes to* CABOT.)

ABBIE. I'm goin' up t' the baby.

CABOT (*with real solicitude*). Air ye able fur the stairs? D'ye want me t' help ye, Abbie?

ABBIE. No. I'm able. I'll be down agen soon.

CABOT. Don't ye git wore out! He needs ye, remember—our son does! (*He grins affectionately, patting her on the back. She shrinks from his touch.*)

ABBIE (*dully*). Don't tech me. I'm goin'—up. (*She goes.* CABOT *looks after* her. *A whisper goes around the room.* CABOT *turns. It ceases. He wipes his forehead streaming with sweat. He is breathing pantingly.*)

CABOT. I'm a-goin' out t' git fresh air. I'm feelin' a mite dizzy. Fiddle up thar! Dance, all o' ye! Here's likker fur them as wants it. Enjoy yerselves. I'll be back. (*He goes, closing the door behind him.*)

FIDDLER (*sarcastically*). Don't hurry none on our account! (*A suppressed laugh. He imitates* ABBIE.) Whar's Eben? (*More laughter.*)

A WOMAN (*loudly*). What's happened in this house is plain as the nose on yer face! (ABBIE *appears in the doorway upstairs and stands looking in surprise and adoration at* EBEN *who does not see her.*)

A MAN. Ssshh! He's li'ble t' be listenin' at the door. That'd be like him. (*Their voices die to an intensive whispering. Their faces are concentrated on this gossip. A noise as of dead leaves in the wind comes from the room.* CABOT *has come out from the porch and stands by the gate, leaning on it, staring at the sky blinkingly.* ABBIE *comes across the room silently.* EBEN *does not notice her until quite near.*)

EBEN (*starting*). Abbie!

ABBIE. Ssshh! (*She throws her arms around him. They kiss—then bend over the cradle together.*) Ain't he purty?— dead spit 'n' image o' yew!

EBEN (*pleased*). Air he? I can't tell none.

ABBIE. E-zactly like!

EBEN (*frowningly*). I don't like this. I don't like lettin' on what's mine's his'n. I been doin' that all my life. I'm gittin' t' the end o' b'arin' it!

ABBIE (*putting her finger on his lips*). We're doin' the best we kin. We got t' wait. Somethin's bound t' happen. (*She puts her arms around him.*) I got t' go back.

EBEN. I'm goin' out. I can't b'ar it

with the fiddle playin' an' the laughin'.

ABBIE. Don't git feelin' low. I love ye, Eben. Kiss me. (*He kisses her. They remain in each other's arms.*)

CABOT (*at the gate, confusedly*). Even the music can't drive it out—somethin'. Ye kin feel it droppin' off the elums, climbin' up the roof, sneakin' down the chimney, pokin' in the corners! They's no peace in houses, they's no rest livin' with folks. Somethin's always livin' with ye. (*With a deep sigh.*) I'll go t' the barn an' rest a spell. (*He goes wearily toward the barn.*)

FIDDLER (*tuning up*). Let's celebrate the old skunk gittin' fooled! We kin have some fun now he's went. (*He starts to fiddle "Turkey in the Straw." There is real merriment now. The young folks get up to dance.*)

SCENE 2

(*A half hour later—Exterior—*EBEN *is standing by the gate looking up at the sky, an expression of dumb pain bewildered by itself on his face.* CABOT *appears, returning from the barn, walking wearily, his eyes on the ground. He sees* EBEN *and his whole mood immediately changes. He becomes excited, a cruel, triumphant grin comes to his lips, he strides up and slaps* EBEN *on the back. From within comes the whining of the fiddle and the noise of stamping feet and laughing voices.*)

CABOT. So har ye be!

EBEN (*startled, stares at him with hatred for a moment—then dully*). Ay-eh.

CABOT (*surveying him jeeringly*). Why hain't ye been in t' dance? They was all axin' fur ye.

EBEN. Let 'em ax!

CABOT. They's a hull passel o' purty gals.

EBEN. T' hell with 'em!

CABOT. Ye'd ought t' be marryin' one o' 'em soon.

EBEN.   I hain't marryin' no one.

CABOT.   Ye might 'arn a share o' a farm that way.

EBEN (*with a sneer*).   Like yew did, ye mean? I hain't that kind.

CABOT (*stung*).   Ye lie! 'Twas yer Maw's folks aimed t' steal my farm from me.

EBEN.   Other folks don't say so. (*After a pause—defiantly.*) An' I got a farm, anyways!

CABOT (*derisively*).   Whar?

EBEN (*stamps a foot on the ground*). Har!

CABOT (*throws his head back and laughs coarsely*).   Ho-ho! Ye hev, hev ye? Waal, that's a good un!

EBEN (*controlling himself—grimly*). Ye'll see!

CABOT (*stares at him suspiciously, trying to make him out—a pause—then with scornful confidence*).   Ay-eh. I'll see. So'll ye. It's ye that's blind—blind as a mole underground. (EBEN *suddenly laughs, one short sardonic bark: "Ha." A pause.* CABOT *peers at him with renewed suspicion.*) What air ye hawin' 'bout? (EBEN *turns away without answering.* CABOT *grows angry.*) God A'mighty, yew air a dumb dunce! They's nothin' in that thick skull o' your'n but noise—like a empty keg it be! (EBEN *doesn't seem to hear.* CABOT'S *rage grows.*) Yewr farm! God A'mighty! If ye wa'n't a born donkey ye'd know ye'll never own stick nor stone on it, specially now arter him bein' born. It's his'n, I tell ye—his'n arter I die—but I'll live a hundred jest t' fool ye all—an' he'll be growed then—yewr age a'most! (EBEN *laughs again his sardonic "Ha." This drives* CABOT *into a fury.*) Ha? Ye think ye kin git 'round that someways, do ye? Waal, it'll be her'n, too—Abbie's—ye won't git 'round her—she knows yer tricks—she'll be too much fur ye—she wants the farm her'n—she was afeerd o' ye—she told me ye was sneakin' 'round tryin' t' make love t' her t' git

her on yer side . . . ye . . . ye mad fool, ye! (*He raises his clenched fists threateningly.*)

EBEN (*is confronting him, choking with rage*).   Ye lie, ye old skunk! Abbie never said no sech thing!

CABOT (*suddenly triumphant when he sees how shaken* EBEN *is*).   She did. An' I says, I'll blow his brains t' the top o' them elums—an' she says no, that hain't sense, who'll ye git t'help ye on the farm in his place—an' then she says yew'n me ought t' have a son—I know we kin, she says—an' I says, if we do, ye kin have anythin' I've got ye've a mind t'. An' she says, I wants Eben cut off so's this farm'll be mine when ye die! (*With terrible gloating.*) An' that's what's happened, hain't it? An' the farm's her'n! An' the dust o' the road— that's your'n! Ha! Now who's hawin'?

EBEN (*has been listening, petrified with grief and rage—suddenly laughs wildly and brokenly*).   Ha-ha-ha! So that's her sneakin' game—all along!— like I suspicioned at fust—t' swaller it all—an' me, too. . . ! (*Madly.*) I'll murder her! (*He springs toward the porch but* CABOT *is quicker and gets in between.*)

CABOT.   No, ye don't!

EBEN.   Git out o' my road! (*He tries to throw* CABOT *aside. They grapple in what becomes immediately a murderous struggle. The old man's concentrated strength is too much for* EBEN. CABOT *gets one hand on his throat and presses him back across the stone wall. At the same moment,* ABBIE *comes out on the porch. With a stifled cry she runs toward them.*)

ABBIE.   Eben! Ephraim! (*She tugs at the hand on* EBEN'S *throat.*) Let go, Ephraim! Ye're chokin' him!

CABOT (*removes his hand and flings* EBEN *sideways full length on the grass, gasping and choking. With a cry,* ABBIE *kneels beside him, trying to take his head on her lap, but he pushes her away.*

CABOT *stands looking down with fierce triumph*). Ye needn't t've fret, Abbie, I wa'n't aimin' t' kill him. He hain't wuth hangin' fur—not by a hell of a sight! (*More and more triumphantly.*) Seventy-six an' him not thirty yit—an' look what he be fur thinkin' his Paw was easy! No, by God, I hain't easy! An' him upstairs, I'll raise him t' be like me! (*He turns to leave them.*) I'm goin' in an' dance!—sing an' celebrate! (*He walks to the porch—then turns with a great grin.*) I don't calc'late it's left in him, but if he gits pesky, Abbie, ye jest sing out. I'll come a-runnin' an' by the Etarnal, I'll put him across my knee an' birch him! Ha-ha-ha! (*He goes into the house laughing. A moment later his loud "whoop" is heard.*)

ABBIE (*tenderly*). Eben. Air ye hurt? (*She tries to kiss him but he pushes her violently away and struggles to a sitting position.*)

EBEN (*gaspingly*). T'hell—with ye!

ABBIE (*not believing her ears*). It's me, Eben—Abbie—don't ye know me?

EBEN (*glowering at her with hatred*). Ay-eh—I know ye—now! (*He suddenly breaks down, sobbing weakly.*)

ABBIE (*fearfully*). Eben—what's happened t' ye—why did ye look at me 's if ye hated me?

EBEN (*violently, between sobs and gasps*). I do hate ye! Ye're a whore—a damn trickin' whore!

ABBIE (*shrinking back horrified*). Eben! Ye don't know what ye're sayin'!

EBEN (*scrambling to his feet and following her—accusingly*). Ye're nothin' but a stinkin' passel o' lies! Ye've been lyin' t' me every word ye spoke, day an' night, since we fust—done it. Ye've kept sayin' ye loved me. . . .

ABBIE (*frantically*). I do love ye! (*She takes his hand but he flings hers away.*)

EBEN (*unheeding*). Ye've made a fool o' me—a sick, dumb fool—a-purpose! Ye've been on'y playin' yer sneakin', stealin' game all along—gittin' me t' lie with ye so's ye'd hev a son he'd think was his'n, an' makin' him promise he'd give ye the farm and let me eat dust, if ye did git him a son! (*Staring at her with anguished, bewildered eyes.*) They must be a devil livin' in ye! T'ain't human t' be as bad as that be!

ABBIE (*stunned—dully*). He told yew. . . ?

EBEN. Hain't it true? It hain't no good in yew lyin'.

ABBIE (*pleadingly*). Eben, listen—ye must listen—it was long ago—afore we done nothin'—yew was scornin' me —goin' t' see Min—when I was lovin' ye—an' I said it t' him t' git vengeance on ye!

EBEN (*unheedingly. With tortured passion*). I wish ye was dead! I wish I was dead along with ye afore this come! (*Ragingly.*) But I'll git my vengeance too! I'll pray Maw t' come back t' help me—t' put her cuss on yew an' him!

ABBIE (*brokenly*). Don't ye, Eben! Don't ye! (*She throws herself on her knees before him, weeping.*) I didn't mean t' do bad t'ye! Fergive me, won't ye?

EBEN (*not seeming to hear her—fiercely*). I'll git squar' with the old skunk—an' yew! I'll tell him the truth 'bout the son he's so proud o'! Then I'll leave ye here t' pizen each other—with Maw comin' out o' her grave at nights—an' I'll go t' the gold fields o' Californi-a where Sim an' Peter be!

ABBIE (*terrified*). Ye won't—leave me? Ye can't!

EBEN (*with fierce determination*). I'm a goin', I tell ye! I'll git rich thar an' come back an fight him fur the farm he stole—an' I'll kick ye both out in the road—t' beg an' sleep in the woods —an' yer son along with ye—t' starve an' die! (*He is hysterical at the end.*)

ABBIE (*with a shudder—humbly*). He's yewr son, too, Eben.

EBEN (*torturedly*). I wish he never

was born! I wish he'd die this minit! I
wish I'd never sot eyes on him! It's him
—yew havin' him—a-purpose t' steal—
that's changed everythin'!

ABBIE (*gently*). Did ye believe I
loved ye—afore he come?

EBEN. Ay-eh—like a dumb ox!

ABBIE. An' ye don't believe no more?

EBEN. B'lieve a lyin' thief! Ha!

ABBIE (*shudders—then humbly*). An'
did ye r'ally love me afore?

EBEN (*brokenly*). Ay-eh—an' ye was
trickin' me!

ABBIE. An' ye don't love me now!

EBEN (*violently*). I hate ye, I tell ye!

ABBIE. An' ye're truly goin' West—
goin' t' leave me—all account o' him
being born?

EBEN. I'm a-goin' in the mornin'—
or may God strike me t' hell!

ABBIE (*after a pause—with a dreadful
cold intensity—slowly*). If that's what
his comin' done t' me—killin' yewr love
—takin' yew away—my on'y joy—the
only joy I ever knowed—like heaven t'
me—purtier'n heaven—then I hate him,
too, even if I be his Maw!

EBEN (*bitterly*). Lies! Ye love him!
He'll steal the farm fur ye! (*Brokenly.*)
But t'ain't the farm so much—not no
more—it's yew foolin' me—gettin' me t'
love ye—lyin' yew loved me—jest t' git
a son t' steal!

ABBIE (*distractedly*). He won't steal!
I'd kill him fust! I do love ye! I'll prove
t' ye. . . !

EBEN (*harshly*). T'ain't no use lyin'
no more. I'm deaf t' ye! (*He turns
away.*) I hain't seein' ye agen. Good-by!

ABBIE (*pale with anguish*). Hain't ye
even goin' t' kiss me—not once—arter
all we loved?

EBEN (*in a hard voice*). I hain't
wantin' t' kiss ye never agen! I'm wantin'
t' forgit I ever sot eyes on ye!

ABBIE. Eben!—ye mustn't—wait a
spell—I want t' tell ye. . . .

EBEN. I'm a-goin' in t' git drunk.
I'm a-goin' t' dance.

ABBIE (*clinging to his arm—with passionate earnestness*). If I could make
it—'s if he'd never come up between us
—if I could prove t' ye I wa'n't schemin'
t' steal from ye—so's everythin' could
be jest the same with us, lovin' each
other jest the same, kissin' an' happy the
same's we've been happy afore he come
—if I could do it—ye'd love me agen,
wouldn't ye? Ye'd kiss me agen? Ye
wouldn't never leave me, would ye?

EBEN (*moved*). I calc'late not.
(*Then shaking her hand off his arm—
with a bitter smile.*) But ye hain't God,
be ye?

ABBIE (*exultantly*). Remember ye've
promised! (*Then with strange intensity.*)
Mebbe I kin take back one thin' God
does!

EBEN (*peering at her*). Ye're gittin
cracked, hain't ye? (*Then going towards
door.*) I'm a-goin' t' dance.

ABBIE (*calls after him intensely*). I'll
prove t' ye! I'll prove I love ye better'n.
. . . (*He goes in the door, not seeming
to hear. She remains standing where she
is, looking after him—then she finishes
desperately.*) Bettern' everythin' else in
the world!

SCENE 3

(*Just before dawn in the morning—
shows the kitchen and* CABOT'S *bedroom.
In the kitchen, by the light of a tallow
candle on the table,* EBEN *is sitting, his
chin propped on his hands, his drawn
face blank and expressionless. His carpet-
bag is on the floor beside him. In the
bedroom, dimly lighted by a small whale-
oil lamp,* CABOT *lies asleep.* ABBIE *is
bending over the cradle, listening, her
face full of terror yet with an undercur-
rent of desperate triumph. Suddenly, she
breaks down and sobs, appears about to
throw herself on her knees beside the
cradle; but the old man turns restlessly,
groaning in his sleep, and she controls
herself, and, shrinking away from the*

cradle with a gesture of horror, backs swiftly toward the door in rear and goes out. A moment later she comes into the kitchen and, running to EBEN, *flings her arms about his neck and kisses him wildly. He hardens himself, he remains unmoved and cold, he keeps his eyes straight ahead.*)

ABBIE (*hysterically*). I done it, Eben! I told ye I'd do it! I've proved I love ye—better'n everythin'—so's ye can't never doubt me no more!

EBEN (*dully*). Whatever ye done, it hain't no good now.

ABBIE (*wildly*). Don't ye say that! Kiss me, Eben, won't ye? I need ye t' kiss me arter what I done! I need ye t' say ye love me!

EBEN (*kisses her without emotion—dully*). That's fur good-by. I'm a-goin' soon.

ABBIE. No! No! Ye won't go—not now!

EBEN (*going on with his own thoughts*). I been a-thinkin'—an' I hain't goin' t' tell Paw nothin'. I'll leave Maw t' take vengeance on ye. If I told him, the old skunk'd jest be stinkin' mean enuf to take it out on that baby. (*His voice showing emotion in spite of him.*) An' I don't want nothin' bad t' happen t' him. He hain't t' blame fur yew. (*He adds with a certain queer pride.*) An' he looks like me! An' by God, he's mine! An' some day I'll be a-comin' back an' . . . !

ABBIE (*too absorbed in her own thoughts to listen to him—pleadingly*). They's no cause fur ye t' go now—they's no sense—it's all the same's it was—they's nothin' come b'tween us now—arter what I done!

EBEN (*something in her voice arouses him. He stares at her a bit frightenedly*). Ye look mad, Abbie. What did ye do?

ABBIE. I—I killed him, Eben.

EBEN (*amazed*). Ye killed him?

ABBIE (*dully*). Ay-eh.

EBEN (*recovering from his astonishment—savagely*). An' serves him right! But we got t' do somethin' quick t' make it look s'if the old skunk'd killed himself when he was drunk. We kin prove by 'em all how drunk he got.

ABBIE (*wildly*). No! No! Not him! (*Laughing distractedly.*) But that's what I ought t' done, hain't it? I oughter killed him instead! Why didn't ye tell me?

EBEN (*appalled*). Instead? What d'ye mean?

ABBIE. Not him.

EBEN (*his face grown ghastly*). Not —not that baby!

ABBIE (*dully*). Ay-eh!

EBEN (*falls to his knees as if he'd been struck—his voice trembling with horror*). Oh God A'mighty! A'mighty God! Maw, whar was ye, why didn't ye stop her?

ABBIE (*simply*). She went back t' her grave that night we fust done it, remember? I hain't felt her about since. (*A pause.* EBEN *hides his head in his hands, trembling all over as if he had the ague. She goes on dully.*) I left the piller over his little face. Then he killed himself. He stopped breathin'. (*She begins to weep softly.*)

EBEN (*rage beginning to mingle with grief*). He looked like me. He was mine, damn ye!

ABBIE (*slowly and brokenly*). I didn't want t' do it. I hated myself fur doin' it. I loved him. He was so purty—dead spit 'n' image o' yew. But I loved yew more—an' yew was goin' away—far off whar I'd never see ye agen, never kiss ye, never feel ye pressed agin me agen—an' ye said ye hated me fur havin' him—ye said ye hated him an' wished he was dead—ye said if it hadn't been fur him comin' it'd be the same's afore between us.

EBEN (*unable to endure this, springs to his feet in a fury, threatening her, his twitching fingers seeming to reach out for her throat*). Ye lie! I never said—I never dreamed ye'd—I'd cut off my 'head afore I'd hurt his finger!

ABBIE (*piteously, sinking on her knees*). Eben, don't ye look at me like that—hatin' me—not after what I done fur ye—fur us—so's we could be happy agen—

EBEN (*furiously now*). Shut up, or I'll kill ye! I see yer game now—the same old sneakin' trick—ye're aimin' t' blame me fur the murder ye done!

ABBIE (*moaning—putting her hands over her ears*). Don't ye, Eben! Don't ye! (*She grasps his legs.*)

EBEN (*his mood suddenly changing to horror, shrinks away from her*). Don't ye tech me! Ye're pizen! How could ye—t' murder a pore little critter— Ye must've swapped yer soul t' hell! (*Suddenly raging.*) Ha! I kin see why ye done it! Not the lies ye jest told—but 'cause ye wanted t' steal agen—steal the last thin' ye'd left me—my part o' him—no, the hull o' him—ye saw he looked like me—ye knowed he was all mine—an' ye couldn't b'ar it—I know ye! Ye killed him fur bein' mine! (*All this has driven him almost insane. He makes a rush past her for the door—then turns—shaking both fists at her, violently.*) But I'll take vengeance now! I'll git the Sheriff! I'll tell him everythin'! Then I'll sing "I'm off to Californi-a!" an' go—gold— Golden Gate—gold sun—fields o' gold in the West! (*This last he half shouts, half croons incoherently, suddenly breaking off passionately.*) I'm a'goin' fur the Sheriff t' come an' git ye! I want ye tuk away, locked up from me! I can't stand t' luk at ye! Murderer an' thief 'r not, ye still tempt me! I'll give ye up t' the Sheriff! (*He turns and runs out, around the corner of house, panting and sobbing, and breaks into a swerving sprint down the road.*)

ABBIE (*struggling to her feet, runs to the door, calling after him*). I love ye, Eben! I love ye! (*She stops at the door*

weakly, swaying, about to fall.) I don't care what ye do—if ye'll on'y love me agen— (*She falls limply to the floor in a faint.*)

SCENE 4

(*About an hour later. Same as Scene 3. Shows the kitchen and* CABOT'S *bedroom. It is after dawn. The sky is brilliant with the sunrise. In the kitchen,* ABBIE *sits at the table, her body limp and exhausted, her head bowed down over her arms, her face hidden. Upstairs,* CABOT *is still asleep but awakens with a start. He looks toward the window and gives a snort of surprise and irritation— throws back the covers and begins hurriedly pulling on his clothes. Without looking behind him, he begins talking to* ABBIE *whom he supposes beside him.*)

CABOT. Thunder 'n' lightin', Abbie! I hain't slept this late in fifty year! Looks 's if the sun was full riz a'most. Must've been the dancin' an' likker. Must be gittin' old. I hope Eben's t' wuk. Ye might've tuk the trouble t' rouse me, Abbie. (*He turns—sees no one there— surprised.*) Waal—whar air she? Gittin' vittles, I calc'late. (*He tiptoes to the cradle and peers down—proudly.*) Mornin', sonny. Purty's a picter! Sleepin' sound. He don't beller all night like most o' 'em. (*He goes quietly out the door in rear—a few moments later enters kitchen —sees* ABBIE—*with satisfaction.*) So thar ye be. Ye got any vittles cooked?

ABBIE (*without moving*). No.

CABOT (*coming to her, almost sympathetically*). Ye feelin' sick?

ABBIE. No.

CABOT (*pats her on shoulder. She shudders*). Ye'd best lie down a spell. (*Half jocularly.*) Yer son'll be needin' ye soon. He'd ought t' wake up with a gnashin' appetite, the sound way he's sleepin'.

ABBIE (*shudders—then in a dead voice*). He hain't never goin' t' wake up.

CABOT (*jokingly*). Takes after me this mornin'. I hain't slept so late in. . . .

ABBIE. He's dead.

CABOT (*stares at her—bewilderedly*). What. . . .

ABBIE. I killed him.

CABOT (*stepping back from her—aghast*). Air ye drunk—'r crazy—'r. . . !

ABBIE (*suddenly lifts her head and turns on him—wildly*). I killed him, I tell ye! I smothered him. Go up an' see if ye don't b'lieve me! (CABOT *stares at her a second, then bolts out the rear door, can be heard bounding up the stairs, and rushes into the bedroom and over to the cradle.* ABBIE *has sunk back lifelessly into her former position.* CABOT *puts his hand down on the body in the crib. An expression of fear and horror comes over his face.*)

CABOT (*shrinking away—tremblingly*). God A'mighty! God A'mighty. (*He stumbles out the door—in a short while returns to the kitchen—comes to* ABBIE, *the stunned expression still on his face—hoarsely.*) Why did ye do it? Why? (*As she doesn't answer, he grabs her violently by the shoulder and shakes her.*) I ax ye why ye done it! Ye'd better tell me 'r . . . !

ABBIE (*gives him a furious push which sends him staggering back and springs to her feet—with wild rage and hatred*). Don't ye dare tech me! What right hev ye t' question me 'bout him? He wa'n't yewr son! Think I'd have a son by yew? I'd die fust! I hate the sight o' ye an' allus did! It's yew I should've murdered, if I'd had good sense! I hate ye! I love Eben. I did from the fust. An' he was Eben's son—mine an' Eben's—not your'n!

CABOT (*stands looking at her dazedly—a pause—finding his words with an effort—dully*). That was it—what I felt—pokin' round the corners—while ye lied—holdin' yerself from me—sayin' ye'd a'ready conceived—. (*He lapses into crushed silence—then with a strange emotion.*) He's dead, sart'n. I felt his heart. Pore little critter! (*He blinks back one tear, wiping his sleeve across his nose.*)

ABBIE (*hysterically*). Don't ye! Don't ye! (*She sobs unrestrainedly.*)

CABOT (*with a concentrated effort that stiffens his body into a rigid line and hardens his face into a stony mask—through his teeth to himself*). I got t' be—like a stone—a rock o' jedgment! (*A pause. He gets complete control over himself—harshly.*) If he was Eben's, I be glad he air gone! An' mebbe I suspicioned it all along. I felt they was somethin' onnateral—somewhars—the house got so lonesome—an' cold—drivin' me down t' the barn—t' the beasts o' the field. . . . Ay-eh. I must've suspicioned somethin'. Ye didn't fool me—not altogether, leastways—I'm too old a bird—growin' ripe on the bough. . . . (*He becomes aware he is wandering, straightens again, looks at* ABBIE *with a cruel grin.*) So ye'd liked t' hev murdered me 'stead o' him, would ye? Waal, I'll live to a hundred! I'll live t' see ye hung! I'll deliver ye up t' the jedgment o' God an' the law! I'll git the Sheriff now. (*Starts for the door.*)

ABBIE (*dully*). Ye needn't. Eben's gone fur him.

CABOT (*amazed*). Eben—gone fur the Sheriff?

ABBIE. Ay-eh.

CABOT. T' inform agen ye?

ABBIE. Ay-eh.

CABOT (*considers this—a pause—then in a hard voice*). Waal, I'm thankful fur him savin' me the trouble. I'll git t' wuk. (*He goes to the door—then turns—in a voice full of strange emotion.*) He'd ought t' been my son, Abbie. Ye'd ought t' loved me. I'm a man. If ye'd loved me, I'd never told no Sheriff on ye no matter what ye did, if they was t' brile me alive!

ABBIE (*defensively*). They's more to it nor yew know, makes him tell.

CABOT (*dryly*). Fur yewr sake, I hope they be. (*He goes out—comes around to the gate—stares up at the sky. His control relaxes. For a moment he is old and weary. He murmurs despairingly.*) God A'mighty, I be lonesomer'n ever! (*He hears running footsteps from the left, immediately is himself again. EBEN runs in, panting exhaustedly, wild-eyed and mad looking. He lurches through the gate. CABOT grabs him by the shoulder. EBEN stares at him dumbly.*) Did ye tell the Sheriff?

EBEN (*nodding stupidly*). Ay-eh.

CABOT (*gives him a push away that sends him sprawling—laughing with withering contempt*). Good fur ye! A prime chip o' yer Maw ye be! (*He goes toward the barn, laughing harshly. EBEN scrambles to his feet. Suddenly CABOT turns—grimly threatening.*) Git off this farm when the Sheriff takes her—or, by God, he'll have t' come back an' git me fur murder, too! (*He stalks off. EBEN does not appear to have heard him. He runs to the door and comes into the kitchen. ABBIE looks up with a cry of anguished joy. EBEN stumbles over and throws himself on his knees beside her—sobbing brokenly.*)

EBEN. Fergive me!

ABBIE (*happily*). Eben! (*She kisses him and pulls his head over against her breast.*)

EBEN. I love ye! Fergive me!

ABBIE (*ecstatically*). I'd fergive ye all the sins in hell fur sayin' that! (*She kisses his head, pressing it to her with a fierce passion of possession.*)

EBEN (*brokenly*). But I told the Sheriff. He's comin' fur ye!

ABBIE. I kin b'ar what happens t' me—now!

EBEN. I woke him up. I told him. He says, wait 'till I git dressed. I was waiting. I got to thinkin' o' yew. I got to thinkin' how I'd loved ye. It hurt like somethin' was bustin' in my chest an' head. I got t' cryin'. I knowed sudden I loved ye yet, an' allus would love ye!

ABBIE (*caressing his hair—tenderly*). My boy, hain't ye?

EBEN. I begun t' run back. I cut across the fields an' through the woods. I thought ye might have time t' run away—with me—an'. . . .

ABBIE (*shaking her head*). I got t' take my punishment—t' pay fur my sin.

EBEN. Then I want t' share it with ye.

ABBIE. Ye didn't do nothin'.

EBEN. I put it in yer head. I wisht he was dead! I as much as urged ye t' do it!

ABBIE. No. It was me alone!

EBEN. I'm as guilty as yew be! He was the child o' our sin.

ABBIE (*lifting her head as if defying God*). I don't repent that sin! I hain't askin' God t' fergive that!

EBEN. Nor me—but it led up t' the other—an' the murder ye did, ye did 'count o' me—an' it's my murder, too, I'll tell the Sheriff—an' if ye deny it, I'll say we planned it t'gether—an' they'll all b'lieve me, fur they suspicion everythin' we've done, an' it'll seem likely an' true to 'em. An' it is true—way down. I did help ye—somehow.

ABBIE (*laying her head on his—sobbing*). No! I don't want yew t' suffer!

EBEN. I got t' pay fur my part o' the sin! An' I'd suffer wuss leavin' ye, goin' West, thinkin' o' ye day an' night, bein' out when yew was in— (*Lowering his voice.*) 'r bein' alive when yew was dead. (*A pause.*) I want t' share with ye, Abbie—prison 'r death 'r hell 'r anythin'! (*He looks into her eyes and forces a trembling smile.*) If I'm sharin' with ye, I won't feel lonesome, leastways.

ABBIE (*weakly*). Eben! I won't let ye! I can't let ye!

EBEN (*kissing her—tenderly*). Ye can't he'p yerself. I got ye beat fur once!

ABBIE (*forcing a smile—adoringly*). I hain't beat—s'long's I got ye!

EBEN (*hears the sound of feet outside*). Ssshh! Listen! They've come t' take us!

ABBIE. No, it's him. Don't give him no chance to fight ye, Eben. Don't say nothin'—no matter what he says. An' I won't, neither. (*It is* CABOT. *He comes up from the barn in a great state of excitement and strides into the house and then into the kitchen.* EBEN *is kneeling beside* ABBIE, *his arm around her, hers around him. They stare straight ahead.*)

CABOT (*stares at them, his face hard. A long pause—vindictively*). Ye make a slick pair o' murderin' turtle doves! Ye'd ought t' be both hung on the same limb an' left thar t' swing in the breeze an' rot—a warnin' t' old fools like me t' b'ar their lonesomeness alone—an fur young fools like ye t' hobble their lust. (*A pause. The excitement returns to his face, his eyes snap, he looks a bit crazy.*) I couldn't work today. I couldn't take no interest. T' hell with the farm! I'm leavin' it! I've turned the cows an' other stock loose! I've druv 'em into the woods whar they kin be free! By freein' 'em, I'm freein' myself! I'm quittin' here today! I'll set fire t' house an' barn an' watch 'em burn, an' I'll leave yer Maw t' haunt the ashes, an' I'll will the fields back t' God, so that nothin' human kin never touch 'em! I'll be a-goin' to Californi'a—t' jine Simeon an' Peter—true sons o' mine if they be dumb fools—an' the Cabots'll find Solomon's Mines t'gether! (*He suddenly cuts a mad caper.*) Whoop! What was the song they sung? "Oh, Californi-a! That's the land fur me." (*He sings this—then gets on his knees by the floorboard under which the money was hid.*) An' I'll sail thar on one o' the finest clippers I kin find! I've

got the money! Pity ye didn't know whar this was hidden so's ye could steal. . . . (*He has pulled up the board. He stares—feels—stares again. A pause of dead silence. He slowly turns, slumping into a sitting position on the floor, his eyes like those of a dead fish, his face the sickly green of an attack of nausea. He swallows painfully several times—forces a weak smile at last.*) So—ye did steal it!

EBEN (*emotionlessly*). I swapped it t' Sim an' Peter fur their share o' the farm—t' pay their passage t' Californi-a.

CABOT (*with one sardonic "Ha!" He begins to recover. Gets slowly to his feet—strangely.*) I calc'late God give it to 'em—not yew! God's hand, not easy! Mebbe they's easy gold in the West but it hain't God's gold. It hain't fur me. I kin hear His voice warnin' me agen t' be hard an' stay on my farm. I kin see his hand usin' Eben t' steal t' keep me from weakness. I kin feel I be in the palm o' His hand, His fingers guidin' me. (*A pause—then he mutters sadly.*) It's a'goin' t' be lonesomer now than ever it war afore—an' I'm gittin' old, Lord—ripe on the bough. . . . (*Then stiffening.*) Waal—what d'ye want? God's lonesome, hain't He? God's hard an' lonesome! (*A pause.* THE SHERIFF *with two men comes up the road from the left. They move cautiously to the door.* THE SHERIFF *knocks on it with the butt of his pistol.*)

SHERIFF. Open in the name o' the law! (*They start.*)

CABOT. They've come fur ye. (*He goes to the rear door.*) Come in, Jim! (*The three men enter.* CABOT *meets them in doorway.*) Jest a minit, Jim. I got 'em safe here. (THE SHERIFF *nods. He and his companions remain in the doorway.*)

EBEN (*suddenly calls*). I lied this mornin', Jim. I helped her do it. Ye kin take me, too.

ABBIE (*brokenly*). No!

CABOT. Take 'em both. (*He comes*

forward—stares at EBEN *with a trace of grudging admiration.*) Purty good—fur yew! Waal, I got t' round up the stock. Good-by.

EBEN. Good-by.

ABBIE. Good-by. (CABOT *turns and strides past the men—comes out and around the corner of the house, his shoulders squared, his face stony, and stalks grimly toward the barn. In the meantime* THE SHERIFF *and men have come into the room.*)

SHERIFF (*embarrassedly*). Waal—we'd best start.

ABBIE. Wait. (*Turns to* EBEN.) I love ye, Eben.

EBEN. I love ye, Abbie. (*They kiss. The three men grin and shuffle embarrassedly.* EBEN *takes* ABBIE's *hand. They go out the door in rear, the men following, and come from the house, walking hand in hand to the gate.* EBEN *stops there and points to the sunrise sky.*) Sun's a-risin'. Purty, hain't it?

ABBIE. Ay-eh. (*They both stand for a moment looking up raptly in attitudes strangely aloof and devout.*)

SHERIFF (*looking around at the farm enviously—to his companion*). It's a jim-dandy farm, no denyin'. Wished I owned it!

(*The curtain falls.*)

FEDERICO GARCÍA LORCA / 1898–1936

Federico García Lorca was born in Granada, Spain, and at twenty-one was studying in Madrid in the experimental, *avant-garde* atmosphere of the 1920's which was producing new art theories and experiments throughout Europe. Lorca was both artist and theorist; he painted, played the piano, and wrote poetry. His first poems were gypsy ballads sung to his own guitar accompaniment; they captivated all of Spain, and his later poetry is quoted and loved. He came to New York City to study at Columbia in 1929, but was unhappy in the mechanized world.

Upon his return to Spain he was put in charge of a traveling theatrical company, *La Barraca,* which went on a protracted tour of the country, playing in remote villages before rural audiences. Drama became a creative mode for him; the complex art of the theater absorbed and unified his poetry, painting, and music.

His first plays were sophisticated comedies: *The Shoemaker's Prodigious Wife* and *The Love of Don Perlimplín for Belissa in the Garden.* Then the life of the fields and villages as he had seen it became the foundation for his poetic folk dramas: *Blood Wedding, Yerma,* and *The House of Bernarda Alba.* All deal with the natural passions curbed and oppressed by traditional restraints and codes. In them, he synthesizes many arts into "free compositions" escaping from realistic bounds, though his stories and their underlying universals have the logic and causality of tragedy. Each of his three folk-tragedies is a distinct and original creation; together, they enlarged the conception and resources of the theater and theatricality.

Blood Wedding

TRAGEDY IN THREE ACTS AND SEVEN SCENES
TRANSLATED BY JAMES GRAHAM-LUJÁN AND
RICHARD L. O'CONNELL

NOTICE

This edition of *Blood Wedding* has been printed with the proper authorization. It was scrupulously revised in accordance with the original manuscript of Federico García Lorca which I have in my possession, and it contains his very latest revisions.

MARGARITA XIRGU

Buenos Aires, July 1938

CHARACTERS

THE MOTHER.
THE BRIDE.
THE MOTHER-IN-LAW.
LEONARDO'S WIFE.
THE SERVANT WOMAN.
THE NEIGHBOR WOMAN.
YOUNG GIRLS.
LEONARDO.
THE BRIDEGROOM.

THE BRIDE'S FATHER.
THE MOON.
DEATH (*as a Beggar Woman*).
WOODCUTTERS.
YOUNG MEN.

Act I

SCENE 1

(*A room painted yellow.*)

BRIDEGROOM (*entering*). Mother.
MOTHER. What?
BRIDEGROOM. I'm going.
MOTHER. Where?
BRIDEGROOM. To the vineyard. (*He starts to go.*)
MOTHER. Wait.
BRIDEGROOM. You want something?
MOTHER. Your breakfast, son.
BRIDEGROOM. Forget it. I'll eat grapes. Give me the knife.
MOTHER. What for?
BRIDEGROOM (*laughing*). To cut the grapes with.
MOTHER (*muttering as she looks for the knife*). Knives, knives. Cursed be all knives, and the scoundrel who invented them.
BRIDEGROOM. Let's talk about something else.
MOTHER. And guns and pistols and the smallest little knife—and even hoes and pitchforks.
BRIDEGROOM. All right.
MOTHER. Everything that can slice a man's body. A handsome man, full of young life, who goes out to the vineyards or to his own olive groves—his own because he's inherited them . . .
BBIDEGROOM (*lowering his head*). Be quiet.
MOTHER. . . . and then that man doesn't come back. Or if he does come back it's only for someone to cover him over with a palm leaf or a plate of rock salt so he won't bloat. I don't know how you dare carry a knife on your body— or how I let this serpent (*she takes a knife from a kitchen chest*) stay in the chest.
BRIDEGROOM. Have you had your say?
MOTHER. If I lived to be a hundred I'd talk of nothing else. First your father; to me he smelled like a carnation and I had him for barely three years. Then your brother. Oh, is it right—how can it be—that a small thing like a knife or a pistol can finish off a man—a bull of a man? No, I'll never be quiet. The months pass and the hopelessness of it stings in my eyes and even to the roots of my hair.
BRIDEGROOM (*forcefully*). Let's quit this talk!
MOTHER. No. No. Let's not quit this talk. Can anyone bring me your father back? Or your brother? Then there's the jail. What do they mean, jail? They eat there, smoke there, play music there! My dead men choking with weeds, silent, turning to dust. Two men like two beautiful flowers. The killers in jail, carefree, looking at the mountains.
BRIDEGROOM. Do you want me to go kill them?
MOTHER. No . . . If I talk about it it's because . . . Oh, how can I help talking about it, seeing you go out that door? It's . . . I don't like you to carry a knife. It's just that . . . that I wish you wouldn't go out to the fields.
BRIDEGROOM (*laughing*). Oh, come now!
MOTHER. I'd like it if you were a woman. Then you wouldn't be going out to the arroyo now and we'd both of us embroider flounces and little woolly dogs.
BRIDEGROOM (*he puts his arm around his mother and laughs*). Mother, what if I should take you with me to the vineyards?
MOTHER. What would an old lady do in the vineyards? Were you going to put me down under the young vines?
BRIDEGROOM (*lifting her in his arms*).

Old lady, old lady—you little old, little old lady!

MOTHER. Your father, he used to take me. That's the way with men of good stock; good blood. Your grandfather left a son on every corner. That's what I like. Men, men; wheat, wheat.

BRIDEGROOM. And I, Mother?

MOTHER. You, what?

BRIDEGROOM. Do I need to tell you again?

MOTHER (seriously). Oh!

BRIDEGROOM. Do you think it's bad?

MOTHER. No.

BRIDEGROOM. Well, then?

MOTHER. I don't really know. Like this, suddenly, it always surprises me. I know the girl is good. Isn't she? Well behaved. Hard working. Kneads her bread, sews her skirts, but even so when I say her name I feel as though someone had hit me on the forehead with a rock.

BRIDEGROOM. Foolishness.

MOTHER. More than foolishness. I'll be left alone. Now only you are left me— I hate to see you go.

BRIDEGROOM. But you'll come with us.

MOTHER. No. I can't leave your father and brother here alone. I have to go to them every morning and if I go away it's possible one of the Félix family, one of the killers, might die—and they'd bury him next to ours. And that'll never happen! Oh, no! That'll never happen! Because I'd dig them out with my nails and, all by myself, crush them against the wall.

BRIDEGROOM (sternly). There you go again.

MOTHER. Forgive me. (Pause.) How long have you known her?

BRIDEGROOM. Three years. I've been able to buy the vineyard.

MOTHER. Three years. She used to have another sweetheart, didn't she?

BRIDEGROOM. I don't know. I don't think so. Girls have to look at what they'll marry.

MOTHER. Yes. I looked at nobody. I looked at your father, and when they killed him I looked at the wall in front of me. One woman with one man, and that's all.

BRIDEGROOM. You know my girl's good.

MOTHER. I don't doubt it. All the same, I'm sorry not to have known what her mother was like.

BRIDEGROOM. What difference does it make now?

MOTHER (looking at him). Son.

BRIDEGROOM. What is it?

MOTHER. That's true! You're right! When do you want me to ask for her?

BRIDEGROOM (happily). Does Sunday seem all right to you?

MOTHER (seriously). I'll take her the bronze earrings, they're very old—and you buy her . . .

BRIDEGROOM. You know more about that . . .

MOTHER. . . . you buy her some open-work stockings—and for you, two suits—three! I have no one but you now!

BRIDEGROOM. I'm going. Tomorrow I'll go see her.

MOTHER. Yes, yes—and see if you can make me happy with six grandchildren—or as many as you want, since your father didn't live to give them to me.

BRIDEGROOM. The first-born for you!

MOTHER. Yes, but have some girls. I want to embroider and make lace, and be at peace.

BRIDEGROOM. I'm sure you'll love my wife.

MOTHER. I'll love her. (She starts to kiss him but changes her mind.) Go on. You're too big now for kisses. Give them to your wife. (Pause. To herself.) When she is your wife.

BRIDEGROOM. I'm going.

MOTHER. And that land around the little mill—work it over. You've not taken good care of it.

BRIDEGROOM. You're right. I will.

MOTHER. God keep you. (THE SON *goes out.* THE MOTHER *remains seated— her back to the door. A* NEIGHBOR WOMAN *with a 'kerchief on her head appears in the door.*) Come in.

NEIGHBOR. How are you?

MOTHER. Just as you see me.

NEIGHBOR. I came down to the store and stopped in to see you. We live so far away!

MOTHER. It's twenty years since I've been up to the top of the street.

NEIGHBOR. You're looking well.

MOTHER. You think so?

NEIGHBOR. Things happen. Two days ago they brought in my neighbor's son with both arms sliced off by the machine. (*She sits down.*)

MOTHER. Rafael?

NEIGHBOR. Yes. And there you have him. Many times I've thought your son and mine are better off where they are— sleeping, resting—not running the risk of being left helpless.

MOTHER. Hush. That's all just something thought up—but no consolation.

NEIGHBOR (*sighing*). Ay!

MOTHER (*sighing*). Ay!

(*Pause.*)

NEIGHBOR (*sadly*). Where's your son?

MOTHER. He went out.

NEIGHBOR. He finally bought the vineyard!

MOTHER. He was lucky.

NEIGHBOR. Now he'll get married.

MOTHER (*as though reminded of something, she draws her chair near* THE NEIGHBOR). Listen.

NEIGHBOR (*in a confidential manner*). Yes. What is it?

MOTHER. You know my son's sweetheart?

NEIGHBOR. A good girl!

MOTHER. Yes, but . . .

NEIGHBOR. But who knows her really well? There's nobody. She lives out there alone with her father—so far away—

fifteen miles from the nearest house. But she's a good girl. Used to being alone.

MOTHER. And her mother?

NEIGHBOR. Her mother I *did* know. Beautiful. Her face glowed like a saint's —but *I* never liked her. She didn't love her husband.

MOTHER (*sternly*). Well, what a lot of things certain people know!

NEIGHBOR. I'm sorry. I didn't mean to offend—but it's true. Now, whether she was decent or not nobody said. That wasn't discussed. She was haughty.

MOTHER. There you go again!

NEIGHBOR. You asked me.

MOTHER. I wish no one knew anything about them—either the live one or the dead one—that they were like two thistles no one even names but cuts off at the right moment.

NEIGHBOR. You're right. Your son is worth a lot.

MOTHER. Yes—a lot. That's why I look after him. They told me the girl had a sweetheart some time ago.

NEIGHBOR. She was about fifteen. He's been married two years now—to a cousin of hers, as a matter of fact. But nobody remembers about their engagement.

MOTHER. How do you remember it?

NEIGHBOR. Oh, what questions you ask!

MOTHER. We like to know all about the things that hurt us. Who was the boy?

NEIGHBOR. Leonardo.

MOTHER. What Leonardo?

NEIGHBOR. Leonardo Félix.

MOTHER. Félix!

NEIGHBOR. Yes, but—how is Leonardo to blame for anything? He was eight years old when those things happened.

MOTHER. That's true. But I hear that name—Félix—and it's all the same. (*Muttering.*) Félix, a slimy mouthful. (*She spits.*) It makes me spit—spit so I won't kill!

NEIGHBOR. Control yourself. What good will it do?

MOTHER. No good. But you see how it is.

NEIGHBOR. Don't get in the way of your son's happiness. Don't say anything to him. You're old. So am I. It's time for you and me to keep quiet.

MOTHER. I'll say nothing to him.

NEIGHBOR (*kissing her*). Nothing.

MOTHER (*calmly*). Such things . . . !

NEIGHBOR. I'm going. My men will soon be coming in from the fields.

MOTHER. Have you ever known such a hot sun?

NEIGHBOR. The children carrying water out to the reapers are black with it. Goodbye, woman.

MOTHER. Goodbye.

(THE MOTHER *starts toward the door at the left. Halfway there she stops and slowly crosses herself.*)

SCENE 2

(*A room painted rose with copper-ware and wreaths of common flowers. In the center of the room is a table with a tablecloth. It is morning.*)

(*Leonardo's* MOTHER-IN-LAW *sits in one corner holding a child in her arms and rocking it. His* WIFE *is in the other corner mending stockings.*)

MOTHER-IN-LAW.
Lullaby, my baby
once there was a big horse
who didn't like water.
The water was black there
under the branches.
When it reached the bridge
it stopped and it sang.
Who can say, my baby,
what the stream holds
with its long tail
in its green parlor?

WIFE (*softly*).
Carnation, sleep and dream,
the horse won't drink from the stream.

MOTHER-IN-LAW.
My rose, asleep now lie,
the horse is starting to cry.
His poor hooves were bleeding,
his long mane was frozen,
and deep in his eyes
stuck a silvery dagger.
Down he went to the river,
Oh, down he went down!
And his blood was running,
Oh, more than the water.

WIFE.
Carnation, sleep and dream,
the horse won't drink from the stream.

MOTHER-IN-LAW.
My rose, asleep now lie,
the horse is starting to cry.

WIFE.
He never did touch
the dank river shore
though his muzzle was warm
and with silvery flies.
So, to the hard mountains
he could only whinny
just when the dead stream
covered his throat.
Ay-y-y, for the big horse
who didn't like water!
Ay-y-y, for the snow-wound
big horse of the dawn!

MOTHER-IN-LAW.
Don't come in! Stop him
and close up the window
with branches of dreams
and a dream of branches.

WIFE.
My baby is sleeping.

MOTHER-IN-LAW.
My baby is quiet.

WIFE.
Look, horse, my baby
has him a pillow.

MOTHER-IN-LAW.
His cradle is metal.

WIFE.
His quilt a fine fabric.

MOTHER-IN-LAW.
Lullaby, my baby.

WIFE.
Ay-y-y, for the big horse
who didn't like the water!
MOTHER-IN-LAW.
Don't come near, don't come in!
Go away to the mountains
and through the grey valleys,
that's where your mare is.
WIFE (*looking at the baby*).
My baby is sleeping.
MOTHER-IN-LAW.
My baby is resting.
WIFE (*softly*).
Carnation, sleep and dream,
The horse won't drink from the stream.
MOTHER-IN-LAW (*getting up, very softly*).
My rose, asleep now lie
for the horse is starting to cry.
(*She carries the child out.* LEONARDO *enters.*)
LEONARDO.　Where's the baby?
WIFE.　He's sleeping.
LEONARDO.　Yesterday he wasn't well. He cried during the night.
WIFE.　Today he's like a dahlia. And you? Were you at the blacksmith's?
LEONARDO.　I've just come from there. Would you believe it? For more than two months he's been putting new shoes on the horse and they're always coming off. As far as I can see he pulls them off on the stones.
WIFE.　Couldn't it just be that you use him so much?
LEONARDO.　No. I almost never use him.
WIFE.　Yesterday the neighbors told me they'd seen you on the far side of the plains.
LEONARDO.　Who said that?
WIFE.　The women who gather capers. It certainly surprised me. Was it you?
LEONARDO.　No. What would I be doing there, in that wasteland?
WIFE.　That's what I said. But the horse was streaming sweat.
LEONARDO.　Did you see him?

WIFE.　No. Mother did.
LEONARDO.　Is she with the baby?
WIFE.　Yes. Do you want some lemonade?
LEONARDO.　With good cold water.
WIFE.　And then you didn't come to eat!
LEONARDO.　I was with the wheat weighers. They always hold me up.
WIFE (*very tenderly, while she makes the lemonade*).　Did they pay you a good price?
LEONARDO.　Fair.
WIFE.　I need a new dress and the baby a bonnet with ribbons.
LEONARDO (*getting up*).　I'm going to take a look at him.
WIFE.　Be careful. He's asleep.
MOTHER-IN-LAW (*coming in*).　Well! Who's been racing the horse that way? He's down there, worn out, his eyes popping from their sockets as though he'd come from the ends of the earth.
LEONARDO (*acidly*).　I have.
MOTHER-IN-LAW.　Oh, excuse me! He's your horse.
WIFE (*timidly*).　He was at the wheat buyers.
MOTHER-IN-LAW.　He can burst for all of me!
(*She sits down. Pause.*)
WIFE.　Your drink. Is it cold?
LEONARDO.　Yes.
WIFE.　Did you hear they're going to ask for my cousin?
LEONARDO.　When?
WIFE.　Tomorrow. The wedding will be within a month. I hope they're going to invite us.
LEONARDO (*gravely*).　I don't know.
MOTHER-IN-LAW.　His mother, I think, wasn't very happy about the match.
LEONARDO.　Well, she may be right. She's a girl to be careful with.
WIFE.　I don't like to have you thinking bad things about a good girl.
MOTHER-IN-LAW (*meaningfully*).　If he does, it's because he knows her.

Didn't you know he courted her for three years?

LEONARDO. But I left her. (*To his* WIFE.) Are you going to cry now? Quit that! (*He brusquely pulls her hands away from her face.*) Let's go see the baby.

(*They go in with their arms around each other. A* GIRL *appears. She is happy. She enters running.*)

GIRL. Señora.

MOTHER-IN-LAW. What is it?

GIRL. The groom came to the store and he's bought the best of everything they had.

MOTHER-IN-LAW. Was he alone?

GIRL. No. With his mother. Stern, tall. (*She imitates her.*) And such extravagance!

MOTHER-IN-LAW. They have money.

GIRL. And they bought some openwork stockings! Oh, such stockings! A woman's dream of stockings! Look: a swallow here, (*she points to her ankle*) a ship here, (*she points to her calf*) and here, (*she points to her thigh*) a rose!

MOTHER-IN-LAW. Child!

GIRL. A rose with the seeds and the stem! Oh! All in silk.

MOTHER-IN-LAW. Two rich families are being brought together.

(LEONARDO *and his* WIFE *appear.*)

GIRL. I came to tell you what they're buying.

LEONARDO (*loudly*). We don't care.

WIFE. Leave her alone.

MOTHER-IN-LAW. Leonardo, it's not that important.

GIRL. Please excuse me. (*She leaves, weeping.*)

MOTHER-IN-LAW. Why do you always have to make trouble with people?

LEONARDO. I didn't ask for your opinion. (*He sits down.*)

MOTHER-IN-LAW. Very well.

(*Pause.*)

WIFE (*to* LEONARDO). What's the matter with you? What idea've you got boiling there inside your head? Don't leave me like this, not knowing anything.

LEONARDO. Stop that.

WIFE. No. I want you to look at me and tell me.

LEONARDO. Let me alone. (*He rises.*)

WIFE. Where are you going, love?

LEONARDO (*sharply*). Can't you shut up?

MOTHER-IN-LAW (*energetically, to her daughter*). Be quiet! (LEONARDO *goes out.*) The baby! (*She goes into the bedroom and comes out again with the baby in her arms. The* WIFE *has remained standing, unmoving.*)

MOTHER-IN-LAW.
His poor hooves were bleeding,
his long mane was frozen,
and deep in his eyes
stuck a silvery dagger.
Down he went to the river,
Oh, down he went down!
And his blood was running,
Oh, more than the water.

WIFE (*turning slowly, as though dreaming*).
Carnation, sleep and dream,
the horse is drinking from the stream.

MOTHER-IN-LAW.
My rose, asleep now lie
the horse is starting to cry.

WIFE.
Lullaby, my baby.

MOTHER-IN-LAW.
Ay-y-y, for the big horse
who didn't like water!

WIFE (*dramatically*).
Don't come near, don't come in!
Go away to the mountains!
Ay-y-y, for the snow-wound,
big horse of the dawn!

MOTHER-IN-LAW (*weeping*).
My baby is sleeping . . .

WIFE (*weeping, as she slowly moves closer*).
My baby is resting . . .

MOTHER-IN-LAW.
Carnation, sleep and dream,
the horse won't drink from the stream.

WIFE (*weeping, and leaning on the table*).
My rose, asleep now lie,
the horse is starting to cry.

SCENE 3

(*Interior of the cave where* THE BRIDE *lives. At the back is a cross of large rose colored flowers. The round doors have lace curtains with rose colored ties. Around the walls, which are of a white and hard material, are round fans, blue jars, and little mirrors.*)

SERVANT. Come right in . . . (*She is very affable, full of humble hypocrisy.* THE BRIDEGROOM *and his* MOTHER *enter.* THE MOTHER *is dressed in black satin and wears a lace mantilla;* THE BRIDEGROOM *in black corduroy with a great golden chain.*) Won't you sit down? They'll be right here.

(*She leaves.* THE MOTHER *and* SON *are left sitting motionless as statues. Long pause.*)

MOTHER. Did you wear the watch?
BRIDEGROOM. Yes. (*He takes it out and looks at it.*)
MOTHER. We have to be back on time. How far away these people live!
BRIDEGROOM. But this is good land.
MOTHER. Good; but much too lonesome. A four hour trip and not one house, not one tree.
BRIDEGROOM. This is the wasteland.
MOTHER. Your father would have covered it with trees.
BRIDEGROOM. Without water?
MOTHER. He would have found some. In the three years we were married he planted ten cherry trees, (*remembering*) those three walnut trees by the mill, a whole vineyard and a plant called Jupiter which had scarlet flowers—but it dried up.
(*Pause.*)
BRIDEGROOM (*referring to* THE BRIDE). She must be dressing.
(THE BRIDE'S FATHER *enters. He is very old, with shining white hair. His head is bowed.* THE MOTHER *and the* BRIDEGROOM *rise. They shake hands in silence.*)

FATHER. Was it a long trip?
MOTHER. Four hours.
(*They sit down.*)
FATHER. You must have come the longest way.
MOTHER. I'm too old to come along the cliffs by the river.
BRIDEGROOM. She gets dizzy.
(*Pause.*)
FATHER. A good hemp harvest.
BRIDEGROOM. A really good one.
FATHER. When I was young this land didn't even grow hemp. We've had to punish it, even weep over it, to make it give us anything useful.
MOTHER. But now it does. Don't complain. I'm not here to ask you for anything.
FATHER (*smiling*). You're richer than I. Your vineyards are worth a fortune. Each young vine a silver coin. But—do you know?—what bothers me is that our lands are separated. I like to have everything together. One thorn I have in my heart, and that's the little orchard there, stuck in between my fields—and they won't sell it to me for all the gold in the world.
BRIDEGROOM. That's the way it always is.
FATHER. If we could just take twenty teams of oxen and move your vineyards over here, and put them down on that hillside, how happy I'd be!
MOTHER. But why?
FATHER. What's mine is hers and what's yours is his. That's why. Just to see it all together. How beautiful it is to bring things together!
BRIDEGROOM. And it would be less work.
MOTHER. When I die, you could sell ours and buy here, right alongside.
FATHER. Sell, sell? Bah! Buy, my friend, buy everything. If I had had sons

I would have bought all this mountain-side right up to the part with the stream. It's not good land, but strong arms can make it good, and since no people pass by, they don't steal your fruit and you can sleep in peace.

(*Pause.*)

MOTHER. You know what I'm here for.

FATHER. Yes.

MOTHER. And?

FATHER. It seems all right to me. They have talked it over.

MOTHER. My son has money and knows how to manage it.

FATHER. My daughter too.

MOTHER. My son is handsome. He's never known a woman. His good name is cleaner than a sheet spread out in the sun.

FATHER. No need to tell you about my daughter. At three, when the morning star shines, she prepares the bread. She never talks: soft as wool, she embroiders all kinds of fancy work and she can cut a strong cord with her teeth.

MOTHER. God bless her house.

FATHER. May God bless it.

(THE SERVANT *appears with two trays. One with drinks and the other with sweets.*)

MOTHER (*to* THE SON). When would you like the wedding?

BRIDEGROOM. Next Thursday.

FATHER. The day on which she'll be exactly twenty-two years old.

MOTHER. Twenty-two! My oldest son would be that age if he were alive. Warm and manly as he was, he'd be living now if men hadn't invented knives.

FATHER. One mustn't think about that.

MOTHER. Every minute. Always a hand on your breast.

FATHER. Thursday, then? Is that right?

BRIDEGROOM. That's right.

FATHER. You and I and the bridal couple will go in a carriage to the church which is very far from here; the wedding party on the carts and horses they'll bring with them.

MOTHER. Agreed.

(THE SERVANT *passes through.*)

FATHER. Tell her she may come in now. (*To the* MOTHER.) I shall be much pleased if you like her.

(THE BRIDE *appears. Her hands fall in a modest pose and her head is bowed.*)

MOTHER. Come here. Are you happy?

BRIDE. Yes, señora.

FATHER. You shouldn't be so solemn. After all, she's going to be your mother.

BRIDE. I'm happy. I've said "yes" because I wanted to.

MOTHER. Naturally. (*She takes her by the chin.*) Look at me.

FATHER. She resembles my wife in every way.

MOTHER. Yes? What a beautiful glance! Do you know what it is to be married, child?

BRIDE (*seriously*). I do.

MOTHER. A man, some children and a wall two yards thick for everything else.

BRIDEGROOM. Is anything else needed?

MOTHER. No. Just that you all live —that's it! Live long!

BRIDE. I'll know how to keep my word.

MOTHER. Here are some gifts for you.

BRIDE. Thank you.

FATHER. Shall we have something?

MOTHER. Nothing for me. (*To* THE SON.) But you?

BRIDEGROOM. Yes, thank you. (*He takes one sweet,* THE BRIDE *another.*)

FATHER (*to* THE BRIDEGROOM). Wine?

MOTHER. He doesn't touch it.

FATHER. All the better.

(*Pause. All are standing.*)

BRIDEGROOM (*to* THE BRIDE). I'll come tomorrow.

BRIDE. What time?

BRIDEGROOM. Five.

BRIDE. I'll be waiting for you.

BRIDEGROOM. When I leave your side I feel a great emptiness, and something like a knot in my throat.

BRIDE. When you are my husband you won't have it any more.

BRIDEGROOM. That's what I tell myself.

MOTHER. Come. The sun doesn't wait. (*To* THE FATHER.) Are we agreed on everything?

FATHER. Agreed.

MOTHER (*to* THE SERVANT). Goodbye, woman.

SERVANT. God go with you!

(THE MOTHER *kisses* THE BRIDE *and they begin to leave in silence.*)

MOTHER (*at the door*). Goodbye, daughter.

(THE BRIDE *answers with her hand.*)

FATHER. I'll go out with you.

(*They leave.*)

SERVANT. I'm bursting to see the presents.

BRIDE (*sharply*). Stop that!

SERVANT. Oh, child, show them to me.

BRIDE. I don't want to.

SERVANT. At least the stockings. They say they're all open work. Please!

BRIDE. I said no.

SERVANT. Well, my Lord. All right then. It looks as if you didn't want to get married.

BRIDE (*biting her hand in anger*). Ay-y-y!

SERVANT. Child, child! What's the matter with you? Are you sorry to give up your queen's life? Don't think of bitter things. Have you any reason to? None. Let's look at the presents. (*She takes the box.*)

BRIDE (*holding her by the wrists*). Let go.

SERVANT. Ay-y-y, girl!

BRIDE. Let go, I said.

SERVANT. You're stronger than a man.

BRIDE. Haven't I done a man's work? I wish I were.

SERVANT. Don't talk like that.

BRIDE. Quiet, I said. Let's talk about something else.

(*The light is fading from the stage. Long pause.*)

SERVANT. Did you hear a horse last night?

BRIDE. What time?

SERVANT. Three.

BRIDE. It might have been a stray horse—from the herd.

SERVANT. No. It carried a rider.

BRIDE. How do you know?

SERVANT. Because I saw him. He was standing by your window. It shocked me greatly.

BRIDE. Maybe it was my fiancé. Sometimes he comes by at that time.

SERVANT. No.

BRIDE. You saw him?

SERVANT. Yes.

BRIDE. Who was it?

SERVANT. It was Leonardo.

BRIDE (*strongly*). Liar! You liar! Why should he come here?

SERVANT. He came.

BRIDE. Shut up! Shut your cursed mouth.

(*The sound of a horse is heard.*)

SERVANT (*at the window*). Look. Lean out. Was it Leonardo?

BRIDE. It was!

(*Quick curtain.*)

Act II

SCENE 1

(*The entrance hall of* THE BRIDE'S *house. A large door in the back. It is night.* THE BRIDE *enters wearing ruffled white petticoats full of laces and embroidered bands, and a sleeveless white bodice.* THE SERVANT *is dressed the same way.*)

SERVANT. I'll finish combing your hair out here.

BRIDE. It's too warm to stay in there.

SERVANT. In this country it doesn't even cool off at dawn.

(THE BRIDE *sits on a low chair and looks into a little hand mirror.* THE SERVANT *combs her hair.*)

BRIDE. My mother came from a place with lots of trees—from a fertile country.

SERVANT. And she was so happy!

BRIDE. But she wasted away here.

SERVANT. Fate.

BRIDE. As we're all wasting away here. The very walls give off heat. Ay-y-y! Don't pull so hard.

SERVANT. I'm only trying to fix this wave better. I want it to fall over your forehead. (THE BRIDE *looks at herself in the mirror.*) How beautiful you are! Ay-y-y!

(*She kisses her passionately.*)

BRIDE (*seriously*). Keep right on combing.

SERVANT (*combing*). Oh, lucky you —going to put your arms around a man; and kiss him; and feel his weight.

BRIDE. Hush.

SERVANT. And the best part will be when you'll wake up and you'll feel him at your side and when he caresses your shoulders with his breath, like a little nightingale's feather.

BRIDE (*sternly*). Will you be quiet?

SERVANT. But, child! What *is* a wedding? A wedding is just that and nothing more. Is it the sweets—or the bouquets or flowers? No. It's a shining bed and a man and a woman.

BRIDE. But you shouldn't talk about it.

SERVANT. Oh, *that's* something else again. But fun enough too.

BRIDE. Or bitter enough.

SERVANT. I'm going to put the orange blossoms on from here to here, so the wreath will shine out on top of your hair. (*She tries on the sprigs of orange blossom.*)

BRIDE (*looking at herself in the mir-ror*). Give it to me. (*She takes the wreath, looks at it and lets her head fall in discouragement.*)

SERVANT. Now what's the matter?

BRIDE. Leave me alone.

SERVANT. This is no time for you to start feeling sad. (*Encouragingly.*) Give me the wreath. (THE BRIDE *takes the wreath and hurls it away.*) Child! You're just asking God to punish you, throwing the wreath on the floor like that. Raise your head! Don't you want to get married? Say it. You can still withdraw.

(THE BRIDE *rises.*)

BRIDE. Storm clouds. A chill wind that cuts through my heart. Who hasn't felt it?

SERVANT. You love your sweetheart, don't you?

BRIDE. I love him.

SERVANT. Yes, yes. I'm sure you do.

BRIDE. But this is a very serious step.

SERVANT. You've got to take it.

BRIDE. I've already given my word.

SERVANT. I'll put on the wreath.

BRIDE (*she sits down*). Hurry. They should be arriving by now.

SERVANT. They've already been at least two hours on the way.

BRIDE. How far is it from here to the church?

SERVANT. Five leagues by the stream, but twice that by the road.

(THE BRIDE *rises and* THE SERVANT *grows excited as she looks at her.*)

SERVANT.

Awake, O Bride, awaken,
On your wedding morning waken!
The world's rivers may all
Bear along your bridal Crown!

BRIDE (*smiling*). Come now.

SERVANT (*enthusiastically kissing her and dancing around her*).

Awake,
with the fresh bouquet
of flowering laurel.
Awake,
by the trunk and branch
of the laurels!

(*The banging of the front door latch is heard.*)

BRIDE. Open the door! That must be the first guests.

(*She leaves.* THE SERVANT *opens the door.*)

SERVANT (*in astonishment*). You!

LEONARDO. Yes, me. Good morning.

SERVANT. The first one!

LEONARDO. Wasn't I invited?

SERVANT. Yes.

LEONARDO. That's why I'm here.

SERVANT. Where's your wife?

LEONARDO. I came on my horse. She's coming by the road.

SERVANT. Didn't you meet anyone?

LEONARDO. I *passed* them on my horse.

SERVANT. You're going to kill that horse with so much racing.

LEONARDO. When he dies, he's dead! (*Pause.*)

SERVANT. Sit down. Nobody's up yet.

LEONARDO. Where's the bride?

SERVANT. I'm just on my way to dress her.

LEONARDO. The bride! She ought to be happy!

SERVANT. (*changing the subject*). How's the baby?

LEONARDO. What baby?

SERVANT. Your son.

LEONARDO (*remembering as though in a dream*). Ah!

SERVANT. Are they bringing him?

LEONARDO. No.

(*Pause.* VOICES *sing distantly.*)

VOICES.
Awake, O Bride, awaken,
On your wedding morning waken!

LEONARDO.
Awake, O Bride, awaken,
On your wedding morning waken!

SERVANT. It's the guests. They're still quite a way off.

LEONARDO. The bride's going to wear a big wreath, isn't she? But it ought not to be so large. One a little smaller would look better on her. Has the groom al-ready brought her the orange blossom that must be worn on the breast?

BRIDE (*appearing, still in petticoats and wearing the wreath*). He brought it.

SERVANT (*sternly*). Don't come out like that.

BRIDE. What does it matter? (*Seriously.*) Why do you ask if they brought the orange blossom? Do you have something in mind?

LEONARDO. Nothing. What would I have in mind? (*Drawing near her.*) You, you know me; you know I don't. Tell me so. What have I ever meant to you? Open your memory, refresh it. But two oxen and an ugly little hut are almost nothing. That's the thorn.

BRIDE. What have you come here to do?

LEONARDO. To see your wedding.

BRIDE. Just as I saw yours!

LEONARDO. Tied up by you, done with your two hands. Oh, they can kill me but they can't spit on me. But even money, which shines so much, spits sometimes.

BRIDE. Liar!

LEONARD. I don't want to talk. I'm hot-blooded and I don't want to shout so all these hills will hear me.

BRIDE. My shouts would be louder.

SERVANT. You'll have to stop talking like this. (*To* THE BRIDE.) You don't have to talk about what's past. (THE SERVANT *looks around uneasily at the doors.*)

BRIDE. She's right. I shouldn't even talk to you. But it offends me to the soul that you come here to watch me, and spy on my wedding, and ask about the orange blossom with something on your mind. Go and wait for your wife at the door.

LEONARDO. But, can't you and I even talk?

SERVANT (*with rage*). No! No, you can't talk.

LEONARDO. Ever since I got married

I've been thinking night and day about whose fault it was, and every time I think about it, out comes a new fault to eat up the old one; but always there's a fault left!

BRIDE. A man with a home knows a lot of things and can do a lot to ride roughshod over a girl stuck out in the desert. But I have my pride. And that's why I'm getting married. I'll lock myself in with my husband and then I'll have to love him above everyone else.

LEONARDO. Pride won't help you a bit. (*He draws near to her.*)

BRIDE. Don't come near me!

LEONARDO. To burn with desire and keep quiet about it is the greatest punishment we can bring on ourselves. What good was pride to me—and not seeing you, and letting you lie awake night after night? No good! It only served to bring the fire down on me! You think that time heals and walls hide things, but it isn't true, it isn't true! When things get that deep inside you there isn't anybody can change them.

BRIDE (*trembling*). I can't listen to you. I can't listen to your voice. It's as though I'd drunk a bottle of anise and fallen asleep wrapped in a quilt of roses. It pulls me along, and I know I'm drowning—but I go on down.

SERVANT (*seizing* LEONARDO *by the lapels*). You've got to go right now!

LEONARDO. This is the last time I'll ever talk to her. Don't you be afraid of anything.

BRIDE. And I know I'm crazy and I know my breast rots with longing; but here I am—calmed by hearing him, by just seeing him move his arms.

LEONARDO. I'd never be at peace if I didn't tell you these things. I got married. Now you get married.

SERVANT. But she *is* getting married! (VOICES *are heard singing, nearer.*)

VOICES.
Awake, O Bride, awaken.
On your wedding morning waken!

BRIDE.
Awake, O Bride, awaken.
(*She goes out, running toward her room.*)

SERVANT. The people are here now. (*To* LEONARDO.) Don't you come near her again.

LEONARDO. Don't worry.
(*He goes out to the left. Day begins to break.*)

FIRST GIRL. (*entering*).
Awake, O Bride, awaken,
the morning you're to marry;
sing round and dance round;
balconies a wreath must carry.

VOICES.
Bride, awaken!

SERVANT (*creating enthusiasm*).
Awake,
with the green bouquet
of love in flower.
Awake,
by the trunk and the branch
of the laurels!

SECOND GIRL (*entering*).
Awake,
with her long hair,
snowy sleeping gown,
patent leather boots with silver—
her forehead jasmines crown.

SERVANT.
Oh, shepherdess,
the moon begins to shine!

FIRST GIRL.
Oh, gallant,
leave your hat beneath the vine!

FIRST YOUNG MAN (*entering holding his hat on high*).
Bride, awaken,
for over the fields
the wedding draws nigh
with trays heaped with dahlias
and cakes piled high.

VOICES.
Bride, awaken!

SECOND GIRL.
The bride
has set her white wreath in place
and the groom

ties it on with a golden lace.

SERVANT.

By the orange tree,
sleepless the bride will be.

THIRD GIRL (*entering*).

By the citron vine,
gifts from the groom will shine.

(*Three* GUESTS *come in.*)

FIRST YOUTH.

Dove, awaken!
In the dawn
shadowy bells are shaken.

GUEST.

The bride, the white bride
today a maiden,
tomorrow a wife.

FIRST GIRL.

Dark one, come down
trailing the train of your silken gown.

GUEST.

Little dark one, come down,
cold morning wears a dewy crown.

FIRST GUEST.

Awaken, wife, awake,
orange blossoms the breezes shake.

SERVANT.

A tree I would embroider her
with garnet sashes wound,
And on each sash a cupid,
with "Long Live" all around.

VOICES.

Bride, awaken.

FIRST YOUTH.

The morning you're to marry!

GUEST.

The morning you're to marry
how elegant you'll seem;
worthy, mountain flower,
of a captain's dream.

FATHER (*entering*).

A captain's wife
the gloom will marry.
He comes with his oxen the treasure to
carry!

THIRD GIRL.

The gloom
is like a flower of gold.
When he walks,
blossoms at his feet unfold.

SERVANT.

Oh, my lucky girl!

SECOND YOUTH.

Bride, awaken.

SERVANT.

Oh, my elegant girl!

FIRST GIRL.

Through the windows
hear the wedding shout.

SECOND GIRL.

Let the bride come out.

FIRST GIRL.

Come out, come out!

SERVANT.

Let the bells
ring and ring out clear!

FIRST YOUTH.

For here she comes!
For now she's near!

SERVANT.

Like a bull, the wedding
is arising here!

(THE BRIDE *appears. She wears a black dress in the style of* 1900, *with a bustle and large train covered with pleated gauzes and heavy laces. Upon her hair, brushed in a wave over her forehead, she wears an orange blossom wreath. Guitars sound.* THE GIRLS *kiss* THE BRIDE.)

THIRD GIRL. What scent did you put on your hair?

BRIDE (*laughing*). None at all.

SECOND GIRL (*looking at her dress*). This cloth is what you can't get.

FIRST YOUTH. Here's the groom!

BRIDEGROOM. Salud!

FIRST GIRL, (*putting a flower behind his ear*).

The groom
is like a flower of gold.

SECOND GIRL.

Quiet breezes
from his eyes unfold.

(THE GROOM *goes to* THE BRIDE.)

BRIDE. Why did you put on those shoes?

BRIDEGROOM. They're gayer than the black ones.

LEONARDO'S WIFE (*entering and kissing* THE BRIDE). Salud!

(*They all speak excitedly.*)

LEONARDO (*entering as one who performs a duty*).
The morning you're to marry
We give you a wreath to wear.

LEONARDO'S WIFE.
So the fields may be made happy
with the dew dropped from your hair!

MOTHER (*to* THE FATHER). Are those people here, too?

FATHER. They're part of the family. Today is a day of forgiveness!

MOTHER. I'll put up with it, but I don't forgive.

BRIDEGROOM. With your wreath, it's a joy to look at you!

BRIDE. Let's go to the church quickly.

BRIDEGROOM. Are you in a hurry?

BRIDE. Yes. I want to be your wife right now so that I can be with you alone, not hearing any voice but yours.

BRIDEGROOM. That's what I want!

BRIDE. And not seeing any eyes but yours. And for you to hug me so hard, that even though my dead mother should call me, I wouldn't be able to draw away from you.

BRIDEGROOM. My arms are strong. I'll hug you for forty years without stopping.

BRIDE (*taking his arm, dramatically*). Forever!

FATHER. Quick now! Round up the teams and carts! The sun's already out.

MOTHER. And go along carefully! Let's hope nothing goes wrong.

(*The great door in the background opens.*)

SERVANT (*weeping*).
As you set out from your house,
oh, maiden white,
remember you leave shining
with a star's light.

FIRST GIRL.
Clean of body, clean of clothes
from her home to church she goes.

(*They start leaving.*)

SECOND GIRL.
Now you leave your home
for the church!

SERVANT.
The wind sets flowers
on the sands.

THIRD GIRL.
Ah, the white maid!

SERVANT.
Dark winds are the lace
of her mantilla.

(*They leave. Guitars, castanets and tambourines are heard.* LEONARDO *and his* WIFE *are left alone.*)

WIFE. Let's go.

LEONARDO. Where?

WIFE. To the church. But not on your horse. You're coming with me.

LEONARDO. In the cart?

WIFE. Is there anything else?

LEONARDO. I'm not the kind of man to ride in a cart.

WIFE. Nor I the wife to go to a wedding without her husband. I can't stand any more of this!

LEONARDO. Neither can I!

WIFE. And why do you look at me that way? With a thorn in each eye.

LEONARDO. Let's go!

WIFE. I don't know what's happening. But I think, and I don't want to think. One thing I do know. I'm already cast off by you. But I have a son. And another coming. And so it goes. My mother's fate was the same. Well, I'm not moving from here.

(VOICES *outside.*)

VOICES.
As you set out from your home
and to the church go
remember you leave shining
with a star's glow.

WIFE (*weeping*).
Remember you leave shining
with a star's glow!
I left my house like that too. They could have stuffed the whole countryside in my mouth. I was that trusting.

LEONARDO (*rising*). Let's go!

WIFE. But you with me!

LEONARDO. Yes. (*Pause.*) Start moving!

(*They leave.*)

VOICES.
As you set out from your home
and to the church go,
remember you leave shining
with a star's glow.

(*Slow curtain.*)

SCENE 2

(*The exterior of* THE BRIDE'S *Cave Home, in white gray and cold blue tones. Large cactus trees. Shadowy and silver tones. Panoramas of light tan tablelands, everything hard like a landscape in popular ceramics.*)

SERVANT (*arranging glasses and trays on a table*).
A-turning,
the wheel was a-turning
and the water was flowing,
for the wedding night comes.
May the branches part
and the moon be arrayed
at her white balcony rail.

(*In a loud voice.*) Set out the table-cloths!

(*In a pathetic voice.*)
A-singing,
bride and groom were singing
and the water was flowing
for their wedding night comes.
Oh, rime-frost, flash!—
and almonds bitter
fill with honey!

(*In a loud voice.*) Get the wine ready!

(*In a poetic tone.*)
Elegant girl,
most elegant in the world,
see the way the water is flowing,
for your wedding night comes.
Hold your skirts close in
under the bridegroom's wing
and never leave your house,
for the Bridegroom is a dove
with his breast a firebrand
and the fields wait for the whisper
of spurting blood.
A-turning
the wheel was a-turning
and the water was flowing
and your wedding night comes.
Oh, water, sparkle!

MOTHER (*entering*). At last!

FATHER. Are we the first ones?

SERVANT. No. Leonardo and his wife arrived a while ago. They drove like demons. His wife got here dead with fright. They made the trip as though they'd come on horseback.

FATHER. That one's looking for trouble. He's not of good blood.

MOTHER. What blood would you expect him to have? His whole family's blood. It comes down from the great grandfather, who started in killing, and it goes on down through the whole evil breed of knife wielding and false smiling men.

FATHER. Let's leave it at that!

SERVANT. But how can she leave it at that?

MOTHER. It hurts me to the tips of my veins. On the forehead of all of them I see only the hand with which they killed what was mine. Can you really see me? Don't I seem mad to you? Well, it's the madness of not having shrieked out all my breast needs to. Always in my breast there's a shriek standing tiptoe that I have to beat down and hold in under my shawls. But the dead are carried off and one has to keep still. And then, people find fault. (*She removes her shawl.*)

FATHER. Today's not the day for you to be remembering these things.

MOTHER. When the talk turns on it, I have to speak. And more so today. Because today I'm left alone in my home.

FATHER. But with the expectation of having someone with you.

MOTHER. That's my hope: grand-children.

(*They sit down.*)

FATHER. I want them to have a lot of them. This land needs hands that aren't hired. There's a battle to be waged against weeds, the thistles, the big rocks that come from one doesn't know where. And those hands have to be the owner's, who chastises and dominates, who makes the seeds grow. Lots of sons are needed.

MOTHER. And some daughters! Men are like the wind! They're forced to handle weapons. Girls never go out into the street.

FATHER (*happily*). I think they'll have both.

MOTHER. My son will cover her well. He's of good seed. His father could have had many sons with me.

FATHER. What I'd like is to have all this happen in a day. So that right away they'd have two or three boys.

MOTHER. But it's not like that. It takes a long time. That's why it's so terrible to see one's own blood spilled out on the ground. A fountain that spurts for a minute, but costs us years. When I got to my son, he lay fallen in the middle of the street. I wet my hands with his blood and licked them with my tongue—because it was my blood. You don't know what that's like. In a glass and topaze shrine I'd put the earth moistened by his blood.

FATHER. Now you must hope. My daughter is wide-hipped and your son is strong.

MOTHER. That's why I'm hoping.

(*They rise.*)

FATHER. Get the wheat trays ready!

SERVANT. They're all ready.

LEONARDO'S WIFE (*entering*). May it be for the best!

MOTHER. Thank you.

LEONARDO. Is there going to be a celebration?

FATHER. A small one. People can't stay long.

SERVANT. Here they are!

(*Guests begin entering in gay groups.* THE BRIDE *and* GROOM *come in arm-in-arm.* LEONARDO *leaves.*)

BRIDEGROOM. There's never been a wedding with so many people!

BRIDE (*sullen*). Never.

FATHER. It was brilliant.

MOTHER. Whole branches of families came.

BRIDEGROOM. People who never went out of the house.

MOTHER. Your father sowed well, and now you're reaping it.

BRIDEGROOM. There were cousins of mine whom I no longer knew.

MOTHER. All the people from the seacoast.

BRIDEGROOM (*happily*). They were frightened of the horses.

(*They talk.*)

MOTHER (*to* THE BRIDE). What are you thinking about?

BRIDE. I'm not thinking about anything.

MOTHER. Your blessings weigh heavily.

(*Guitars are heard.*)

BRIDE. Like lead.

MOTHER (*stern*). But they shouldn't weigh so. Happy as a dove you ought to be.

BRIDE. Are you staying here tonight?

MOTHER. No. My house is empty.

BRIDE. You ought to stay!

FATHER (*to* THE MOTHER). Look at the dance they're forming. Dances of the far away seashore.

(LEONARDO *enters and sits down. His* WIFE *stands rigidly behind him.*)

MOTHER. They're my husband's cousins. Stiff as stones at dancing.

FATHER. It makes me happy to watch them. What a change for this house! (*He leaves.*)

BRIDEGROOM (*to* THE BRIDE). Did you like the orange blossom?

BRIDE (*looking at him fixedly*). Yes.

BRIDEGROOM. It's all of wax. It will last forever. I'd like you to have had them all over your dress.

BRIDE. No need of that.

(LEONARDO *goes off to the right.*)

FIRST GIRL. Let's go and take out your pins.

BRIDE (*to* THE GROOM). I'll be right back.

LEONARDO'S WIFE. I hope you'll be happy with my cousin!

BRIDEGROOM. I'm sure I will.

LEONARDO'S WIFE. The two of you here; never going out; building a home. I wish I could live far away like this, too!

BRIDEGROOM. Why don't you buy land? The mountainside is cheap and children grow up better.

LEONARDO'S WIFE. We don't have any money. And at the rate we're going . . . !

BRIDEGROOM. Your husband is a good worker.

LEONARDO'S WIFE. Yes, but he likes to fly around too much; from one thing to another. He's not a patient man.

SERVANT. Aren't you having anything? I'm going to wrap up some wine cakes for your mother. She likes them so much.

BRIDEGROOM. Put up three dozen for her.

LEONARDO'S WIFE. No. no. A half-dozen's enough for her!

BRIDEGROOM. But today's a day!

LEONARDO'S WIFE (*to* THE SERVANT). Where's Leonardo?

BRIDEGROOM. He must be with the guests.

LEONARDO'S WIFE. I'm going to go see. (*She leaves.*)

SERVANT (*looking off at the dance*). That's beautiful there.

BRIDEGROOM. Aren't you dancing?

SERVANT. No one will ask me.

(*Two* GIRLS *pass across the back of the stage; during this whole scene the background should be an animated crossing of figures.*)

BRIDEGROOM (*happily*). They just don't know anything. Lively old girls like you dance better than the young ones.

SERVANT. Well! Are you tossing me a compliment, boy? What a family yours is! Men among men! As a little girl I saw your grandfather's wedding. What a figure! It seemed as if a mountain were getting married.

BRIDEGROOM. I'm not as tall.

SERVANT. But there's the same twinkle in your eye. Where's the girl?

BRIDEGROOM. Taking off her wreath.

SERVANT. Ah! Look. For midnight, since you won't be sleeping, I have prepared ham for you, and some large glasses of old wine. On the lower shelf of the cupboard. In case you need it.

BRIDEGROOM (*smiling*). I won't be eating at midnight.

SERVANT (*slyly*). If not you, maybe the bride. (*She leaves.*)

FIRST YOUTH (*entering*). You've got to come have a drink with us!

BRIDEGROOM. I'm waiting for the bride.

SECOND YOUTH. You'll have her at dawn!

FIRST YOUTH. That's when it's best!

SECOND YOUTH. Just for a minute.

BRIDEGROOM. Let's go.

(*They leave. Great excitement is heard.* THE BRIDE *enters. From the opposite side two* GIRLS *come running to meet her.*)

FIRST GIRL. To whom did you give the first pin; me or this one?

BRIDE. I don't remember.

FIRST GIRL. To me, you gave it to me here.

SECOND GIRL. To me, in front of the altar.

BRIDE (*uneasily, with a great inner struggle*). I don't know anything about it.

FIRST GIRL. It's just that I wish you'd . . .

BRIDE (*interrupting*). Nor do I care. I have a lot to think about.

SECOND GIRL. Your pardon.

(LEONARDO *crosses at the rear of the stage.*)

BRIDE (*she sees* LEONARDO). And this is an upsetting time.

FIRST GIRL. We wouldn't know anything about that!

BRIDE. You'll know about it when your time comes. This step is a very hard one to take.

FIRST GIRL. Has she offended you?

BRIDE. No. You must pardon me.

SECOND GIRL. What for? But *both* the pins are good for getting married, aren't they?

BRIDE. Both of them.

FIRST GIRL. Maybe now one will get married before the other.

BRIDE. Are you so eager?

SECOND GIRL (*shyly*). Yes.

BRIDE. Why?

FIRST GIRL. Well . . .

(*She embraces* THE SECOND GIRL. *Both go running off.* THE GROOM *comes in very slowly and embraces* THE BRIDE *from behind.*)

BRIDE (*in sudden fright*). Let go of me!

BRIDEGROOM. Are you frightened of me?

BRIDE. Ay-y-y! It's you?

BRIDEGROOM. Who else would it be? (*Pause.*) Your father or me.

BRIDE. That's true!

BRIDEGROOM. Of course, your father would have hugged you more gently.

BRIDE (*darkly*). Of course!

BRIDEGROOM (*embracing her strongly and a little bit brusquely*). Because he's old.

BRIDE (*curtly*). Let me go!

BRIDEGROOM. Why? (*He lets her go.*)

BRIDE. Well . . . the people. They can see us.

(THE SERVANT *crosses at the back of the stage again without looking at* THE BRIDE *and* BRIDEGROOM.)

BRIDEGROOM. What of it? It's consecrated now.

BRIDE. Yes, but let me be . . . Later.

BRIDEGROOM. What's the matter with you? You look frightened!

BRIDE. I'm all right. Don't go.

(LEONARDO'S WIFE *enters.*)

LEONARDO'S WIFE. I don't mean to intrude . . .

BRIDEGROOM. What is it?

LEONARDO'S WIFE. Did my husband come through here?

BRIDEGROOM. No.

LEONARDO'S WIFE. Because I can't find him, and his horse isn't in the stable either.

BRIDEGROOM (*happily*). He must be out racing it.

(THE WIFE *leaves, troubled.* THE SERVANT *enters.*)

SERVANT. Aren't you two proud and happy with so many good wishes?

BRIDEGROOM. I wish it were over with. The bride is a little tired.

SERVANT. That's no way to act, child.

BRIDE. It's as though I'd been struck on the head.

SERVANT. A bride from these mountains must be strong. (*To* THE GROOM.) You're the only one who can cure her, because she's yours. (*She goes running off.*)

BRIDEGROOM (*embracing* THE BRIDE). Let's go dance a little. (*He kisses her.*)

BRIDE (*worried*). No. I'd like to stretch out on my bed a little.

BRIDEGROOM. I'll keep you company.

BRIDE. Never! With all these people here? What would they say? Let me be quiet for a moment.

BRIDEGROOM. Whatever you say! But don't be like that tonight!

BRIDE (*at the door*). I'll be better tonight.

BRIDEGROOM. That's what I want.

(THE MOTHER *appears*.)

MOTHER. Son.

BRIDEGROOM. Where've you been?

MOTHER. Out there—in all that noise. Are you happy?

BRIDEGROOM. Yes.

MOTHER. Where's your wife?

BRIDEGROOM. Resting a little. It's a bad day for brides!

MOTHER. A bad day? The only good one. To me it was like coming into my own. (THE SERVANT *enters and goes toward* THE BRIDE'S *room*.) Like the breaking of new ground; the planting of new trees.

BRIDEGROOM. Are you going to leave?

MOTHER. Yes. I ought to be at home.

BRIDEGROOM. Alone.

MOTHER. Not alone. For my head is full of things: of men, and fights.

BRIDEGROOM. But now the fights are no longer fights.

(THE SERVANT *enters quickly; she disappears at the rear of the stage, running*.)

MOTHER. While you live, you have to fight.

BRIDEGROOM. I'll always obey you!

MOTHER. Try to be loving with your wife, and if you see she's acting foolish or touchy, caress her in a way that will hurt her a little: a strong hug, a bite and then a soft kiss. Not so she'll be angry, but just so she'll feel you're the man, the boss, the one who gives orders. I learned that from your father. And since you don't have him. I have to be the one to tell you about these strong defenses.

BRIDEGROOM. I'll always do as you say.

FATHER (*entering*). Where's my daughter?

BRIDEGROOM. She's inside.

(THE FATHER *goes to look for her*.)

FIRST GIRL. Get the bride and groom! We're going to dance a round!

FIRST YOUTH (*to the* BRIDEGROOM). You're going to lead it.

FATHER (*entering*). She's not there.

BRIDEGROOM. No?

FATHER. She must have gone up to the railing.

BRIDEGROOM. I'll go see! (*He leaves. A hubbub of excitement and guitars is heard*.)

FIRST GIRL. They've started it already! (*She leaves*.)

BRIDEGROOM (*entering*). She isn't there.

MOTHER (*uneasily*). Isn't she?

FATHER. But where could she have gone?

SERVANT (*entering*). But where's the girl, where is she?

MOTHER (*seriously*). That we don't know.

(THE BRIDEGROOM *leaves. Three guests enter*.)

FATHER (*dramatically*). But, isn't she in the dance?

SERVANT. She's not in the dance.

FATHER (*with a start*). There are a lot of people. Go look!

SERVANT. I've already looked.

FATHER (*tragically*). Then where is she?

BRIDEGROOM (*entering*). Nowhere. Not anywhere.

MOTHER (*to* THE FATHER). What does this mean? Where is your daughter?

(LEONARDO'S WIFE *enters*.)

LEONARDO'S WIFE. They've run away! They've run away! She and Leonardo. On the horse. With their arms around each other, they rode off like a shooting star!

FATHER. That's not true! Not my daughter!

MOTHER. Yes, your daughter! Spawn of a wicked mother, and he, he too. But now she's my son's wife!

BRIDEGROOM (*entering*). Let's go after them! Who has a horse?

MOTHER. Who has a horse? Right away! Who has a horse? I'll give him all I have—my eyes, my tongue even. . . .

VOICE. Here's one.

MOTHER (*to* THE SON). Go! After them! (*He leaves with two young men.*) No. Don't go. Those people kill quickly and well . . . but yes, run, and I'll follow!

FATHER. It couldn't be my daughter. Perhaps she's thrown herself in the well.

MOTHER. Decent women throw themselves in water; not that one! But now she's my son's wife. Two groups. There are two groups here. (*They all enter.*) My family and yours. Everyone set out from here. Shake the dust from your heels! We'll go help my son. (*The people separate into two groups.*) For he has his family: his cousins from the sea, and all who came from inland. Out of here! On all roads. The hour of blood has come again. Two groups! You with yours and I with mine. After them! After them!

Act III

SCENE 1

(*A forest. It is nighttime. Great moist tree trunks. A dark atmosphere. Two violins are heard. Three* WOODCUTTERS *enter.*)

FIRST WOODCUTTER. And have they found them?

SECOND WOODCUTTER. No. But they're looking for them everywhere.

THIRD WOODCUTTER. They'll find them.

SECOND WOODCUTTER. Sh-h-h!

THIRD WOODCUTTER. What?

SECOND WOODCUTTER. They seem to be coming closer on all the roads at once.

FIRST WOODCUTTER. When the moon comes out they'll see them.

SECOND WOODCUTTER. They ought to let them go.

FIRST WOODCUTTER. The world is wide. Everybody can live in it.

THIRD WOODCUTTER. But they'll kill them.

SECOND WOODCUTTER. You have to follow your passion. They did right to run away.

FIRST WOODCUTTER. They were deceiving themselves but at the last blood was stronger.

THIRD WOODCUTTER. Blood!

FIRST WOODCUTTER. You have to follow the path of your blood.

SECOND WOODCUTTER. But blood that sees the light of day is drunk up by the earth.

FIRST WOODCUTTER. What of it? Better dead with the blood drained away than alive with it rotting.

THIRD WOODCUTTER. Hush!

FIRST WOODCUTTER. What? Do you hear something?

THIRD WOODCUTTER. I hear the crickets, the frogs, the night's ambush.

FIRST WOODCUTTER. But not the horse.

THIRD WOODCUTTER. No.

FIRST WOODCUTTER. By now he must be loving her.

SECOND WOODCUTTER. Her body for him; his body for her.

THIRD WOODCUTTER. They'll find them and they'll kill them.

FIRST WOODCUTTER. But by then they'll have mingled their bloods. They'll be like two empty jars, like two dry arroyos.

SECOND WOODCUTTER. There are many clouds and it would be easy for the moon not to come out.

THIRD WOODCUTTER. The bridegroom will find them with or without the moon. I saw him set out. Like a raging star. His face the color of ashes. He looked the fate of all his clan.

FIRST WOODCUTTER. His clan of dead men lying in the middle of the street.

SECOND WOODCUTTER. There you have it!

THIRD WOODCUTTER. You think they'll be able to break through the circle?

SECOND WOODCUTTER. It's hard to. There are knives and guns for ten leagues 'round.

THIRD WOODCUTTER. He's riding a good horse.

SECOND WOODCUTTER. But he's carrying a woman.

FIRST WOODCUTTER. We're close by now.

SECOND WOODCUTTER. A tree with forty branches. We'll soon cut it down.

THIRD WOODCUTTER. The moon's coming out now. Let's hurry.

(*From the left shines a brightness.*)

FIRST WOODCUTTER.

O rising moon!
Moon among the great leaves.

SECOND WOODCUTTER.

Cover the blood with jasmines!

FIRST WOODCUTTER.

O lonely moon!
Moon among the great leaves.

SECOND WOODCUTTER.

Silver on the bride's face.

THIRD WOODCUTTER.

O evil moon!
Leave for their love a branch in shadow.

FIRST WOODCUTTER.

O sorrowing moon!
Leave for their love a branch in shadow.

(*They go out.* THE MOON *appears through the shining brightness at the left.* THE MOON *is a young woodcutter with a white face. The stage takes on an intense blue radiance.*)

MOON.

Round swan in the river
and a cathedral's eye,
false dawn on the leaves,
they'll not escape; these things am I!
Who is hiding? And who sobs
in the thornbrakes of the valley?
The moon sets a knife
abandoned in the air
which being a leaden threat
yearns to be blood's pain.
Let me in! I come freezing
down to walls and windows!
Open roofs, open breasts
where I may warm myself!
I'm cold! My ashes
of somnolent metals
seek the fire's crest
on mountains and streets.
But the snow carries me
upon its mottled back
and pools soak me
in their water, hard and cold.
But this night there will be
red blood for my cheeks,
and for the reeds that cluster
at the wide feet of the wind.
Let there be neither shadow nor bower,
and then they can't get away!
O let me enter a breast
where I may get warm!
A heart for me!
Warm! That will spurt
over the mountains of my chest;
let me come in, oh let me!

(*To the branches.*)

I want no shadows. My rays
must get in everywhere,
even among the dark trunks I want
the whisper of gleaming lights,
so that this night there will be
sweet blood for my cheeks,
and for the reeds that cluster
at the wide feet of the wind.
Who is hiding? Out, I say!
No! They will not get away!
I will light up the horse
with a fever bright as diamonds.

(*He disappears among the trunks, and the stage goes back to its dark lighting. An* OLD WOMAN *comes out completely covered by thin green cloth. She is barefooted. Her face can barely be seen among the folds. This character does not appear in the cast.*)

BEGGAR WOMAN.

That moon's going away, just when they're
     near.

They won't get past here. The river's
     whisper

and the whispering tree trunks will muffle

the torn flight of their shrieks.

It has to be here, and soon. I'm worn
     out.

The coffins are ready, and white sheets

wait on the floor of the bedroom

for heavy bodies with torn throats.

Let not one bird awake, let the breeze,
     gathering their moans in her skirt,

fly with them over black tree tops

or bury them in soft mud.

     (*Impatiently.*)

Oh, that moon! That moon!

     (THE MOON *appears. The intense blue
     light returns.*)

MOON.   They're coming. One band
through the ravine and the other along
the river. I'm going to light up the boulders. What do you need?

BEGGAR WOMAN.   Nothing.

MOON.   The wind blows hard now,
with a double edge.

BEGGAR WOMAN.   Light up the waistcoat and open the buttons; the knives
will know the path after that.

MOON.

But let them be a long time a-dying. So
     the blood

will slide its delicate hissing between my
     fingers.

Look how my ashen valleys already are
     waking

in longing for this fountain of shudder-
     ing gushes!

BEGGAR WOMAN.   Let's not let them
get past the arroyo. Silence!

MOON.   There they come! (*He goes.
The stage is left dark.*)

BEGGAR WOMAN.   Quick! Lots of
light! Do you hear me? They can't get
away!

     (THE BRIDEGROOM *and* THE FIRST
YOUTH *enter.* THE BEGGAR WOMAN *sits
down and covers herself with her cloak.*)

BRIDEGROOM.   This way.

FIRST YOUTH.   You won't find them.

BRIDEGROOM (*angrily*).   Yes, I'll find
them.

FIRST YOUTH.   I think they've taken
another path.

BRIDEGROOM.   No. Just a moment ago
I felt the galloping.

FIRST YOUTH.   It could have been another horse.

BRIDEGROOM (*intensely*).   Listen to
me. There's only one horse in the whole
world, and this one's it. Can't you understand that? If you're going to follow
me, follow me without talking.

FIRST YOUTH.   It's only that I want
to . . .

BRIDEGROOM.   Be quiet. I'm sure of
meeting them there. Do you see this
arm? Well, it's not my arm. It's my
brother's arm, and my father's, and that
of all the dead ones in my family. And
it has so much strength that it can pull
this tree up by the roots, if it wants to.
And let's move on, because here I feel
the clenched teeth of all my people in
me so that I can't breathe easily.

BEGGAR WOMAN (*whining*).   Ay-y-y!

FIRST YOUTH.   Did you hear that?

BRIDEGROOM.   You go that way and
then circle back.

FIRST YOUTH.   This is a hunt.

BRIDEGROOM.   A hunt. The greatest
hunt there is.

     (THE YOUTH *goes off.* THE BRIDE-
GROOM *goes rapidly to the left and stumbles over* THE BEGGAR WOMAN, DEATH.)

BEGGAR WOMAN.   Ay-y-y!

BRIDEGROOM.   What do you want?

BEGGAR WOMAN.   I'm cold.

BRIDEGROOM.   Which way are you
going?

BEGGAR WOMAN (*always whining like
a beggar*).   Over there, far away . . .

BRIDEGROOM.   Where are you from?

BEGGAR WOMAN.   Over there . . .
very far away.

BRIDEGROOM.   Have you seen a man
and a woman running away on a horse?

BEGGAR WOMAN (*awakening*). Wait a minute . . . (*She looks at him.*) Handsome young man. (*She rises.*) But you'd be much handsomer sleeping.

BRIDEGROOM. Tell me; answer me. Did you see them?

BEGGAR WOMAN. Wait a minute . . . What broad shoulders! How would you like to be laid out on them and not have to walk on the soles of your feet which are so small?

BRIDEGROOM (*shaking her*). I asked you if you saw them! Have they passed through here?

BEGGAR WOMAN (*energetically*). No. They haven't passed; but they're coming from the hill. Don't you hear them?

BRIDEGROOM. No.

BEGGAR WOMAN. Do you know the road?

BRIDEGROOM. I'll go, whatever it's like!

BEGGAR WOMAN. I'll go along with you. I know this country.

BRIDEGROOM (*impatiently*). Well, let's go! Which way?

BEGGAR WOMAN (*dramatically*). This way!

(*They go rapidly out. Two violins, which represent the forest, are heard distantly. The* WOODCUTTERS *return. They have their axes on their shoulders. They move slowly among the tree trunks.*)

FIRST WOODCUTTER.

O rising death!
Death among the great leaves.

SECOND WOODCUTTER.

Don't open the gush of blood!

FIRST WOODCUTTER.

O lonely death!
Death among the dried leaves.

THIRD WOODCUTTER.

Don't lay flowers over the wedding!

SECOND WOODCUTTER.

O sad death!
Leave for their love a green branch.

FIRST WOODCUTTER.

O evil death!

Leave for their love a branch of green!

(*They go out while they are talking.* LEONARDO *and* THE BRIDE *appear.*)

LEONARDO.

Hush!

BRIDE.

From here I'll go on alone.
You go now! I want you to turn back.

LEONARDO.

Hush, I said!

BRIDE.

With your teeth, with your hands, any-
　　way you can,
take from my clean throat
the metal of this chain,
and let me live forgotten
back there in my house in the ground.
And if you don't want to kill me
as you would kill a tiny snake,
set in my hands, a bride's hands,
the barrel of your shotgun.
Oh, what lamenting, what fire,
sweeps upward through my head!
What glass splinters are stuck in my
　　tongue!

LEONARDO.

We've taken the step now; hush!
because they're close behind us,
and I must take you with me.

BRIDE.

Then it must be by force!

LEONARDO.

By force? Who was it first
went down the stairway?

BRIDE.

I went down it.

LEONARDO.

And who was it put
a new bridle on the horse?

BRIDE.

I myself did it. It's true.

LEONARDO.

And whose were the hands
strapped spurs to my boots?

BRIDE.

The same hands, these that are yours,
but which when they see you would like
to break the blue branches
and sunder the purl of your veins.

I love you! I love you! But leave me!
For if I were able to kill you
I'd wrap you 'round in a shroud
with the edges bordered in violets.
Oh, what lamenting, what fire,
sweeps upward through my head!
    LEONARDO.
What glass splinters are stuck in my
    tongue!
Because I tried to forget you
and put a wall of stone
between your house and mine.
It's true. You remember?
And when I saw you in the distance
I threw sand in my eyes.
But I was riding a horse
and the horse went straight to your
    door.
And the silver pins of your wedding
turned my red blood black.
And in me our dream was choking
my flesh with its poisoned weeds.
Oh, it isn't my fault—
the fault is the earth's—
and this fragrance that you exhale
from your breasts and your braids.
    BRIDE.
Oh, how untrue! I want
from you neither bed nor food,
yet there's not a minute each day
that I don't want to be with you,
because you drag me, and I come,
then you tell me to go back
and I follow you,
like chaff blown on the breeze.
I have left a good, honest man,
and all his people,
with the wedding feast half over
and wearing my bridal wreath.
But you are the one will be punished
and that I don't want to happen.
Leave me alone now! You run away!
There is no one who will defend you.
    LEONARDO.
The birds of early morning
are calling among the trees.
The night is dying
on the stone's ridge.
Let's go to a hidden corner

where I may love you forever,
for to me the people don't matter,
nor the venom they throw on us.
    (*He embraces her strongly.*)
    BRIDE.
And I'll sleep at your feet,
to watch over your dreams.
Naked, looking over the fields,
as though I were a bitch.
Because that's what I am! Oh, I look at
    you
and your beauty sears me.
    LEONARDO.
Fire is stirred by fire.
The same tiny flame
will kill two wheat heads together.
Let's go!
    BRIDE.
Where are you taking me?
    LEONARDO.
Where they cannot come,
these men who surround us.
Where I can look at you!
    BRIDE (*sarcastically*).
Carry me with you from fair to fair,
a shame to clean women,
so that people will see me
with my wedding sheets
on the breeze like banners.
    LEONARDO.
I, too, would want to leave you
if I thought as men should.
But wherever you go, I go.
You're the same. Take a step. Try.
Nails of moonlight have fused
my waist and your thighs.
    (*This whole scene is violent, full of
great sensuality.*)
    BRIDE.
Listen!
    LEONARDO.
They're coming.
    BRIDE.
              Run!
It's fitting that I should die here,
with water over my feet,
with thorns upon my head.
And fitting the leaves should mourn me,
a woman lost and virgin.

LEONARDO.
Be quiet. Now they're appearing.
    BRIDE.   Go now!
    LEONARDO.
Quiet. Don't let them hear us.
    (*The Bride hesitates.*)
    BRIDE.
Both of us!
    LEONARDO (*embracing her*).
                Any way you want!
If they separate us, it will be
because I am dead.
    BRIDE.
             And I dead too.
    (*They go out in each other's arms.*)
    (THE MOON *appears very slowly. The
stage takes on a strong blue light. The
two violins are heard. Suddenly two long,
ear-splitting shrieks are heard, and the
music of the two violins is cut short. At
the second shriek* THE BEGGAR WOMAN
*appears and stands with her back to the
audience. She opens her cape and stands
in the center of the stage like a great
bird with immense wings.* THE MOON
*halts. The curtain comes down in ab-
solute silence.*

SCENE 2

(*The Final Scene.*)

    (*A white dwelling with arches and
thick walls. To the right and left, are
white stairs. At the back, a great arch
and a wall of the same color. The floor
also should be shining white. This simple
dwelling should have the monumental
feeling of a church. There should not be
a single gray nor any shadow, not even
what is necessary for perspective.*)

    (*Two* GIRLS *dressed in dark blue are
winding a red skein.*)

    FIRST GIRL.
Wool, red wool,
what would you make?
    SECOND GIRL.
Oh, jasmine for dresses,
fine wool like glass.
At four o'clock born,

at ten o'clock dead.
A thread from this wool yarn,
a chain 'round your feet
a knot that will tighten
the bitter white wreath.
    LITTLE GIRL (*singing*).
Were you at the wedding?
    FIRST GIRL.
No.
    LITTLE GIRL.
Well, neither was I!
What could have happened
'midst the shoots of the vineyards?
What could have happened
'neath the branch of the olive?
What really happened
that no one came back?
Were you at the wedding?
    SECOND GIRL.
We told you once, no.
    LITTLE GIRL (*leaving*).
Well, neither was I!
    SECOND GIRL.
Wool, red wool,
what would you sing?
    FIRST GIRL.
Their wounds turning waxen
balm-myrtle for pain.
Asleep in the morning,
and watching at night.
    LITTLE GIRL (*in the doorway*).
And then, the thread stumbled
on the flinty stones,
but mountains, blue mountains,
are letting it pass.
Running, running, running,
and finally to come
to stick in a knife blade,
to take back the bread.
    (*She goes out.*)
    SECOND GIRL.
Wool, red wool,
what would you tell?
    FIRST GIRL.
The lover is silent,
crimson the groom,
at the still shoreline
I saw them laid out.
    (*She stops and looks at the skein.*)

LITTLE GIRL (*appearing in the doorway*).
Running, running, running,
the thread runs to here.
All covered with clay
I feel them draw near.
Bodies stretched stiffly
in ivory sheets!

(THE WIFE *and* MOTHER-IN-LAW *of* LEONARDO *appear. They are anguished.*)

FIRST GIRL.   Are they coming yet?

MOTHER-IN-LAW (*harshly*).   We don't know.

SECOND GIRL.   What can you tell us about the wedding?

FIRST GIRL.   Yes, tell me.

MOTHER-IN-LAW (*curtly*).   Nothing.

LEONARDO'S WIFE.   I want to go back and find out all about it.

MOTHER-IN-LAW (*sternly*).
You, back to your house.
Brave and alone in your house.
To grow old and to weep.
But behind closed doors.
Never again. Neither dead nor alive.
We'll nail up our windows
and let rains and nights
fall on the bitter weeds.

LEONARDO'S WIFE.   What could have happened?

MOTHER-IN-LAW.
It doesn't matter what.
Put a veil over your face.
Your children are yours,
that's all. On the bed
put a cross of ashes
where his pillow was.

(*They go out.*)

BEGGAR WOMAN (*at the door*).   A crust of bread, little girls.

LITTLE GIRL.   Go away!

(*The* GIRLS *huddle close together.*)

BEGGAR WOMAN.   Why?

LITTLE GIRL.   Because you whine; go away!

FIRST GIRL.   Child!

BEGGAR WOMAN.
I might have asked for your eyes! A cloud

of birds is following me. Will you have one?

LITTLE GIRL.   I want to get away from here!

SECOND GIRL (*to the* BEGGAR WOMAN).   Don't mind her!

FIRST GIRL.   Did you come by the road through the arroyo?

BEGGAR WOMAN.   I came that way!

FIRST GIRL (*timidly*).   Can I ask you something?

BEGGAR WOMAN.
I saw them: they'll be here soon; two torrents
still at last, among the great boulders,
two men at the horse's feet.
Two dead men in the night's splendor.
(*With pleasure.*)
Dead, yes, dead.

FIRST GIRL.   Hush, old woman, hush!

BEGGAR WOMAN.
Crushed flowers for eyes, and their teeth
two fistfuls of hard-frozen snow.
Both of them fell, and the Bride returns
with bloodstains on her skirt and hair.
And they come covered with two sheets
carried on the shoulders of two tall boys.
That's how it was; nothing more. What was fitting.
Over the golden flower, dirty sand.
(*She goes. The* GIRLS *bow their heads and start going out rhythmically.*)

FIRST GIRL.
Dirty sand.

SECOND GIRL.
Over the golden flower.

LITTLE GIRL.
Over the golden flower
they're bringing the dead from the arroyo.
Dark the one,
dark the other.
What shadowy nightingale flies and weeps
over the golden flower!
(*She goes. The stage is left empty.* THE MOTHER *and a* NEIGHBOR WOMAN *appear.* THE NEIGHBOR *is weeping.*)

MOTHER. Hush.

NEIGHBOR. I can't.

MOTHER. Hush, I said. (*At the door.*) Is there nobody here? (*She puts her hands to her forehead.*) My son ought to answer me. But now my son is an armful of shrivelled flowers. My son is a fading voice beyond the mountains now. (*With rage, to* THE NEIGHBOR.) Will you shut up? I want no wailing in this house. Your tears are only tears from your eyes, but when I'm alone mine will come—from the soles of my feet, from my roots—burning more than blood.

NEIGHBOR. You come to my house; don't you stay here.

MOTHER. I want to be here. Here. In peace. They're all dead now: and at midnight I'll sleep, sleep without terror of guns or knives. Other mothers will go to their windows, lashed by rain, to watch for their sons' faces. But not I. And of my dreams I'll make a cold ivory dove that will carry camellias of white frost to the graveyard. But no; not graveyard, not graveyard: the couch of earth, the bed that shelters them and rocks them in the sky. (*A woman dressed in black enters, goes toward the right, and there kneels. To* THE NEIGHBOR.) Take your hands from your face. We have terrible days ahead. I want to see no one. The earth and I. My grief and I. And these four walls. Ay-y-y! Ay-y-y! (*She sits down, overcome.*)

NEIGHBOR. Take pity on yourself!

MOTHER (*pushing back her hair*). I must be calm. (*She sits down.*) Because the neighbor women will come and I don't want them to see me so poor. So poor! A woman without even one son to hold to her lips.

(THE BRIDE *appears. She is without her wreath and wears a black shawl.*)

NEIGHBOR (*with rage, seeing* THE BRIDE). Where are you going?

BRIDE. I'm coming here.

MOTHER (*to* THE NEIGHBOR). Who is it?

NEIGHBOR. Don't you recognize her?

MOTHER. That's why I asked who it was. Because I don't want to recognize her, so I won't sink my teeth in her throat. You snake! (*She moves wrathfully on* THE BRIDE, *then stops. To* THE NEIGHBOR.) Look at her! There she is, and she's crying, while I stand here calmly and don't tear her eyes out. I don't understand myself. Can it be I didn't love my son? But, where's his good name? Where is it now? Where is it? (*She beats* THE BRIDE *who drops to the floor.*)

NEIGHBOR. For God's sake! (*She tries to separate them.*)

BRIDE (*to* THE NEIGHBOR). Let her; I came here so she'd kill me and they'd take me away with them. (*To* THE MOTHER.) But not with her hands; with grappling hooks, with a sickle—and with force—until they break on my bones. Let her! I want her to know I'm clean, that I may be crazy, but that they can bury me without a single man ever having seen himself in the whiteness of my breasts.

MOTHER. Shut up, shut up; what do I care about that?

BRIDE. Because I ran away with the other one; I ran away! (*With anguish.*) You would have gone, too. I was a woman burning with desire, full of sores inside and out, and your son was a little bit of water from which I hoped for children, land, health; but the other one was a dark river, choked with brush, that brought near me the undertone of its rushes and its whispered song. And I went along with your son who was like a little boy of cold water—and the other sent against me hundreds of birds who got in my way and left white frost on my wounds, my wounds of a poor withered woman, of a girl caressed by fire. I didn't want to; remember that! I didn't want to. Your son was my destiny

and I have not betrayed him, but the
other one's arm dragged me along like
the pull of the sea, like the head toss of
a mule, and he would have dragged me
always, always, always—even if I were
an old woman and all your son's sons
held me by the hair!

(*A* NEIGHBOR *enters.*)

MOTHER. She is not to blame; nor
am I! (*Sarcastically.*) Who is, then? It's
a delicate, lazy, sleepless woman who
throws away an orange blossom wreath
and goes looking for a piece of bed
warmed by another woman!

BRIDE. Be still! Be still! Take your
revenge on me; here I am! See how soft
my throat is; it would be less work for
you than cutting a dahlia in your garden.
But never that! Clean, clean as a new-
born little girl. And strong enough to
prove it to you. Light the fire. Let's
stick our hands in; you, for your son, I,
for my body. *You'll* draw yours out first.

(*Another* NEIGHBOR *enters.*)

MOTHER. But what does your good
name matter to me? What does your
death matter to me? What does anything about anything matter to me?
Blessèd be the wheat stalks, because my
sons are under them; blessèd be the
rain, because it wets the face of the dead.
Blessèd be God, who stretches us out
together to rest.

(*Another* NEIGHBOR *enters.*)

BRIDE. Let me weep with you.

MOTHER. Weep. But at the door.

(THE GIRL *enters.* THE BRIDE *stays at
the door.* THE MOTHER *is at the center
of the stage.*)

LEONARDO'S WIFE (*entering and going to the left*).
He was a beautiful horseman,
now he's a heap of snow.
He rode to fairs and mountains
and women's arms.
Now, the night's dark moss
crowns his forehead.

MOTHER.
A sunflower to your mother,

a mirror of the earth.
Let them put on your breast
the cross of bitter rosebay;
and over you a sheet
of shining silk;
between your quiet hands
let water form its lament.

WIFE.
Ay-y-y, four gallant boys
come with tired shoulders!

BRIDE.
Ay-y-y, four gallant boys
carry death on high!

MOTHER.
Neighbors.

LITTLE GIRL (*at the door*).
They're bringing them now.

MOTHER.
It's the same thing.
Always the cross, the cross.

WOMEN.
Sweet nails,
cross adored,
sweet name
of Christ our Lord.

BRIDE. May the cross protect both
the quick and the dead.

MOTHER.
Neighbors: with a knife,
with a little knife,
on their appointed day, between two and
    three,
these two men killed each other for
    love.
With a knife,
with a tiny knife
that barely fits the hand,
but that slides in clean
through the astonished flesh
and stops at the place
where trembles, enmeshed,
the dark root of a scream.

BRIDE.
And this is a knife,
a tiny knife
that barely fits the hand;
fish without scales, without river,
so that on their appointed day, between
    two and three,

with this knife,
two men are left stiff,
with their lips turning yellow.
    MOTHER.
And it barely fits the hand
but it slides in clean

through the astonished flesh
and stops there, at the place
where trembles enmeshed
the dark root of a scream.
    (THE NEIGHBORS, *kneeling on the floor, sob.*)

JEAN ANOUILH / 1910–

"I have no biography, and I am very glad of it." So Jean Anouilh prefaced a short biographical sketch, the point of which was that what little life lay beyond his plays was private. Anouilh was born in Bordeaux, of a tailor father and a mother who played the violin in an orchestra. His schooling, chiefly in Paris, ended with a year or so in law studies, after which he wrote for an advertising agency. He was writing plays at an early age, wrote for the motion pictures while in advertising, and gave all his time to the theater as soon as he could afford to. Molière, Pirandello, and Giraudoux were influential in his development. Anouilh was secretary to a theatrical company at twenty-one, then a playwright, finally a director of his own plays and a force in the modern theater. In all, he has had some thirty plays produced.

Le Voyageur sans bagage (*Traveller Without Luggage*) succeeded on the stage in 1937; since then Anouilh has been a consistently successful dramatist, producing a new play almost every year. Popularity outside France followed upon his *Antigone,* produced in Paris during the German occupation and taken by the French as propaganda for resistance (Antigone) to collaboration (Creon). The play may be and has been otherwise interpreted; it is possible that its political overtones were the product rather of the French audiences than of the play. Anouilh is certainly not a political dramatist; the themes of *Antigone* appear in his work both before and after the German occupation.

Anouilh's plays were published in collections whose titles indicate something (not all) about their tone and temper: *Pièces noires* (*Black Plays*), *Nouvelles pièces noires* (*New Black Plays*), *Pièces roses* (*Rose Plays*), *Pièces brillantes* (*Brilliant Plays*), and *Pièces grinçantes* (*Grating Plays*). Anouilh has developed a variety of themes. A strain of pessimism or world-weary cynicism about the powers of the individual and the honesty of life runs through his dramatizations of the classes, of the sexes, and of the family. He has reinterpreted Greek classics and historical characters, and explored appearance and reality, rôle and identity. His dramatic modes range from unrelieved realism, through fantasy and realism in conjunction, to complete abandonment to the fantastic and grotesque. He is of the theater, with a theatrical sense of unity and projection which gives his plays individuality and dramatic character.

Among Anouilh's more important plays are *Antigone, Le Bal des voleurs* (*Thieves' Carnival*), *L'Invitation au château* (titled *Ring Round the Moon* in its Christopher Fry adaptation), *La Valse des toréadors* (*Waltz of the Toreadors*), *L'Alouette* (*The Lark*), and *Becket ou L'Honneur de Dieu* (*Becket or The Honor of God*).

In a charming account of how he came to write *Becket,* Anouilh speaks of "this drama of friendship between two men, between the king and his friend, his companion in pleasure and in work (and this is what had gripped me about the story), this friend whom he could not cease to love though he became his worst enemy the night he was named archbishop. . . ."

Becket or The Honor of God

TRANSLATED BY LUCIENNE HILL

CHARACTERS

(*In order of appearance*)

HENRY II.
THOMAS BECKET.
ARCHBISHOP OF CANTERBURY.
GILBERT FOLLIOT.
BISHOP OF YORK.
SAXON PEASANT.
HIS SON.
GWENDOLEN.
1ST ENGLISH BARON.
2ND ENGLISH BARON.
3RD ENGLISH BARON.
4TH ENGLISH BARON.
QUEEN MOTHER.
THE QUEEN.
LOUIS, KING OF FRANCE.
THE POPE.

Act I

(*An indeterminate set, with pillars. We are in the cathedral. Center stage:* BECKET'S *tomb; a stone slab with a name carved on it. Two* SENTRIES *come in and take up their position upstage. Then the* KING *enters from the back. He is wearing his crown, and is naked under a big cloak. A* PAGE *follows at a distance. The* KING *hesitates a moment before the tomb; then removes his cloak with a swift movement and the* PAGE *takes it away. He falls to his knees on the stone floor and prays, alone, naked, in the middle of the stage. Behind the pillars, in the shadows, one senses the disquieting presence of unseen lookers-on.*)

KING. Well, Thomas Becket, are you satisfied? I am naked at your tomb and your monks are coming to flog me. What an end to our story! You, rotting in this tomb, larded with my barons' dagger thrusts, and I, naked, shivering in the draughts, and waiting like an idiot for those brutes to come and thrash me. Don't you think we'd have done better to understand each other?

(BECKET *in his Archbishop's robes, just as he was on the day of his death, has appeared on the side of the stage, from behind a pillar. He says softly:*)

BECKET. Understand each other? It wasn't possible.

KING. I said, "In all save the honor of the realm." It was you who taught me that slogan, after all.

BECKET. I answered you, "In all save the honor of God." We were like two deaf men talking.

KING. How cold it was on that bare plain at La Ferté-Bernard, the last time we two met! It's funny, it's always been cold, in our story. Save at the beginning, when we were friends. We had a few fine summer evenings together, with the girls . . . (*He says suddenly:*) Did you love Gwendolen, Archbishop? Did you hate me, that night when I said, "I am the King," and took her from you? Perhaps that's what you never could forgive me for?

BECKET (*quietly*). I've forgotten.

KING. Yet we were like two brothers, weren't we—you and I? That night it was a childish prank—a lusty lad shouting "I am the King!" . . . I was so young . . . And every thought in my head came from you, you know that.

BECKET (*gently, as if to a little boy*). Pray, Henry, and don't talk so much.

KING (*irritably*). If you think I'm

in the mood for praying at the moment
. . . (BECKET *quietly withdraws into the*
darkness and disappears during the
KING'S *next speech.*) I can see them
through my fingers, spying on me from
the aisles. Say what you like, they're an
oafish lot, those Saxons of yours! To give
oneself over naked to those ruffians!
With my delicate skin . . . Even you'd be
afraid. Besides, I'm ashamed. Ashamed
of this whole masquerade. I need them
though, that's the trouble. I have to rally
them to my cause, against my son, who'll
gobble up my kingdom if I let him. So
I've come to make my peace with their
Saint. You must admit it's funny. You've
become a Saint and here am I, the King,
desperately in need of that great amor-
phous mass which could do nothing,
up till now, save lie inert beneath its
own enormous weight, cowering under
blows, and which is all-powerful now.
What use are conquests, when you stop
to think? They are England now, because of their vast numbers, and the
rate at which they breed—like rabbits,
to make good the massacres. But one
must always pay the price—that's another thing you taught me, Thomas
Becket, when you were still advising
me . . . You taught me everything . . .
(*Dreamily.*) Ah, those were happy
times . . . At the peep of dawn—well,
our dawn that is, around noon, because
we always went to bed very late—you'd
come into my room, as I was emerging
from the bathhouse, rested, smiling, debonair, as fresh as if we'd never spent
the entire night drinking and whoring
through the town. (*He says a little*
sourly:) That's another thing you were
better at than me . . .

(*The* PAGE *has come in. He wraps a*
white towel around the KING *and pro-*
ceeds to rub him down. Off stage is heard
for the first time—we will hear it often
—the gay, ironical Scottish marching
song which BECKET *is always whistling.*)

(*The lighting changes. We are still in*
the empty cathedral. Then, a moment
or so later, BECKET *will draw aside a*
curtain and reveal the KING'S *room.*
Their manner, his and the KING'S*, far-*
away at first like a memory relived, will
gradually become more real.)

(THOMAS BECKET, *dressed as a noble-*
man, elegant, young, charming, in his
short doublet and pointed, upturned
shoes, comes in blithely and greets the
KING.)

BECKET.   My respects, my Lord!

KING (*his face brightening*).   Oh,
Thomas . . . I thought you were still
asleep.

BECKET.   I've already been for a
short gallop to Richmond and back, my
Lord. There's a divine nip in the air.

KING (*his teeth chattering*).   To
think you actually like the cold! (*To the*
PAGE.) Rub harder, pig! (*Smiling,*
BECKET *pushes the* PAGE *aside and pro-*
ceeds to rub the KING *himself.*) (*To the*
PAGE.) Throw a log on the fire and get
out. Come back and dress me later.

BECKET.   My Prince, I shall dress you
myself.

(*The* PAGE *goes.*)

KING.   Nobody rubs me down the
way you do. Thomas, what would I do
without you? You're a nobleman, why
do you play at being my valet? If I
asked my barons to do this, they'd start
a civil war!

BECKET (*smiling*).   They'll come
round to it in time, when Kings have
learnt to play their role. I am your servant, my prince, that's all. Helping you
to govern or helping you get warm
again is part of the same thing to me.
I like helping you.

KING (*with an affectionate little ges-*
ture).   My little Saxon! At the beginning, when I told them I was taking you
into my service, do you know what they
all said? They said you'd seize the chance
to knife me in the back one day.

BECKET (*smiling as he dresses him*).
Did you believe them, my prince?

KING. N . . . no. I was a bit scared at first. You know I scare easily . . . But you looked so well brought up, beside those brutes. However did you come to speak French without a trace of an English accent?

BECKET. My parents were able to keep their lands by agreeing to "collaborate," as they say, with the King your father. They sent me to France as a boy to acquire a good French accent.

KING. To France? Not to Normandy?

BECKET (*still smiling*). That was their one patriotic conceit. They loathed the Norman accent.

KING (*distinctly*). Only the accent?

BECKET (*lightly and inscrutably*). My father was a very severe man. I would never have taken the liberty of questioning him on his personal convictions while he was alive. And his death shed no light on them, naturally. He managed, by collaborating, to amass a considerable fortune. As he was also a man of rigid principles, I imagine he contrived to do it in accordance with his conscience. That's a little piece of sleight of hand that men of principle are very skillful at in troubled times.

KING. And you?

BECKET (*feigning not to understand the question*). I, my Lord?

KING (*putting a touch of contempt into his voice, for despite his admiration for Thomas or perhaps because of it, he would like to score a point against him occasionally*). The sleight of hand, were you adept at it too?

BECKET (*still smiling*). Mine was a different problem. I was a frivolous man, you'll agree? In fact, it never came up at all. I adore hunting and only the Normans and their protégés had the right to hunt. I adore luxury and luxury was Norman. I adore life and the Saxons' only birthright was slaughter. I'll add that I adore honor.

KING (*with faint surprise*). And was honor reconciled with collaboration too?

BECKET (*lightly*). I had the right to draw my sword against the first Norman nobleman who tried to lay hands on my sister. I killed him in single combat. It's a detail, but it has its points.

KING (*a little slyly*). You could always have slit his throat and fled into the forest, as so many did.

BECKET. That would have been uncomfortable, and not a lot of use. My sister would immediately have been raped by some other Norman baron, like all the Saxon girls. Today, she is respected. (*Lightly.*) My Lord, did I tell you?— My new gold dishes have arrived from Florence. Will my Liege do me the honor of christening them with me at my house?

KING. Gold dishes! You lunatic!

BECKET. I'm setting a new fashion.

KING. I'm your King and I eat off silver!

BECKET. My prince, your expenses are heavy and I have only my pleasures to pay for. The trouble is I'm told they scratch easily. Still, we'll see. I received two forks as well—

KING. Forks?

BECKET. Yes. It's a new instrument, a devilish little thing to look at—and to use too. It's for pronging meat with and carrying it to your mouth. It saves you dirtying your fingers.

KING. But then you dirty the fork?

BECKET. Yes. But it's washable.

KING. So are your fingers. I don't see the point.

BECKET. It hasn't any, practically speaking. But it's refined, it's subtle. It's very un-Norman.

KING (*with sudden delight*). You must order me a dozen! I want to see my great fat barons' faces, at the first court banquet, when I present them with that! We won't tell them what they're for. We'll have no end of fun with them.

BECKET (*laughing*). A dozen! Easy

now, my Lord! Forks are very expensive you know! My prince, it's time for the Privy Council.

KING (*laughing too*). They won't make head nor tail of them! I bet you they'll think they're a new kind of dagger. We'll have a hilarious time!

(*They go out, laughing, behind the curtain, which draws apart to reveal the same set, with the pillars. The Council Chamber. The Councilors stand waiting. The* KING *and* BECKET *come in, still laughing.*)

KING (*sitting in a chair*). Gentlemen, the Council is open. I have summoned you here today to deal with this refusal of the clergy to pay the absentee tax. We really must come to an understanding about who rules this kingdom, the Church—(*The* ARCHBISHOP *tries to speak.*) just a moment, Archbishop!— or me! But before we quarrel, let us take the good news first. I have decided to revive the office of Chancellor of England, keeper of the Triple Lion Seal and to entrust it to my loyal servant and subject Thomas Becket.

(BECKET *rises in surprise, the color draining from his face.*)

BECKET. My Lord . . . !

KING (*roguishly*). What's the matter, Becket? Do you want to go and piss already? True, we both had gallons to drink last night! (*He looks at him with delight.*) Well, that's good! I've managed to surprise you for once, little Saxon.

BECKET (*dropping on one knee, says gravely*). My Liege, this is a token of your confidence of which I fear I may not be worthy. I am very young, frivolous perhaps—

KING. I'm young too. And you know more than all of us put together. (*To the others.*) He's read books, you know. It's amazing the amount he knows. He'll checkmate the lot of you! Even the Archbishop! As for his frivolity, don't let him fool you! He drinks strong wine,

he likes to enjoy himself, but he's a lad who thinks every minute of the time! Sometimes it embarrasses me to feel him thinking away beside me. Get up, Thomas. I never did anything without your advice anyway. Nobody knew it, now everybody will, that's all. (*He bursts out laughing, pulls something out of his pocket and gives it to* BECKET.) There. That's the Seal. Don't lose it. Without the Seal, there's no more England and we'll all have to go back to Normandy. Now, to work!

(*The* ARCHBISHOP *rises, all smiles, now the first shock is over.*)

ARCHBISHOP. May I crave permission to salute, with my Lord's approval, my young and learned archdeacon here? For I was the first—I am weak enough to be proud of pointing it out—to notice him and take him under my wing. The presence at this Council, with the preponderant title of Chancellor of England, of one of our brethren—our spiritual son in a sense—is a guarantee for the Church of this country, that a new era of agreement and mutual understanding is dawning for us all and we must now, in a spirit of confident cooperation—

KING (*interrupting*). Etc., etc. . . . Thank you, Archbishop! I knew this nomination would please you. But don't rely too much on Becket to play your game. He is my man. (*He turns to* BECKET, *beaming.*) Come to think of it, I'd forgotten you were a deacon, little Saxon.

BECKET (*smiling*). So had I, my prince.

KING. Tell me—I'm not talking about wenching, that's a venial sin—but on the odd occasions when I've seen you fighting, it seems to me you have a mighty powerful sword arm, for a priest! How do you reconcile that with the Church's commandment forbidding a priest to shed blood?

BISHOP OF OXFORD (*prudently*). Our young friend is only a deacon, he has not yet taken all his vows, my Lord. The Church in its wisdom knows that youth must have its day and that—under the sacred pretext of a war—a holy war, I mean, of course, young men are permitted to—

KING (*interrupting*). All wars are holy wars, Bishop! I defy you to find me a serious belligerent who doesn't have Heaven on his side, in theory. Let's get back to the point.

ARCHBISHOP. By all means, your Highness.

KING. Our customs demand that every landowner with sufficient acreage to maintain one must send a man-at-arms to the quarterly review of troops, fully armed and shield in hand, or pay a tax in silver. Where is my tax?

BISHOP OF OXFORD. *Distingo,* your Highness.

KING. Distinguish as much as you like. I've made up my mind. I want my money. My purse is open, just drop it in. (*He sprawls back in his chair and picks his teeth. To* BECKET.) Thomas, I don't know about you, but I'm starving. Have them bring us something to eat.

(BECKET *makes a sign to the* SENTRY *who goes out. A pause. The* ARCHBISHOP *rises.*)

ARCHBISHOP. A layman who shirks his duty to the State, which is to assist his Prince with arms, should pay the tax. Nobody will question that.

KING (*jovially*). Least of all the clergy!

ARCHBISHOP (*continuing*). A churchman's duty to the State is to assist his Prince in his prayers, and in his educational and charitable enterprises. He cannot therefore be liable to such a tax unless he neglects those duties.

BISHOP OF OXFORD. Have we refused to pray?

KING (*rising in fury*). Gentlemen! Do you seriously think that I am going to let myself be swindled out of more than two thirds of my revenues with

arguments of that sort? In the days of the Conquest, when there was booty to be had, our Norman abbots tucked up their robes all right. And lustily too! Sword in fist, hams in the saddle, at cockcrow or earlier! "Let's go to it, Sire! Out with the Saxon scum! It's God's will! It's God's will!" You had to hold them back then! And on the odd occasions when you wanted a little Mass, they never had the time. They'd mislaid their vestments, the churches weren't equipped—any excuse to put it off, for fear they'd miss some of the pickings while their backs were turned!

ARCHBISHOP. Those heroic days are over. It is peacetime now.

KING. Then pay up! I won't budge from that. (*Turning to* BECKET.) Come on, Chancellor, say something! Has your new title caught your tongue?

BECKET. May I respectfully draw my Lord Archbishop's attention to one small point?

KING (*grunting*). Respectfully, but firmly. You're the Chancellor now.

BECKET (*calmly and casually*). England is a ship.

KING (*beaming*). Why, that's neat! We must use that, sometime.

BECKET. In the hazards of seafaring, the instinct of self-preservation has always told men that there must be one and only one master on board ship. Mutinous crews who drown their captain always end up, after a short interval of anarchy, by entrusting themselves body and soul to one of their number, who then proceeds to rule over them, more harshly sometimes than their drowned captain.

ARCHBISHOP. My Lord Chancellor— my young friend—there is in fact a saying—the captain is sole master after God. (*He thunders suddenly, with a voice one did not suspect from that frail body:*) After God!

(*He crosses himself. All the* BISHOPS *follow suit. The wind of excommunica-*

tion shivers through the Council. The KING, *awed, crosses himself too and mumbles, a little cravenly.*)

KING. Nobody's trying to question God's authority, Archbishop.

BECKET (*who alone has remained unperturbed*). God steers the ship by inspiring the captain's decisions. But I never heard tell that He gave His instructions directly to the helmsman.

(GILBERT FOLLIOT, *Bishop of London, rises. He is a thin-lipped, venomous man.*)

FOLLIOT. Our young Chancellor is only a deacon—but he is a member of the Church. The few years he has spent out in the tumult of the world cannot have made him forget so soon that it is through His Church Militant and more particularly through the intermediary of our Holy Father the Pope and his Bishops—his qualified representatives—that God dictates His decisions to men!

BECKET. There is a chaplain on board every ship, but he is not required to determine the size of the crew's rations, nor to take the vessel's bearings. My Reverend Lord the Bishop of London—who is the grandson of a sailor they tell me—cannot have forgotten that point either.

FOLLIOT (*yelping*). I will not allow personal insinuations to compromise the dignity of a debate of this importance! The integrity and honor of the Church of England are at stake!

KING (*cheerfully*). No big words, Bishop. You know as well as I do that all that's at stake is its money. I need money for my wars. Will the Church give me any, yes or no?

ARCHBISHOP (*cautiously*). The Church of England has always acknowledged that it was its duty to assist the King, to the best of its ability, in all his needs.

KING. There's a fine speech. But I don't like the past tense, Archbishop. There's something so nostalgic about it.

I like the present. And the future. Are you going to pay up?

ARCHBISHOP. Your Highness, I am here to defend the privileges which your illustrious forefather William granted to the Church of England. Would you have the heart to tamper with your forefather's work?

KING. May he rest in peace. His work is inviolable. But where he is now he doesn't need money. I'm still on earth unfortunately, and I do.

FOLLIOT. Your Highness, this is a question of principle!

KING. I'm levying troops, Bishop! I have sent for 1,500 German foot soldiers, and three thousand Swiss infantry to help fight the King of France. And nobody has ever paid the Swiss with principles.

BECKET (*rises suddenly and says incisively*): I think, your Highness, that it is pointless to pursue a discussion in which neither speaker is listening to the other. The law and custom of the land give us the means of coercion. We will use them.

FOLLIOT (*beside himself*). Would you dare—you whom she raised from the obscurity of your base origins—to plunge a dagger in the bosom of your Mother Church?

BECKET. My Lord and King has given me his Seal with the Three Lions to guard. My mother is England now.

FOLLIOT (*frothing, and slightly ridiculous*). A deacon! A miserable deacon nourished in our bosom! Traitor! Little viper! Libertine! Sycophant! Saxon!

KING. My Reverend friend, I suggest you respect my Chancellor, or else I'll call my guards. (*He has raised his voice a little toward the end of this speech. The* GUARDS *come in.*) (*Surprised.*) Why, here they are! Oh, no, it's my snack. Excuse me, gentlemen, but around noon I need something to peck at or I tend to feel week. And a King has no right to weaken. I needn't tell you that. I'll have it in my chapel, then I can pray directly afterwards. Come and sit with me, son.

(*He goes out taking* BECKET *with him. The three prelates have risen, deeply offended. They move away, murmuring to one another, with sidelong glances in the direction in which the* KING *went out.*)

FOLLIOT. We must appeal to Rome! We must take a firm line!

YORK. My Lord Archbishop, you are the Primate of England. Your person is inviolate and your decisions on all matters affecting the Church are law in this country. You have a weapon against such intransigence: excommunication.

BISHOP OF OXFORD. We must not use it save with a great deal of prudence, Reverend Bishop. The Church has always triumphed over the centuries, but it has triumphed prudently. Let us bide our time. The King's rages are terrible, but they don't last. They are fires of straw.

FOLLIOT. The little self-seeker he has at his elbow now will make it his business to kindle them. And I think, like the Reverend Bishop, that only the excommunication of that young libertine can reduce him to impotence.

(BECKET *comes in.*)

BECKET. My Lords, the King has decided to adjourn his Privy Council. He thinks that a night of meditation will inspire your Lordships with a wise and equitable solution—which he authorizes you to come and submit to him tomorrow.

FOLLIOT (*with a bitter laugh*). You mean it's time for the hunt.

BECKET (*smiling*). Yes, my Lord Bishop, to be perfectly frank with you, it is. Believe me, I am personally most grieved at this difference of opinion and the brutal form it has taken. But I cannot go back on what I said as Chancellor of England. We are all bound, laymen as well as priests, by the same

feudal oath we took to the King as our Lord and Sovereign; the oath to preserve his life, limbs, dignity and honor. None of you, I think, has forgotten the words of that oath?

ARCHBISHOP (*quietly*). We have not forgotten it, my son. No more than the other oath we took, before that—the oath to God. You are young, and still uncertain of yourself, perhaps. Yet you have, in those few words, taken a resolution the meaning of which has not escaped me. Will you allow an old man, who is very close to death, and who, in this rather sordid argument, was defending more perhaps than you suspect—to hope, as a father, that you will never know the bitterness of realizing, one day, that you made a mistake. (*He holds out his ring and* BECKET *kisses it.*) I give you my blessing, my son.

(BECKET *has knelt. Now he rises and says lightly:*)

BECKET. An unworthy son, Father, alas. But when is one worthy? And worthy of what? (*He pirouettes and goes out, insolent and graceful as a young boy.*)

FOLLIOT (*violently*). Such insults to your Grace cannot be tolerated. This young rake's impudence must be crushed!

ARCHBISHOP (*thoughtfully*). He was with me for a long time. His is a strange, elusive nature. Don't imagine he is the ordinary libertine that outward appearances would suggest. I've had plenty of opportunity to observe him, in the bustle of pleasure and daily living. He is as it were detached. As if seeking his real self.

FOLLIOT. Break him, my Lord, before he finds it! Or the clergy of this country will pay dearly.

ARCHBISHOP. We must be very circumspect. It is our task to see into the hearts of men. And I am not sure that this one will always be our enemy.

(*The* ARCHBISHOP *and the three* BISHOPS *go out. The* KING *is heard calling off stage.*)

KING. Well, son, have they gone? Are you coming hunting?

(*Trees come down from the flies. The black velvet curtain at the back opens on a clear sky, transforming the pillars into the leafless trees of a forest in winter. Bugles. The lights have gone down. When they go up again, the* KING *and* BECKET *are on horseback, each with a hawk on his gauntleted wrist. Torrential rain is heard.*)

KING. Here comes the deluge. (*Unexpectedly.*) Do you like hunting this way, with hawks?

BECKET. I don't much care to delegate my errands. I prefer to feel a wild boar on the end of my spear. When he turns and charges there's a moment of delicious personal contact when one feels, at last, responsible for oneself.

KING. It's odd, this craving for danger. Why are you all so hell-bent on risking your necks for the most futile reasons?

BECKET. One has to gamble with one's life to feel alive.

KING. Or dead! You make me laugh. (*To his hawk:*) Quiet, my pretty, quiet! We'll take your hood off in a minute. You couldn't give much of a performance under all these trees. I'll tell you one creature that loves hawking anyway, and that's a hawk! It seems to me we've rubbed our backsides sore with three hours' riding, just to give them this royal pleasure.

BECKET (*smiling*). My Lord, these are Norman hawks. They belong to the master race. They have a right to it.

KING (*suddenly, as he reins his horse*). Do you love me, Becket?

BECKET. I am your servant, my prince.

KING. Did you love me when I made you Chancellor? I wonder sometimes if you're capable of love. Do you love Gwendolen?

BECKET. She is my mistress, my prince.

KING. Why do you put labels onto everything to justify your feelings?

BECKET. Because, without labels, the world would have no shape, my prince.

KING. Is it so important for the world to have a shape?

BECKET. It's essential, my prince, otherwise we can't know what we're doing. (*Bugles in the distance.*) The rain is getting heavier, my Lord! Come, let us shelter in that hut over there.

(*He gallops off. After a second of confused indecision, the* KING *gallops after him, holding his hawk high and shouting:*)

KING. Becket! You didn't answer my question!

(*He disappears into the forest. Bugles again. The four* BARONS *cross the stage, galloping after them, and vanish into the forest. Thunder. Lightning. A hut has appeared to one side of the stage.* BECKET *is heard shouting:*)

BECKET. Hey there! You! Fellow! Can we put the horses under cover in your barn? Do you know how to rub down a horse? And have a look at the right forefoot of messire's horse. I think the shoe is loose. We'll sit out the storm under your roof.

(*After a second, the* KING *enters the hut, followed by a hairy Saxon who, cap in hand, bows repeatedly, in terrified silence.*)

KING (*shaking himself*). What a soaking! I'll catch my death! (*He sneezes.*) All this just to keep the hawks amused! (*Shouting at the* MAN.) What are you waiting for? Light a fire, dog! It's freezing cold in this shack. (*The* MAN, *terror-stricken, does not move. The* KING *sneezes again. To* BECKET.) What is he waiting for?

BECKET. Wood is scarce, my Lord. I don't suppose he has any left.

KING. What—in the middle of the forest?

BECKET. They are entitled to two

measures of dead wood. One branch more and they're hanged.

KING (*astounded*). Really? And yet people are always complaining about the amount of dead wood in the forests. Still, that's a problem for my intendants, not me. (*Shouting at the* MAN.) Run and pick up all the wood you can carry and build us a roaring fire! We won't hang you this time, dog!

(*The peasant, terrified, dares not obey.* BECKET *says gently:*)

BECKET. Go, my son. Your King commands it. You've the right.

(*The* MAN *goes out, trembling, bowing to the ground, repeatedly.*)

KING. Why do you call that old man your son?

BECKET. Why not? You call him dog, my prince.

KING. It's a manner of speaking. Saxons are always called "dog." I can't think why, really. One could just as well have called them "Saxon"! But that smelly old ragbag your son! (*Sniffing.*) What on earth can they eat to make the place stink so—dung?

BECKET. Turnips.

KING. Turnips—what are they?

BECKET. Roots.

KING (*amused*). Do they eat roots?

BECKET. Those who live in the forests can't grow anything else.

KING. Why don't they move out into the open country then?

BECKET. They would be hanged if they left their area.

KING. Oh, I see. Mark you, that must make life a lot simpler, if you know you'll be hanged at the least show of initiative. You must ask yourself far fewer questions. They don't know their luck! But you still haven't told me why you called the fellow your son?

BECKET (*lightly*). My prince, he is so poor and so bereft and I am so strong beside him, that he really is my son.

KING. We'd go a long way with that theory!

BECKET. Besides, my prince, you're appreciably younger than I am and you call me "son" sometimes.

KING. That's got nothing to do with it. It's because I love you.

BECKET. You are our King. We are all your sons and in your hands.

KING. What, Saxons too?

BECKET (*lightly, as he strips off his gloves*). England will be fully built, my prince, on the day the Saxons are your sons as well.

KING. You are a bore today! I get the feeling that I'm listening to the Archbishop. And I'm dying of thirst. Hunt around and see if you can't find us something to drink. Go on, it's your son's house! (BECKET *starts looking, and leaves the room after a while. The* KING *looks around too, examining the hut with curiosity, touching things with grimaces of distaste. Suddenly he notices a kind of trap door at the foot of a wall. He opens it, thrusts his hand in and pulls out a terrified* GIRL. *He shouts:*) Hey, Thomas! Thomas!

(BECKET *comes in.*)

BECKET. Have you found something to drink, Lord?

KING (*holding the* GIRL *at arm's length*). No. Something to eat. What do you say to that, if it's cleaned up a bit?

BECKET (*coldly*). She's pretty.

KING. She stinks a bit, but we could wash her. Look, did you ever see anything so tiny? How old would you say it was—fifteen, sixteen?

BECKET (*quietly*). It can talk, my Lord. (*Gently, to the* GIRL.) How old are you?

(*The* GIRL *looks at them in terror and says nothing.*)

KING. You see? Of course it can't talk! (*The* MAN *has come back with the wood and stops in the doorway, terrified.*) How old is your daughter, dog? (*The* MAN *trembles like a cornered animal and says nothing.*) He's dumb as well, that son of yours. How did you get him—with a deaf girl? It's funny the amount of dumb people I meet the second I set foot out of my palace. I rule over a kingdom of the dumb. Can you tell me why?

BECKET. They're afraid, my prince.

KING. I know that. And a good thing too. The populace must live in fear, it's essential. The moment they stop being afraid they have only one thought in mind—to frighten other people instead. And they adore doing that! Just as much as we do! Give them a chance to do it and they catch up fast, those sons of yours! Did you never see a peasants' revolt? I did once, in my father's reign, when I was a child. It's not a pretty sight. (*He looks at the* MAN, *exasperated.*) Look at it, will you? It's tongue-tied, it's obtuse, it stinks and the country is crawling with them! (*He seizes the* GIRL *who was trying to run away.*) Stay here, you! (*To* BECKET.) I ask you, what use is it?

BECKET (*smiling*). It scratches the soil, it makes bread.

KING. Pooh, the English eat so little of it . . . At the French Court, yes, I daresay—they fairly stuff it down! But here!

BECKET (*smiling*). The troops have to be fed. For a King without troops . . .

KING (*struck by this*). True enough! Yes, that makes sense. There must be some sort of reason in all these absurdities. Very well, you little Saxon philosopher, you! I don't know how you do it, but you'll turn me into an intelligent man yet! The odd thing is, it's so ugly and yet it makes such pretty daughters. How do you explain that, you who can explain it all?

BECKET. At twenty, before he lost his teeth and took on that indeterminate age the common people have, that man may have been handsome. He may have had one night of love, one minute when

he too was a King, and shed his fear. Afterwards, his pauper's life went on, eternally the same. And he and his wife no doubt forgot it all. But the seed was sown.

KING (*dreamily*). You have such a way of telling things . . . (*He looks at the* GIRL.) Do you think she'll grow ugly too?

BECKET. For sure.

KING. If we made her a whore and kept her at the palace, would she stay pretty?

BECKET. Perhaps.

KING. Then we'd be doing her a service, don't you think?

BECKET (*coldly*). No doubt.

(*The* MAN *stiffens. The* GIRL *cowers, in terror. The* BROTHER *comes in, somber-faced, silent, threatening.*)

KING. Would you believe it? They understand every word, you know! Who's that one there?

BECKET (*taking in the situation at a glance*). The brother.

KING. How do you know?

BECKET. Instinct, my Lord. (*His hand moves to his dagger.*)

KING (*bawling suddenly*). Why are they staring at me like that? I've had enough of this! I told you to get something to drink, dog!

(*Terrified, the* MAN *scuttles off.*)

BECKET. Their water will be brackish. I have a gourd of juniper juice in my saddlebag. (*To the* BROTHER.) Come and give me a hand, you! My horse is restive.

(*He seizes the boy roughly by the arm and hustles him out into the forest, carelessly whistling his little marching song. Then, all of a sudden, he hurls himself onto him. A short silent struggle.* BECKET *gets the boy's knife away; he escapes into the forest.* BECKET *watches him go for a second, holding his wounded hand. Then he walks around the back of the hut. The* KING *has settled himself on a bench, with his feet up on another, whistling to himself. He lifts the* GIRL'S *skirts with his cane and examines her at leisure.*)

KING (*in a murmur*). All my sons! . . . (*He shakes himself.*) That Becket! He wears me out. He keeps making me think! I'm sure it's bad for the health. (*He gets up,* BECKET *comes in followed by the* MAN.) What about that water? How much longer do I have to wait?

BECKET. Here it is, my Lord. But it's muddy. Have some of this juniper juice instead.

KING. Drink with me. (*He notices* BECKET'S *hand, wrapped in a blood-stained cloth.*) What's the matter? You're wounded!

BECKET (*hiding his hand*). No doubt about it, that horse of mine is a nervous brute. He can't bear his saddle touched. He bit me.

KING (*with a hearty, delighted laugh*). That's funny! Oh, that's very funny! Milord is the best rider in the Kingdom! Milord can never find a stallion with enough spirit for him! Milord makes us all look silly at the jousts, with his fancy horsemanship, and when he goes to open his saddlebags he gets himself bitten! Like a page! (*He is almost savagely gleeful. Then suddenly, his gaze softens.*) You're white as a sheet, little Saxon . . . Why do I love you? . . . It's funny, I don't like to think of you in pain. Show me that hand. A horse bite can turn nasty. I'll put some of that juniper gin on it.

BECKET (*snatching his hand away*). I already have, my Lord, it's nothing.

KING. Then why do you look so pale? Show me your hand.

BECKET (*with sudden coldness*). It's an ugly wound and you know you hate the sight of blood.

KING (*steps back a little, then exclaims with delight*). All this just to fetch me a drink! Wounded in the serv-ice of the King! We'll tell the others you defended me against a wild boar and I'll present you with a handsome gift this evening. What would you like?

BECKET (*softly*). This girl. (*He adds after a pause.*) I fancy her.

(*A pause.*)

KING (*his face clouding over*). That's tiresome of you. I fancy her too. And where that's concerned, friendship goes by the board. (*A pause. His face takes on a cunning look.*) All right, then. But favor for favor. You won't forget, will you?

BECKET. No, my prince.

KING. Favor for favor; do you give me your word as a gentleman?

BECKET. Yes, my prince.

KING (*draining his glass, suddenly cheerful*). Done! She's yours. Do we take her with us or shall we have her sent?

BECKET. I'll send two soldiers to fetch her. Listen. The others have caught up.

(*A troop of men-at-arms have come riding up behind the shack during the end of the scene.*)

KING (*to the* MAN). Wash your daughter, dog, and kill her fleas. She's going to the palace. For Milord here, who's a Saxon too. You're pleased about that, I hope? (*To* BECKET *as he goes.*) Give him a gold piece. I'm feeling generous this morning.

(*He goes out. The* MAN *looks at* BECKET *in terror.*)

BECKET. No one will come and take your daughter away. Keep her better hidden in future. And tell your son to join the others, in the forest, he'll be safer there, now. I think one of the soldiers saw us. Here!

(*He throws him a purse and goes out. When he has gone, the* MAN *snatches up the purse, then spits venomously, his face twisted with hate.*)

MAN. God rot your guts! Pig!

GIRL (*unexpectedly*). He was handsome, that one. Is it true he's taking me to the palace?

MAN. You whore! You Norman's trollop!

(*He hurls himself onto her and beats her savagely. The* KING, BECKET *and the* BARONS *have galloped off, amid the sound of bugles. The hut and the forest backcloth disappear. We are in* BECKET'S *palace.*)

(FOOTMEN *push on a kind of low bed-couch, with cushions and some stools. Upstage, between two pillars, a curtain behind which can be seen the shadows of banqueting guests. Singing and roars of laughter. Downstage, curled up on the bed,* GWENDOLEN *is playing a string instrument. The curtain is drawn aside.* BECKET *appears. He goes to* GWENDOLEN *while the banqueting and the laughter, punctuated by hoarse incoherent snatches of song, go on upstage.* GWENDOLEN *stops playing.*)

GWENDOLEN. Are they still eating?

BECKET. Yes. They have an unimaginable capacity for absorbing food.

GWENDOLEN (*softly, beginning to play again*). How can my Lord spend his days and a large part of his nights with such creatures?

BECKET (*crouching at her feet and caressing her*). If he spent his time with learned clerics debating the sex of angels, your Lord would be even more bored, my kitten. They are as far from the true knowledge of things as mindless brutes.

GWENDOLEN (*gently, as she plays*). I don't always understand everything my Lord condescends to say to me . . . What I do know is that it is always very late when he comes to see me.

BECKET (*caressing her*). The only thing I love is coming to you. Beauty is one of the few things which don't shake one's faith in God.

GWENDOLEN. I am my Lord's war captive and I belong to him body and soul. God has willed it so, since He gave the Normans victory over my people. If the Welsh had won the war I would have married a man of my own race, at my father's castle. God did not will it so.

BECKET (*quietly*). That belief will do as well as any, my kitten. But, as I belong to a conquered race myself, I have a feeling that God's system is a little muddled. Go on playing.

(GWENDOLEN *starts to play again. Then she says suddenly:*)

GWENDOLEN. I'm lying. You are my Lord, God or no God. And if the Welsh had been victorious, you could just as easily have stolen me from my father's castle. I should have come with you. (*She says this gravely.* BECKET *rises abruptly and moves away. She looks up at him with anguished eyes and stops playing.*) Did I say something wrong? What is the matter with my Lord?

BECKET. Nothing. I don't like being loved. I told you that.

(*The curtain opens. The* KING *appears.*)

KING (*a little drunk*). Well, son, have you deserted us? It worked! I told you! They've tumbled to it! They're fighting with your forks! They've at last discovered that they're for poking one another's eyes out. They think it's a most ingenious little invention. You'd better go in, son, they'll break them in a minute. (BECKET *goes behind the curtain to quieten his guests. He can be heard shouting.*) Gentlemen, gentlemen! No, no, they aren't little daggers. No, truly—they're for pronging meat . . . Look, let me show you again.

(*Huge roars of laughter behind the curtain. The* KING *has moved over to* GWENDOLEN. *He stares at her.*)

KING. Was that you playing, while we were at table?

GWENDOLEN (*with a deep curtsy*). Yes, my Lord.

KING. You have every kind of accomplishment, haven't you? Get up.

(*He lifts her to her feet, caressing her as he does so. She moves away, ill at ease. He says with a wicked smile:*)

KING. Have I frightened you, my heart? We'll soon put that right. (*He pulls the curtain aside.*) Hey there, Becket! That's enough horseplay, my fat lads! Come and hear a little music. When the belly's full, it's good to elevate the mind a bit. (*To* GWENDOLEN.) Play! (*The four* BARONS, *bloated with food and drink, come in with* BECKET. GWENDOLEN *has taken up her instrument again. The* KING *sprawls on the bed, behind her. The* BARONS, *with much sighing and puffing, unclasp their belts and sit down on stools, where they soon fall into a stupor.* BECKET *remains standing.*) Tell her to sing us something sad. I like sad music after dinner, it helps the digestion. (*He hiccups.*) You always feed us far too well, Thomas. Where did you steal that cook of yours?

BECKET. I bought him, Sire. He's a Frenchman.

KING. Really? Aren't you afraid he might poison you? Tell me, how much does one pay for a French cook?

BECKET. A good one, like him, costs almost as much as a horse, my Lord.

KING (*genuinely outraged*). It's outrageous! What is the country coming to! No man is worth a horse! If I said "favor for favor"—remember?—and I asked you to give him to me, would you?

BECKET. Of course, my Lord.

KING (*with a smile, gently caressing* GWENDOLEN). Well, I won't. I don't want to eat too well every day; it lowers a man's morale. Sadder, sadder, my little doe. (*He belches.*) Oh, that venison! Get her to sing that lament they composed for your mother, Becket. It's my favorite song.

BECKET. I don't like anyone to sing that lament, my Lord.

KING. Why not? Are you ashamed of being a Saracen girl's son? That's half your charm, you fool! There must be some reason why you're more civilized than all the rest of us put together! I adore that song. (GWENDOLEN *looks uncertainly at* BECKET. *There is a pause. Then the* KING *says coldly.*) That's an order, little Saxon.

BECKET (*inscrutably, to* GWENDOLEN.) Sing.

(*She strikes a few opening chords, while the* KING *makes himself comfortable beside her, belching contentedly. She begins.*)

GWENDOLEN (*singing*).
Handsome Sir Gilbert
Went to the war
One fine morning in May
To deliver the heart
Of Lord Jesus our Saviour,
From the hands of the Saracens.

Woe! Woe! Heavy is my heart
At being without love!
Woe! Woe! Heavy is my heart
All the livelong day!
KING (*singing*).
All the livelong day! Go on!
GWENDOLEN.
As the battle raged
He swung his mighty sword
And many a Moor fell dead
But his trusty charger
Stumbled in the fray
And Sir Gilbert fell.

Woe! Woe! Heavy is my heart!
At being without love!
Woe! Woe! Heavy is my heart
All the livelong day.

Wounded in the head
Away Gilbert was led
To the Algiers market
Chained hand and foot
And sold there as a slave.
KING (*singing, out of tune*).
All the livelong day!
GWENDOLEN.
A Saracen's daughter
Lovely as the night

Lost her heart to him
Swore to love him always
Vowed to be his wife.

Woe! Woe! Heavy is my heart
At being without love!
Woe! Woe! Heavy is my heart
All the livelong day—

KING (*interrupting*). It brings tears to my eyes, you know, that story. I look a brute but I'm soft as swansdown really. One can't change one's nature. I can't imagine why you don't like people to sing that song. It's wonderful to be a love child. When I look at my august parents' faces, I shudder to think what must have gone on. It's marvelous to think of your mother helping your father to escape and then coming to join him in London with you inside her. Sing us the end, girl. I adore the end.

GWENDOLEN (*softly*).
Then he asked the holy Father
For a priest to baptize her
And he took her as his wife
To cherish with his life
Giving her his soul
To love and keep alway.

Gay! Gay! Easy is my heart
At being full of love
Gay! Gay! Easy is my heart
To be loved alway.

KING (*dreamily*). Did he really love her all his life? Isn't it altered a bit in the song?

BECKET. No, my prince.

KING (*getting up, quite saddened*). Funny, it's the happy ending that makes me feel sad . . . Tell me, do you believe in love, Thomas?

BECKET (*coldly*). For my father's love for my mother, Sire, yes.

(*The* KING *has moved over to the* BARONS *who are now snoring on their stools. He gives them a kick as he passes.*)

KING. They've fallen asleep, the hogs. That's their way of showing their finer feelings. You know, my little Saxon, sometimes I have the impression that you and I are the only sensitive men in England. We eat with forks and we have infinitely distinguished sentiments, you and I. You've made a different man of me, in a way . . . What you ought to find me now, if you loved me, is a girl to give me a little polish. I've had enough of whores. (*He has come back to* GWENDOLEN. *He caresses her a little and then says suddenly:*) Favor for favor—do you remember?

(*A pause.*)

BECKET (*pale*). I am your servant, my prince, and all I have is yours. But you were also gracious enough to say I was your friend.

KING. That's what I mean! As one friend to another it's the thing to do! (*A short pause. He smiles maliciously, and goes on caressing* GWENDOLEN *who cowers, terrified.*) You care about her then? Can you care for something? Go on, tell me, tell me if you care about her? (BECKET *says nothing. The* KING *smiles.*) You can't tell a lie. I know you. Not because you're afraid of lies—I think you must be the only man I know who isn't afraid of anything—not even Heaven—but because it's distasteful to you. You consider it inelegant. What looks like morality in you is nothing more than esthetics. Is that true or isn't it?

BECKET (*meeting his eyes, says softly*). It's true, my Lord.

KING. I'm not cheating if I ask for her, am I? I said "favor for favor" and I asked you for your word of honor.

BECKET (*icily*). And I gave it to you.

(*A pause. They stand quite still. The* KING *looks at* BECKET *with a wicked smile.* BECKET *does not look at him. Then the* KING *moves briskly away.*)

KING. Right. I'm off to bed. I feel like an early night tonight. Delightful evening, Becket. You're the only man in England who knows how to give your friends a royal welcome. (*He kicks the slumbering* BARONS.) Call my guards and help me wake these porkers. (*The*

BARONS *wake with sighs and belches as the* KING *pushes them about, shouting:*) Come on, Barons, home! I know you're connoisseurs of good music, but we can't listen to music all night long. Happy evenings end in bed, eh Becket?

BECKET (*stiffly*). May I ask your Highness for a brief moment's grace?

KING. Granted! Granted! I'm not a savage. I'll wait for you both in my litter. You can say good night to me downstairs.

(*He goes out, followed by the* BARONS. BECKET *stands motionless for a while under* GWENDOLEN'S *steady gaze. Then he says quietly.*)

BECKET. You will have to go with him, Gwendolen.

GWENDOLEN (*composedly*). Did my Lord promise me to him?

BECKET. I gave him my word as a gentleman that I would give him anything he asked for. I never thought it would be you.

GWENDOLEN. If he sends me away tomorrow, will my Lord take me back?

BECKET. No.

GWENDOLEN. Shall I tell the girls to put my dresses in the coffer?

BECKET. He'll send over for it tomorrow. Go down. One doesn't keep the King waiting. Tell him I wish him a respectful good night.

GWENDOLEN (*laying her viol on the bed*). I shall leave my Lord my viol. He can almost play it now. (*She asks, quite naturally:*) My Lord cares for nothing, in the whole world, does he?

BECKET. No.

GWENDOLEN (*moves to him and says gently*). You belong to a conquered race too. But through tasting too much of the honey of life, you've forgotten that even those who have been robbed of everything have one thing left to call their own.

BECKET (*inscrutably*). Yes, I daresay I had forgotten. There is a gap in me where honor ought to be. Go now.

(GWENDOLEN *goes out.* BECKET *stands quite still. Then he goes to the bed, picks up the viol, looks at it, then throws it abruptly away. He pulls off the fur coverlet and starts to unbutton his doublet. A* GUARD *comes in, dragging the* SAXON GIRL *from the forest, whom he throws down in the middle of the room. The* KING *appears.*)

KING (*hilariously*). Thomas, my son! You'd forgotten her! You see how careless you are! Luckily I think of everything. It seems they had to bully the father and the brother a tiny bit to get her, but anyway, here she is. You see? —I really am a friend to you, and you're wrong not to love me. You told me you fancied her. I hadn't forgotten that, you see. Sleep well, son!

(*He goes out, followed by the* GUARD. *The* GIRL, *still dazed, looks at* BECKET *who has not moved. She recognizes him, gets to her feet and smiles at him. A long pause, then she asks with a kind of sly coquetry:*)

GIRL. Shall I undress, my Lord?

BECKET (*who has not moved*). Of course. (*The* GIRL *starts to undress.* BECKET *looks at her coldly, absentmindedly whistling a few bars of his little march. Suddenly he stops, goes to the* GIRL, *who stands there dazed and half naked, and seizes her by the shoulders.*) I hope you're full of noble feelings and that all this strikes you as pretty shabby?

(*A* SERVANT *runs in wildly and halts in the doorway speechless. Before he can speak, the* KING *comes stumbling in.*)

KING (*soberly*). I had no pleasure with her, Thomas. She let me lay her down in the litter, limp as a corpse, and then suddenly she pulled out a little knife from somewhere. There was blood everywhere . . . I feel quite sick. (BECKET *has let go of the* GIRL. *The* KING *adds, haggard:*) She could easily have killed me instead! (*A pause. He says abruptly:*) Send that girl away. I'm sleeping in your room tonight. I'm frightened. (BECKET *motions to the* SERVANT, *who takes away the half-naked* GIRL. *The* KING *has thrown himself, fully dressed, onto the bed with an animal-like sigh.*) Take half the bed.

BECKET. I'll sleep on the floor, my prince.

KING. No. Lie down beside me. I don't want to be alone tonight. (*He looks at him and murmurs:*) You loathe me, I shan't even be able to trust you now . . .

BECKET. You gave me your Seal to keep, my prince. And the Three Lions of England which are engraved on it keep watch over me too. (*He snuffs out the candles, all save one. It is almost dark.*)

KING (*his voice already thick with sleep*). I shall never know what you're thinking . . .

(BECKET *has thrown a fur coverlet over the* KING. *He lies down beside him and says quietly:*)

BECKET. It will be dawn soon, my prince. You must sleep. Tomorrow we are crossing to the Continent. In a week we will face the King of France's army and there will be simple answers to everything at last.

(*He has lain down beside the* KING. *A pause, during which the* KING'S *snoring gradually increases. Suddenly, the* KING *moans and tosses in his sleep.*)

KING (*crying out*). They're after me! They're after me! They're armed to the teeth! Stop them! Stop them!

(BECKET *sits up on one elbow. He touches the* KING, *who wakes up with a great animal cry.*)

BECKET. My prince . . . my prince . . . sleep in peace. I'm here.

KING. Oh . . . Thomas, it's you . . . They were after me.

(*He turns over and goes back to sleep with a sigh. Gradually he begins to snore again, softly.* BECKET *is still on one elbow. Almost tenderly, he draws the coverlet over the* KING.)

BECKET. My prince . . . If you were my true prince, if you were one of my race, how simple everything would be. How tenderly I would love you, my

prince, in an ordered world. Each of us bound in fealty to the other, head, heart and limbs, with no further questions to ask of oneself, ever. (*A pause. The* KING'S *snores grow louder.* BECKET *sighs and says with a little smile:*) But I cheated my way, a twofold bastard, into the ranks and found a place among the conquerors. You can sleep peacefully though, my prince. So long as Becket is obliged to improvise his honor, he will serve you. And if one day, he meets it face to face . . . (*A short pause.*) But where is Becket's honor?

(*He lies down with a sigh, beside the* KING. *The* KING'S *snores grow louder still. The candle sputters. The lights grow even dimmer . . .*)

Act II

(*The curtain rises on the same set of arching pillars, which now represents a forest in France. The* KING'S *tent, not yet open for the day, is set up among the trees. A* SENTRY *stands some way off.*)

(*It is dawn. Crouched around a camp-fire, the four* BARONS *are having their morning meal, in silence. After a while, one of them says:*)

1ST BARON. This Becket then, who is he?

(*A pause. All four are fairly slow in their reactions.*)

2ND BARON (*surprised at the question*). The Chancellor of England.

1ST BARON. I know that! But who is he, exactly?

2ND BARON. The Chancellor of England, I tell you! The Chancellor of England is the Chancellor of England! I don't see what else there is to inquire into on that score.

1ST BARON. You don't understand. Look, supposing the Chancellor of England were some other man. Me, for instance . . .

2ND BARON. That's plain idiotic.

1ST BARON. I said supposing. Now, I would be Chancellor of England but I wouldn't be the same Chancellor of England as Becket is. You can follow that, can you?

2ND BARON (*guardedly*). Yes . . .

1ST BARON. So, I *can* ask myself the question.

2ND BARON. What question?

1ST BARON. Who is this man Becket?

2ND BARON. What do you mean, who is this man Becket? He's the Chancellor of England.

1ST BARON. Yes. But what I'm asking myself is who is he, as a man?

2ND BARON (*looks at him and says sorrowfully*). Have you got a pain?

1ST BARON. No, why?

2ND BARON. A Baron who asks himself questions is a sick Baron. Your sword—what's that?

1ST BARON. My sword?

2ND BARON. Yes.

1ST BARON (*putting his hand to the hilt*). It's my sword! And anyone who thinks different—

2ND BARON. Right. Answered like a nobleman. We peers aren't here to ask questions. We're here to give answers.

1ST BARON. Right then. Answer me.

2ND BARON. Not to questions! To orders. You aren't asked to think in the army. When you're face to face with a French man-at-arms, do you ask yourself questions?

1ST BARON. No.

2ND BARON. Does he?

1ST BARON. No.

2ND BARON. You just fall to and fight. If you started asking each other questions like a pair of women, you might as well bring chairs onto the battlefield. If there are any questions to be asked you can be sure they've been asked already, higher up, by cleverer heads than yours.

1ST BARON (*vexed*). I meant I didn't like him, that's all.

2ND BARON. Why couldn't you say so then? That we'd have understood. You're entitled not to like him. I don't like him either, come to that. To begin with, he's a Saxon.

1ST BARON. To begin with!

3RD BARON. One thing you can't say though. You can't say he isn't a fighter. Yesterday when the King was in the thick of it, after his squire was killed, he cut his way right through the French, and he seized the King's banner and drew the enemy off and onto himself.

1ST BARON. All right! He's a good fighter!

3RD BARON (*to* 2ND BARON). Isn't he a good fighter?

2ND BARON (*stubbornly*). Yes. But he's a Saxon.

1ST BARON (*to the* 4TH BARON, *who has so far said nothing*). How about you, Regnault? What do you think of him?

4TH BARON (*placidly, swallowing his mouthful of food*). I'm waiting.

1ST BARON. Waiting for what?

4TH BARON. Till he shows himself. Some sorts of game are like that; you follow them all day through the forest, by sounds, or tracks, or smell. But it wouldn't do any good to charge ahead with drawn lance; you'd just spoil everything because you don't know for sure what sort of animal it is you're dealing with. You have to wait.

1ST BARON. What for?

4TH BARON. For whatever beast it is to show itself. And if you're patient it always does in the end. Animals know more than men do, nearly always, but a man has something in him that an animal hasn't got: he knows how to wait. With this man Becket—I'll wait.

1ST BARON. For what?

4TH BARON. For him to show himself. For him to break cover. (*He goes on eating.*) The day he does, we'll know who he is.

(BECKET's *little whistle march is heard off stage.* BECKET *comes in, armed.*)

BECKET. Good morning to you, gentlemen. (*The four* BARONS *rise politely, and salute.*) Is the King still asleep?

1ST BARON (*stiffly*). He hasn't called yet.

BECKET. Has the camp marshal presented his list of losses?

1ST BARON. No.

BECKET. Why not?

2ND BARON (*surlily*). He was part of the losses.

BECKET. Oh?

1ST BARON. I was nearby when it happened. A lance knocked him off his horse. Once on the ground, the foot soldiers dealt with him.

BECKET. Poor Beaumont. He was so proud of his new armor.

2ND BARON. There must have been a chink in it then. They bled him white. On the ground. French swine!

BECKET (*with a slight shrug*). That's war.

1ST BARON. War is a sport like any other. There are rules. In the old days, they took you for ransom. A Knight for a Knight. That was proper fighting!

BECKET (*smiling*). Since one has taken to sending the foot soldiery against the horses with no personal protection save a cutlass, they're a little inclined to seek out the chink in the armor of any Knight unwise enough to fall off his horse. It's repulsive, but I can understand them.

1ST BARON. If we start understanding the common soldiery war will be butchery plain and simple.

BECKET. The world is certainly tending towards butchery, Baron. The lesson of this battle, which has cost us far too much, is that we will have to form platoons of cutthroats too, that's all.

1ST BARON. And a soldier's honor, my Lord Chancellor, what of that?

BECKET (*dryly*). A soldier's honor, Baron, is to win victories. Let us not be hypocritical. The Norman nobility lost no time in teaching those they conquered that little point. I'll wake the King. Our entry into the city is timed for eight o'clock and the *Te Deum* in the cathedral for a quarter past nine. It would be bad policy to keep the French Bishop waiting. We want these people to collaborate with a good grace.

1ST BARON (*grunting*). In my day, we slaughtered the old and marched in afterwards.

BECKET. Yes, into a dead city! I want to give the King living cities to increase his wealth. From eight o'clock this morning, I am the French people's dearest friend.

1ST BARON. What about England's honor, then?

BECKET (*quietly*). England's honor, Baron, in the final reckoning, has always been to succeed.

(*He goes into the* KING's *tent smiling. The four* BARONS *look at each other, hostile.*)

1ST BARON (*muttering*). What a mentality!

4TH BARON (*sententiously*). We must wait for him. One day, he'll break cover.

(*The four* BARONS *move away.* BECKET *lifts the tent flap and hooks it back. The* KING *is revealed, in bed with a girl.*)

KING (*yawning*). Good morning, son. Did you sleep well?

BECKET. A little memento from the French on my left shoulder kept me awake, Sire. I took the opportunity to do some thinking.

KING (*worriedly*). You think too much. You'll suffer for it, you know! It's because people think that there are problems. One day, if you go on like this, you'll think yourself into a dilemma, your big head will present you with a solution and you'll jump feet first into a hopeless mess—which you'd have done far better to ignore, like the majority of fools, who know nothing and live to a ripe old age. What do you think of my little French girl? I must say, I adore France.

BECKET (*smiling*). So do I, Sire, like all Englishmen.

KING. The climate's warm, the girls are pretty, the wine is good. I intend to spend at least a month here every winter.

BECKET. The only snag is, it's expensive! Nearly 2,000 casualties yesterday.

KING. Has Beaumont made out his total?

BECKET. Yes. And he added himself to the list.

KING. Wounded? (BECKET *does not answer. The* KING *shivers. He says somberly:*) I don't like learning that people I know have died. I've a feeling it may give Death ideas.

BECKET. My prince, shall we get down to work? We haven't dealt with yesterday's dispatches.

KING. Yesterday we were fighting! We can't do everything.

BECKET. That was a holiday! We'll have to work twice as hard today.

KING. Does it amuse you—working for the good of my people? Do you mean to say you love all those folk? To begin with they're too numerous. One can't love them, one doesn't know them. Anyway, you're lying, you don't love anything or anybody.

BECKET (*tersely*). There's one thing I do love, my prince, and that I'm sure of. Doing what I have to do and doing it well.

KING (*grinning*). Always the es—es . . . What's your word again? I've forgotten it.

BECKET. Esthetics?

KING. Esthetics! Always the esthetic side, eh?

BECKET. Yes, my prince.

KING (*slapping the* GIRL's *rump*). And isn't that esthetic too? Some people go into ecstasies over cathedrals. But this is a work of art too! Look at that—round as an apple . . . (*Quite naturally, as if* he were offering him a sweetmeat:*) Want her?

BECKET (*smiling*). Business, my Lord!

KING (*pouting like a schoolboy*). All right. Business. I'm listening. Sit down.

(BECKET *sits down on the bed, beside the* KING, *with the* GIRL *like a fascinated rabbit in between them.*)

BECKET. The news is not good, my prince.

KING (*with a careless wave of the hand*). News never is. That's a known fact. Life is one long web of difficulties. The secret of it—and there is one, brought to perfection by several generations of worldly-wise philosophers—is to give them no importance whatever. In the end one difficulty swallows up the other and you find yourself ten years later still alive with no harm done. Things always work out.

BECKET. Yes. But badly. My prince, when you play tennis, do you simply sit back and let things work out? Do you wait for the ball to hit your racket and say "It's bound to come this way eventually"?

KING. Ah, now just a minute. You're talking about things that matter. A game of tennis is important, it amuses me.

BECKET. And suppose I were to tell you that governing can be as amusing as a game of tennis? Are we going to let the others smash the ball into our court, my prince, or shall we try to score a point, both of us, like two good English sportsmen?

KING (*suddenly roused by his sporting instinct*). The point, Begod, the point! You're right! On the court, I sweat and strain, I fall over my feet, I half kill myself, I'll cheat if need be, but I never give up the point!

BECKET. Well then, I'll tell you what the score is, so far. Piecing together all the information I have received from London since we've been on the Continent, one thing strikes me, and that is: that there exists in England a power which has grown until it almost rivals yours, my Lord. It is the power of your clergy.

KING. We did get them to pay the tax. That's something!

BECKET. Yes, it's a small sum of money. And they know that Princes can always be pacified with a little money. But those men are past masters at taking back with one hand what they were forced to give with the other. That's a little conjuring trick they've had centuries of practice in.

KING (to the GIRL). Pay attention, my little sparrow. Now's your chance to educate yourself. The gentleman is saying some very profound things!

BECKET (in the same flippant way). Little French sparrow, suppose you educate us instead. When you're married— if you do marry despite the holes in your virtue—which would you prefer, to be mistress in your own house or to have your village priest laying down the law there?

(The KING, a little peeved, gets up on his knees on the bed and hides the bewildered GIRL under an eiderdown.)

KING. Talk sense, Becket! Priests are always intriguing, I know that. But I also know that I can crush them any time I like.

BECKET. Talk sense, Sire. If you don't do the crushing now, in five years' time there will be two Kings in England, the Archbishop of Canterbury and you. And in ten years' time there will be only one.

KING (a bit shamefaced). And it won't be me?

BECKET (coldly). I rather fear not.

KING (with a sudden shout). Oh, yes, it will! We Plantagenets hold on to our own! To horse, Becket, to horse! For England's glory! War on the faithful! That will make a change for us!

(The eiderdown starts to toss. The GIRL emerges, disheveled, and red in the face.)

GIRL (pleadingly). My lord! I can't breathe!

(The KING looks at her in surprise. He had clearly forgotten her. He bursts out laughing.)

KING. What are you doing there? Spying for the clergy? Be off. Put your clothes on and go home. Give her a gold piece, Thomas.

(The GIRL picks up her rags and holds them up in front of her.)

GIRL. Am I to come back to the camp tonight, my Lord?

KING (exasperated). Yes. No. I don't know! We're concerned with the Archbishop now, not you! Be off. (The GIRL disappears into the back portion of the tent. The KING cries:) To horse, Thomas! For England's greatest! With my big fist and your big brain we'll do some good work, you and I! (With sudden concern.) Wait a second. You can never be sure of finding another one as good in bed. (He goes to the rear of the tent and cries:) Come back tonight, my angel! I adore you! You have the prettiest eyes in the world! (He comes downstage and says confidentially to BECKET:) You always have to tell them that, even when you pay for it, if you want real pleasure with them. That's high politics, too! (Suddenly anxious, as his childish fear of the clergy returns.) What will God say to it all, though? After all, they're His Bishops!

BECKET (with an airy gesture). We aren't children. You know one can always come to some arrangement with God, on this earth. Make haste and dress, my prince. We're going to be late.

KING (hurrying out). I'll be ready in a second. Do I have to shave?

BECKET (smiling). It might be as well, after two days' fighting.

KING. What a fuss for a lot of conquered Frenchmen! I wonder sometimes if you aren't a bit too finicky, Thomas.

(*He goes out.* BECKET *closes the tent just as two* SOLDIERS *bring on a* YOUNG MONK, *with his hands tied.*)

BECKET. What is it?

SOLDIER. We've just arrested this young monk, my Lord. He was loitering round the camp. He had a knife under his robe. We're taking him to the Provost.

BECKET. Have you got the knife? (*The* SOLDIER *hands it to him.* BECKET *looks at it, then at the little* MONK.) What use do you have for this in your monastery?

MONK. I cut my bread with it!

BECKET (*amused*). Well, well. (*To the* SOLDIERS.) Leave him to me. I'll question him.

SOLDIER. He's turbulent, my Lord. He struggled like a very demon. It took four of us to get his knife away and tie him up. He wounded the Sergeant. We'd have finished him there and then, only the Sergeant said there might be some information to be got out of him. That's why we're taking him to the Provost. (*He adds:*) That's just to tell you he's a spiteful devil.

BECKET (*who has not taken his eyes off the little* MONK). Very well. Stand off. (*The* SOLDIERS *move out of earshot.* BECKET *goes on looking at the boy, and playing with the knife.*) What are you doing in France? You're a Saxon.

MONK (*crying out despite himself*). How do you know?

BECKET. I can tell by your accent. I speak Saxon very well, as well as you speak French. Yes, you might almost pass for a Frenchman—to unpracticed ears. But I'd be careful. In your predicament, you'd do as well to be taken for a Frenchman as a Saxon. It's less unpopular.

(*A pause.*)

MONK (*abruptly*). I'm prepared to die.

BECKET (*smiling*). After the deed. But before, you'll agree it's stupid. (*He looks at the knife which he is still hold-ing between two fingers.*) Where are you from?

MONK (*venomously*). Hastings!

BECKET. Hastings. And who was this kitchen implement intended for? (*No answer.*) You couldn't hope to kill more than one man with a weapon of this sort. You didn't make the journey for the sake of an ordinary Norman soldier, I imagine. (*The little* MONK *does not answer.*) (*Tersely.*) Listen to me, my little man. They're going to put you to the torture. Have you ever seen that? I'm obliged to attend professionally from time to time. You think you'll have the necessary strength of spirit, but they're terribly ingenious and they have a knowl-edge of anatomy that our imbecilic doctors would do well to emulate. One always talks. Believe me, I know. If I can vouch that you've made a full con-fession, it will go quicker for you. That's worth considering. (*The* MONK *does not answer.*) Besides, there's an amusing detail to this affair. You are directly under my jurisdiction. The King gave me the deeds and livings of all the abbeys in Hastings when he made me Chancellor.

MONK (*stepping back*). Are you Becket?

BECKET. Yes. (*He looks at the knife with a faint distaste.*) You didn't only use it to cut your bread. Your knife stinks of onion, like any proper little Saxon's knife. They're good, aren't they, the Hastings onions? (*He looks at the knife again with a strange smile.*) You still haven't told me who it was for. (*The* MONK *says nothing.*) If you meant it for the King, there was no sense in that, my lad. He has three sons. Kings spring up again like weeds. Did you imagine you could liberate your race singlehanded?

MONK. No. (*He adds dully:*) Not my race. Myself.

BECKET. Liberate yourself from what?

MONK. My shame.

BECKET (*with sudden gravity*). .How old are you?

MONK. Sixteen.

BECKET (*quietly*). The Normans have occupied the island for a hundred years. Shame is an old vintage. Your father and your grandfather drank it to the dregs. The cup is empty now.

MONK (*shaking his head*). No.

(*A shadow seems to cross* BECKET's *eyes. He goes on, quietly:*)

BECKET. So, one fine morning, you woke in your cell to the bell of the first offices, while it was still dark. And it was the bells that told you, a boy of sixteen, to take the whole burden of shame onto yourself?

MONK (*with the cry of a cornered animal*). Who told you that?

BECKET (*softly*). I told you I was a polyglot. (*Indifferently.*) I'm a Saxon too, did you know that?

MONK (*stonily*). Yes.

BECKET (*smiling*). Go on. Spit. You're dying to. (*The* MONK *looks at him, a little dazed, and then spits.*)

BECKET (*smiling*). That felt good, didn't it? (*Tersely.*) The King is waiting. And this conversation could go on indefinitely. But I want to keep you alive, so we can continue it one of these days. (*He adds lightly:*) It's pure selfishness, you know. Your life hasn't any sort of importance for me, obviously, but it's very rare for Fate to bring one face to face with one's own ghost, when young. (*Calling.*) Soldier! (*The* SOLDIER *comes back and springs clanking to attention.*) Fetch me the Provost. Run! (*The* SOLDIER *runs out.* BECKET *comes back to the silent young* MONK.) Delightful day, isn't it? This early-morning sun, hot already under this light veil of mist . . . A beautiful place, France. But I'm like you, I prefer the solid mists of the Sussex downs. Sunshine is luxury. And we belong to a race which used to despise luxury, you and I. (*The* PROVOST MARSHAL *of the camp comes in, followed by the* SOLDIER. *He is an important personage, but* BECKET *is inaccessible, even for a* PROVOST MARSHAL, *and the man's behavior shows it.*) Sir Provost, your men have arrested this monk who was loitering around the camp. He is a lay brother from the convent of Hastings and he is directly under my jurisdiction. You will make arrangements to have him sent back to England and taken to the convent, where his Abbot will keep him under supervision until my return. There is no specific charge against him, for the moment. I want him treated without brutality, but very closely watched. I hold you personally responsible for him.

PROVOST. Very good, my Lord.

(*He motions to the* SOLDIERS. *They surround the little* MONK *and take him away without a further glance from* BECKET. *Left alone,* BECKET *looks at the knife, smiles, wrinkles his nose and murmurs, with faint distaste:*)

BECKET. It's touching, but it stinks, all the same. (*He flings the knife away, and whistling his little march goes toward the tent. He goes in, calling out lightheartedly:*) Well, my prince, have you put on your Sunday best? It's time to go. We mustn't keep the Bishop waiting!

(*A sudden joyful peal of bells. The tent disappears as soon as* BECKET *has gone in. The set changes. A backcloth representing a street comes down from the flies. The permanent pillars are there, but the* SOLDIERS *lining the route have decorated them with standards. The* KING *and* BECKET *advance into the city, on horseback, preceded by two* TRUMPETERS; *the* KING *slightly ahead of* BECKET *and followed by the four* BARONS. *Acclamations from the crowd. Bells, trumpets throughout the scene.*)

KING (*beaming as he waves*). Listen to that! They adore us, these French!

BECKET. It cost me quite a bit. I had money distributed among the populace this morning. The prosperous classes are at home, sulking, of course.

KING. Patriots?

BECKET. No. But they would have cost too much. There are also a certain number of your Highness' soldiers among the crowd, in disguise, to encourage any lukewarm elements.

KING. Why do you always make a game of destroying my illusions? I thought they loved me for myself! You're an amoral man, Becket. (*Anxiously.*) Does one say amoral or immoral?

BECKET (*smiling*). It depends what one means.

KING. She's pretty, look—the girl on the balcony to the right there. Suppose we stopped a minute . . .

BECKET. Impossible. The Bishop is waiting in the cathedral.

KING. It would be a lot more fun than going to see a Bishop!

BECKET. My Lord, do you remember what you have to say to him ?

KING (*waving to the crowd*). Yes, yes, yes! As if it mattered what I say to a French Bishop, whose city I've just taken by force!

BECKET. It matters a great deal. For our future policy.

KING. Am I the strongest or am I not?

BECKET. You are, today. But one must never drive one's enemy to despair. It makes him strong. Gentleness is better politics. It saps virility. A good occupational force must not crush, it must corrupt.

KING (*waving graciously*). What about my pleasure then? Where does that enter into your scheme of things? Suppose I charged into this heap of frog-eaters now instead of acting the goat at their *Te Deum?* I can indulge in a bit of pleasure, can't I? I'm the conqueror.

BECKET. That would be a fault. Worse, a failing. One can permit oneself anything, Sire, but one must never indulge.

KING. Yes, Papa, right, Papa. What a bore you are today. Look at that little

redhead there, standing on the fountain! Give orders for the procession to follow the same route back.

(*He rides on, turning his horse to watch the girl out of sight. They have gone by, the four* BARONS *bringing up the rear. Organ music. The standards disappear, together with the* SOLDIERS. *We are in the cathedral. The stage is empty.*

The organ is heard. Swelling chords. The organist is practicing in the empty cathedral. Then a sort of partition is pushed on, which represents the sacristy.

The KING, *attired for the ceremony, the* BARONS, *an unknown* PRIEST *and a* CHOIRBOY *come in. They seem to be waiting for something. The* KING *sits impatiently on a stool.*)

KING. Where's Becket? And what are we waiting for?

1ST BARON. He just said to wait, my Lord. It seems there's something not quite in order.

KING (*pacing about ill-humoredly*). What a lot of fuss for a French Bishop! What do I look like, I ask you, hanging about in this sacristy like a village bridegroom!

4TH BARON. I quite agree, my Lord! I can't think why we don't march straight in. After all, it's your cathedral now. (*Eagerly.*) What do you say, my Lord? Shall we just draw our swords and charge?

KING (*going meekly back to his stool with a worried frown*). No. Becket wouldn't like it. And he's better than we are at knowing the right thing to do. If he told us to wait, there must be a good reason. (BECKET *hurries in.*) Well, Becket, what's happening? We're freezing to death in here! What do the French think they're at, keep us moldering in this sacristy?

BECKET. The order came from me, Sire. A security measure. My police are certain that a French rising was to break out during the ceremony.

(*The* KING *has risen. The* 2ND BARON

has drawn his sword. The other three follow suit.)

2ND BARON.   God's Blood!

BECKET.   Put up your swords. The King is safe in here. I have put guards on all the doors.

2ND BARON.   Have we your permission to go in and deal with it, my Lord? We'll make short work of it!

3RD BARON.   Just say the word, Sire! Shall we go?

BECKET (*curtly*).   I forbid you. There aren't enough of us. I am bringing fresh troops into the city and having the cathedral evacuated. Until that is done, the King's person is in your keeping, gentlemen. But sheathe your swords. No provocation, please. We are at the mercy of a chance incident and I still have no more than the fifty escort men-at-arms in the city.

KING (*tugging at* BECKET's *sleeve*). Becket! Is that priest French?

BECKET.   Yes. But he is part of the Bishop's immediate entourage. And the Bishop is our man.

KING.   You know how reliable English Bishops are! So I leave you to guess how far we can trust a French one! That man has a funny look in his eyes.

BECKET.   Who, the Bishop?

KING.   No. That priest.

BECKET (*glances at the* PRIEST *and laughs*).   Of course, my prince; he squints! I assure you that's the only disturbing thing about him! It would be tactless to ask him to leave. Besides, even if he had a dagger, you have your coat of mail and four of your Barons. I must go and supervise the evacuation of the nave.

(*He starts to go. The* KING *runs after him.*)

KING.   Becket! (BECKET *stops.*) The choirboy?

BECKET (*laughing*).   He's only so high!

KING.   He may be a dwarf. You never know with the French. (*Drawing*

BECKET *aside.*) Becket, we talked a little flippantly this morning. Are you sure God isn't taking his revenge?

BECKET (*smiling*).   Of course not. I'm afraid it's simply my police force taking fright and being a little over-zealous. Policemen have a slight tendency to see assassins everywhere. They only do it to make themselves important. Bah, what does it matter? We'll hear the *Te Deum* in a deserted church, that's all.

KING (*bitterly*).   And there was I thinking those folk adored me. Perhaps you didn't give them enough money.

BECKET.   One can only buy those who are for sale, my prince. And those are just the ones who aren't dangerous. With the others, it's wolf against wolf. I'll come back straightaway and set your mind at rest.

(*He goes out. The* KING *darts anxious looks on the* PRIEST *as he paces up and down muttering his prayers.*)

KING.   Baron!

(*The* 4TH BARON *is nearest the* KING. *He steps forward.*)

4TH BARON (*bellowing as usual*). My Lord?

KING.   Shush! Keep an eye on that man, all four of you, and at the slightest move, leap on him. (*There follows a little comic dumbshow by the* KING *and the* PRIEST, *who is beginning to feel uneasy too. A sudden violent knocking on the sacristy door. The* KING *starts.*) Who is it?

(*A* SOLDIER *comes in.*)

SOLDIER.   A messenger from London, my Lord. They sent him on here from the camp. The message is urgent.

KING (*worried*).   I don't like it. Regnault, you go and see.

(*The* 4TH BARON *goes out and comes back again, reassured.*)

4TH BARON.   It's William of Corbeil, my Lord. He has urgent letters.

KING.   You're sure it *is* him? It wouldn't be a Frenchman in disguise? That's an old trick.

4TH BARON (*roaring with laughter*). I know him, Sire! I've drained more tankards with him than there are whiskers on his face. And the old goat has plenty!

(*The* KING *makes a sign. The* 4TH BARON *admits the* MESSENGER, *who drops on one knee and presents his letters to the* KING.)

KING. Thank you. Get up. That's a fine beard you have, William of Corbeil. Is it well stuck on?

MESSENGER (*rising, bewildered*). My beard, Sire?

(*The* 4TH BARON *guffaws and slaps him on the back.*)

4TH BARON. You old porcupine you!

(*The* KING *has glanced through the letters.*)

KING. Good news, gentlemen! We have one enemy less. (BECKET *comes in. The* KING *cries joyfully.*) Becket!

BECKET. Everything is going according to plan, my prince. The troops are on their way. We've only to wait here quietly, until they arrive.

KING (*cheerfully*). You're right, Becket, everything is going according to plan. God isn't angry with us. He has just recalled the Archbishop.

BECKET (*in a murmur*). That little old man . . . How could that feeble body contain so much strength?

KING. Now, now, now! Don't squander your sorrow, my son. I personally consider this an excellent piece of news!

BECKET. He was the first Norman who took an interest in me. He was a true father to me. God rest his soul.

KING. He will! After all the fellow did for Him, he's gone to Heaven, don't worry. Where he'll be definitely more use to God than he was to us. So it's definitely for the best. (*He pulls* BECKET *to him.*) Becket! My little Becket, I think the ball's in our court now! This is the time to score a point. (*He seizes his arm, tense and quite transformed.*) An extraordinary idea is just creeping into my mind, Becket. A master stroke! I can't think what's got into me this morning, but I suddenly feel extremely intelligent. It probably comes of making love with a French girl last night. I am subtle, Becket, I am profound! So profound it's making my head spin. Are you sure it isn't dangerous to think too hard? Thomas, my little Thomas! Are you listening to me?

BECKET (*smiling at his excitement*). Yes, my prince.

KING (*as excited as a little boy*). Are you listening carefully? Listen, Thomas! You told me once that the best ideas are the stupidest ones, but the clever thing is to think of them! Listen, Thomas! Tradition prevents me from touching the privileges of the Primacy. You follow me so far?

BECKET. Yes, my prince . . .

KING. But what if the Primate is my man? If the Archbishop of Canterbury is for the King, how can his power possibly incommodate me?

BECKET. That's an ingenious idea, my prince, but you forget that his election is a free one.

KING. No! You're forgetting the Royal Hand! Do you know what that is? When the candidate is displeasing to the Throne the King sends his Justicer to the Conclave of Bishops and it's the King who has the final say. That's an old custom too, and for once, it's in my favor! It's fully a hundred years since the Conclave of Bishops has voted contrary to the wishes of the King!

BECKET. I don't doubt it, my Lord. But we all know your Bishops. Which one of them could you rely on? Once the Primate's miter is on their heads, they grow dizzy with power.

KING. Are you asking me, Becket? I'll tell you. Someone who doesn't know what dizziness means. Someone who isn't even afraid of God. Thomas, my son, I need your help again and this time it's important. I'm sorry to deprive you of French girls and the fun of battle, my son, but pleasure will come later. You are going over to England.

BECKET. I am at your service, my prince.

KING. Can you guess what your mission will be?

(*A tremor of anguish crosses* BECKET'S *face at what is to come.*)

BECKET. No, my prince.

KING. You are going to deliver a personal letter from me to every Bishop in the land. And do you know what those letters will contain, my Thomas, my little brother? My royal wish to have you elected Primate of England.

(BECKET *has gone deathly white. He says with a forced laugh:*)

BECKET. You're joking, of course, my Lord. Just look at the edifying man, the saintly man whom you would be trusting with these holy functions! (*He has opened his fine coat to display his even finer doublet.*) Why, my prince, you really fooled me for a second! (*The* KING *bursts out laughing.* BECKET *laughs too, rather too loudly in his relief.*) A fine Archbishop I'd have made! Look at my new shoes! They're the latest fashion in Paris. Attractive, that little upturned toe, don't you think? Quite full of unction and compunction, isn't it, Sire?

KING (*suddenly stops laughing.*) Shut up about your shoes, Thomas! I'm in deadly earnest. I shall write those letters before noon. You will help me.

(BECKET, *deathly pale, stammers:*)

BECKET. But my Lord, I'm not even a priest!

KING (*tersely*). You're a deacon. You can take your final vows tomorrow and be ordained in a month.

BECKET. But have you considered what the Pope will say?

KING (*brutally*). I'll pay the price!

(BECKET, *after an anguished pause, murmurs:*)

BECKET. My Lord, I see now that you weren't joking. Don't do this.

KING. Why not?

BECKET. It frightens me.

KING (*his face set and hard*). Becket, this is an order!

(BECKET *stands as if turned to stone. A pause. He murmurs:*)

BECKET (*gravely*). If I become Archbishop, I can no longer be your friend.

(*A burst of organ music in the cathedral. Enter an* OFFICER.)

OFFICER. The church is now empty, my Lord. The Bishop and his clergy await your Highness' good pleasure.

KING (*roughly to* BECKET). Did you hear that, Becket? Pull yourself together. You have an odd way of taking good news. Wake up! They say we can go in now.

(*The procession forms with the* PRIEST *and the* CHOIRBOY *leading.* BECKET *takes his place, almost reluctantly, a pace or so behind the* KING.)

BECKET (*in a murmur*). This is madness, my Lord. Don't do it. I could not serve both God and you.

KING (*looking straight ahead, says stonily*). You've never disappointed me, Thomas. And you are the only man I trust. You will leave tonight. Come, let's go in.

(*He motions to the* PRIEST. *The procession moves off and goes into the empty cathedral, as the organ swells.*)

(*A moment's darkness. The organ continues to play. Then a dim light reveals* BECKET's *room. Open chests into which two* SERVANTS *are piling costly clothes.*)

2ND SERVANT (*who is the younger of the two*). The coat with the sable trimming as well?

1ST SERVANT. Everything! You heard what he said!

2ND SERVANT (*grumbling*). Sables! To beggars! Who'll give them alms if they beg with that on their backs! They'll starve to death!

1ST SERVANT (*cackling*). They'll eat the sables! Can't you understand, you idiot! He's going to sell all this and give them the money!

2ND SERVANT. But what will he wear himself? He's got nothing left at all!

(BECKET *comes in, wearing a plain gray dressing gown.*)

BECKET. Are the chests full? I want them sent over to the Jew before tonight. I want nothing left in this room but the bare walls. Gil, the fur coverlet!

1ST SERVANT (*regretfully*). My Lord will be cold at night.

BECKET. Do as I say. (*Regretfully, the* 1ST SERVANT *takes the coverlet and puts it in the chest.*) Has the steward been told about tonight's meal? Supper for forty in the great hall.

1ST SERVANT. He says he won't have enough gold plate, my Lord. Are we to mix it with the silver dishes?

BECKET. Tell him to lay the table with the wooden platters and earthenware bowls from the kitchens. The plate has been sold. The Jew will send over for it late this afternoon.

1ST SERVANT (*dazed*). The earthenware bowls and the wooden platters. Yes, my Lord. And the steward says could he have your list of invitations fairly soon, my Lord. He only has three runners and he's afraid there won't be time to—

BECKET. There are no invitations. The great doors will be thrown open and you will go out into the street and tell the poor they are dining with me tonight.

1ST SERVANT (*appalled*). Very good, my Lord.

(*He is about to go.* BECKET *calls him back.*)

BECKET. I want the service to be impeccable. The dishes presented to each guest first, with full ceremony, just as for princes. Go now. (*The two* SERVANTS *go out.* BECKET, *left alone, casually looks over one or two articles of clothing in the chests. He murmurs:*) I must say it was all very pretty stuff. (*He drops the lid and bursts out laughing.*) A prick of vanity! The mark of an upstart. A truly saintly man would never have done the whole thing in one day. Nobody will ever believe it's genuine. (*He turns to the jeweled crucifix above the bed and says simply:*) I hope You haven't inspired me with all these holy resolutions in order to make me look ridiculous, Lord. It's all so new to me. I'm setting about it a little clumsily perhaps. (*He looks at the crucifix and with a swift gesture takes it off the wall.*) And you're far too sumptuous too. Precious stones around your bleeding Body . . . I shall give you to some poor village church. (*He lays the crucifix on the chest. He looks around the room, happy, light-hearted, and murmurs:*) It's like leaving for a holiday. Forgive me, Lord, but I never enjoyed myself so much in my whole life. I don't believe You are a sad God. The joy I feel in shedding all my riches must be part of Your divine intentions.

(*He goes behind the curtain into the antechamber where he can be heard gaily whistling an old English marching song. He comes back a second later, his bare feet in sandals, and wearing a monk's coarse woolen robe. He draws the curtain across again and murmurs:*)

BECKET. There. Farewell, Becket. I wish there had been something I had regretted parting with, so I could offer it to You. (*He goes to the crucifix and says simply:*) Lord, are You sure You are not tempting me? It all seems far too easy.

(*He drops to his knees and prays.*)

Act III

(*A room in the* KING'S *palace. The two* QUEENS, *the* QUEEN MOTHER *and the* YOUNG QUEEN, *are on stage, working at their tapestry. The* KING'S *two* SONS, *one considerably older than the other, are playing in a corner, on the floor. The* KING *is in another corner, playing at cup-and-ball. After several unsuccessful attempts to catch the ball in the cup, he throws down the toy and exclaims irritably:*)

KING. Forty beggars! He invited forty beggars to dinner!

QUEEN MOTHER. The dramatic gesture, as usual! I always said you had misplaced your confidence, my son.

KING (*pacing up and down*). Madam, I am very particular where I place my confidence. I only ever did it once in my whole life and I am still convinced I was right. But there's a great deal we don't understand! Thomas is ten times more intelligent than all of us put together.

QUEEN MOTHER (*reprovingly*). You are talking about royalty, my son.

KING (*grunting*). What of it? Intelligence has been shared out on a different basis.

YOUNG QUEEN. It seems he has sold his gold plate and all his rich clothes to a Jew. He wears an ordinary homespun habit now.

QUEEN MOTHER. I see that as a sign of ostentation, if nothing worse! One can become a saintly man, certainly, but not in a single day. I've never liked the man. You were insane to make him so powerful.

KING (*crying out*). He is my friend!

QUEEN MOTHER (*acidly*). More's the pity.

YOUNG QUEEN. He is your friend in debauchery. It was he who lured you away from your duty towards me. It was he who first took you to the whorehouses!

KING (*furious*). Rubbish, Madam! I didn't need anybody to lure me away from my duty towards you. I made you three children, very conscientiously. Phew! My duty is done for a while.

YOUNG QUEEN (*stung*). When that libertine loses the evil influence he has on you, you will come to appreciate the joys of family life again. Pray Heaven he disobeys you!

KING. The joys of family life are limited, Madam. To be perfectly frank, you bore me. You and your eternal back-biting, over your everlasting tapestry, the pair of you! That's no sustenance for a man! (*He trots about the room, furious, and comes to a halt behind their chairs.*) If at least it had some artistic merit. My ancestress Mathilda, while she was waiting for her husband to finish carving out his kingdom, now *she* embroidered a masterpiece —which they left behind in Bayeux, more's the pity. But that! It's beyond belief it's so mediocre.

YOUNG QUEEN (*nettled*). We can only use the gifts we're born with.

KING. Yes. And yours are meager. (*He glances out of the window once more to look at the time, and says with a sigh:*) I've been bored to tears for a whole month. Not a soul to talk to. After his nomination, not wanting to seem in too indecent a hurry, I leave him alone to carry out his pastoral tour. Now, back he comes at last, I summon him to the palace and he's late. (*He looks out of the window again and exclaims:*) Ah! Someone at the sentry post! (*He turns away, disappointed.*) No, it's only a monk. (*He wanders about the room, aimlessly. He goes over to join the children, and watches them playing for a while.*) (*Sourly.*) Charming babes. Men in the making. Sly and obtuse already. And to think one is expected to be dewy-eyed over creatures like that, merely because they aren't yet big enough to be hated or despised. Which is the elder of you two?

ELDER BOY (*rising*). I am, Sir.

KING. What's your name again?

ELDER BOY. Henry III.

KING (*sharply*). Not yet, Sir! Number II is in the best of health. (*To the* QUEEN.) You've brought them up well! Do you think of yourself as Regent already? And you wonder that I shun your bedchamber? I don't care to make love with my widow.

(*An* OFFICER *comes in.*)

OFFICER. A messenger from the Archbishop, my Lord.

KING (*beside himself with rage*). A messenger! A messenger! I summoned the Archbishop Primate in person! (*He turns to the women, suddenly uneasy, almost touching.*) Perhaps he's ill? That would explain everything.

QUEEN MOTHER (*bitterly*). That's too much to hope for.

KING (*raging*). You'd like to see him dead, wouldn't you, you females—because he loves me? If he hasn't come, it's because he's dying! Send the man in, quickly! O my Thomas . . . (*The* OF-FICER *goes and admits the* MONK. *The* KING *hurries over to him.*) Who are you? Is Becket ill?

MONK (*falling on one knee*). My Lord, I am William son of Etienne, secretary to his Grace the Archbishop.

KING. Is your master seriously ill?

MONK. No, my Lord. His Grace is in good health. He has charged me to deliver this letter with his deepest respects—and to give your Highness this. (*He bows lower and hands something to the* KING.)

KING (*stunned*). The Seal? Why has he sent me back the Seal? (*He unrolls the parchment and reads it in silence. His face hardens. He says curtly, without looking at the* MONK.) You have carried out your mission. Go.

(*The* MONK *rises and turns to go.*)

MONK. Is there an answer from your Highness for his Grace the Archbishop?

KING (*harshly*). No!

(*The* MONK *goes out. The* KING *stands still a moment, at a loss, then flings himself onto his throne, glowering. The women exchange a conspiratorial look. The* QUEEN MOTHER *rises and goes to him.*)

QUEEN MOTHER (*insidiously*). Well, my son, what does your friend say in his letter?

KING (*bawling*). Get out! Get out, both of you! And take your royal vermin with you! I am alone! (*Frightened, the* QUEENS *hurry out with the children, The* KING *stands there a moment, reeling a little, as if stunned by the blow. Then he collapses onto the throne and sobs like a child.*) (*Moaning.*) O my Thomas! (*He remains a moment prostrate, then collects himself and sits up. He looks at the Seal in his hand and says between clenched teeth:*) You've sent me back the Three Lions of England, like a little boy who doesn't want to play with me any more. You think you have God's honor to defend now! I would have gone to war with all England's might behind me, and against England's interests, to defend you, little Saxon. I would have given the honor of the Kingdom laughingly . . . for you . . . Only I loved you and you didn't love me . . . that's the difference. (*His face hardens. He adds between clenched teeth:*) Thanks all the same for this last gift as you desert me. I shall learn to be alone. (*He goes out. The lights dim.* SERVANTS *remove the furniture. When the lights go up again, the permanent set, with the pillars, is empty.*)

(*A bare church; a man half hidden under a dark cloak is waiting behind a pillar. It is the* KING. *Closing chords of organ music. Enter* GILBERT FOLLIOT, *Bishop of London, followed by his* CLERGY. *He has just said Mass. The* KING *goes to him.*)

KING. Bishop . . .

FOLLIOT (*stepping back*). What do you want, fellow? (*His acolytes are about to step between them, when he exclaims:*) The King!

KING. Yes.

FOLLIOT. Alone, without an escort, and dressed like a common squire?

KING. The King nevertheless. Bishop, I would like to make a confession.

FOLLIOT (*with a touch of suspicion*). I am the Bishop of London. The King has his own Confessor. That is an important Court appointment and it has its prerogatives.

KING. The choice of priest for Holy Confession is open, Bishop, even for a King. (FOLLIOT *motions to his* CLERGY, *who draw away*.) Anyway, my confession will be short, and I'm not asking for absolution. I have something much worse than a sin on my conscience, Bishop: a mistake. A foolish mistake. (FOLLIOT *says nothing*.) I ordered you to vote for Thomas Becket at the Council of Clarendon. I repent of it.

FOLLIOT. (*inscrutably*). We bowed before the Royal Hand.

KING. Reluctantly, I know. It took me thirteen weeks of authority and patience to crush the small uncrushable opposition of which you were the head, Bishop. On the day the Council met you looked green. They told me you fell seriously ill afterwards.

FOLLIOT (*impenetrably*). God cured me.

KING. Very good of Him. But He is rather inclined to look after His own, to the exclusion of anyone else. He let me fall ill without lifting a finger! And I must cure myself without divine intervention. I have the Archbishop on my stomach. A big hard lump I shall have to vomit back. What does the Norman clergy think of him?

FOLLIOT (*reserved*). His Grace seems to have the reins of the Church of England well in hand. Those who are in close contact with him even say that he behaves like a holy man.

KING (*with grudging admiration*). It's a bit sudden, but nothing he does ever surprises me. God knows what the brute is capable of, for good or for evil. Bishop, let us be frank with each other. Is the Church very interested in holy men?

FOLLIOT (*with the ghost of a smile*). The Church has been wise for so long, your Highness, that she could not have failed to realize that the temptation of

saintliness is one of the most insidious and fearsome snares the devil can lay for her priests. The administration of the realm of souls, with the temporal difficulties it carries with it, chiefly demands, as in all administrations, competent administrators. The Roman Catholic Church has its Saints, it invokes their benevolent intercession, it prays to them. But it has no need to create others. That is superfluous. And dangerous.

KING. You seem to be a man one can talk to, Bishop. I misjudged you. Friendship blinded me.

FOLLIOT (*still impenetrable*). Friendship is a fine thing.

KING (*suddenly hoarse*). It's a domestic animal, a living, tender thing. It seems to be all eyes, forever gazing at you, warming you. You don't see its teeth. But it's a beast with one curious characteristic. It is only after death that it bites.

FOLLIOT (*prudently*). Is the King's friendship for Thomas Becket dead, your Highness?

KING. Yes, Bishop. It died quite suddenly. A sort of heart failure.

FOLLIOT. A curious phenomenon, your Highness, but quite frequent.

KING (*taking his arm suddenly*). I hate Becket now, Bishop. There is nothing more in common between that man and me than this creature tearing at my guts. I can't bear it any more. I shall have to turn it loose on him. But I am the King; what they conventionally call my greatness stands in my way. I need somebody.

FOLLIOT (*stiffening*). I do not wish to serve anything but the Church.

KING. Let us talk like grown men, Bishop. We went in hand in hand to conquer, pillage and ransom England. We quarrel, we try to cheat each other of a penny or two, but Heaven and Earth still have one or two common interests. Do you know what I have just obtained from the Pope? His Blessing to go and murder Catholic Ireland, in the name of the Faith. Yes, a sort of crusade to impose Norman barons and clergy on the Irish, with our swords and standards solemnly blessed as if we were off to give the Turks a drubbing. The only condition: a little piece of silver per household per year, for St. Peter's pence, which the native clergy of Ireland is loath to part with and which I have undertaken to make them pay. It's a mere pittance. But at the end of the year it will add up to a pretty sum. Rome knows how to do her accounts.

FOLLIOT (*terror-stricken*). There are some things one should never say, your Highness: one should even try not to know about them, so long as one is not directly concerned with them.

KING (*smiling.*) We are alone, Bishop, and the church is empty.

FOLLIOT. The church is never empty. A little red lamp burns in front of the High Altar.

KING (*impatiently*). Bishop, I like playing games, but only with boys of my own age! Do you take me for one of your sheep, holy pastor? The One whom that little red lamp honors read into your innermost heart and mine a long time ago. Of your cupidity and my hatred, He knows all there is to know. (FOLLIOT *withdraws into his shell. The* KING *cries irritably:*) If that's the way you feel you must become a monk, Bishop! Wear a hair shirt on your naked back and go and hide yourself in a monastery to pray! The Bishopric of London, for the pure-hearted son of a Thames waterman, is too much, or too little!

(*A pause.*)

FOLLIOT (*impassively*). If, as is my duty, I disregard my private feelings, I must admit that his Grace the Archbishop has so far done nothing which has not been in the interests of Mother Church.

KING (*eying him, says jovially*). I can see your game, my little friend. You mean to cost me a lot of money. But I'm rich—thanks to Becket, who has succeeded in making you pay the Absentee Tax. And it seems to me eminently ethical that a part of the Church's gold should find its way, via you, back to the Church. Besides, if we want to keep this on a moral basis, Holy Bishop, you can tell yourself that as the greatness of the Church and that of the State are closely linked, in serving me, you will in the long run be working for the consolidation of the Catholic Faith.

FOLLIOT (*contemplating him with curiosity*). I had always taken your Highness for a great adolescent lout who cared only for his pleasure.

KING. One can be wrong about people, Bishop. I made the same mistake. (*With a sudden cry.*) O my Thomas . . .

FOLLIOT (*fiercely*). You love him, your Highness! You still love him! You love that mitered hog, that impostor, that Saxon bastard, that little guttersnipe!

KING (*seizing him by the throat*). Yes, I love him! But that's my affair, priest! All I confided to you was my hatred. I'll pay you to rid me of him, but don't ever speak ill of him to me. Or we'll fight it out as man to man!

FOLLIOT. Highness, you're choking me!

KING (*abruptly releasing him*). We will meet again tomorrow, my Lord Bishop, and we'll go over the details of our enterprise together. You will be officially summoned to the palace on some pretext or other—my good works in your London Diocese, say—where I am your chief parishioner. But it won't be the poor and needy we'll discuss. My poor can wait. The Kingdom they pin their hopes on is eternal.

(*The* KING *goes out.* GILBERT FOLLIOT *remains motionless. His* CLERGY *join him timidly. He takes his crook and goes out with dignity, but not before one of his*

*Canons has discreetly adjusted his miter,
which was knocked askew in the recent
struggle. They have gone out.*)

(*The lighting changes. Curtains between the pillars. The episcopal palace.*)

(*Morning. A* PRIEST *enters, leading
two* MONKS *and the* YOUNG MONK *from
the convent of Hastings.*)

PRIEST. His Grace will receive you
here.

(*The two* MONKS *are impressed. They
push the* YOUNG MONK *about a little.*)

1ST MONK. Stand up straight. Kiss
his Grace's ring and try to answer his
questions with humility, or I'll tan your
backside for you!

2ND MONK. I suppose you thought
he'd forgotten all about you? The great
never forget anything. And don't you
act proud with him or you'll be sorry.

(*Enter* BECKET, *wearing a coarse
monk's robe.*)

BECKET. Well, brothers, is it fine
over in Hastings?

(*He gives them his ring to kiss.*)

1ST MONK. Foggy, my Lord.

BECKET (*smiling*). Then it's fine in
Hastings. We always think fondly of
our Abbey there and we intend to visit
it soon, when our new duties grant us a
moment's respite. How has this young
man been behaving? Has he given our
Abbot much trouble?

2ND MONK. A proper mule, my
Lord. Father Abbot tried kindness, as
you recommended, but he soon had to
have recourse to the dungeon and bread
and water, and even to the whip. Nothing
has any effect. The stubborn little wretch
is just the same; all defiance and insults.
He has fallen into the sin of pride. Nothing I know of will pull him out of that!

1ST MONK. Save a good kick in the
rump perhaps—if your Grace will pardon the expression. (*To the boy.*) Stand
up straight.

BECKET (*to the boy*). Pay attention
to your brother. Stand up straight. As a
rule the sin of pride stiffens a man's

back. Look me in the face. (*The* YOUNG
MONK *looks at him.*) Good. (BECKET
*looks at the boy for a while, then turns
to the* MONKS.) You will be taken to the
kitchens where you can refresh yourselves before you leave, brothers. They
have orders to treat you well. Don't
spurn our hospitality; we relieve you, for
today, of your vows of abstinence, and
we fondly hope you will do honor to our
bill of fare. Greet your father Abbot in
Jesus on our behalf.

2ND MONK (*hesitantly*). And the
lad?

BECKET. We will keep him here.

1ST MONK. Watch out for him, your
Grace. He's vicious.

BECKET (*smiling*). We are not
afraid. (*The* MONKS *go out.* BECKET
and the YOUNG MONK *remain, facing
each other.*) Why do you hold yourself
so badly?

YOUNG MONK. I don't want to look
people in the face any more.

BECKET. I'll teach you. That will be
your first lesson. Look at me. (*The boy
gives him a sidelong glance.*) Better than
that. (*The boy looks at him.*) Are you
still bearing the full weight of England's
shame alone? Is it that shame which
bends your back like that?

YOUNG MONK. Yes.

BECKET. If I took over half of it,
would it weigh less heavy? (*He motions
to the* PRIEST.) Show in their Lordships
the Bishops. You'll soon see that being
alone is not a privilege reserved entirely
for you. (*The* BISHOPS *come in.* BECKET
leads the YOUNG MONK *into a corner.*)
You stay here in the corner and hold
my tablets. I ask only one thing. Don't
leap at their throats; you'd complicate
everything.

(*He motions to the* BISHOPS *who remain standing.*)

FOLLIOT. Your Grace, I am afraid
this meeting may be a pointless one.
You insisted—against our advice—on
attacking the King openly. Even before

the three excommunications which you asked us to sanction could be made public, the King has hit back. His Grand Justicer Richard de Lacy has just arrived in your antechamber and is demanding to see you in the name of the King. He is the bearer of an official order summoning you to appear before his assembled Council within twenty-four hours and there to answer the charges made against you.

BECKET. Of what is the King accusing me?

FOLLIOT. Prevarication. Following the examination of accounts by his Privy Council, his Highness demands a considerable sum still outstanding on your administration of the Treasury.

BECKET. When I resigned the Chancellorship I handed over my ledgers to the Grand Justicer who acquitted me of all subsequent dues and claims. What does the King demand?

OXFORD. Forty thousand marks in fine gold.

BECKET (*smiling*). I don't believe there was ever as much money in all the coffers of all England in all the time I was Chancellor. But a clever clerk can soon change that . . . The King has closed his fist and I am like a fly inside it. (*He smiles and looks at him.*) I have the impression, gentlemen, that you must be feeling something very akin to relief.

YORK. We advised you against open opposition.

BECKET. William of Aynsford, incited by the King, struck down the priest I had appointed to the Parish of his Lordship's See, on the pretext that his Highness disapproved of my choice. Am I to look on while my priests are murdered?

FOLLIOT. It is not for you to appoint a priest to a free fief! There is not a Norman, layman or cleric, who will ever concede that. It would mean reviewing the entire legal system of the Conquest.

Everything can be called into question in England except the fact that it was conquered in 1066. England is the land of law and of the most scrupulous respect for the law; but the law begins at that date only, or England as such ceases to exist.

BECKET. Bishop, must I remind you that we are men of God and that we have an Honor to defend, which dates from all eternity?

OXFORD (*quietly*). This excommunication was bad policy, your Grace. William of Aynsford is a companion of the King.

BECKET (*smiling*). I know him very well. He's a charming man. I have drained many a tankard with him.

YORK (*yelping*). And his wife is my second cousin!

BECKET. That is a detail I deplore, my Lord Bishop, but he has killed one of my priests. If I do not defend my priests, who will? Gilbert of Clare has indicted before his court of justice a churchman who was under our exclusive jurisdiction.

YORK. An interesting victim I must say! He deserved the rope a hundred times over. The man was accused of rape and murder. Wouldn't it have been cleverer to let the wretch hang—and have peace?

BECKET. "I bring not peace but the sword." Your Lordship must I'm sure have read that somewhere. I am not interested in what this man is guilty of. If I allow my priests to be tried by a secular tribunal; if I let Robert de Vere abduct our tonsured clerics from our monasteries, as he has just done, on the grounds that the man was one of his serfs who had escaped land bondage, I don't give much for freedom and our chances of surivival in five years' time, my Lord. I have excommunicated Gilbert of Clare, Robert de Vere and William of Aynsford. The Kingdom of God must be defended like any other Kingdom. Do you think that Right has only to show its handsome face for everything to drop in its lap? Without Might, its old enemy, Right counts for nothing.

YORK. What Might? Let us not indulge in empty words. The King is Might and he is the law.

BECKET. He is the written law, but there is another, unwritten law, which always makes Kings bend the neck eventually. (*He looks at them for a moment and smiles.*) I was a profligate, gentlemen, perhaps a libertine, in any case, a worldly man. I loved living and I laughed at all these things. But you passed the burden on to me and now I have to carry it. I have rolled up my sleeves and taken it on my back and nothing will ever make me set it down again. I thank your Lordships. The council is adjourned and I have made my decision. I shall stand by these three excommunications. I shall appear tomorrow before the King's supreme court of Justice. (*The* BISHOPS *look at one another in surprise, then bow and go out.* BECKET *turns to the* YOUNG MONK.) Well, does the shame weigh less heavy now?

YOUNG MONK. Yes.

BECKET (*leading him off and laughing*). Then stand up straight!

(*The drapes close. Distant trumpets. The* KING *comes out from behind the curtains and turns to peep through them at something. A pause. Then* GILBERT FOLLIOT *comes hurrying in.*)

KING. What's happening? I can't see a thing from up here.

FOLLIOT. Legal procedure is taking its course, your Highness. The third summons has been delivered. He has not appeared. In a moment he will be condemned in absentia. Once prevarication is established, our Dean the Bishop of Chichester will go to see him and communicate according to the terms of the ancient Charter of the Church of England, our corporated repudiation of allegiance, absolving us of obedience to him—and our intention to report him

to our Holy Father the Pope. I shall then, as Bishop of London, step forward and publicly accuse Becket of having celebrated, in contempt of the King, a sacrilegious Mass at the instigation of the Evil Spirit.

KING (*anxiously*). Isn't that going rather far?

FOLLIOT. Of course. It won't fool anyone, but it always works. The assembly will then go out to vote, in order of precedence, and return a verdict of imprisonment. The sentence is already drawn up.

KING. Unanimously?

FOLLIOT. We are all Normans. The rest is your Highness' concern. It will merely be a matter of carrying out the sentence.

KING (*staggering suddenly*). O my Thomas!

FOLLIOT (*impassively*). I can still stop the machine, your Highness.

KING (*hesitates a second then says*). No. Go.

(FOLLIOT *goes out. The* KING *goes back to his place, behind the curtain.*)

(*The two* QUEENS *come into the room, and join the* KING. *All three stand and peer through the curtain. A pause.*)

YOUNG QUEEN. He's doomed, isn't he?

KING (*dully*). Yes.

YOUNG QUEEN. At last!

(*The* KING *turns on her, his face twisted with hate.*)

KING. I forbid you to gloat!

YOUNG QUEEN. At seeing your enemy perish—why not?

KING (*frothing*). Becket is my enemy, but in the human balance, bastard as he is, and naked as his mother made him, he weighs a hundred times more than you do, Madam, with your crown and all your jewels and your august father the Emperor into the bargain. Becket is attacking me and he has betrayed me. I am forced to fight him and crush him, but at least he gave me, with open hands, everything that is at all good in me. And you have never given me anything but your carping mediocrity, your everlasting obsession with your puny little person and what you thought was due to it. That is why I forbid you to smile as he lies dying!

YOUNG QUEEN. I gave you my youth! I gave you your children!

KING (*shouting*). I don't like my children! And as for your youth—that dusty flower pressed in a hymnbook since you were twelve years old, with its watery blood and its insipid scent—you can say farewell to that without a tear. With age, bigotry and malice may perhaps give some spice to your character. Your body was an empty desert, Madam!— which duty forced me to wander in alone. But you have never been a wife to me! And Becket was my friend, red-blooded, generous and full of strength! (*He is shaken by a sob.*) O my Thomas!

(*The* QUEEN MOTHER *moves over to him.*)

QUEEN MOTHER (*haughtily*). And I, my son, I gave you nothing either, I suppose?

KING (*recovers his composure, glares at her and says dully*). Life. Yes. Thank you. But after that I never saw you save in a passage, dressed for a Ball, or in your crown and ermine mantle, ten minutes before official ceremonies, where you were forced to tolerate my presence. I have always been alone, and no one on this earth has ever loved me except Becket!

QUEEN MOTHER (*bitterly*). Well, call him back! Absolve him, since he loves you! Give him supreme power then! But do something!

KING. I am. I'm learning to be alone again, Madam. As usual. (*A* PAGE *comes in, breathless.*) Well? What's happening? How far have they got?

PAGE. My Liege, Thomas Becket appeared just when everyone had given him up; sick, deathly pale, in full pontifical regalia and carrying his own heavy silver cross. He walked the whole length of the hall without anyone daring to stop him, and when Robert Duke of Leicester, who was to read out his sentence, began the consecrated words, he stopped with a gesture and forbade him, in God's name, to pronounce judgment against him, his spiritual Father. Then he walked back through the crowd, which parted for him in silence. He has just left.

KING (*unable to hide his delight*). Well played, Thomas! One point to you. (*He checks himself, embarrassed, and then says:*) And what about my Barons?

PAGE. Their hands flew to their swords with cries of "Traitor! Perjurer! Arrest him! Miserable wretch! Hear your sentence!" But not one of them dared move, or touch the sacred ornaments.

KING (*with a roar*). The fools! I am surrounded by fools and the only intelligent man in my Kingdom is against me!

PAGE (*continuing his story*). Then, on the threshold, he turned, looked at them coldly as they shouted in their impotence, and he said that not so long ago he could have answered their challenge sword in hand. Now he could no longer do it, but he begged them to remember that there was a time when he met strength with strength.

KING (*jubilantly*). He could beat them all! All, I tell you! On horseback, on foot, with a mace, with a lance, with a sword! In the lists they fell to him like ninepins!

PAGE. And his eyes were so cold, and so ironic—even though all he had in his hand was his episcopal crook—that one by one, they fell silent. Only then did he turn and go out. They say he has given orders to invite all the beggars of the city to sup at his house tonight.

KING (*somberly*). And what about the Bishop of London, who was going to reduce him to powder? What about my busy friend Gilbert Folliot?

PAGE. He had a horrible fit of rage trying to incite the crowd, he let out a screech of foul abuse and then he fainted. They are bringing him round now.

(*The* KING *suddenly bursts into a shout of irrepressible laughter, and, watched by the two outraged* QUEENS, *collapses into the* PAGE'S *arms, breathless and helpless with mirth.*)

KING. It's too funny! It's too funny!

QUEEN MOTHER (*coldly*). You will laugh less heartily tomorrow, my son. If you don't stop him, Becket will reach the coast tonight, ask asylum of the King of France and jeer at you, unpunished, from across the Channel.

(*She sweeps out with the* YOUNG QUEEN. *Suddenly, the* KING *stops laughing and runs out.*)

(*The light changes. Curtains part. We are at the Court of* LOUIS, KING OF FRANCE. *He is sitting in the middle of the courtroom, very erect on his throne. He is a burly man with intelligent eyes.*)

LOUIS (*to his* BARONS). Gentlemen, we are in France and a fart on England's King—as the song goes.

1ST BARON. Your Majesty cannot *not* receive his Ambassadors Extraordinary!

LOUIS. Ordinary, or extraordinary, I am at home to all ambassadors. It's my job. I shall receive them.

1ST BARON. They have been waiting in your Majesty's anteroom for over an hour, Sire.

LOUIS. Let them wait. That's *their* job. An ambassador is made for pacing about an antechamber. I know what they are going to ask me.

2ND BARON. The extradition of a felon is a courtesy due from one crowned head to another.

LOUIS. My dear man, crowned heads can play the little game of courtesy but nations owe each other none. My right to play the courteous gentleman stops where France's interests begin. And France's interests consist in making things as difficult as possible for England —a thing England never hesitates to do to us. The Archbishop is a millstone round Henry Plantagenet's neck. Long

live the Archbishop! Anyway, I like the fellow.

2ND BARON. My gracious sovereign is master. And so long as our foreign policy permits us to expect nothing of King Henry—

LOUIS. For the time being, it is an excellent thing to stiffen our attitude. Remember the Montmirail affair. We only signed the peace treaty with Henry on condition that he granted to spare the lives of the refugees from Brittany and Poitou whom he asked us to hand over to him. Two months later all of them had lost their heads. That directly touched my personal honor. I was not strong enough at the time, so I had to pretend I hadn't heard of these men's execution. And I continued to lavish smiles on my English cousin. But praise God our affairs have taken a turn for the better. And today *he* needs *us.* So I will now proceed to remember my honor. Show in the ambassadors.

(*Exit* 1ST BARON. *He comes back with* FOLLIOT *and the* DUKE OF ARUNDEL.)

1ST BARON. Permit me to introduce to your Majesty the two envoys extraordinary from his Highness Henry of England; his Grace the Bishop of London and the Duke of Arundel.

LOUIS (*with a friendly wave to the* DUKE). Greetings to you, Milord. I have not forgotten your amazing exploits at the last tournament at Calais. Do you still wield a lance as mightily as you did, Milord?

ARUNDEL (*with a gratified bow*). I hope so, Sire.

LOUIS. We hope that our friendly relations with your gracious master will allow us to appreciate your jousting skill again before long, on the occasion of the forthcoming festivities. (FOLLIOT *has unrolled a parchment.*) Bishop, I see you have a letter for us from your master. We are listening.

FOLLIOT (*bows again and starts to read*). "To my Lord and friend Louis, King of the French; Henry, King of

England, Duke of Normandy, Duke of Aquitaine and Count of Anjou: Learn that Thomas, former Archbishop of Canterbury, after a public trial held at my court by the plenary assembly of the Barons of my realm has been found guilty of fraud, perjury and treason towards me. He has forthwith fled my Kingdom as a traitor, and with evil intent. I therefore entreat you not to allow this criminal, nor any of his adherents, to reside upon your territories, nor to permit any of your vassals to give help, support or counsel to this my greatest enemy. For I solemnly declare that your enemies or those of your Realm would receive none from me or my subjects. I expect you to assist me in the vindication of my honor and the punishment of my enemy, as you would wish me to do for you, should the need arise."

(*A pause.* FOLLIOT *bows very low and hands the parchment to the* KING *who rolls it up casually and hands it to one of the* BARONS.)

LOUIS. Gentlemen, we have listened attentively to our gracious cousin's request and we take good note of it. Our chancellery will draft a reply which will be sent to you tomorrow. All we can do at the moment, is express our surprise. No news had reached us of the presence of the Archbishop of Canterbury on our domains.

FOLLIOT (*tersely*). Sire, the former Archbishop has taken refuge at the Abbey of St. Martin, near Saint-Omer.

LOUIS (*still gracious*). My Lord Bishop, we flatter ourselves that there is some order in our Kingdom. If he were there, we would certainly have been informed. (*He makes a gesture of dismissal. The ambassadors bow low and go out backwards, ushered out by the* 1ST BARON. *Immediately,* LOUIS *says to the* 2ND BARON:) Show in Thomas Becket and leave us. (*The* 2ND BARON *goes out and a second later admits* THOMAS *dressed in a monk's robe.*

THOMAS *drops onto one knee. The* BARON *goes out.*) (*Kindly.*) Rise, Thomas Becket. And greet us as the Primate of England. The bow is enough —and if I know my etiquette, you are entitled to a slight nod of the head from me. There, that's done. I would even be required to kiss your ring, if your visit were an official one. But I have the impression that it isn't, am I right?

BECKET (*with a smile*). No, Sire. I am only an exile.

LOUIS (*graciously*). That too is an important title, in France.

BECKET. I am afraid it is the only one I have left. My property has been seized and distributed to those who served the King against me, letters have been sent to the Duke of Flanders and all his Barons enjoining them to seize my person. John, Bishop of Poitiers, who was suspected of wanting to grant me asylum, has just been poisoned.

LOUIS (*smiling*). In fact you are a very dangerous man.

BECKET. I'm afraid so.

LOUIS (*unperturbed*). We like danger, Becket. And if the King of France started being afraid of the King of England, there would be something sadly amiss in Europe. We grant you our royal protection on whichever of our domains it will please you to choose.

BECKET. I humbly thank your Majesty. I must, however, tell you that I cannot buy this protection with any act hostile to my country.

LOUIS. You do us injury. That was understood. You may be sure we are practiced enough in the task of Kingship not to make such gross errors in our choice of spies and traitors. The King of France will ask nothing of you. But . . . There is always a but, as I'm sure you are aware, in politics. (BECKET *looks up. The* KING *rises heavily onto his fat legs, goes to him and says familiarly:*) I am only responsible for France's interests, Becket. I really can't afford to shoulder those of Heaven. In a month or a year I can summon you back here and tell you, just as blandly, that my dealings with the King of England have taken a different turn and that I am obliged to banish you. (*He slaps him affably on the back, his eyes sparkling with intelligence and asks, with a smile:*) I believe you have dabbled in politics too, Archbishop?

BECKET (*smiling*). Yes, Sire. Not so very long ago.

LOUIS (*jovially*). I like you very much. Mark you, had you been a French Bishop, I don't say I wouldn't have clapped you in prison myself. But in the present circumstances, you have a right to my royal protection. Do you value candor, Becket?

BECKET. Yes, Sire.

LOUIS. Then we are sure to understand each other. Do you intend to go to see the Holy Father?

BECKET. Yes, Sire, if you give me your safe conduct.

LOUIS. You shall have it. But a word in your ear—as a friend. (Keep this to yourself, won't you?—don't go and stir up trouble for me with Rome.) Beware of the Pope. He'll sell you for thirty pieces of silver. The man needs money.

(*The lights dim. A curtain closes. Two small rostra, bearing the* POPE *and the* CARDINAL, *are pushed on stage, to a light musical accompaniment.*)

(*The* POPE *is a thin, fidgety little man with an atrocious Italian accent. The* CARDINAL *is swarthy, and his accent is even worse. The whole effect is a little grubby, among the gilded splendor.*)

POPE. I don't agree, Zambelli! I don't agree at all! It's a very bad plan altogether. We will forfeit our honor all for 3,000 silver marks.

CARDINAL. Holy Father, there is no question of forfeiting honor, but merely of taking the sum offered by the King of England and thereby gaining time. To lose that sum and give a negative answer right away would solve neither the prob-

lems of the Curia, nor those of Thomas Becket—nor even, I am afraid, those of the higher interests of the Church. To accept the money—the sum is meager, I agree, and cannot be viewed as a factor in our decision—is merely to make a gesture of appeasement in the interests of peace in Europe. Which has always been the supreme duty of the Holy See.

POPE (*concerned*). If we take money from the King, I cannot possibly receive the Archbishop, who has been waiting here in Rome for a whole month for me to grant him an audience.

CARDINAL. Receive the money from the King, Very Holy Father, and receive the Archbishop too. The one will neutralize the other. The money will remove all subversive taint from the audience you will grant the Archbishop and on the other hand, the reception of the Archbishop will efface whatever taint of humiliation there may have been in accepting the money.

POPE (*gloomily*). I don't want to receive him at all. I gather he is a sincere man. I am always disconcerted by people of that sort. They leave me with a bad taste in my mouth.

CARDINAL. Sincerity is a form of strategy, just like any other, Holy Father. In certain very difficult negotiations, when matters are not going ahead and the usual tactics cease to work, I have been known to use it myself. The great pitfall, of course, is if your opponent starts being sincere at the same time as you. Then the game becomes horribly confusing.

POPE. You know what they say Becket's been meaning to ask me?—in the month he's spent pacing about my antechamber?

CARDINAL (*innocently*). No, Holy Father.

POPE (*impatiently*). Zambelli! Don't play the fox with me! It was you who told me!

CARDINAL (*caught out*). I beg your pardon, Holy Father, I had forgotten.

Or rather, as your Holiness asked me the question, I thought you had forgotten and so I took a chance and—

POPE (*irritably*). Zambelli, if we start outmaneuvering each other to no purpose, we'll be here all night!

CARDINAL (*in confusion*). Force of habit, your Holiness. Excuse me.

POPE. To ask me to relieve him of his rank and functions as Archbishop of Canterbury—that's the reason Becket is in Rome! And do you know why he wants to ask me that?

CARDINAL (*candidly for once*). Yes, Holy Father.

POPE (*irritably*). No, you do not know! It was your enemy Rapallo who told me!

CARDINAL (*modestly*). Yes, but I knew it just the same, because I have a spy in Rapallo's palace.

POPE (*with a wink*). Culograti?

CARDINAL. No. Culograti is only my spy in his master's eyes. By the man I have spying on Culograti.

POPE (*cutting short the digression*). Becket maintains that the election of Clarendon was not a free one, that he owes his nomination solely to the royal whim and that consequently the honor of God, of which he has now decided he is the champion, does not allow him to bear this usurped title any longer. He wishes to be nothing more than an ordinary priest.

CARDINAL (*after a moment's thought*). The man is clearly an abyss of ambition.

POPE. And yet he knows that we know that his title and functions are his only safeguard against the King's anger. I don't give much for his skin wherever he is, when he is no longer Archbishop!

CARDINAL (*thoughtfully*). He's playing a deep game. But I have a plan. Your Holiness will pretend to believe in his scruples. You will receive him and relieve him of his titles and functions as Primate, then, immediately after, as a reward for his zeal in defending the Church of England, you will reappoint him Archbishop, in right and due form this time. We thus avert the danger, we score a point against him—and at the same time a point against the King.

POPE. That's a dangerous game. The King has a long arm.

CARDINAL. We can cover ourselves. We will send secret letters to the English court explaining that this new nomination is a pure formality and that we herewith rescind the excommunications pronounced by Becket; on the other hand, we will inform Becket of the existence of these secret letters, swearing him to secrecy and begging him to consider them as null and void.

POPE (*getting muddled*). In that case, perhaps there isn't much point in the letters being secret?

CARDINAL. Yes, there is. Because that will allow us to maneuver with each of them as if the other was ignorant of the contents, while taking the precaution of making it known to them both. The main thing is for them not to know that we know they know. It's so simple a child of twelve could grasp it!

POPE. But Archbishop or no, what are we going to do with Becket?

CARDINAL (*with a lighthearted wave of his hand*). We will send him to a convent. A French convent, since King Louis is protecting him—to the Cistercians, say, at Pontigny. The monastic rule is a strict one. It will do that onetime dandy a world of good! Let him learn real poverty! That will teach him to be the comforter of the poor!

POPE. That sounds like good advice, Zambelli. Bread and water and nocturnal prayers are an excellent remedy for sincerity. (*He muses a moment.*) The only thing that puzzles me, Zambelli, is why you should want to give me a piece of good advice . . .

(*The* CARDINAL *looks a little embarrassed.*)

(*The little rostra go as they came and the curtain opens revealing a small, bare cell, center stage.*)

(BECKET *is praying before a humble wooden crucifix. Crouching in a corner, the* YOUNG MONK *is playing with a knife.*)

BECKET. Yet it would be simple enough. Too simple perhaps. Saintliness is a temptation too. Oh, how difficult it is to get an answer from You, Lord! I was slow in praying to You, but I cannot believe that others, worthier than I, who have spent years asking You questions, have been better than myself at deciphering Your real intentions. I am only a beginner and I must make mistake after mistake, as I did in my Latin translations as a boy, when my riotous imagination made the old priest roar with laughter. But I cannot believe that one learns Your language as one learns any human tongue, by hard studying, with a dictionary, a grammar and a set of idioms. I am sure that to the hardened sinner, who drops to his knees for the first time and murmurs Your name, marveling, You tell him all Your secrets, straightaway, and that he understands. I have served You like a dilettante, surprised that I could still find my pleasure in Your service. And for a long time I was on my guard because of it. I could not believe this pleasure would bring me one step nearer You. I could not believe that the road could be a happy one. Their hair shirts, their fasting, their bells in the small hours summoning one to meet You, on the icy paving stones, in the sick misery of the poor ill-treated human animal—I cannot believe that all these are anything but safeguards for the weak. In power and in luxury, and even in the pleasures of the flesh, I shall not cease to speak to You, I feel this now. You are the God of the rich man and the happy man too, Lord, and therein lies Your profound justice. You do not turn away Your eyes from the man who was given everything from birth. You have not abandoned him, alone in his ensnaring facility. And he may be Your true lost sheep. For Your scheme of things, which we mistakenly call Justice, is secret and profound and You plumb the hidden depths of poor men's puny frames as carefully as those of Kings. And beneath those outward differences, which blind us, but which to You are barely noticeable; beneath the diadem or the grime, You discern the same pride, the same vanity, the same petty, complacent preoccupation with oneself. Lord, I am certain now that You meant to tempt me with this hair shirt, object of so much vapid self-congratulation! this bare cell, this solitude, this absurdly endured winter cold—and the conveniences of prayer. It would be too easy to buy You like this, at so low a price. I shall leave this convent, where so many precautions hem You round. I shall take up the miter and the golden cope again, and the great silver cross, and I shall go back and fight in the place and with the weapons it has pleased You to give me. It has pleased You to make me Archbishop and to set me, like a solitary pawn, face to face with the King, upon the chessboard. I shall go back to my place, humbly, and let the world accuse me of pride, so that I may do what I believe is my life's work. For the rest, Your will be done.

(*He crosses himself.*)

(*The* YOUNG MONK *is still playing with his knife. Suddenly he throws it and watches as it quivers, embedded in the floor.*)

Act IV

(*The King of France's Court.*)

(KING LOUIS *comes in, holding* BECKET *familiarly by the arm.*)

LOUIS. I tell you, Becket, intrigue is an ugly thing. You keep the smell about you for ages afterwards. There is a return of good understanding between the Kingdom of England and Ourselves.

Peace in that direction assures me of a great advantage in the struggle which I will shortly have to undertake against the Emperor. I must protect my rear by a truce with Henry Plantagenet, before I march towards the East. And, needless to say, you are one of the items on the King's bill of charges. I can even tell you, that apart from yourself, his demands are negligible. (*Musingly.*) Curious man. England's best policy would have been to take advantage of the Emperor's aggressive intentions and close the other jaw of the trap. He is deliberately sacrificing this opportunity for the pleasure of seeing you driven out. He really hates you, doesn't he?

BECKET (*simply*). Sire, we loved each other and I think he cannot forgive me for preferring God to him.

LOUIS. Your King isn't doing his job properly, Archbishop. He is giving way to passion. However! He has chosen to score a point against you, instead of against me. You are on his bill, I have to pay his price and banish you. I do not do so without a certain shame. Where are you thinking of going?

BECKET. I am a shepherd who has remained too long away from his flock. I intend to go back to England. I had already made my decision before this audience with your Majesty.

LOUIS (*surprised*). You have a taste for martyrdom? You disappoint me. I thought you more healthy-minded.

BECKET. Would it be healthy-minded to walk the roads of Europe, and beg a refuge where my carcass would be safe? Besides, where would I be safe? I am a Primate of England. That is a rather showy label on my back. The honor of God and common sense, which for once coincide, dictate that instead of risking the knife thrust of some hired assassin, on the highway, I should go and have myself killed—if killed I must be— clad in my golden cope, with my miter on my head and my silver cross in my

hand, among my flock in my own cathedral. That place alone befits me.

(*A pause.*)

LOUIS. I daresay you're right. (*He sighs.*) Ah, what a pity it is to be a King, sometimes, when one has the surprise of meeting a man! You'll tell me, fortunately for me, that men are rare. Why weren't you born on this side of the Channel, Becket? (*He smiles.*) True, you would no doubt have been a thorn in *my* side then! The honor of God is a very cumbersome thing. (*He muses for a moment and then says abruptly:*) Who cares, I'll risk it! I like you too much. I'll indulge in a moment's humanity. I am going to try something, even if your master does seize on the chance to double his bill. After all, banishing you would merely have cost me a small slice of honor . . . I am meeting Henry in a day or two, at La Ferté-Bernard, to seal our agreement. I shall try to persuade him to make his peace with you. Should he agree, will you be willing to talk with him?

BECKET. Sire, ever since we stopped seeing each other, I have never ceased to talk to him.

(*Blackout. Prolonged blare of trumpets. The set is completely removed. Nothing remains but the cyclorama around the bare stage. A vast, arid plain, lashed by the wind. Trumpets again.*)

(*Two* SENTRIES *are on stage, watching something in the distance.*)

SENTRY. Open those eyes of yours, lad! And drink it all in. You're new to the job, but you won't see something like this every day! This a historic meeting!

YOUNG SENTRY. I daresay, but it's perishing cold! How long are they going to keep us hanging about?

SENTRY. We're sheltered by the wood here, but you can bet they're even colder than we are, out there in the plain.

YOUNG SENTRY. Look! They've come up to each other! I wonder what they're talking about?

SENTRY. What do you think they're talking about, muttonhead? Inquiring how things are at home? Complaining about their chilblains? The fate of the world, that's what they're arguing about! Things you and I won't ever understand. Even the words those bigwigs use—why, you wouldn't even know what they meant!

(*They go off. The lights go up.* BECKET *and the* KING, *on horseback, are alone in the middle of the plain, facing each other.*)

(*Throughout the scene, the winter blizzard wails like a shrill dirge beneath their words. And during their silences, only the wind is heard.*)

KING. You look older, Thomas.

BECKET. You too, Highness. Are you sure you aren't too cold?

KING. I'm frozen stiff. You love it of course! You're in your element, aren't you? And you're barefooted as well!

BECKET (*smiling*). That's my latest affectation.

KING. Even with these fur boots on, my chilblains are killing me. Aren't yours, or don't you have any?

BECKET (*gently*). Of course.

KING (*cackling*). You're offering them up to God, I hope, holy monk?

BECKET (*gravely*). I have better things to offer Him.

KING (*with a sudden cry*). If we start straightaway, we're sure to quarrel! Let's talk about trivial things. You know my son is fourteen? He's come of age.

BECKET. Has he improved at all?

KING. He's a little idiot and sly like his mother. Becket, don't you ever marry!

BECKET (*smiling*). The matter has been taken out of my hands. By you, Highness! It was you who had me ordained!

KING (*with a cry*). Let's not start yet, I tell you! Talk about something else!

BECKET (*lightly*). Has your Highness done much hunting lately?

KING (*snarling*). Yes, every day! And it doesn't amuse me any more.

BECKET. Have you any new hawks?

KING (*furiously*). The most expensive on the market! But they don't fly straight.

BECKET. And your horses?

KING. The Sultan sent me four superb stallions for the tenth anniversary of my reign. But they throw everyone! Nobody has managed to mount one of them, yet!

BECKET (*smiling*). I must see what I can do about that some day.

KING. They'll throw you too! And we'll see your buttocks under your robe! At least, I hope so, or everything would be too dismal.

BECKET (*after a pause*). Do you know what I miss most, Sire? The horses.

KING. And the women?

BECKET (*simply*). I've forgotten.

KING. You hypocrite! You turned into a hypocrite when you became a priest. (*Abruptly.*) Did you love Gwendolen?

BECKET. I've forgotten her too.

KING. You did love her! That's the only way I can account for it.

BECKET (*gravely*). No, my prince, in my soul and conscience, I did not love her.

KING. Then you never loved anything, that's worse! (*Churlishly.*) Why are you calling me your prince, like in the old days?

BECKET (*gently*). Because you have remained my prince.

KING (*crying out*). Then why are you doing me harm?

BECKET (*gently*). Let's talk about something else.

KING. Well, what? I'm cold.

BECKET. I always told you, my prince, that one must fight the cold with the cold's own weapons. Strip naked and splash yourself with cold water every morning.

KING. I used to when you were there

to force me into it. I never wash now. I stink. I grew a beard at one time. Did you know?

BECKET (*smiling*). Yes. I had a hearty laugh over it.

KING. I cut it off because it itched. (*He cries out suddenly, like a lost child:*) Becket, I'm bored!

BECKET (*gravely*). My prince. I do so wish I could help you.

KING. Then what are you waiting for? You can see I'm dying for it!

BECKET (*quietly*). I'm waiting for the honor of God and the honor of the King to become one.

KING. You'll wait a long time then!

BECKET. Yes. I'm afraid I will.

(*A pause. Only the wind is heard.*)

KING (*suddenly*). If we've nothing more to say to each other, we might as well go and get warm!

BECKET. We have everything to say to each other, my prince. The opportunity may not occur again.

KING. Make haste, then. Or there'll be two frozen statues on this plain making their peace in a frozen eternity! I am your King, Becket! And so long as we are on this earth you owe me the first move! I'm prepared to forget a lot of things but not the fact that I am King. You yourself taught me that.

BECKET (*gravely*). Never forget it, my prince. Even against God. You have a different task to do. You have to steer the ship.

KING. And you—what do you have to do?

BECKET. Resist you with all my might, when you steer against the wind.

KING. Do you expect the wind to be behind me, Becket? No such luck! That's the fairy-tale navigation! God on the King's side? That's never happened yet! Yes, once in a century, at the time of the Crusades, when all Christendom shouts "It's God's will!" And even then! You know as well as I do what private greeds a Crusade covers up, in nine

cases out of ten. The rest of the time, it's a head-on wind. And there must be somebody to keep the watch!

BECKET. And somebody else to cope with the absurd wind—and with God. The tasks have been shared out, once and for all. The pity of it is that it should have been between us two, my prince—who were friends.

KING (*crossly*). The King of France —I still don't know what he hopes to gain by it—preached at me for three whole days for me to make my peace with you. What good would it do you to provoke me beyond endurance?

BECKET. None.

KING. You know that I am the King, and that I must act like a King! What do you expect of me? Are you hoping I'll weaken?

BECKET. No. That would prostrate me.

KING. Do you hope to conquer me by force then?

BECKET. You are the strong one.

KING. To win me round?

BECKET. No. Not that either. It is not for me to win you round. I have only to say no to you.

KING. But you must be logical, Becket!

BECKET. No. That isn't necessary, my Liege. We must only do—absurdly —what we have been given to do—right to the end.

KING. Yet I know you well enough, God knows. Ten years we spent together, little Saxon! At the hunt, at the whorehouse, at war; carousing all night long the two of us; in the same girl's bed, sometimes . . . and at work in the Council Chamber too. Absurdly. That word isn't like you.

BECKET. Perhaps. I am no longer like myself.

KING (*derisively*). Have you been touched by grace?

BECKET (*gravely*). Not by the one you think. I am not worthy of it.

KING. Did you feel the Saxon in you coming out, despite Papa's good collaborator's sentiments?

BECKET. No. Not that either.

KING. What then?

BECKET. I felt for the first time that I was being entrusted with something, that's all—there in that empty cathedral, somewhere in France, that day when you ordered me to take up this burden. I was a man without honor. And suddenly I found it—one I never imagined would ever become mine—the honor of God. A frail, incomprehensible honor, vulnerable as a boy-King fleeing from danger.

KING (*roughly*). Suppose we talked a little more precisely, Becket, with words I understand? Otherwise we'll be here all night. I'm cold. And the others are waiting for us on the fringes of this plain.

BECKET. I am being precise.

KING. I'm an idiot! Talk to me like an idiot! That's an order. Will you lift the excommunication which you pronounced on William of Aynsford and others of my liegemen?

BECKET. No, Sire, because that is the only weapon I have to defend this child, who was given, naked, into my care.

KING. Will you agree to the twelve proposals which my Bishops have accepted in your absence at Northampton, and notably to forego the much-abused protection of Saxon clerics who get themselves tonsured to escape land bondage?

BECKET. No, Sire. My role is to defend my sheep. And they are my sheep. (*A pause.*) Nor will I concede that the Bishops should forego the right to appoint priests in their own dioceses, nor that churchmen should be subject to any but the Church's jurisdiction. These are my duties as a pastor—which it is not for me to relinquish. But I shall agree to the nine other articles in a spirit of peace, and because I know that you must

remain King—in all save the honor of God.

(*A pause.*)

KING (*coldly*). Very well. I will help you defend your God, since that is your new vocation, in memory of the companion you once were to me—in all save the honor of the Realm. You may come back to England, Thomas.

BECKET. Thank you, my prince. I meant to go back in any case and give myself up to your power, for on this earth, you are my King. And in all that concerns this earth, I owe you obedience.

(*A pause.*)

KING (*ill at ease*). Well, let's go back now. We've finished. I'm cold.

BECKET (*dully*). I feel cold too, now.

(*Another pause. They look at each other. The wind howls.*)

KING (*suddenly*). You never loved me, did you, Becket?

BECKET. In so far as I was capable of love, yes, my prince, I did.

KING. Did you start to love God? (*He cries out:*) You mule! Can't you ever answer a simple question?

BECKET (*quietly*). I started to love the honor of God.

KING (*somberly*). Come back to England. I give you my royal peace. May you find yours. And may you not discover you were wrong about yourself. This is the last time I shall come begging to you. (*He cries out:*) I should never have seen you again! It hurts too much.

(*His whole body is suddenly shaken by a sob.*)

BECKET (*goes nearer to him; moved*). My prince—

KING (*yelling*). No! No pity! It's dirty. Stand away from me! Go back to England! It's too cold out here!

(BECKET *turns his horse and moves nearer to the* KING.)

BECKET (*gravely*). Farewell, my prince. Will you give me the kiss of peace?

KING. No! I can't bear to come near you! I can't bear to look at you! Later! Later! When it doesn't hurt any more!

BECKET. I shall set sail tomorrow. Farewell, my prince. I know I shall never see you again.

KING (*his face twisted with hatred*). How dare you say that to me after I gave you my royal word? Do you take me for a traitor?

(BECKET *looks at him gravely for a second longer, with a sort of pity in his eyes. Then he slowly turns his horse and rides away. The wind howls.*)

KING. Thomas!

(*But* BECKET *has not heard. The* KING *does not call a second time. He spurs his horse and gallops off in the other direction. The lights fade. The wind howls.*)

(*The lights change. Red curtains fall.* BECKET'S *whistled march is heard off stage during the scene change.*)

(*The curtains open. Royal music. King Henry's palace somewhere in France. The two* QUEENS, *the* BARONS *and Henry's* SON *are standing around the dinner table, waiting. The* KING, *his eyes gleaming maliciously, looks at them and then exclaims:*)

KING. Today, gentlemen, I shall not be the first to sit down! (*To his* SON, *with a comic bow.*) You are the King, Sir. The honor belongs to you. Take the high chair. Today I shall wait on *you!*

QUEEN MOTHER (*with slight irritation*). My son!

KING. I know what I'm doing, Madam! (*With a sudden shout.*) Go on, you great loon, look sharp! You're the King, but you're as stupid as ever! (*The boy flinches to avoid the blow he was expecting and goes to sit in the* KING'S *chair, sly and rather ill at ease.*) Take your places, gentlemen! I shall remain standing. Barons of England, here is your second King. For the good of our vast domains, a kingly colleague had become a necessity. Reviving an ancient custom, we have decided to have our successor crowned during our lifetime and to share our responsibilities with him. We ask you now to give him your homage and to honor him with the same title as Ourself.

(*He makes a sign. Two* SERVANTS *have brought in a haunch of venison on a silver charger. The* KING *serves his* SON.)

YOUNG QUEEN (*to her* SON). Sit up straight! And try to eat properly for once, now that you've been raised to glory!

KING (*grunting as he serves him*). He hasn't the face for it! He's a little sly-boots and dim-witted at that. However, he'll be your King in good earnest one day, so you may as well get used to him. Besides, it's the best I had to offer.

QUEEN MOTHER (*indignantly*). Really, my son! This game is unworthy of you and of us. You insisted on it—against my advice—at least play it with dignity!

KING (*rounding on her in fury*). I'll play the games that amuse me, Madam, and I'll play them the way I choose! This mummery, gentlemen, which is, incidentally, without any importance at all —(if your new King fidgets, let me know, I'll give him a good kick up his train)—will at the very least have the appreciable result of showing our new friend, the Archbishop, that we can do without him. If there was one ancient privilege the Primacy clung to, tooth and nail, it was its exclusive right to anoint and consecrate the Kings of this realm. Well, it will be that old toad the Archbishop of York—with letters from the Pope authorizing him to do so—I paid the price!—who, tomorrow, will crown our son in the cathedral! What a joke that's going to be! (*He roars with laughter amid the general silence.*) What a tremendous, marvelous joke! I'd give anything to see that Archbishop's face when he has to swallow that! (*To his*

Son.) Get down from there, you imbecile! Go back to the bottom of the table and take your victuals with you! You aren't officially crowned until tomorrow. (*The boy picks up his plate and goes back to his place, casting a cowed, smoldering look at his father.*) (*Watching him, says jovially.*) What a look! Filial sentiments are a fine thing to see, gentlemen! You'd like to be the real King, wouldn't you, you young pig? You'd like that number III after your name, eh, with Papa good and stiff under his catafalque! You'll have to wait a bit! Papa is well. Papa is very well indeed!

QUEEN MOTHER. My son, God knows I criticized your attempts at reconciliation with that wretch, who has done us nothing but harm . . . God knows I understand your hatred of him! But do not let it drag you into making a gesture you will regret, merely for the sake of wounding his pride. Henry is still a child. But you were not much older when you insisted on reigning by yourself, and in opposition to me. Ambitious self-seekers—and there is never any scarcity of those around Princes—can advise him, raise a faction against you and avail themselves of this hasty coronation to divide the Kingdom! Think it over, there is still time.

KING. We are still alive, Madam, and in control! And nothing can equal my pleasure in imagining my proud friend Becket's face when he sees the fundamental privilege of the Primacy whisked from under his nose! I let him cheat me out of one or two articles the other day, but I had something up my sleeve for him!

QUEEN MOTHER. Henry! I bore the weight of state affairs longer than you ever have. I have been your Queen and I am your mother. You are answerable for the interests of a great Kingdom, not for your moods. You already gave far too much away to the King of France, at La Ferté-Bernard. It is England you must think of, not your hatred—or disappointed love—for that man.

KING (*in a fury*). Disappointed love —disappointed love? What gives you the right, Madam, to meddle in my loves and hates?

QUEEN MOTHER. You have a rancor against the man which is neither healthy nor manly. The King your father dealt with his enemies faster and more summarily than that. He had them killed and said no more about it. If Thomas Becket were a faithless woman whom you still hankered after, you would act no differently. Sweet Jesu, tear him out of your heart once and for all! (*She bawls suddenly:*) Oh, if I were a man!

KING (*grinning*). Thanks be to God, Madam, he gave you dugs. Which I never personally benefited from. I suckled a peasant girl.

QUEEN MOTHER (*acidly*). That is no doubt why you have remained so lumpish, my son.

YOUNG QUEEN. And haven't I a say in the matter? I tolerated your mistresses, Sir, but do you expect me to tolerate everything? Have you ever stopped to think what kind of woman I am? I am tired of having my life encumbered with this man. Becket! Always Becket! Nobody ever talks about anything else here! He was almost less of a hindrance when you loved him. I am a woman. I am your wife and your Queen. I refuse to be treated like this! I shall complain to my father, the Duke of Aquitaine! I shall complain to my uncle, the Emperor! I shall complain to all the Kings of Europe, my cousins! I shall complain to God!

KING (*shouting rather vulgarly*). I should start with God! Be off to your private chapel, Madam, and see if He's at home. (*He turns to his mother, fuming.*) And you, the other Madam, away to your chamber with your secret councilors and go and spin your webs! Get out, both of you! I can't stand the sight of you! I retch with boredom whenever I set eyes on you! And young Henry III too! Go on, get out! (*He chases him out with kicks, yelling:*) Here's my royal foot in your royal buttocks! And to the devil with my whole family, if he'll have you! Get out, all of you! Get out! Get out! Get out! (*The* QUEENS *scurry out, with a great rustling of silks. He turns to the* BARONS *who all stand watching him, terror-stricken.*) (*More calmly.*) Let us drink, gentlemen. That's about all one can do in your company. Let us get drunk, like men, all night; until we roll under the table, in vomit and oblivion. (*He fills their glasses and beckons them closer.*) Ah, my four idiots! My faithful hounds! It's warm beside you, like being in a stable. Good sweat! Comfortable nothingness! (*He taps their skulls.*) Not the least little glimmer inside to spoil the fun. And to think that before he came I was like you! A good fat machine for belching after drink, for pissing, for mounting girls and punching heads. What the devil did you put into it, Becket, to stop the wheels from going round? (*Suddenly to the* 2ND BARON.) Tell me, do you think sometimes, Baron?

2ND BARON. Never, Sire. Thinking has never agreed with an Englishman. It's unhealthy. Besides, a gentleman has better things to do.

KING (*sitting beside them, suddenly quite calm*). Drink up, gentlemen. That's always been considered a healthy thing to do. (*He fills the goblets.*) Has Becket landed? I'm told the sea has been too rough to cross these last few days.

1ST BARON (*somberly*). He has landed, Sire, despite the sea.

KING. Where?

1ST BARON. On a deserted stretch of coast, near Sandwich.

KING. So God did not choose to drown him?

1ST BARON. No.

KING (*he asks in his sly, brutish way*).

Was nobody there waiting for him? There must be one or two men in England whom he can't call his friends!

1ST BARON. Yes. Gervase, Duke of Kent, Regnouf de Broc and Regnault de Garenne were waiting for him. Gervase had said that if he dared to land he'd cut off his head with his own hands. But the native Englishmen from all the coastal towns had armed themselves to form an escort for the Archbishop. And the Dean of Oxford went to meet the Barons and charged them not to cause bloodshed and make you look a traitor, seeing that you had given the Archbishop a safe conduct.

KING (*soberly*). Yes, I gave him a safe conduct.

1ST BARON. All along the road to Canterbury, the peasants, the artisans and the small shopkeepers came out to meet him, cheering him and escorting him from village to village. Not a single rich man, not a single Norman, showed his face.

KING. Only the Saxons?

1ST BARON. Poor people armed with makeshift shields and rusty lances. Riff-raff. Swarms of them though, all camping around Canterbury, to protect him. (*Gloomily*) Who would have thought there were so many people in England!

(*The* KING *has remained prostrate without uttering a word. Now he suddenly jumps up and roars.*)

KING. A miserable wretch who ate my bread! A man I raised up from nothing! A Saxon! A man I loved! (*Shouting like a madman.*) I loved him! Yes, I loved him! And I believe I still do! Enough, O God! Enough! Stop, stop, O God, I've had enough!

(*He flings himself down on the couch, sobbing hysterically; tearing at the horse-hair mattress with his teeth, and eating it. The* BARONS, *stupefied, go nearer to him.*)

1ST BARON (*timidly*). Your High-ness . . .

KING (*moaning, with his head buried*

in the mattress). I can do nothing!
Nothing! I'm as limp and useless as a
girl! So long as he's alive, I'll never be
able to do a thing. I tremble before him
astonished. And I am the King! (*With
a sudden cry.*) Will no one rid me of
him? A priest! A priest who jeers at me
and does me injury! Are there none but
cowards like myself around me? Are
there no men left in England? Oh, my
heart! My heart is beating too fast to
bear!

(*He lies, still as death on the torn
mattress. The four* BARONS *stand around
speechless. Suddenly, on a percussion
instrument, there rises a rhythmic beating, a sort of muffled tom-tom which is
at first only the agitated heartbeats of
the* KING, *but which swells and grows
more insistent. The four* BARONS *look at
each other. Then they straighten, buckle
their sword belts, pick up their helmets
and go slowly out, leaving the* KING
*alone with the muffled rhythm of the
heartbeats, which will continue until the
murder. The* KING *lies there prostrate,
among the upturned benches, in the deserted hall. A torch splutters and goes
out. He sits up, looks around, sees
they have gone and suddenly realizes
why. A wild, lost look comes into his
eyes. A moment's pause; then he collapses on the bed with a long broken
moan.*)

KING.   O my Thomas!

(*A second torch goes out. Total darkness. Only the steady throb of the heartbeats is heard. A dim light. The forest
of pillars again. Canterbury Cathedral.
Upstage a small altar, with three steps
leading up to it, half screened by a grill.
In a corner downstage* BECKET, *and the*
YOUNG MONK, *who is helping him on
with his vestments. Nearby, on a stool,
the Archbishop's miter. The tall silver
cross is leaning against a pillar.*)

BECKET.   I must look my best today.
Make haste.

(*The* MONK *fumbles with the vestments. The muffled tom-tom is heard
distantly at first, then closer.*)

MONK.   It's difficult with all those
little laces. It wants a girl's hands.

BECKET (*softly*).   A man's hands are
better today. Never mind the laces. The
alb, quickly. And the stole. And then
the cope.

MONK (*conscientiously*).   If it's worth
doing it's worth doing well.

BECKET.   You're quite right. If it's
worth doing it's worth doing well. Do up
all the little laces, every one of them.
God will give us time. (*A pause. The boy
struggles manfully on, putting out his
tongue in concentration. The throbbing
grows louder.*) (*Smiling.*) Don't pull
your tongue out like that!

(*He watches the boy as he works
away.*)

MONK (*sweating but content*).   There.
That's all done. But I'd rather have
cleaned out our pigsty at home! It's not
half such hard work!

BECKET.   Now the alb. (*A pause.*)
Were you fond of your pigs?

MONK (*his eyes lighting up*).   Yes,
I was.

BECKET.   At my father's house, we
had some pigs too, when I was a child.
(*Smiling.*) We're two rough lads from
Hastings, you and I! Give me the chasuble. (BECKET *kisses the chasuble and
slips it over his head. He looks at the
boy and says gently:*) Do you miss your
knife?

MONK.   Yes. (*Pause.*) Will it be
today?

BECKET (*gravely*).   I think so, my
son. Are you afraid?

MONK.   Oh, no. Not if we have time
to fight. All I want is the chance to strike
a few blows first; so I shan't have done
nothing but receive them all my life. If
I can kill one Norman first—just one, I
don't want much—one for one, that will
seem fair and right enough to me.

BECKET (*with a kindly smile*).   Are
you so very set on killing one?

MONK. One for one. After that, I don't much care if I *am* just a little grain of sand in the machine. Because I know that by putting more and more grains of sand in the machine, one day it will come grinding to a stop.

BECKET (*gently*). And on that day, what then?

MONK. We'll set a fine, new, well-oiled machine in the place of the old one and this time we'll put the Normans into it instead. (*He asks, quite without irony:*) That's what justice means, isn't it?

(BECKET *smiles and does not answer him.*)

BECKET. Fetch me the miter. (*He says quietly, as the boy fetches it:*) O Lord, You forbade Peter to strike a blow in the Garden of Olives. But I shall not deprive him of that joy. He has had too few joys in his short span on earth. (*To the boy.*) Now give me my silver cross. I must hold it.

MONK (*passing it to him*). Lord, it's heavy! A good swipe with that and they'd feel it! My word, I wish I could have it!

BECKET (*stroking his hair*). Lucky little Saxon! This black world will have been in order to the end, for you. (*He straightens, grave once more.*) There. I'm ready, all adorned for Your festivities, Lord. Do not, in this interval of waiting, let one last doubt enter my soul.

(*During this scene, the throbbing has grown louder. Now it mingles with a loud knocking on the door. A* PRIEST *runs in wildly.*)

PRIEST. Your Grace! There are four armed men outside! They say they must see you on behalf of the King. I've barricaded the door but they're breaking it in! They've got hatchets! Quickly! You must go into the back of the church and have the choir gates closed! They're strong enough, they'll hold!

BECKET (*calmly*). It is time for Vespers, William. Does one close the choir gates during Vespers? I never heard of such a thing.

PRIEST (*nonplused*). I know, but . . .

BECKET. Everything must be the way it should be. The choir gates will remain open. Come, boy, let us go up to the altar. This is no place to be.

(*He goes toward the altar, followed by the* YOUNG MONK. *A great crash. The door has given way. The four* BARONS *come in, in their helmets. They fling down their hatchets and draw their swords.* BECKET *turns to face them, grave and calm, at the foot of the altar. They stop a moment, uncertain and disconcerted; four statues, huge and threatening. The tom-tom has stopped. There is nothing now but a heavy silence.* BECKET *says simply:*) Here it comes. The supreme folly. This is its hour. (*He holds their eyes. They dare not move. He says coldly:*) One does not enter armed into God's house. What do you want?

1ST BARON (*thickly*). Your death.

(*A pause.*)

2ND BARON (*thickly*). You bring shame to the King. Flee the country or you're a dead man.

BECKET (*softly*). It is time for the service. (*He turns to the altar and faces the tall crucifix without paying any further attention to them. The throbbing starts again, muffled. The four men close in like automata. The* YOUNG MONK *suddenly leaps forward brandishing the heavy silver cross in order to protect* BECKET, *but one of the* BARONS *swings his sword and fells him to the ground.* BECKET *murmurs, as if in reproach.*) Not even one! It would have given him so much pleasure, Lord. (*With a sudden cry.*) Oh how difficult You make it all! And how heavy Your honor is to bear! (*He adds, very quietly:*) Poor Henry.

(*The four men hurl themselves onto him. He falls at the first blow. They hack at his body, grunting like woodcutters. The* PRIEST *has fled with a long scream, which echoes in the empty cathedral. Blackout.*)

(*On the same spot. The* KING, *naked,*

on bended knees at BECKET'S *tomb, as in the first scene. Four* MONKS *are whipping him with ropes, almost duplicating the gestures of the* BARONS *as they killed* BECKET.)

KING (*crying out*). Are you satisfied now, Becket? Does this settle our account? Has the honor of God been washed clean? (*The four* MONKS *finish beating him, then kneel down and bow their heads. The* KING *mutters—one feels it is part of the ceremony:*) Thank you. Yes, yes, of course, it was agreed, I forgive you. Many thanks. (*The* PAGE *comes forward with a vast cloak, which the* KING *wraps around himself. The* BARONS *surround the* KING *and help him to dress, while the* BISHOPS *and the* CLERGY, *forming a procession, move away solemnly upstage to the strains of the organ. The* KING *dresses hurriedly, with evident bad temper, aided by his* BARONS. *He grimaces ill humoredly and growls:*) The pigs! The Norman Bishops just went through the motions, but those little Saxon monks—my word, they had their money's worth!

(*A* BARON *comes in. A joyful peal of bells is heard.*)

BARON. Sire, the operation has been successful! The Saxon mob is yelling with enthusiasm outside the cathedral, acclaiming your Majesty's name in the same breath as Becket's! If the Saxons are on our side now, Prince Henry's followers look as though they have definitely lost the day.

KING (*with a touch of hypocritical majesty beneath his slightly loutish manner*). The honor of God, gentlemen, is a very good thing, and taken all in all, one gains by having it on one's side. Thomas Becket, who was our friend, used to say so. England will owe her ultimate victory over chaos to him, and it is our wish that, henceforward, he should be honored and prayed to in this Kingdom as a saint. Come, gentlemen. We will determine, tonight, in Council, what posthumous honors to render him and what punishment to deal out to his murderers.

1ST BARON (*imperturbably*). Sire, they are unknown.

KING (*impenetrably*). Our justice will seek them out, Baron, and you will be specially entrusted with this inquiry, so that no one will be in any doubt as to our Royal desire to defend the honor of God and the memory of our friend from this day forward.

(*The organ swells triumphantly, mingled with the sound of the bells and the cheering of the crowds as they file out.*)

EUGENE IONESCO / 1912–

Born in Romania of a Romanian father and a French mother, educated chiefly in France, and for a time employed as a teacher of French in Bucharest, Ionesco along with Samuel Beckett projected "the theater of the absurd" or "the anti-theater" into fashionable prominence. From obscure beginnings on the Left Bank, where *The Bald Soprano* had an audience of three, Ionesco's plays have become successful throughout the world. Somewhat ironically, an *avant garde* experimentalist has become a bourgeois success.

Taken seriously, the theater of the absurd is based on a philosophy of nihilism: the ordering of reality by science and reason has reached a final bankruptcy in an empty universe; individuality and communication are illusory; the whole scheme of things has been reason-driven to absurdity. Taken theatrically, illogicality dictates that such logical means as plot, causal sequence, and, especially, intelligible language are to be discarded. Beckett's *Act Without Words* and Ionesco's *The New Tenant* are pantomimes. Language, however, can be employed illogically—fragmented, made into mechanical nonsense, kept *non sequitur*, kept banal and worn-out. Once the sense of association and congruity necessary to keep language communicative has been removed, the attempt at communication itself becomes an absurdity.

Ionesco is a theatrical artificer of the absurd; he calculates and synthesizes the resources of theater for an antirealistic unity as intensely as the realistic playwrights have worked to create a unity rooted in logic and causality. Language and characters, treated in the absurd, are still the most important of his resources, although pantomime, symbolism, and a free use of primitive and sophisticated means in combination contribute essentially to the whole.

Dramatic structure as evolved by playwrights interpreting societies which have confidence in reason and order is of course a target for fragmentation and destruction by the theater of the absurd. The absurd plays demand from the reader his traditional dramatic expectation, so that by baffling and shocking his expectation the play may lead him to perceive the absurd nature of life. Ionesco's *The Rhinoceros* was suspected by his enthusiasts of having a too discernible plot and they complained that he was recanting or compromising with rational theater. Some critics feel that the steps in basic dramatic structure may still be discerned in the absurd plays, and in a parodied or parasitic sense they may be, but they are not, perhaps, trustworthy enough guides to the individual unity of each play to be profitably followed by the reader or theater audience.

A fair range of the messages and methods of the theater of the absurd will be found in Samuel Beckett's *Waiting for Godot, Endgame,* and *Happy Days,* and in the following plays of Ionesco: *The Bald Soprano* (*La Cantatrice chauve*), *The Future Is in Eggs, or It Takes All Sorts to Make a World* (*L'Avenir est dans les oeufs, ou Il faut de tout pour faire un monde*), *The Killer* (*Tueur sans gages*), and *The Rhinoceros* (*Le Rhinocéros*).

Of *The Chairs,* Ionesco wrote, "I have tried to deal with the themes that obsess me; with emptiness, with frustration, with this world, at once fleeting and crushing, with despair and death. The characters I have used are not fully conscious of their spiritual rootlessness, but they feel it instinctively and emotionally."

The Chairs

A TRAGIC FARCE
TRANSLATED BY DONALD M. ALLEN

CHARACTERS

OLD MAN, *aged 95.*
OLD WOMAN, *aged 94.*
THE ORATOR, *aged 45 to 50.*
And many other characters.

SCENE: *Circular walls with a recess upstage center. A large, very sparsely furnished room. To the right, going upstage from the proscenium, three doors. Then a window with a stool in front of it; then another door. In the center of the back wall of the recess, a large double door, and two other doors facing each other and bracketing the main door: these last two doors, or at least one of them, are almost hidden from the audience. To the left, going upstage from the proscenium, there are three doors, a window with a stool in front of it, opposite the window on the right, then a blackboard and a dais. See the plan below. Downstage are two chairs, side by side. A gas lamp hangs from the ceiling.*

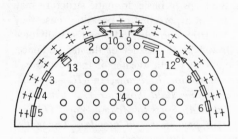

1: Main double door.
2, 3, 4, 5: Side doors on the right.
6, 7, 8: Side doors on the left.
9, 10: Two doors hidden in the recess.
11: Dais and blackboard.

12, 13: Windows, with stools, left and right.
14: Empty chairs.
XXX Corridor, in wings.

(*The curtain rises. Half-light.* THE OLD MAN *is up on the stool, leaning out the window on the left.* THE OLD WOMAN *lights the gas lamp. Green light. She goes over to* THE OLD MAN *and takes him by the sleeve.*)

OLD WOMAN. Come my darling, close the window. There's a bad smell from that stagnant water, and besides the mosquitoes are coming in.

OLD MAN. Leave me alone!

OLD WOMAN. Come, come, my darling, come sit down. You shouldn't lean out, you might fall into the water. You know what happened to François I. You must be careful.

OLD MAN. Still more examples from history! Sweetheart, I'm tired of French history. I want to see—the boats on the water making blots in the sunlight.

OLD WOMAN. You can't see them, there's no sunlight, it's nighttime, my darling.

OLD MAN. There are still shadows. (*He leans out very far.*)

OLD WOMAN (*pulling him in with all her strength*). Oh! . . . you're frightening me, my darling . . . come sit down, you won't be able to see them come, anyway. There's no use trying. It's dark . . .

(THE OLD MAN *reluctantly lets himself be pulled in.*)

OLD MAN. I wanted to see—you know how much I love to see the water.

OLD WOMAN. How can you, my darling? . . . It makes me dizzy. Ah! this house, this island, I can't get used to it. Water all around us . . . water under the windows, stretching as far as the horizon.

(THE OLD WOMAN *drags* THE OLD MAN *down and they move towards the two chairs downstage;* THE OLD MAN *seats himself quite naturally on the lap of* THE OLD WOMAN.)

OLD MAN. It's six o'clock in the evening . . . it is dark already. It wasn't like this before. Surely you remember, there was still daylight at nine o'clock in the evening, at ten o'clock, at midnight.

OLD WOMAN. Come to think of it, that's very true. What a remarkable memory you have!

OLD MAN. Things have certainly changed.

OLD WOMAN. Why is that, do you think?

OLD MAN. I don't know, Semiramis, sweetheart . . . Perhaps it's because the further one goes, the deeper one sinks. It's because the earth keeps turning around, around, around, around . . .

OLD WOMAN. Around, around, my little pet. (*Silence.*) Ah! yes, you've certainly a fine intellect. You are very gifted, my darling. You could have been head president, head king, or even head doctor, or head general, if you had wanted to, if only you'd had a little ambition in life . . .

OLD MAN. What good would that have done us? We'd not have lived any better . . . and besides, we have a position here. I am a general, in any case, of the house, since I am the general factotum.

OLD WOMAN (*caressing* THE OLD MAN *as one caresses a child*). My darling, my pet.

OLD MAN. I'm very bored.

OLD WOMAN. You were more cheerful when you were looking at the water . . . Let's amuse ourselves by making

believe, the way you did the other evening.

OLD MAN. Make believe yourself, it's your turn.

OLD WOMAN. It's your turn.

OLD MAN. Your turn.

OLD WOMAN. Your turn.

OLD MAN. Your turn.

OLD WOMAN. Your turn.

OLD MAN. Drink your tea, Semiramis.

(*Of course there is no tea.*)

OLD WOMAN. Come on now, imitate the month of February.

OLD MAN. I don't like the months of the year.

OLD WOMAN. Those are the only ones we have, up till now. Come on, just to please me . . .

OLD MAN. All right, here's the month of February. (*He scratches his head like Stan Laurel.*)

OLD WOMAN (*laughing, applauding*). That's just right. Thank you, thank you, you're as cute as can be, my darling. (*She hugs him.*) Oh, you are so gifted, you could have been at least a head general, if you had wanted to . . .

OLD MAN. I am a general, general factotum. (*Silence.*)

OLD WOMAN. Tell me the story, you know *the* story: "Then at last we arrived . . ."

OLD MAN. Again? . . . I'm sick of it . . . "Then at last we arrived"? That again . . . you always ask for the same thing! . . . "Then at last we arrived . . ." But it's monotonous . . . For all of the seventy-five years that we've been married, every single evening, absolutely every blessed evening, you've made me tell the same story, you've made me imitate the same people, the same months . . . always the same . . . let's talk about something else . . .

OLD WOMAN. My darling, I'm not tired of it . . . it's your life, it fascinates me.

OLD MAN. You know it by heart.

OLD WOMAN. It's as if suddenly I'd forgotten everything . . . it's as though my mind were a clean slate every evening . . . Yes, my darling, I do it on purpose, I take a dose of salts . . . I become new again, for you, my darling, every evening . . . Come on, begin again, please.

OLD MAN. Well, if you want me to.

OLD WOMAN. Come on then, tell your story . . . It's also mine; what is yours is mine! Then at last we arrived . . .

OLD MAN. Then at last we arrived . . . my sweetheart . . .

OLD WOMAN. Then at last we arrived . . . my darling . . .

OLD MAN. Then at last we arrived at a big fence. We were soaked through, frozen to the bone, for hours, for days, for nights, for weeks . . .

OLD WOMAN. For months . . .

OLD MAN. . . . In the rain . . . Our ears, our feet, our knees, our noses, our teeth were chattering . . . that was eighty years ago . . . They wouldn't let us in . . . they might at least have opened the gate of the garden . . . (*Silence.*)

OLD WOMAN. In the garden the grass was wet.

OLD MAN. There was a path which led to a little square and in the center, a village church . . . Where was this village? Do you recall?

OLD WOMAN. No, my darling, I've forgotten.

OLD MAN. How did we reach it? Where is the road? This place was called Paris, I think . . .

OLD WOMAN. Paris never existed, my little one.

OLD MAN. That city must have existed because it collapsed . . . It was the city of light, but it has been extinguished, extinguished, for four hundred thousand years . . . Nothing remains of it today, except a song.

OLD WOMAN. A real song? That's odd. What song?

OLD MAN. A lullaby, an allegory: "Paris will always be Paris."

OLD WOMAN. And the way to it was through the garden? Was it far?

OLD MAN (*dreaming, lost*). The song? . . . the rain? . . .

OLD WOMAN. You are very gifted. If you had had a little ambition in life you could have been head king, head journalist, head comedian, head general . . . All that's gone down the drain, alas . . . down the old black drain . . . down the old drain, I tell you. (*Silence.*)

OLD MAN. Then at last we arrived . . .

OLD WOMAN. Ah! yes, go on . . . tell me . . .

OLD MAN (*while* THE OLD WOMAN *begins to laugh softly, senilely, then progressively in great bursts,* THE OLD MAN *laughs, too, as he continues*). Then at last we arrived, we laughed till we cried, the story was so idiotic . . . the idiot arrived full speed, bare-bellied, the idiot was pot-bellied . . . he arrived with a trunk chock full of rice; the rice spilled out on the ground . . . the idiot on the ground too, belly to ground . . . then at last we laughed, we laughed, we laughed, the idiotic belly, bare with rice on the ground, the trunk, the story of sick from rice belly to ground, bare-bellied, all with rice, at last we laughed, the idiot at last arrived all bare, we laughed . . .

OLD WOMAN (*laughing*). At last we laughed like idiots, at last arrived all bare, we laughed, the trunk, the trunk full of rice, the rice on the belly, on the ground . . .

OLD MAN AND OLD WOMAN (*laughing together*). At last we laughed. Ah! . . . laughed . . . arrived . . . arrived . . . Ah! . . . Ah! . . . rived . . . arrived . . . arrived . . . the idiotic bare belly . . . arrived with the rice . . . arrived with the rice . . . (*This is all we hear.*) At last we . . . bare-bellied . . . arrived . . . the trunk . . . (*Then* THE OLD MAN *and* OLD WOMAN *calm down little by little.*) We lau . . . Ah! . . . aughed . . . Ah! . . . arrived . . . Ah! . . . arrived . . . aughed . . . aughed.

OLD WOMAN. So that's the way it was, your wonderful Paris.

OLD MAN. Who could put it better?

OLD WOMAN. Oh! my darling, you are so really fine. Oh! so really, you know, so really, so really, you could have been anything in life, a lot more than general factotum.

OLD MAN. Let's be modest . . . we should be content with the little . . .

OLD WOMAN. Perhaps you've spoiled your career?

OLD MAN (*weeping suddenly*). I've spoiled it? I've spilled it? Ah, where are you, Mamma, Mamma, where are you, Mamma? . . . hi, hi, hi, I'm an orphan. (*He moans.*) . . . an orphan, dworfan.

OLD WOMAN. Here I am, what are you afraid of?

OLD MAN. No, Semiramis, my sweetheart, you're not my mamma . . . orphan, dworfan, who will protect me?

OLD WOMAN. But I'm here, my darling!

OLD MAN. It's not the same thing . . . I want my mamma, na, you, you're not my mamma, you . . .

OLD WOMAN (*caressing him*). You're breaking my heart, don't cry, my little one.

OLD MAN. Hi, hi, let me go, hi, hi, I'm all spoiled, I'm wet all over, my career is spilled, it's spoiled.

OLD WOMAN. Calm down.

OLD MAN (*sobbing, his mouth wide open like a baby*). I'm an orphan . . . dworfan.

OLD WOMAN (*trying to console him by cajoling him*). My orphan, my darling, you're breaking my heart, my orphan. (*She rocks* THE OLD MAN *who is sitting on her knees again.*)

OLD MAN (*sobbing*). Hi, hi, hi! My mamma! Where is my mamma? I don't have a mamma anymore.

OLD WOMAN. I am your wife, I'm the one who is your mamma now.

OLD MAN (*giving in a little*). That's not true, I'm an orphan, hi, hi.

OLD WOMAN (*still rocking him*). My pet, my orphan, dworfan, worfan, morphan, orphan.

OLD MAN (*still sulky, but giving in more and more*). No . . . I don't want; I don't wa-a-a-ant.

OLD WOMAN (*crooning*). Orphan-ly, orphan-lay, orphan-lo, orphan-loo.

OLD MAN. No-o-o . . . No-o-o.

OLD WAMAN (*same business*). Li lon lala, li lon la lay, orphan-ly, orphan-lay, relee-relay, orphan-li-relee-rela . . .

OLD MAN. Hi, hi, hi, hi. (*He sniffles, calming down little by little.*) Where is she? My mamma.

OLD WOMAN. In heavenly paradise . . . she hears you, she sees you, among the flowers; don't cry anymore, you will only make me weep!

OLD MAN. That's not even true-ue . . . she can't see me . . . she can't hear me. I'm an orphan, on earth, you're not my mamma . . .

OLD WOMAN (*he is almost calm*). Now, come on, calm down, don't get so upset . . . you have great qualities, my little general . . . dry your tears; the guests are sure to come this evening and they mustn't see you this way . . . all is not lost, all is not spoiled, you'll tell them everything, you will explain, you have a message . . . you always say you are going to deliver it . . . you must live, you have to struggle for your message . . .

OLD MAN. I have a message, that's God's truth, I struggle, a mission, I have something to say, a message to communicate to humanity, to mankind . . .

OLD WOMAN. To mankind, my daring, your message! . . .

OLD MAN. That's true, y,es, it's true . . .

OLD WOMAN (*she wipes* THE OLD MAN's *nose, dries his tears*). That's it . . . you're a man, a soldier, a general factotum . . .

OLD MAN (*he gets off* THE OLD WOMAN's *lap and walks with short, agitated steps*). I'm not like other people, I have an ideal in life. I am perhaps gifted, as you say, I have some talent, but things aren't easy for me. I've served well in my capacity as general factotum, I've always been in command of the situation, honorably, that should be enough . . .

OLD WOMAN. Not for you, you're not like other people, you are much greater, and moreover you'd have done much better if you had got along with other people, like other people do. You've quarreled with all your friends, with all the directors, with all the generals, with your own brother.

OLD MAN. It's not my fault, Semiramis, you know very well what he said.

OLD WOMAN. What did he say?

OLD MAN. He said: "My friends, I've got a flea. I'm going to pay you a visit in the hope of leaving my flea with you."

OLD WOMAN. People say things like that, my dear. You shouldn't have paid any attention to it. But with Carel, why were you so angry with him. Was it his fault too?

OLD MAN. You're going to make me angry, you're going to make me angry. Na. Of course it was his fault. He came one evening, he said: "I know just the word that fits you. I'm not going to say it, I'll just think it." And he laughed like a fool.

OLD WOMAN. But he had a warm heart, my darling. In this life, you've got to be less sensitive.

OLD MAN. I don't care for jokes like that.

OLD WOMAN. You could have been head admiral, head cabinet-maker, head orchestra conductor.

(*Long silence. They remain immobile for a time, completely rigid on their chairs.*)

OLD MAN (*as in a dream*). At the end of the garden there was . . . there was . . . there was . . . there was . . . was what, my dear?

OLD WOMAN. The city of Paris!

OLD MAN. At the end, at the end of the end of the city of Paris, there was, there was, was what?

OLD WOMAN. My darling, was what, my darling, was who?

OLD MAN. The place and the weather were beautiful . . .

OLD WOMAN. The weather was so beautiful, are you sure?

OLD MAN. I don't recall the place . . .

OLD WOMAN. Don't tax your mind then . . .

OLD MAN. It's too far away, I can no longer . . . recall it . . . where was this?

OLD WOMAN. But what?

OLD MAN. What I . . . what I . . . where was this? And who?

OLD WOMAN. No matter where it is —I will follow you anywhere, I'll follow you, my darling.

OLD MAN. Ah! I have so much difficulty expressing myself . . . but I must tell it all.

OLD WOMAN. It's a sacred duty. You've no right to keep your message from the world. You must reveal it to mankind, they're waiting for it . . . the universe waits only for you.

OLD MAN. Yes, yes, I will speak.

OLD WOMAN. Have you really decided? You must.

OLD MAN. Drink your tea.

OLD WOMAN. You could have been head orator, if you had more will power in life . . . I'm proud, I'm happy that you have at last decided to speak to every country, to Europe, to every continent!

OLD MAN. Unfortunately, I have so

much difficulty expressing myself, it isn't easy for me.

OLD WOMAN. It's easy once you begin, like life and death . . . it's enough to have your mind made up. It's in speaking that ideas come to us, words, and then we, in our own words, we find perhaps everything, the city too, the garden, and then we are orphans no longer.

OLD MAN. It's not I who's going to speak, I've hired a professional orator, he'll speak in my name, you'll see.

OLD WOMAN. Then, it really is for this evening? And have you invited everyone, all the characters, all the property owners, and all the intellectuals?

OLD MAN. Yes, all the owners and all the intellectuals. (*Silence.*)

OLD WOMAN. The janitors? the bishops? the chemists? the tinsmiths? the violinists? the delegates? the presidents? the police? the merchants? the buildings? the pen holders? the chromosomes?

OLD MAN. Yes, yes, and the post-office employees, the innkeepers, and the artists, everybody who is a little intellectual, a little proprietary!

OLD WOMAN. And the bankers?

OLD MAN. Yes, invited.

OLD WOMAN. The proletarians? the functionaries? the militaries? the revolutionaries? the reactionaries? the alienists and their alienated?

OLD MAN. Of course, all of them, all of them, all of them, since actually everyone is either intellectual or proprietary.

OLD WOMAN. Don't get upset, my darling, I don't mean to annoy you, you are so very absent-minded, like all great geniuses. This meeting is important, they must all be here this evening. Can you count on them? Have they promised?

OLD MAN. Drink your tea, Semiramis. (*Silence.*)

OLD WOMAN. The papacy, the papayas, and the papers?

OLD MAN. I've invited them. (*Silence.*) I'm going to communicate the message to them . . . All my life, I've felt that I was suffocating; and now, they will know all, thanks to you and to the Orator, you are the only ones who have understood me.

OLD WOMAN. I'm so proud of you . . .

OLD MAN. The meeting will take place in a few minutes.

OLD WOMAN. It's true then, they're going to come, this evening? You won't feel like crying any more, the intellectuals and the proprietors will take the place of papas and mammas? (*Silence.*) Couldn't you put off this meeting? It won't be too tiring for us?

(*More violent agitation. For several moments* THE OLD MAN *has been turning around* THE OLD WOMAN *with the short, hesitant steps of an old man or of a child. He takes a step or two towards one of the doors, then returns and walks around her again.*)

OLD MAN. You really think this might tire us?

OLD WOMAN. You have a slight cold.

OLD MAN. How can I call it off?

OLD WOMAN. Invite them for another evening. You could telephone.

OLD MAN. No, my God, I can't do that, it's too late. They're probably already embarked!

OLD WOMAN. You should have been more careful.

(*We hear the sound of a boat gliding through the water.*)

OLD MAN. I think someone is coming already . . . (*The gliding sound of a boat is heard more clearly.*) . . . Yes, they're coming! . . .

(THE OLD WOMAN *gets up also and walks with a hobble.*)

OLD WOMAN. Perhaps it's the Orator.

OLD MAN. He won't come so soon. This must be somebody else. (*We hear the doorbell ring.*) Ah!

OLD WOMAN. Ah!

(*Nervously,* THE OLD MAN *and* THE OLD WOMAN *move towards the con-*

cealed door in the recess to the right. As they move upstage, they say.)

OLD MAN. Come on . . .

OLD WOMAN. My hair must look a sight . . . wait a moment . . .

(She arranges her hair and her dress as she hobbles along, pulling up her thick red stockings.)

OLD MAN. You should have gotten ready before . . . you had plenty of time.

OLD WOMAN. I'm so badly dressed . . . I'm wearing an old gown and it's all rumpled . . .

OLD MAN. All you had to do was to press it . . . hurry up! You're making our guests wait.

(The OLD MAN, *followed by* THE OLD WOMAN *still grumbling, reaches the door in the recess; we don't see them for a moment; we hear them open the door, then close it again after having shown someone in.)*

VOICE OF OLD MAN. Good evening, madam, won't you please come in. We're delighted to see you. This is my wife.

VOICE OF OLD WOMAN. Good evening, madam, I am very happy to make your acquaintance. Take care, don't ruin your hat. You might take out the hatpin, that will be more comfortable. Oh! no, no one will sit on it.

VOICE OF OLD MAN. Put your fur down there. Let me help you. No, nothing will happen to it.

VOICE OF OLD WOMAN. Oh! what a pretty suit . . . and such darling colors in your blouse . . . Won't you have some cookies . . . Oh, you're not fat at all . . . no . . . plump . . . just leave your umbrella there.

VOICE OF OLD MAN. Follow me, please.

OLD MAN *(back view).* I have only a modest position . . .

(THE OLD MAN *and* OLD WOMAN *re-enter together, leaving space between them for their guest. She is invisible.* THE OLD MAN *and* OLD WOMAN *ad-*

vance, downstage, facing the audience and speaking to the invisible LADY, *who walks between them.)*

OLD MAN *(to the invisible* LADY*).* You've had good weather?

OLD WOMAN *(to the* LADY*).* You're not too tired? . . . Yes, a little.

OLD MAN *(to the* LADY*).* At the edge of the water . . .

OLD WOMAN *(to the* LADY*).* It's kind of you to say so.

OLD MAN *(to the* LADY*).* Let me get you a chair.

(OLD MAN goes to the left, he exits by door No. 6.)

OLD WOMAN *(to the* LADY*).* Take this one, for the moment, please. *(She indicates one of the two chairs and seats herself on the other, to the right of the invisible* LADY*.)* It seems rather warm in here, doesn't it? *(She smiles at the* LADY*.)* What a charming fan you have! My husband . . . *(THE* OLD MAN *re-enters through door No. 7, carrying a chair.)* . . . gave me one very like it, that must have been seventy-three years ago . . . and I still have it . . . *(THE* OLD MAN *places the chair to the left of the invisible* LADY*.)* . . . it was for my birthday! . . .

(THE OLD MAN *sits on the chair that he has just brought onstage, so that the invisible* LADY *is between the old couple.* THE OLD MAN *turns his face towards the* LADY*, smiles at her, nods his head, softly rubs his hands together, with the air of following what she says.* THE OLD WOMAN *does the same business.)*

OLD MAN. No, madam, life is never cheap.

OLD WOMAN *(to the* LADY*).* You are so right . . . *(The* LADY *speaks.)* As you say, it is about time all that changed . . . *(Changing her tone.)* Perhaps my husband can do something about it . . . he's going to tell you about it.

OLD MAN *(to* THE OLD WOMAN*).* Hush, hush, Semiramis, the time hasn't come to talk about that yet. *(To the*

LADY.) Excuse me, madam, for having aroused your curiosity. (*The* LADY *reacts.*) Dear madam, don't insist . . .

(THE OLD MAN *and* THE OLD WOMAN *smile. They even laugh. They appear to be very amused by the story the invisible* LADY *tells them. A pause, a moment of silence in the conversation. Their faces lose all expression.*)

OLD MAN (*to the invisible* LADY). Yes, you're quite right . . .

OLD WOMAN. Yes, yes, yes . . . Oh! surely not.

OLD MAN. Yes, yes, yes. Not at all.

OLD WOMAN. Yes?

OLD MAN. No!?

OLD WOMAN. It's certainly true.

OLD MAN (*laughing*). It isn't possible.

OLD WOMAN (*laughing*). Oh! well. (*To* THE OLD MAN.) She's charming.

OLD MAN (*to* THE OLD WOMAN). Madam has made a conquest. (*To the invisible* LADY.) My congratulations! . . .

OLD WOMAN (*to the invisible* LADY). You're not like the young people today . . .

OLD MAN (*bending over painfully in order to recover an invisible object that the invisible* LADY *has dropped*). Let me . . . don't disturb yourself . . . I'll get it . . . Oh! you're quicker than I . . . (*He straightens up again.*)

OLD WOMAN (*to* THE OLD MAN). She's younger than you!

OLD MAN (*to the invisible* LADY). Old age is a heavy burden. I can only wish you an eternal youth.

OLD WOMAN (*to the invisible* LADY). He's sincere, he speaks from the heart. (*To* THE OLD MAN.) My darling!

(*Several moments of silence.* THE OLD MAN *and* OLD WOMAN, *heads turned in profile, look at the invisible* LADY, *smiling politely; they then turn their heads towards the audience, then look again at the invisible* LADY, *answering her smile with their smiles, and her questions with their replies.*)

OLD WOMAN. It's very kind of you to take such an interest in us.

OLD MAN. We live a retired life.

OLD WOMAN. My husband's not really misanthropic, he just loves solitude.

OLD MAN. We have the radio, I get in some fishing, and then there's fairly regular boat service.

OLD WOMAN. On Sundays there are two boats in the morning, one in the evening, not to mention privately chartered trips.

OLD MAN (*to the invisible* LADY). When the weather's clear, there is a moon.

OLD WOMAN (*to the invisible* LADY). He's always concerned with his duties as general factotum . . . they keep him busy . . . On the other hand, at his age, he might very well take it easy.

OLD MAN (*to the invisible* LADY). I'll have plenty of time to take it easy in my grave.

OLD WOMAN (*to* THE OLD MAN). Don't say that, my little darling . . . (*To the invisible* LADY.) Our family, what's left of it, my husband's friends, still came to see us, from time to time, ten years ago . . .

OLD MAN (*to the invisible* LADY). In the winter, a good book, beside the radiator, and the memories of a lifetime.

OLD WOMAN (*to the invisible* LADY). A modest life but a full one . . . he devotes two hours every day to work on his message.

(*The doorbell rings. After a short pause, we hear the noise of a boat leaving.*)

OLD WOMAN (*to* THE OLD MAN). Someone has come. Go quickly.

OLD MAN (*to the invisible* LADY). Please excuse me, madam. Just a moment! (*To* THE OLD WOMAN.) Hurry and bring some chairs!

(*Loud ringing at the doorbell.*)

OLD MAN (*hastening, all bent over,*

towards door No. 2 to the right, while
THE OLD WOMAN *goes towards the con-*
cealed door on the left, hurrying with
difficulty, hobbling along). It must be
someone important. (*He hurries, opens
door No. 2, and the invisible* COLONEL
*enters. Perhaps it would be useful for us
to hear discreetly several trumpet notes,
several phrases, like "Hail the Chief."
When he opens the door and sees the
invisible* COLONEL, THE OLD MAN *stiffens into a respectful position of attention.*) Ah! . . . Colonel! (*He lifts his
hand vaguely towards his forehead, so as
to roughly sketch a salute.*) Good evening, my dear Colonel . . . This is a
very great honor for me . . . I . . . I
. . . I was not expecting it . . . although
. . . indeed . . . in short, I am most
proud to welcome you, a hero of your
eminence, into my humble dwelling . . .
(*He presses the invisible hand that the
invisible* COLONEL *gives him, bending
forward ceremoniously, then straightening up again.*) Without false modesty,
nevertheless, I permit myself to confess
to you that I do not feel unworthy of the
honor of your visit! Proud, yes . . . unworthy, no! . . .

(*The* OLD WOMAN *appears with a
chair, entering from the right.*)

OLD WOMAN. Oh! What a handsome uniform! What beautiful medals!
Who is it, my darling?

OLD MAN (*to* THE OLD WOMAN).
Can't you see that it's the Colonel?

OLD WOMAN (*to* THE OLD MAN).
Ah!

OLD MAN (*to* THE OLD WOMAN).
Count his stripes! (*To the* COLONEL.)
This is my wife, Semiramis. (*To* THE
OLD WOMAN.) Come here so that I can
introduce you to the Colonel. (THE
OLD WOMAN *approaches, dragging the
chair by one hand, and makes a curtsey,
without letting go of the chair. To the*
COLONEL.) My wife. (*To* THE OLD
WOMAN.) The Colonel.

OLD WOMAN. How do you do, Colonel. Welcome. You're an old comrade of
my husband's, he's a general . . .

OLD MAN (*annoyed*). Factotum,
factotum . . .

(*The invisible* COLONEL *kisses the
hand of* THE OLD WOMAN. *This is apparent from the gesture she makes as she
raises her hand toward his lips. Overcome with emotion,* THE OLD WOMAN
lets go of the chair.)

OLD WOMAN. Oh! He's most polite
. . . you can see that he's really superior,
a superior being! . . . (*She takes hold
of the chair again. To the* COLONEL.)
This chair is for you . . .

OLD MAN (*to the invisible* COLONEL).
This way, if you please . . . (*They move
downstage,* THE OLD WOMAN *dragging
the chair. To the* COLONEL.) Yes, one
guest has come already. We're expecting
a great many more people! . . .

(THE OLD WOMAN *places the chair
to the right.*)

OLD WOMAN (*to the* COLONEL). Sit
here, please.

(THE OLD MAN *introduces the two
invisible guests to each other.*)

OLD MAN. A young lady we know
. . .

OLD WOMAN. A very dear friend . . .

OLD MAN (*same business*). The
Colonel . . . a famous soldier.

OLD WOMAN (*indicating the chair she
has just brought in to the* COLONEL).
Do take this chair . . .

OLD MAN (*to* THE OLD WOMAN).
No, no, can't you see that the Colonel
wishes to sit beside the Lady! . . .

(*The* COLONEL *seats himself invisibly
on the third chair from the left; the invisible* LADY *is supposedly sitting on the
second chair; seated next to each other
they engage in an inaudible conversation;* THE OLD WOMAN *and* OLD MAN
*continue to stand behind their chairs, on
both sides of their invisible guests;* THE
OLD MAN *to the left of the* LADY, THE

OLD WOMAN *to the right of the* COLONEL.)

OLD WOMAN (*listening to the conversation of the two guests*). Oh! Oh! That's going too far.

OLD MAN (*same business*). Perhaps. (THE OLD MAN *and* THE OLD WOMAN *make signs to each other over the heads of their guests, while they follow the inaudible conversation which takes a turn that seems to displease them. Abruptly.*) Yes, Colonel, they are not here yet, but they'll be here. And the Orator will speak in my behalf, he will explain the meaning of my message . . . Take care, Colonel, this Lady's husband may arrive at any moment.

OLD WOMAN (*to* THE OLD MAN). Who is this gentleman?

OLD MAN (*to* THE OLD WOMAN). I've told you, it's the Colonel.

(*Some embarrassing things take place, invisibly.*)

OLD WOMAN (*to* THE OLD MAN). I knew it. I knew it.

OLD MAN. Then why are you asking?

OLD WOMAN. For my information. Colonel, no cigarette butts on the floor!

OLD MAN (*to* COLONEL). Colonel, Colonel, it's slipped my mind—in the last war did you win or lose?

OLD WOMAN (*to the invisible* LADY). But my dear, don't let it happen!

OLD MAN. Look at me, look at me, do I look like a bad soldier? One time, Colonel, under fire . . .

OLD WOMAN. He's going too far! It's embarrassing! (*She seizes the invisible sleeve of the* COLONEL.) Listen to him! My darling, why don't you stop him!

OLD MAN (*continuing quickly*). And all on my own, I killed 209 of them; we called them that because they jumped so high to escape, however there weren't so many of them as there were flies; of course it is less amusing, Colonel, but thanks to my strength of character, I have . . . Oh! no, I must, please.

OLD WOMAN (*to* COLONEL). My husband never lies; it may be true that we are old, nevertheless we're respectable.

OLD MAN (*violently, to the* COLONEL). A hero must be a gentleman too, if he hopes to be a complete hero!

OLD WOMAN (*to the* COLONEL). I've known you for many years, but I'd never have believed you were capable of this. (*To the* LADY, *while we hear the sound of boats.*) I'd never have believed him capable of this. We have our dignity, our self-respect.

OLD MAN (*in a quavering voice*). I'm still capable of bearing arms. (*Doorbell rings.*) Excuse me, I must go to the door. (*He stumbles and knocks over the chair of the invisible* LADY.) Oh! pardon.

OLD WOMAN (*rushing forward*). You didn't hurt yourself? (THE OLD MAN *and* OLD WOMAN *help the invisible* LADY *onto her feet.*) You've got all dirty, there's some dust. (*She helps brush the* LADY. *The doorbell rings again.*)

OLD MAN. Forgive me, forgive me. (*To* THE OLD WOMAN.) Go bring a chair.

OLD WOMAN (*to the two invisible guests*). Excuse me for a moment.

(*While* THE OLD MAN *goes to open door No. 3,* THE OLD WOMAN *exits through door No. 5 to look for a chair, and she re-enters by door No. 8.*)

OLD MAN (*moving towards the door*). He was trying to get my goat. I'm almost angry. (*He opens the door.*) Oh! madam, you're here! I can scarcely believe my eyes, and yet, nevertheless . . . I didn't really dare to hope . . . really it's . . . Oh! madam, madam . . . I have thought about you, all my life, all my life, madam, they always called you La Belle . . . it's your husband . . . someone told me, certainly . . . you haven't changed a bit . . . Oh! yes, yes, your nose *has* grown longer, maybe it's a little swollen . . . I didn't notice it

when I first saw you, but I see it now
. . . a lot longer . . . ah! how unfortunate!
You certainly didn't do it on purpose
. . . how did it happen? . . . little by
little . . . excuse me, sir and dear friend,
you'll permit me to call you "dear
friend," I knew your wife long before
you . . . she was the same, but with a
completely different nose . . . I congratulate you, sir, you seem to love each
other very much. (THE OLD WOMAN
*re-enters through door No. 8 with a
chair.*) Semiramis, two guests have arrived, we need one more chair . . .
(THE OLD WOMAN *puts the chair behind the four others, then exits by door
No. 8 and re-enters by door No. 5, after
a few moments, with another chair that
she places beside the one she has just
brought in. By this time,* THE OLD MAN
and the two guests have moved near
THE OLD WOMAN.) Come this way,
please, more guests have arrived. I'm
going to introduce you . . . now then,
madam . . . Oh! Belle, Belle, Miss Belle,
that's what they used to call you . . .
now you're all bent over . . . Oh! sir, she
is still Belle to me, even so; under her
glasses, she still has pretty eyes; her hair
is white, but under the white one can
see brown, and blue, I'm sure of that . . .
come nearer, nearer . . . what is this,
sir, a gift for my wife? (*To* THE OLD
WOMAN, *who has just come on with the
chair.*) Semiramis, this is Belle, you
know, Belle . . . (*To the* COLONEL *and
the invisible* LADY.) This is Miss, pardon,
Mrs. Belle, don't smile . . . and her
husband . . . (*To* THE OLD WOMAN.)
A childhood friend, I've often spoken
of her to you . . . and her husband.
(*Again to the* COLONEL *and to the invisible* LADY.) And her husband . . .
OLD WOMAN (*making a little curtsey*).
He certainly makes good introductions.
He has fine manners. Good evening,
madam, good evening, sir. (*She indicates
the two first guests to the newly arrived
couple.*) Our friends, yes . . .

OLD MAN (*to* THE OLD WOMAN).
He's brought you a present.

(THE OLD WOMAN *takes the present.*)

OLD WOMAN. Is it a flower, sir? or
a cradle? a pear tree? or a crow?

OLD MAN (*to* THE OLD WOMAN).
No, no, can't you see that it's a painting?

OLD WOMAN. Oh! how pretty!
Thank you, sir . . . (*To the invisible*
LADY.) Would you like to see it, dear
friend?

OLD MAN (*to the invisible* COLONEL).
Would you like to see it?

OLD WOMAN (*to* BELLE'S HUSBAND).
Doctor, Doctor, I feel squeamish, I have
hot flashes, I feel sick, I've aches and
pains, I haven't any feeling in my feet,
I've caught cold in my eyes, I've a cold
in my fingers, I'm suffering from liver
trouble, Doctor, Doctor! . . .

OLD MAN (*to* THE OLD WOMAN).
This gentleman is not a doctor, he's a
photo-engraver.

OLD WOMAN (*to the first invisible*
LADY). If you've finished looking at it,
you might hang it up. (*To* THE OLD
MAN.) That doesn't matter, he's charming even so, he's dazzling. (*To the*
PHOTO-ENGRAVER.) Without meaning to
flatter you . . .

(THE OLD MAN *and* THE OLD WOMAN
*now move behind the chairs, close to
each other, almost touching, but back
to back; they talk:* THE OLD MAN *to*
BELLE, THE OLD WOMAN *to the* PHOTO-
ENGRAVER; *from time to time their replies, as shown by the way they turn
their heads, are addressed to one or the
other of the two first guests.*)

OLD MAN (*to* BELLE). I am very
touched . . . You're still the same, in
spite of everything . . . I've loved you,
a hundred years ago . . . But there's
been such a change . . . No, you haven't
changed a bit . . . I loved you, I love
you . . .

OLD WOMAN (*to the* PHOTO-EN-
GRAVER). Oh! Sir, sir, sir . . .

OLD MAN (*to the* COLONEL). I'm

in complete agreement with you on that point.

OLD WOMAN (*to the* PHOTO-ENGRAVER). Oh! certainly, sir, certainly, sir, certainly . . . (*To the first* LADY.) Thanks for hanging it up . . . Forgive me if I've inconvenienced you.

(*The light grows stronger. It should grow stronger and stronger as the invisible guests continue to arrive.*)

OLD MAN (*almost whimpering to* BELLE). Where are the snows of yesteryear?

OLD WOMAN (*to the* PHOTO-ENGRAVER). Oh! Sir, sir, sir . . . Oh! sir . . .

OLD MAN (*pointing out the first lady to* BELLE). She's a young friend . . . she's very sweet . . .

OLD WOMAN (*pointing the* COLONEL *out to the* PHOTO-ENGRAVER). Yes, he's a mounted staff colonel . . . a comrade of my husband . . . a subaltern, my husband's a general . . .

OLD MAN (*to* BELLE). Your ears were not always so pointed! . . . My Belle, do you remember?

OLD WOMAN (*to the* PHOTO-ENGRAVER, *simpering grotesquely; she develops this manner more and more in this scene; she shows her thick red stockings, raises her many petticoats, shows an underskirt full of holes, exposes her old breast; then, her hands on her hips, throws her head back, makes little erotic cries, projects her pelvis, her legs spread apart; she laughs like an old prostitute; this business, entirely different from her manner heretofore as well as from that she will have subsequently, and which must reveal the hidden personality of* THE OLD WOMAN, *ceases abruptly*). So you think I'm too old for that, do you?

OLD MAN (*to* BELLE, *very romantically*). When we were young, the moon was a living star. Ah! yes, yes, if only we had dared, but we were only children. Wouldn't you like to recapture those bygone days . . . is it still possible? Is it still possible? Ah! no, no, it is no longer possible. Those days have flown away as fast as a train. Time has left the marks of his wheels on our skin. Do you believe surgeons can perform miracles? (*To the* COLONEL.) I am a soldier, and you too, we soldiers are always young, the generals are like gods . . . (*To* BELLE.) It ought to be that way . . . Alas! Alas! We have lost everything. We could have been so happy, I'm sure of it, we could have been, we could have been; perhaps the flowers are budding again beneath the snow! . . .

OLD WOMAN (*to* PHOTO-ENGRAVER). Flatterer! Rascal! Ah! Ah! I look younger than my years? You're a little savage! You're exciting.

OLD MAN (*to* BELLE). Will you be my Isolde and let me be your Tristan? Beauty is more than skin deep, it's in the heart . . . Do you understand? We could have had the pleasure of sharing, joy, beauty, eternity . . . an eternity . . . Why didn't we dare? We weren't brave enough . . . Everything is lost, lost, lost.

OLD WOMAN (*to* PHOTO-ENGRAVER). Oh no, Oh! no, Oh! la la, you give me the shivers. You too, are you ticklish? To tickle or be tickled? I'm a little embarrassed . . . (*She laughs.*) Do you like my petticoat? Or do you like this skirt better?

OLD MAN (*to* BELLE). A general factotum has a poor life!

OLD WOMAN (*turning her head towards the first invisible* LADY). In order to make crepes de Chine? A leaf of beef, an hour of flour, a little gastric sugar. (*To the* PHOTO-ENGRAVER.) You've got clever fingers, ah . . . all the sa-a-a-me! . . . Oh-oh-oh-oh.

OLD MAN (*to* BELLE). My worthy helpmeet, Semiramis, has taken the place of my mother. (*He turns towards the* COLONEL.) Colonel, as I've often observed to you, one must take the truth as one finds it. (*He turns back towards* BELLE.)

OLD WOMAN (*to* PHOTO-ENGRAVER). Do you really really believe that one could have children at my age? Any age children?

OLD MAN (*to* BELLE). It's this alone that has saved me: the inner life, peace of mind, austerity, my scientific investigations, philosophy, my message . . .

OLD WOMAN (*to* PHOTO-ENGRAVER). I've never yet betrayed my husband, the general . . . not so hard, you're going to make me fall . . . I'm only his poor mamma! (*She sobs.*) A great, great (*she pushes him bac*k), great . . . mamma. My conscience causes these tears to flow. For me the branch of the apple tree is broken. Try to find somebody else. I no longer want to gather rosebuds . . .

OLD MAN (*to* BELLE). . . . All the preoccupations of a superior order . . .

(THE OLD MAN *and* OLD WOMAN *lead* BELLE *and the* PHOTO-ENGRAVER *up alongside the two other invisible guests, and seat them.*)

OLD MAN *and* OLD WOMAN (*to the* PHOTO-ENGRAVER *and* BELLE). Sit down, please sit down.

(THE OLD MAN *and* OLD WOMAN *sit down too, he to the left, she to the right, with the four empty chairs between them. A long mute scene, punctuated at intervals with "no," "yes," "yes."* THE OLD MAN *and* OLD WOMAN *listen to the conversation of the invisible guests.*)

OLD WOMAN (*to the* PHOTO-ENGRAVER). We had one son . . . of course, he's still alive . . . he's gone away . . . it's a common story . . . or, rather, unusual . . . he abandoned his parents . . . he had a heart of gold . . . that was a long time ago . . . We loved him so much . . . he slammed the door . . . My husband and I tried to hold him back with all our might . . . he was seven years old, the age of reason, I

called after him: "My son, my child, my son, my child." . . . He didn't even look back . . .

OLD MAN. Alas, no . . . no, we've never had a child . . . I'd hoped for a son . . . Semiramis, too . . . we did everything . . . and my poor Semiramis is so maternal, too. Perhaps it was better that way . . . As for me I was an ungrateful son myself . . . Ah! . . . grief, regret, remorse, that's all we have . . . that's all we have left . . .

OLD WOMAN. He said to me: "You kill birds! Why do you kill birds?" . . . But we don't kill birds . . . we've never harmed so much as a fly . . . His eyes were full of big tears. He wouldn't let us dry them. He wouldn't let me come near him. He said: "Yes, you kill all the birds, all the birds." . . . He showed us his little fists . . . "You're lying, you've betrayed me! The streets are full of dead birds, of dying baby birds." It's the song of the birds! . . . "No, it's their death rattle. The sky is red with blood." . . . No, my child, it's blue. He cried again: "You've betrayed me, I adored you, I believed you to be good . . . the streets are full of dead birds, you've torn out their eyes . . . Papa, mamma, you're wicked! . . . I refuse to stay with you." . . . I threw myself at his feet . . . His father was weeping. We couldn't hold him back. As he went we could still hear him calling: "It's you who are responsible" . . . What does that mean, "responsible"?

OLD MAN. I let my mother die all alone in a ditch. She called after me, moaning feebly: "My little child, my beloved son, don't leave me to die all alone . . . Stay with me. I don't have much time left." Don't worry, Mamma, I told her, I'll be back in a moment . . . I was in a hurry . . . I was going to the ball, to dance. I will be back in a minute. But when I returned, she was already dead, and they had buried her deep . . . I broke open the grave, I searched for her . . . I couldn't find her . . . I know, I know, sons, always, abandon their mothers, and they more or less kill their fathers . . . Life is like that . . . but I, I suffer from it . . . and the others, they don't . . .

OLD WOMAN. He cried: "Papa, Mamma, I'll never set eyes on you again."

OLD MAN. I suffer from it, yes, the others don't. . . .

OLD WOMAN. Don't speak of him to my husband. He loved his parents so much. He never left them for a single moment. He cared for them, coddled them . . . And they died in his arms, saying to him: "You have been a perfect son. God will be good to you."

OLD MAN. I can still see her stretched out in the ditch, she was holding a lily of the valley in her hand, she cried: "Don't forget me, don't forget me" . . . her eyes were full of big tears, and she called me by my baby name: "Little Chick," she said, "Little Chick, don't leave me here all alone."

OLD WOMAN (*to the* PHOTO-ENGRAVER). He has never written to us. From time to time, a friend tells us that he's been seen here or there, that he is well, that he is a good husband . . .

OLD MAN (*to* BELLE). When I got back, she had been buried a long time. (*To the first invisible* LADY.) Oh, yes. Oh! yes, madam, we have a movie theatre in the house, a restaurant, bathrooms . . .

OLD WOMAN (*to the* COLONEL). Yes, Colonel, it is because he . . .

OLD MAN. Basically that's it.

(*Desultory conversation, getting bogged down.*)

OLD WOMAN. If only!

OLD MAN. Thus, I've not . . . I, it . . . certainly . . .

OLD WOMAN (*dislocated dialogue, exhaustion*). All in all.

OLD MAN. To ours and to theirs.

OLD WOMAN. So that.

OLD MAN. From me to him.

OLD WOMAN. Him, or her?

OLD MAN. Them.

OLD WOMAN. Curl-papers . . . After all.

OLD MAN. It's not that.

OLD WOMAN. Why?

OLD MAN. Yes.

OLD WOMAN. I.

OLD MAN. All in all.

OLD WOMAN. All in all.

OLD MAN (*to the first invisible* LADY). What was that, madam?

(*A long silence,* THE OLD MAN *and* OLD WOMAN *remain rigid on their chairs. Then the doorbell rings.*)

OLD MAN (*with increasing nervousness*). Someone has come. People. Still more people.

OLD WOMAN. I thought I heard some boats.

OLD MAN. I'll go to the door. Go bring some chairs. Excuse me, gentlemen, ladies. (*He goes towards door No. 7.*)

OLD WOMAN (*to the invisible guests who have already arrived*). Get up for a moment, please. The Orator will be here soon. We must ready the room for the meeting. (THE OLD WOMAN *arranges the chairs, turning their backs towards the audience.*) Lend me a hand, please. Thanks.

OLD MAN (*opening door No. 7*). Good evening, ladies, good evening, gentlemen. Please come in.

(*The three or four invisible persons who have arrived are very tall, and* THE OLD MAN *has to stand on his toes in order to shake hands with them.* THE OLD WOMAN, *after placing the chairs as indicated above, goes over to* THE OLD MAN.)

OLD MAN (*making introductions*). My wife . . . Mr. . . . Mrs. . . . my wife . . . Mr. . . . Mrs. . . . my wife . . .

OLD WOMAN. Who are all these people, my darling?

OLD MAN (*to* OLD WOMAN). Go find some chairs, dear.

OLD WOMAN. I can't do everything! . . .

(*She exits, grumbling, by door No. 6 and re-enters by door No. 7, while* THE OLD MAN, *with the newly arrived guests, moves downstage.*)

OLD MAN. Don't drop your movie camera. (*More introductions.*) The Colonel . . . the Lady . . . Mrs. Belle . . . the Photo-engraver . . . These are the newspapermen, they have come to hear the Orator too, who should be here any minute now . . . Don't be impatient . . . You'll not be bored . . . all together now . . . (THE OLD WOMAN *re-enters through door No. 7 with two chairs.*) Come along, bring the chairs more quickly . . . we're still short one.

(THE OLD WOMAN *goes to find another chair, still grumbling, exiting by door No. 3, and re-entering by door No. 8.*)

OLD WOMAN. All right, and so . . . I'm doing as well as I can . . . I'm not a machine, you know . . . Who are all these people? (*She exits.*)

OLD MAN. Sit down, sit down, the ladies with the ladies, and the gentlemen with the gentlemen, or vice versa, if you prefer . . . We don't have any more nice chairs . . . we have to make do with what we have . . . I'm sorry . . . take the one in the middle . . . does anyone need a fountain pen? Telephone Maillot, you'll get Monique . . . Claude is an angel. I don't have a radio . . . I take all the newspapers . . . that depends on a number of things; I manage these buildings, but I have no help . . . we have to economize . . . no interviews, please, for the moment . . . later, we'll see . . . you'll soon have a place to sit . . . what can she be doing? (THE OLD WOMAN *enters by door No. 8 with a chair.*) Faster, Semiramis . . .

OLD WOMAN. I'm doing my best . . . Who are all these people?

OLD MAN. I'll explain it all to you later.

OLD WOMAN. And that woman? That woman, my darling?

OLD MAN. Don't get upset . . . (*To the* COLONEL.) Colonel, journalism is a profession too, like a fighting man's . . . (*To* THE OLD WOMAN.) Take care of the ladies, my dear . . . (*The doorbell rings.* THE OLD MAN *hurries towards door No. 8.*) Wait a moment . . . (*To* THE OLD WOMAN.) Bring chairs!

OLD WOMAN. Gentlemen, ladies, excuse me . . .

(*She exits by door No. 3, re-entering by door No. 2;* THE OLD MAN *goes to open concealed door No. 9, and disappears at the moment* THE OLD WOMAN *re-enters by door No. 2.*)

OLD MAN (*out of sight*). Come in . . . come in . . . come in . . . come in. (*He reappears, leading in a number of invisible people, including one very small child he holds by the hand.*) One doesn't bring little children to a scientific lecture . . . the poor little thing is going to be bored . . . if he begins to cry or to peepee on the ladies' dresses, that'll be a fine state of affairs! (*He conducts them to stage center;* THE OLD WOMAN *comes on with two chairs.*) I wish to introduce you to my wife, Semiramis; and these are their children.

OLD WOMAN. Ladies, gentlemen . . . Oh! aren't they sweet!

OLD MAN. That one is the smallest.

OLD WOMAN. Oh, he's so cute . . . so cute . . . so cute!

OLD MAN. Not enough chairs.

OLD WOMAN. Oh! dear, oh dear, oh dear . . .

(*She exits, looking for another chair, using now door No. 2 as exit and door No. 3 on the right to re-enter.*)

OLD MAN. Hold the little boy on your lap . . . The twins can sit together in the same chair. Be careful, they're not very strong . . . they go with the house, they belong to the landlord. Yes, my children, he'd make trouble for us, he's a bad man . . . he wants us to buy them from him, these worthless chairs. (THE OLD WOMAN *returns as quickly as she can with a chair.*) You don't all know each other . . . you're seeing each other for the first time . . . you knew each other by name . . . (*To* THE OLD WOMAN.) Semiramis, help me make the introductions . . .

OLD WOMAN. Who are all these people? . . . May I introduce you, excuse me . . . May I introduce you . . . but who are they?

OLD MAN. May I introduce you . . . Allow me to introduce you . . . permit me to introduce you . . . Mr., Mrs., Miss . . . Mr. . . . Mrs. . . . Mrs. . . . Mr.

OLD WOMAN (*to* OLD MAN). Did you put on your sweater? (*To the invisible guests.*) Mr., Mrs., Mr. . . .

(*Doorbell rings again.*)

OLD MAN. More people!

(*Another ring of doorbell.*)

OLD WOMAN. More people!

(*The doorbell rings again, then several more times, and more times again;* THE OLD MAN *is beside himself; the chairs, turned towards the dais, with their backs to the audience, form regular rows, each one longer as in a theatre;* THE OLD MAN *is winded, he mops his brow, goes from one door to another, seats invisible people, while* THE OLD WOMAN, *hobbling along, unable to move any faster, goes as rapidly as she can, from one door to another, hunting for chairs and carrying them in. There are now many invisible people on stage; both* THE OLD MAN *and* OLD WOMAN *take care not to bump into people and to thread their way between the rows of chairs. The movement could go like this:* THE OLD MAN *goes to door No. 4,* THE OLD WOMAN *exits by door No. 3, returns by door No. 2;* THE OLD MAN *goes to open door*

No. 7, THE OLD WOMAN *exits by door No. 8, re-enters by door No. 6 with chairs, etc., in this manner making their way around the stage, using all the doors.*)

OLD WOMAN. Beg pardon . . . excuse me . . . what . . . oh, yes . . . beg pardon . . . excuse me . . .

OLD MAN. Gentlemen . . . come in . . . ladies . . . enter . . . it is Mrs. . . . let me . . . yes . . .

OLD WOMAN (*with more chairs*). Oh dear . . . Oh dear . . . there are too many . . . There really are too, too . . . too many, oh dear, oh dear, oh dear . . .

(*We hear from outside, louder and louder and approaching nearer and nearer, the sounds of boats moving through the water; all the noises come directly from the wings.* THE OLD WOMAN *and* THE OLD MAN *continue the business outlined above; they open the doors, they carry in chairs. The doorbell continues to ring.*)

OLD MAN. This table is in our way. (*He moves a table, or he sketches the business of moving it, without slowing down his rhythm, aided by* THE OLD WOMAN.) There's scarcely a place left here, excuse us . . .

OLD WOMAN (*making a gesture of clearing the table, to* THE OLD MAN). Are you wearing your sweater?

(*Doorbell rings.*)

OLD MAN. More people! More chairs! More people! More chairs! Come in, come in, ladies and gentlemen . . . Semiramis, faster . . . We'll give you a hand soon . . .

OLD WOMAN. Beg pardon . . . beg pardon . . . good evening, Mrs. . . . Mrs. . . . Mr. . . . Mr. . . . yes, yes, the chairs . . .

(*The doorbell rings louder and louder and we hear the noises of boats striking the quay very close by, and more and more frequently.* THE OLD MAN *flounders among the chairs; he has scarcely enough time to go from one door to another, so rapidly do the ringings of the doorbell succeed each other.*)

OLD MAN. Yes, right away . . . are you wearing your sweater? Yes, yes . . . immediately, patience, yes, yes . . . patience . . .

OLD WOMAN. Your sweater? My sweater? . . . Beg pardon, beg pardon.

OLD MAN. This way, ladies and gentlemen, I request you . . . I re you . . . pardon . . . quest . . . enter, enter . . . going to show . . . there, the seats . . . dear friend . . . not there . . . take care . . . you, my friend?

(*Then a long moment without words. We hear waves, boats, the continuous ringing of the doorbell. The movement culminates in intensity at this point. The doors are now opening and shutting all together ceaselessly. Only the main door in the center of the recess remains closed.* THE MAN *and* OLD WOMAN *come and go, without saying a word, from one door to another; they appear to be gliding on roller skates.* THE OLD MAN *receives the people, accompanies them, but doesn't take them very far, he only indicates seats to them after having taken one or two steps with them; he hasn't enough time.* THE OLD WOMAN *carries in chairs.* THE OLD MAN *and* THE OLD WOMAN *meet each other and bump into each other, once or twice, without interrupting their rhythm. Then,* THE OLD MAN *takes a position upstage center, and turns from left to right, from right to left, etc., towards all the doors and indicates the seats with his arms. His arms move very rapidly. Then, finally* THE OLD WOMAN *stops, with a chair in one hand, which she places, takes up again, replaces, looks as though she, too, wants to go from one door to another, from right to left, from left to right, moving her head and neck very rapidly. This must not interrupt the rhythm;* THE OLD MAN *and* OLD WOMAN *must still give the impression of not stopping,*

even while remaining almost in one place; their hands, their chests, their heads, their eyes are agitated, perhaps moving in little circles. Finally, there is a progressive slowing down of movement, at first slight: the ringings of the doorbell are less loud, less frequent; the doors open less and less rapidly; the gestures of THE OLD MAN *and* OLD WOMAN *slacken continuously. At the moment when the doors stop opening and closing altogether, and the ringings cease to be heard, we have the impression that the stage is packed with people.*)

OLD MAN. I'm going to find a place for you . . . patience . . . Semiramis, for the love of . . .

OLD WOMAN (*with a large gesture, her hands empty*). There are no more chairs, my darling. (*Then, abruptly, she begins to sell invisible programs in a full hall, with the doors closed.*) Programs, get your programs here, the program of the evening, buy your program!

OLD MAN. Relax, ladies and gentlemen, we'll take care of you . . . Each in his turn, in the order of your arrival . . . You'll have a seat. I'll take care of you.

OLD WOMAN. Buy your programs! Wait a moment, madam, I cannot take care of everyone at the same time, I haven't got thirty-three hands, you know, I'm not a cow . . . Mister, please be kind enough to pass the program to the lady next to you, thank you . . . my change, my change . . .

OLD MAN. I've told you that I'd find a place for you! Don't get excited! Over here, it's over here, there, take care . . . oh, dear friend . . . dear friends . . .

OLD WOMAN. . . . Programs . . . get your grams . . . grams . . .

OLD MAN. Yes, my dear, she's over there, further down, she's selling programs . . . no trade is unworthy . . . that's her . . . do you see her? . . . you have a seat in the second row . . . to the right . . . no, to the left . . . that's it! . . .

OLD WOMAN. . . . gram . . . gram . . . program . . . get your program . . .

OLD MAN. What do you expect me to do? I'm doing my best! (*To invisible seated people.*) Push over a little, if you will please . . . there's still a little room, that will do for you, won't it, Mrs. . . . come here. (*He mounts the dais, forced by the pushing of the crowd.*) Ladies, gentlemen, please excuse us, there are no more seats available . . .

OLD WOMAN (*who is now on the opposite side of the stage, across from* THE OLD MAN, *between door No. 3 and the window*). Get your programs . . . who wants a program? Eskimo pies, caramels . . . fruit drops . . . (*Unable to move,* THE OLD WOMAN, *hemmed in by the crowd, scatters her programs and candies anywhere, above the invisible heads.*) Here are some! There they are!

OLD MAN (*standing on the dais, very animated; he is jostled as he descends from the dais, remounts it, steps down again, hits someone in the face, is struck by an elbow, says*). Pardon . . . please excuse us . . . take care . . . (*Pushed, he staggers, has trouble regaining his equilibrium, clutches at shoulders.*)

OLD WOMAN. Why are there so many people? Programs, get your program here, Eskimo pies.

OLD MAN. Ladies, young ladies, gentlemen, a moment of silence, I beg you . . . silence . . . it's very important . . . those people who've no seats are asked to clear the aisles . . . that's it . . . don't stand between the chairs.

OLD WOMAN (*To* THE OLD MAN, *almost screaming*). Who are all these people, my darling? What are they doing here?

OLD MAN. Clear the aisles, ladies and gentlemen. Those who do not have seats must, for the convenience of all,

stand against the wall, there, along the right or the left . . . you'll be able to hear everything, you'll see everything, don't worry, you won't miss a thing, all seats are equally good!

(*There is a great hullabaloo. Pushed by the crowd.* THE OLD MAN *makes almost a complete turn around the stage and ends up at the window on the right, near to the stool.* THE OLD WOMAN *makes the same movement in reverse, and ends up at the window on the left, near the stool there.*)

OLD MAN (*making this movement*). Don't push, don't push.

OLD WOMAN (*same business*). Don't push, don't push.

OLD MAN (*same business*). Don't push, don't push.

OLD WOMAN (*same business*). Don't push, ladies and gentlemen, don't push.

OLD MAN (*same business*). Relax . . . take it easy . . , be quiet . . . what's going on here?

OLD WOMAN (*same business*). There's no need to act like savages, in any case.

(*At last they reach their final positions. Each is near a window.* THE OLD MAN *to the left, by the window which is beside the dais.* THE OLD WOMAN *on the right. They don't move from these positions until the end.*)

OLD WOMAN (*calling to* THE OLD MAN). My darling . . . I can't see you, anymore . . . where are you? Who are they? What do all these people want? Who is that man over there?

OLD MAN. Where are you? Where are you, Semiramis?

OLD WOMAN. My darling, where are you?

OLD MAN. Here, beside the window . . . Can you hear me?

OLD WOMAN. Yes, I hear your voice! . . . there are so many . . . but I can make out yours . . .

OLD MAN. And you, where are you?

OLD WOMAN. I'm beside the window too! . . . My dear, I'm frightened, there are too many people . . . we are very far from each other . . . at our age we have to be careful . . . we might get lost . . . We must stay close together, one never knows, my darling, my darling . . .

OLD MAN. Ah! . . . I just caught sight of you . . . Oh! . . . We'll find each other, never fear . . . I'm with friends. (*To the friends*.) I'm happy to shake your hands . . . But of course, I believe in progress, uninterrupted progress, with some jolts, nevertheless . . .

OLD WOMAN. That's fine, thanks . . . What foul weather! Yes, it's been nice! (*Aside*.) I'm afraid, even so . . . What am I doing here? . . . (*She screams*.) My darling, my darling!

(THE OLD MAN *and* OLD WOMAN *individually speak to guests near them*.)

OLD MAN. In order to prevent the exploitation of man by man, we need money, money, and still more money!

OLD WOMAN. My darling! (*Then, hemmed in by friends*.) Yes, my husband is here, he's organizing everything . . . over there . . . Oh! you'll never get there . . . you'd have to go across, he's with friends . . .

OLD MAN. Certainly not . . . as I've always said . . . pure logic does not exist . . . all we've got is an imitation.

OLD WOMAN. But you know, there are people who are happy. In the morning they eat breakfast on the plane, at noon they lunch in the pullman, and in the evening they dine aboard the liner. At the night they sleep in the trucks that roll, roll, roll . . .

OLD MAN. Talk about the dignity of man! At least let's try to save face. Dignity is only skin deep.

OLD WOMAN. Don't slink away into the shadows . . . (*She bursts out laughing in conversation*.)

OLD MAN. Your compatriots ask of me.

OLD WOMAN. Certainly . . . tell me everything.

OLD MAN. I've invited you . . . in order to explain to you . . . that the individual and the person are one and the same.

OLD WOMAN. He has a borrowed look about him. He owes us a lot of money.

OLD MAN. I am not myself. I am another. I am the one in the other.

OLD WOMAN. My children, take care not to trust one another.

OLD MAN. Sometimes I awaken in the midst of absolute silence. It's a perfect circle. There's nothing lacking. But one must be careful, all the same. Its shape might disappear. There are holes through which it can escape.

OLD WOMAN. Ghosts, you know, phantoms, mere nothings . . . The duties my husband fulfills are very important, sublime.

OLD MAN. Excuse me . . . that's not at all my opinion! At the proper time, I'll communicate my views on this subject to you . . . I have nothing to say for the present! . . . We're waiting for the Orator, he'll tell you, he'll speak in my behalf, and explain everything that we hold most dear . . . he'll explain everything to you . . . when? . . . when the moment has come . . . the moment will come soon . . .

OLD WOMAN (*on her side to her friends*). The sooner, the better . . . That's understood . . . (*Aside*.) They're never going to leave us alone. Let them go, why don't they go? . . . My poor darling, where is he? I can't see him any more . . .

OLD MAN (*same business*). Don't be so impatient. You'll hear my message. In just a moment.

OLD WOMAN (*aside*). Ah! . . . I hear his voice! . . . (*To her friends*.) Do you know, my husband has never been understood. But at last his hour has come.

OLD MAN. Listen to me, I've had a rich experience of life. In all walks of life, at every level of thought . . . I'm not an egotist: humanity must profit by what I've learned.

OLD WOMAN. Ow! You stepped on my foot . . . I've got chilblains!

OLD MAN. I've perfected a real system. (*Aside.*) The Orator ought to be here. (*Aloud.*) I've suffered enormously.

OLD WOMAN. We have suffered so much. (*Aside.*) The Orator ought to be here. It's certainly time.

OLD MAN. Suffered much, learned much.

OLD WOMAN (*like an echo*). Suffered much, learned much.

OLD MAN. You'll see for yourselves, my system is perfect.

OLD WOMAN (*like an echo*). You'll see for yourselves, his system is perfect.

OLD MAN. If only my instructions are carried out.

OLD WOMAN (*echo*). If only his instructions are carried out.

OLD MAN. We'll save the world! . . .

OLD WOMAN (*echo*). Saving his own soul by saving the world! . . .

OLD MAN. One truth for all!

OLD WOMAN (*echo*). One truth for all!

OLD MAN. Follow me! . . .

OLD WOMAN (*echo*). Follow him! . . .

OLD MAN. For I have absolute certainty! . . .

OLD WOMAN (*echo*). He has absolute certainty!

OLD MAN. Never . . .

OLD WOMAN (*echo*). Ever and ever . . .

(*Suddenly we hear noises in the wings, fanfares.*)

OLD WOMAN. What's going on?

(*The noises increase, then the main door opens wide, with a great crash; through the open door we see nothing but a very powerful light which floods onto the stage through the main door and the windows, which at the entrance of the* EMPEROR *are brightly lighted.*)

OLD MAN. I don't know . . . I can scarcely believe . . . is it possible . . . but yes . . . but yes . . . incredible . . . and still it's true . . . yes . . . if . . . yes . . . it is the Emperor! His Majesty the Emperor!

(*The light reaches its maximum intensity, through the open door and through the windows; but the light is cold, empty; more noises which cease abruptly.*)

OLD MAN. Stand up! . . . It's His Majesty the Emperor! The Emperor in my house, in our house . . . Semiramis . . . do you realize what this means?

OLD WOMAN (*not understanding*). The Emperor . . . the Emperor? My darling! (*Then suddenly she understands.*) Ah, yes, the Emperor! Your Majesty! Your Majesty! (*She wildly makes countless grotesque curtsies.*) In our house! In our house!

OLD MAN (*weeping with emotion*). Your Majesty! . . . Oh! Your Majesty! . . . Your little, Your great Majesty! . . . Oh! what a sublime honor . . . it's all a marvelous dream.

OLD WOMAN (*like an echo*). A marvelous dream . . . arvelous . . .

OLD MAN (*to the invisible crowd*). Ladies, gentlemen, stand up, our beloved sovereign, the Emperor, is among us! Hurrah! Hurrah! (*He stands up on the stool; he stands on his toes in order to see the* EMPEROR; THE OLD WOMAN *does the same on her side.*)

OLD WOMAN. Hurrah! Hurrah!

(*Stamping of feet.*)

OLD MAN. Your Majesty! . . . I'm over here! . . . Your Majesty! Can you hear me? Can you see me? Please tell his Majesty that I'm here! Your Majesty! Your Majesty!!! I'm here, your most faithful servant! . . .

OLD WOMAN (*still echoing*). Your most faithful servant, Your Majesty!

OLD MAN. Your servant, your slave, your dog, arf, arf, your dog, Your Majesty! . . .

OLD WOMAN (*barking loudly like a dog*). Arf . . . arf . . . arf . . .

OLD MAN (*wringing his hands*). Can you see me? . . . Answer, Sire! . . . Ah, I can see you, I've just caught sight of Your Majesty's august face . . . your divine forehead . . . I've seen you, yes, in spite of the screen of courtiers . . .

OLD WOMAN. In spite of the courtiers . . . we're here, Your Majesty!

OLD MAN. Your Majesty! Your Majesty! Ladies, gentlemen, don't keep him —His Majesty standing . . . you see, Your Majesty, I'm truly the only one who cares for you, for your health, I'm the most faithful of all your subjects . . .

OLD WOMAN (*echoing*). Your Majesty's most faithful subjects!

OLD MAN. Let me through, now, ladies and gentlemen . . . how can I make my way through such a crowd? . . . I must go to present my most humble respects to His Majesty, the Emperor . . . let me pass . . .

OLD WOMAN (*echo*). Let him pass . . . let him pass . . . pass . . . ass . . .

OLD MAN. Let me pass, please, let me pass. (*Desperate.*) Ah! Will I ever be able to reach him?

OLD WOMAN (*echo*). Reach him . . . reach him . . .

OLD MAN. Nevertheless, my heart and my whole being are at his feet, the crowd of courtiers surrounds him, ah! ah! they want to prevent me from approaching him . . . They know very well that . . . oh! I understand, I understand . . . Court intrigues, I know all about it . . . They hope to separate me from Your Majesty!

OLD WOMAN. Calm yourself, my darling . . . His Majesty sees you, he's looking at you . . . His Majesty has given me a wink . . . His Majesty is on our side! . . .

OLD MAN. They must give the Emperor the best seat . . . near the dais . . . so that he can hear everything the Orator is going to say.

OLD WOMAN (*hoisting herself up on the stool, on her toes, lifting her chin as high as she can, in order to see better*). At last they're taking care of the Emperor.

OLD MAN. Thank heaven for that! (*To the* EMPEROR.) Sire . . . Your Majesty may rely on him. It's my friend, it's my representative who is at Your Majesty's side. (*On his toes, standing on the stool.*) Gentlemen, ladies, young ladies, little children, I implore you.

OLD WOMAN (*echoing*). Plore . . . plore . . .

OLD MAN. . . . I want to see . . . move aside . . . I want . . . the celestial gaze, the noble face, the crown, the radiance of His Majesty . . . Sire, deign to turn your illustrious face in my direction, toward your humble servant . . . so humble . . . Oh! I caught sight of him clearly that time . . . I caught sight . . .

OLD WOMAN (*echo*). He caught sight that time . . . he caught sight . . . caught . . . sight . . .

OLD MAN. I'm at the height of joy . . . I've no more words to express my boundless gratitude . . . in my humble dwelling, Oh! Majesty! Oh! radiance! . . . here . . . here . . . in the dwelling where I am, true enough, a general . . . but within the hierarchy of your army, I'm only a simple general factotum . . .

OLD WOMAN (*echo*). General factotum . . .

OLD MAN. I'm proud of it . . . proud and humble, at the same time . . . as I should be . . . alas! certainly, I am a general, I might have been at the imperial court, I have only a little court here to take care of . . . Your Majesty . . . I . . . Your Majesty, I have difficulty expressing myself . . . I might have had . . . many things, not a few possessions if I'd known, if I'd wanted, if I . . . if we . . . Your Majesty, forgive my emotion . . .

OLD WOMAN. Speak in the third person!

OLD MAN (*sniveling*). May Your Majesty deign to forgive me! You are

here at last . . . We had given up hope
. . . you might not even have come . . .
Oh! Savior, in my life, I have been humiliated . . .

OLD WOMAN (*echo, sobbing*). . . .
miliated . . . miliated . . .

OLD MAN. I've suffered much in my
life . . . I might have been something,
if I could have been sure of the support
of Your Majesty . . . I have no other
support . . . if you hadn't come, everything would have been too late . . . you
are, Sire, my last recourse . . .

OLD WOMAN (*echo*). Last recourse
. . . Sire . . . ast recourse . . . ire . . .
recourse . . .

OLD MAN. I've brought bad luck to
my friends, to all those who have helped
me . . . Lightning struck the hand which
was held out toward me . . .

OLD WOMAN (*echo*). . . . hand that
was held out . . . held out . . . out . . .

OLD MAN. They've always had good
reasons for hating me, bad reasons for
loving me . . .

OLD WOMAN. That's not true, my
darling, not true. *I* love you, I'm your
little mother . . .

OLD MAN. All my enemies have been
rewarded and my friends have betrayed
me . . .

OLD WOMAN (*echo*). Friends . . .
betrayed . . . betrayed . . .

OLD MAN. They've treated me badly.
They've persecuted me. If I complained,
it was always they who were in the right
. . . Sometimes I've tried to revenge
myself . . . I was never able to, never
able to revenge myself . . . I have too
much pity . . . I refused to strike the
enemy to the ground, I have always been
too good.

OLD WOMAN (*echo*). He was too
good, good, good, good, good . . .

OLD MAN. It is my pity that has
defeated me.

OLD WOMAN (*echo*). My pity . . .
pity . . . pity . . .

OLD MAN. But they never pitied me.
I gave them a pin prick, and they repaid

me with club blows, with knife blows,
with cannon blows, they've crushed my
bones . . .

OLD WOMAN (*echo*). . . . My bones
. . . my bones . . . my bones . . .

OLD MAN. They've supplanted me,
they've robbed me, they've assassinated
me . . . I've been the collector of in-
justices, the lightning rod of catastrophes . . .

OLD WOMAN (*echo*). Lightning rod
. . . catastrophe . . . lightning rod . . .

OLD MAN. In order to forget, Your
Majesty, I wanted to go in for sports . . .
for mountain climbing . . . they pulled
my feet and made me slip . . . I wanted
to climb stairways, they rotted the steps
. . . I fell down . . . I wanted to travel,
they refused me a passport . . . I wanted
to cross the river, they burnt my
bridges . . .

OLD WOMAN (*echo*). Burnt my
bridges.

OLD MAN. I wanted to cross the
Pyrenees, and there were no more Pyrenees.

OLD WOMAN (*echo*). No more Pyrenees . . . He could have been, he too,
Your Majesty, like so many others, a
head editor, a head actor, a head doctor,
Your Majesty, a head king . . .

OLD MAN. Furthermore, no one has
ever shown me due consideration . . .
no one has ever sent me invitations . . .
However, I, hear me, I say this to you,
I alone could have saved humanity, who
is so sick. Your Majesty realizes this as
do I . . . or, at the least, I could have
spared it the evils from which it has
suffered so much this last quarter of a
century, had I had the opportunity to
communicate my message; I do not despair of saving it, there is still time, I
have a plan . . . alas, I express myself
with difficulty . . .

OLD WOMAN (*above the invisible
heads*). The Orator will be here, he'll
speak for you. His Majesty is here, thus
you'll be heard, you've no reason to despair, you hold all the trumps, everything

has changed, everything has changed . . .

OLD MAN. I hope Your Majesty will excuse me . . . I know you have many other worries . . . I've been humiliated . . . Ladies and gentlemen, move aside just a little bit, don't hide His Majesty's nose from me altogether, I want to see the diamonds of the imperial crown glittering . . . But if Your Majesty has deigned to come to our miserable home, it is because you have condescended to take into consideration my wretched self. What an extraordinary reward. Your Majesty, if corporeally I raise myself on my toes, this is not through pride, this is only in order to gaze upon you! . . . morally, I throw myself at your knees.

OLD WOMAN (*sobbing*). At your knees, Sire, we throw ourselves at your knees, at your feet, at your toes . . .

OLD MAN. I've had scabies. My employer fired me because I did not bow to his baby, to his horse. I've been kicked in the ass, but all this, Sire, no longer has any importance . . . since . . . since . . . Sir . . . Your Majesty . . . look . . . I am here . . . here . . .

OLD WOMAN (*echo*). Here . . . here . . . here . . . here . . . here . . . here . . .

OLD MAN. Since Your Majesty is here . . . since Your Majesty will take my message into consideration . . . But the Orator should be here . . . he's making His Majesty wait . . .

OLD WOMAN. If Your Majesty will forgive him. He's surely coming. He will be here in a moment. They've telephoned us.

OLD MAN. His Majesty is so kind. His Majesty wouldn't depart just like that, without having listened to everything, heard everything.

OLD WOMAN (*echo*). Heard everything . . . heard . . . listened to everything . . .

OLD MAN. It is he who will speak in my name . . . I, I cannot . . . I lack the talent . . . he has all the papers, all the documents . . .

OLD WOMAN (*echo*). He has all the documents . . .

OLD MAN. A little patience, Sire, I beg of you . . . he should be coming.

OLD WOMAN. He should be coming in a moment.

OLD MAN (*so that the* EMPEROR *will not grow impatient*). Your Majesty, hear me, a long time ago I had the revelation . . . I was forty years old . . . I say this also to you, ladies and gentlemen . . . one evening, after supper, as was our custom, before going to bed, I seated myself on my father's knees . . . my mustaches were longer than his and more pointed . . . I had more hair on my chest . . . my hair was graying already, but his was still brown . . . There were some guests, grownups, sitting at table, who began to laugh, laugh.

OLD WOMAN (*echo*). Laugh . . . laugh . . .

OLD MAN. I'm not joking, I told them, I love my papa very much. Someone replied: It is midnight, a child shouldn't stay up so late. If you don't go beddy-bye, then you're no longer a kid. But I'd still not have believed them if they hadn't addressed me as an adult.

OLD WOMAN (*echo*). An adult.

OLD MAN. Instead of as a child . . .

OLD WOMAN (*echo*). A child.

OLD MAN. Nevertheless, I thought to myself, I'm not married. Hence, I'm still a child. They married me off right then, expressly to prove the contrary to me . . . Fortunately, my wife has been both father and mother to me . . .

OLD WOMAN. The Orator should be here, Your Majesty . . .

OLD MAN. The Orator will come.

OLD WOMAN. He will come.

OLD MAN. He will come.

OLD WOMAN. He will come.

OLD MAN. He will come.

OLD WOMAN. He will come.

OLD MAN. He will come, he will come.

OLD WOMAN.   He will come, he will come.

OLD MAN.   He will come.

OLD WOMAN.   He is coming.

OLD MAN.   He is coming.

OLD WOMAN.   He is coming, he is here.

OLD MAN.   He is coming, he is here.

OLD WOMAN.   He is coming, he is here.

OLD MAN AND OLD WOMAN.   He is here . . .

OLD WOMAN.   Here he is!

(*Silence; all movement stops. Petrified, the two old people stare at door No. 5; this immobility lasts rather long—about thirty seconds; very slowly, very slowly the door opens wide, silently; then the* ORATOR *appears. He is a real person. He's a typical painter or poet of the nineteenth century; he wears a large black felt hat with a wide brim, loosely tied bow tie, artist's blouse, mustache and goatee, very histrionic in manner, conceited; just as the invisible people must be as real as possible, the* ORATOR *must appear unreal. He goes along the wall to the right, gliding, softly, to upstage center, in front of the main door, without turning his head to right or left; he passes close by* THE OLD WOMAN *without appearing to notice her, not even when* THE OLD WOMAN *touches his arm in order to assure herself that he exists. It is at this moment that* THE OLD WOMAN *says: "Here he is!"*).

OLD MAN.   Here he is!

OLD WOMAN (*following the* ORATOR *with her eyes and continuing to stare at him*).   It's really he, he exists. In flesh and blood.

OLD MAN (*following him with his eyes*).   He exists. It's really he. This is not a dream!

OLD WOMAN.   This is not a dream, I told you so.

(THE OLD MAN *clasps his hands, lifts his eyes to heaven; he exults silently. The* ORATOR, *having reached upstage center, lifts his hat, bends forward in silence, saluting the invisible* EMPEROR *with his hat with a Musketeer's flourish and somewhat like an automaton. At this moment.*)

OLD MAN.   Your Majesty . . . May I present to you, the Orator . . .

OLD WOMAN.   It is he!

(*Then the* ORATOR *puts his hat back on his head and mounts the dais from which he looks down on the invisible crowd on the stage and at the chairs; he freezes in a solemn pose.*)

OLD MAN (*to the invisible crowd*).   You may ask him for autographs. (*Automatically, silently, the* ORATOR *signs and distributes numberless autographs.* THE OLD MAN *during this time lifts his eyes again to heaven, clasping his hands, and exultantly says.*)   No man, in his lifetime, could hope for more . . .

OLD WOMAN (*echo*).   No man could hope for more.

OLD MAN (*to the invisible crowd*).   And now, with the permission of Your Majesty, I will address myself to all of you, ladies, young ladies, gentlemen, little children, dear colleagues, dear compatriots, Your Honor the President, dear comrades in arms . . .

OLD WOMAN (*echo*).   And little children . . . dren . . . dren . . .

OLD MAN.   I address myself to all of you, without distinction of age, sex, civil status, social rank, or business, to thank you, with all my heart.

OLD WOMAN (*echo*).   To thank you . . .

OLD MAN.   As well as the Orator . . . cordially, for having come in such large numbers . . . silence, gentlemen! . . .

OLD WOMAN (*echo*).   . . . Silence, gentlemen . . .

OLD MAN.   I address my thanks also to those who have made possible the meeting this evening, to the organizers . . .

OLD WOMAN.   Bravo!

(*Meanwhile, the* ORATOR *on the dais remains solemn, immobile, except for*

his hand, which signs autographs auto-
matically.)

OLD MAN. To the owners of this
building, to the architect, to the masons
who were kind enough to erect these
walls! . . .

OLD WOMAN (*echo*). . . . walls . . .

OLD MAN. To all those who've dug
the foundations . . . Silence, ladies and
gentlemen . . .

OLD WOMAN. . . . 'adies and gentlemen . . .

OLD MAN. Last but not least I address my warmest thanks to the cabinet-
makers who have made these chairs on
which you have been able to sit, to the
master carpenter . . .

OLD WOMAN (*echo*). . . . penter . . .

OLD MAN. . . . Who made the arm-
chair in which Your Majesty is sinking
so softly, which does not prevent you,
nevertheless, from maintaining a firm
and manly attitude . . . Thanks again to
all the technicians, machinists, electrocu-
tioners . . .

OLD WOMAN (*echoing*). . . . cutioners . . . cutioners . . .

OLD MAN. . . . To the paper manu-
facturers and the printers, proofreaders,
editors to whom we owe the programs,
so charmingly decorated, to the universal
solidarity of all men, thanks, thanks, to
our country, to the State (*He turns
toward where the* EMPEROR *is sitting.*)
whose helm Your Majesty directs with
the skill of a true pilot . . . thanks to
the usher . . .

OLD WOMAN (*echo*). . . . usher . . .
rusher . . .

OLD MAN (*pointing to* THE OLD
WOMAN). Hawker of Eskimo pies and
programs . . .

OLD WOMAN (*echo*). . . . grams . . .

OLD MAN. . . . My wife, my helpmeet . . . Semiramis! . . .

OLD WOMAN (*echo*). . . . ife . . .
meet . . . mis . . . (*Aside.*) The darling,
he never forgets to give me credit.

OLD MAN. Thanks to all those who

have given me their precious and expert,
financial or moral support, thereby contributing to the overwhelming success of
this evening's gathering . . . thanks again,
thanks above all to our beloved sovereign, His Majesty the Emperor . . .

OLD WOMAN (*echo*). . . . jesty the
Emperor . . .

OLD MAN (*in a total silence*). . . . A
little silence . . . Your Majesty . . .

OLD WOMAN (*echo*). . . . jesty . . .
jesty . . .

OLD MAN. Your Majesty, my wife
and myself have nothing more to ask of
life. Our existence can come to an end
in this apotheosis . . . thanks be to
heaven who has granted us such long
and peaceful years . . . My life has been
filled to overflowing. My mission is accomplished. I will not have lived in vain,
since my message will be revealed to the
world . . . (*Gesture towards the* ORATOR,
who does not perceive it; the ORATOR
*waves off requests for autographs, very
dignified and firm.*) To the world, or
rather to what is left of it! (*Wide gesture
toward the invisible crowd.*) To you,
ladies and gentlemen, and dear comrades, who are all that is left from humanity, but with such leftovers one can
still make a very good soup . . . Orator,
friend . . . (*The* ORATOR *looks in another
direction.*) If I have been long unrecog-
nized, underestimated by my contemporaries, it is because it had to be . . .
(THE OLD WOMAN *sobs.*) What matters
all that now when I am leaving to you,
to you, my dear Orator and friend (*The
ORATOR rejects a new request for an
autograph, then takes an indifferent pose,
looking in all directions.*) . . . the responsibility of radiating upon posterity
the light of my mind . . . thus making
known to the universe my philosophy.
Neglect none of the details of my private
life, some laughable, some painful or
heartwarming, of my tastes, my amusing
gluttony . . . tell everything . . . speak
of my helpmeet . . . (THE OLD WOMAN

redoubles her sobs.) . . . of the way she prepared those marvelous little Turkish pies, of her potted rabbit à la Norman-dabbit . . . speak of Berry, my native province . . . I count on you, great master and Orator . . . as for me and my faithful helpmeet, after our long years of labor in behalf of the progress of humanity during which we fought the good fight, nothing remains for us but to withdraw . . . immediately, in order to make the supreme sacrifice which no one demands of us but which we will carry out even so . . .

OLD WOMAN (*sobbing*). Yes, yes, let's die in full glory . . . let's die in order to become a legend . . . At least, they'll name a street after us . . .

OLD MAN (*to* OLD WOMAN). O my faithful helpmeet! . . . you who have believed in me, unfailingly, during a whole century, who have never left me, never . . . alas, today, at this supreme moment, the crowd pitilessly separates us . . .

> Above all I had hoped
> that together we might lie
> with all our bones together
> within the selfsame skin
> within the same sepulchre
> and that the same worms
> might share our old flesh
> that we might rot together . . .

OLD WOMAN. . . . Rot together . . .
OLD MAN. Alas! . . . alas! . . .
OLD WOMAN. Alas! . . . alas! . . .
OLD MAN. . . . Our corpses will fall far from each other, and we will rot in an aquatic solitude . . . Don't pity us over much.

OLD WOMAN. What will be, will be!
OLD MAN. We shall not be forgotten. The eternal Emperor will remember us, always.

OLD WOMAN (*echo*). Always.
OLD MAN. We will leave some traces, for we are people and not cities.

OLD MAN AND OLD WOMAN (*together*). We will have a street named after us.

OLD MAN. Let us be united in time and in eternity, even if we are not together in space, as we were in adversity: let us die at the same moment . . . (*To the* ORATOR, *who is impassive, immobile.*) One last time . . . I place my trust in you . . . I count on you. You will tell all . . . bequeath my message . . . (*To the* EMPEROR.) If Your Majesty will excuse me . . . Farewell to all. Farewell, Semiramis.

OLD WOMAN. Farewell to all! . . . Farewell, my darling!

OLD MAN. Long live the Emperor!
(*He throws confetti and paper streamers on the invisible* EMPEROR; *we hear fanfares; bright lights like fireworks.*)

OLD WOMAN. Long live the Emperor!
(*Confetti and streamers thrown in the direction of the* EMPEROR, *then on the immobile and impassive* ORATOR, *and on the empty chairs.*)

OLD MAN (*same business*). Long live the Emperor!

OLD WOMAN (*same business*). Long live the Emperor!

(THE OLD WOMAN *and* OLD MAN *at the same moment throw themselves out the windows, shouting "Long Live the Emperor." Sudden silence; no more fireworks; we hear an "Ah" from both sides of the stage, the sea-green noises of bodies falling into the water. The light coming through the main door and the windows has disappeared; there remains only a weak light as at the beginning of the play; the darkened windows remain wide open, their curtains floating on the wind.*)

ORATOR (*he has remained immobile and impassive during the scene of the double suicide, and now, after several moments, he decides to speak. He faces the rows of empty chairs; he makes the invisible crowd understand that he is deaf and dumb; he makes the signs of a*

deaf-mute; desperate efforts to make him-
self understood; then he coughs, groans,
utters the guttural sounds of a mute).
He, mme, mm, mm. Ju, gou, hou, hou.
Heu, heu, gu gou, gueue.

(*Helpless, he lets his arms fall down*
alongside his body; suddenly, his face
lights up, he has an idea, he turns toward
the blackboard, he takes a piece of chalk
out of his pocket, and writes, in large
capitals:)

ANGELFOOD

(*Then:*)

NNAA NNM NWNWNW V

(*He turns around again, towards the*
invisible crowd on the stage, and points
with his finger to what he's written on
the blackboard.)

ORATOR.   Mmm, Mmm, Gueue, Gou,
Gu. Mmm, Mmm, Mmm, Mmm.

(*Then, not satisfied, with abrupt ges-*
tures he wipes out the chalk letters, and
replaces them with others, among which
we can make out, still in large capitals:)

ΛADIEU   ΛDIEU   ΛPΛ

(*Again, the* ORATOR *turns around to*
face the crowd; he smiles, questions, with
an air of hoping that he's been under-
stood, of having said something; he in-
dicates to the empty chairs what he's
just written. He remains immobile for a
few seconds, rather satisfied and a little
solemn; but then, faced with the absence
of the hoped-for reaction, little by little
his smile disappears, his face darkens; he
waits another moment; suddenly he bows
petulantly, brusquely, descends from the
dais; he goes toward the main door up-
stage center, gliding like a ghost; before
exiting through this door, he bows cere-
moniously again to the rows of empty
chairs, to the invisible EMPEROR. *The*
stage remains empty with only the chairs,
the dais, the floor covered with streamers
and confetti. The main door is wide open
onto darkness.

We hear for the first time the human
noises of the invisible crowd; these are
bursts of laughter, murmurs, shh's, ironi-
cal coughs; weak at the beginning, these
noises grow louder, then, again, progres-
sively they become weaker. All this should
last long enough for the audience—the
real and visible audience—to leave with
this ending firmly impressed on its mind.
The curtain falls very slowly.)[1]

[1] In the original production the curtain fell
on the mumblings of the mute ORATOR. The
blackboard was not used.

Index of Authors, Titles, and Literary Terms

Abbey Theatre, 17, 391
Absurd, Theater of the, 22, 517
Action, 7
Allegory, 80
Amphitryon (Plautus), 49
ANOUILH, JEAN, 466
Antagonist, 14
Antagonistic force, 14
Antigone (Sophocles), 26
Antirealistic style, 22
Antitheater, 517
Arena staging, 22
Aristotle, 3, 13, 19

Becket or The Honor of God (Anouilh), 467
Bergson, Henri, 165
Blood Wedding (Lorca), 436

Catastrophe, 10, 13
Chairs, The (Ionesco), 518
Characters, 13-15
CHEKHOV, ANTON, 318
Cherry Orchard, The (Chekhov), 319
Chester Cycle, 80
Chorus, 26
Climax, 10, 13
Comedy, 18, 165
Commedia dell' arte, 165
Complication, 10, 13
Confidant (confidante), 14
Conflict, 10
Conventions, dramatic, 5
Corpus Christi, 80
Coventry Cycle, 80

Dénouement, 10, 13
Desire Under the Elms (O'Neill), 400
Deus ex machina, 13
Dialogue, 7
Dionysus, 26
Dramatic present, 2

Drame, 19

Everyman, 80
Exposition, 10
Expressionism, 22

Farce, 17
Foil, 14
Folk drama, 436

Ghosts (Ibsen), 251
Globe Theatre, 4

Hamlet (Shakespeare), 97
Hobbes, Thomas, 165

IBSEN, HENRIK, 251
Inciting force, 10, 12
IONESCO, EUGÈNE, 517
Irish Literary Theatre, The, 391
Irony, 15-16
   dramatic, 16
   Sophoclean, 16
It Is So! (If You Think So) (Pirandello), 351

James, Henry, 6

Katharsis, 20

LORCA, FEDERICO GARCIA, 436

Man of Destiny, The (Shaw), 291
Melodrama, 18
Miracles, 80
Misanthrope, The (Molière), 166
MOLIÈRE, 165
Morality plays, 80
Moscow Art Theatre, The, 21, 318

Naturalism, 21

O'NEILL, EUGENE, 399

PIRANDELLO, LUIGI, 350
PLAUTUS, 49
Plot, 10-13
    parts of, 10
Presentational style, 22
Problem play, 19, 251
Prologue, 11
Protagonist, 14, 19
Purposive will, 10

Realism, 21-22
Resolution, 10, 13
Riders to the Sea (Synge), 391
Rising action, 10

Satire, 18, 165
School for Scandal, The (Sheridan), 200
SHAKESPEARE, WILLIAM, 96
SHAW, GEORGE BERNARD, 290

SHERIDAN, RICHARD BRINSLEY, 200
SOPHOCLES, 26
Story, 6
Surrealism, 22
Symbolism, 22
SYNGE, JOHN MILLINGTON, 391

Theater in the round, 22
Theatricalism, 22
Theme, 15
Tragedy, 19-21
Trope, 80
Turning Point, 10, 13
Types of plays, 16

Unity, 16

Wakefield Cycle, 80

York Cycle, 80